AF834037

THE ENVIRONMENTAL RULE OF LAW FOR OCEANS

Our oceans need a strong and effective environmental rule of law to protect them against increased pressures and demands, including climate change, pollution, fisheries, shipping and more. The environmental rule of law for oceans requires the existence of a set of rules and policies at multiple governance levels that appropriately regulate human activities at sea and ensure that pressures on the marine ecosystem are tackled effectively. Adhering to the rule of law through clear, predictable, coherent and legitimate rules, and their implementation and enforcement, is timely and urgent. In this book, we are searching for ways to improve, strengthen and further develop the environmental rule of law for oceans. The book provides future-oriented perspectives on how law should evolve to better preserve the oceans. All chapters incorporate novel insights and ideas for legal solutions that might inspire scholars, actors, authorities, citizens and communities around the globe. This title is Open Access.

FROUKJE MARIA PLATJOUW is a Senior researcher at the Norwegian Institute for Water Research (NIVA), Oslo. She is an expert in EU and international law, specialized in environmental law, ocean law and ecosystem-based governance. She is the coordinator of the Horizon Europe funded 'CrossGov' project on Coherent and cross-compliant ocean governance for delivering the EU Green Deal for European Seas.

ALLA POZDNAKOVA is Professor of Law at the Scandinavian Institute for Maritime Law, University of Oslo. Her areas of research and teaching are public international law, law of the sea, outer space law, environmental law, Arctic and EU/EEA law. She is a board member of the International Law Association, Norway, and a member of the International Institute for Space Law and of the expert committee for Norwegian space law.

The Environmental Rule of Law for Oceans

DESIGNING LEGAL SOLUTIONS

Edited by

FROUKJE MARIA PLATJOUW

Norwegian Institute for Water Research

ALLA POZDNAKOVA

University of Oslo

CAMBRIDGE
UNIVERSITY PRESS

CAMBRIDGE
UNIVERSITY PRESS

Shaftesbury Road, Cambridge CB2 8EA, United Kingdom

One Liberty Plaza, 20th Floor, New York, NY 10006, USA

477 Williamstown Road, Port Melbourne, VIC 3207, Australia

314–321, 3rd Floor, Plot 3, Splendor Forum, Jasola District Centre, New Delhi – 110025, India

103 Penang Road, #05–06/07, Visioncrest Commercial, Singapore 238467

Cambridge University Press is part of Cambridge University Press & Assessment, a department of the University of Cambridge.

We share the University's mission to contribute to society through the pursuit of education, learning and research at the highest international levels of excellence.

www.cambridge.org
Information on this title: www.cambridge.org/9781009253727

DOI: 10.1017/9781009253741

First published 2023
First paperback edition 2026

A catalogue record for this publication is available from the British Library

Library of Congress Cataloging-in-Publication data
NAMES: Platjouw, Froukje Maria, editor. | Pozdnakova, Alla, editor.
TITLE: The environmental rule of law for oceans : designing legal solutions / edited by Froukje Maria Platjouw, University of Oslo; Alla Pozdnakova, University of Oslo.
DESCRIPTION: Cambridge, United Kingdom ; New York, ny : Cambridge University Press, 2022. | Includes bibliographical references and index.
IDENTIFIERS: LCCN 2022033787 (print) | LCCN 2022033788 (ebook) | ISBN 9781009253741 (epub) | ISBN 9781009253765 (hardback) | ISBN 9781009253727 (paperback)
SUBJECTS: LCSH: United Nations Convention on the Law of the Sea (1982 December 10) | Law of the sea. | Maritime law. | Marine resources conservation–Law and legislation. | Marine pollution–Law and legislation. | Shipping–environmental aspects. | Climatic changes–Law and legislation. | Environmental law, International.
CLASSIFICATION: LCC KZA1145 (ebook) | LCC KZA1145 .E59 2022 (print) | DDC 341.4/5 23/eng/20220–dc21
LC record available at https://lccn.loc.gov/2022033787

ISBN 978-1-009-25376-5 Hardback
ISBN 978-1-009-25372-7 Paperback

Contents

Contributors

Vasco Becker-Weinberg is Professor at the Faculty of Law of the Universidade Lusófona and at NOVA School of Law, and President of the IPDM – The Portuguese Institute of the Law of the Sea. He is also Law Clerk at the Portuguese Constitutional Court.

Brita Bohman is Senior Lecturer in Environmental Law at Stockholm University. Her main research is focused on legal aspects of social-ecological resilience and ecosystem approach. She is also specialized in Baltic Sea law.

Carlos A. Cruz Carrillo is a PhD researcher at the University of Basel. He holds a master's degree in international law from the Graduate Institute of Geneva (IHEID) and an LLB from the National Autonomous University of Mexico (UNAM).

Agnes Chong is Assistant Professor at the Chinese University of Hong Kong. Dr. Chong's research interests include international law, watercourses law, environmental law and human rights law. She obtained her PhD from the University of Hong Kong and, after that, was a visiting scholar at the University of Cambridge.

Jakub Ciesielczuk is a lecturer in public international law at Neapolis University Pafos. He obtained his LLB in English law with German from the University of Dundee. He also holds an LLM in public international law from Leiden University. Ciesielczuk is currently finalizing his PhD in public international law at the University of Lincoln.

Pierre Cloutier de Repentigny is an assistant professor at the Department of Law and Legal Studies, Carleton University. Their research revolves around law and marine biodiversity, political ecology, trans justice and critical theory.

Sarah Ryan Enright is an Irish qualified lawyer with more than fifteen years' experience in European and International Law. She is currently a researcher in ocean law and marine governance at MaREI: the SFI Research Centre for Energy,

Climate and Marine, University College Cork, where she completed a PhD on the international legal framework for transboundary Marine Protected Areas.

Solène Guggisberg is a senior research associate at Utrecht University, currently working on the regulation of Antarctic tourism. She has previously undertaken postdoctoral research on international fisheries law, and worked for international governmental and nongovernmental organizations involved in fisheries and maritime affairs as well as for international courts and tribunals.

Leonila Guglya is a counsel leading the International Trade / WTO Law Practice of the SwissLegal Rouiller et Associés office in Geneva and a Professor at Business School Lausanne (BSL) and International Institute in Geneva (IIG). She holds a PhD in international trade law from the University of Geneva (2017) and an SJD in international arbitration from Central European University (2010), both summa cum laude.

Rozemarijn J. Roland Holst is Assistant Professor in International Environmental Law at Durham University. She previously taught at Utrecht University, where she also obtained her PhD (cum laude). She holds an LLM with distinction from the University of Edinburgh and an LLB (cum laude) from the University of Amsterdam.

Dawoon Jung is a research fellow at the Centre for International Law, the National University of Singapore. She is also an associate editor of the *Asian Journal of International Law*. She holds law degrees from the University of Edinburgh (PhD) and Korea University (LLM, LLB).

David Langlet is currently a professor of environmental law at Uppsala University, and has previously held positions as a professor of ocean governance law at Gothenburg University and research fellow at the University of Oxford. He has researched a wide range of topics in the fields of environmental law, law of the sea and energy law.

Mitchell Lennan is a Lecturer in Law (Energy & Environment) at the University of Aberdeen. He joined Aberdeen in December 2022 after completing a PhD in law of the sea at the University of Strathclyde. His research focuses on the regulation of marine resources in the face of climate change.

Froukje Maria Platjouw is a Senior researcher at the Norwegian Institute for Water Researcher, specialized in environmental and marine law and governance. Her research aims to strengthen the effectiveness, harmonization and coherence of legal frameworks for a better protection of the environment. She obtained her PhD at the University of Oslo, Faculty of Law. She coordinates the Horizon Europe funded research and innovation project 'CrossGov'.

Alla Pozdnakova has researched and published broadly on law of the sea and maritime safety, environmental law, outer space law, Arctic, and European law. She is a board member of the International Law Association (Norway), and member of the International Institute for Space Law and of the expert committee for Norwegian space law.

Henrik Ringbom is Professor of Marine Law at Åbo Akademi University (Finland) and holds a part-time professorship at the Scandinavian Institute of Maritime Law (University of Oslo). His career also includes eleven years as an EU civil servant, at the European Commission in Brussels and the European Maritime Safety Agency in Lisbon.

Aref Shams is a PhD student in international law at University College London. He holds a master's degree in international law from the Graduate Institute of International and Development Studies in Switzerland, and a bachelor of laws from the University of Waikato in New Zealand.

Anastasia Telesetsky's research focuses on marine environmental protection, food security, disaster risk reduction and ecological restoration . She is the co-author of *Ecological Restoration in International Environmental* Law, the textbook *Comparative and Global Environmental Law and Policy*, and the Ocean and Coastal Management Law in a Nutshell.

David Testa is a legal counsel at the London office of Det Norske Veritas. He has a PhD in shipping, law of the sea and marine environment protection from the University of Nottingham and an LLM in public international law from the University of Cambridge.

Andrey Todorov is a postdoctoral research fellow at the Harvard Kennedy School's Arctic Initiative, and Senior Researcher at the Primakov Institute of World Economy and International Relations (Russian Academy of Sciences). He holds a PhD with interests in Arctic Ocean governance and the international Law of the Sea.

Christina Voigt is an expert in international environmental law and works in particular on legal issues of climate change, biodiversity conservation, environmental multilateralism and sustainability. She is also chair of the IUCN World Commission on Environmental Law and co-chair of the Paris Agreement Implementation and Compliance Committee.

Pieter van Welzen is a senior legal consultant with CMS South Africa, advising on financial markets transactions. He is also a PhD student at the University of Hamburg, researching the international legal regime applying to illegal fishing, with a particular focus on West Africa.

Kirsi White is a doctoral candidate at the University of Turku Law School, Finland, with research interest in environmental regulation at regional sea level. She currently works at the Finnish Ministry of the Environment as a Senior Officer, Legal Affairs. She holds law degrees from the University of Hertfordshire (LLM, GDL) and BPP University College London (LPC).

Maurus Wollensak is currently a master's degree student in international law at the Geneva Graduate Institute. He holds a First State Exam in law with a specialization in European and public international law undertaken at the University of Hamburg.

Constantinos Yiallourides is a lecturer in international law at Macquarie University Sydney, specializing in the law of the sea, and the intersection of sustainability and energy transformation. He is concurrently the Arthur Watts research fellow in law of the sea at the British Institute of International and Comparative Law (BIICL) where he leads the Institute's Watts Programme of research and training in the law of the sea, energy and natural resources law.

Foreword

We live in unprecedented times in human history. In this difficult and uncertain era, few will dispute that the marine environment, ocean processes and ecosystem services have never been more vital for the collective wellbeing and future progress of humans on planet Earth. In many ways, the existentialist and current predicaments faced by humanity in ocean affairs provide the general context for the daunting task taken on by the editors and contributors to this book, which is to explore the best solutions for sustainability and the protection of the marine environment. In light of their commendable endeavours in this regard, it is indeed a singular honour to pen the foreword to this very fine compendium of chapters published under the title, *The Environmental Rule of Law for Oceans: Designing Legal Solutions*.

Many of the chapters were first delivered at a memorable symposium convened by the research group on International Law and Governance in collaboration with the Norwegian Institute for Water Research and held in the Professorboligen in Oslo University in November 2019. This proved to be an enchanting venue for two days of thought-provoking deliberations on the academic papers that now form the core of these edited proceedings. In one volume, the collection draws together a range of incisive contributions made by leading law of the sea and environmental law scholars, diplomats and practitioners, who write with great authority and clarity about the protection, sustainable use and restoration of the marine environment, as well as its associated resources and ecosystems.

At the time of the symposium, no one foresaw that the world would change irrevocably shortly thereafter. Since then, many of the intergovernmental processes that are so crucial for the progressive development of the law of the sea have been delayed or postponed. Virtual and hybrid meetings have become the order of the day. Despite these constraints, the search for regulatory and policy responses to engender greater marine environmental stewardship has gathered pace and taken on a new sense of urgency. In light of these developments, the publication of this volume could not be more timely, as it marks the fortieth anniversary of the adoption of the 1982 United Nations Convention on the Law of the Sea (UNCLOS), as well as the seventieth anniversary of the 1972 United Nations Conference on the Human Environment, which led to the adoption of the Stockholm Declaration and Action Plan for the Human Environment. As is well known, these instruments were also adopted at a time of heightened international discord and concern about the degradation of the marine environment. Nonetheless, they managed to usher in a new era of intergovernmental cooperation and stability in the rule of law as it applies to ocean affairs and environmental matters more generally. The publication of this volume is therefore first and foremost a curt reminder of the resilience of the international community when faced with adversity in protecting and preserving the environment. At the same time, it signals the potency of the rule of law in setting priorities and delivering solutions that deftly balance competing interests in the use of ocean space and the conservation of natural resources.

The negotiators of UNCLOS intended the Convention to be comprehensive in substance and scope, as well as of universal application. Indeed, one has to go no further than the Preamble of UNCLOS to see that they were extravagantly optimistic as they sought to settle 'all issues relating to the law of the sea' by establishing a 'legal order for the seas and oceans which will facilitate international communication, and will promote the peaceful uses of the seas and oceans, the equitable and efficient utilisation of their resources, the conservation of their living resources, and the study, protection and preservation of the marine environment'. In the four decades since the adoption of the Convention, many of the chapters reveal, however, that the law of the sea has not stood still. Today, the discrete field of law concerning the protection of the marine environment is made up of a complex and highly dynamic framework of specialist rules and standards. In addition, the jurisprudence of international courts and tribunals has added greatly to this framework in contentious and advisory proceedings concerning the interpretation and implementation of the Convention and related instruments. As the reader will see, this progression in normative development forms the backbone of much of the analysis undertaken in the volume. In shining the spotlight on contentious issues, the selection and treatment of topics is wide-ranging and cutting-edge, embracing as it does climate change and vessel source pollution, plastic pollution, space debris, living and non-living resources including biodiversity beyond national jurisdiction, environmental crimes, fisheries law, WTO Law, EU maritime governance, ecosystem-based management of the Arctic, the resumption of commercial whaling by Japan, as well as the perennial problems associated with the rule of law and the South China Sea. Significantly, the diffuse nature of individual chapter topics is structured creatively by the editors around five interwoven strands that bind the collection together, namely tackling multiple pressures on the oceans; balancing the exploitation and preservation of ocean resources; paths towards effective ocean governance, implementation and compliance; and strengthening the rule of law in regional seas and oceans. The collection is book-ended by two discrete chapters authored by the joint editors that set the scene in the search for novel approaches to protecting the ocean, which conclude the compendium by charting out a compelling range of legal solutions for more sustainable uses of the oceans in an era of what often appears as unabated environmental change.

A fascinating question that pervades the entire narrative relates to the effectiveness and strength of the rule of law in meeting contemporary challenges as they pertain to the marine environment. In exploring various potential answers to this enquiry, many of the authors deconstruct the laws, science and policies in discrete fields, and by doing so make the topics at hand accessible and insightful to read. This approach will be welcomed by all readers, including specialist and non-specialist alike. As evident from the title of the volume, the narrative underpinning the collection does not only focus on the successes and failures of the environmental rule of law for the ocean but also tenders viable solutions to some of the most intractable challenges faced by humanity in the twenty-first century. The discussion reveals that many of the contemporary difficulties encountered in managing human impacts on the marine environment are not entirely new. The pressures are, however, intensifying due to a confluence of factors, including the climate emergency, extreme weather events and perhaps most acutely in relation to the tragic consequences of the recent Covid-19 pandemic. Furthermore, the impacts are most severe in countries in the Global South, where much remains to be done to address global inequalities, as well as to protect the human and natural environment.

In delving into the functions and the limits of the law, many of the contributions demonstrate that the normative might of instruments that protect the marine environment vary considerably and perhaps inevitably. Overall, what is also clearly evident is that the whole process of normative development is increasingly disparate. As such, it demands the creation of new mandates and new forms of engagement by intergovernmental bodies and other actors. Crucially, the authors point the way to strengthening the rule of law and the institutional setting for decision-making on the protection of the marine environment. In addition, on the basis of in-depth evaluation and analysis undertaken in the chapters, the editors provide a blueprint in the final chapter for the future development of the law and the road to ocean sustainability, which is to be applauded. Indeed, at the time of writing, several of the most pressing issues concerning the protection of the marine environment are subject to further regulatory developments with the elaboration of a new legally binding instrument on the conservation and sustainable use of biodiversity beyond national jurisdiction, as well as nascent steps to adopt a multilateral instrument aimed at controlling plastic pollution. Increasingly, we see the convergence of climate change and human rights considerations in law of the sea instruments, especially those concerned with forced migration and illegal, unreported and unregulated fishing. Moreover, the year of 2022 promises a new era of international engagement on ocean issues and will see the convening of an Ocean Summit in France, Our

Ocean Conference in Palau, the ninth World Ocean Summit and Expo in Portugal, the fourth session of the biodiversity beyond national jurisdiction intergovernmental conference at the United Nations, the fifteenth Conference of the Parties of the Convention on Biological Diversity, and the second UN Ocean Conference in Lisbon. One anticipates that the scientific basis for decision-making will become more assured in the years ahead, as we progress with the UN Decade of Ocean Science for Sustainable Development (2021–2030). We can also expect that the three institutions established by UNCLOS – the International Tribunal for the Law of the Sea, the International Seabed Authority, and the Commission on the Limits of the Continental Shelf – will continue to make steady progress in discharging their mandates and contribute to the progressive development and implementation of the law of the sea. All of the aforementioned show that marine environmental law commands broad international engagement and support. Furthermore, it will continue to flourish and remain a priority for legal scholarship.

In the regulatory and policy efforts ahead, we can be confident that the analysis undertaken in this volume will provide invaluable guidance to judges, diplomats, practitioners, academics and policymakers, who face the inevitable task of interpreting and applying the law, including mediating scientific evidence concerning the conservation and sustainable use of the marine environment, as well as its associated resources and ecological services. In doing so, this volume will make its own contribution to the maintenance of peace, stability and progress in human affairs. Permit me, therefore, to express my appreciation and congratulations to the editors and contributors for adding greatly to scholarship on the environmental rule of law for oceans, as well as to the international law of the sea more generally.

Professor Ronán Long,
Director of the Sasakawa Global Ocean Institute
and the Nippon Foundation Chair in
Ocean Governance and the Law of the Sea,
World Maritime University, Malmö, Sweden,
7 January 2022

Preface

This book crystallized in the aftermath of the Rule of Law for Oceans conference held at the University of Oslo's Faculty of Law in November 2019. The conference was organized by the faculty's research group on International Law and Governance in collaboration with the Norwegian Institute for Water Research. Scientific research on challenges and pressures on the marine environment, the role and functioning of environmental and international law, as well as the law of the sea, all culminated in the understanding that it is high time to critically examine the environmental rule of law for oceans. Many oceans and seas around the world are currently under threat. Strengthening the environmental rule of law is therefore urgent.

This book brings together a variety of perspectives from an extremely knowledgeable and intellectually creative group of scholars. Each author presents unique perspectives on the environmental rule of law for oceans (or the lack of such) and proposes legal solutions that might contribute to better protection and sustainable use of our oceans and seas. We would like to thank the authors for their patience and positive collaboration during the entire book process, and especially during the review of individual chapters. The majority of writing and editing took place during the Covid-19 pandemic, which may have slightly slowed down the process but never stopped any of us. It has been an intellectually inspiring and exciting journey.

In addition to all authors, we would also like to thank several others who have contributed to the success of this book project. First and foremost, for academic, practical and financial support in the organization of the conference and accomplishment of the book project we owe major thanks to the Faculty of Law's research group on International Law and Governance, the Scandinavian Institute of Maritime Law, as well as the Norwegian Institute for Water Research. Others who have contributed with financial support are the Fridtjof Nansen Foundation (Nansenfondet) for language editing, and the Norwegian Institute for Water Research and the law faculty of the University of Oslo for covering Open Access expenses related to publication of this book. Special thanks go to Christopher Goddard for proofreading all chapters thoroughly and consistently. Finally, we would like to express our gratitude to Cambridge University Press for their highly constructive and positive collaboration, and especially to Tom Randall, who has always been supportive and helpful throughout the entire process.

International Instruments

1946 Convention on the Privileges and Immunities of the United Nations, New York, 13 February 1946, in force 17 September 1946, 1 UNTS 15

1948 Convention on the International Maritime Organization, Geneva, 6 March 1948, in force 17 March 1958, 289 UNTS 3

1949 Convention between the United States of America and the Republic of Costa Rica for the Establishment of an Inter-American Tropical Tuna Commission, Washington, 31 May 1949, in force 3 March 1950, 80 UNTS 3

1969 Vienna Convention on the Law of Treaties, Vienna, 23 May 1969, in force 27 January 1980, 1155 UNTS 331; (1969) 8 ILM 679; UKTS (1980) 58

1972 Convention on the Prevention of Marine Pollution by Dumping of Wastes and Other Matter, Washington/Moscow/London/Mexico City, adopted 29 December 1972, in force 30 August 1975, 1046 UNTS 120

1973 Convention on International Trade in Endangered Species of Wild Fauna and Flora, Washington, 3 March 1973, in force 1 July 1975, 993 UNTS 243

1973 International Convention for the Prevention of Pollution from Ships, London, 2 November 1973, 1340 UNTS 184, as Amended by the Protocol of 1978 Relating to the International Convention for the Prevention of Pollution from Ships of 1973, 17 February 1978, 1340 UNTS 61 (MARPOL)

1974 Helsinki Convention on the Protection of the Marine Environment of the Baltic Sea Area, Helsinki, 22 March 1974, in force 3 May 1980, 1507 UNTS 166

1975 Convention for the Establishment of a European Space Agency, Paris, adopted 30 May 1975, in force 30 October 1980, 1297 UNTS 161

1978 International Convention on Standards of Training, Certification and Watchkeeping for Seafarers, 1978, London, 7 July 1978, in force 28 April 1984, 1361 UNTS 2, 1362 UNTS 2

1979 Convention on the Conservation of Migratory Species of Wild Animals (CMS), Bonn, 23 June 1979 in force 1 November 1983, 1651 UNTS 333

1980 Convention on the Conservation of Antarctic Marine Living Resources, Canberra, 20 May 1980, in force 4 April 1982, 1329 UNTS 47
1981 Convention for the Protection of the Marine Environment and Coastal Area of the South-East Pacific (Lima Convention), adopted on 12 November 1981
1982 United Nations Convention on the Law of the Sea (UNCLOS), Montego Bay, 10 December 1982, in force 16 November 1994, 1833 UNTS 397
1987 Basel Convention on the Control of Transboundary Movements of Hazardous Wastes and Their Disposal (Basel Convention) Basel, 22 March 1987, in force 5 May 1993, 1673 UNTS 57
1987 Montreal Protocol on Substances That Deplete the Ozone Layer, Montreal, 16 September 1987, in force 1 January 1989, 1522 UNTS 3
1992 Convention for the Protection of the Marine Environment of the North-East Atlantic, Paris, 22 September 1992, in force 25 March 1998 1993 2354 UNTS 67 (OSPAR Convention)
1992 Convention on the Protection of the Marine Environment of the Baltic Sea Area, Helsinki, 9 April 1992, in force 17 January 2000, 2009 UNTS 197
1992 United Nations Framework Convention on Climate Change, New York, 9 May 1992, in force 21 March 1994, 1771 UNTS 107
1992 Convention on Biological Diversity, Rio de Janeiro, 5 June 1992, in force 29 December 1993, 1760 UNTS 69
1992 Convention for the Protection of the Marine Environment of the North-East Atlantic, Paris, 22 September 1992, in force 25 March 1998, 2354 UNTS 67
1993 Convention for the Conservation of Southern Bluefin Tuna, Canberra, 10 May 1993, in force 20 May 1994, 1819 UNTS 359
1993 Agreement to Promote Compliance with International Conservation and Management Measures by Fishing Vessels on the High Seas, Rome, 24 November 1993, in force 24 April 2003, 2221 UNTS 120
1993 Agreement for the Implementation of the Provisions of the United Nations Convention on the Law of the Sea of 10 December 1982 Relating to the Conservation and Management of Straddling Fish Stocks and Highly Migratory Fish Stocks (UNFSA), New York, 4 August 1995, in force 11 December 2001, 2167 UNTS 88
1995 Convention for the Protection of the Marine Environment and the Coastal Region of the Mediterranean, Barcelona, 10 June 1995, in force 9 July 2004, 1102 UNTS 27
1996 International Law Commission Draft Code of Crimes against the Peace and Security of Mankind (1996), Yearbook of the International Law Commission, 1996, vol. II
1997 Convention on the Law of the Non-Navigational Uses of International Watercourses, New York, 21 May 1997, in force 17 August 2014, 2999 UNTS
1997 Kyoto Protocol to the United Nations Framework Convention on Climate Change, Kyoto, 11 December 1997, in force 16 February 2005, 2303 UNTS 162

1998 1998 Convention on Access to Information, Public Participation in Decision-Making and Access to Justice in Environmental Matters (Aarhus Convention), Aarhus, 25 June 1998, in force 30 October 2001, 2161 UNTS 447

1998 The Rome Statute of the International Criminal Court, Rome, 17 July 1998, in force 1 July 2002, 2187 UNTS 90

2000 United Nations Convention against Transnational Organized Crime, Palermo, 12 December 2000, in force 29 September 2003, 2225 UNTS 209, 40 ILM 335 (2001)

2001 International Treaty on Plant Genetic Resources for Food and Agriculture, Rome, 3 November 2001, in force 29 June 2004, 2400 UNTS 303

2001 Responsibility of States for Internationally Wrongful Acts (2001), Yearbook of the International Law Commission, 2001, vol. II (Part Two)

2002 Convention for Cooperation in the Protection and Sustainable Development of the Marine and Coastal Environment of the Northeast Pacific, Antigua, 18 February 2002 (Not yet in force). Available online at: www.ecolex.org (TRE-001350)

2009 Agreement on Port State Measures to Prevent, Deter and Eliminate Illegal, Unreported and Unregulated Fishing, Rome, 22 November 2009, in force 5 June 2016, 55 ILM 1157

2012 Convention on the Determination of the Minimal Conditions for Access and Exploitation of Marine Resources within the Maritime Areas under Jurisdiction of the Member States of the Sub-Regional Fisheries Commission, Dakar, 8 June 2012, in force 16 September 2012

2013 Protocol No. 16 to the Convention for the Protection of Human Rights and Fundamental Freedoms, Strasbourg, 2 October 2013, in force 1 August 2018, Council of Europe Treaty Series – No. 214

2014 Agreement for the Establishment of the General Fisheries Commission for the Mediterranean as Amended by the General Fisheries Council for the Mediterranean at Its First Special Session (May 1963), at Its Thirteenth Session (July 1976), at Its Twenty-Second Session (October 1997) and by the General Fisheries Commission for the Mediterranean at Its Thirty-Eighth Session (May 2014), Rome, 20 May 2014, in force 20 May 2014, 3041 UNTS A-1691

2015 Paris Agreement to the United Nations Framework Convention on Climate Change, Paris, 12 December 2015, in force 4 November 2016

2019 Convention on the Law of the Sea on the Conservation and Sustainable Use of Marine Biological Diversity of Areas beyond National Jurisdiction, Revised Draft Text of an Agreement under the United Nations Convention on the Law of the Sea on the Conservation and Sustainable Use of Marine Biological Diversity of Areas beyond National Jurisdiction, 4th sess., Annex, UN Doc A/CONF.232/2020/3, 18 November 2019 (Draft BBNJ Agreement)

2022 WTO Agreement on Fisheries Subsidies, 17 June 2022, WT/MIN(22)/33WT/L/1144 (not yet in force)

EU LEGAL ACTS

Treaty on the Functioning of the European Union, Official Journal C 326, 26/10/2012 P. 1 – 390

REGULATIONS

Regulation (EC) No 1367/2006 of the European Parliament and of the Council of 6 September 2006 on the application of the provisions of the Aarhus Convention on Access to Information, Public Participation in Decision-Making and Access to Justice in Environmental Matters to Community institutions and bodies

Council Regulation (EC) No 1005/2008 of 29 September 2008 establishing a Community system to prevent, deter and eliminate illegal, unreported and unregulated fishing, amending Regulations (EEC) No 2847/93, (EC) No 1936/2001 and (EC) No 601/2004 and repealing Regulations (EC) No 1093/94 and (EC) No 1447/1999, OJ 2008 No. L 286, 29 October 2008 (EU IUU Regulation)

DIRECTIVES

Directive 2000/60/EC of the European Parliament and of the Council of 23 October 2000 establishing a framework for Community action in the field of water policy: https://ec.europa.eu/environment/aarhus/legislation.htm (last accessed August 2021)

Directive 2001/42/EC of the European Parliament and of the Council of 27 June 2001 on the assessment of the effects of certain plans and programmes on the environment

Directive 2003/4/EC of the European Parliament and of the Council of 28 January 2003 on public access to environmental information and repealing Council Directive 90/313/EEC

Directive 2003/35/EC of the European Parliament and of the Council of 26 May 2003 providing for public participation in respect of the drawing up of certain plans and programmes relating to the environment and amending with regard to public participation and access to justice Council Directives 85/337/EEC and 96/61/EC

Directive 2009/123/EC of the European Parliament and of the Council of 21 October 2009, amending Directive 2005/35/EC on ship-source pollution and on the introduction of penalties for infringements

Table of Cases

The Case of the S.S. 'Lotus' (France v. *Turkey)* [1927] PCIJ Rep. (Ser. A no. 10) 4
Interpretation of the Greco-Turkish Agreement, Final Protocol, Article IV (Advisory Opinion) [1928] PCIJ Rep (Ser. B no 16) 18
Trail Smelter Arbitration (1941) RIAA vol. III, 1905–82
Interpretation of Peace Treaties with Bulgaria, Hungary and Romania (First Phase) (Advisory Opinion) [1950] ICJ Rep. 65
Nottebohm (Liechtenstein v. *Guatemala) case* (Preliminary Objections, Judgment) [1953] ICJ Rep. 111
North Sea Continental Shelf cases (Federal Republic of Germany v. *Denmark and Netherlands)* (Judgment) [1969] ICJ Rep. 3
Case concerning the Barcelona Traction, Light and Power Company, Limited (Belgium v. *Spain)* Second Phase (Judgment) [1970] ICJ Rep. 3
Application for Review of Judgement No. 158 of the United Nations Administrative Tribunal (Advisory Opinion) [1973] ICJ Rep. 166
Fisheries Jurisdiction (United Kingdom v. *Iceland)* (Merits, Judgment) [1974] ICJ Rep. 3
Nuclear Tests (Australia v. *France)* (Judgment) [1974] ICJ Rep. 253
Western Sahara (Request for Advisory Opinion) (Order) [1975] ICJ Rep. 6
Western Sahara (Advisory Opinion) [1975] ICJ Rep. 12
Request for an Examination of the Situation in Accordance with paragraph 63 of the Court's Judgment of 20 December 1974 in the Nuclear Tests (New Zealand v. *France) case* (Order) [1995] ICJ Rep. 288
Legality of the Use by a State of Nuclear Weapons in Armed Conflict (Advisory Opinion) [1996] ICJ Rep. 66
Legality of the Threat or Use of Nuclear Weapons (Advisory Opinion) [1996] ICJ Rep. 226

Gabčíkovo–Nagymaros Project (Hungary v. *Slovakia)* (Judgment) [1997] ICJ Rep. 7, 37 ILM 162 (1998)

Southern Bluefin Tuna (New Zealand v. *Japan; Australia* v. *Japan)* (Provisional Measures, Order of 27 August 1999) [1999] ITLOS Rep. 280, 38 ILM 1624 (1999)

Case Concerning the Conservation and Sustainable Exploitation of Swordfish Stocks in the Southern-Eastern Pacific Ocean (Chile v. *European Community)* (Order of 20 December 2000) [2000] ITLOS Rep. 146, 40 ILM 475 (2001)

The MOX Plant Case (Ireland v. *United Kingdom)* (Provisional Measures, Order of 3 December 2001) [2001] ITLOS Rep. 95, 41 ILM 405 (2002)

Kyrtatos v. *Greece* (ECtHR Judgment of 22 August 2003) Application no. 41666/98 [2003] HRCD 14

Legal Consequences of the Construction of a Wall in the Occupied Palestinian Territory (Advisory Opinion) [2004] ICJ Rep. 136

United States – Subsidies on Upland Cotton (WTO Appellate Body Report of 3 March 2005), WT/DS267/AB/R, DSR 2005:I

Pulp Mills on the River Uruguay (Argentina v. *Uruguay)* (Judgment) [2010] ICJ Rep. 14

Accordance with International Law of the Unilateral Declaration of Independence in respect of Kosovo (Advisory Opinion) [2010] ICJ Rep. 403

European Communities and Certain Member States – Measures Affecting Trade in Large Civil Aircraft (WTO Appellate Body Report of 18 May 2011) WT/DS316/AB/R, DSR 2011:I

M/V "Louisa" Case (*Saint Vincent and the Grenadines* v. *Kingdom of Spain)* (Provisional Measures, Order of 23 December 2010) [2008–2010] ITLOS Rep. 58

Mangouras v. *Spain* (ECtHR Grand Chamber Judgment, Merits) [2010] ECHR 1364, IHRL 1816

Application of the International Convention on the Elimination of All Forms of Racial Discrimination (Georgia v. *Russian Federation)* (Preliminary Objections, Judgment) [2011] ICJ Rep. 70

Responsibilities and obligations of States sponsoring persons and entities with respect to activities in the Area (Request for Advisory Opinion submitted to the Seabed Disputes Chamber) (Advisory Opinion) [2011] ITLOS Rep. 7

Judgment No. 2867 of the Administrative Tribunal of the International Labour Organization upon a Complaint Filed against the International Fund for Agricultural Development (Advisory Opinion) [2012] ICJ Rep. 10

Questions relating to the obligation to prosecute or extradite (Belgium v. *Senegal)* (Judgment) [2012] ICJ Rep. 422

Whaling in the Antarctic (Australia v. *Japan: New Zealand intervening)* (Judgment) [2014] ICJ Rep. 226

Rights and Guarantees of Children in the Context of Migration and/or in Need of International Protection (Advisory Opinion OC-21/14 of 19 August 2014) [2014] IACtHR Series A No. 21, www.refworld.org/cases,IACRTHR,54129c854.html

Chagos Marine Protected Area Arbitration (Mauritius v. *United Kingdom)* (Award of 18 March 2015) [2015] PCA Case No. 2011-03 https://files.pca-cpa.org/pcadocs/MU-UK%2020150318%20Award.pdf

Request for an Advisory Opinion submitted by the Sub-Regional Fisheries Commission (SRFC) (Advisory Opinion) [2015] ITLOS Rep. 1

Construction of a Road in Costa Rica along the San Juan River (Nicaragua v. *Costa Rica) and Certain Activities Carried Out by Nicaragua in the Border Area (Costa Rica* v. *Nicaragua)* (Judgment) [2015] ICJ Rep. 665

The South China Sea Arbitration (Philippines v. *China)* (Award of 12 July 2016) PCA Case No 2013-19 https://pcacases.com/web/sendAttach/2086

Timor-Leste v. *Australia (Decision on Australia's Objections to Competence of* 19 September 2016*)* PCA Conciliation Commission Case No 2016-10 https://pcacases.com/web/sendAttach/10052

Case C-461/13 *Bund für Umwelt und Naturschutz Deutschland* v. *Bundesrepublik Deutschland* (The Weser Case) (Judgment of 1 July 2015) ECLI:EU:C:2015:433

Obligations concerning Negotiations relating to Cessation of the Nuclear Arms Race and to Nuclear Disarmament (Marshall Islands v. *India)* (Jurisdiction and Admissibility, Judgment) [2016] ICJ Rep. 255

Obligations concerning Negotiations relating to Cessation of the Nuclear Arms Race and to Nuclear Disarmament (Marshall Islands v. *Pakistan)* (Jurisdiction and Admissibility, Judgment) [2016] ICJ Rep. 552

Obligations concerning Negotiations relating to Cessation of the Nuclear Arms Race and to Nuclear Disarmament (Marshall Islands v. *United Kingdom)* (Preliminary Objections, Judgment) [2016] ICJ Rep. 833

The Obligations in Matters of Human Rights of a State That Has Denounced the American Convention on Human Rights and the Charter of the Organization of American States (Advisory Opinion OC-22/16 of 26 February 2016) [2016] IACtHR Series A No. 22

Maritime Delimitation in the Indian Ocean (Somalia v. *Kenya)*, Preliminary Objections, Judgment, ICJ Reports 2017, 3, 161-20170202-ORD-01-00-BI.pdf (icj-cij.org)

The Environment and Human Rights (State Obligation in relation to the environment in the context of the protection and guarantee of the rights to life and to personal integrity interpretation and scope of articles 4(1) and 5 (1) in relation to Articles 1(1) and 2 of the American Convention on Human

Rights) (Advisory Opinion OC-23/17 of 15 November 2017) [2017] IACtHR Series A No. 23 www.corteidh.or.cr/docs/opiniones/seriea_23_ing.pdf

Certain Activities Carried Out by Nicaragua in the Border Area (Costa Rica v. *Nicaragua)* (Compensation, Judgment) [2018] ICJ Rep. 15

The M/V "Norstar" case (Panama v. *Italy)* (Judgment of 10 April 2019) [2918–2918] ITLOS Rep. 10

Legal Consequences of the Separation of the Chagos Archipelago from Mauritius in 1965 (Advisory Opinion) [2019] ICJ Rep. 95

Dispute concerning delimitation of the maritime boundary between Mauritius and Maldives in the Indian Ocean (Mauritius/Maldives) (Preliminary Objections, Judgment of 28 January 2021) ITLOS Rep. 2020-2021, p. 17.

Abbreviations

AB	appellate body (WTO)
ABNJ	areas beyond national jurisdiction
ABPMM	area-based protection and management measures
ABS	access and benefit-sharing
AC	Arctic Council
AHTEG	The Ad Hoc Technical Expert Group
AMOC	Atlantic meridional overturning circulation
AOA	agreement on agriculture (WTO)
ATS	Antarctic Treaty System
Basel Convention	Convention on the Control of Transboundary Movements of Hazardous Wastes and Their Disposal
BBNJ	biodiversity beyond national jurisdiction
BMSY	biomass that enables a fish stock to deliver the maximum sustainable yield
BSAP	Baltic Sea Action Plan
CBD	Convention on Biological Diversity
CCAMLR	Commission for the Conservation of Antarctic Marine Living Resources
CCSBT	Convention for the Conservation of Southern Bluefin Tuna
CIGI	Centre for International Governance Innovation
CJEU	Court of Justice of the European Union
CLCS	Commission on the Limits of the Continental Shelf
CMAR	The Eastern Tropical Pacific Marine Corridor
CMM	conservation and management measures
CMS	Convention on Migratory Species of Wild Animals

CO_2	carbon dioxide
COC	ASEAN code of conduct
COFI	The FAO Committee on Fisheries
COLREG	Convention on the International Regulations for Preventing Collisions at Sea, 1972 (COLREGs)
COP	conference of parties
COPUOS	UN Committee on the Peaceful Uses of Outer Space
COSIS	Commission of Small Island States on Climate Change and International Law
CPPS	Permanent Commission for the South Pacific (Comisión Permanente del Pacifico Sur)
CTE	Committee on Trade and Environment (WTO)
DNA	deoxyribonucleic acid
DOALOS	United Nations Division for Ocean Affairs and the Law of the Sea
DOC	China–ASEAN Declaration on Conduct of the Parties in the South China Sea
DSI	digital sequence information
DSM	dispute settlement mechanism
EA	ecosystem approach
EAF	ecosystem approach to fisheries
EBSA	ecologically and biologically significant area
ECHR	European Convention on Human Rights
ECtHR	European Court of Human Rights
EEZ	exclusive economic zone
EIA	environmental impact assessment
ESA	European Space Agency
Espoo Convention	Convention on Environmental Impact Assessment in a Transboundary Context
ETP	Eastern Tropical Pacific
ETPO	Eastern Tropical Pacific Ocean
EU	European Union
EU IUU Regulation	Council Regulation (EC) No 1005/2008 of 29 September 2008 establishing a Community system to prevent, deter and eliminate illegal, unreported and unregulated fishing, amending Regulations (EEC) No 2847/93, (EC) No 1936/2001 and (EC) No 601/2004 and repealing Regulations (EC) No 1093/94 and (EC) No 1447/1999
FAA	fisheries access agreement

FAO	Food and Agricultural Organization of the United Nations
FMSY	fishing mortality consistent with achieving Maximum Sustainable Yield (MSY)
FTA	free trade agreement
GATT	General Agreement on Tariffs and Trade
GES	good environmental status
GESAMP	Joint Group of Experts on the Scientific Aspects of Marine Environmental Protection
GFCM	General Fisheries Commission for the Mediterranean
GHG	green house gas emissions
GLT	green legal theory
GPA	The Global Programme of Action for Protection of the Marine Environment from Land-Based Activities
Gt	gross tonnage
HELCOM	Helsinki Commission / Baltic Marine Environment Protection Commission
HRCD	Human Rights Case Digest
IACtHR	Inter-American Court of Human Rights
IASC	International Arctic Science Committee
IASS	Institute for Advanced Sustainability Studies
IATTC	Inter-American Tropical Tuna Commission
IAU	International Astronomic Union
ICC	International Chamber of Commerce
ICES	International Council for the Exploration of the Sea
ICISS	International Commission on Intervention and State Sovereignty
ICJ	International Court of Justice
ICJ Rep.	ICJ reports of judgments, advisory opinions and orders
ICRW	International Convention for the Regulation of Whaling
IDDRI	Institute for Sustainable Development and International Relations
IEBMM	integrated ecosystem-based marine management
IHRL	international human rights law
ILC	International Law Commission
ILM	international legal materials

IMO	International Maritime Organization
INTERPOL	The International Criminal Police Organization
IOC	Intergovernmental Oceanographic Commission of UNESCO
IPBES	Intergovernmental Science-Policy Platform on Biodiversity and Ecosystem Services
IPCC	Intergovernmental Panel on Climate Change
IPOA IUU	FAO international plan of action to prevent, deter, and eliminate illegal, unreported and unregulated fishing
ISA	International Seabed Authority
ITLOS	International Tribunal for the Law of the Sea
ITLOS Rep.	ITLOS reports of judgments, advisory opinions and orders
ITPGRFA	The International Treaty on Plant Genetic Resources for Food and Agriculture
IUCN	International Union for Conservation of Nature
IUCN-ELC	IUCN Environmental Law Centre
IUU fishing	illegal, unreported and unregulated fishing
IWC	International Whaling Commission
Kyoto Protocol	Kyoto Protocol to the United Nations Framework Convention on Climate Change
LDC	least developed country
LME	large marine ecosystem
London Convention	Convention on the Prevention of Marine Pollution by Dumping of Wastes and Other Matter
MAFF	Ministry of Agriculture, Forestry and Fisheries
MARPOL	International Convention for the Prevention of Pollution from Ships
MC	ministerial conference (WTO)
MGRs	marine genetic resources
MLRs	marine living resources
Montreal Protocol	Montreal Protocol on Substances that deplete the ozone layer
MPAs	marine protected areas
MSFD	marine strategy framework directive
MSP	maritime spatial planning
MSPD	maritime spatial planning directive
MSR	marine scientific research
MSY	maximum sustainable yield
NAMCCO	North Atlantic Marine Mammal Commission

NDC	nationally determined contribution
NEAFC	North East Atlantic Fisheries Commission
NGR	negotiating group on rules (WTO)
nm	nautical miles
NOAA	The United States National Oceanic and Atmospheric Administration
NPS	UN principles relevant to the use of nuclear power in outer space
OECD	Organisation for Economic Cooperation and Development
OJ	*Official Journal of the European Union*
OSPAR Convention	Convention for the Protection of the Marine Environment of the North-East Atlantic
OZ	ocean zoning
PA	Paris Agreement to the United Nations Framework Convention on Climate Change
PAG	Pacific Arctic Group
PAME	Arctic Council Working Group on Protection of the Arctic Marine Environment
PCA	Permanent Court of Arbitration
PCIJ	Permanent Court of International Justice
PCIJ Rep.	PCIJ collection of judgment and advisory opinions
PICES	North Pacific Marine Science Organization
PSMA	agreement on port state measures
PSSA	particularly sensitive sea areas
RCRA	Resource Conservation and Recovery Act (US Law)
RECIEL	*Review of European, Comparative & International Environmental Law*
RFB	regional fisheries bodies
RFMA	regional fisheries management arrangement
RFMO	Regional Fisheries Management Organisation
RIIA	United Nations, Reports of International Arbitral Awards
RMC	regional ministerial committee
RMP	revised management procedure
RNA	ribonucleic acid
ROG	regional ocean governance
RSP	Regional Seas Programme
RTC	regional technical committee
SBT cases	southern bluefin tuna cases
SCM	subsidies and countervailing measures

SCS	South China Sea
SDG	sustainable development goal
SDT	special and differential treatment
SJD	San José Declaration
SOLAS	International Convention for the Safety of Life at Sea
SPS	sanitary and phytosanitary measures
TAC	ASEAN Treaty of Amity and Cooperation in Southeast Asia
TBT	technical barriers to trade
TFEU	Treaty on the Functioning of the European Union
TMG	think tank for sustainability
TOC	the ocean cleanup
TRIPS Agreement	The Agreement on Trade-Related Aspects of Intellectual Property Rights
UKTS	The United Kingdom Treaty Series
UN	United Nations
UNCLOS	United Nations Convention on the Law of the Sea
UNCLOS III	The 3rd United Nations Conference on the Law of the Sea (1973–1982)
UNCTAD	United Nations Conference on Trade and Development
UNEA	United Nations Environmental Assembly
UNECE	United Nations Economic Commission for Europe
UNEP	United Nations Environment Programme
UNEP-WCMC	UNEP World Conservation Monitoring Centre
UNESCO	United Nations Educational, Scientific and Cultural Organization
UNFCCC	United Nations Framework Convention on Climate Change
UNFSA	United Nations Agreement Relating to the Conservation and Management of Straddling Fish Stocks and Migratory Fish Stocks
UNGA	United Nations General Assembly
UNISPACE	United Nations Conference on the Exploration and Peaceful Uses of Outer Space
UNODC	United Nations Office on Drugs and Crime
UNTOC	United Nations Convention against Transnational Organized Crime
UNTS	United Nations Treaty Series

USC	United States code
USCA	United States code annotated
USD	United States dollar
VLCT	Vienna Convention on the Law of Treaties
WFD	Water Framework Directive
WTO	World Trade Organization
WWF	World Wide Fund for Nature

PART I

Introduction

1

The Environmental Rule of Law for Oceans

Froukje Maria Platjouw and Alla Pozdnakova

1.1 INTRODUCTION: OCEANS UNDER THREAT

Various economic activities have severe impacts on marine ecosystems. These impacts include habitat destruction; visible pollution such as plastic litter, particles and oil spills; invisible pollution such as microplastics, underwater noise, chemicals and nutrients; and hydro-morphological changes to the seabed. Additionally, climate change and greenhouse gas emissions adversely impact seas, coasts and people living in those areas. Climate change leads to changes in water temperature, acidification, intensifying algae blooms, rising sea levels and more frequent and intense flooding and erosion. In combination with threats posed by biodiversity loss, which is driven by climate change, pollution, over-exploitation of resources and the destruction of natural habitats, these impacts will severely challenge the resilience of marine ecosystems, and consequently, of societies around coastlines. Without urgent and coherent action, our oceans face an uncertain future. We still have a chance to protect and restore marine ecosystems if we act decisively and coherently and strike a sustainable balance between how we use our seas and how we protect them.

Clearly, strengthening the rule of law for oceans is urgent. Many of our seas are among the busiest marine regions in the world, where multiple maritime sectors are competing for increased space. Complex multi-level and multi-sector governance landscapes have unfolded over several decades, resulting in a situation where existing legal and policy frames of reference contain overlaps, gaps, weaknesses and inconsistencies.[1] Authorities responsible for implementation and compliance are affected by institutional challenges, and actors may face a lack of clarity and predictability, while local communities and other stakeholder groups may not be

[1] UN General Assembly (2018) Gaps in international environmental law and environment-related instruments: towards a global pact for the environment. 30 November.

sufficiently or effectively included in planning, policymaking and decision-making, negatively affecting legitimacy and inclusiveness. Challenges also arise in the context of difficult science–policy–society interfaces, where a lack of sound methods and mechanisms to systematically handle incomplete scientific knowledge, uncertainty and contested knowledge, and the broader institutional challenges related to environmental policy integration and coordination, easily lead to unsustainable outcomes and failure to prioritize preservation of the environment and oceans.

After many decades of intensive law-making, we now face highly comprehensive, multi-level and multi-sector policy and legal frameworks that apply to the marine domain. Arguably, this strengthens the rule of law, in that the overall picture appears to provide a web of laws and regulations that could provide clarity and predictability with regard to the rights and duties of citizens, private actors, authorities and States, fostering predictability, accountability, clarity, legal certainty and coherence. The question is, though, whether this backdrop also ensures the *environmental* rule of law for oceans. Is law effective enough and strong enough to ensure protection of our oceans against increasing pressures and demands?

This book explores the environmental rule of law for oceans from a range of different perspectives. As an overarching question we ask whether existing legal frameworks are sufficiently effective, dynamic and robust enough to address new challenges and pressures in light of advanced scientific knowledge and understanding of oceans. Do we have adequate governance and compliance mechanisms and solutions in place to ensure satisfactory implementation of the law in its existing and evolving dimensions? And how can we further strengthen the rule of law for better protection of our oceans. The book provides future-oriented perspectives on how law should evolve to better preserve the oceans. All chapters incorporate novel insights and ideas for legal solutions that might inspire scholars, actors, authorities, citizens and communities around the globe.

1.2 FROM RULE OF LAW TO ENVIRONMENTAL RULE OF LAW FOR OCEANS

The rule of law is essential for democracy and good governance. Multiple approaches to and understandings of the rule of law have evolved at the national level, and notion(s) of the rule of law are accordingly influenced by (and adjusted to) national legal contexts.[2] The traditional meaning of the rule of law, though, is a system of governance based on generally applicable abstract rules and limited state discretion, in which the government is subject to the same law as individual citizens. This means that governments are bound by rules fixed and announced beforehand. As such, these rules enable foreseeing with fair certainty how authorities will

[2] For an overview of these main approaches see, e.g., Henk Addink, *Good Governance: Concept and Context* (Oxford: Oxford University Press 2019), 75–76.

implement legislation and policies.[3] The formal elements of the rule of law therefore encompass the notions that law must be set forth in advance (be prospective), be made public, be general, be clear, be stable and certain and be applied to everyone according to its terms.[4] Application of laws should be administered by impartial and independent courts that are reasonably accessible to all, and people and governments ought to be given adequate opportunity to comply with the law.[5]

Probably the best-known aspects of the rule of law are the eight formal principles of Lon Fuller's 'inner morality of law'. Fuller's account of the rule of law requires that the State should do whatever it wants to do in an orderly and predictable way, giving us plenty of advance notice by publicizing the general norms on which its actions will be based, and that it should then stick to those norms and not arbitrarily depart from them even if it seems politically advantageous to do so.[6] More specifically, Fuller suggested the following principles:

1. *Generality*: Legal prescriptions must be issued at some level of generality. No legal system can function by addressing its prescriptions to individuals, one by one, or by addressing each particular act separately.
2. *Promulgation*: For the law to be able to guide human conduct, it must be promulgated to its subjects. People can only be guided by rules or prescriptions if they know about the existence of the rule or prescription.
3. *No retroactive rules*: For the law to be able to guide human conduct, it must prescribe modes of behaviour prospectively. Retroactive rules, which purport to affect behaviour which had already occurred prior to promulgation of a rule, cannot achieve the purpose of actually guiding human conduct.
4. *Clarity*: Rules or prescriptions can only guide human conduct if the subjects understand what the rule requires. Promulgation is not enough. A certain level of understanding of the rule is essential in order to follow the rule.
5. *No contradictory rules*: For similar reasons, if a rule prescribes one thing and at the same time prescribes a contradictory or inconsistent rule, people cannot follow it. Or if people are required to do x by one rule and not-x by another rule, then there is no way in which they are able to follow both.
6. *No impossible prescriptions*: A rule or prescription may be comprehensible and not inconsistent but, in practice, impossible to follow. A rule

[3] Friedrich A. Hayek, *The Road to Serfdom* (Chicago: University of Chicago Press 1944).

[4] Brian Z. Tamanaha, 'A Concise Guide to the Rule of Law', in Neil Walker and Gianluggi Palombella (eds.), *Florence Workshop on the Rule of Law* (Oxford: Hart Publishing 2007), 3.

[5] Andrei Marmor, 'The Ideal of the Rule of Law', *USC Legal Studies Research Paper* No. 08-6 (2008) 1.

[6] Ibid., 6; see further Lon Fuller, *The Morality of Law* (New Haven: Yale University Press 1969), 46–90.

that people cannot follow is a rule that cannot guide human conduct, even if it is understood perfectly well. To guide human conduct, rules must require conduct that is feasible for the rule subjects.

7. *Stability*: It is generally assumed that some level of stability over time is essential for the law to achieve its purposes, whatever they are. The law can change, of course, but the assumption is that if changes are too frequent, people cannot follow the law. This stems partly from the fact that many of our actions that the law purports to regulate require advance planning, preparation and a certain level of guaranteed expectations about the future normative environment.
8. *Consistent application*: For the law to be able to guide human conduct, it must maintain considerable congruence between the rules promulgated and their actual application to specific cases. In other words, the law cannot guide human conduct if actual deviations from it are not treated as such, namely as deviations from the rule. This is actually a highly complex requirement, which entails a whole range of principles and practices. Generally speaking, it requires that agencies dealing with enforcing and applying law to specific cases actually apply rules promulgated by the law.[7]

These are the formal aspects of the rule of law because they concern the form of those norms that are applied to our conduct: generality, prospectivity, stability, publicity, clarity and so on.[8] An important benefit of the rule of law is thus that it enhances legal certainty, predictability and legitimacy.[9] It restricts the discretion of government officials, reducing wilfulness and arbitrariness. Government officials may be unduly influenced in their government actions by inappropriate considerations – by prejudice, by whim, by arbitrariness, by passion, by ill will or a foul disposition or by any of the many factors that warp human decision-making and actions.[10] The rule of law constrains these factors by insisting that government officials act pursuant to and consistent with applicable legal rules. Government officials are required to consult and conform to the law both before and during

[7] Andrei Marmor, 'The Rule of Law and Its Limits', *USC Public Policy Research Paper No. 03-16* (2003) 6–8.
Referring to Lon Fuller in his book *The Morality of Law*, ch. 2. Many others have basically endorsed Fuller's list, for example: John Finnis, *Natural Law and Natural Rights* (2nd ed., Oxford: Oxford University Press 2011), 270–276; N. MacCormick, 'Natural Law and the Separation of Law and Morals', in Robert P. George (ed.), *Natural Law Theory: Modern Essays* (Oxford: Clarendon Press 1992); and Joseph Raz, *The Authority of Law* (Oxford: Oxford University Press 2009), ch.11.

[8] Jeremy Waldron, 'The Concept of and the Rule of Law', *Public Law & Legal Theory Research Paper Series Working Papers No. 08-5* (2008) 8.

[9] Ibid., 1.

[10] Ibid., 9.

actions, and legal rules provide publicly available requirements and standards that can be used to hold government officials accountable during and after their actions.[11]

1.2.1 *The International Dimension*

The rule of law is also highly relevant at the international level. The notion of the international rule of law has been critically examined in the scholarly literature. On the one hand, the international rule of law has to a large extent evolved from concepts and practices of the rule of law at the national level. This is evident in some of the essential aspects of the international rule of law as formulated by the UN, international courts and legal scholars (accountability, non-arbitrariness, predictability, certainty and so on).[12] On the other hand, the absence in international law of certain normative and institutional qualities characteristic of the national legal order,[13] alongside concerns pertaining to the (seeming or real) disruption of the unity of the international legal order,[14] gives reasons to doubt the very existence of the international rule of law.

In the international legal system, all States are sovereigns and equals. No legislative, executive or judicial powers exist with competence to bind States, or non-State actors, or take enforcement or coercive measures against those not complying with international law.[15] Moreover, the UN speaks of the 'rule of law at the international level', not 'international rule of law'; however, it seeks to promote 'an international order based on the rule of law and international law'.[16] These aspects have also been acknowledged by the United Nations Security Council, which stresses that the rule of law requires 'measures to ensure adherence to the principles of supremacy of law, equality before the law, accountability to the law, fairness in application of the law, separation of powers, participation in decision-making, legal certainty, avoidance of arbitrariness, and procedural and legal transparency'.[17]

It has been suggested that the various components of the rule of law at the international level may be of a different character from those at the national level.[18] Notwithstanding, some common requirements of the rule of law acceptable to all

[11] Ibid.

[12] See, e.g., discussion by Noora Arajärvi, 'The Core Requirements of the International Rule of Law in the Practice of States', *Hague Journal on the Rule of Law* (2021) 13: 173–193.

[13] Simon Chesterman, 'An International Rule of Law?', *The American Journal of Comparative Law* (2008) 56(2): 331–361.

[14] Arajärvi (n 12), 173–193.

[15] Robert McCorquodale, 'Defining the International Rule of Law: Defying Gravity?', *International and Comparative Law Quarterly* (2016) 65: 277–304.

[16] Ibid.

[17] United Nations Security Council, *The Rule of Law and Transitional Justice in Conflict and Post-Conflict Societies: Report of the Secretary General*, document no. S/2004/616 (United Nations 2004).

[18] McCorquodale (n 15), 277–304, 290.

States can be identified, such as non-arbitrariness, consistency and predictability (as minimum core requirements).[19]

At the international level, the rule of law presupposes at the very least that norm-creating behaviour and compliance with environmental obligations are not incidental, *ad hoc* actions guided by random considerations of power interplay or self-interest on the part of actors. Indeed, the rule of law implies that actors operate under a shared understanding that their actions (or abstention from action) are required and controlled by certain principles and norms. Thus, actors are guided by a common perception of legal obligations and a sense of legal commitment to shared values.[20] Such a shared, reciprocal commitment to law is crucial for the existence and effectiveness of law, because problems are mostly not local, but international and global, including transboundary pollution of oceans and climate change.

For that reason, as argued by Brunnée and Toope, who build on the views of Fuller, '[l]aw does not depend on hierarchy between law-givers and subjects, but on reciprocity between all participants in the enterprise. By "reciprocity" we mean that law is not a "one-way street". It can exist only when actors collaborate to build shared understandings and uphold a practice of legality.'[21] They view the notion of reciprocity as standing at the very heart of the interactional account of international law.

1.2.2 *The Rule of Law for Oceans*

In addition to these formal requirements of the rule of law, the concept also contains a substantive content requiring that law complies with internationally recognized human rights norms and standards regarding fundamental rights and freedoms, personal security and protection of personal integrity.[22] The substantive dimension of the rule of law may be particularly important for protection of our oceans. In the context of environmental and ecosystem degradation, the concept of the rule of law has also been given a more specific understanding through introducing the concept of the 'rule of law for nature'.[23] This refers to a 'system of governance in which all persons, institutions and entities, public and private, including the State itself, are accountable to laws that aim at protecting the health, integrity and security of the

[19] e.g., Arajärvi (n 12), 173–193.
[20] See, e.g., Fuller (n 6).
[21] Jutta Brunnée and Stephen J. Toope, *Legitimacy and Legality in International Law: An Interactional Account* (Cambridge: Cambridge University Press 2013), 7, https://doi.org/10.1017/CBO9780511781261
[22] Hans Christian Bugge, 'Twelve Fundamental Challenges in Environmental Law', in Christina Voigt (ed.), *Rule of Law for Nature: New Dimensions and Ideas in Environmental Law* (Cambridge: Cambridge University Press 2013), 6–7.
[23] Christina Voigt (ed.), *Rule of Law for Nature: New Dimensions and Ideas in Environmental Law* (Cambridge: Cambridge University Press 2013).

environment'.[24] As such, the concept encompasses local, national, regional and international levels of governance. Given the transversal nature of many types of ecosystems, including oceans, this partly blurs the distinction between national and international rule of law.[25] Environmental issues have always transcended national borders and existed even in those areas where the borderlines between the national and international legal order become unclear, that is, areas beyond national jurisdiction.[26] For that reason, both dimensions are equally relevant for the protection of our oceans.

Bugge explains that the rule of law for nature means better legal protection of nature from human activities that may threaten or damage nature. Substantially, it aims at the integrity and security of nature.[27] This means that nature and natural values are protected by law from encroachments, deterioration and destruction in fundamentally the same way as citizens are protected by law. Of course, this does not mean that nature and its values must be protected at any price, regardless of other conflicting goals or interests. But those goals or interests must be strong enough to justify environmental damage, and procedural rules must be available to ensure that the trade-off is made with due regard to nature's value and all other relevant facts. Rule of law for nature means predictability, security and the absence of arbitrariness and bias in decisions that affect nature, as well as a full accounting of environmental values in decision-making – be it by private or public authorities.[28] In essence, a legal system would not be adhering to the rule of law if it fails to prevent people from destroying the functioning of ecosystems.[29] Likewise, Bosselmann notices that connecting the rule of law to the ecological challenge is very timely and that law has been complicit in the sense of legitimizing and legalizing excessive growth and environmental destruction.[30]

The importance of the rule of law for environmental protection and sustainable development has received significant impetus through adoption of the Agenda 2030, and particularly through Sustainable Development Goal (SDG) 16. As described in the 2016 UNDP Annual Report on The Rule of Law and Human Rights, SDG 16 – for peaceful, just and inclusive societies – ushers a new kind of development: one where people have the opportunity to influence decisions that affect their lives and create communities that thrive. SDG 16 articulates the key role that governance and the rule of law play in promoting peaceful, just and inclusive societies and in ensuring sustainable development. As such, adhering to the rule of law will enhance the implementation of, for example, SDG 14, which aims to

[24] Bugge (n 22), 5.
[25] Arajärvi (n 12), 173–193.
[26] Ibid., 177.
[27] Voigt (ed.) (n 23).
[28] Bugge (n 22), 7–8.
[29] Cormac Cullinan, 'The Rule of Nature's Law', in Voigt (ed.) (n 23), 100.
[30] Klaus Bosselmann, 'Grounding the Rule of Law', in Voigt (ed.) (n 23), 76.

conserve and – sustainably – exploit the oceans, seas and marine resources with a view to sustainable development.

1.3 AIM OF THE BOOK

At present, our oceans need a strong and effective environmental rule of law. Adhering to the rule of law through clear, predictable, coherent and legitimate rules will contribute to the protection of our oceans against increased pressures and demands. In this book, we are searching for ways to improve, strengthen and further develop the environmental rule of law for oceans. In short, the environmental rule of law for oceans requires the existence of a set of rules and policies at multiple governance levels that appropriately regulate human activities at sea and ensure that pressures on the marine ecosystem are tackled effectively. As such, law should contribute to ensuring the long-term functioning of our marine ecosystems and ocean resilience.

Throughout the book, we identify and critically examine different areas of law that need to change or evolve to respond to pressures on our oceans and future challenges in terms of governing the oceans in times to come. The authors examine whether current legal frameworks are sufficiently effective to address new challenges and pressures in light of advanced scientific knowledge and understanding of oceans. They thereby also shed light on whether we have adequate governance and compliance mechanisms and solutions in place to ensure the effectiveness of the law in its existing and evolving dimensions. The authors address different rule of law norms, such as legitimacy, coherence, clarity and legal certainty and accountability. In addition, they propose solutions to identified regulatory weaknesses, gaps or other barriers that adversely affect protection of the oceans. In some areas, existing laws may need to evolve, adapt and improve, while in other areas we need to think afresh. Together, the twenty-five chapters in this book seek to contribute to the overarching question, namely what new legal solutions are needed to strengthen the environmental rule of law for oceans?

1.4 STRUCTURE OF THE BOOK

The book consists of six parts. Part I introduces the concept of the rule of law and more specifically the environmental rule of law for oceans. Part II focuses on a selection of current pressures on the marine environment and assesses regulatory and governance aspects from a rule of law perspective. Part III discusses the challenge of balancing conservation of the oceans in light of new demands and interests. Part IV presents proposals for innovative governance approaches that contribute to effectiveness, legitimacy and other rule of law values. Part V encompasses diverse regional regulatory and governance practices and experiences.

Finally, Part VI presents conclusions and solutions in terms of strengthening the environmental rule of law for oceans.

1.4.1 *Part II: Tackling Multiple Pressures on the Oceans*

Part II of the book addresses selected pressures on the oceans, including shipping, fishing, spaceflight-source pollution, plastic pollution and climate change. *Christina Voigt* addresses the impacts of climate change and greenhouse gas emissions on marine life and biodiversity and assesses to what extent this interlinkage is appropriately addressed in the UNCLOS and UNFCCC regimes. She goes on to discuss the opportunities for comprehensive and synergetic regulation in this regard. *David Testa* examines whether UNCLOS is fit-for-purpose in terms of addressing the problem of GHG emissions from shipping. To increase effectiveness, he notes that current provisions need to be complemented by more technical rules and measures that also need to be integrated with the wider international environmental law framework. This will enhance coherence, comprehensiveness and effectiveness. *Dawoon Jung* examines how the rule of law could be enhanced in relation to regulation of marine plastics and microplastics pollution. She stresses the need for cooperation and coordination between sector-specific instruments and between the multiple layers of regulations at global, regional and national levels, as well as adoption of a life-cycle approach to plastics. *Anastasia Telesetsky* sheds light on the problem of single-use plastic packaging and identifies several current weaknesses, including a lack of comprehensive and effective regulation as well as lack of accountability mechanisms. She urges States to agree to a single-use plastic product waste tariff and a fishing gear tariff to increase legal accountability for plastic pollution. Finally, *Alla Pozdnakova* presents an innovative perspective on pollution of the marine environment from spaceflight activities. In the absence of specific environmental provisions in the international law of outer space, she discusses the effectiveness of the applicable environmental law provisions from general environmental laws and multilateral environmental agreements such as the UN Convention on the Law of the Sea.

1.4.2 *Part III: Balancing the Exploitation and Preservation of Ocean Resources*

Part III of the book presents a variety of perspectives on resources or challenges in need of a proper balance between use and preservation. It also examines the usefulness of the precautionary principle for the management of living resources and problems pertaining to the use of resources beyond national jurisdiction. *Rozemarijn Roland Holst* addresses the problem of marine plastic pollution and specifically discusses the legal challenges raised by the use of new technologies for marine environmental restoration purposes, using The Ocean Cleanup's plastic clean-up activities in areas beyond national jurisdiction as a case study. Next, *Brita Bohman and Henrik Ringbom* analyze the challenges to the rule of law related to different types of risks and benefits of activities and related uncertainty. The authors shed light on the challenge posed by novel technologies to combat eutrophication in the Baltic Sea, thereby also exploring how marine environmental law operates in the absence of specific rules and how environmental law principles manage to fill legal gaps. In particular, they discuss the case of 'sea-based measures' to target pollution that has already been released into the sea, as a complement to land-based measures to prevent marine pollution. In view of the purely environmental objectives behind these technologies and the scientific uncertainty that surrounds their effectiveness, the case study presents particular challenges in terms of balancing the interests at stake, thereby establishing the content and role of law in this field. *Aref Shams* analyses utilization of icebergs for fresh water and discusses the legality of proposed plans for such action. Despite a gap in the regulatory capacities of international law, this is an example of emerging demands on the oceans, which need to be regulated by an adequate rule of law. *Maurus Wollensak* studies the management of living resources under the United Nations Convention on the Law of the Sea, in particular considering the so-called precautionary principle/approach. He discusses to what extent application of the precautionary principle/approach is required and fit-for-purpose in respect to management of living resources *vel non*. *Pierre Cloutier de Repentigny* discusses law's capacity to adequately protect marine biodiversity through green legal theory. He demonstrates the entanglement of the UNCLOS marine conservation framework with economic growth and reflects on how to move past the limitations of this framework to build better rules for the protection of marine life, including beyond national jurisdiction. *Mitchell Lennan* addresses whether and to what extent the international legal framework adequately places an obligation on States to adapt to the complexities caused by marine living resources shifting their location (redistribution of fish stocks under climate change). He points out that despite a general obligation on States, there are gaps in law and governance with respect to addressing fluctuating or changing distributions of fish stocks. *Jakub Ciesielczuk* stresses the importance of the legal definition of marine genetic resources for the legal certainty and clarity of international legal regimes, and goes on to provide a working, legal definition of marine genetic resources. A compass in the form of a working definition of MGRs helps navigate the sea of uncertainties and strenghtens the rule of law.

1.4.3 *Part IV: Paths towards Effective Ocean Governance, Implementation and Compliance*

Part IV of the book examines a variety of tools and mechanisms – and the gaps in existing tools and mechanisms – to ensure implementation and compliance with the law. Different issues require different solutions and tools, so this Part consists of chapters addressing litigation and the role of international courts; regulation of environmental crimes and the need for international law development in this field; and the role of the international trade organization – the WTO – with regard to sustainable fisheries. *David Langlet* assesses and compares the extent to which and how legitimacy is considered in the three main legal instruments making up the EU regulatory framework for marine conservation, blue growth and efficient use of marine space, that is, the Water Framework Directive, the Marine Strategy Framework Directive and the Maritime Spatial Planning Directive. He identifies various legitimacy challenges in this regard and potential for strengthening these. *Vasco Becker-Weinberg* focuses on maritime environmental crimes as one of the main causes of the destruction of marine ecosystems and devastation of marine life, also discussing the lack of a joint international regulatory approach to these crimes. He emphasizes the need for a new global paradigm that is also aligned with international law. *Pieter van Welzen* discusses illegal fisheries as a pressure on global marine resources as well as on the economies and societies of many developing coastal States. He questions the effectiveness of fisheries regulations and in particular their enforcement in tackling illegal fisheries. *Carlos A. Cruz Carrillo* examines the potential of the advisory jurisdiction of the plenary of the International Tribunal for the Law of the Sea (ITLOS) to strengthen ocean governance. Since its conception, the legal basis of this judicial function has been unclear. Nevertheless, these instruments could assist in adapting the UNCLOS to new challenges such as climate change or technological developments. *Leonila Guglya* assesses the potential contribution of the WTO to the rule of law for oceans through prohibitions of subsidies contributing to overcapacity and overfishing; subsidies for fishing on overfished stocks; and subsidies to vessels and/or operators involved in IUU fishing. Finally, *Solène Guggisberg* sheds light on litigation as a tool to improve compliance with international fisheries law. The traditional regime regulating international fisheries appears inadequate at ensuring the rule of law, since many States are unwilling or unable to respect their relevant obligations. She stresses that recourse to international courts and tribunals is an option that should be considered by States, in that it could bring an end to specific violations, hence tackling the most egregious cases of non-compliance, as well as enabling clarification of certain obligations.

1.4.4 *Part V: Strengthening the Rule of Law in Regional Seas and Oceans*

Part V of the book provides regional solutions to environmental pressures and challenges to governance from a rule of law perspective. This part covers case studies from the Baltic Sea, Africa, the Eastern Tropical Pacific, the South China Sea and Northeast Asia. *Sarah Enright* analyses State-led regional cooperation efforts in the Eastern Tropical Pacific Ocean to create a transboundary marine corridor linking five Marine Protected Areas (MPAs) across four jurisdictions. This might potentially overcome challenges related to lack of a legally binding cooperation agreement, limited sectoral participation, the vast scale of the project and lack of a cohesive regional ocean governance framework. *Kirsi White* discusses oil Pollution Control Regulations in the Baltic Sea and discusses the potential effects of institutional interplay on implementation of the ecosystem approach. She suggests that development of institutional interlinkages may facilitate common policy objectives, decision-making and implementation of sectoral measures, also shedding light on the role of soft modes of governance from a rule of law perspective. *Andrey Todorov* addresses the ecosystem-based approach to Arctic Ocean governance. He discusses how to make regional measures in areas beyond national jurisdiction binding and ensure compliance by non-Arctic States; and how the ecosystem-based approach correlates with sectoral environmental measures regarding, in particular, fisheries, exploitation of resources in the Area and vessel traffic in the Arctic, adopted by relevant sectoral international organizations. *Constantinos Yiallourides* offers an overview of the Japanese legal system governing marine environmental conservation and Japan's approach towards the management, conservation and sustainable use of marine living resources, including whales. Commercial whaling is part of the broader international environmental law debate – ensuring environmental protection while facilitating sustainable use of the natural resources of the sea – and the author discusses the use of scientific knowledge and the precautionary principle. Finally, *Agnes Chong* takes a look at the South China Sea, where the rule of law is failing to protect the marine environment. Maritime claims and competition for resources often disregard conservation and sustainability, undermining cooperation on environmental protection. She discusses the requirements for cooperation and due regard, and the potential for a binding ASEAN Code of Conduct as a possible way forward.

1.4.5 *Part VI: Concluding Remarks*

Part VI concludes the book, wherein the editors reflect on legal solutions for changing oceans in light of the discussions throughout the book. Several cross-cutting rule of law challenges are discussed, including the absence of fit-for-purpose law, vagueness and ambiguity, lack of coordination and cooperation, lack of effective and enforceable law, the conflicting need for both specificity and generality under different circumstances, and so forth. The editors discuss the legal solutions identified throughout the book to these cross-cutting challenges and propose a way forward. The Part concludes with some answers and reflections related to the four main questions as identified in this chapter as key for the Rule of Law for Oceans.

PART II

Tackling Multiple Pressures on the Oceans

2

Oceans and Climate Change

Implications for UNCLOS and the UN Climate Regime

Christina Voigt

2.1 INTRODUCTION

The projected impacts of climate change on the oceans pose a significant threat to marine fisheries and biodiversity that might outpace other stress factors.[1] Increases in anthropogenic greenhouse gas (GHG) emissions and the consequential increase in GHG concentrations in the atmosphere have significant direct and indirect impacts on oceans and marine life.[2] Ocean warming might affect fish stocks, their health and migratory routes.[3] Ocean acidification linked to increased uptake of CO_2 as well as de-oxygenation due to increasing ocean stratification and less ventilation between surface and deeper waters are another two phenomena that could affect certain marine species as well as entire marine ecosystems.[4] At the same time, the global biomass of marine animals as well as the maximum catch potential of fisheries are both projected to decline.[5] Rebuilding overexploited and depleted fisheries and managing them sustainably is already being addressed under the United Nations Convention on the Law of the Sea (UNCLOS),[6] though much still needs to be done. However, using the oceans in a way that helps mitigate climate change provides an opportunity to address both concerns – climate change and declining ocean biomass – at the same time. It will require comprehensive governance structures for port, flag, coastal and market States, structures which also address

1 Intergovernmental Panel on Climate Change (IPCC), 2019, Summary for Policymakers. In: H.-O. Poertner et al. (eds.), *IPCC Special Report on the Ocean and Cryosphere in a Changing Climate*.
2 Intergovernmental Science-Policy Platform on Biodiversity and Ecosystem Services (IPBES), Report of the Plenary of the Intergovernmental Science-Policy Platform on Biodiversity and Ecosystem Services on the work of its seventh session (Report, IPBES/7/10/Add.1, 29 May 2019).
3 IPCC, *IPCC Special Report on the Ocean and Cryosphere in a Changing Climate* (n 1).
4 Ibid.
5 Ibid.
6 Montego Bay, 10 December 1982, in force 16 November 1994, 1833 UNTS 397.

the causes and impacts of climate change. This raises the question if and to what extent the international legal regime under UNCLOS and the UN climate regime can be coordinated and integrated, and how they can support one another in fully addressing the critical issue of the 'oceans and climate change nexus'.

The United Nations Framework Convention on Climate Change (UNFCCC)[7] was negotiated when the impacts of climate change on the oceans were not well understood and studied. However, we are facing the dilemma that, on the one hand, UNCLOS provides a comprehensive framework that is intended to cover all matters related to the oceans but does not expressly refer to climate change. On the other hand, we have an international regime – consisting of the UNFCCC, the Kyoto Protocol[8] and the Paris Agreement[9] – which is intended to cover matters related to climate change but which is territorial and atmospheric in scope, with very limited application to the ocean.

Addressing both concerns could open the way to opportunities for comprehensive and synergetic regulation. Such regulation contributes to strengthening the rule of law, in terms of enhancing effectiveness and legal certainty for marine protection. Compliance with both marine law and climate law could reinforce the targets and objectives of both regimes, so that the effects of climate change on the oceans decrease (for example, through setting climate targets) and the climate-mitigating capacity of oceans increases (for example, by conservation of a marine biology and ecosystems through marine protection measures). Appropriate synergy and coherence at a legal level between the marine and climate regimes will contribute to better protection of oceans in implementation at national, regional and local levels, thereby enhancing the rule of law for oceans.

2.2 SCIENTIFIC BACKGROUND

The interrelationship between the oceans and climate change is twofold. On the one hand, oceans are crucially important for regulating the global climate. They serve as the most important and biggest sink of anthropogenic CO_2, which is the strongest driver of climate change. Over millennia, they have been absorbing and storing CO_2 from the atmosphere, including about 30 per cent of emitted anthropogenic CO_2.[10] Ocean water also absorbs large quantities of energy (i.e., heat). More than 90 per cent of the excess heat in the climate system accumulated between

[7] New York, 9 May 1992, in force 21 March 1994, 1771 UNTS 107, https://unfccc.int/resource/docs/convkp/conveng.pdf.

[8] Kyoto Protocol to the United Nations Framework Convention on Climate Change, 11 December 1997, in force 16 February 2005, 2303 UNTS 162.

[9] Paris, 12 December 2015, in force 4 November 2016, https://unfccc.int/sites/default/files/english_paris_agreement.pdf.

[10] IPCC, *IPCC Special Report on the Ocean and Cryosphere in a Changing Climate* (n 1).

1971 and 2010 was absorbed by ocean waters, with only 1 per cent stored in the atmosphere.

On the other hand, oceans are significantly affected by the impacts of climate change, which can already be observed. Ocean properties are changing due to climate change, especially temperature, pH, oxygen content, salinity, carbon, ice sheet and albedo. The Intergovernmental Panel on Climate Change (IPPC) in its 2019 special report on oceans notes with virtual certainty that oceans are warming and that the rate of warming has doubled since 1993.[11]

The absorption of anthropogenic CO_2 is causing increasing surface acidification (decrease in pH). Moreover, de-oxygenation is occurring due to increasing ocean stratification, that is, reduced vertical exchanges of heat, salinity, oxygen, carbon and nutrients. Also, the conveyor belt of the Atlantic Meridional Overturning Circulation (AMOC) has started to weaken.[12]

Global sea levels are rising due to climate change caused by increasing ice loss from the Greenland and Antarctic ice sheets, as well as glaciers melting and ocean thermal expansion. From 2007 to 2016, the mass loss from the Antarctic ice sheet tripled compared to the previous decade, while loss from the Greenland ice sheet doubled and is accelerating. Ice loss from Antarctica has the potential to lead to a sea level rise of several metres within a few centuries. The IPCC warns that the changes already observed may mark the onset of irreversible ice sheet instability.

Ocean warming contributes to an overall decrease in maximum catch potential, compounding the impacts from illegal fishing and overfishing. This phenomenon also impacts biodiversity and ecosystem functioning, including impacts on catches, economic benefits, livelihoods, local and indigenous culture.[13] Given the close interconnection between oceans and climate change, this chapter aims to analyse the mutual links between the international regulatory framework for the oceans as expressed in UNCLOS and the UN regulatory framework to address climate change contained in the UNFCCC and the Paris Agreement. Through both regimes, the 'ocean-and-climate nexus' is governed by the rule of law. Its effectiveness in addressing the challenges of climate change, however, depends on how well these two regimes 'speak to each other'.

2.3 A WAY FORWARD?

The IPCC offers a number of strong suggestions for responses to the current and projected scenarios. Foremost among them are deep and rapid GHG emission

[11] Ibid.
[12] Ibid., at A 2.7.
[13] IPCC, *IPCC Special Report on the Ocean and Cryosphere in a Changing Climate* (n 1).

reductions in the coming decades[14] and ambitious adaptation of low-lying and other vulnerable or exposed areas. A central aspect, reiterated in all the latest IPCC reports, as well as the Intergovernmental Science-Policy Platform on Biodiversity and Ecosystem Services (IPBES) report on biodiversity, is that such rapid and deep reductions in emissions are unprecedented and require transformative governance changes.[15] The temporal scales of climate change impacts exceed the time horizons of most governance arrangements, which lack the ability to prepare for and respond to long-term changes. Governance arrangements such as marine protected areas, spatial plans and coastal management systems are largely ineffective to address such long-term challenges, as they are too fragmented across administrative boundaries and sectors to provide integrated responses to the cascading risks from climate change.[16]

However, these reports stress that such transformation requires the fundamental system-wide reorganization of all sectors and across economic, social and technological factors, including paradigms, goals and values. Both reports call for strengthening the global response and enhancing international cooperation. Climate change, global biodiversity loss and ocean impacts as collective action problems can only be effectively addressed through a system of international cooperation, management and implementation support, and through comprehensive and synergetic legislation. In other words, a crucial role exists for international law, and the rule of law, not only in creating a global level playing field that avoids free riding but also in creating the legal structure for a coordinated response commensurate with these global challenges.

2.4 CLIMATE CHANGE AND THE LAW OF THE SEA (UNCLOS)

In ocean governance, what is needed is a profound economic and institutional transformative change to enable climate-resilient development pathways for the oceans. The IPCC calls for intensifying cooperation and coordination among governing authorities across scales, jurisdictions, sectors, policy domains and

[14] IPCC, 2021, Summary for Policymakers. In: V. Masson-Delmotte et al. (eds.), *Climate Change 2021: The Physical Science Basis.*
Contribution of Working Group I to the Sixth Assessment Report of the Intergovernmental Panel on Climate Change.

[15] IPCC, 2018, Summary for Policymakers. In: *Global Warming of 1.5°C*. An IPCC Special Report on the impacts of global warming of 1.5°C above pre-industrial levels and related global greenhouse gas emission pathways, in the context of strengthening the global response to the threat of climate change, sustainable development and efforts to eradicate poverty (Report, October 2018), 3–24; and Intergovernmental Science-Policy Platform on Biodiversity and Ecosystem Services IPBES (n 3).

[16] Froukje Platjouw, *Environmental Law and the Ecosystem Approach: Maintaining Ecological Integrity through Consistency in Law* (London: Routledge 2016).

planning horizons in order to enable effective responses to ocean changes.[17] This requires compatible and coherent legal frameworks.

Climate change impacts will affect marine life and biodiversity, fisheries, shipping routes and maritime zones. It is, therefore, opportune to assess to what extent climate change has been addressed within the legal framework of the law of the sea, or could be brought within its embrace. It might not have been the intention at the time of developing the UNCLOS, but climate change issues could be addressed through contemporary and dynamic interpretation.

The UN General Assembly has successively reiterated its serious concern over the current and projected adverse effects of climate change on the marine environment and marine biodiversity, including coral reefs as well as the vulnerability of the environment and the fragile ecosystems of the polar regions, emphasizing the urgency of addressing this issue.[18] However, UNCLOS was negotiated during a period where concerns about climate change were not known or barely known. Consequently, despite the importance the Convention gave in Part XII to protection and preservation of the marine environment, understandably it does not explicitly refer to the adverse impacts of climate change on the ocean and the marine environment or the role that ocean governance could play in addressing climate change.

This situation does not mean that UNCLOS is not of relevance with respect to climate change. Under Article 192, States have the obligation to protect and preserve the marine environment. This applies to all areas of the oceans and to all impacts on the oceans. This obligation arguably also includes the duty to protect against climate change impacts. The Permanent Court of Arbitration, in the South China Sea Arbitration, stated clearly that the obligation to 'protect' the marine environment under UNCLOS includes protection from any future damage, while 'preserve' means to maintain or improve the existing condition of the marine environment. The Tribunal stated that these two elements included the obligation to take active measures and to prevent degradation of the existing marine environment.[19]

Such an approach would, at the very least, be applicable to the increased uptake of anthropogenic CO_2 leading to ocean acidification. Pollution, as widely defined in Article 1(1)(4) of UNCLOS, is 'the introduction by man, directly or indirectly, of

[17] IPCC, *IPCC Special Report on the Ocean and Cryosphere in a Changing Climate* (n 1), 41. In addition to regulation under UNCLOS, regional cooperation, including through regional treaties and conventions, can support effective action. Institutional arrangements that provide strong multiscale linkages would be beneficial in this situation. Coordination between national and transboundary regional policies and measures can address risks to resource security and management, such as for fisheries.

[18] UN A/RES/64/71 (https://undocs.org/en/A/RES/64/71); A/RES/66/231 (https://undocs.org/A/RES/66/231); A/RES/71/257 (https://undocs.org/en/A/RES/71/257).

[19] The South China Sea Arbitration (*Philippines* v. *China*) (Award of 12 July 2016) PCA Case no. 2013-19, para 941.

substances or energy into the marine environment, which results or is likely to result in such deleterious effects as harm to living resources and marine life, hazards to human health'. Anthropogenic CO_2 fits the definition in UNCLOS and therefore would come within its scope of application.

Further, Article 194 sets out the duty to adopt necessary measures to prevent, reduce and control pollution from any source, including transboundary pollution. This is a duty on all States to adopt measures to prevent transboundary pollution from sources or activities under their jurisdiction or control. Furthermore, Article 194(5) includes the duty to protect rare or fragile ecosystems and habitat or depleted, threatened or endangered species and other forms of marine life. This would also include a duty to protect against the impacts of climate change. In sum, the argument is that anthropogenic CO_2 is a transboundary source of pollution and that Articles 192 and 194 include the duty to protect the marine environment against climate change impacts.

The standard of conduct under Article 194 was elaborated by the International Tribunal for the Law of the Sea (ITLOS), which recognized that use of the language 'to ensure' creates an obligation of due diligence.[20] Such standard means that States need to adopt appropriate rules and measures, exercise vigilance in their enforcement and monitor the activities of private and public operators. It is an obligation to 'take all appropriate measures to enforce its relevant regulations on a public or private operator under its jurisdiction'[21] and to 'deploy adequate means, to exercise best possible efforts, to do the utmost, to obtain [the required result]'.[22]

It remains, however, somewhat uncertain how far such duty imposes an obligation. For example, do States have a general due diligence obligation under Article 194 to regulate and control activities such as permitting GHG-emitting installations, for example, oil or gas-based power plants, oil extraction industries or coal mining, if such activities are carried out under their jurisdiction or control? Articles 207 and 212 focus, in particular, on pollution of the marine environment from land-based sources and through the atmosphere, respectively, requiring parties to 'prevent, reduce, and control' marine pollution from these sources. Again, the same pertinent questions arise here.

In sum, while UNCLOS contains no reference to the adverse impacts of climate change on the ocean and the marine environment, it is a matter of interpretation of

[20] International Tribunal for the Law of the Sea (ITLOS), Advisory Opinion of 2 April 2015 (Request for an Advisory Opinion submitted by the sub-regional fisheries commission (SRFC)) (Request for Advisory Opinion submitted to the Tribunal) Case no. 21 (2015) ITLOS Reports p. 1.

[21] Ibid., para. 131.

[22] ITLOS Seabed Disputes Chamber, Advisory opinion on the responsibilities and obligations of states sponsoring persons and entities with respect to activities in the Area, 1 February 2011 (2001) ITLOS Report 10, at 41, paras. 110–112.

the Convention to clarify the scope of existing duties.[23] While further normative clarification (or dynamic development) could be obtained through jurisprudence, for example, by an Advisory Opinion from the ITLOS, it is also a possibility to work on an implementing agreement, which could focus in particular on climate change-relevant aspects of the Convention, if member States so wanted.

Finally, the recent development of a new implementing agreement under UNCLOS to protect and conserve biological diversity beyond national jurisdiction (BBNJ) does (still) foresee a particular role of area-based management and environmental impact assessment in addressing climate change. The current draft negotiating text sets out as one of the guiding principles an approach that builds ecosystem resilience to the adverse effects of climate change and ocean acidification and restores ecosystem integrity.[24] In this context, area-based management tools, such as marine protected areas, should be established, inter alia, in order to rehabilitate and restore biodiversity and ecosystems. This might enhance their productivity and health and build resilience to stressors, such as those related to climate change, ocean acidification and marine pollution.[25] Climate impacts might also be considered part of 'cumulative impacts' on the same ecosystem and could fall under the scope of environmental impact assessments. Still, it remains to be seen to what extent parties will be willing to integrate adequate responses to climate change and its impacts in the BBNJ agreement.

2.5 UN CLIMATE CHANGE REGIME AND THE OCEANS

The UNFCCC establishes as its ultimate objective the stabilization of GHG concentrations in the atmosphere at a level that would prevent dangerous interference with the climate system.[26] In general, this includes the role of oceans in stabilizing atmospheric GHG concentrations. Accordingly, Article 4, paragraph 1 (d) sets out the commitment of UNFCCC parties to 'promote and cooperate in the conservation and enhancement, as appropriate, of sinks and reservoirs of ... greenhouse gases ... including biomass, forests and oceans as well as other terrestrial, coastal and marine ecosystems'. However, while the scope of the UNFCCC is arguably not limited to territorial emission, the rather general obligations of member States set out in Article 4 apply only to activities under their jurisdiction or control. While States could include ocean-based emissions or removals in their

23 See D. Bodansky, The Ocean and Climate Change Law: Exploring the Relationships. In: Richard Barnes and Ronan Long (eds.), *Frontiers in International Law: Oceans and Climate Challenges, Essays in Honor of David Freestone* (Boston: Brill 2020).

24 Art. 5.(h) Revised draft text of an agreement under the United Nations Convention on the Law of the Sea on the conservation and sustainable use of marine biological diversity of areas beyond national jurisdiction, 27 November 2019 (www.un.org/bbnj/sites/www.un.org.bbnj/files/revised_draft_text_a.conf_.232.2020.11_advance_unedited_version.pdf).

25 Ibid., Art. 14.(e).

26 Art. 2 UNFCCC.

national plans, programs, policies or measures, the reality is that so far very few, have done so.

The Paris Agreement, adopted under the UNFCCC, recognizes in its preamble the importance of conservation and enhancement, as appropriate, of sinks and reservoirs of the greenhouse gases referred to in the UNFCCC, and explicitly notes the importance of ensuring the integrity of all ecosystems, *including oceans*, and protection of biodiversity. Its main goal is set out in Article 2, according to which, inter alia, the increase in the global average temperature should be limited to well below 2°C above pre-industrial levels, while pursuing efforts to limit the increase to 1.5°C.[27] Oceans play a significant part in the global climate system, as described previously. However, the measures that parties include in their Nationally Determined Contributions (NDCs) under the agreement, and will be accounted for and reported on, remain within parties' territorial jurisdiction. The National GHG Inventory of each party only contains territorial GHG emissions and removals. It is therefore unclear how oceans – especially the high seas – fit into the scope of measures under the Paris Agreement.

However, as an exception to the territorial focus, inter-party tradable emission units can either increase or decrease the national volume of GHG emissions. Including cross-border carbon trading in NDCs, therefore, adds an 'extra-national jurisdictional element' to the scope of NDCs. Similarly, some of those parties that include REDD+ in their NDC also allow for cross-border transactions, thereby widening territorial capture to elements that lie outside the strict territorial jurisdiction of each party. Along the same lines, it is possible for a party to include ocean-based mitigation activities within its own jurisdiction or control, or implement activities jointly with other parties with respect to ocean-based climate change mitigation, for example, ocean fertilization or vessel-based direct air capture of CO_2, or certain CCS activities.

The Paris Agreement further encourages parties, in Article 5, paragraph 1, 'to take action to conserve and enhance, as appropriate, sinks and reservoirs of greenhouse gases as referred to in Article 4, paragraph 1(d), of the Convention, including forests'. Article 4, paragraph 1(d) of the UNFCCC refers to conservation and enhancement of sinks and reservoirs, including oceans, and coastal and marine ecosystems. Accordingly, there is a recognition of the important role of oceans as carbon sinks and reservoirs, but the challenge, as mentioned previously, is how to link the extra-jurisdictional scope of oceans to the NDCs by parties and to the atmospheric levels of GHG concentrations or temperature increases, as recognized in the context of the Convention and the Paris Agreement, respectively.

To sum up, it could be argued that the degree of consistency and synergy between the climate and ocean regimes is dynamic and invites further elaboration and rule development. For the ocean rule of law, this means that a dynamic interpretation of

[27] Art. 2 Paris Agreement.

the existing rules is necessary in order to comprehensively address the role of ocean governance in addressing climate change. For the climate change regime, in turn, this means that the scope and potential for ocean-based solutions to climate change, their inclusion in NDCs as well as their robust and accurate reporting and accounting requires further consideration. Still, significant potential exists for synergies that could both improve the effectiveness of ocean governance as well as enhance the scope for climate change mitigation measures. The following section presents three implementation measures that could reinforce this synergy and provides some suggestions on how to recognize the role of oceans more effectively in climate change mitigation.

2.6 THE OCEANS AS A SOLUTION TO CLIMATE CHANGE: SOME SUGGESTIONS

Several suggestions have been made as to how the oceans can contribute to solving the climate challenge. Several options have recently been put forth by civil society,[28] which together could save the world 4Gt CO_2 emissions yearly from 2030, and more than 11Gt in 2050. In the following sections, three examples are discussed in more detail.

2.6.1 *Ocean-Based Renewable Energy*

While recognizing that most emission reductions must happen from deep decarbonization of terrestrial activities, ocean-based activities can and should be included in the NDCs of parties to the Paris Agreement. While some parties have already included some marine activities and policies, more could follow suit with the next round of NDCs in 2025.

NDCs can play a critical role in supporting acceleration of renewable energy by sending clear, consistent signals to the private sector. Importantly, however, NDCs are to be implemented through effective domestic planning and regulatory as well as enforcement measures. By including ocean-based solutions in NDCs, greater legal and regulatory machinery will be set in motion. Also, reporting on the implementation and achievement of NDCs is mandatory under the Paris Agreement,[29] and all reports are subject to an independent technical expert review. NDCs can further help to stimulate further investment, research and development for less mature technologies such as tidal, current and geothermal energy.

[28] World Resources Institute, *The Ocean as a Solution to Climate Change*, Hoegh-Guldberg et al. (WRI Report 2019) (http://oceanpanel.org/sites/default/files/2019-10/HLP_Report_Ocean_Solution_Climate_Change_final.pdf).

[29] Paris Agreement (n 9), Art. 13, para. 7 b.

A recent report by the World Research Institute suggests several options for including ocean-based renewable energy in new or updated NDCs, such as:

- Expanding and increasing the ambition of existing economy-wide GHG targets by including emission reductions from ocean-based renewable energy production.
- Defining capacity and generation targets for ocean-based renewable energy (e.g., offshore wind within Exclusive Economic Zones (EEZ), and tidal and wave energy). Such targets could be expressed as absolute quantities, as a percentage increase from current levels or as a share of the total energy or electricity mix.
- Committing to developing inclusive national marine spatial planning frameworks and integrated ocean management to map ocean-based activities and area-based management tools. This will help identify opportunities for expanding offshore renewable energy that balances the needs of other ocean users and sustainability of coastal and marine ecosystems.
- Committing to research and development to explore opportunities to align ocean-based renewable energy with efforts to decarbonize marine transport and aquaculture and support coastal and marine ecosystems.[30]

Further examples might also include fixed and floating offshore wind and solar installations and ocean thermal energy conversion installations. This would help in addressing the significant gap between the aggregate effect of parties' mitigation efforts and the emissions pathway needed to hold temperature increases to well below 2°C above pre-industrial levels and in pursuing efforts to limit temperature increases to 1.5°C.[31] Moreover, parties to the Paris Agreement are expected to reflect their highest possible ambition in their NDC[32] – a due diligence requirement, which means taking all appropriate measures, which for many coastal states would include ocean-based activities.

2.6.2 *Decarbonizing Ocean-Based Transport*

Decarbonization of ocean transport is another way by which ocean-related aspects might contribute to climate solutions. Ocean transport currently makes up about

[30] E. Northrop and M. Finch, *4 Ocean-Based Solutions to Advance Climate Action through NDCs* (2021) (www.wri.org/blog/2021/01/4-ocean-based-solutions-advance-climate-action-through-ndcs)

[31] UNFCCC secretariat, Nationally Determined Contributions under the Paris Agreement, Synthesis Report, FCCC/PA/CMA/2021/8, 17 September 2021.

[32] Art. 4, para. 3 Paris Agreement (n 9); see also Decision 1/CMA.2, paras. 6 and 7. See: Christina Voigt and Felipe Ferreira (2016) "Dynamic Differentiation": The Principles of CBDR-RC, Progression and Highest Possible Ambition in the Paris Agreement, 5 *Transnational Environmental Law* 2, 285–303.

3 per cent of global GHG emissions, with a rising trend.[33] Increased energy efficiency, maximizing the overall operational efficiency of new and existing ships and promoting or prescribing low and zero carbon fuels could mitigate this contribution. International work through the International Maritime Organization and regional organizations might be necessary, which should also increase possibilities for enforcement of norms.

Additionally, the inclusion of ocean transport in parties' NDCs could be an effective way forward. This might involve, for example, setting a specific GHG target for domestic shipping and domestic fleets; aiming to phase out GHG emissions from coastal passenger transport through technology transfer and research and development in battery- and wind-powered ferries; developing cross-sectoral decarbonization plans that link strategies to transition land-based energy sources and supply chains with ports and marine fleets; or financing technology transfer and research and development for the transition to zero-emission passenger and freight transport.[34]

2.6.3 *Coastal and Marine Ecosystem Protection*

Protecting coastal and marine ecosystems is necessary to maintain and enhance the CO2 and reservoir capacities of oceans. This might include enhancing protection measures for mangroves, kelp forests, seaweed beds under the CBD and other legal instruments, and inclusion of such 'marine-based natural solutions' as a nature-based solution in parties' NDCs.[35]

Moreover, providing incentives for 'blue carbon' similar to 'green carbon' under REDD+ could be a necessary tool to engage more States in ocean-based natural protection for climate purposes. This might require enhancing carbon accounting for mangroves, sea grass and seaweed or kelp forests and other ocean sinks within national GHG Inventories, and the improvement of monitoring technologies and capacities for 'blue carbon' (under the UNFCCC and Paris Agreement).[36]

National and global mapping of blue carbon ecosystems (especially seaweed) and development of legal mechanisms for long-term preservation of blue carbon are significant steps that are necessary in order to include the conservation and enhancement of ocean sinks and reservoirs in the scope of nature-based solutions in NDCs.

[33] S. Widjaja, T. Long, H. Wirajuda et al., *Illegal, Unreported and Unregulated Fishing and Associated Drivers* (Washington, DC: World Resources Institute 2019, 38).

[34] Northrop and Finch (n 30).

[35] 151 parties to the Paris Agreement have already included addressed some aspects of ocean carbon in their NDCs. See: The Blue Carbon Initiative (www.thebluecarboninitiative.org/policy-guidance).

[36] See also: Martin R. Stuchtey, Adrien Vincent, Andreas Merkl and Maximilian Bucher, *Ocean Solutions That Benefit People, Nature and the Economy* (Washington, DC: World Resources Institute (oceanpanel.org) 2020).

2.6.4 *Management of Fisheries and Aquaculture*

Another important aspect is elimination of harmful subsidies[37] and strengthening of tools to eliminate illegal, unreported and unregulated (IUU) fishing.[38] The climate challenge is significant and the role of oceans as the real 'lungs of the Earth' is crucial in maintaining a carbon balance. This understanding, while backed up by science, is only slowly moving into political decisions and appropriate legal responses.

One principal way in which ocean-based foods can contribute significantly to climate change mitigation is in reduction of the carbon footprint of ocean-derived food production, especially fisheries. For example, changing fuel sources in vessels and technological advances in production techniques can alter the emissions associated with seafood from both fisheries and ocean-based aquaculture. However, reducing emissions by improving fish catch efficiency as well as increasing fishery yields will require significant governance changes, including design of appropriate international and regional legal frameworks. In this context, existing tools within the international framework to address IUU fishing should be strengthened and streamlined into a global framework.[39]

2.7 CONCLUSIONS

Oceans are under threat from climate change, and the question is whether the interrelated ocean and climate change dynamics have been sufficiently recognized in UNCLOS and UN climate change law. So far, there is no clear legal regime under international law addressing both climate change and the oceans in a comprehensive manner. The UN climate change regime is severely limited in its capacity to address ocean issues because of its terrestrial and atmospheric focus. The UN regime for the Law of the Sea already has certain components and established obligations for its parties, including for land-based source activities that cause ocean pollution. The relatively weak legal synergy between the two regimes

[37] SDG14.6, www.un.org/ga/search/view_doc.asp?symbol=A/RES/70/1&Lang=E (page 23).

[38] SDG14.5, www.un.org/ga/search/view_doc.asp?symbol=A/RES/70/1&Lang=E (page 23).

[39] Currently, this framework consists of both binding agreements and voluntary instruments that facilitate the management of fisheries at the global, regional and national levels.

Within this framework, a number of provisions and requirements specifically address IUU fishing, with provisions and guidance relating to port State measures, flag State performance, coastal State responsibilities, market State measures or a combination of all or some of these (e.g., UNCLOS, FAO Compliance Agreement, UN Fish Stocks Agreement, Code of Conduct for Responsible Fisheries, IPOA-IUU, Agreement on Port State Measures (PSMA), Voluntary Guidelines for Flag State Performance, Voluntary Guidelines for Catch Documentation Schemes, and the Global Record of Fishing Vessels, Refrigerated Transport Vessels and Supply Vessels). For an overview, see: www.fao.org/iuu-fishing/international-framework/en/.

could pose a challenge to the rule of law for protection of oceans and the climate system; if not improved.

As this chapter has shown, ample possibility exists for parties to include ocean-related mitigation aspects in their NDCs under the Paris Agreement. The advantage of such inclusion would not only be that oceans would become part and parcel of parties' climate strategies. In addition, the inclusion of ocean transport, blue carbon, fishery regulation and/or ocean-based renewable energy and other ocean-based climate mitigation activities in NDCs would also require parties to adopt effective domestic implementation measures, such as regulations, laws, acts and other implementation instruments as well as ensure their compliance and enforcement.[40] Furthermore, parties would also be under the legal obligation to provide a biennial transparency report on the implementation and achievement of their NDCs, which would be public and accessible to everyone.[41] In this report, parties need to provide information on legal, institutional, administrative and procedural arrangements for domestic implementation, monitoring, reporting and achievement as well as stakeholder engagement.[42] In other words, inclusion of ocean-based mitigation measures in an NDC would draw ocean governance under the transparency requirements of the Paris Agreement, enhancing their visibility, legitimacy and, potentially, coordination.

However, further legal developments in international law (i.e., law-making, jurisprudence) might be necessary to adequately reflect the important role of oceans in the global governance framework, in order to address climate change and its impacts. The current BBNJ negotiations could provide a part of this framework by setting out criteria for identifying areas for area-based management, criteria that consider the carbon density and climate relevance of certain marine and coastal ecosystems, such as kelp forests and seaweed beds.

An alternative avenue is dynamic development and interpretation of UNCLOS provisions with relevance to climate change or consideration of a new implementing agreement under UNCLOS, which provides for clarification and specification of States' duties with respect to climate change and its impact on oceans. In the absence of such development, or in addition to it, it is possible to seek an advisory opinion from, for example, ITLOS on the obligation of States with respect to climate change impacts on the oceans.

The solutions offered by the oceans should, and most likely must, play a more prominent role in climate policy and regulation. In order to achieve the global goal of climate neutrality around 2050 and global net-negative emissions thereafter until the end of this century,[43] oceans form an indispensable part of the solution. While more and more States are currently adopting climate neutrality targets, their reliance

40 Paris Agreement (n 9) Art. 4, para. 2, sentence 2.

41 Paris Agreement (n 9) Art. 13, para. 7(b).

42 Decision 18/CMA, 1, annex, para. 62, https://unfccc.int/sites/default/files/resource/cma2018_3_add2_new_advance.pdf (page 28).

43 IPCC, *Climate Change 2021: The Physical Science Basis* (n 14).

on ocean-based measures is expected to rise. However, ocean-based solutions are not the whole solution. They must happen alongside, but not replace, rapid, deep and sustained emission reductions in terrestrial energy sectors and from land-based sources, as well as protection of natural terrestrial sinks.

Holding temperature increases to well below 2°C requires unprecedented action in scope and scale. This is a call for innovation and change – including how to integrate two-thirds of this planet into the solution.

3

Controlling GHG Emissions from Shipping

The Role, Relevance and Fitness for Purpose of UNCLOS

David Testa

3.1 INTRODUCTION

At less than 3 per cent of global Greenhouse Gas (GHG) emissions,[1] it may be tempting to argue that shipping emissions do not constitute a particularly alarming or significant component of the global climate change problem. This would be a mistaken approach. According to one estimate, if the international shipping industry were a country, it would be ranked as the sixth largest emitter of energy-related CO_2, just above Germany.[2] Moreover, according to the International Maritime Organisation (IMO) Fourth GHG Study, maritime CO_2 emissions are projected to increase considerably in the coming decades. Projections vary widely, depending on future economic and energy developments, but the IMO predicts that emissions are projected to increase from about 90 per cent of 2008 emissions in 2018 to 90–130 per cent of 2008 emissions by 2050.[3] Given these statistics and projections, there can be no doubt that GHG emissions from shipping need to be decisively addressed as part of international efforts to combat climate change.

Considering that the United Nations Convention on the Law of the Sea (UNCLOS)[4] was negotiated between 1972 and 1982, it should come as no surprise that the Convention makes no express reference to climate change. This does not mean that UNCLOS has no role to play in the context of climate change generally or in the more specific context of efforts to regulate GHG emissions from shipping.

1 See IMO, 'Fourth IMO GHG Study 2020: Executive Summary' (2021) <wwwcdn.imo.org/localresources/en/OurWork/Environment/Documents/Fourth%20IMO%20GHG%20Study%202020%20Executive-Summary.pdf> accessed 28 June 2021. (Fourth IMO GHG Study).

2 International Council on Clean Transportation, 'GHG Emission from Global Shipping, 2013–2015' <https://theicct.org/sites/default/files/publications/Global-shipping-GHG-emissions-2013-2015_ICCT-Report_17102017_vF.pdf> accessed 19 February 2020.

3 Fourth IMO GHG Study (n 1), 3.

4 Montego Bay, 10 December 1982, in force 16 November 1994, 1833 UNTS 3.

The drafters of UNCLOS intended to establish a comprehensive regime for the oceans. This is clear from the Convention's preamble, which speaks of a desire to create:

> . . . a legal order for the seas and oceans which will facilitate international communication, and will promote the peaceful uses of the seas and oceans, the equitable and efficient utilization of their resources, the conservation of their living resources, and the study, protection and preservation of the marine environment.[5]

While the aspiration to comprehensive coverage is clear, when applied to UNCLOS comprehensiveness is a term that must be understood in a limited sense; it denotes the sheer breadth of coverage, rather than coverage in considerable detail of all substantive matters that may conceivably arise in practice.[6] Such detail would have rendered UNCLOS an unwieldy document and would have made the negotiation process immeasurably harder. A different approach was adopted by the Convention's drafters. The basic rules and the jurisdictional framework are authoritatively set out in UNCLOS, whereas matters of substantive technical detail are left to be fleshed out in a variety of international instruments such as the International Convention for the Prevention of Pollution by Ships (MARPOL).[7] The extent of development that can be registered therefore depends on the willingness of States to be proactive in developing the relevant rules and standards that are contained in instruments associated with UNCLOS, such as the MARPOL Convention.

This chapter examines the role, relevance and fitness for purpose of UNCLOS in relation to ongoing efforts to tackle GHG emissions from shipping. It asks whether UNCLOS is adequate and considers what further steps need to be taken. Following this introduction, Sections 3.2 and 3.3 provide a brief overview of the UN Climate Change Regime and of the Initial IMO Strategy on Reduction of GHG Emissions from Ships. Section 3.4 examines UNCLOS's various points of relevance. It starts with a brief examination of the Convention definition of 'marine pollution' and proceeds with an analysis of Articles 192 and 194 and of Articles 211 and 212, which establish important obligations for States to regulate pollution from vessels and pollution from or through the atmosphere. It then examines flag, coastal and port State jurisdiction to regulate GHG emissions from shipping. Section 3.5 provides some concluding comments and considers whether UNCLOS can be considered as fit for purpose in this context.

5 UNCLOS (n 4), Preamble, para. 4.

6 UNCLOS 'has a wide coverage of topics; but it is not a comprehensive code – a full grammar'. See Vaughan Lowe, 'Was It Worth the Effort?' (2012) 27 *IJMCL* 875, 877.

7 The International Convention for the Prevention of Pollution from Ships (adopted 2 November 1973, entered into force 2 October 1983) and its Protocol of 1978 (adopted 17 February 1978, entered into force 1 October 1983) 1340 UNTS 62.

3.2 THE UN CLIMATE CHANGE REGIME

Efforts to reduce GHG emissions from shipping are happening as part of a concerted global effort to reduce GHG emissions generally. Alongside UNCLOS and specialist shipping instruments such as MARPOL, a distinct yet related regime has developed to address climate change. While an in-depth examination of this regime would be well beyond the scope of this chapter, a brief overview must be provided to contextualise efforts to reduce GHG emissions from shipping as well as to better understand external pressures that are being faced by the shipping industry.

The United Nations Framework Convention on Climate Change (UNFCCC)[8] is 'the primary international, intergovernmental forum for negotiating the global response to climate change'.[9] Its overall objective is to '[stabilize] greenhouse gas concentrations in the atmosphere at a level that would prevent dangerous anthropogenic interference with the climate system'.[10] The Kyoto Protocol[11] was the first substantive international agreement to be adopted under the UNFCCC. It established binding emissions reduction targets for the developed countries listed in Annex I of the UNFCCC.[12] Article 2(2) of the Kyoto Protocol obliges Annex 1 parties to 'pursue limitation or reduction of emissions of greenhouse gases . . . from aviation and marine bunker fuels, working through the International Civil Aviation Organization and the International Maritime Organization, respectively'.[13]

The Paris Agreement[14] entered into force on 4 November 2016. It brings all State parties into a common cause to undertake ambitious efforts to combat climate change. The parties agreed a long-term goal to hold the increase in the global average temperature to well below 2°C above pre-industrial levels and to pursue efforts to limit the temperature increase to 1.5°C above pre-industrial levels.[15] Each State must prepare, communicate and maintain successive Nationally Determined Contributions (NDCs) that it intends to achieve.[16] NDCs are to be strengthened every five years in light of a global stocktaking exercise undertaken by the meeting of the parties to the Paris Agreement.[17]

[8] United Nations Framework Convention on Climate Change, New York, 9 May 1992, in force 21 March 1994, 1771 UNTS 107.

[9] UNGA, 'Transforming our world: The 2030 Agenda for Sustainable Development' (25 September 2015) UN Doc A/Res/70/1 Preamble para. 31.

[10] UNFCCC (n 8), Art. 2.

[11] Kyoto Protocol to the United Nations Framework Convention on Climate Change, Kyoto, 11 December 1997, in force 16 February 2005, 2303 UNTS 162, 37 ILM 22 (1998).

[12] Ibid., Art. 3.

[13] Ibid., Art. 2(2).

[14] UNFCCC (n 8), 'Adoption of the Paris Agreement' (FCCC/CP/2015/L.9/Rev.1, 12 December 2015) <https://undocs.org/FCCC/CP/2015/L.9/Rev.1> accessed 30 September 2019.

[15] Paris Agreement, Paris, 12 December 2015, in force 4 November 2016, Art. 2(1)(a).

[16] Paris Agreement, Art. 4(2).

[17] Paris Agreement, Art. 14.

3.3 THE INITIAL IMO STRATEGY ON REDUCTION OF GHG EMISSIONS FROM SHIPS

The IMO has been dealing with the question of air pollution from ships in some form or other since the 1980s.[18] Central to the IMO's efforts in this regard is the MARPOL Convention. Annex VI of the convention, which deals with the Prevention of Air Pollution from Ships, is the most relevant. It regulates emissions of sulphur oxide and nitrogen oxide, ozone-depleting substances, volatile organic compounds and shipboard incineration.[19] In 2011, the IMO's Marine Environment Protection Committee (MEPC) adopted a package of technical measures for new ships and operational reduction measures for all ships. This package of measures was included in a new Chapter 4 of MARPOL Annex VI, titled 'Regulations on Energy Efficiency for Ships', and includes two main measures: the Energy Efficiency Design Index (EEDI) and the Ship Energy Efficiency Plan (SEEMP). The EEDI aims to stimulate continued innovation and technical development of all those components that influence the fuel efficiency of a ship from its design stage. The SEEMP establishes a mechanism for shipowners to improve the energy efficiency of both new and existing ships using operational measures such as speed optimisation and just-in-time arrival in ports.

On 13 April 2018, the MEPC adopted the Initial IMO Strategy on Reduction of GHG Emissions from Ships.[20] The Strategy identifies three levels of ambition. First, the carbon intensity of ships is to decline through implementation of further phases of the Energy Efficiency Design Index (EEDI) for new ships. Second, the carbon intensity of international shipping is to decline to reduce average CO_2 emissions by at least 40 per cent by 2030 while pursuing efforts to reduce average CO_2 emissions towards 70 per cent by 2050, compared to 2008. Third, to peak GHG emissions from international shipping as soon as possible and to reduce the total annual GHG emissions by at least 50 per cent by 2050 compared to 2008 while pursuing efforts towards phasing them out.

The Initial IMO Strategy signals a willingness to address GHG emissions from international shipping and, for the first time, establishes levels of ambition in this regard. At the same time, there can be no doubts about the fact that the Strategy is an initial strategy; a political document of an aspirational nature that needs to be followed up by substantive action and measures over the coming years.

18 For a detailed historic account of IMO efforts see Aldo Chircop, Meinhard Doelle and Ryan Gauvin, 'Shipping and Climate Change: International Law and Policy Considerations' 36 onwards, Centre for International Governance Innovation Special Report 2018 (hereinafter 'CIGI Special Report') <www.cigionline.org/sites/default/files/documents/Shipping%27s%20contribution%20to%20climate%20change%202018web_0.pdf> accessed 30 September 2019.

19 MARPOL (n 7) Annex IV, Chapter 3.

20 Resolution MEPC.304(72), 'Initial IMO Strategy on Reduction of GHG Emissions from Ships' (13 April 2018) (IMO GHG Strategy).

The Strategy has also been criticised for not being ambitious enough. Doelle and Chircop, for instance, have argued that '[i]t is hard to see how full decarbonization well after 2050 can be considered a fair contribution to the long-term goals of the Paris Agreement, which ultimately calls for efforts to keep global average temperature increases to within 1.5% of pre-industrial levels'.[21] The IMO Strategy, like current nationally stated mitigation ambitions submitted under the Paris Agreement,[22] will therefore need to be revised if it is to contribute fairly to and be consistent with the Paris Agreement temperature goals.

3.4 THE LAW OF THE SEA CONVENTION

3.4.1 *Pollution of the Marine Environment*

Article 1(1)(4) of the Convention defines 'pollution of the marine environment' as:

> the introduction by man, directly or indirectly, of substances or energy into the marine environment . . . which results or is likely to result in such deleterious effects as harm to living resources and marine life, hazards to human health, hindrance to marine activities, including fishing and other legitimate uses of the sea, impairment of quality for use of sea water and reduction of amenities.[23]

The UNCLOS definition of marine pollution is a wide and comprehensive one that is subject to evolutionary interpretation.[24] By design, it 'provides an open definition on marine pollution which may include all sources of marine pollution in the present and future'.[25]

Considering that the definition encompasses the introduction of both 'substances' and 'energy' into the marine environment, it is difficult to argue in good faith that GHG emissions from shipping do not constitute 'pollution of the marine environment'. The warming of the oceans introduces 'energy' into the marine environment that results or is likely to result in deleterious effects. The introduction of CO_2 into the water column results in deleterious effects through ocean acidification. Given all this, Bodansky finds no difficulty in concluding that 'emissions from maritime shipping clearly constitute "pollution of the marine environment" within the

[21] Meinhard Doelle and Aldo Chircop, 'Decarbonizing International Shipping: An Appraisal of the IMO's Initial Strategy' (2019) 28 *RECEIL* 268–277, 273.

[22] The IPCC's 'Global Warming of 1.5°C Special Report' concluded that '[p]athways reflecting [current nationally stated mitigation ambitions] would not limit global warming to 1.5° C, even if supplemented by very challenging increases in the scale and ambition of emissions reductions after 2030 (*high confidence*)'. See IPCC, 'Global warming of 1.5°C' (2019) <www.ipcc.ch/site/assets/uploads/sites/2/2019/06/SR15_Full_Report_Low_Res.pdf> accessed 22 October 2019.

[23] UNCLOS (n 4), Art. 1(4).

[24] Alan Boyle, 'Further Development of the Law of the Sea Convention: Mechanisms for Change' (2005) 54 *ICLQ* 563, 573.

[25] Alexander Proelss (ed.), *United Nations Convention on the Law of the Sea: A Commentary* (München/Oxford/Baden-Baden: Beck/Hart/Nomos 2017) 23.

meaning of Article 1.1(4)',[26] and similar views have been expressed by other authors.[27] Since GHG emissions therefore amount to 'pollution of the marine environment', the question that must be answered next is: which precise provisions of the Convention are engaged by GHG emissions and what are the implications of these provisions in practice?

3.4.2 *General Provisions: Articles 192 and 194*

Article 192 establishes a general obligation on all States to protect and preserve the marine environment. As noted in the *South China Sea* arbitration, 'the content of the general obligation in Article 192 is further detailed in the subsequent provisions of Part XII ... as well as by reference to specific obligations set out in other international agreements'.[28] On this basis, in the *South China Sea* arbitration, the arbitral tribunal integrated the definition of 'ecosystem' from the Convention on Biological Diversity[29] as well as aspects of the CITES Convention[30] into its reasoning, enabling it to reach the conclusion that 'Article 192 includes a due diligence obligation to prevent the harvesting of species that are recognised internationally as being at risk of extinction and requiring international protection'.[31] In a similar manner, it is submitted that Article 192 serves to bring the UN Climate Change Regime into the scope of UNCLOS and that the Paris Agreement effectively sets the standard for giving effect to Article 192 insofar as State obligations in the context of climate change are concerned.[32] This is in line with the principle of systemic integration enshrined in Article 31(3)(c) of the Vienna Convention on the Law of Treaties (VCLT).[33] According to Article 31(3)(c), in interpreting a treaty, together with the context, account shall be taken of 'any relevant rules of international law applicable in the relations between the parties'.[34] As Bowman observes,

[26] Daniel Bodansky, 'Regulating Greenhouse Gas Emissions from Ships: The Role of the International Maritime Organisation' (2016) 9 <https://papers.ssrn.com/sol3/papers.cfm?abstract_id=2813785>.

[27] See, e.g., James Harrison, *Saving the Oceans through Law: The International Legal Framework for the Protection of the Marine Environment* (Oxford: Oxford University Press 2017) 26–27; Alan Boyle, 'Climate Change, Ocean Governance and UNCLOS' in *Law of the Sea: UNCLOS as a Living Treaty* (London: BIICL 2016) 211, 218; Yoshifumi Tanaka, 'Regulation of Greenhouse Gas Emissions from International Shipping and Jurisdiction of States' (2016) 25 *RECIEL* 337.

[28] *South China Sea Arbitration (Philippines v China)*, PCA, Award on the Merits, 12 July 2016 para. 942.

[29] Convention on Biological Diversity (adopted 5 June 1992, entered into force 29 December 1993) 1760 UNTS 79.

[30] Convention on International Trade in Endangered Species of Wild Fauna and Flora (adopted 3 March 1973, entered into force 1 July 1975) 993 UNTS 243.

[31] *South China Sea Arbitration* (n 28), para. 956.

[32] For a similar view see Boyle (n 27), 220.

[33] Vienna Convention on the Law of Treaties (adopted 23 May 1969, entered into force 27 January 1980) 1155 UNTS 331.

[34] Ibid., Art. 31(3)(c).

what systemic integration requires is that 'interpretation of each individual provision ... be woven into the broader fabric not only of the treaty as a whole, but of the wider legal system'.[35]

The nature of the Article 192 obligation to protect and preserve the marine environment as a due diligence obligation can have important ramifications in the context of tackling GHG emissions from shipping. As affirmed in the *Responsibilities in the Area* opinion, the concept of due diligence can 'change over time as measures considered sufficiently diligent at a certain moment may become not diligent enough in light, for instance, of new scientific or technological knowledge'.[36] Paragraph 7 of the IMO GHG Strategy establishes an obligation for the Strategy to be revised every five years after its final adoption in 2023. Re-assessment should not be restricted to aspects of the Strategy such as short, medium and long-term measures but should include careful consideration of all the relevant elements, including the all-important levels of ambition. These should be re-evaluated considering the latest scientific and technical knowledge available and maintained in line with the global effort under the Paris Agreement to keep temperature increases to within 1.5 per cent of pre-industrial levels.

Article 194(1) obliges States to take all measures necessary to prevent, reduce and control pollution of the marine environment from any source. As Boyle notes, although Article 194 makes no express reference to GHG emissions, 'it is entirely possible to read Article 194(3) as covering atmospheric depositions of CO_2 resulting in marine pollution'.[37] Atmospheric pollution is mentioned specifically in Article 194(3)(a), which provides that measures taken pursuant to Part XII must include measures designed to minimise to the fullest extent possible 'the release of toxic, harmful or noxious substances, especially those which are persistent, from land-based sources, *from or through the atmosphere* or by dumping'.[38] Article 194(3)(b) then tackles vessel-source pollution specifically by requiring that measures taken pursuant to Part XII must include measures designed to minimise to the fullest extent possible pollution from vessels.[39]

3.4.3 *More Specific Provisions: Articles 211 and 212*

Article 211 expands on the obligation contained in Article 194(3)(b) and addresses both national and international law-making. Insofar as international law-making is concerned, Article 211(1) provides that 'States, acting through the competent

35 Michael Bowman, 'Normalizing the International Convention for the Regulation of Whaling' (2008) 29 *Michigan Journal of International Law* 293, 343.

36 *Responsibilities and Obligations of States Sponsoring Persons and Entities with Respect to Activities in the Area* (Advisory Opinion) ITLOS No. 17 (1 February 2011) para. 117.

37 Boyle (n 27), 217.

38 UNCLOS (n 4), Art. 194(3)(a) – emphasis added.

39 UNCLOS (n 4), Art. 194(3)(b).

international organization or general diplomatic conference, shall establish international rules and standards to prevent, reduce and control pollution of the marine environment from vessels'.[40] Article 211(1) requires that '[s]uch rules and standards ... be re-examined from time to time as necessary'. The obligation to re-examine rules is an important one that complements the construal of Article 192 in the preceding section as an obligation of due diligence. Article 211(2) deals with national law-making and provides that:

> States shall adopt laws and regulations for the prevention, reduction and control of pollution of the marine environment from vessels flying their flag or of their registry. Such laws and regulations shall at least have the same effect as that of generally accepted international rules and standards established through the competent international organization or general diplomatic conference.[41]

Article 211(2) establishes an important prescriptive obligation in relation to flag States. Given the phrasing of Article 211(2), a crucial question is whether the Regulations on Energy Efficiency for Ships that are contained in MARPOL Annex VI Chapter 4 can be considered as Generally Accepted International Rules and Standards (GAIRS). A problem with MARPOL Annex VI Chapter 4 is that the relevant amending resolution in terms of which Chapter 4 was added to Annex VI was not adopted by consensus, as is typically the case with IMO decisions, but by a vote in which forty-nine out of fifty-nine MARPOL State parties at the time voted in favour, but Brazil, Chile, China, Kuwait and Saudi Arabia voted against.[42] The fact that five States with a significant number of ships in their registries voted against gives Harrison reason to believe that the relevant Regulations 'may not qualify as being generally accepted for the purposes of Article 211(2)'.[43] This may have been true at the time of adoption but, as has been noted in other contexts, the fact that a number of States at some point opposed a given measure does not disqualify the same measure from becoming generally accepted at a later point.[44] All those States that opposed the adoption of Chapter 4 eventually ratified Annex VI,[45] and, as of October 2019, MARPOL Annex VI has ninety-five contracting parties representing 96.71 per cent of world tonnage between them.[46] It is therefore submitted that the energy efficiency regulations contained in MARPOL Annex VI Chapter 4 can be considered as GAIRS for the purpose of Article 211(2). Whether it will be possible to

40 UNCLOS (n 4), Art. 211(1).

41 UNCLOS (n 4), Art. 211(2).

42 Report of the MEPC on its 62nd Session (MEPC 62/24, 26 July 2011) 57.

43 James Harrison, 'Recent Development and Continuing Challenges in the Regulation of Greenhouse Gas Emissions from International Shipping' (2013) *Ocean Yearbook* 379.

44 Hugo Caminos and Vincent Cogliati-Bantz, *The Legal Regime of Straits: Contemporary Challenges and Solutions* (Cambridge: Cambridge University Press 2014) 308.

45 Tanaka (n 27), 339.

46 IMO, 'Status of Conventions' (constantly updated) <www.imo.org/en/About/Conventions/StatusOfConventions/Pages/Default.aspx> accessed 8 October 2019.

state the same for future rules on GHG emissions from shipping will largely depend on the circumstances of their adoption.

While Article 211(2) establishes a prescriptive obligation for flag States, Article 217 establishes a corresponding obligation of enforcement: 'States shall ensure compliance by vessels flying their flag or of their registry with applicable international rules and standards, established through the competent international organization or general diplomatic conference, and with their laws and regulations adopted in accordance with this Convention for the prevention, reduction and control of pollution of the marine environment from vessels . . .'[47]

Article 212(3) requires States to 'endeavour to establish global and regional rules, standards and recommended practices and procedures to prevent, reduce and control [atmospheric] pollution'.[48] Insofar as atmospheric pollution from ships in particular is concerned, UNCLOS State parties have fulfilled this responsibility through the adoption of MARPOL Annex VI. In relation to national law-making, Article 212(1) requires States to: 'adopt laws and regulations to prevent, reduce and control pollution of the marine environment from or through the atmosphere, applicable to the air space under their sovereignty and to vessels flying their flag or vessels or aircraft of their registry, *taking into account* internationally agreed rules, standards and recommended practices and procedures'.[49]

Two main distinctions exist between Article 211(2) and Article 212(1). First, Article 212(1) refers not to GAIRS but to 'internationally agreed rules, standards and recommended practices and procedures'.[50] This means that 'Article 212(1) does not require a rule or standard to be "generally accepted" before it is relevant'.[51] Second, unlike Article 211(2), which requires flag States to adopt laws and regulations that 'shall at least have the same effect as that of generally accepted international rules and standards', Article 212(1) requires States to 'tak[e] into account internationally agreed rules, standards and recommended practices and procedures'. As a result, 'States are free to adopt less or more stringent national instruments under this reference'.[52] As argued above, there can be little doubt today that the rules contained in MARPOL Annex VI Chapter 4 are generally accepted. That said, it is not entirely possible to exclude the possibility of such doubts resurfacing in relation to future rules, especially if the IMO will once again have to resort to majority voting. In such an eventuality, Article 212 will ensure that States are obliged to 'tak[e] into account internationally agreed rules, standards and recommended practices and procedures', at least until clarity can be obtained about whether the relevant rules can be considered as GAIRS under Article 211(2).

47 UNCLOS (n 4), Art. 217.
48 UNCLOS (n 4), Art. 212(3).
49 UNCLOS (n 4), Art. 212(1) – emphasis added.
50 UNCLOS (n 4), Art. 212(1).
51 Harrison (n 43), 379.
52 Proelss (n 25), 1448.

Article 222 requires States to 'enforce, within the air space under their sovereignty or with regard to vessels flying their flag or vessels or aircraft of their registry, their laws and regulations adopted in accordance with article 212, paragraph 1 . . .'[53]

3.4.4 *Prescriptive and Enforcement Jurisdiction*

The forthcoming sub-sections analyse the jurisdiction and obligations pertaining to flag, coastal and port States under UNCLOS in regard to GHG emissions from ships.

3.4.4.1 Flag State Jurisdiction

Flag States have primary jurisdiction over their vessels, and, on the high seas, they enjoy practically exclusive jurisdiction.[54] The privileged position that flag States enjoy is subject to corresponding duties. In Article 94(1) UNCLOS obliges flag States to 'effectively exercise [their] jurisdiction and control in administrative, technical and social matters over ships flying [their] flag'.[55]

The enforcement jurisdiction of flag States is regulated by Article 217, which requires States to 'ensure compliance by vessels flying their flag . . . with applicable international rules and standards, established through the competent international organization or general diplomatic conference, and with their laws and regulations adopted in accordance with this Convention for the prevention, reduction and control of pollution of the marine environment from vessels . . . '[56] Flag States are obliged to ensure such enforcement irrespective of where a violation occurs.[57] Article 217 establishes an obligation of due diligence. As the ITLOS Seabed Disputes Chamber held in the *Responsibilities in the Area* Opinion, an obligation of due diligence is an 'obligation to deploy adequate means, to exercise best possible efforts, to do the utmost, to obtain this result . . . this obligation may be characterized as an obligation "of conduct" and not "of result"'.[58] In practice, flag States fulfil their enforcement obligations under Article 217 by issuing certificates indicating compliance with the relevant rules and regulations and by investigating and prosecuting suspected infringements of international standards.[59]

Doubts have often been expressed about the efficacy of flag State control. Effective enforcement of the relevant regulations can be costly, and some flag States may be primarily interested in the registration fees and taxes that they obtain

[53] UNCLOS (n 4), Art. 222.
[54] UNCLOS (n 4), Art. 92.
[55] UNCLOS (n 4), Art. 94(1).
[56] UNCLOS (n 4), Art. 217.
[57] Ibid.
[58] *Responsibilities and Obligations in the Area* (n 36), para. 110.
[59] Harrison (n 27), 142.

from their ship registries. UNCLOS seeks to deal with flag State failure to exercise effective jurisdiction and control over its vessels primarily through Article 94(6), which provides that '[a] State which has clear grounds to believe that proper jurisdiction and control with respect to a ship have not been exercised may report the facts to the flag State'.[60] A flag State that receives such a report is obliged to investigate the matter and to take any remedial action that may be necessary.[61] Moreover, according to Article 211(7), the flag State must promptly inform the requesting State and the competent international organisation of the action taken and its outcome.[62] If a reporting State remains unsatisfied with flag State action, it will have the option of instituting dispute settlement proceedings against the flag State in accordance with the dispute settlement provisions of UNCLOS.[63] In practice, however, 'there are no cases in which a flag State has been held to account in this manner, and the effect of these procedures has thus been limited'.[64]

3.4.4.2 Coastal State Jurisdiction

TERRITORIAL SEA In the territorial Sea, a coastal State may adopt laws and regulations relating to preservation of the environment of the coastal State and prevention, reduction and control of pollution thereof.[65] This right is considerably restricted by Article 21(2), which prescribes that such laws and regulations 'shall not apply to the design, construction, manning or equipment of foreign ships unless they are giving effect to [GAIRS]'.[66] Chircop et al. argue that '[t]he logical consequence [of this] is that unilateral rules and standards on atmospheric emissions inconsistent with MARPOL Annex VI may not be legislated and enforced'.[67] While this is generally correct, there appears to be no reason why a coastal State should not be able to use the prescriptive jurisdiction that is conferred on it by Article 21 to unilaterally adopt operational measures (such as speed reduction requirements) to reduce GHG emissions from ships in its territorial sea.

According to Article 19, 'any act of *wilful* and *serious* pollution'[68] contrary to the Convention strips passage of its innocent character[69] and can be the subject of coastal State enforcement jurisdiction.[70] UNCLOS does not offer any guidance as

60 UNCLOS (n 4), Art. 94(6).
61 Ibid.
62 UNCLOS (n 4), Art. 217(7). See also *Request for an Advisory Opinion Submitted by the Sub-Regional Fisheries Commission* (Advisory Opinion) ITLOS No. 21 (2 April 2015), para. 118.
63 UNCLOS (n 4), Art. 286.
64 Harrison (n 27), 143. See also Proelss (n 25), 713.
65 UNCLOS (n 4), Art. 21(1)(f).
66 UNCLOS (n 4), Art. 21(2).
67 CIGI Report (n 18), 18.
68 UNCLOS (n 4), Art. 19(2)(h) – emphasis added.
69 UNCLOS (n 4), Art. 19(1).
70 UNCLOS (n 4), Art. 25(1).

to how the terms 'wilful' and 'serious' are to be interpreted. Whether pollution is serious or not will to some extent need to be determined on a case-by-case basis,[71] but it is submitted that an infringement of rules on atmospheric emissions from ships is not the best example of an act of pollution serious enough to render passage non-innocent under Article 19 of UNCLOS.[72] In practice, and unless there are particularly compelling circumstances, States are likely to be reluctant to take enforcement action in the territorial sea for fear of unjustifiably interfering with innocent passage and will likely consider port State jurisdiction as a safer and more appropriate way to deal with rules on atmospheric pollution from ships.

EXCLUSIVE ECONOMIC ZONE The general rule in regard to prescriptive coastal State jurisdiction to prevent vessel-source pollution in the Exclusive Economic Zone (EEZ) is set out in Article 211(5), which determines that coastal States '… may adopt laws and regulations for the prevention, reduction and control of pollution from vessels conforming to and giving effect to generally accepted international rules and standards established through the competent international organisation or general diplomatic conference'.[73] In requiring domestic legislation to conform and give effect to Generally Accepted International Rules and Standards (GAIRS), Article 211(5) limits the prescriptive jurisdiction of coastal States and reaffirms the pre-eminence of the international level for rule-setting. The implication of Article 211(5) in the case of GHG emissions from ships is that the prescriptive entitlement of coastal States is presently restricted to incorporating the provisions of MARPOL Annex VI into their domestic law and to making the said provisions applicable to their respective EEZs.

Article 220 provides coastal States with graduated enforcement competence in the EEZ proportionate to the perceived severity of pollution damage involved.[74] An infringement of rules on atmospheric pollution from vessels cannot realistically be classified as a discharge 'causing major damage or threat of major damage to the coastline'[75] and it is unlikely that such an infringement would ordinarily be considered as 'causing or threatening significant pollution of the marine environment'.[76] It would therefore appear that, insofar as GHG emissions from ships are concerned, the coastal State's enforcement powers in the EEZ are in practice restricted to requesting information from a vessel, and this only where there are

[71] Proelss (n 25), 195 – Barnes notes that 'some waters may be more sensitive to pollution than others, or subject to prevailing high levels of pollution such that there is no tolerance to further pollution'.

[72] For a similar view see Tanaka (n 27), 339.

[73] UNCLOS (n 4), Art. 211(5).

[74] Shabtai Rosenne, Alexander Yankov and Myron Nordquist (eds.), *United Nations Convention on the Law of the Sea, 1982: A Commentary* (Vol IV, Dordrecht: Martinus Nijhoff 1991) 282.

[75] UNCLOS (n 4), Art. 220(6).

[76] UNCLOS (n 4), Art. 220(5).

clear grounds for believing that the vessel has committed a violation of applicable international rules and standards.

3.4.4.3 Port State Jurisdiction

Article 218(1) establishes the general principle of port State enforcement of international rules and standards.[77] When a vessel is voluntarily within a port or at an offshore terminal of a State, that State may undertake investigations and, where the evidence so warrants, institute proceedings in respect of any discharge from that vessel *outside* the internal waters, territorial sea or EEZ of that State in violation of applicable international rules and standards.[78]

Although the term 'discharge' is nowhere defined in UNCLOS, it has been suggested[79] that this term should be interpreted by reference to MARPOL, which defines it as 'any release howsoever caused from a ship and includes any escape, disposal, spilling, leaking, pumping, emitting or emptying'.[80] This is a wide definition that encompasses accidental as well as operational pollution. Port States are therefore entitled to exercise extraterritorial jurisdiction in relation to discharge infringements caused by the emission of substances such as sulphur and nitrogen dioxide. It is good to keep in mind, however, that in practice port States may be reluctant to initiate costly legal proceedings and may in any case not be in a position to gather strong enough evidence to prosecute.

In addition to the jurisdiction that is made available by Article 218, States have a largely unfettered[81] right to deny vessels entry into their ports. On the basis of the reasoning that 'who can do more can also do less',[82] it is possible to take a wider view of port-State jurisdiction and to consider it as including a right to prescribe and enforce conditions for entry. The existence of this right is confirmed by Article 211 (3) of UNCLOS, which requires States that establish requirements for the prevention, reduction and control of marine pollution as a condition for the entry of foreign vessels into their ports or internal waters to publicise such requirements and to communicate them to the competent international organisation.[83] Requirements for entry into ports need to be adopted on a non-discriminatory basis[84] and in good faith.[85]

77 Proelss (n 25), 1489.
78 UNCLOS (n 4), Art. 218(1) – emphasis added.
79 Proelss (n 25), 1493.
80 MARPOL (n 7), Art. 2(3)(a).
81 Although largely unfettered, a port State's right to deny entry is subject to some limitations. See Erik Molenaar, 'Port-State Jurisdiction: Towards Comprehensive, Mandatory and Global Coverage' (2007) 38 *Ocean Development and International Law* 225, 228.
82 Molenaar (n 81), 228. See also Bevan Marten, *Port-State Jurisdiction and the Regulation of International Merchant Shipping* (Cham: Springer 2014).
83 UNCLOS (n 4), Art. 211(3).
84 UNCLOS (n 4), Art. 227.
85 UNCLOS (n 4), Art. 300.

3.4.4.4 Port State Control

Port State control is a proactive and preventive mechanism whereby port States verify whether a given vessel's condition and its documentation comply with international rules and standards. Unlike port State jurisdiction proper, port State control is not geared towards institution of proceedings but is restricted to taking administrative measures of verification, potentially including detention of the vessel.

The conduct of port State control inspections is envisaged by MARPOL, Article 5 (2) of which provides that any such inspection 'shall be limited to verifying that there is on board a valid certificate, unless there are clear grounds for believing that the condition of the ship or its equipment does not correspond substantially with the particulars of that'.[86] In that case, or if the ship does not carry a valid certificate, the port State 'shall take such steps as will ensure that the ship shall not sail until it can proceed to sea without presenting an unreasonable threat of harm to the marine environment'.[87] More specific rules for port State control on Annex VI requirements are set out in Regulations 10 and 11 of Annex VI. Port State control is also envisaged by and consistent with the Law of the Sea Convention.[88]

3.5 FITNESS FOR PURPOSE AND THE WAY AHEAD

It is appropriate to conclude this chapter by considering whether UNCLOS can be considered as 'fit for purpose'. The answer to this question depends largely on the purpose that we expect UNCLOS to fulfil.

As it does in other contexts, in the context of GHG emissions from shipping UNCLOS adequately fulfils its designated function as a constitution for the oceans. This is evident in several ways. First, as seen in Section 3.4.1, the Convention provides a flexible definition of marine pollution that comfortably encompasses GHG emissions from shipping. Second, the Convention is conducive to harmonious coexistence between the different regimes that apply in this area. Article 192 allows for systemic integration of the UN climate change regime into the scope of the Convention, with the Paris Agreement effectively setting the standard for giving effect to Article 192 insofar as State obligations in the context of climate change are concerned.[89] Third, the Convention establishes clear rules in relation to flag, coastal and port State jurisdiction.[90] Flag and port State jurisdiction (including port State control) are arguably the two most important forms of jurisdiction for successful implementation of existing and future measures.

[86] MARPOL (n 7), Art. 5(2).
[87] Ibid.
[88] See UNCLOS (n 4), Arts. 219 and 226.
[89] Section 3.4.2.
[90] Section 3.4.4.

But if we expect UNCLOS to be a comprehensive solution on its own, then we will invariably be disappointed. This should not be surprising. The basic rules that are set out in UNCLOS were by design intended to be complemented by more comprehensive and detailed technical rules and regulations. This is at once an advantage of UNCLOS – in light of the flexibility and dynamism that it allows – and a potential pitfall of long-term stagnation as a result of State inaction.

The IMO's Initial Strategy is very much a tentative and preliminary step towards giving meaningful content and substance to UNCLOS's general provisions. Moving ahead, it is clear, however, that the Strategy will need to be followed up by substantive GHG emission reduction measures that are sufficiently ambitious in nature. In line with UNCLOS, these measures will need to be systemically integrated with the wider international environmental law framework and will need to be informed by the relevant goals under the UN Climate Change regime. UNCLOS offers the basic rules, the necessary structure and flexibility to deal with today's environmental problems, including GHG emission from ships, but it is up to the international community to make use of this flexibility and to fulfil common and individual obligations under UNCLOS to develop and then enforce adequate rules and standards. Only in this way can an effective regime for GHG emissions reduction in shipping be established and the rule of law truly be allowed to prevail.

4

An International Legal Framework for Marine Plastics Pollution

Time for a Change to Regulate the Lifecycle of Plastics

Dawoon Jung

4.1 INTRODUCTION

Plastics have become a popular material for use in a wide range of applications due to their characteristics of being safe, durable, inexpensive, and capable of being formed into a great variety of shapes. As a result of the explosion in the use of single-use and disposable plastics, the amount of plastic waste discharged into the oceans has become one of the most pressing environmental issues of our time. More than eight million tonnes of plastic waste are discarded into the oceans every year. And with the ever-increasing global consumption of plastic, research suggests that the oceans could contain, by weight, more plastic than fish by 2050.[1] Indeed, the Covid-19 pandemic has resulted in an additional issue with regard to marine plastics waste. The widespread use of single-use plastic products (e.g., masks and gloves) to provide protection against the spread of this infectious disease has generated and continues to generate millions of tons of plastic waste.[2]

Marine plastic litter and microplastics have become serious threats to the marine environment.[3] For example, marine species are suffering from entanglement, ingestion of plastic chemical substances and destruction of their marine habitats. Microplastics, which are fragments of plastic less than 5 mm in size, raise additional concerns. They cause potential threats not only to marine species but also to human health, via the food chain. The non-degradable nature of plastics and the ability of

[1] Graeme Wearden, 'More plastic than fish in the sea by 2050, says Ellen MacArthur', *The Guardian*, 19 January 2016. Available at: www.theguardian.com/business/2016/jan/19/more-plastic-than-fish-in-the-sea-by-2050-warns-ellen-macarthur (accessed 30 November 2021).

[2] Ana L. Patrício Silva, Joana C. Prata, Tony R. Walker, Armando C. Duarte, Wei Ouyang, Damià Barcelò and Teresa Rocha-Santos, 'Increased Plastic Pollution Due to COVID-19 Pandemic: Challenges and Recommendations' (2021) 405 *Chemical Engineering Journal* 1–9.

[3] See, GESAMP, *Proceedings of the GESAMP International Workshop on Assessing the Risks Associated with Plastics and Microplastics in the Marine Environment* (2020), 3–12; UN, *The Second World Ocean Assessment* Volume II, (2021) Chapter 12, 151–183.

plastic waste to travel long distances across the oceans from its origin can also cause a serious issue. The Great Pacific garbage patch is an example of this, as it comprises a floating plastic accumulation far from any point of origin, which is more than 1.6 million square km in size and contains around 80,000 tonnes of plastic.[4]

Whilst a number of treaties and legal instruments deal with marine plastics pollution, nevertheless, millions of tons of marine plastic waste are being discharged into the oceans on a continuous basis. This raises the question whether these regulations are adequate to address the situation, or whether the extent of plastics pollution taking place is due to poor implementation of these existing instruments.[5] The rule of law, an indispensable foundation for ocean governance, requires both legal certainty in law-making and also effective implementation.[6] Thus, the problem of marine plastics pollution raises a challenge in terms of maintenance of the rule of law. This chapter will examine how the rule of law could be enhanced in relation to regulation of marine plastics and microplastics pollution. It will provide an overview of the current legal framework that addresses marine plastics and microplastics and analyses what gaps remain within it. Then it will discuss how to enhance the current legal framework to promote the rule of law.

4.2 THE CURRENT LEGAL FRAMEWORK GOVERNING MARINE PLASTIC LITTER AND MICROPLASTICS

4.2.1 *Fragmented Nature of International Instruments*

No international treaty has the primary objective of preventing and regulating marine plastics pollution. The United Nations Convention on the Law of the Sea (UNCLOS)[7] provides an overarching legal framework regulating all activities in the oceans. In addition to a general obligation under Article 192 to protect the marine environment, Article 194 requires States to take all measures to prevent, reduce and control pollution of the marine environment. UNCLOS also regulates specific sources that have caused pollution, such as land-based sources,[8] dumping[9] and vessels.[10] However, UNCLOS does not provide detailed regulations on prevention of marine plastic litter and microplastics.

4 *National Geographic*, 'Great pacific garbage patch'. Available at: www.nationalgeographic.org/encyclopedia/great-pacific-garbage-patch/ (accessed 30 November 2021).

5 Karen Raubenheimer, Alistair McIlgorm and Nilüfer Oral, 'Towards an Improved International Framework to Govern the Life Cycle of Plastics' (2018) 27 *Review of European, Comparative & International Environmental Law* 210 at 216.

6 UNGA Resolution 67/1, 'Declaration of the high-level meeting of the general assembly on the rule of law at the national and international level', A/RES/67/1 (2012).

7 Montego Bay, 10 December 1982, in force 16 November 1994, 1833 UNTS 397.

8 UNCLOS (n. 7), Art. 207.

9 UNCLOS (n. 7), Art. 210.

10 UNCLOS (n. 7), Art. 211.

A wide range of legal instruments address issues relating to marine plastics. First, various treaties regulate different sources of marine plastics. For land-based sources, which are responsible for 80 per cent of the plastics disposed of in the oceans, UNCLOS remains the only binding treaty that regulates them in these terms.[11] Although Article 207 of UNCLOS is of particular importance, it allows States wide discretion in regulating land-based pollution to reconcile national economic interests and protection of the marine environment from land-based sources.[12] The Global Programme of Action for Protection of the Marine Environment from Land-based Activities (GPA), which is not legally binding, provides guidance on taking action to prevent land-based sources of pollution. In 2012, UNEP introduced the 'Honolulu Strategy: a Global Framework for Prevention and Management of Marine Debris' to support implementation of the GPA by a set of goals and strategies.

Sea-based sources that generate marine plastic litter and microplastics by fishing, dumping and shipping should also be regulated. The United Nations Agreement for Implementation of the Provisions of the United Nations Convention on the Law of the Sea of 10 December 1982 relating to the Conservation and Management of Straddling Fish Stocks and Highly Migratory Fish Stocks (UNFSA)[13] regulates abandoned, lost or otherwise discarded fishing gear, which forms a significant component of sea-based sources of marine plastics pollution. It requires States to minimise waste, discards and catch by lost or abandoned gear through taking appropriate measures.[14] In addition, the 1972 Convention on the Prevention of Marine Pollution by Dumping of Wastes and Other Matter[15] and its 1996 Protocol[16] regulates and strengthens the obligation to prohibit dumping under Article 210 of UNCLOS. The International Convention for the Prevention of Pollution from Ships (MARPOL),[17] which regulates ship-based sources of pollution, is linked to the obligation under Article 211 of UNCLOS. In particular, Annex

11 Nilufer Oral, 'From the Plastics Revolution to the Marine Plastics Crisis: A Patchwork of International Law', in Richard Barnes and Ronán Long (eds.), *Frontiers in International Environmental Law: Oceans and Climate Challenges: Essays in Honour of David Freestone* (Leiden: Brill 2021), 288.

12 Yoshifumi Tanaka, 'Regulation of Land-Based Marine Pollution in International Law: A Comparative Analysis between Global and Regional Legal Frameworks' (2006) 66 *ZaöRV* 535 at 547–548.

13 New York, 4 August 1995, in force 11 December 2001, 2167 UNTS 88.

14 UNFSA, ibid., Art. 5(f).

15 Washington/Moscow/London/Mexico City, adopted 29 December 1972, in force 30 August 1975, 1046 UNTS 120.

16 1996 Protocol to the Convention on the Prevention of Marine Pollution by Dumping of Wastes and Other Matter, 1972 (as amended in 2006).

17 International Convention for the Prevention of Pollution from Ships, London, 2 November 1973, 1340 UNTS 184, as Amended by the Protocol of 1978 Relating to the International Convention for the Prevention of Pollution from Ships of 1973, 17 February 1978, 1340 UNTS 61.

V on the prevention of pollution by garbage from ships prohibits all kinds of discharges into the sea, including plastics. Such plastic wastes include 'synthetic ropes, synthetic fishing nets, plastic garbage bags and incinerator ashes from plastic products'.[18]

Second, treaties regulating the impact of marine plastics on biodiversity and species include the Convention on Biological Diversity (CBD)[19] and the Convention on the Conservation of Migratory Species of Wild Animals (CMS).[20] Each conference of parties has adopted a series of decisions relating to the management of marine debris. These decisions are non-legally binding, but they contribute to identifying knowledge gaps regarding the impacts of marine plastics on biodiversity and to developing best practices that States can apply.[21]

Third, with regard to hazardous wastes, the Basel Convention on the Control of Transboundary Movements of Hazardous Wastes and Their Disposal (Basel Convention)[22] and the Stockholm Convention on Persistent Organic Pollutants (Stockholm Convention)[23] should be considered. The Basel Convention requires States to reduce hazardous waste generation, undertake environmentally sound management of hazardous wastes and restrict transboundary movements of hazardous wastes.[24] In 2019, the COP to the Basel Convention adopted a decision on the plastic waste amendment, which is notable progress in regulation of marine plastic waste.[25] The amendment has expanded the scope of 'hazardous waste' (Annex VIII) and 'other waste' (Annex II) so that most plastic wastes are subject to the Basel Convention. The amendment entered into force on 1 January 2021. Norway, which initially proposed the amendment, explains that the amendment will result in 'less marine plastic litter, increased traceability, more control and less illegal dumping of plastic waste'.[26] States should minimise generation of plastic waste and manage it in an environmentally sound manner.[27] Although the amendment to the Basel Convention expanded the scope to encompass regulation of plastic wastes, it has

18 MARPOL (n. 17) Annex V, Reg. 1(13).

19 Convention on Biological Diversity, Rio de Janeiro, 5 June 1992, 1760 UNTS 69.

20 Bonn, 23 June 1979, in force 1 November 1983, 1651 UNTS 333.

21 For example, CBD Decision XIII/10 on Addressing impacts of marine debris and anthropogenic underwater noise on marine and coastal biodiversity, CBD/COP/DEC/XIII/10 (2016) and Annex on 'Voluntary practical guidance on preventing and mitigating: the impacts of marine debris on marine and coastal biodiversity and habitats'; CMS Resolution 12.20 on Management of Marine Debris monitoring the effects (2017).

22 Basel, 22 March 1987, in force 5 May 1993, 1673 UNTS 57.

23 Stockholm, 22 May 2001, in force 17 May 2004, 2256 UNTS 119.

24 Basel Convention (n. 22) Art. 4.

25 Decision BC-14/12: Amendments to Annexes II, VIII and IX to the Basel Convention (n. 22), UNEP/CHW.14/28 (11 May 2019).

26 UNEP/CHW/OEWG.11/INF/36 (9 August 2018).

27 Basel Convention (n. 22), Art. 4(2). Art. 2(8) defines environmentally sound management of hazardous wastes or other wastes as 'taking all practicable steps to ensure that hazardous wastes or other wastes are managed in a manner which will protect human health and the environment against the adverse effects which may result from such wastes'.

been argued that there are still gaps, such as lack of national targets, relating to reducing the quantity of plastic waste in addition to no compliance system.[28] The plastic waste amendment does, nevertheless, represent notable progress in regulation of marine plastics pollution.[29] Indeed, the Stockholm Convention regulates plastics containing or adsorbing persistent organic pollutants that pose a hazard to marine ecosystems and humans.

Moreover, a regional legal framework provides an additional layer of regulation of marine plastic pollution. UNCLOS highlights the importance of regional cooperation in regulating pollution from land-based sources, which account for more than 80 per cent of marine plastic pollution.[30] The UNEP Regional Seas Programmes for the protection of the marine environment contribute to facilitating effective implementation of obligations, taking into account regional characteristics. Several regions have adopted regional seas conventions and legally binding instruments on different sources of pollution, such as land-based sources in the form of an annex or protocol.[31] In addition, some regions have adopted Action Plans on marine litter, recognising marine plastics as the main sources.[32] Although Action Plans are usually non-legally binding instruments – except the Regional Plan on Marine Litter Management in the Mediterranean – they demonstrate member States' consensus on regional priorities, develop best practices and promote compliance with international obligations.

However, despite a plethora of international instruments to regulate marine plastics pollution, they provide only limited obligations within their mandate. Not all regions have binding regional instruments relating to marine plastic litter and microplastics. In this regard, it has been argued that the current international instruments are 'rather patchy and subject to prudentially competing norms of behaviour'.[33] Fragmentation undermines legal certainty and reliable application of the laws in question.[34] It prevents effective implementation of relevant treaties, so resulting in weakening the rule of law.

[28] Karen Raubenheimer and Alistair McIlgorm, 'Can the Basel and Stockholm Conventions Provide a Global Framework to Reduce the Impact of Marine Plastic Litter?' (2018) 96 *Marine Policy* 285 at 286.

[29] Sabaa Ahmad Khan, 'Clearly Hazardous, Obscurely Regulated: Lessons from the Basel Convention on Waste Trade' (2020) 114 *American Journal of International Law* 200 at 200–205.

[30] UNCLOS, Art. 207.

[31] See Nilufer Oral, 'Forty Years of the UNEP Regional Seas Programmes: From Past to Future', in Rosemary Rayfuse (ed.), *Research Handbook on International Marine Environmental Law* (Cheltenham: Edward Elgar Publishing 2015), 339–362.

[32] For example, the Baltic Sea; East Asian Seas; the Mediterranean; the Northeast Atlantic; Northwest Pacific; the Wider Caribbean Region.

[33] Elizabeth A. Kirk and Naporn Popattanachai, 'Marine Plastics: Fragmentation, Effectiveness and Legitimacy in International Law-Making' (2018) 27 *Review of European, Comparative & International Environmental Law* 222 at 227.

[34] Anne Peters, 'The Refinement of International Law: From Fragmentation to Regime Interaction and Politicization' (2017) 15 *International Journal of Constitutional Law* 671 at 679.

4.2.2 *Lack of Consideration of the Lifecycle of Plastics*

The current legal framework on marine plastics pollution still does not provide a holistic approach governing all the lifecycle phases of plastics. The approach focusing on waste management will not be able to prevent generation of plastics, especially since the use of plastics causes significant negative environmental impacts on the marine environment at each stage of the plastics lifecycle.[35] On the other hand, a lifecycle approach of plastics seeks sustainable solutions based on the entire lifecycle of plastics rather than focusing on waste management at the end of their life. Therefore, the need is to take a lifecycle approach. This suggests adopting measures from the early phases of plastic production, such as a sustainable design for reuse, recycling or composting, and reducing the use of harmful substances to the end-of-life phase.[36] This is closely linked to a circular economy for plastics, which represents a shift from waste management to resource management.[37]

There are a few instruments regulating the entire lifecycle of plastics, including upstream activities, such as manufacturing, materials used and product design.[38] For example, CBD guidance covers the full lifecycle of plastic pollution, addressing production design, limiting consumption of plastic, promoting recycling and best practices along with the whole of plastics manufacturing. The COP of the Basel Convention discusses updating Technical Guidelines for the Identification and Environmentally Sound Management of Plastic Wastes and for Their Disposal to reflect the entire lifecycle of plastic wastes. It recognises that 'waste prevention or reduction involves both upstream alterations in product design, including use of alternative materials or technologies … '.[39] It recommends measures at the early stages of plastic production, including adopting a sustainable design for reuse, recycling or composting, and reducing the use of harmful substances.[40] Extended producer responsibility addressed in the technical guidelines is closely linked to a lifecycle approach as it promotes waste minimisation from product design through to disposal of plastics by allocating a significant responsibility to producers.[41] Although the guidelines do not impose obligations on States, they provide general guidance for developing national waste management strategies and best practices with respect to environmentally sound management of plastic waste.

35 Giulia Carlini and Konstantin Kleine, 'Advancing the International Regulation of Plastic Pollution beyond the United Nations Environment Assembly Resolution on Marine Litter and Microplastics' (2018) 27 *Review of European, Comparative & International Environmental Law* 234 at 243.

36 UNEP/CHW.14/INF/29/Add.1; UNEP/POPS/COP.9/INF/28/Add.1 (15 March 2019), para. 12.

37 Ibid.

38 CBD/COP/DEC/XIII/10 (2016), (n. 21), para. 8.

39 UNEP/CHW/OEWG.12/INF/14 (15 May 2020), 31, para. 98.

40 Ibid., 32, para. 102.

41 Ibid., 35–36, paras. 117–126.

There is increasing recognition of a lifecycle approach beyond the limit of waste management in tackling marine plastic pollution. It is interesting to note that UNEA Resolution 3/7 on marine plastic litter and microplastics highlights that 'preventive action through waste minimization and environmentally sound waste management' is the highest priority.[42] However, UNEA Resolution 4/6 moves forward from waste management by underlining 'the importance of more sustainable management of plastics throughout their lifecycle in order to increase sustainable consumption and production patterns … '.[43] A lifecycle approach will contribute to minimising plastic waste generation, including microplastics, and reduce the use of hazardous substances through the entire plastics lifecycle, so as to closely link to the obligation to prevent under Article 192 of UNCLOS and to increase zero waste at the end-of-life phase of plastic.

4.3 STRENGTHENING THE EXISTING REGULATORY FRAMEWORK

4.3.1 *Cooperation and Coordination between International Instruments*

The fragmentation that exists between regulations remains an obstacle to tackling marine plastic litter and microplastics pollution. Cooperation and coordination between international instruments at the global level would help to reduce unnecessary overlap and duplication between existing regulations and improve implementation of legal instruments, consequently strengthening the rule of law. Since existing instruments often have overlapping objectives in terms of protecting the marine environment from marine plastic pollution within each sectoral interest, they are closely related to each other, and thus should be considered comprehensively and in a coordinated manner. The COP to the Basel Convention is a good example: it adopted guidance in collaboration with the IMO on how to improve the sea–land interface to ensure that waste offloaded from a ship, which previously fell within the scope of MARPOL, is managed in an environmentally sound manner.[44]

In this regard, UNEP, as 'the entity providing secretariat functions' for a number of multilateral environmental agreements, could be used as an overarching body to coordinate different institutions.[45] UNEP is neither a superior institution with the authority to override decisions adopted by other institutions nor one that could impose legally binding decisions on States.[46] Yet it could encourage inter-sectoral coordination for the effective development and implementation of regulations

[42] UNEP/EA.3/Res.7 (30 January 2018), preamble.

[43] UNEP/EA.4/Res.6 (28 March 2019), preamble.

[44] UNEP/CHW.13/18 and UNEP/CHW.13/INF/37/Rev.1 (8 May 2018); UNEP/CHW.13/INF/37 (6 April 2017).

[45] UNEP/EA.1/INF/8 (30 May 2014), 7–10.

[46] Elvira Pushkareva, 'United Nations Environment Programme (UNEP)' (2014) *Max Planck Encyclopaedia of International Law*, para. 21.

intended for prevention of marine plastics and microplastics pollution. The coordinating role of UNEP in regulating marine plastic pollution has been recognised in several instruments. For example, Decision 14/13 adopted by COP to the Basel Convention stresses 'the importance of cooperation and coordination with other international organizations and activities through existing mechanisms, and in particular the multi-stakeholder platform within the UNEP'.[47]

4.3.2 *Importance of Regional Cooperation*

Regional conventions and action plans adopted in several regions are only applicable within a specific geographical scope. However, these could still serve as a significant platform to develop guidelines and best practices to prevent marine plastic pollution, taking into account its regional characteristics. The transboundary nature of plastic waste also requires a coordinated response across the regions. Interregional cooperation contributes to developing harmonised standards and promoting effective implementation at national levels.[48] The Regional Plan on Marine Litter Management in the Mediterranean could be considered a good example. Although it aims to address marine litter in general, including both land-based and sea-based sources, it is also applicable to marine plastic waste. The binding nature of the plan includes self-determined national targets and timelines that States should meet, which are applicable to marine plastic waste and countervail the weakness of international instruments.[49] It also requires regional cooperation by establishing institutional cooperation with various relevant regional institutions.[50]

Some action plans expand broad aspects of regulation of marine litter, reflecting the lifecycle of plastic. For example, the action plan in the Mediterranean region states that 'the entire lifecycle of the product with measures prioritizing the hierarchy of waste management to encourage companies to design products with long durability for reuse, recycling and materials reduction in weight and toxicity'.[51] It includes an extensive producer responsibility strategy aiming at ensuring the entire lifecycle of the product and advocates establishment of manufacturing methodologies in cooperation with the plastics industry.[52] The OSPAR[53] Regional Action Plan

47 UNEP/CHW.14/13, Decision BC-14/13 (2019), para. 4.

48 Youna Lyons, MeiLin Neo, Amanda Lim, Yuke Ling Tay and Vu Hai Dang, 'Status of research, legal and policy efforts on marine plastics in ASEAN+3: A gap analysis at the interface of science, law and policy', COBSEA and NUS, (2020), 348–349. Available at: https://cil.nus.edu.sg/research/special-projects/#polllution-from-marine-plastics-in-the-seas-of-asean-plus-three (accessed 30 November 2021), 349.

49 The Regional Plan on Marine Litter Management in the Mediterranean (adopted in December 2013; entered into force 8 July 2014), Art. 7 and Annex II.

50 Ibid., Art. 18.

51 Ibid., Art. 9(3)(a).

52 Ibid., paras. 3(a) and (g).

53 Convention for the Protection of the Marine Environment of the North-East Atlantic (OSPAR Convention), Paris, 22 September 1992, in force 25 March 1998, 2354 UNTS 67.

also provides upstream measures, including development of design improvements in sustainable packaging and the phase-out of microplastics in certain industries.[54] Considering that fishing gear is one of the major sources of marine plastic pollution, OSPAR adopted the Scoping Study on Best Practices for the Design and Recycling of Fishing Gear. This is consistent with a lifecycle approach as it addresses the design and recycling of fishing gear throughout the supply chain.[55] Thus, these regional action plans indicate that they complement implementation of international obligations taking into account the lifecycle of plastics and promote consistent action at regional and national levels.

Moreover, a monitoring system under the UNEP Regional Seas Programme should be highlighted.[56] This will contribute to monitoring compliance of international obligations by filling in the gaps in the data on marine plastics, such as the impact of marine plastics on regional seas, on plastic material flow and the quantity of marine plastic waste. It will assist in developing a global monitoring assessment on marine plastic pollution.[57] Monitoring in regions where the largest number of marine plastics are discarded could also provide a scientific basis for enhancing efficient decision-making and subsequently taking concrete measures.

4.3.3 *Engagement of Multi-Stakeholders*

Multi-stakeholders play a significant role in achieving a lifecycle approach in a circular economy. In particular, the plastics industry can contribute to developing technical standards and certificates relating to, for instance, labelling, recyclability and biodegradability. Development of industry standards relating to production, consumption, recycling and the final treatment of plastic is crucial to promoting implementation at national, regional and global levels. Yet there are regulatory and technical challenges to be faced throughout the lifecycle of plastics. They include substitution with no alternatives (product design phase), chemical release from plastic products (use phase), difficulties of chemical risk assessment and emission of potentially toxic substances (end-of-life phase).[58]

54 OSPAR Regional Action Plan (RAP) for Marine Litter (2014–2021).

55 OSPAR, OSPAR scoping study on best practices for the design and recycling of fishing gear as a means to reduce quantities of fishing gear found as marine litter in the North-East Atlantic (2020), 68–69.

56 UNEP, 'Summary of the analysis of the effectiveness of existing and potential response options and activities on marine litter and microplastics at all levels to determine the contribution in solving the global problem', UNEP/AHEG/4/4 (28 September 2020), 9–12.

57 Nicole Wienrich, Laura Weiand and Sebastian Unger, 'Stronger together, the role of regional instruments in strengthening global governance of marine plastic pollution', Institute for Advanced Sustainability Studies (2021), 36–39.

58 UNEP/CHW.14/INF/29/Add.1; UNEP/POPS/COP.9/INF/28/Add.1 (15 March 2019) (n. 36), para. 12.

Multi-stakeholder partnerships can fill regulatory gaps and assist in tackling these challenges. For example, the Global Partnership on Marine Litter is a multi-stakeholder partnership to facilitate international cooperation through implementation of the Honolulu Strategy.[59] It serves as a global platform for multi-stakeholders that can contribute to information sharing, development of new technologies and capacity building. It provides a useful forum for discussing industry standards and developing harmonised best practices to be implemented in collaboration with private actors. Indeed, the Basel Convention recently established a new Partnership on Plastic Waste to promote environmentally sound management of plastic waste in cooperation with multi-stakeholders, including 'governments, regional and local authorities, Regional Seas Programmes, intergovernmental organizations, private sector, non-governmental organizations and academia'.[60] These partnerships can contribute to building synergies in collaboration with other international and regional organisations and the private sector.

Moreover, multi-stakeholder partnerships can play a significant role in enhancing the rule of law by providing opportunities for participation in salient law-making. They will be critical in decision-making and implementation of regulations and standards to achieve a circular economy for plastics. In this regard, whilst the international framework governing plastics should move towards a circular economy, cooperation with multi-stakeholders at multiple levels should be enhanced.

4.4 TOWARDS A GLOBAL TREATY ON THE LIFECYCLE OF PLASTICS

The United Nations Environment Assembly has discussed marine plastic litter and microplastics, and has recently adopted a series of resolutions on this matter.[61] In particular, the Assembly also established the ad hoc open-ended expert group on marine litter and microplastics to 'identify the range of national, regional and international response options, including actions and innovative approaches, and voluntary and *legally binding governance strategies and approaches*'.[62] Recognising the fragmented nature of the current legal framework on marine plastics pollution, the group suggested possible options for improved global governance to tackle marine plastics pollution. These options broadly include (1) to maintain the status quo which should not be considered; (2) to revise and strengthen the existing

[59] See, Global Partnership on Marine Litter: Purpose, Function and Organization, Framework Document (2018).

[60] UNEP/CHW.14/INF/16/Rev.1 (11 June 2019).

[61] UNEP/EA.1/Res.6 (27 June 2014); UNEP/EA.2/Res.11 (4 August 2016); UNEP/EA.3/Res.7 (30 January 2018); UNEP/EA.4/Res.6 (28 March 2019).

[62] Ibid., UNEP/EA.3/Res.7 (30 January 2018), para. 10(d) (emphasis added).

framework; and (3) to adopt a new treaty that encompasses both enforced and voluntary measures.[63]

At the fourth meeting of the ad hoc open-ended expert group on marine litter and microplastics in 2020, the third option, adoption of a new treaty on marine plastics, was strongly supported by many delegates.[64] Various delegates highlighted the key elements that should be considered in a new treaty, such as measurable targets or timelines; global industry standards, such as for design, labelling and recycling; harmonised monitoring procedures; effective compliance mechanisms; and capacity building.[65] Delegates also declared that these key elements should be developed in alignment with the entire lifecycle of plastics approach.

In 2022, UNGA adopted a resolution to develop a legally binding global instrument on plastic pollution 'based on a comprehensive approach that addresses the full life cycle of plastic' by 2024.[66] A new treaty could improve legal certainty and increase compliance with international standards, thus enhancing the rule of law. Yet a new treaty would not be a one-stop solution for preventing and managing marine plastics pollution. The legally binding nature of such a treaty and an effective enforcement mechanism for it have yet to be confirmed. Not all countries have expressed their support for adoption of a new treaty. If the States that produce most of the plastics waste were to refuse to ratify a new global treaty, the effectiveness of such a treaty could not be guaranteed. Therefore, whilst a new treaty aims to close the gaps in the existing legal framework, it should be mutually supportive of it, and not undermine obligations under existing treaties.[67] Adoption of a new treaty should not replace existing legal instruments. Rather, it should reinforce and strengthen existing rules and standards, thereby enhancing the rule of law for oceans.

4.5 CONCLUSION

Marine plastics litter and microplastics pose one of the most serious challenges to the marine environment today. Whilst UNCLOS provides an overarching legal framework to deal with marine plastics issues, which should be supplemented by multiple layers of global and regional regulations, a range of treaties and non-binding instruments regulate marine plastics, with a particular focus on their respective specific mandates. Although the 2019 amendment of the annexes to the

[63] UNEP, 'Combating marine plastic litter and microplastics: an assessment of the effectiveness of relevant international, regional and sub regional governance strategies and approaches – a summary for policymakers', UNEP/AHEG/2018/1/INF/3 (20 April 2018).

[64] UNEP, 'Report on the work of the ad hoc open-ended expert group on marine litter and microplastics at its fourth meeting', UNEP/AHEG/4/7 (18 November 2020), 17–22, paras. 129–160.

[65] Ibid.

[66] UNEP/EA.5/Res.14 (07 March 2022).

[67] Raubenheimer et al. 219.

Basel Convention is notable progress in regulating plastic waste, the current legal framework for marine plastics pollution is still criticised as a patchwork of instruments that are fragmented and ineffective in tackling the marine plastics issue. Marine plastics pollution is among those issues that indicate challenges to the rule of law in the sense that the fragmented nature of legal instruments regulating marine plastics and microplastics weakens legal certainty and effective implementation.

Existing legal instruments at global and regional levels remain an important aspect in terms of tackling marine plastics pollution. Cooperation and coordination between sector-specific instruments and between multiple layers of regulations at global, regional and national levels will promote coherent regulations and implementation. Meanwhile, a new paradigm revolving around adopting a lifecycle approach should be considered. This could significantly contribute to prevention of marine plastics litter and microplastics. There is growing awareness regarding issues of pollution 'upstream', which requires prevention and minimisation of plastic waste generation at an early stage of plastic production. Although a lifecycle approach has not been fully reflected in the current legal framework, it has recently been increasingly referred to as momentum for sustainable production and consumption. Multi-stakeholder partnership should be promoted in order to facilitate development of initiative solutions throughout the entire lifecycle of plastics from design to recyclability.

Despite urgent and widespread threats to the marine environment from marine plastics pollution, there is no one-stop shop solution. While discussion at the United Nations Environment Assembly clearly expressed support for adoption of a global agreement, development of a new international agreement and strengthening of the current legal framework should be mutually reinforced. The rule of law will be maintained only through comprehensive efforts to enhance legal certainty and to facilitate implementation of legal obligations at global, regional and national levels, taking into account the lifecycle of plastics.

5

The 'Thin Law' of Plastic Regulation and a Proposal for a Regional or Global Waste Tariff

Anastasia Telesetsky

5.1 INTRODUCTION

In general, effective rule of law relies on certain general attributes, including predictability, stability and accountability. In several ocean law areas including the subject of this chapter – marine plastic pollution – States have attempted to implement basic rule of law principles through laws, regulations and codes. In practice, however, the existing marine plastic pollution laws have failed to achieve an effective environmental rule of law, and this will continue to be so until States require some accountability from the primary producers and users of plastics. While the plastic packaging industry, especially the single-use plastic market, will continue to increase output, the industry has generally been able to avoid legal accountability for the harms associated with its products by shifting attention to consumers' 'desire' for convenience and municipalities' responsibilities to manage solid waste.

This chapter suggests that much of existing law that could address marine plastic packaging waste operates as a smokescreen for continued industry operations. This has consequences for both the plastic waste challenge and capping existing carbon emissions. As this chapter will argue, the problem is 'thin law', where the law exists but either fails to tackle the most difficult management aspects of the problem or attempts to tackle difficult issues but allows numerous exceptions.

Section 5.2 offers a brief introduction to an increasingly well-known problem: the saturation of plastic packaging waste into marine spaces. Section 5.3 identifies gaps and challenges with existing plastic management legal tools using several examples. And Section 5.4 offers a potential solution to the 'thin law' problem with the introduction of tariffs to stimulate a transition to a circular economy where packaging remains a resource and not waste.

5.2 PROBLEM: THE PLASTOCENE

Chronic plastic pollution in the oceans from packaging has attracted global attention. One estimate posits 50–80 per cent of marine litter as plastic in origin.[1] Impacts on living systems include entanglement, ingestion, smothering and transport of toxins and non-endemic species.[2] In the 1960s, early marine litter research pointed to the lethality of many of these fishing-related plastics for seabirds, turtles and sea mammals.[3] By the 1970s and 1980s, continued research indicated that the problems associated with plastic had intensified. In some instances, plastic has changed the physical environment with unknown implications for species depending on coastal currents and beaches.[4] Researchers continue to locate plastic not just along inhabited coastal areas but also the world's remotest islands, such as Henderson Island in the Pitcairn Island chain, and the world's deepest sea features, including the Marianas Trench.[5]

The Pew Foundation estimates that continuing 'business as usual' practices in current management of plastic waste will result in increased use of our shared oceans as an 'oceanfill'.[6] Known chronic impacts of marine plastics on the ocean ecosystem such as entrapment and ingestion are well-documented by researchers and non-governmental organizations. Less-researched impacts of marine plastics may also include long-term negative consequences for ecosystems, commerce, national security and food security.[7] The impact on human health of ingested microplastics from food sources such as fish remains uncertain. It is possible that

1 D. Barnes et al., Accumulation and fragmentation of plastic debris in global environments (2009) 364 *Philosophical Transactions of the Royal Society B: Biological Sciences* 1985–1998.

2 M. R. Gregory, Environmental implications of plastic debris in marine settings: Entanglement, ingestion, smothering, hangers-on, hitch-hiking and alien invasions (2009) 364 *Philosophical Transactions of the Royal Society B* 2013–2025.

3 P. G. Ryan, A brief history of marine litter research, in M. Bergmann et al. (eds.), *Marine Anthropogenic Litter* (Cham: Springer 2015) 1–25.

4 H. S. Carson et al., Small plastic debris changes water movement and heat transfer through beach sediments (2011) 62 *Marine Pollution Bulletin* 1708–1713.

5 J. Lavers and A. Bond, Exceptional and rapid accumulation of anthropogenic debris on one of the world's most remote and pristine islands (6 June 2017) 114 (23) *PNAS* 6052–6055; Reis Thebault, 'He went where no human had gone before. Our trash had already beaten him there' (14 May 2019), *The Washington Post*.

6 Pew Foundation, 'Breaking the plastic, wave' (2020), www.pewtrusts.org/-/media/assets/2020/07/breakingtheplasticwave_report.pdf

7 Sunwook Hong et al., Navigational threats by derelict fishing gear to navy ships in the Korean seas (June 2017) 119 *Marine Pollution Bulletin* 100–105 (plastic fishing gear entangles propellers on vessels, including navy ships); Anne Nash, Impacts of marine debris on subsistence fishermen: An exploratory study (March 1992) 24 *Marine Pollution Bulletin* 150–156; P. Farrell and K. Nelson, Trophic level transfer of microplastic: *Mytilus edulis* (L.) to *Carcinus maenas* (L.) (2013) 177 *Environmental Pollution* 1–3; Ana Markic et al., Plastic ingestion by marine fish in the wild (2020) 50 *Critical Reviews in Environmental Science and Technology* 657–697. (Researchers reviewing 93 papers on plastic ingestion in fish found microplastic ingestion in 67 per cent of the 391 commercial fish species.)

these microplastics concentrate toxins in the environment.[8] Equally alarming and inadequately researched, plastics release greenhouse gases as they disintegrate in the ocean, and microplastics may be interrupting the ability of the ocean to operate efficiently as a carbon sink.[9]

In response to unsettling media images of sea turtles with straws in their noses, rivers clogged with plastic waste and villages burning imported plastic waste, global norms had begun to slowly shift towards reducing virgin plastic packaging output. Young people have been particularly committed crusaders to ending ocean plastic pollution.[10] While normative shifts can be identified in the demands of some consumer groups and the actions of some corporations, have these normative shifts been reflected in the law? Does the rule of law as applied to oceans compel legal reform that will slow or reverse 'business as usual' trends? Or is the existing law 'thin law' that will be unable to shift the packaging industry because application of the law will only replicate the status quo?

5.3 GAPS AND CHALLENGES: TOO MUCH 'THIN LAW' FOR A THICK LAW PROBLEM

As observed in the previous section, the global community has had decades of awareness of the problem of plastics. The global community has been addressing known problems with marine plastics for almost five decades since adoption of the Convention on the Prevention of Pollution by Dumping of Wastes and Other Matters (London Convention). In 1988, with a focus on vessel operations, States passed Annex V of the International Convention for the Prevention of Pollution from Ships to prevent intentional garbage disposal. These laws, if fully complied with, would reduce at least one known source of marine pollution. Vessel-based plastic pollution remains, however, a problem, as indicated by the registration of 10,000 pollution incidents in the Western and Central Pacific Ocean between 2003 and 2015; 37 per cent of these incidents were intentional discharges of plastic.[11]

8 US Environmental Protection Agency, Toxicological Threats of Plastic, www.epa.gov/trash-free-waters/toxicological-threats-plastic (Observing that 'When PBTs [persistent, bioaccumulative and toxic substances] encounter plastic debris, they tend to preferentially sorb (take up or hold) to the debris. In effect plastics are like magnets for PBTs.')

9 Sarah-Jean Royer et al., Production of methane and ethylene from plastic in the environment (1 August 2018) *PLOS ONE*, http://dx.doi.org.ezproxy.uio.no/10.1371/journal.pone.0200574; Alina Wieczorek et al., Microplastic ingestion by gelatinous zooplankton may lower efficiency of the biological pump (April 2019) 53 *Environmental Science & Technology* 5387–5395; Cai Zhang et al., Toxic effect of microplastic on marine microalgae *Skeletonema costatum*: Interactions between microplastic and algae (January 2017) 220(B) *Environmental Pollution* 1282–1288.

10 See e.g., Ocean Heroes Network, Ocean Heroes Bootcamp, https://oceanheroes.blue/ (asserting that 'This bootcamp turns kids into plastic-fighting superheroes.')

11 K. Richardson et al., Marine pollution original from purse seine and longline fishing vessel operations in the Western and Central Pacific Ocean 2003–2015 (March 2017) 46(2) *Ambio*

As problematic as 'at-sea' plastics are, land-based plastic garbage poses risks that have yet to be addressed comprehensively through law. The United Nations Convention on the Law of the Sea (UNCLOS) that requires States to prohibit pollution from land-based sources is weak. States only committed themselves to adopt laws and regulations 'taking into account internationally agreed rules, standards and recommended practices and procedures' designed to prevent, reduce or control toxic, harmful or noxious substances from land-based sources.[12] As of 2020, there are no international rules, standards or recommended practices and procedures for land-based plastics unless States were to legislate based on emerging industry trends towards reducing the amount of virgin plastic being used in packaging.[13]

To avoid offshoring of plastic pollution problems, the Basel Convention parties adopted amendments that became effective on 1 January 2021, requiring shippers to obtain prior informed consent for particular shipments of plastic waste deemed to be hazardous.[14] At the regional level, States have also attempted to address land-based pollution through a variety of instruments calling on them to take action. For example, the Cartagena Convention's Protocol Concerning Pollution from Land-Based Sources and Activities urges State participants to reduce solid waste/marine litter by developing National Programmes of Action for Watershed and Coastal Management as well as developing marine management plans to reduce marine pollution.[15] The Protocol serves an important coordination role to assist the Caribbean Sea States in tackling the reality that the Caribbean region is home to the second most plastic-contaminated sea after the Mediterranean Sea.[16] While the Protocol itself will not eliminate marine litter, it is expected to catalyse national legislation.

What is needed to eliminate marine litter is regulation of source material and production. The challenge for the 'rule of law' in this area is how to achieve this type of regulation without being outmanoeuvred by a powerful industry of fossil fuel, chemical and plastic corporations. Most States in response to public concerns have offered some form of legislation designed to address plastic waste. Many of these responses are 'thin', and by 'thin' this chapter refers to responses that do not directly address the problem at hand, or when they do address the problem at hand are

190–200. (Reporting that most of the incidents were from Papua New Guinea and six water fishing nations: Taiwan, United States, Korea, Philippines, Japan and China.)

12 Montego Bay, 10 December 1982, in force 16 November 1994, 1833 U.N.T.S. 397.

13 Unilever Announces Ambitious New Commitments for a Waste-Free World (7 October 2019), www.unilever.com/news/press-releases/2019/unilever-announces-ambitious-new-commitments-for-a-waste-free-world.html

14 Basel Convention on the Control of Transboundary Movements of Hazardous Wastes and their Disposal (Basel Convention) Basel, 22 March 1987, in force 5 May 1993, 1673 UNTS 57. Basel Convention Plastic Waste Amendments to Annex IX, OEWG-11/7 (2019).

15 Available at www2.ecolex.org/server2neu.php/libcat/docs/TRE/Full/En/TRE-001331.txt

16 Report on Status of Styrofoam and Plastic Bag Bans in the Wider Caribbean, UNEP – Caribbean Environment Programme (May 2019), https://gpml-caribe.org/download/32/reports/1486/status-of-styrofoam-and-plastic-bans-in-the-caribbean.pdf

engulfed in exceptions that allow operations to continue according to the existing status quo. What this means is that even though there is law on the books, the law as conceived is unable to address the scale of the problem. Looking at the examples in the next sections, one might conclude that 'thin law' is the best that one can expect from political compromise. While this may be the pragmatic reality of the authority of modern legislative institutions, these 'thin' laws fail to offer any possibility of shifting the environmental paradigm as they continue to encourage ongoing investments in conventional fossil fuel-based plastic production.

5.3.1 *Thin National Laws*

Three examples illustrate this 'thin law approach. First, the United States as a major plastic producer has no national approach to reducing packaging sources that contribute to marine litter. While, on the one hand, persistent plastic that becomes waste could be characterized as hazardous waste under the Resource Conservation and Recovery Act (RCRA) depending on ecological toxicity associated with accumulated marine litter,[17] this law has never been applied consistently across industries to reduce mismanaged waste. For example, even though researchers in 2010 working in the Puget Sound region recovered 870 gillnets that had arguably become waste containing plastic filaments that entrapped thousands of fish, hundreds of birds and dozens of mammals, no attempt has been made to hold the fishing industry or fishing net manufacturers accountable for failing to manage a potentially dangerous waste material because this would have required the regulators or courts to be creative in applying the RCRA.[18] Nor are plastic beverage container manufacturers considered to be generators of waste for the purposes of the RCRA even though only minimal numbers of bottles are ever recycled. The RCRA law, despite setting national standards, is not 'fit' to address marine debris or the amassing of post-consumer plastics except to ensure that landfills are properly designed.

More specific attempts to address Marine Debris in US legislation fare no better in terms of delivering outcomes capable of addressing the scale of the challenge. The Marine Debris Act as amended by the Save our Seas Act provided for the National Oceanic and Atmospheric Administration to work with other federal agencies to address marine debris sources, to assist in facilitating a response to a 'severe marine debris event' and to develop international action.[19] Not unsurprisingly, given the growth of the plastics industry in the United States and the strength

[17] M. J. Bean, Legal strategies for reducing persistent plastics in marine environments (1987) 18 *Marine Pollution Bulletin* 357–360.

[18] T. P. Good et al., Derelict fishing nets in Puget Sound and the Northwest Straits: Patterns and threats to marine fauna (2010) 60 *Marine Pollution Bulletin* 39–50.

[19] Save Our Seas Act of 2018, P.L. 115–265, https://marinedebris.noaa.gov/sites/default/files/2018%20Save%20our%20Seas%20Act%2C%20Title%20I%20%28S.%203508%29.pdf

of the industry lobby,[20] the law fails to specifically address unabated plastic manufacturing for ends such as single-use packaging as one of the unmitigated sources of marine pollution.

A second 2020 Save Our Seas 2.0 Act that passed the partisan US House and Senate extends financing for a trust fund and a prize competition.[21] While the prize competition offers an improvement over the existing 2018 Save our Seas law by rewarding one or more individuals for the development of ocean-degradable packaging materials and other packaging innovations, the law remains quite 'thin' because it fails to recognize the existence of numerous viable ocean-degradable packaging materials and to mandate for better packaging standards using these existing materials. Instead, the proposed US law presumes that the market will boost the prize winner's innovation, plastic production will shift to new materials on a schedule that is amenable to plastic producers and Congress will not need to intervene. Equally 'thin' are the provisions on addressing the proliferation of ocean-bound plastic in the fishing industry, where government administrators 'shall encourage United States efforts, such as the Fishing for Energy net disposal program'.[22]

The United States' approach is a 'thin' approach because it offers nothing more than a potential indirect fix through the possible development of a new market niche. There are no affirmative steps designed to transform existing supply chains. The United States could have attempted a 'thick' law fix that would address the heart of the problem, as it attempted to do with the 1970 Clean Air Act mandating 'technology-forcing' that required the automobile industry to design higher efficiency vehicles and better emission control systems.[23] The 'thinness' of US efforts is unsurprising given the powerful lobbying support from the Grocery Manufacturers Association, the America Chemistry Council and the Plastic Industry Association.

A second example of a 'thin' approach is taken by Uganda whose legislation, at first glance, seems to be on target to address the issue of plastic production. Uganda extended a ban on plastic bags, but a closer review of the ban illustrates that a large sector of single-use plastic packaging production remains intentionally unregulated. When Uganda opted in 2010 to ban the importation, sale and use of plastic bags in response to the waste challenges faced by the nation, the government adopted a set of regulations that allowed for extensive exceptions to the more general prohibition

20 Thomas Hundertmark et al., Accelerating plastic recovery in the United States (22 December 2019) McKinsey & Company Chemicals, www.mckinsey.com/industries/chemicals/our-insights/accelerating-plastic-recovery-in-the-united-states# (Estimating that demand for plastics may grow in the United States by 35 per cent above current levels by 2040).

21 Save our Seas 2.0 Act (2020) (n 19) P.L. 116–224.

22 Ibid. at Sec. 133(b).

23 Clean Air Act, Section 110, 42 U.S.C.A. 7410(a)(2)(A) and Section 202(b)19)(A), 42 U.S.C.A. 7521(b)(1)(A).

against plastic bags, including 'plastic for packaging of toilet paper', 'shrink sleeves made of plastic for labelling of water bottles, cosmetic bottles, and jars', 'plastic bags used for packaging of candy sweets, biscuits, pasta, sugar… and any other food or cosmetic product requiring moisture barrier properties' and 'plastic sheeting for agricultural, horticultural or floricultural use'.[24] When the schedule to the regulations listing the exceptions to the ban is read *in toto*, the list of exceptions encompasses a broad array of potentially problematic packaging and industrial materials, where alternative packaging materials are likely to exist though they may be more costly. While these exceptions that were negotiated into the law reflect the reality of stakeholders who have already sunk costs into packaging materials and packaging machinery, they also reflect a 'thin' approach to law, as the status quo for plastic manufacturing remains for much of Uganda.[25]

Finally, even where a State imposes a ban on plastic importation or production, laws may appear tough on their face but are unable to be implemented due to unenforceability. As UNEP authors noted in a recent report on the legal limits of single-use plastics, 'the majority of bans do not contain specific enforcement provisions, such as fines or prosecutions'.[26] For countries where the normative push in support of the legal ban framework lacks broad community support, lack of enforcement means that the law may become 'ultrathin', as it depends on persuasion for implementation rather than authority.

5.3.2 *Thicker Laws?*

A couple of 'thick' laws have yet to be fully tested but could change production paradigms if broadly adopted and with the intention of innovating in the existing packaging market. What constitutes a 'thick law' for the purposes of marine plastic waste is a law with enough substantive content and implementation to lead to a fundamental change in the current packaging economy that sells a million conventionally produced plastic bottles every minute and expects to grow by 20 per cent.[27] As of today, few countries are prepared to experiment with these laws. On 29 July 2019, Tuvalu introduced an import ban on single-use bottles under 1.5 litres and food

[24] Government of Uganda, The finance (permitted plastic bags and other plastics for exceptional use) regulations 2010 No. 32 (20 August 2010).

[25] Uganda's president vocalized an intention to implement a ban in June 2018, but there has been limited political will to stop plastic manufacturing. Attention has shifted to plastic recycling. Pritish Behuria, The comparative political economy of plastic bag bans in East Africa: Why implementation, has varied in Rwanda, Kenya, and Uganda, The University of Manchester Global Development Institute (February 2019), http://hummedia.manchester.ac.uk/institutes/gdi/publications/workingpapers/GDI/gdi-working-paper-2019037-behuria.pdf

[26] UNEP, Legal limits on single-use plastics and microplastics: A review of national laws and regulations (2018) 48, https://wedocs.unep.org/bitstream/handle/20.500.11822/27113/plastics_limits.pdf

[27] Sandra Laville and Matthew Taylor, A million bottles a minute: World's plastic binge 'as dangerous as climate change', *The Guardian* (28 June 2017).

wrap as well as bags, straws, cutlery and plates.[28] Failure to comply could lead to an individual fine of up to US$3420 or a corporate fine of up to US$6840 for a first offence and/or imprisonment of up to two months. Depending on how regulators interpret 'food wrap', these laws could change how locally produced food is distributed and packaged. Tuvalu is, however, a very small market for global trade.

As of mid-2020 Costa Rica is in the process of implementing a law requiring importers, producers, marketers and distributors of single-use plastic bottles and products that are packaged in single-use bottles to engage in either: using recycled resins, recovering bottles in an extended producer responsibility scheme, designing products minimizing waste or working with municipalities to recover waste.[29] Violations of the law would be subject to fines and an obligation to compensate and restore environmental damage. Implementation of this law could substantially change packaging practices within Costa Rica, but there is no requirement that any of the packaging be marine biodegradable.

In the Caribbean Sea and Pacific Ocean region, several 'thicker' laws have been proposed with a ban focused on particular packaging and single-use items including single-use plastic bags, Styrofoam containers, plastic utensils and plastic straws.[30] For each of these items, there are readily available alternatives that are less damaging in terms of generating potential marine pollution. As of 2020, Canada is in the process of proposing a 'thicker' law to reduce plastic packaging in the market by banning additional products beyond the Caribbean and Pacific States, including beverage six-pack rings and food packaging made from plastics that are difficult to recycle. Many other products, including garbage bags, snack food wrappers, disposable personal care items and beverage containers, are not proposed for inclusion in the single-use plastics ban due to a lack of existing readily available alternative packaging.[31]

The paradigm that needs to shift is from single-use disposable materials to some version of a circular packaging economy where materials selected for use by the industry do not contribute to toxicity or other serious long-term impacts on the environment. The challenge for countries that have adopted these rules is that, as States with limited market share, it may take time before products can be shifted to marine-friendly packaging. Whether there would be consumer backlash due to the

[28] Government of Tuvalu Waste Management (Prohibition on the importation of single-use plastic) regulation 2019, https://tuvalu-data.sprep.org/system/files/bothregulationstouploadenvironmentportalinform.zip

[29] Government of Costa Rica, Law No. 9786 Law to combat pollution by plastic and protect the environment (6 December 2019) (Art. 5).

[30] See e.g., Bahamas, Barbados, Belize, the Dominican Republic, Grenada, Jamaica, Trinidad and Tobago, Guyana, Vanuatu, Fiji.

[31] Government of Canada, A proposed integrated management approach to plastic products to prevent waste and pollution, www.canada.ca/en/environment-climate-change/services/canadian-environmental-protection-act-registry/plastics-proposed-integrated-management-approach.html#toc12

unavailability of products leading to legislative retraction remains to be seen with the recently adopted Caribbean laws. In Saint Vincent and the Grenadines, the ban on distribution, sale and use of disposable plastic shopping bags has been suspended until after the Christmas season in part because of COVID-19 but also allegedly to allow businesses the ability to deplete their stocks of plastic bags.[32]

For either 'thin' laws or 'thick' laws, implementation can always pose a challenge. Even where a given regulation provides for administrative penalties such as Uganda's 2010 regulations prohibiting the import or use of plastic carrier bags measuring less than 30 microns in thickness,[33] state institutions appear to lack the political will to pursue enforcement activities due to special interests. A 2018 commentary in a Uganda newspaper observed that the law 'has for the last 8 years almost had no legal force' despite commitments by the National Environmental Management Authority, Kampala Capital City Authority, the President and the Finance Minister to make progress.[34] The High Court of Uganda even weighed in on the matter with a 2012 legal opinion indicating that the continued proliferation of unmanaged plastic garbage across Uganda, including some items that were deemed permissible under the government regulation, violated the rights of Ugandan citizens to a clean and healthy environment.[35] The Ugandan government, as a whole, has proved to be less than resolute in implementing its law because of constant pressure from plastic manufacturers in Uganda, who argue that the ban is destroying their livelihood and that the problem is not high rates of manufacturing but low rates of recycling.[36]

The gaps in the law operate more like a sieve. While certain products are subject to regulation, including bans designed in part to shift the packaging industry to less environmentally damaging materials, the status quo remains largely in place for

32 Ban on Use of Disposable Plastic Bags Suspended- PM, Searchlight (15 August 2020), https://searchlight.vc/searchlight/breaking-news/2020/08/15/ban-on-use-of-disposable-plastic-bags-suspended-pm/

33 Government of Uganda (n 24) at Section 6 and 7 (Specifying penalties of 120,000 Uganda shillings per day for initial violations, which is approximately USD$32.50 per day, and 70,000 shillings for each day of continuing violations, which is about US$19).

34 Wetaya Richard, Enforcement frustrate Uganda's efforts to ban Polythene bags, *Masaaba Chronicle* (6 July 2018), https://masaabachronicle.com/news/commentary/commentary/enforcement-frustrates-uganda-s-efforts-to-ban-polythene-bags

35 Greenwatch v. Attorney General and National Environmental Management Agency, High Court of Uganda (Misc. Cause No. 140 of 2002) UGHC 205 (5 October 2012), https://ulii.org/ug/judgment/high-court/2012/205 ('All this court can say is that whoever is involved in the process of enacting a law towards the protection of the environment should do so as a matter of urgency because the damage is likely to be extremely costly. Given this observation, the best this court can do is make a declaration that the manufacture, distribution, use, sale, sell [sic] disposal of plastic bags, plastic containers, plastic food wrappers, and all other forms of plastic commonly referred to as "kaveera" violates the rights of citizens of Uganda to a clean and healthy environment as acknowledged by both parties.')

36 Richard (n 34) (quoting from National Environmental Management Agency staff).

most containers. Single-use plastics remain a 'wicked problem'[37] that is hard to resolve because the problems associated with production and consumption continue to accrue across a dispersed landscape.

Ideally, a global instrument will emerge to fill this gap. Some discussions have advanced. In 2019, UNEP launched a project 'Protecting the Marine Environment from Land-Based Pollution Through Strengthened Coordination of Global Action' that includes linking implementation of the Global Programme of Action to the UN Environment Assembly (UNEA), which is the 'world's highest-level decision-making body on the environment'.[38] During the third session of the UNEA in 2018, States convened an ad hoc open-ended expert group on marine litter and plastics that has continued proposing global responses. As the scale of marine plastic waste challenges expands, the Assembly may in coming meetings 'consider the need for international rules, as well as recommended practices and procedures, to further the objectives of the Global Programme of Action' and offer some essential rules or standards.[39]

In 2020, the expert group collected nine potential State and regional governance responses for future Assembly action. Responses varied greatly across geographical groups. The African Group called for a new internationally legally binding agreement that would include reduction targets, national action plans, reporting (including plastic production, plastic use, plastic waste management), monitoring of national discharge by an international scientific body, a financial mechanism to support implementation, technology transfer and capacity building and adopting 'uniform regulatory measures ... [for] those categories of plastic products that are most prone to leakage and that pose a particular risk to the environment, including single-use plastics, fishing gear and primary microplastics'.[40] Norway agreed with the idea for a new instrument but recommended that the focus be on enhancing cooperation and coordination between States to minimize plastic waste, better management of recycling, designing sustainable plastic products, sharing responsibility for plastic waste management fairly, creating targeted measures for microplastics and developing a clearinghouse of knowledge around marine plastic.[41]

37 Tod Hardin, The magnificent 7 elements of plastics as a 'wicked problem' (8 December 2015), https://plasticoceans.org/magnificent-7-elements-plastics-wicked-problem/; H. Rittel and M. Webber, Dilemmas in a general theory of planning (1973) 4 *Policy Science* 155–169.

38 www.unenvironment.org/explore-topics/oceans-seas/what-we-do/addressing-land-based-pollution/global-action-protect-marine; https://environmentassembly.unenvironment.org/

39 Global Programme of Action for the Protection of the Marine Environment from Land-Based Activities, UNEP(OCA)(LBA)/IG.2/7 (3 December 1985), Para. 77, https://papersmart.unon.org/resolution/uploads/1995-gpa.pdf

40 Draft Outline of Summary of Submissions on Potential Response for Continued Work for Consideration by the United Nations Environment Assembly (2020), http://wedocs.unep.org/bitstream/handle/20.500.11822/31980/Draft%20outline%20for%20response%20options%2023%20March.pdf?sequence=7

41 Ibid.

Vietnam offered an even more specific and ambitious vision of a future treaty. The States' draft instrument that would include binding measures to regulate subsidies to the fossil-fuel industry, identify alternative materials to replace plastics, reduce production of low density polyethylene, introduce eco-labelling standards, improve compliance with Basel Convention on any trade in plastic waste, ban certain uses of low density polyethylene and 'problematic plastics', implement Extended Producer Responsibility schemes for private industry, set international standards on waste management practices for export and import of recycled waste, create an international financial mechanism for waste management and recovery, mandate national action on marine cleanup, create a Regional-level Plastic Study Center, implement an international or regional mechanism for monitoring and reporting of transboundary plastic waste flows, regulate import and export of plastic materials and waste, adopt national action plans that match global obligations, adopt regular reporting, generate global rules and standards on extended producer responsibility, implement the 'polluter pays' principle and create capacity building programmes.[42]

The United States' submission sought more cooperation between States but did not support new international obligations. Rather it supported better local implementation. The United States called for better use of existing instruments and institutions to manage marine litter through regional seas programmes, regional fisheries bodies and river basin committees.[43]

Is existing law fit for purpose to protect oceans from unmanaged marine plastics? Regrettably, no. Existing law is simply too 'thin' because the laws either fail to address the essential challenge of marine litter, like the proposed US law, or the substantive components of laws appear not to be systematically implemented, as in Uganda. International law conversations at the UNEA offer hope that States might be able to coordinate a global response to be implemented nationally, but as of yet there is no common vision beyond agreement that marine plastic litter must be reduced. While not every large plastic-producing or using country participated in submitting responses, the existing responses illustrate two important framings of existing marine plastic pollution issues. For some entities such as the United States who are eager to protect their industries, marine plastic pollution is understood not as a consumption problem but as a waste management challenge. There is no political interest in a paradigm shift. For other entities such as the African group, Norway or Vietnam, there appears to be substantial political interest in transforming the status quo of plastic production to create a paradigm shift allowing for wholesale reimagination of aspects of our economy that have become conventional. Even so, there are differences in approach.

42 Ibid.
43 Ibid.

While concluding any global instrument to specifically address marine plastics will be fraught with political difficulties given the numerous populist/nationalist politicians governing certain States who have historically operated as bottlenecks to international cooperation, allowing business as usual for the conventional plastic industry will only continue to undermine the object and purpose of existing legal regimes such as the Law of the Sea Convention. If law is going to be part of any potential paradigm shift to change what plastic is produced and how it will be used, there need to be stronger market signals. Section 5.4 builds on what Vietnam proposed indirectly in its submission to the ad hoc commission in terms of regulating 'subsidies' for fossil-fuel based primary feedstocks. In addition to any possible re-examination of fossil fuel subsidies, States across the globe need to apply a reasonable global carbon tax on plastic manufacturing from fossil fuel derivatives to achieve both a reduction of marine plastic litter but also a reduction of greenhouse gas emissions.

5.4 SOLUTION: OVERDUE SINGLE-USE WASTE TARIFFS AND PLASTIC FISHING GEAR TARIFFS TO ADDRESS MAJOR SOURCES OF MARINE PLASTICS

As suggested by the ongoing challenges of regulating through 'thin' and 'thicker' rules, there are yawning gaps in existing legislation to reduce the amount of single-use plastic in circulation. Most notably, the piecemeal approach taken by the 'thicker' rules that ban the importation or sale of certain single-use items still fails to change the larger paradigm of relying on single-use plastic for daily necessities.

In the past decade, States and some enterprises have begun to promote the concept of a 'circular economy', which is understood as an economy designed to reduce waste and pollution by designing 'cradle to cradle' products that do not rely on non-renewable feedstocks and can be either reused or more fully recycled.[44] Certain products such as single-use products generally do not conform to the principles of a 'circular economy'. How do we take a linear economy and create a 'circular economy'?

One tool for advancing the 'circular economy' might be global tariffs. Environmental economists are fond of suggesting that environmental issues can be handled by proper pricing so that goods reflect the costs of environmental externalities. Yet as the ongoing carbon tax debates have continued to unspool over the last two decades, there has been little agreement on how to multilaterally deploy economic instruments to achieve global change. Every country and municipality is left to its own devices.

[44] UN Industrial Development Organization, Circular Economy, www.unido.org/sites/default/files/2017-07/Circular_Economy_UNIDO_0.pdf

This failure to develop a multilateral response ignores the interactions among global enterprises, target markets and environmental externalities. In our global system of capitalism, fossil fuel industries and plastic manufacturers are continually seeking to identify and create new markets, with particular growth targeted for the Middle East, China and the United States – all entities that have shown historical intransigence on reducing emissions.[45] The lack of any multilateral waste tariff enables this global growth.

Economic instruments such as tariffs offer additional instrument choices beyond direct regulation and voluntary instruments.[46] While truly international tariffs have not been negotiated, they would provide an efficient means of pricing externalities that States are being forced to absorb either in the form of additional investments in waste management or in damage to marine resources. Adopting an international tariff would be politically challenging but would address the gap in the existing rule of law where there is no real accountability to address single-use plastics as a growing source of carbon emissions or a global environmental and public health threat.

The work of the United Nations Environmental Assembly in the years to come would have the most impact on curbing plastic pollution by focusing political will on tackling the upstream aspects of drivers of plastic waste, which includes production of single-use plastic products that have not been designed to be part of a 'cradle to cradle' system. While the downstream aspects of plastic waste are the most visible aspects of the problem in the form of trash-strewn beaches and garbage-clogged rivers, it will not be possible to alleviate these problems if production continues to accelerate. Affluent countries already struggle with locating space for landfilling, and incineration has its own public health costs.[47] Certain regions such as the EU are already attempting essential policy investments to make these changes to focus on upstream production.[48]

To curb production, the economics of single-use plastic production would need to change. One means of changing production is through taxes. A multilateral

[45] Center for International Environmental Law, *How Fracked Gas, Cheap Oil, and Unburnable Coal are Driving the Plastics Boom* (2017), www.ciel.org/wp-content/uploads/2017/09/Fueling-Plastics-How-Fracked-Gas-Cheap-Oil-and-Unburnable-Coal-are-Driving-the-Plastics-Boom.pdf

[46] Niko Soininen and Froukje Maria Platjouw, Resilience and adaptive capacity of aquatic environmental law in the EU: An evaluation and comparison of the WFD, MSFD, and MSPD, in David Langlet and Rosemary Rayfuse (eds.), *The Ecosystem Approach in Ocean Planning and Governance* (Leiden: Brill, 2019), 17–79.

[47] Cole Rosengren, Public companies increased control of $74B US waste industry in 2018 (4 June 2019), www.wastedive.com/news/public-companies-increased-control-of-74b-us-waste-industry-in-2018/556079/

[48] See e.g. European Commission, *A European Strategy for Plastics in a Circular Economy* (2018), https://ec.europa.eu/environment/circular-economy/pdf/plastics-strategy-brochure.pdf (Providing an overview of Europe's 'New Plastics Economy' and calling for improved design of products, regulation of what constitutes biodegradable and compostable, and reduction in single-use plastics.)

carbon tax would be a good start but is politically challenging.[49] As of 2020, some forty-six countries have some form of carbon tax, including the EU Member States, the (pre-Brexit) United Kingdom, Switzerland, Iceland, Canada, Mexico, Argentina, Chile, New Zealand, Australia, Singapore, Japan, South Korea and Kazakhstan.[50] Most analysis of the impact of carbon taxes has focused on the cost increases for certain resources. The impact of these taxes on reduction of marine pollution from plastic sources has yet to be measured. Many of these taxes have only recently been adopted.

Despite all of the merits of a carbon tax system in terms of its efficiency and fairness (e.g., focusing payments at the level where decisions can be made about production), few countries appear to be pricing carbon high enough to create the types of reduction needed to reduce emissions to the 'safe' level urged by the Intergovernmental Panel on Climate Change. In the European Union, the epicentre for the most countries engaged in a carbon tax, excess carbon allowance permits have been on the market for years, resulting in low carbon prices.[51] The United Kingdom recognized some of this failing and enacted a carbon price floor for certain carbon-intensive industries designed to financially incentivize a shift to cleaner energy production.[52] Even with the current low prices for carbon allowances in the EU, researchers have still observed a reduction in carbon emissions across the EU as part of Europe's oft-criticized Emissions Trading Scheme, suggesting that a carbon tax system would deliver even more reductions if the price of carbon is uniform.[53]

It has been, however, politically difficult to have a carbon tax that is more than simply window-dressing since voters in at least some parts of the world are unwilling to accept that the 'polluter pays' principle also applies to consumers. In Australia, the Labor Government introduced a carbon tax but then lost the elections to the Liberal party, who gutted the programme in favour of industry interests.[54]

Some countries such as Canada are using a revenue-neutral approach to appease voters. For Canadian provinces that do not have a carbon pricing policy that meets

[49] John Kemp, Carbon taxes will be needed to reduce CO_2 emissions (7 November 2019), *Reuters*, www.reuters.com/article/us-climatechange-taxation-kemp-column/carbon-taxes-will-be-needed-to-reduce-co2-emissions-kemp-idUSKBN1XH242

[50] World Bank, https://carbonpricingdashboard.worldbank.org/

[51] Organisation for Economic Cooperation and Development, Effective carbon rates 2018: Pricing carbon emissions through taxes and emissions trading (2018). www.oecd.org/tax/effective-carbon-rates-2018-9789264305304-en.htm

[52] David Hirst, Carbon Price Floor and Price Support mechanism, Briefing paper (8 January 2018), https://researchbriefings.files.parliament.uk/documents/SN05927/SN05927.pdf

[53] Patrick Bayer and Michael Aklin, The European Union Emissions Trading System reduces CO_2 emissions despite low prices (21 April 2020) 117 *PNAS* 16, 8804–8812.

[54] Australian Government, Department of Industry, Science, Energy, and Resources, 'Repealing the carbon tax', https://publications.industry.gov.au/publications/climate-change/climate-change/government/repealing-carbon-tax.html

certain benchmarks, Canada collected a fuel tax, beginning in 2019, starting at around 4.42 cents per litre. For most of the affected provinces, 90 per cent of revenues are redistributed to individual Canadians through Climate Action Incentive payments to offset higher costs for individuals who use less fuel.[55] Ten per cent is returned to small businesses, schools, hospitals, cities, non-profits and indigenous communities. Canada also initiated a parallel system for large industries with global competition that were not charged the fuel tax but instead were required to purchase carbon credits for excess emissions in a programme called the 'output-based pricing system'.

A truly global carbon tax could change the calculus of operation for major energy-intensive industries such as the chemicals and plastics sectors. One estimate by researchers calculates that a consumption tax on fossil fuel-derived plastic would shrink the plastic market by 7.24 per cent through reducing global demand.[56] The bazillion dollar multilateral question is how to set a global carbon tax that is politically palatable but also effective. A carbon tax is desirable and would directly address greenhouse gas emissions and, indirectly, pollution. By raising the costs of plastics so that single-use plastic would no longer be the cheapest packaging option, manufacturers would presumably seek alternative packaging approaches for goods that are presently in single-use plastic containers. The increase in cost associated with plastic packaging should decrease the amount of plastic waste being generated and the potential for plastic to prejudice both the terrestrial and marine environments.

In the interim before a global carbon tax catalyses system-wide changes across all industries, States should respond to citizen demands for a first step towards implementing the circular economy in the packaging industry and the fishing industry by placing tariffs on specific non-essential plastic products that contribute to marine pollution. An international waste tariff would focus attention on the externalities associated with the global trade in non-essential single-use plastics and problematic plastic fishing gear. A non-essential plastic should be defined in a harmonized fashion to include excess packaging such as double wrapping for advertising purposes (e.g., a plastic drink bottle with a plastic sleeve advertising the brand) as well as containers that could be manufactured from alternative sources (e.g., plastic milk jugs that could be manufactured from glass). States could agree to levy General Agreement on Tariffs and Trade-compliant import tariffs on certain plastics items from other member States to cover not just carbon-related costs (e.g., carbon is

55 Government of Canada, Implementing Canada's plan to address climate change and grow the economy: Putting a price on carbon pollution, Technical briefing, 22 October 2018, www.canada.ca/content/dam/eccc/documents/pdf/climate-change/pricing-pollution/ECCC_Technical_Deck_En.pdf

56 Neus Escobar et al., Land use mediated ghg emissions and spillovers from increased consumption of bioplastics (2018) 13(12) *Environmental Research Letters*.

released when plastics begin to decompose)[57] but, more importantly, adequate disposal costs.[58] Non-discriminatory tariffs will require similar levies to be placed on domestic plastics. To prevent leakage of non-tariffed plastics from non-member States into a member's market, members should refuse imports of plastics from non-member States that would not otherwise be subject to levies unless the non-member State agrees bilaterally to be subject to the same levies. This approach has legal precedents found in the Basel Convention[59] and the Montreal Protocol.[60]

Critics might argue that focusing on drafting a multilateral trade-focused treaty in the middle of a waste crisis contributes too little too late and that available political attention should instead be focused on national and local efforts to reduce plastic consumption.[61] While possibly appropriate for certain situations such as domestic production of plastics for domestic markets, this critique ignores the global supply chain aspects of single-use plastic markets. As noted earlier in this chapter, the growth in petrochemical production infrastructure in the Middle East, China and the United States is intended for expansion of surplus plastic production into international markets, not just for national markets.

Tariffs strengthen the rule of environmental law by offering more predictability for economic actors seeking to enter an alternative packaging market as well as some financial accountability from those producers who continue to sell non-essential plastics into the marketplace. Tariffs are 'thick' because they have a substantive content that can be operationalized through customs and revenue agents. If these waste tariffs are set at an appropriate level to cover the long-term costs of plastics to environmental and human health, then implementation of waste tariffs could lead to a fundamental change in the current packaging economy. Under the rules of non-discrimination, a tariff must not give an advantage to domestic producers over foreign producers. This would mean that States with tariffs in place on imported plastic goods would be expected to have similar measures in place for domestic

57 Sarah-Jeanne Royer et al., Production of methane and ethylene from plastic in the environment (2018) 13 *PLOS ONE* 8. (Finding an acceleration of greenhouse gas emissions as plastics photochemically degrade).

58 Highly recyclable plastics could be assigned minimal waste disposal costs while low recyclable plastics or plastics that cannot be recycled would be assigned high costs. In theory, if these costs are passed on to consumers, then consumers would, if pure financial costs matter to them, opt to select more recyclable plastics when given a choice to avoid packaging costs.

59 Basel Convention (n 14) Art. 4(5) 'A Party shall not permit hazardous wastes or other wastes to be exported to a non-Party or to be imported from a non-Party'.

60 Montreal Protocol on Substances That Deplete the Ozone Layer, Montreal, 16 September 1987, in force 1 January 1989, 1522 UNTS 3, Art. 4(1) 'Within one year of the entry into force of this Protocol, each Party shall ban the import of controlled substances from any State not party to this Protocol'.

61 Some States are pursuing their own 'plastic taxes'. Civil society groups and recycling management companies submitted the California Recycling and Plastic Pollution Reduction Act in 2020 to raise a 1 cent tax on non-recyclable and non-compostable packaging to support waste management through subsidies to the recycling industry.

producers. The key to success of any waste tariff will be setting the tariff at a rate capable of helping state markets to shift towards new packaging and fishing gear materials.

Some States, such as many African countries, Vietnam and Norway, have been publicly outspoken about the need to take system-wide steps to promote a circular economy capable of addressing plastic pollution. These States can take leadership in a different direction than the current effort to address marine plastic pollution, which has largely depended on ad hoc efforts by individual States to improve waste management. While more can certainly be done to improve waste management through capacity building and financing, focusing on waste management alone will not achieve the principles of the circular economy. States must give attention to ongoing plastic production and what role the market plays in creating conditions for what has become a persistent problem. Unlike the 'thin and 'thicker' national laws that have attempted to address production concerns provisionally by regulating easy-to-regulate products, a multilateral trade tariff offers a State committed to systematically reducing plastic pollution the ability to raise the ceiling across manufacturers to demand better design and fewer sources of waste.[62]

5.5 CONCLUSION

This chapter has reviewed the increasingly well-understood problem of marine plastic pollution while noting that conventional single-use plastic production is also compounding our emissions crisis. Existing international responses have been insufficient to curb plastic pollution. Well-intended national legal responses have failed to address plastic pollution by focusing only on waste management or allowing exceptions to swallow rules. As States attempt to practically achieve circular economy principles in relation to plastic usage, they will need to eliminate competition in their markets from cheap and unnecessary plastics. One means of doing this is by properly setting prices to reflect the long-term environmental and social costs of plastics within a given State. To shift markets unilaterally is very difficult, as evidenced by the government of Kenya, which struggles with leakage of banned plastic materials from neighbouring States.[63] Global cooperation is essential to support the transition to a circular economy, with States collectively seeking new solutions to both packaging challenges and marine fishing efforts. A trade treaty

[62] This chapter has focused on the reduction of single-use plastics in particular. Some researchers argue for a reduction of all single-use packaging and not just plastics because of other environmental costs associated with such packaging. Timo Herberz, Claire Barlow and Matthias Finkbeiner, 'Sustainability assessment of a single-use plastics ban' 12(9) (2020) 3746 *Sustainability* www.mdpi.com/2071-1050/12/9/3746.

[63] Duncan Moore, UN Environment (16 May 2018), 'How smuggling threatens to undermine Kenya's plastic bag ban', www.unenvironment.org/news-and-stories/story/how-smuggling-threatens-undermine-kenyas-plastic-bag-ban (alleging an illegal trade in plastic bags from Uganda).

focused on pricing external costs associated with plastics between interested parties such as the African Group, Norway and Vietnam – who have politically indicated some ambition to eliminate plastic waste streams – could prove transformative for limiting new sources of marine litter, while having much-needed spillover effects on reducing emissions.

The rule of law plays a critical role in achieving the post-Plastocene era. A waste tariff addresses the accountability gap that exists in current approaches to systematically addressing marine plastic pollution. It does so by changing basic assumptions that all products entering a particular market should be regarded as functionally equivalent and environmentally neutral.

6

Pollution of the Marine Environment by Spaceflights

Alla Pozdnakova[*]

6.1 INTRODUCTION

Like other industrial activities, launches and returns of man-made space objects inevitably take a toll on the Earth's environment. For example, emissions from space launches may result in atmospheric pollution, ozone layer depletion, impact on wildlife and biodiversity, and pollution of land and water by emissions of carbon soot, alumina or water vapour, as well as by jettisoned parts (worked-off lower stages) of the launch vehicle. The impact from launching involves multiple explosive emissions of combustion products and thermal energy, as well as strong acoustic oscillation on the launch pad.[1] At the same time, developments in the space sector suggest that space launches will continue to grow as new commercial satellite launch facilities emerge in coastal areas around the world. Deposition into the sea of materials jettisoned during the launch of space vehicles is an activity expected to rise sharply in frequency in the coming years.[2]

Although environmental concerns in the space sector were raised decades ago, legal aspects of protection of the Earth's environment from pollution by spaceflights have received relatively little international attention. International treaty-based space law only indirectly addresses this problem through provisions on state liability for

* I would like to thank Steven Freeland, Henrik Ringbom, Froukje Maria Platjouw and Jenni Tapio for their valuable comments on earlier versions of this chapter.

1 Tatyana V. Koroleva, Pavel P. Krechetov, Ivan N. Semenkov et al., The environmental impact of space transport (2018) 58 *Transportation Research Part D* 54–69; World Meteorological Organization Global Ozone Research and Monitoring Project–Report No. 58 (2018) *Scientific Assessment of Ozone Depletion* ES.50, available at https://public.wmo.int/en/resources

2 Report of the Scientific Group of the London Convention and the 13th meeting of the Scientific Group of the London Protocol LC/SG 42/16, *Progress of the Correspondence Group on the Marine Environmental Effects of Jettisoned Waste from Commercial Spaceflight Activities* (LC/SG 42/8/1), available at www.unoosa.org

damage caused by space objects on another State's territory or aircraft.[3] To tackle the challenges pertaining to the use of nuclear power sources in outer space, including protection of the Earth's biosphere, the United Nations (UN) has adopted non-binding instruments.[4] However, contamination of the environment resulting from normal operation of launches and other spaceflight-related activities has largely remained within the national domain of States.[5]

Several reasons may explain scarce international development on this issue. The total impact of space activities on the Earth's environment has been viewed as insignificant, short-term and local, whereas the focus of international environmental law has traditionally been placed on serious transboundary pollution. However, the environmental impact of spaceflight may indeed be transboundary, affecting maritime areas both within and outside national jurisdiction of States. Even launches from inland-located spaceports may produce a long-range and transboundary environmental impact on maritime areas located far away from the launching site.[6] The use of highly toxic fuels or nuclear power for propulsion of spacecraft could multiply environmental harm in the case of a launch accident, or of radioactively contaminated space objects returning to Earth.

3 Convention on International Liability for Damage Caused by Space Objects, London/Moscow/Washington, 29 March 1972, in force 1 September 1972, 961 UNTS 187 (Liability Convention). On the Cosmos 954 accident, see, e.g., Francis Lyall and Paul B. Larsen, *Space Law: A Treatise*, 2nd edition (London: Routledge 2018) 106. It is arguable whether pure environmental damage is included in the liability regime: see, e.g., He Qizhi, Environmental impact of space activities and measures for international protection (1988) 16 *Journal of Space Law* 117–127, at 124.

4 The Scientific and Technical Subcommittee of the United Nations Committee on the Peaceful Uses of Outer Space and the International Atomic Energy Agency, *Safety Framework for Nuclear Power Source Applications in Outer Space*, 19 May 2009, A/AC.105/934, available at www.un-ilibrary.org; UN Resolution 47/68, *Principles Relevant to the Use of Nuclear Power Sources in Outer Space* (NPS Principles), A/47/20, available at www.unoosa.org. See also Lotta Viikari, *The Environmental Element in Space Law: Assessing the Present and Charting the Future* (Leiden: Martinus Nijhoff Publishers 2008).

5 On UN concerns with the impact of increasing space launch activities on the Earth environment and the ozone layer: see The 1982 Report of the 2nd United Nations Conference on the exploration and peaceful use of outer space (A/CONF.101/10), paras. 290–291, available at www.digitallibrary.un.org, and The 1999 Recommendation on the protection of the Earth environment (A/CONF.184/6), 7 point 1(a)(v), available at https://undocs.org/A/CONF.184/6. Another step forward was taken by the initiative of the International Astronomic Union (IAU) on Dark and Quiet Skies, Recommendations, COPUOS (2021), A/AC.105/C.1/2021/CRP.17, available at www.unoosa.org, highlighting the issue of the environmental protection of the Earth from light pollution created by space activities.

6 The Rockot incident is described in Michael Byers and Cameron Byers, Toxic splash: Russian rocket stages dropped in Arctic waters raise health, environmental and legal concerns (2017) 53 (6) *Polar Record* 580–591; see also He Qizhi (n 3); Vito de Lucia and Viviana Iavicoli, From outer space to ocean depths: The 'Spacecraft Cemetery' and the protection of the marine environment in areas beyond national jurisdiction (2018) 49(2) *California Western International Law Journal* Art. 4, 346–389.

As the contemporary space sector is characterized by active participation of commercial, non-state actors, appropriate regulations at the national level are indispensable to ensure environmentally responsible conduct by private actors in the space sector.[7] At the same time, the question arises whether an approach based on unilateral environmental regulations and standards of individual States is sufficient to tackle environmental pressures from spaceflight, especially pressures on maritime areas.

A feasible explanation for the lack of international legal measures to tackle spaceflight pollution lies in a weak environmental rule of law in the space sector. In principle, protection of the marine environment from pollution by spaceflights is governed by general international environmental law,[8] and by two treaty-based regimes: space law and the law of the sea. General environmental law suffers from inherent weaknesses, notably vague environmental obligations of States, uncertain legal status of principles (e.g., the precautionary principle) and absence of an adequate institutional framework allowing for inter-state dialogue and cooperation.[9] These issues remain largely unresolved in the special regimes of space law and the law of the sea. Neither space law nor the law of the sea expressly addresses protection of the Earth's environment from pollution by space-related activities. In the absence of specific provisions, the applicable obligations have to be derived from generally applicable environmental provisions and principles, resulting in a vague and fragmented legal framework. This is insufficient to address complex issues of environmental protection effectively and comprehensively in the space sector.[10]

This chapter argues that further development of international regulation of the environmental dimension of spaceflights is imperative in order to tackle existing and future pressures that such activities may cause the Earth's environment. The focus of the discussion in this chapter is international legal solutions for tackling spaceflight pollution of the marine environment, resulting from normal (operational) discharges during launch activities. It is pointed out that international cooperation needs to clarify and strengthen the relationship between the space

7 See Annette Froehlich and Vincent Seffinga (eds.), *National Space Legislation: A Comparative and Evaluative Analysis*, Studies in Space Policy 15 (Cham: Springer International Publishing AG 2018), https://doi.org/10.1007/978-3-319-70431-9_3

8 See Viikari (n 4); Lyall and Larsen (n 3), 254 et seq.

9 See, e.g., James R. May and J. Patrick Kelly, The environment and international society: Issues, concepts and context, in Shawkat Alam, Md Jahid Hossain Bhuiyan, Tareq M. R. Chowdhury and Erika J. Techera (eds.), *Routledge Handbook of International Environmental Law* (London: Routledge 2013) 16–17.

10 Claudia Cinelli and Katarzyna Pogorzelska, The current international legal setting for the protection of the outer space environment: The precautionary principle avant la lettre (2013) 22 (2) *RECIEL* 186–201, at 187; Steven Freeland and Donna Lawler, Whose mess is it anyway? Regulating the environmental consequences of commercial launch activities, *Proceedings of the International Institute of Space Law* 2011, The Hague: Eleven International Publishing, 3.

law and law-of-the sea regimes through developing a more effective normative and institutional framework.

Further discussion starts in Section 6.2 by assessing international space law and the law of the sea as normative frameworks for the marine environmental dimension of spaceflight, with focus on the Outer Space Treaty and United Nations Convention on the Law of the Sea (UNCLOS)[11] Part XII. Then in Section 6.3 the discussion turns to the question of how the environmental rule of law should be strengthened and developed to tackle marine pollution in the space sector more effectively. Section 6.4 concludes.

6.2 THE INTERNATIONAL ENVIRONMENTAL FRAMEWORK GOVERNING SPACEFLIGHT POLLUTION

6.2.1 *International Space Law*

The Outer Space Treaty is a universal treaty establishing a legal regime for state activities in the exploration and use of outer space.[12] Importantly, the Outer Space Treaty places responsibility on State Parties for their national governmental and non-governmental activities in outer space, and for assuring that national activities are carried out in conformity with the Treaty provisions. It further provides that the 'activities of non-governmental entities in outer space, including the Moon and other celestial bodies, shall require authorization and continuing supervision by the appropriate State Party to the Treaty'.[13] The State of registration of a space object 'shall retain jurisdiction and control over such object', and over any personnel thereof, while in outer space or on a celestial body.[14]

General obligations of States in the space sector should be interpreted in light of applicable international environmental law provisions.[15] The Treaty contains relevant principles of law such as the principle of cooperation and mutual assistance, and the duty to report on potentially hazardous activities.[16] Such fundamental rules of international environmental law as the duty to prevent transboundary environmental harm and the duty to notify of imminent danger had already been articulated

[11] Montego Bay, 10 December 1982, in force 16 November 1994, 1833 UNTS 397.

[12] Treaty on Principles Governing the Activities of States in the Exploration and Use of Outer Space, including the Moon and other celestial bodies (the Outer Space Treaty) London/Moscow/Washington, 19 December 1966, in force 10 October 1967, 610 UNTS 205. The Outer Space Treaty is ratified by over 100 States and signed by around twenty States. Outer Space Treaty, ibid., Art. IX.

[13] Art. VI Outer Space Treaty (n 12).

[14] Art. VIII.

[15] Art. III Outer Space Treaty (n 12). See also Viikari, (n 4) 190; Ian H. Rowlands, Atmosphere and outer space, in Daniel Bodansky, Jutta Brunnée and Ellen Hey (eds.), *The Oxford Handbook of International Environmental Law* (Oxford: Oxford University Press 2008) 332.

[16] Arts. IX and XI Outer Space Treaty (n 12).

in international environmental law at the time when the space treaties were developed.[17] With regard to nuclear safety, the UN Principles Relevant to the Use of Nuclear Power in Outer Space (NPS Principles) are accepted as part of customary international law.[18]

Further, the contours of the principle of prevention are arguably detectable in international space law instruments, including the Outer Space Treaty and the Liability Convention. In 1999, the UN recognized that 'action should be taken to ensure, to the extent possible, that all space activities, in particular those which may have harmful effects on the local and global environment, are carried out in a manner that limits such effects and to take appropriate measures to achieve that objective'.[19] This confirms the existence of a state obligation to take relevant measures to prevent and combat environmental degradation by spaceflights. However, the specific aspects of this obligation, including the criteria for determining environmental 'harm' triggering the duty to take measures are unclear.[20]

Other questions that also remain are what kind of state measures would be required to achieve this objective, and whether existing international space law is adequate for this purpose. The ambiguity of state obligations laid down in space law instruments and the absence of expressly formulated provisions on protection of the Earth's environment – other than Article IX of the Outer Space Treaty addressing protection of the Earth's environment from pollution by extraterrestrial matter – results in challenges for the effectiveness of the environmental rule of law in the space sector. For example, international space law is silent on the duty to conduct an environmental impact assessment before starting a space activity. There are also no jointly developed standards of environmental safety and emission levels.

The legal relevance of the precautionary approach in the face of scientific uncertainty with regard to the environmental effect of spaceflights, including their terrestrial dimension, is not articulated explicitly in outer space law instruments, with the exception of the NPS Principles. These Principles require States to conduct safety assessments and take other relevant measures, indicating the importance of the precautionary approach (if not the precautionary principle) in the nuclear sector of outer space activities.[21] The overall legal status of the precautionary principle – or at least the relevance of the precautionary approach – in outer space law is not yet

[17] Trail Smelter Arbitration (1941), RIAA, vol. III, 1905–82.

[18] See Rowlands (n 15).

[19] Report of the Third United Nations Conference on the Exploration and Peaceful Uses of Outer Space (UNISPACE III), Recommendation on the protection of the Earth environment (A/CONF.184/6) point 1(a)(v), available at www.unoosa.org.

[20] See, e.g., Martha Mejía-Kaiser, Space law and hazardous space debris, planetary science, 30 January 2020, https://doi.org/10.1093/acrefore/9780190647926.013.70.

[21] Principles Relevant to the Use of Nuclear Power Sources in Outer Space (NPS Principles) (n 4).

commonly agreed.[22] This may be partly explained by the continuing uncertainty of the precautionary principle and its legal status in international environmental law generally.[23]

An important condition for effective environmental rule of law in the space sector is the existence of an adequate international institutional framework. International governance of outer space, including its environmental dimension, takes place at several levels. The global space governance institution, the UN Committee on the Peaceful Uses of Outer Space (COPUOS),[24] has contributed significantly to development of policy on the long-term sustainability of outer space and mitigation of space debris.[25] Other international and regional organizations have also played an increasingly significant role in space governance. Importantly, the European Space Agency (ESA)[26] contributes to the formation of space law as it develops its own internal procedures, negotiates international agreements in the space sector and implements international space practices.[27] The ESA has been working on a green fuel project to replace toxic space propellants such as hydrazine.[28] However, COPUOS and other international space institutions do not have a specific environmental law-making mandate, nor are they explicitly given competence to monitor and supervise member States' measures regulating the terrestrial dimension of environmental protection in the space sector.

6.2.2 *Law of the Sea as a Normative Basis for Regulating Marine Pollution by Spaceflights*

UNCLOS provides a comprehensive legal framework on marine environmental protection.[29] A general obligation of States to protect the marine environment from

[22] Viikari (n 4) 172.

[23] See, however, Nicolas de Sadeleer, *Environmental Principles: From Political Slogans to Legal Rules* (Oxford: Oxford University Press 2020) 139, arguing that the precautionary principle is a general principle of international law and a general principle of environmental (or even administrative) national law.

[24] Established by UN General Assembly (UNGA) Res. 1348 (XIII), Question of the peaceful use of outer space, 13 December 1948. See also Lyall and Larsen (n 3), 14.

[25] E.g., COPUOS Space Debris Mitigation Guidelines and Guidelines for long-term sustainability of space activities, 16 June 2016, A/AC.105/2016/CRP.17, available at www.unoosa.org. See also Jenni Tapio and Alexander Soucek, National implementation of non-legally binding instruments: Managing uncertainty in space law? (2019) 44(6) *Air & Space Law* 565–582.

[26] Convention for the Establishment of a European Space Agency, Paris, adopted 30 May 1975, in force 30 October 1980, 1297 UNTS 161.

[27] Lyall and Larsen (n 3), 21.

[28] ESA, 'Green' Satellite Fuel designed to make space safer 16 March 2010, available at www.esa.int/Our_Activities/Space_Engineering_Technology/Green_satellite_fuel_designed_to_make_space_safer

[29] On UNCLOS and third States see, e.g., J. Ashley Roach, Today's customary international law of the sea (2014) 45 *Ocean Development & International Law* 239–259, at 250–251.

the harmful impact of space activities follows from Article 192 UNCLOS. Crucially, UNCLOS requires States to exercise due diligence in environmental matters by adopting appropriate measures and showing adequate levels of vigilance in their enforcement and control.[30]

Article 192 also encompasses potential impacts on the marine environment, transboundary and non-transboundary alike,[31] the duty to protect the oceans from future threats and to take positive action with a view to maintaining and improving their present condition.[32] The obligation to protect the marine environment from pollution is set out in Article 194 UNCLOS and detailed in several further provisions of Part XII. Although UNCLOS does not expressly include spaceflight pollution in its scope, it seeks to address 'all issues relating to the law of the sea' and requires States to protect and preserve the marine environment from all sources of pollution.

In general, the definition of pollution envisages actual or likely 'deleterious effects' on the marine environment such as harm to living resources or hazards to human health.[33] While the general threshold for harm is relatively low, some effect (even if only potential) on the marine environment is required. The focus appears to be not on changes in the marine environment in general but on harm to some more or less specific interests or resources.[34] Article 194 also envisages a nuanced approach, by requiring more stringent control of activities that may harm 'rare or fragile ecosystems'.[35]

Effective application of Article 194 is thus conditioned on the availability of knowledge about the effects of spaceflights on the marine environment, allowing State(s) to rely on some scientific outputs in order to determine whether and what 'adequate' and 'necessary' measures are to be adopted to tackle such pollution.[36] Still, existing research on the marine environmental effects of spaceflight appears rather piecemeal. These information gaps result in significant uncertainty about the risks and extent of environmental degradation that accelerating spaceflights may bring about, calling for use of the precautionary approach to protection of the marine environment from spaceflight-source pollution. In this author's view, the hazardous character of spaceflight activities calls for application of the precautionary

[30] Request for Advisory Opinion submitted by the Sub-Regional Fisheries Commission (Advisory Opinion) ITLOS Reports (2 April 2015), para. 131; South China Sea Arbitration (*The Philippines* v. *China*) PCA Case No 2013-19 (12 July 2016), para. 944.

[31] James Harrison, *Making the Law of the Sea: A Study in the Development of International Law* (Cambridge: Cambridge University Press 2011) 24–25.

[32] South China Sea Arbitration (n 30), para. 941; Harrison (n 31).

[33] See De Lucia and Iavicoli (n 6).

[34] See also Allen L. Springer, Towards a meaningful concept of pollution in international law (1977) 26 *The International & Comparative Law Quarterly*. 531.

[35] Art. 194(5); South China Sea Arbitration (n 30), para. 945.

[36] On the precautionary approach in the law of the sea, see, e.g., Rosemary Rayfuse, Precaution and the protection of marine biodiversity in areas beyond national jurisdiction (2012) 27 *The International Journal of Marine and Coastal Law* 773–781.

approach as part of the duty of due diligence. However, while precaution is envisaged in several multilateral environmental agreements and has also been accepted by international courts with regard to specific activities and sectors, the general relevance of the precautionary approach in the law of the sea remains unclear.[37]

Significant information gaps on the marine environmental impact of spaceflight highlight the particular importance of provisions addressing research cooperation (Article 200), establishment of scientific criteria (Article 201), monitoring the risks or effects of pollution and publishing reports (Articles 204 and 205) and assessing the potential effects of activities on the environment (Article 206). By comparison, no corresponding provisions with regard to environmental research are included in space treaties and other space law instruments developed at the international level.

Furthermore, UNCLOS also contains an overview of types of measures to be applied by States to prevent or minimize marine pollution.[38] However, UNCLOS grants States a considerable degree of discretion in their choice of appropriate measures. In particular, it does not require that environmental protection measures must always be adopted by States at the international level: States may adopt 'individual or joint measures as appropriate' to address marine pollution.[39] Further, international measures do not need take the shape of binding regulations or agreements: 'soft law' measures such as rules, standards or recommendations are also acceptable (if 'appropriate') and may indeed be preferable for States for a number of reasons. However, to meet its duty of due diligence, a State must actually consider what regulation, and at what level – individual, joint, global or regional, binding or not – will be adequate to address spaceflight pollution.

Article 194 clarifies that responsibility for taking measures is vested in the State holding 'jurisdiction or control' over activities that may cause damage to the marine environment of other States.[40] The State in whose territory the spaceport is located would clearly hold 'jurisdiction or control' over spaceflight activities within the meaning of Article 194. This would also be consistent with Article VI of the Outer Space Treaty, which assigns central responsibilities to the 'appropriate' State, which must authorize and properly supervise space activities by non-governmental entities in outer space.[41]

The notion of 'jurisdiction or control' may also include spaceflights conducted extraterritorially, that is, from launch sites located in other States or from the high

[37] The International Tribunal for the Law of the Sea has implicitly applied the precautionary principle but still has not endorsed the principle in general. See, e.g., Annecoos Wiersema, The precautionary principle in environmental governance, in Douglas Fisher (ed.), *Research Handbook on Fundamental Concepts of Environmental Law* (Cheltenham: Edward Elgar Publishing 2016) 464–466.

[38] UNCLOS Art. 194.

[39] UNCLOS Art. 194(1).

[40] UNCLOS Art. 194(2).

[41] See Section 6.2.1.

seas. This is in line with the Outer Space Treaty.[42] The duty to take appropriate measures to protect the marine environment thus also applies to spaceflight activities conducted from another State's territory or from the high seas. Article 192 also requires a State (or States) to take measures with regard to marine pollution by space debris re-entering the Earth, including pollution of the high seas. However, identifying the State(s) holding 'jurisdiction or control' over an extraterritorially located object or activity resulting in marine pollution may be difficult. It is questionable whether Article 194 UNCLOS should be interpreted in light of the relevant space law provisions, at least where such interpretation may result in narrowing down the application of Part XII UNCLOS.

Further, it is problematic that UNCLOS does not clarify the competences and responsibilities of other States whose EEZs may be affected by spaceflights. As the Rockot case illustrates, a coastal State in whose EEZ spaceflight produces environmental impacts may find itself in a vulnerable and unclear legal position.[43] In this author's view, the provisions of UNCLOS Part V entitle a coastal State to regulate or ban the use of its EEZ for jettisoning spaceflight residues by a foreign State, by virtue of coastal State jurisdiction over the EEZ.[44] Moreover, in light of the Part XII obligations described earlier, both the coastal State and the launching State(s) are under a positive obligation to take measures to prevent environmental harm to the EEZ.

Nevertheless, UNCLOS Part V does not provide for an obvious allocation of jurisdiction in such cases, challenging the coastal State's jurisdiction to regulate pollution resulting from spaceflight of foreign origin. A relevant legal basis for resolving conflicts arising from lack of clear allocation of rights and jurisdiction in UNCLOS may be found in Article 59 UNCLOS. This provision addresses cases where UNCLOS does not expressly attribute rights or jurisdiction by requiring resolution of a problem 'on the basis of equity and in the light of all the relevant circumstances, taking into account the respective importance of the interests involved to the parties as well as to the international community as a whole'. Protection of the marine environment from jettisoned space waste may, in principle, be one of the relevant interests under Article 59 (both of the coastal State and the international community). However, effective application of this provision is, in this author's view, conditional on cooperation to facilitate interaction and conflict resolution between the States concerned and to include the interests of the 'international community as a whole' in this work.

[42] Bin Cheng, Article VI of the 1967 Space Treaty revisited: 'International responsibility', 'national activities' and 'the appropriate state' (1998) 26 *Journal of Space Law* 7.

[43] Byers and Byers (n 6), 585.

[44] Alla Pozdnakova, Oceans as spaceports: State jurisdiction and responsibility for space launch projects at sea (2020) 26 *Journal of International Maritime Law* 267.

6.2.3 *Relevance of the Dumping Regime to Tackling Marine Pollution in the Space Sector*

Section 5 of Part XII UNCLOS addresses specific sources of marine pollution and details the general rules of Article 194. Arguably, some of these provisions may provide a relevant normative basis to strengthen marine environmental protection from spaceflight pollution. This part examines Article 210, which requires States to take measures to prevent, reduce and control pollution of the marine environment by dumping. Importantly, according to this provision, States must ensure that national laws, regulations and measures prevent dumping from being carried out without permission from the competent authorities.

States are required to adopt relevant national rules and measures to prevent marine pollution by dumping that are no less effective in preventing, reducing and controlling such pollution than global rules and standards.[45] These international rules are laid down in the London Convention on Dumping (the London Convention)[46] as amended by the 1996 Protocol. The latter instrument extends the Convention provisions to include aircraft and imposes a prohibition on marine dumping, with a narrow exception.[47] The provisions of Article 210 UNCLOS are further detailed and strengthened in the London Convention with the 1996 Protocol, which transforms a 'right' into an 'obligation'. In addition, dumping is regulated at the regional level, for example, by the Convention for the Protection of the Marine Environment of the North-East Atlantic (OSPAR Convention).[48]

International rules on protection of the marine environment from pollution by dumping are potentially relevant for spaceflight-source pollution. First, provisions on marine dumping may be relevant to governing de-orbiting of end-of-life space objects and regulating pollution caused by jettisoned space residues on the high seas.[49] Second, the marine dumping regime may also be useful for regulation of spaceflight-source pollution within maritime zones under jurisdiction of a coastal State, including situations when spaceflight residues generated by launches of space objects from another State's territory fall into maritime areas under national jurisdiction of a coastal State.[50]

Thus, Article 210(5) UNCLOS precludes dumping within the territorial sea and the exclusive economic zone or onto the continental shelf without the express prior

45 Art. 120(1) and (6) UNCLOS.
46 Convention on the Prevention of Marine Pollution by Dumping of Wastes and Other Matter, Washington/Moscow/London/Mexico City, adopted 29 December 1972, in force 30 August 1975, 1046 UNTS 120.
47 1996 Protocol to the Convention on the Prevention of Marine Pollution by Dumping of Wastes and Other Matter, 1972 (as amended in 2006).
48 Paris, 22 September 1992, in force 25 March 1998, 2354 UNTS 67, www.ospar.org/convention.
49 See also De Lucia and Iavicoli (n 6), 379 et seq.
50 Cf. Rockot case (n 6).

approval of the coastal State. The coastal State also has a right to regulate dumping within its maritime zones through a system of permits, regulations and controls. The wording of this provision may allow a coastal State to prohibit third States from using its EEZ for jettisoning spaceflight residues. It also specifies that a coastal State's right to issue permits and regulate and control such dumping is subject to the duty to bring the matter up for 'due consideration' by those States that, by reason of their geographical situation, may be adversely affected by dumping.[51] These may arguably be neighbouring States and States dependent on navigation or other activities in the waters where jettisoning is taking place.[52]

The question is whether a coastal State within the meaning of the dumping regime may also be viewed as the 'appropriate' State for the purposes of Article VI of the Outer Space Treaty. The latter requires that the appropriate State must authorize and supervise space activities by its non-governmental entities.[53] This question is relevant for situations when a coastal State is acting as a launching State (from whose territory the launch is taking place), or as a State whose maritime zones are used by another State for jettisoning spaceflight residues. As pointed out earlier, the coastal State's rights and obligations in the latter situation are not fully clear under general UNCLOS provisions and the Outer Space Treaty. If applicable, provisions on marine dumping laid down in Article 210 and the London Convention with Protocol would spell out a coastal State's competences to regulate such cases more clearly.

Regrettably, spaceflight-source pollution is not included in the definition of dumping in UNCLOS and the London Convention.[54] The regime only regulates dumping from vessels, platforms and other man-made structures, or from aircraft at sea. While Article 4.2 of the 1996 Protocol also includes 'any deliberate disposal at sea *of* vessels, aircraft, platforms or other man-made structures *at sea*' (author's italics), it is arguable whether jettisoned parts of space rockets and other space objects, including end-of-mission/de-orbited spacecraft, may be viewed as 'aircraft'.[55] In any case, the definition of dumping expressly excludes disposal of wastes or other matter 'incidental to, or derived from the normal operations' of vessels, aircraft, platforms or other man-made structures at sea and their equipment.[56] Spaceflight-source pollution in the shape of jettisoned launch waste is part of a normal launch

[51] Art. VIII London Convention (n 46).

[52] Compare, however, with Art. 59 UNCLOS, which encompasses the international community as a whole, not just geographically relevant States.

[53] UNCLOS Art. 210(3). The latter requirement is more far-reaching than Arts. 207, 211 and 212, which do not envisage a requirement to regulate polluting activities through permits. Art. 210 UNCLOS does not distinguish between governmental and non-governmental entities.

[54] Art. 1(5) UNCLOS.

[55] International law does not, however, contain a generally accepted definition of an aircraft: Lisa Tomas, 'Air Law', in Anne Peters (ed.), *Max Planck Encyclopedia of Public International Law* (Oxford Public International Law), available at opil.oplaw.com.

[56] Art. 1(5) UNCLOS.

operation,[57] much like so-called operational discharges from ships. The marine dumping rules also differentiate between 'deliberate' and 'incidental' pollution, albeit without detailing what constitutes either type of pollution. Pollution resulting from an accident such as a space rocket explosion following a launch is likely not to be viewed as 'dumping' within the meaning of these regulations.

6.3 ASSESSMENT AND PATHWAYS TO MORE EFFECTIVE INTERNATIONAL REGULATION OF SPACEFLIGHT-SOURCE MARINE POLLUTION

6.3.1 *Overview*

The discussion in the previous section shows that the international environmental regime governing the space sector is fragmented and does not adequately regulate state responsibility for environmental measures in the spaceflight sector. Admittedly, UNCLOS establishes more far-reaching environmental obligations on States engaged with space activities than does the Outer Space Treaty, which only imposes a duty on States to conduct international consultations before starting activities with potentially harmful interference with activities by other States in outer space.[58] UNCLOS clarifies that States are responsible for protection of maritime areas, including the high seas, from any pollution, which would include spaceflight-source pollution.

However, the normative relevance and effectiveness of UNCLOS for spaceflight-source pollution is challenged by several factors. It often remains unclear which State should be responsible for taking appropriate measures to protect the marine environment from spaceflight-source pollution. It is also not clear what provisions would be feasible to develop, in what kind of instrument and what issues require international, rather than national, regulation. This may be partly explained by the absence of spaceflight-specific environmental provisions in UNCLOS and other international instruments, and the inherent ambiguity and normative weakness of general international environmental law, which is unable to fill the gaps in the space law and law of the sea regimes.

In this author's view, the first step is to clarify and strengthen the relationship between international space law and the law of the sea. Currently, adequate interaction between the space law and law of the sea regimes is lacking at the normative and institutional level, which in turn stands in the way of developing environmental regulation in the space sector. Further, with regard to development of substantive environmental provisions in the spaceflight sector, unilateral

[57] Report of the Scientific Group (n 2), pkt 1.
[58] Art. IX Outer Space Treaty (n 12).

(national) measures should arguably be supplemented by joint (international) state measures. To enable progress in this area, it is necessary to obtain sufficient knowledge about the environmental effects of spaceflight and to develop an adequate institutional framework to back up the normative and procedural dimension of environmental protection in the space sector.

6.3.2 *Strengthening Knowledge about the Marine Environmental Impact of Spaceflight*

UNCLOS Part XII Sections 2–3, which lay down provisions on inter-state cooperation on gathering and exchange of knowledge about spaceflight pollution, should be used actively by States responsible for spaceflights as well as by States affected by spaceflight pollution. The necessity for measures to protect the marine environment is normally determined by means of establishing appropriate scientific criteria for the formulation of rules (Article 201 UNCLOS), by advice from international bodies such as the International Council for the Exploration of the Sea (ICES), and by monitoring and assessing the environmental impact of spaceflights (Articles 204–206).

As pointed out earlier, an important impediment is the absence of sufficient knowledge on the environmental impact of the spaceflight sector, as available research on the marine environmental effects of space activities is rather scarce and appears unsatisfactory.[59] States should more actively apply UNCLOS provisions requiring them to gather and exchange knowledge on spaceflight pollution of the marine environment. This may ensure the necessary scientific basis for assessment of space launch effects on the marine environment and enable development of a systematic international approach to problems revealed.

Arguably, the present under-utilization by States of UNCLOS provisions on scientific research on the environmental impact of spaceflight may even lead to infringement of the due diligence obligation with regard to protection of the marine environment. It is generally recognized that the duty to conduct an environmental impact assessment (EIA) follows from general international environmental law as part of a State's due diligence obligation, and is necessary for fulfilment of the international environmental law principle of prevention.[60] As EIA is an important – although not in itself sufficient – step towards collection and sharing of knowledge

[59] Greenpeace International submitted to the Scientific group of the London Convention that a gap exists in assessment and control of launch activities, de facto disposals of wastes at sea is taking place and access is limited to publicly available information and assessments: see Greenpeace, 'Concerns relating to de facto disposal at sea of jettisoned space vehicle components', available at www.greenpeace.to/greenpeace/wp-content/uploads/2018/09/LC-SG-41-8-2.pdf.

[60] Responsibilities and obligations of states with respect to activities in the area (Advisory Opinion, 11 February 2011) ITLOS case no. 17, ITLOS Reports (2011), para. 145.

on the cumulative environmental effects of spaceflight, it is hence essential for the future development of environmental standards and requirements in the space sector.[61]

With regard to the marine environment, the duty to assess the potential effects of planned space activities would follow from Article 206 UNCLOS. The duty to conduct EIA also applies to activities with an impact on the environment in areas beyond the limits of national jurisdiction.[62] UNCLOS also requires States to publish reports with the results of such assessment or communicate the results to a competent international organization.[63]

However, UNCLOS leaves it to the responsible State to evaluate whether there are 'reasonable grounds for believing' that the threshold for EIA – 'substantial pollution of or significant and harmful changes to the marine environment' – is reached.[64] Thus, States enjoy wide discretion to determine whether an EIA should be required for spaceflight, and what activities more specifically form part of such assessment. For example, some States require an EIA for launch activities; however, there exists no consistent and uniform international approach to the scope of this requirement.[65]

It is arguably necessary to harmonize approaches to EIA among spaceflight-active States by expressly including spaceflight pollution in the scope of relevant activities and by detailing the conditions and requirements for EIAs. In this respect, it would be more effective to address the issue through a global, rather than a regional, measure such as the forthcoming legally binding instrument on biodiversity in areas beyond national jurisdiction.

The Convention on Environmental Impact Assessment in a Transboundary Context (Espoo Convention)[66] also sets out more detailed rules for EIA, including rules on the duty to notify and consult each other and important procedural provisions. Regrettably, the Espoo Convention does not expressly include spaceflight and, in any case, does not have global reach in terms of its ratification status. Amendment of the Espoo Convention would be an important step forward. In the EU context, a corresponding change could arguably be achieved by amending existing secondary legislation.[67]

[61] See also the IAU report to the 64th session of COPUOS (n 5), including statement by astronomers on the need to mitigate the adverse impacts of mega-constellations.

[62] Responsibilities and obligations of States with respect to activities in the area (n 60) para. 148.

[63] Art. 205.

[64] Cf. Art. 2(3) Espoo Convention (n 66).

[65] On the scope of EIAs in national jurisdictions (US example), see also Joosung Lee, Legal analysis of Sea Launch license: National security and environmental concerns (2008) 24 *Space Policy* 104–112, at 107, who points out that the long-term effects on the environment remain undetermined.

[66] Espoo, 25 February 1991, in force 10 September 1997, available at https://unece.org.

[67] Directive 2011/92/EU of the European Parliament and of the Council of 13 December 2011 on the assessment of the effects of certain public and private projects on the environment, OJ L 26, 28 January 2012, 1.

6.3.3 *Developing the Institutional Framework in the Space Sector to Include Environmental Matters*

To meet their due diligence obligations to protect the environment from spaceflight-source pollution, it is also crucial for States to establish environmental cooperation in the spaceflight sector. Outer space law is based on the premise of 'broad international cooperation in the scientific as well as the legal aspects of the exploration and use of outer space for peaceful purposes'.[68] UNCLOS explicitly requires States to cooperate directly or through 'competent international organizations' on matters of the law of the sea. Cooperation through an organization or an institution, in addition to direct bilateral or multilateral cooperation on an ad hoc basis, has a number of advantages for regulating issues of global concern. For example, in the shipping sector, States acting through the International Maritime Organisation (IMO) have over time developed international safety and environmental standards, obligations and procedures. In the space sector, development of international emission and other environmental safety standards comparable to those adopted under the auspices of IMO (e.g., MARPOL) would be far too premature.[69] It would be feasible to begin by tackling the lack of an adequate institutional framework necessary to facilitate inter-state dialogue and to support cooperation on research, harmonization and monitoring of environmental legal standards in the space sector.[70] Presently, there are no international institutions that hold a clear mandate to address pollution of the marine environment by spaceflights. Better interaction between space law and the law of the sea may be achieved by stronger institutions with clearer competence for protection of the marine environment from pollution caused by spaceflight. This could also preclude unnecessary fragmentation of the environmental legal framework in the spaceflight sector, ensuring that international legal solutions consider protection of the Earth's environment as a whole.

An internationally coordinated approach through an institution responsible for international legal development in the space sector such as COPUOS, supplemented by inter-institutional cooperation with other competent international organizations, is indispensable to pave the way for prospective harmonization steps. It may also be feasible to adjust and strengthen the existing regulatory and institutional framework for spaceflight pollution, for example, by expanding the marine dumping

[68] Outer Space Treaty (n 12), Preamble.

[69] However, ESA is working on the project of 'greening' space launches, notably through developing more environmentally friendly types of fuel. See ESA, 'Green' Satellite Fuel designed to make space safer, available at www.esa.int/Our_Activities/Space_Engineering_Technology/Green_satellite_fuel_designed_to_make_space_safer

[70] See Samuel Barrows, Racing to the top ... at last: The regulation of safety in shipping, in Walter Mattli and Ngaire Woods (eds.), *The Politics of Global Regulation* (Princeton: Princeton University Press 2009) 196, who points out that the institutional context at the supranational level has been crucial in facilitating regulatory change in international shipping.

regime. As pointed out earlier, the London Convention and related instruments contain important regulatory tools that are not present in the space treaties or UNCLOS. Expanding the marine dumping regime to include 'operational' (normal) pollution by jettisoned components of space objects and by de-orbited end-of-mission spacecraft may contribute to strengthening legal protection of the marine environment from spaceflight pollution. The relevance of the dumping regime for the spaceflight sector has been under examination via the auspices of the IMO since 2016, but this work has not yet been concluded.[71] It is advisable to continue the work initiated by the IMO and UN COPUOS to evaluate expansion of the London Convention to the spaceflight sector and accordingly to amend the 1996 Protocol in order to include disposal of jettisoned space objects into the maritime environment.

6.4 CONCLUSIONS

Spaceflight-source pollution of the marine environment is not yet perceived by States as a problem that requires immediate international measures. A likely explanation is lack of sufficient knowledge about cumulative, long-term and transboundary effects on the oceans of space launches and other spaceflight-related activities. This may partly be explained by a lack of clear environmental competences of international outer space governance institutions. Although some marginal steps have been taken in the right direction, namely, to assess application of the international dumping regime to jettisoned space launch waste, the issue is not a priority for inter-state cooperation and the competent institutions in the maritime and space sector. Thus, international environmental rule of law remains at an embryotic stage of development in the space sector. There is a clear need for development of a more comprehensive, international framework to tackle the environmental impact of spaceflights.

International environmental law requires States to exercise due diligence in taking adequate measures to protect the environment from pollution by all kinds of industrial activities. However, an unclear and fragmented international legal context may hardly help States meet their obligations to protect the marine environment from spaceflight pollution. A more pro-active approach is nevertheless required from States at the individual and international level. Here, initial steps should be aimed at gathering and sharing knowledge about the marine environmental effects of spaceflight. To enable development of environmental rule of law in the space sector, including its maritime dimension, it is also crucial to build up an adequate institutional framework at the international level that can support the

[71] Report of the Scientific Groups (n 2). See also Andrew Birchenough and Fredrik Haag, The London convention and London protocol and their expanding mandate (2020) 34 *Ocean Yearbook* 255–278, 274.

development of harmonized substantive provisions and facilitate cooperation on environmental matters. Such an institutional framework should be anchored in the existing international institutions – importantly, COPUOS and the IMO – but their responsibility for environmental matters needs to be clarified and, if necessary, strengthened. Last but not least, cross-institutional cooperation is indispensable to ensure that legal solutions are holistic, protecting the ocean environment, marine ecosystems and the Earth's environment as a whole.

PART III

Balancing the Exploitation and Preservation of Ocean Resources

7

Restoration Activities in the Marine Environment

Balancing Diverging Perceptions of 'Risk'

Rozemarijn J. Roland Holst

7.1 INTRODUCTION

The idea that, in addition to mitigation and adaptation action, we might also need to look at actively restoring some of the damage that has already been done is a relatively novel notion in the context of the marine environment.[1] It is prompted by a growing awareness of the unprecedented scale of cumulative human impacts on the oceans.[2] The Intergovernmental Panel on Climate Change (IPCC) Special Report on Oceans and the Cryosphere identifies marine habitat restoration as a means of enhancing ecosystem-based adaptation to changing conditions.[3] The UN General Assembly recently declared 2021–2030 the 'UN Decade on Ecosystem Restoration' in order to address climate change, enhance water and food security, and protect biodiversity.[4] Restoration also plays a role under various multilateral environmental agreements, including the Convention on Biological Diversity (CBD).[5] Often, restoration is mentioned in the same breath as the need to build ecosystem resilience. For example, the draft negotiating text of the Agreement under the UN Convention on the Law of the Sea (UNCLOS) on the conservation and sustainable use of marine biological diversity of areas beyond national jurisdiction

[1] This chapter is based on R. J. Roland Holst, *Change in the Law of the Sea: Context, Mechanisms and Practice* (Leiden: Brill 2022) ch. 6 section 4. Emerging scholarship on restoration and the law has predominantly been terrestrial in focus. See for an overview e.g., B. J. Richardson, 'The Emerging Age of Ecological Restoration Law' (2016) 25 *Review of European, Comparative & International Environmental Law* 277; A. Akhtar-Khavari and B. J. Richardson (eds.), *Ecological Restoration Law: Concepts and Case Studies* (New York: Routledge 2019).

[2] See extensively United Nations, 'The Second World Ocean Assessment' (2021).

[3] H. O. Pörtner and others, 'IPCC Special Report on the Ocean and Cryosphere in a Changing Climate' (2019) <www.ipcc.ch/srocc/download-report-2/>. Summary for Policymakers, para. C.2.2.

[4] UNGA Resolution A/RES/73/248 (6 March 2019).

[5] CBD Arts. 8(f) and 9(c) and Aichi Targets 14 and 15, CBD COP Decision X/2, Strategic Plan for Biodiversity 2011–2020 (2010).

(ABNJ) includes references to 'restoration of ecosystem integrity' as a general principle or approach,[6] to 'rehabilitating and restoring biodiversity and ecosystems' as an objective of area-based management tools,[7] as well as to a potential trust fund to finance 'rehabilitation and ecological restoration' of marine biodiversity in ABNJ.[8]

Does this suggest that we may be seeing a surge in restoration activities in the marine environment over the coming decades? It should be emphasised that restoring marine ecosystems and ecosystem services remains a highly complicated task, and a subject of ongoing scientific research.[9] Most restoration efforts are furthermore extremely expensive, and feasibility is often questionable. However, this does not seem to deter the most avid proponents. Interestingly, private actors are leading recent developments. A noteworthy example is The Ocean Cleanup (TOC): a private actor taking to the high seas with a new technology to systematically clean up plastic pollution. While the objective of both proponents and opponents of such technological 'solutions' is ultimately the same – protection of the marine environment – the underlying conceptions of 'risk' or 'harm' to the marine environment seem to diverge. When seeking guidance from the rule of law on how to assess or balance these different approaches, challenges may arise in issue-areas where the law in turn relies on extra-legal knowledge, such as scientific data, to give content to legal standards.

This chapter will explore this interaction by taking emerging state practice in relation to TOC as a case-study. It will briefly position the notion of restoration within the context of the law of the sea more broadly before zooming in on the example of TOC to illustrate how state practice deals with interpretative questions under UNCLOS in the absence of dedicated legislation. The focus will be on several key outstanding questions regarding the standard of due diligence required from States exercising jurisdiction over such restoration activities, and the difficulties involved in balancing the risks inherent in technological interventions in the absence of knowledge of both the environmental benefits and potential risks. Finally, some conclusions will be drawn as to what guidance, if any, is provided by existing rules and principles of (environmental) law in this context.

7.2 RESTORATION ACTIVITIES UNDER UNCLOS

The term 'restoration' means slightly different things in different contexts.[10] A general distinction is often drawn between restoration in the sense of positive

6 Revised Draft Text, UN Doc A/CONF.232/2020/3 (18 November 2019), draft Art. 5(h).

7 Ibid., draft Art. 14(e).

8 Ibid., draft Art. 52(5)(d).

9 See e.g., the EU-funded MERCES Project on the restoration of degraded marine habitats <www.merces-project.eu/>.

10 A distinction has been drawn between 'environmental restoration' in discrete contexts of a more limited scope (such as a spill site) and the broader notion of structural 'ecological restoration'. See for a discussion, e.g., Richardson (n 1).

measures to improve the degraded condition of the environment affected by past activities and 'remediation' or 're-instalment' action to repair damage for which there is legal liability.[11] Yet, in the *Costa Rica/Nicaragua compensation* case the International Court of Justice (ICJ) used the term 'restoration' in its finding that when natural recovery cannot return an environment to the state it was in before the damage occurred, then 'active restoration measures' may be required in order to return the environment to its prior condition, in so far as that is possible.[12] To avoid confusion, and leaving aside questions of liability and compensation for environmental damage attributable to a particular actor, restoration activities of the kind discussed here do not depend on questions of legal attribution or a causal link.[13] The focus is on restoration activities that consist of deliberate intervention aiming to (partly) restore damage or degradation of the marine environment for the purpose of improving the condition of the environment *per se*.

That the common objective of enhanced marine environmental protection is inherently linked to strengthening the rule of law is evidenced by the very existence of Part XII of UNCLOS, which provides a central framework for protection of the marine environment.[14] It has been observed that one of the most significant contributions of UNCLOS to strengthening the rule of law lies in the *process* rather than the substance of many of its provisions.[15] Again, Part XII is a case in point. By setting out a general obligation to protect the marine environment, which has been interpreted and applied as an obligation of 'due diligence',[16] it enables an ever-evolving balance of interests to be struck, as well as incorporation of more detailed environmental (procedural) duties and standards that respond to developments in law and in fact. This obligation of due diligence to protect and preserve the marine

[11] This distinction is drawn, e.g., under EU Directive 2004/35/CE on Environmental liability with regard to the prevention and remedying of environmental damage (2004). See also R. Long, 'Restoring Marine Environmental Damage: Can the "*Costa Rica* v *Nicaragua*" Compensation Case Influence the BBNJ Negotiations?' (2019) 28 *Review of European, Comparative & International Environmental Law* 244, 9.

[12] *Certain Activities Carried Out by Nicaragua in the Border Area (Costa Rica* v. *Nicaragua)* Compensation, Judgement, ICJ Reports 2018, 15, para. 43.

[13] See for a discussion of these issues, e.g., Long (n 11).

[14] See also B. H. Oxman, 'The Rule of Law and the United Nations Convention on the Law of the Sea' (1996) 7 *European Journal of International Law* 353, 364; and more generally J. Harrison, *Saving the Oceans through Law: The International Legal Framework for the Protection of the Marine Environment* (Oxford: Oxford University Press 2017).

[15] Oxman (n 14) 356; P. Allott, 'Mare Nostrum: A New International Law of the Sea' (1992) 86 *The American Journal of International Law* 764, 785.

[16] See UNCLOS Art. 192 et seq. See also *South China Sea Arbitration (Philippines* v. *China)*, Award on the Merits, 12 July 2016, para. 944; *Request for an Advisory Opinion Submitted by the Sub-Regional Fisheries Commission*, Advisory Opinion, 2 April 2015, ITLOS Reports 2015, 4, para. 131; *Pulp Mills on the River Uruguay (Argentina* v. *Uruguay)* Judgment, ICJ Reports 2010 (I), 14, para. 197.

environment does not impose an explicit duty to proactively restore parts of the marine environment that are damaged or degraded in the absence of legal liability for such damage.[17] However, the general obligation has been interpreted to include both protection from future damage and 'preservation in the sense of maintaining *or improving* its present condition'.[18] While this does not quite amount to an obligation of result to restore or improve the condition of the marine environment in order to comply with the general obligation of due diligence, restoration activities are in principle clearly consistent with the object and purpose of Part XII.

Various kinds of restoration activities are already taking place in the marine environment, primarily on a local scale in areas within national jurisdiction, for example, revegetation of seagrass meadows or coral farming for the purposes of re-planting and restoring natural reefs.[19] These are relatively small-scale and non-invasive activities that, when successful, can reap multi-user benefits by increasing species abundance, thereby supporting local livelihoods. Proactive restoration measures are also being explored on the regional level. In the Baltic Sea, a serious environmental threat is posed by eutrophication and the resultant oxygen depletion caused by excessive nutrient runoff from land.[20] As a result, large parts of the seabed can no longer sustain any plant or animal life.[21] Among the measures proposed to address this issue is sea-based engineering that purposefully targets the pollution that is already out there; either by dredging phosphorus-rich sediments, or by chemically treating those sediments.[22] These proposals have proven controversial; both due to concerns about the environmental risks involved in the technologies themselves, as well as concerns about the implications of sea-based measures for the overall governance approach to eutrophication in the region.[23] Furthermore, while the Baltic Sea is one of the most densely regulated seas on the planet, the absence of a specific legal framework for the proposed engineering techniques and the resultant questions of legal qualification under the various layers of law, make it a significantly more complex activity from a regulatory point of view, compared to the non-invasive

17 UNCLOS only contains an obligation to 'maintain or restore' populations of harvested species for the specific purpose of maintaining the maximum sustainable yield, see Arts. 61 for the EEZ and 119 for the high seas.

18 *South China Sea* (n 16), para. 941. Emphasis added.

19 See e.g. <www.coralrestoration.org/>.

20 Eutrophication and oxygen depletion concentrate at the seabed, where a chemical process occurs through which additional phosphorus is released from sediments. As the Baltic is a semi-enclosed sea, this means that limited amounts of oxygen-rich waters can reach its central parts. See next chapter and H. Ringbom, B. Bohman and S. Ilvessalo, *Combatting Eutrophication in the Baltic Sea: Legal Aspects of Sea-Based Engineering Measures* (Leiden: Brill 2019) 2–3.

21 Ibid.

22 For an extensive legal study of these proposals, see Ringbom, Bohman and Ilvessalo (n 20).

23 Most Baltic countries strongly emphasise the potential of (enhanced) land-based measures. Only Sweden and Finland are openly positive towards exploring sea-based measures further. Ibid., 3–4.

small-scale restoration projects under a single jurisdiction mentioned above.[24] Yet another type of applicable law questions is raised by restoration activities that take place entirely in areas beyond national jurisdiction. The latter will be the focus of the remainder of this chapter, for which TOC serves as an example.

7.3 THE OCEAN CLEANUP: A NOVEL USE OF THE HIGH SEAS

TOC is a private entity with a unique agenda: a Dutch non-profit organisation on a mission to rid the oceans of plastic. In October 2018, TOC towed the first cleanup system (System 001) into the Great Pacific Garbage Patch (GPGP) for an operational trial. The GPGP is an oceanic gyre situated on the high seas off the coast of North America where ocean currents naturally accumulate plastic debris and other matter, and it is the largest plastic accumulation zone on the planet according to research conducted by TOC.[25] System 001 consisted of a 600-metre-long U-shaped passively floating boom with a three-metre underwater curtain to retain plastics within the system.[26] The latest iteration of the system (System 002) uses a similar contraption, but with a closed retention net, while the system will now be actively towed by two vessels.[27] TOC's ambition is to eventually scale up to a fleet of such devices, to be operated in all five subtropical gyres where currents concentrate ocean-borne plastic waste.[28]

As TOC is a legal entity incorporated under Dutch law, the Dutch Government not only has an obligation of due diligence under UNCLOS and general international law to ensure that activities under its jurisdiction and control do not cause harm to other States or the marine environment,[29] but it has also expressed a willingness to actively 'facilitate and support' TOC's activities.[30] However, owing to the unique nature of the activity, it is not self-evident which international legal

[24] Applicable are national laws, regional rules under the Helsinki Convention and EU law, as well as international law under UNCLOS, the London Convention/London Protocol and CBD. See for an extensive and comprehensive legal analysis of all these aspects Ringbom, Bohman and Ilvessalo (n 20).

[25] It is estimated to contain over 79 thousand tonnes of plastic, which does not form a solid floating 'trash island', as is sometimes suggested, but is rather widely dispersed, see L. Lebreton and others, 'Evidence That the Great Pacific Garbage Patch Is Rapidly Accumulating Plastic' (2018) 8 *Scientific Reports* 4666.

[26] See <https://theoceancleanup.com/oceans/>.

[27] Ibid.

[28] i.e., the North Pacific Gyre, South Pacific Gyre, Indian Ocean Gyre, North Atlantic Gyre and South Atlantic Gyre. See for detailed cleanup projections <www.theoceancleanup.com/technology/>

[29] UNCLOS Art. 194(2) and customary international law as confirmed in e.g., *Pulp Mills* (n 16) para. 101; *Certain Activities Carried Out by Nicaragua in the Border Area (Costa Rica* v. *Nicaragua) and Construction of a Road in Costa Rica Along the San Juan River (Nicaragua* v. *Costa Rica)* Judgment ICJ Reports 2015, 665, para. 104.

[30] See Explanatory Notes to the *Agreement between the State of the Netherlands and The Ocean Cleanup concerning the deployment of systems designed to clean up plastic floating in the upper*

frameworks are directly applicable, nor is dedicated domestic legislation in place. In order to ensure that TOC's activities are at least conducted in accordance with general international law on maritime safety, protection of the marine environment and other legitimate uses of the high seas, the Dutch government entered into an agreement with TOC on 8 June 2018 (the Agreement).[31] In this Agreement the parties chose to draw 'by analogy' on the provisions of Part XIII of UNCLOS on marine scientific research (MSR).[32] The next sections will consider how the Agreement interprets and applies UNCLOS to TOC's activities, and what legal questions remain outstanding.

7.3.1 *The 2018 Agreement between the Netherlands and The Ocean Cleanup*

The legal qualification of the cleanup system is not immediately obvious.[33] The Agreement does not specify its status as a 'vessel', 'installation' or otherwise. The system does carry identification markings to indicate its connection to the Netherlands;[34] however, these depictions of the flag are based on UNCLOS Article 262 and are not intended to identify the Netherlands as the flag State within the meaning of Article 94.[35] It is interesting to note that the Agreement uses the term 'system' in the singular, and defines it as 'one *or more* floating systems developed by [TOC] and designed to capture plastic floating in the upper surface layer of the high seas'.[36] Yet, as will be considered in more detail later, none of the Agreement's provisions substantively differentiate between the operation of a single system or the envisaged fleet.

UNCLOS Article 87 provides a non-exhaustive list of high seas freedoms, including the freedom to construct 'installations permitted under international law', which would logically entail the right to deploy such installations. There is no apparent reason why the system could not be regarded an 'installation'.[37] A further point of

surface layer of the high seas (The Hague, 8 June 2018) Staatscourant 2018 nr. 31907, 6 July 2018, at paras. A1–2.

31 Agreement between the State of the Netherlands and The Ocean Cleanup concerning the deployment of systems designed to clean up plastic floating in the upper surface layer of the high seas (The Hague, 8 June 2018) Staatscourant 2018 nr. 31907, 6 July 2018. Full text of the Agreement in English reproduced in R. Roland Holst, 'The 2018 Agreement between The Ocean Cleanup and the Netherlands' (2019) 34 *The International Journal of Marine and Coastal Law* 351. The next section draws partly on this earlier work by the author.

32 Explanatory Notes (n 30), at para. A1.

33 See more extensively Roland Holst (n 31) 353–354.

34 Agreement (n 31), Art. 1.5

35 See Explanatory Notes (n 30) to Art. 1.5. The system is not registered in the Dutch flag registry at the time of writing, but the Agreement leaves this option open for the future. See also the Agreement, Art. 6.4.

36 Agreement (n 31), Art. 1.1(c). Emphasis added.

37 UNCLOS Art. 87(1)(d), the Convention does not define either of the terms. Note that the terminology for 'installations' is not consistent throughout the various parts of UNCLOS: Arts. 56, 60 and 80 of the EEZ and Continental Shelf regimes refer to 'installations and

reference for the deployment and use of installations on the high seas can then be found in Part XIII of UNCLOS on MSR, which contains provisions relating to the legal status of installations (and equipment) and maritime safety-related aspects of their deployment in general. Without using the term 'MSR' in the text of the Agreement, the parties chose to apply UNCLOS provisions on MSR 'by analogy', which, according to the Explanatory Notes, allows the Dutch government to 'sufficiently fulfil its duty of care and provide for a recognisable context in the international arena'.[38] Yet, the Agreement not only transposes those obligations from Part XIII that relate to the deployment of installations but also more MSR-related ones, such as the obligation on the TOC to publish scientifically relevant findings.[39] This may give the impression that the Agreement in effect treats TOC's activities as MSR (which is another recognised high seas freedom); however, the reluctance to explicitly qualify it as such bears witness to the fact that this is not an obvious fit.[40] The choice to model the Agreement on Part XIII appears to be a pragmatic one. As the Agreement was concluded shortly before the scheduled trial of System 001, it enabled compliance by TOC without requiring major changes to the setup of its activities, while providing the Dutch government with a sufficiently recognisable legal basis to take responsibility for TOC's activities in international fora.[41]

The Agreement's provisions remain of a very general character and focus on the system's interaction with other uses of the high seas and maritime safety,[42] as well as protection of the marine environment.[43] The provisions on maritime safety and other uses of the high seas require TOC to take the necessary precautionary measures to prevent hindrance caused by the system,[44] and to consult with affected parties to seek a joint solution, in line with UNCLOS Article 87.[45] As for the safety of the system at sea, the Agreement is drafted, where applicable, in accordance with legislation applicable to ships flying the Dutch flag.[46] The system thus needs to be equipped with traceability and visibility instruments that are standard on sea-going vessels; a requirement that is furthermore analogous to Article 262 of UNCLOS and the general requirement that MSR is conducted in compliance with other relevant

structures'; Art. 87(1)(d) refers to 'other installations permitted under international law' and Arts. 258–262 on MSR refer to 'installations or equipment'. There is no indication, however, that installations need to be 'fixed'.

38 Explanatory Notes (n 30), para. A3.

39 See Agreement (n 31), Art. 6.1 and Explanatory Notes (n 30) to Art. 6.1, referring to UNCLOS Art. 244.

40 See more extensively Roland Holst (n 31) 355–357.

41 Explanatory Notes (n 30), para. A3 and Arts. 1.1–1.2.

42 In accordance with UNCLOS Art. 240(c).

43 In accordance with UNCLOS Art. 240(d).

44 Agreement (n 31), Art. 4.1. See more extensively Roland Holst (n 31) 357–358.

45 Agreement (n 31), Art. 4.2.

46 Explanatory Notes (n 30), para. A3.

rules of international law.[47] Finally, and importantly for the Netherlands, the Agreement stipulates that any damage caused to third parties by the system, including damage resulting from pollution or maritime accidents for which the Netherlands is held liable under international law, can be recovered from TOC.[48]

The provisions on protection of the marine environment from any (accidental) damage caused by the cleanup itself recognise the Netherlands' general obligation to protect the marine environment under Part XII of UNCLOS.[49] TOC is required to take precautionary measures, and is bound to remove any parts of the system from the high seas when they are no longer used.[50] A second article requires precautionary measures to be taken specifically for the protection of species in the area of operation, including establishment of a monitoring plan, which is curiously limited to the first year of deployment on the high seas.[51] A final provision concerns the processing of captured plastic, and it requires TOC to ensure that this is done in accordance with applicable domestic and international legislation.[52] Other than 'best efforts' obligations in terms of precautionary measures, the Agreement does not set out any concrete environmental standards or obligations in addition to those TOC claims to have already incorporated in the system's basic design, nor does it deal with the process of collecting the plastic, or the support vessels' interaction with the system. Noteworthy in particular is the fact that the need for an environmental impact assessment (EIA) is not mentioned anywhere in the Agreement. The next section will consider the implications of some of these outstanding issues in more detail.[53]

7.3.2 *Outstanding Questions: What Standard of Due Diligence?*

The Agreement does not differentiate in any of its provisions between operating a single system and the envisaged scale-up. This is particularly remarkable considering the possible impacts of the system(s) on the marine environment, as the monitoring obligation is limited to one year, and there is no provision for a (renewed) EIA. TOC published an EIA on its own initiative in July 2018 before towing the first system to

[47] This applies to the exercise of all high seas freedoms, UNCLOS Art. 87(1), as well as to MSR in particular, Art. 240(d). Other relevant rules of international law, to the extent applicable to the system, include provisions of COLREGS, SOLAS and MARPOL.

[48] Agreement (n 31), Art. 2.5(2), analogous to UNCLOS Arts. 263(3) and 235.

[49] See UNCLOS Arts. 192; 194(2) and 240(d).

[50] Agreement (n 31), Art. 3.1.

[51] Ibid., Art. 3.2. Monitoring is to include the interaction between the system and species, and the impact of captured plastic on species.

[52] Agreement (n 31), Art. 3.3. It is interesting to note in this respect that TOC's zero-waste policy treats the captured plastic as raw material, rather than waste. Explanatory Notes (n 30), Art. 3.3.

[53] It should be noted that an annual meeting between the parties is provided for to evaluate the effectiveness of the Agreement, and to make any future amendments. Hence outstanding or emerging issues may have to be addressed in a responsive manner as TOC's activities progress. Agreement (n 31), Art. 6.3; and Explanatory Notes (n 30).

the high seas, and a second one in July 2021 for System 002.[54] Presumably for this reason and the fact that the initial EIA did not establish a risk of significant harm to the marine environment,[55] the Agreement does not mention the need for an EIA. Nevertheless, this is an apparent lacuna. While the first trial of a single system may not reasonably be expected to pose any significant risks, the proposed scale-up to a fleet of systems may significantly change potential (cumulative) environmental impacts in the future. Reasonable grounds to expect that significant harm may occur could well arise at a later stage of the project, in which case the Netherlands is required as part of its obligation of due diligence under Part XII and general international law to (re)assess these risks by means of a new EIA, take any necessary measures to reduce the risk and notify any potentially affected States.[56]

This notion of environmental risk is not just hypothetical. Experts have raised a number of concerns, including the cleanup's impacts on particular (endangered) species living in the surface layer of the gyre,[57] and the risk of 'by-catch', nor has an approach been developed to deal with biofouling in an effective and environmentally sound way.[58] A unique but little-known floating sea-surface ecosystem called 'the neuston' can be found in the GPGP, exactly because of the same currents that concentrate the plastic there.[59] Apart from being home to a range of specific surface-dwelling creatures, the neuston is intimately connected to the wider marine ecosystem as a nursery for species of larval fish, and a crucial hunting ground for a diverse range of predators.[60] This surface ecosystem has been compared in function to an 'upside-down coral reef'.[61] Owing to its unique area of operation, TOC is quite possibly the first actor and activity to come into direct interaction with this ecosystem. Whereas TOC's first EIA notably omitted potential impacts on the neuston from the assessment altogether, the second EIA established moderate to high impacts of routine operation of the system on the neuston due to entrapment

54 CSA Ocean Sciences, 'The Ocean Cleanup Environmental Impact Assessment' (2018) <https://assets.theoceancleanup.com/app/uploads/2019/04/TOC_EIA_2018.pdf>; CSA Ocean Sciences, 'The Ocean Cleanup: Final Environmental Impact Assessment' (2021) <https://assets.theoceancleanup.com/app/uploads/2021/07/TOC_FL_21_3648_EIA_FINREV01_12July2021.pdf>.

55 CSA Ocean Sciences, (n 54) ES-3.

56 See UNCLOS Art. 206, and customary international law as confirmed in *Pulp Mills* (n 16) para. 204; *Construction of a Road in Costa Rica* (n 29) paras. 104, 106.

57 R. Helm, 'How Plastic Cleanup Threatens the Ocean's Living Islands', *The Atlantic* (22 January 2019) <www.theatlantic.com/science/archive/2019/01/ocean-cleanup-project-could-destroy-neuston/580693/>. For a response by the Ocean Cleanup see B Slat, 'The Ocean Cleanup and the Neuston' (6 February 2019), available at <www.theoceancleanup.com/updates/the-ocean-cleanup-and-the-neuston/>.

58 For a critical review of an earlier feasibility study see K. Martini and M. Goldstein, 'The Ocean Cleanup, Part 2: Technical Review of the Feasibility Study' (Deep Sea News, 14 July 2014) <www.deepseanews.com/2014/07/the-ocean-cleanup-part-2-technical-review-of-the-feasibility-study/>.

59 See for a discussion Helm (n 57).

60 Ibid.

61 Ibid.

resulting in injury or death.[62] The concern of scientists is thus that if TOC is going to be successful at catching the plastic, it is going to be equally successful at catching the neuston; potentially harming or destroying an important ecosystem before it was properly understood.

These considerations are relevant for the standard of care required from the Netherlands as part of its obligation of due diligence. If the neuston can indeed be considered an important 'rare and fragile ecosystem' or even the habitat of 'depleted, threated or endangered species' this would raise the standard of care and precautionary measures required *vis-à-vis* the neuston in accordance with UNCLOS,[63] but also, for example, the CBD,[64] and potentially the future Implementing Agreement on BBNJ.[65] Yet, similar to the Baltic eutrophication measures mentioned previously,[66] determining the standard of due diligence and the exact measures required involves a different balancing exercise than most traditional activities.

7.4 BALANCING UNKNOWN RISKS

A key function of the rule of law in general is to constrain the arbitrary use of power,[67] and for a broad legal framework like UNCLOS that governs a spatially shared realm this means that a multitude of different interests need to be accommodated and balanced.[68] Whereas many UNCLOS provisions – especially in an exploitation context – typically balance particular sovereign rights and interests, on the one hand, with (common) environmental interests on the other, restoration activities such as TOC involve balancing one environmental concern (the impacts of plastic debris on the marine environment) against another environmental concern (impacts of the cleanup system itself on the neuston and biodiversity). The objective is the same: protecting and conserving the marine environment, but the two types of 'harm' or 'risk' involved are weighed differently, depending on one's position. This involves a novel type of balancing exercise for which existing legal principles do not necessarily provide any concrete benchmarks or guidance.

62 CSA Ocean Sciences, 'The Ocean Cleanup: Final Environmental Impact Assessment' (n 54) ES-7.
63 See UNCLOS, Art. 194(5).
64 See also *South China Sea* arbitration (n 16), paras. 945, 956.
65 The future Implementing Agreement may well contain more specific obligations on environmental impact assessment vis-à-vis biodiversity beyond national jurisdiction, see e.g., Revised Draft Text (n 6), Part IV.
66 See also Ringbom, Bohman and Ilvessalo (n 20) 54, 85.
67 See e.g. J. H. H. Weiler, 'The Geology of International Law: Governance, Democracy and Legitimacy' (2004) 64 *Heidelberg Journal of International Law* 547.
68 P. Allott, 'Power Sharing in the Law of the Sea' (1983) 77 *The American Journal of International Law* 1.

What technology-driven 'solutions' to environmental problems such as TOC or engineering measures to combat eutrophication have in common is that the regulator is confronted with complex 'risk/risk trade-offs'.[69] These 'trade-offs' occur when an intervention to reduce the target risk (knowingly or inadvertently) creates another new risk.[70] Complexity arises where scientific uncertainty remains as to both the potential *benefits* of the technology addressing the target risk and the potential *risks* involved in deploying the technology.[71] Owing to this uncertainty, environmental standards and principles can work both ways in providing guidance on how a balance should be struck. For example, the need to apply the precautionary approach is not controversial in cases where uncertainty persists, but its precise implications are undetermined. The precautionary principle can be used as a regulatory principle in the sense that it prompts regulatory action in the absence of concrete evidence or scientific certainty surrounding a technology, but – based on that same precautionary principle – the technology may still either be authorised or prohibited.[72] That said, even when a permissive approach is taken, the principle requires at the very least a thorough risk assessment before deployment, as well as continuous monitoring.

The general obligation to protect the marine environment under Part XII, and principles such as the no-harm principle or even the ecosystem approach can also work both ways, either to provide support for TOC's continuous cleanup efforts, or as an argument not to do so – depending on how the (short- and long-term) impacts of the activity on the ecosystem versus its benefits are understood and weighed. Application of the environmental rules and principles mentioned above presupposes at least some knowledge of a technology, its consequences, risks and possible alternatives. When this is not available, the rules and principles are effectively 'drained of their substantive content'.[73] Tools and principles such as 'best available technology', 'best available science' or 'best practices' that are commonly used to give content to, for example, the precautionary approach and general due diligence, are of little help when no comparison can be made because there is no relevant 'science' or 'practice' available in the first place.

69 The dilemma is that 'whilst the seriousness of a given problem may call for immediate and targeted intervention, the ensuing uncertain impacts on other elements of inter-connected systems may be equally deleterious, necessitating a gradual, considered, and holistic approach'. F. M. Fleurke, 'Catastrophic Climate Change, Precaution, and the Risk/Risk Dilemma' in M. Ambrus, R. Rayfuse and W. Werner (eds.), *Risk and the Regulation of Uncertainty in International Law* (Oxford: Oxford University Press 2017) 197, 200.

70 S. F. Hansen, M. K. von Krauss and J. A. Tickner, 'The Precautionary Principle and Risk-Risk Tradeoffs' (2008) 11 *Journal of Risk Research* 423, 424–426; J. D. Graham and J. B. Wiener, *Risk vs Risk Tradeoffs in Protecting Health and the Environment* (Cambridge: Harvard University Press 1997) 23.

71 See also Fleurke (n 69) 203; Ringbom, Bohman and Ilvessalo (n 20) 54.

72 Fleurke (n 69) 205–208.

73 Also Ringbom, Bohman and Ilvessalo (n 20) 47–48, 86.

The current lack of knowledge and baseline data concerning the neuston is also precisely what makes a proper risk and impact assessment for TOC so difficult at this stage.[74] This is arguably as much a challenge as it is an opportunity, as novel types of activities such as TOC may also prompt the study and acquisition of data in relation to little-known ecosystems and thereby inform the governance of (future) activities in areas beyond national jurisdiction. That said, given the current uncertainty and knowledge gaps that remain, a restoration activity such as TOC with uncertain benefits, feasibility and (potentially) significant risks may well meet some resistance based on environmental rules and principles, despite their best intentions.[75] Particular weight should be attached to the precautionary principle, at least in the form of prioritising knowledge-enhancement before any significant scale-up of the activity takes place.

An adaptive approach would furthermore be warranted, through which newly acquired knowledge is continuously integrated into the management of the activity.[76] If the Netherlands is to be considered to have taken 'all necessary measures' required as part of its general obligation of due diligence, it would thus be advisable to at the very least spell out dedicated EIA and continuous monitoring requirements before TOC's activities move into the next phase. Any arguments and future decisions on how the various risks involved are to be balanced can only be developed (and challenged) on the basis of such extra-legal knowledge and data.

7.5 CONCLUSIONS

TOC is a new actor and user of the high seas for restoration purposes. Whether it ushers in a time of private actor-led cleanup efforts and technological interventions in the marine environment only time will tell. TOC's objective to restore the marine environment is in line with the object and purpose of the Convention, as well as with general international policy on plastic pollution,[77] yet its means could prove controversial. While the analogous application of Part XIII under the 2018 Agreement may provide a suitable model to establish core responsibilities and liabilities and to ensure that TOC's activities are conducted in line with relevant international law, several important legal questions remain outstanding, notably concerning the standard of due diligence required from the Netherlands – the

[74] Furthermore, its location far out on the high seas makes monitoring and studying the neuston technically challenging and very expensive. R. Helm, Keynote Lecture at Ocean Cleanup Symposium, University of Liverpool, 17 December 2019.

[75] See for similar considerations with regard to sea-based eutrophication measures, Ringbom, Bohman and Ilvessalo (n 20) 84.

[76] Similarly, Ringbom, Bohman and Ilvessalo (n 20), 56–57.

[77] See e.g. UNEP's 'war on plastics', www.unenvironment.org/news-and-stories/press-release/nations-commit-fight-plastic-pollution-together-during-un-general. Also UNGA Resl 74/19 (2019), paras. 216–227, and UNEP/EA Resl 4/6 (2019).

content of which depends on the availability and assessment of extra-legal knowledge that is currently lacking.

Perhaps the biggest challenge for the rule of law in governing restoration activities such as TOC lies in dealing with uncertainty and knowledge gaps regarding both the benefits and risks involved in employing a new technology in a complex environment, and how to approach environmental risk/risk trade-offs when perceptions of these risks diverge. In such instances, general rules and principles such as the precautionary approach do not provide concrete directions. This chapter has sought to uncover a particular challenge for the rule of law in terms of its relationship with scientific knowledge, or the absence thereof, in times defined by cumulative pressures on marine ecosystems, significant measures of uncertainty and diverging perceptions of 'risk'.

8

Marine Geoengineering to Abate Eutrophication in the Baltic Sea

How to Address Regulatory Voids and Uncertainty

Brita Bohman and Henrik Ringbom

8.1 INTRODUCTION

Sea-based measures represent a new way of dealing with eutrophication in the Baltic Sea. In brief, they refer to different technological innovations that could be implemented at sea to target pollution that has already been released, in contrast to reducing discharges from the original source on land. These measures are not directly subject to any specific regulation. It is therefore interesting to study what rules apply for such activities but also to explore more generally how marine environmental law operates in the absence of specific rules, and how environmental principles manage to fill those gaps. The topic thus serves as a case study on how the rule of law functions in the absence of specific legal rules and how environmental principles may serve to fill such gaps. Moreover, sea-based measures raise interesting issues linked to the balancing of interests, as the arguments both against and in favour of the measures are based on environmental protection, and as their environmental impact is uncertain. Eutrophication is the main environmental problem in the Baltic Sea. This is the result of excessive inputs of nutrients, mainly phosphorus and nitrogen, from a variety of sources, including industry, agriculture and wastewater. These nutrients stimulate growth of aquatic plant life. Yet, overgrowth of plants and algae blocks sunlight and, in the degradation phase, consumes oxygen from the sea, thereby contributing to a state of hypoxia. This lack of oxygen at the bottom of the sea, in turn, initiates a chemical process whereby phosphorus (from historical excess inputs) tied to the seabed sediments is released, thereby causing another source of nutrients in the sea.[1]

Over recent decades a broad range of initiatives have been taken to mitigate eutrophication in the Baltic Sea. As many steps have already been taken to reduce

[1] See, e.g., Vahanen Environment Oy and Centrum Balticum, *Speeding up the Ecological Recovery of the Baltic Sea* (Report for Ministry of the Environment of Finland, Helsinki, 2018) 29–31, https://vahanen.com/app/uploads/2018/05/Speeding_up_the_ecological_recovery_of_the_ Baltic_Sea.pdf

nutrient input into the sea through land-based measures, attention is increasingly turning to new forms of reduction measures, including sea-based measures to target phosphorus leakage from the seabed. The sea-based measures that are currently envisaged for the Baltic Sea can be broadly grouped into three main categories: (1) those focusing on removal of the phosphorus-rich parts of sediments (through dredging or 'skimming'), (2) those influencing the chemical composition of sediments through treating the seabed with chemicals and (3) those seeking to improve oxygen levels in the seabed through different forms of oxygenation (notably by pumping oxygen-rich surface water down to the bottom). For reasons of convenience the three categories are generally referred to as 'dredging', 'chemical treatment' and 'oxygenation'.

All sea-based measures include some environmental risks, albeit that the nature and magnitude of the risk varies between techniques.[2] For all three main groups of techniques, the longer-term risks and effects on the marine ecosystem are significantly under-studied, in particular with respect to larger-scale and off-shore operations. Establishing the polluting impact of sea-based measures is therefore coupled with serious challenges from a scientific perspective, which also affects their legal status, for example, as to whether the measures themselves qualify as 'pollution'. At the same time, the whole idea behind sea-based measures is to function as a potentially important cure for the eutrophication problem of the Baltic Sea.

Based on this concrete example, this chapter explores how environmental law (Section 8.2) and environmental principles (Section 8.3) apply to and operate in the absence of specific regulation of a given activity, and where a high degree of uncertainty exists about the effects of the activity. The chapter ends with some concluding thoughts on the format of potential future regulation of marine geoengineering measures in the Baltic Sea (Section 8.4).

8.2 RULES APPLICABLE TO SEA-BASED OR GEOENGINEERING MEASURES?

8.2.1 *The International Legal Framework*

At the time of writing, there are no rules specifically regulating sea-based measures, at any regulatory level (global, regional, EU or national regulation). This section very briefly summarizes some of the key rules in this respect and how they relate to the three categories of sea-based measures.[3]

2 See e.g., ibid.

3 The review here is by no means exhaustive. For more details, see e.g., H. Ringbom, B. Bohman and S. Ilvessalo, 'Combatting Eutrophication in the Baltic Sea: Legal Aspects of Sea-Based Engineering Measures', *Legal Perspectives, The Law of the Sea*, Issue 2.4, 2019, 1–96.

Being the global 'constitution for the oceans', covering all usages of the sea, the United Nations Convention on the Law of the Sea (UNCLOS)[4] is the obvious starting point for any legal inquiry into maritime activities. In the Baltic Sea, maritime delimitation as provided by UNCLOS is nearly complete, that is, apart from a few minor exceptions, the maritime borders are settled between the littoral countries. In terms of jurisdiction, the entire sea is covered by coastal zones (internal waters, territorial seas and exclusive economic zones) of the coastal States, as far as environmental protection is concerned.[5]

UNCLOS Part XII includes obligations for States to protect and preserve the marine environment.[6] Notably, all States have an obligation inter alia to protect the marine environment and must not cause damage by pollution. Furthermore, States individually or jointly are to prevent, reduce and control pollution of the marine environment from any source.[7]

'Pollution of the marine environment' is broadly defined to include 'the introduction by man of substance or energy into the marine environment', which would encompass any of the sea-based measures discussed. However, the definition also includes a requirement with respect to the environmental effect of such activity,[8] which performs a legal assessment as to whether or not the measures are to be considered pollution, dependent on their harmful impact. Ultimate assessment of whether sea-based measures qualify as 'pollution of the marine environment', or 'dumping' for that matter,[9] depends on the level of environmental risk linked to those measures. On the basis of the uncertainties related to sea-based measures, it seems prudent to assume that the measures fall within these definitions. This does not in itself rule out such activities but involves a range of consequential obligations in UNCLOS and other instruments that specifically relate to pollution.[10]

Apart from UNCLOS, the London Dumping Regime, composed of the 1972 London Dumping Convention and its 1996 Protocol,[11] is also applicable.

4 Montego Bay, 10 December 1982, in force 16 November 1994, 1833 UNTS 397.

5 As to jurisdiction in the EEZ, see UNCLOS, Art. 56(1)(a) and (b)). On the maritime delimitation of the Baltic Sea, see E. Franckx, 'Gaps in Baltic Sea Maritime Boundaries', in H. Ringbom (ed.), *Regulatory Gaps in Baltic Sea Governance: Selected Issues* (Cham: Springer, 2018), 7.

6 UNCLOS, Part XII, Arts. 192–195.

7 UNCLOS, Art. 194(1).

8 Under UNCLOS Art. 1(4), the definition focuses on the environmental perspective and is not dependent on matters such as the intention behind the act that caused it. See also P. Birnie, A. Boyle and C. Redgwell, *International Law and the Environment*, 3rd ed. (Oxford: Oxford University Press, 2009) 188–189.

9 For more details, see Ringbom et al. (n 3).

10 E.g., UNCLOS Arts. 194(2) and (4), 195, 199, 204 and 205.

11 The 1972 Convention on the Prevention of Marine Pollution by Dumping of Wastes and Other Matter, Washington/Moscow/London/Mexico City, adopted 29 December 1972, in force 30 August 1975, 1046 UNTS 120 (the London Convention); 1996 Protocol to the Convention on the Prevention of Marine Pollution by Dumping of Wastes and Other Matter 36 ILM 1. Dumping is also regulated in UNCLOS, but in less detailed terms.

These instruments are most relevant with regard to measures in the form of chemical treatment of the seabed and sediments, which may qualify as 'dumping' according to the relevant legal definitions but have recently gained a potentially more general relevance with respect to sea-based measures, through the adoption of rules and principles relating to 'marine geoengineering'.

The applicability of dumping obligations to chemical treatment depends on the effects, including the environmental effects, of such measures. The greater risk they constitute for the marine environment, the more likely it is that they will be considered to work against the aims of the conventions and hence included in the definition of dumping, independently of whether or not the purpose is to dispose of chemicals. However, even if an activity falls within the definition of dumping, it does not necessarily follow that it is completely prohibited.

In this respect, the rules differ significantly between the Convention and the Protocol. The Protocol is stricter, imposing a general prohibition on dumping, with the exception of wastes and other matters listed in its Annex I. The Protocol also introduces a specific obligation for the States parties to apply a precautionary approach to environmental protection from dumping.[12]

In the subsequent practice of the international dumping regime, certain environmental measures that were not foreseen by its drafters have been considered to be dumping and therefore ruled out by the governing bodies. A particularly relevant example is ocean fertilization for mitigation of climate change, which was not considered to be permitted under the Protocol, except for legitimate scientific research purposes, with reference to the precautionary approach required by the Protocol.[13] Many, if not all, proposed sea-based measures to reduce the amount of phosphorus in the Baltic Sea include important similarities to such geoengineering activities.

8.2.2 *Regional Rules: The Helsinki Convention and EU Law*

The key regional environmental instrument covering the Baltic Sea is the Helsinki Convention on the Protection of the Marine Environment of the Baltic Sea Area (Helsinki Convention),[14] which operates through the so-called Helsinki Commission (HELCOM). In addition, all Baltic Sea coastal States, except Russia,

[12] London Protocol, Art. 3. Both instruments apply to all coastal waters, except to the internal waters of States, hence including both the EEZ and the territorial sea of the States parties. In addition, the Protocol extends certain parts of its permit procedures to internal waters.

[13] London Protocol, Art. 3(1); Resolution LC-LP.1(2008) on the Regulation of Ocean Fertilization, adopted on the Thirtieth Meeting of the Contracting Parties to the London Convention and the Third Meeting of the Contracting Parties to the London Protocol; see also P. Sands and J. Peel, *Principles of International Environmental Law*, 3rd ed. (Cambridge: Cambridge University Press, 2012) 187ff , 396.

[14] Helsinki, 22 March 1974, in force 3 May 1980, 1507 UNTS 166.

are Member States of the European Union (EU), which plays an increasingly important role in the regulation and governance of the Baltic Sea.[15]

The legal relationship between the HELCOM regime and the EU is complex. On the one hand, the EU, alongside some of its Member States, is a party to the Helsinki Convention, signifying that the Convention, at least in part, forms an integral part of EU law, including being subject to review by EU institutions. On the other hand, certain key HELCOM measures, notably the Baltic Sea Action Plan (BSAP), represent a means of implementing EU maritime legislation at regional level. The two regulatory layers are hence increasingly intertwined and need to be considered together.

The Helsinki Convention covers a wide range of activities within its scope, but includes no direct rules on sea-based measures. Complementing the requirements found in the Convention and its annexes, substantive standards are commonly introduced in the form of recommendations, which is the main regulatory tool of HELCOM. Apart from a series of HELCOM recommendations on agricultural discharges and wastewater treatment adopted over the years, the revised BSAP of 2021 places further emphasis on certain key issues, including eutrophication, and establishes a country-by-country nutrient reduction scheme through a system of maximum allowable inputs (MAI).[16]

The revised BSAP includes references to the internal load of nutrients, but there are no concrete actions connected to this in the BSAP. Most requirements and approaches taken to combat eutrophication to date have focused on land-based sources and measures to reduce pollution from the land,[17] which is consistent with the fact that most eutrophic pollution comes from the land.

A similar focus on land-based measures has been dominating EU legislation. At EU level, some key rules from the early 1990s place ceilings on release into the sea of certain types of nutrients, notably the Nitrates Directive (91/676/EEC) and the Urban Wastewater Treatment Directive (91/271/EEC). However, since the turn of the Millennium the focus of EU marine policy has been on more holistic, goal-based legal instruments. Today the key EU measures for addressing eutrophication in the Baltic Sea are the EU Marine Strategy Framework Directive (MSFD)[18] and

[15] See e.g., H. Ringbom and M. Joas, 'Concluding Remarks: Regulatory Gaps and Broader Governance Patterns in the Baltic Sea', *Marine Policy*, Volume 98, 2018, 317.

[16] 'The aim is to reach HELCOM's vision for good environmental status in the Baltic Sea', BSAP Eutrophication segment, the BSAP Preamble, para. 3. See also: *'HELCOM Ecological Objectives for an Ecosystem Approach'*, document for HELCOM Stakeholder Conference on the Baltic Sea Action Plan, Helsinki, Finland, 7 March 2006.

[17] See, e.g., the HELCOM Copenhagen Ministerial Declaration, 'Taking Further Action to Implement the Baltic Sea Action Plan: Reaching Good Environmental Status for a Healthy Baltic Sea', Copenhagen, Denmark, 3 October 2013, including the acts adopted, 'HELCOM Palette of optional agro-environmental measures and Recommendations'.

[18] Directive 2008/56/EC of the European Parliament and of the Council of 17 June 2008 establishing a framework for community action in the field of marine environmental policy, OJ L 164/19.

the Water Framework Directive (WFD).[19] Both instruments set out general environmental goals, and each establishes a procedural framework for identifying and adopting measures required to reach those goals but include few precise obligations for the Member States. The MSFD is applicable to marine areas, including EEZ,[20] but has a significant focus on the land–sea interplay and thus mainly on land-based sources of eutrophication. The focus of the WFD is more land-based and mainly concerns sea areas only up to one nautical mile from the coast/baseline.

The provisions in the MSFD also include a requirement to restore marine ecosystems where they have been adversely affected,[21] which could be taken as a positive obligation to undertake, inter alia, sea-based measures. Both directives include a rule aimed at preventing environmental deterioration.[22] The Court of Justice of the EU has interpreted this rule strictly in its case law on the WFD, by ruling that any activity that will lead to deterioration, even on a temporary basis, is prohibited in accordance with the non-deterioration rule.[23] This ruling significantly limits the scope for EU Member States to approve sea-based measures to abate eutrophication in their internal and coastal waters, but it is unlikely that a similar interpretation would apply to the MSFD.[24]

Apart from these two directives, certain EU environmental rules of more horizontal applicability will be of relevance for sea-based measures. This is notably the case for the directives aimed at protecting biodiversity and nature, that is, the Habitats and Birds Directives,[25] to the extent that sea-based measures take place in or affect areas covered by those directives, which are not further discussed here.

19 Directive 2000/60/EC of the European Parliament and of the Council of 23 October 2000 establishing a framework for Community action in the field of water policy, OJ L327/1 (the WFD).

20 MSFD, Art. 3(1)(a) and (b).

21 MSFD, Art.1(2)(b).

22 MSFD, Art. 1(2)(a) and WFD Art. 4.

23 Case C-461/13 *Bund* v. *Germany* (the *Weser* case). The Court also ruled (at para. 68) that the balancing between long-term and short-term consequences in relation to activities that deteriorate the ecological surface status should only be undertaken through the derogations foreseen in Article 4(7) of the Directive. See also T. Paloniitty, 'Analysis: The Weser Case: Case C-461/13 Bund v Germany', *Journal of Environmental Law*, Volume 28, Issue 1, 2016, 157.

24 Like the WFD, the MSFD includes a non-deterioration rule, which could suggest that the interpretations in the *Weser* ruling could be applied analogously. However, many key aspects are designed rather differently in the MSFD. Another important difference is that the areas protected by the MSFD are much larger than in the WFD and are also more difficult to monitor and control. Hence, the link between a specific plan or project and deterioration is much more uncertain under the MSFD. While the general principles of the *Weser* ruling could perhaps be seen as parallel in relation to the aim and application of MSFD, the general conclusions are probably, therefore, not directly transferable.

25 Directive 2009/147/EC of the European Parliament and of the Council of 30 November 2009 on the conservation of wild birds (the Birds Directive) OJ L 20/7; Directive 92/43/EEC of 21 May 1992 on the conservation of natural habitats and of wild fauna and flora (the Habitats Directive) OJ L 206/7.

8.2.3 *Conclusions*

It follows from the brief review in the preceding sections that some aspects of sea-based measures are subject to international regulation, while others are not. At the jurisdictional level, things are reasonably clear. It is the coastal State that exercises sovereignty over measures, independently of the coastal zone concerned. In most coastal States, such measures are supposedly subject to some form of permit, and it is accordingly for the permit authorities of the coastal State concerned to decide whether the measures may take place and impose more precise conditions.

In the absence of specific rules, reliance has to be directed to general environmental obligations, which essentially make the legality of measures dependent on their effectiveness. If sea-based measures are successful in improving the environment without posing major short-term risks, the law presents few obstacles for their introduction. Indeed, it may even oblige them to undertake such measures as part of their general environmental due diligence duties. Conversely, if the benefits are limited and the environmental risks are significant, a whole range of legal obstacles present themselves across all legal levels. In the end, the legality of any kind of sea-based measure, in any sea area, depends on the risks it presents – in both the short and long term – balanced against their long-term benefits. In view of this, one particular category of measures cannot be legally preferred over another without having regard to their performance and environmental impact.

A peculiarity with sea-based measures, however, is the scientific uncertainty that surrounds them. The knowledge required for determining their risks and benefits – and hence the applicable legal constraints – is simply not available.[26] This state of affairs prompts the question as to how environmental law deals with scientific uncertainty. The matter is addressed through general principles of environmental law, the most relevant of which are addressed in the next section.

8.3 ENVIRONMENTAL LAW PRINCIPLES

8.3.1 *General*

Just like environmental law generally, environmental law principles are primarily focused on the balance between prevention or protection against environmental harm and other interests, such as exploitation of natural resources. Compared to the rules discussed in the previous section, international environmental law principles are designed to play a more flexible role to ensure regulatory proactivity and precaution in relation to the changing environment and changing knowledge.[27]

[26] See e.g., Ringbom et al. (n 3), 3–5, 48.

[27] Sands and Peel (n 13) 187ff. See also the Treaty on the Functioning of the European Union, Art. 191.

'Principles' in this context refers more to function than legal status. All principles discussed here, at least in some measure, feature in the Helsinki Convention or its annexes. This ensures their applicability as binding law throughout the Baltic Sea.[28] As always, however, acceptance of the applicability of a certain principle does not necessarily guarantee agreement on what the principle actually provides in substantive terms, whether in general or in the specific case.

8.3.2 *The Principle of Prevention*

One of the main and most long-standing principles of international environmental law is that States must not permit their territory or operations under their jurisdiction to harm the interests of other States or territories beyond their jurisdiction (the 'no harm' principle). It has since been supplemented by the principle of prevention, which is broader as it is not limited to transboundary harm.[29] The principle requires prevention of damage to the environment, including within national borders, or, otherwise, to reduce, limit or control harmful activities.

This does not amount to a duty to prevent any environmental harm, however. It is an obligation of conduct, rather than of result, and the key standard of care required is to exercise due diligence to prevent harm. International case law has further specified, inter alia, that harm which is merely potential must also be considered if it is significant (even if not serious or irreversible)[30] and that the standard of diligence expected is higher with respect to riskier activities.[31]

Despite this, the no-harm and preventive principles will not, as such, prevent sea-based measures. Their application depends on assessing whether any of the suggested sea-based measures would cause (potentially significant) harm to the environment, within or beyond the territory of the State where the measure takes place. As already noted, sea-based measures are difficult to assess in this respect. They do not pose obvious immediate threats to the environment – within or beyond national borders – which would rule them out on that basis alone. However, the consequences of sea-based measures may not be sufficiently known to justify application of the prevention principle.

Yet the matter can also be reversed. Sea-based measures are aimed at repairing the environment, which also opens up application of the principles in favour of the measure. In this perspective, sea-based measures could be regarded as a necessary

[28] Helsinki Convention, Art. 3(2).

[29] N. De Sadeleer, *Environmental Principles: From Political Slogans to Legal Rules* (Oxford: Oxford University Press, 2002) 63–64.

[30] ICJ Judgment in *Pulp Mills on the River Uruguay* (*Argentina* v. *Uruguay*) 20 April, 2010 ICJ Rep. 14, para. 101.

[31] Responsibilities and obligations of States sponsoring persons and entities with respect to activities in the Area (Request for Advisory Opinion submitted to the Seabed Disputes Chamber), International Tribunal for the Law of the Sea, Case No. 17, para. 117.

preventive measure to mitigate damage caused by past polluters. The validity of that argument, however, depends on their consequences and effect, which, again, leads to the question of their factual effectiveness and impact, which is surrounded by uncertainty.

In summary, assessment eventually comes down to scientific uncertainty regarding threats versus possible positive longer-term effects for the environment.

8.3.3 *'Best Available Technology'*

The principle of best available technology (BAT) is a requirement that keeps evolving with the development of new technology.[32] The flexibility of the principle lies in this way of continuously raising the bar. The BAT principle is generally acknowledged and is closely connected to the prevention principle as a tool for acting cautiously.

In the Helsinki Convention the BAT principle, together with best environmental practice (BEP), is laid down in Article 3(3). The wording requires the use of BAT and BEP to 'prevent and eliminate pollution'. The general approach of the Helsinki Convention framework has been to emphasize land-based sources and reducing input of pollution.[33] However, the terms 'prevent and eliminate' in this paragraph might just as well be interpreted more broadly as also including minimization of the 'internal load' by means of sea-based measures.

BAT is further defined in Annex II of the Helsinki Convention. Here it is established that this principle refers to '… the latest stage of development (state of the art) of processes, of facilities or of methods of operation which indicate the practical suitability of a particular measure for limiting discharges',[34] coupled with a list of criteria to be applied when determining BAT.

Sea-based measures definitively represent a new technology for addressing eutrophication. However, that novelty does not in itself make it the best technology for the purpose. For establishing whether a technology is 'best' for this purpose, the criteria of Annex II must be taken into account. Some of the listed criteria may strengthen the position of sea-based measures over land-based reduction measures (e.g., low waste technology), while others (time limits, economic feasibility and the precautionary principle) could work in the opposite direction. A related issue is whether sea-based measures should be assessed and compared in this context to other forms of sea-based measures or whether the reference point in this respect should be technologies for land-based phosphorus reduction measures.

Naturally, assessment may also vary between different types of sea-based measures. The risks, uncertainties and general knowledge vary significantly between, say,

[32] De Sadeleer, (n 29), 84–86.

[33] See e.g., B. Bohman, 'Lessons from the Regulatory Approaches to Combat Eutrophication in the Baltic Sea Region', *Marine Policy*, Volume 98, 2018, 229–230.

[34] Helsinki Convention, Annex II, Regulation 3, para. 1.

oxygenation and chemical treatment, and between small-scale operations in bay areas and measures applied in the open sea. In the end, a key issue is weighing the potential risks of sea-based measures with potential gains. This, in combination with the limited scientific certainty of those risks, leads to the precautionary principle, which is also acknowledged as a key consideration under the Helsinki Convention in determining whether a particular process, facility or method constitutes BAT.[35]

8.3.4 *The Precautionary Principle*

8.3.4.1 General

The precise content of the precautionary principle is not settled.[36] In view of this uncertainty, international courts, including the International Court of Justice (ICJ), have been reluctant to acknowledge the principle as forming part of customary law.[37] But for present purposes, all principles discussed are adopted in the Helsinki Convention and it suffices to note that the principle is laid down in relatively similar terms in both the Helsinki Convention and the London Protocol.

> The Contracting Parties shall apply the precautionary principle, i.e., to take preventive measures when there is reason to assume that substances or energy introduced, directly or indirectly, into the marine environment may create hazards to human health, harm living resources and marine ecosystems, damage amenities or interfere with other legitimate uses of the sea even when there is no conclusive evidence of a causal relationship between inputs and their alleged effects.[38]

The definition makes it clear that application of the principle is not facultative, but States are to apply preventive measures when a certain activity may harm the marine environment. Reference to the absence of conclusive evidence of harm presupposes that some evidence exists to suggest that the activity is harmful, but not enough to provide certainty on the matter.

8.3.4.2 Application to Sea-Based Measures

The precautionary principle suggests that States must 'take preventive measures'. This presumably involves significant restraints or caution in authorizing the activity. Furthermore, in relation to sea-based measures this principle would, in contrast to

35 Helsinki Convention, Annex II, Regulation 3, para. 2.

36 World Charter for Nature, 1982, UN General Assembly, UNGA Res. 37/7, 22 ILM 455 (1983), Art. 11(b).

37 E.g., the *Pulp Mills* case (n 30), 14. However, a Special Chamber of the International Tribunal for the Law of the Sea in 2011 declared that the inclusion of Rio Principle 15 into several international conventions 'has initiated a trend towards making this approach part of customary international law'. SDC Advisory Opinion (n 31) para. 135.

38 Helsinki Convention, Art. 3(2). See also London Protocol, Art. 3(1) and TFEU, Art. 191(2).

other principles and rules discussed earlier, prevent them from being applied, due to scientific uncertainty and the potential risks surrounding them.

On the other hand, the environmental objectives of sea-based measures need to be acknowledged here, too. It may be argued that the state of eutrophication in the Baltic Sea requires further mitigation measures and that all options to ameliorate the ecological state of the sea have to be examined. The precautionary approach should not, accordingly, be used as an excuse for not further exploring new options of interest. At the very least, the fact of a significant knowledge gap – which triggers the precautionary principle – should not be used as an excuse for not undertaking the kind of research necessary to gain that missing knowledge.[39] Application of the precautionary approach in the London Convention provides an example of how this delicate balance could be maintained.

8.3.4.3 The Precedent in the London Dumping Regime

The London dumping regime recently addressed ocean geoengineering measures used to mitigate climate change. This may be of significant value for how sea-based measures could be tackled from a governance point of view in relation to the precautionary principle. The amendment to the London Protocol is not yet in force, but it represents an example of a way to balance the different risks and interests involved in novel measures to address environmental concerns, where the risks are not fully understood, and, hence, entails many similarities to sea-based measures.

The framework for dealing with geoengineering measures under the London Protocol has been developed to deal specifically with ocean fertilization to abate climate change. However, it may be extended to other geoengineering activities.[40] The parties to the London Convention first confirmed the applicability of the dumping regime to ocean fertilization in a joint resolution in 2008. This provided for a precautionary approach by stating that 'given the present state of knowledge, ocean fertilization activities other than legitimate scientific research should not be allowed'.[41] The parties further agreed that in order to provide for legitimate scientific

39 See also: V. Galaz, 'Geo-engineering, Governance, and Social-Ecological Systems: Critical Issues and Joint Research Needs', *Ecology and Society* , Volume 17, Issue 1, 2012, 24, http://dx .doi.org/ 10.5751/ES-04677-170124; K. Güssow et al., 'Ocean Iron Fertilization: Why Further Research Is Needed', *Marine Policy*, Volume 34, Issue 5, 2010, 911–918.

40 The London Protocol defines marine geoengineering, see LC 36/16, Annex 5, 1, Guidance for Consideration of Marine Geoengineering Activities, Section 2, para. 2. *Proceedings of the 2015 Science Day Symposium on Marine Geoengineering*, held on 23 April 2015 at IMO Headquarters, London, United Kingdom.

41 Resolution LC-LP.1(2008) on the Regulation of Ocean Fertilization, para. 8. Even if the resolution is not binding as such, it can be seen as a subsequent agreement or practice between the parties under the Vienna Convention on the Law of Treaties, Vienna, 23 May 1969, in force 27 January 1980, 1155 UNTS 331, Art. 31(3) and, through that, have implications for the interpretation of the London Convention and Protocol.

research, and hence to gain more knowledge about ocean fertilization, an assessment framework should be adopted in order to define projects for research purposes. That framework was to include, inter alia, tools for determining whether or not the proposed activity is contrary to the aims of the Convention and Protocol,[42] hence setting out a new way to respect and operationalize the precautionary principle, while still providing a pathway to promote further knowledge through scientific research. A new resolution was adopted in 2010, known as the 'Assessment Framework for Scientific Research Involving Ocean Fertilization',[43] which guides the parties on how to assess proposals they receive for ocean fertilization research and provides criteria for an initial assessment of such proposals.[44]

In 2013 a resolution was adopted on the 'Amendment to the London Protocol to regulate the placement of matter for ocean fertilization and other marine geoengineering activities'.[45] The amendment provides that 'Contracting Parties shall not allow the placement of matter into the sea from vessels, aircraft, platforms or other man-made structures at sea for marine geoengineering activities listed in Annex 4, unless the listing provides that the activity or the sub-category of an activity may be authorized under a permit'.[46]

'Marine geoengineering' is defined to mean deliberate intervention in the marine environment to manipulate natural processes, including to counteract anthropogenic climate change and/or its impacts, and that has the potential to result in deleterious effects, especially where those effects may be 'widespread, long lasting and severe'.[47] A new Annex 5 also adds an Assessment Framework that lists a number of points to be described, following an initial assessment of whether the activity falls within the definition of dumping at all and hence can be considered within the framework.[48]

If a project is accepted under the Assessment Framework, a thorough monitoring mechanism has to be established to consider both the long-term and short-term impacts of the activity. This forms a safeguard for the general lack of knowledge that remains, despite the review process, and bridges the risks that cannot be accounted for due to the fact that these are methods still under research. While the 2013 amendment is not formally in force, it provides an interesting model for operationalizing the precautionary principle for activities aimed at environmental protection that entail uncertain risks. It could, therefore, also serve as a model for addressing sea-based measures more generally in the specific Baltic Sea context with a view to

42 Resolution LC-LP.1(2008) on the Regulation of Ocean Fertilization, para. 5.

43 Resolution LC-LP.2(2010).

44 *Proceedings of the 2015 Science Day Symposium on Marine Geoengineering*, held on 23 April 2015 at IMO Headquarters, London, United Kingdom.

45 LP.4(8), see circular LC-LP.1/Circ.61.

46 Art. 6bis.

47 Art. 1(5bis).

48 An arrangement of such experts in the consultation process was adopted by the governing bodies in 2014 as Annex 4 to document LC 36/16.

gaining more knowledge about the effects of such measures.[49] This has partly materialized, through endorsement of the 'HELCOM Guidelines for sea-based measures to manage internal nutrient reserves' by the Heads of Delegation in June 2021.[50] The aim of the guidelines is to 'to provide guidance for researchers planning to undertake research projects and for operators and environmental managers planning to implement activities' related to sea-based measures, but also to 'provide decision support for relevant authorities when administering consultations and environmental permitting'.[51] The new BSAP adopted in October 2021 makes specific reference to these Guidelines, adding that through their application, 'measures to manage these internal nutrient reserves should utilize the best available scientific knowledge and minimize potential risks'.[52]

8.3.5 *Conclusions on the Role of Environmental Law Principles*

The environmental law principles, too, leave many questions open as to how and when sea-based measures should be assessed and permitted. The first issue is that the environmental principles discussed in this chapter may be used both ways. Sea-based measures do not – as indeed many of the principles implicitly seem to assume – relate to the balance between environmental objectives as against other objectives, such as economic benefits. They do not even balance different environmental objectives against each other, as in the case of marine geoengineering measures to mitigate climate change. Instead, both the arguments in favour of and against the measures centre on very similar concerns for the marine environment and the long-term survivability of the marine ecosystems. This raises issues on how the principles operate, and those issues cannot be addressed without a proper analysis of the effect of the measures. Thus, these principles, like the rules discussed in Section 8.2, presuppose some degree of knowledge of the risks and/or dangers linked to a certain activity before they can provide useful guidance.

A second problem with sea-based measures is that this knowledge is not available. Generally speaking, the impact and effectiveness of sea-based measures in achieving their objectives are not well understood. Their effectiveness is highly disputed, and there is no certainty or consensus among scientists as to the likely environmental outcome of sea-based measures, in particular for large-scale measures. Indeed, marine biologists in the Baltic Sea region have voiced strong concerns about the

[49] Such research cooperation, and harmonization of permit policies, is also called for in Art. 24(1) of the Helsinki Convention.

[50] HELCOM Doc. HOD 60, 5-3 (Guidelines for Sea-Based Measures to Manage Internal Nutrient Reserves in the Baltic Sea Region); See also HELCOM Doc. HOD 60-2021 (Outcome of the HOD 60), para. 5.26.

[51] HELCOM Doc. HOD 60, 5-3, para. 1.

[52] BSAP 2021 (Helcom 2021), 22.

negative impact that the measures may have and questioned whether they have any benefits at all in the longer term.[53]

The precautionary principle should be able to navigate through the seas of this kind of scientific uncertainty and the principle has an unusually clear legal foundation in the Helsinki Convention. Nevertheless, it turns out that similar uncertainties that pertain to the other principles apply to the precautionary principle as well. These, too, could be used both ways while waiting for scientific data to build up. Halting sea-based measures across the board based on existing scientific uncertainty would ignore the differences between different types of measures. More importantly, it would effectively also halt research and development of more effective measures to deal with the internal load. This, in turn, would mean that a potentially useful tool for improving the environmental status of the Baltic Sea would already be lost at the outset, which does not correspond well with the rationale of the precautionary or other principles discussed previously.

In view of these dilemmas, it seems that the only way forward is to gain more knowledge about the effectiveness of sea-based measures through cautious and controlled measures. One way of achieving this would be to limit permits to scientific purposes and imposing particular criteria for the purpose. The approach adopted by the London Protocol could serve as an important example but needs some further refinement for sea-based measures in the Baltic Sea context in view of the many features that distinguish sea-based measures from most other marine geoengineering measures. The benefits of a tailor-made solution for the Baltic Sea are further emphasized by the legal setting in the region, where the entire sea area is covered by zones where coastal States enjoy jurisdiction over environmental matters, and a strong governance framework in place, with a long tradition of close cooperation in environmental matters, centring around the Helsinki Commission.

8.4 CONCLUDING OBSERVATIONS

No specific laws apply to any of the sea-based measures. Further, the more generic laws that exist do not generally provide much guidance in the matter, except where the measures fall within the scope of the dumping regime. The relevant rights and obligations depend on the environmental effects, both positive and negative. Since sea-based measures present potential risks, while at the same time being potential problem-solvers in relation to eutrophication, weighing their effect is not obvious and leaves much depending on scientific results, which are currently not available.

The same dilemma persists when analysing sea-based measures in the light of various environmental law principles. These principles are generally designed to balance environmental risks against the need for exploitation, by steering away from

[53] See e.g., Swedish newspaper *Svenska Dagbladet*, 1 September 2015: 'Det finns ingen mirakelmedicin för Östersjön' (There is no miracle cure for the Baltic Sea).

the most apparent environmental risks. In this case, where the alternative is not exploitation, where geographical flexibility is limited and the measures to be assessed are actually aiming to solve the very same environmental problems that its opponents are criticizing it for contributing to, clearly much of the balancing will have to centre on scientific knowledge and certainty. The key issue to be balanced is weighing the risk of further escalating eutrophication with all its consequences, and to continue only with land-based measures, against the risks that sea-based measures may have on the ecosystem – due to their novelty and the fact that they have not been sufficiently tested in relation to risks. However, the fact that other methods are available to combat eutrophication, namely land-based measures, that do not involve corresponding environmental risks, that directly aim at stopping the discharges at source and that are proven to work, affects this balance. The availability of land-based measures as an alternative also affects the role of principles such as BAT or BEP. Sea-based measures may definitely represent the most novel techniques in the field, but is it the best available technology? The fact that other measures are available, involving lower risks, will also put the risk assessment in another light since the necessity for the measures is likely to be reduced.

In short, the legality of any kind of sea-based measures, in any sea area, depends on the risks they present – in the short- and long-term – balanced against their long-term benefits. In that light, one particular category of measures cannot be legally preferred over another without having regard to their performance and environmental impact. If a particular measure improves the marine environment without much risk, it is legally easy to justify, while, conversely, a measure with uncertain benefits and large risks meets resistance in a variety of applicable legal rules and principles across many levels.

Lack of scientific certainty about the risks and effects of sea-based measures significantly complicates assessment in this regard, in connection to the precautionary principle. Yet that uncertainty should not be used to dismiss sea-based measures altogether. Rather, it calls for further research into the matter, guided by the precautionary principle.

As sea-based measures are receiving increased focus in the Baltic Sea context, it is important to acknowledge the number of uncertainties involved without giving up potential useful tools to fight eutrophication in the future. At this stage, we conclude that it is both important and appropriate to focus on developing a new framework or guidelines, inspired by the Assessment Framework developed under the London dumping regime, to coordinate policies among the Baltic Sea States, thereby helping permit authorities in their tasks. With the recent adoption of the HELCOM Guidelines, this process appears to be well under way.

9

Filling an Iceberg-Sized Gap in the Law of the Sea

Addressing an Emerging Demand on Oceans

Aref Shams

9.1 INTRODUCTION

The United Nations Environment Programme has stated that water scarcity is fast becoming one of the most prominent challenges of the twenty-first century. Population growth and economic development coupled with climate change are reducing the per capita availability of freshwater around the world, which will likely lead to increasing droughts and famines.[1] The intensification of problems means that as States search for innovative solutions, the oceans and seas are increasingly being looked at to address water scarcity, for instance with the proliferation of large-scale water desalination.[2] It is in this context that there have been recent proposals to tow icebergs from Antarctica to alleviate the water shortages of cities in South Africa and the United Arab Emirates. These plans claim to be cheaper and allegedly more environmentally friendly alternatives to water desalination.[3] This chapter seeks to examine whether international law is able to adequately regulate – that is balancing

* An earlier version of this chapter was written during an internship with the International Tribunal for the Law of the Sea. The views expressed herein are expressed by the author in his personal capacity and do not reflect the views of the International Tribunal for the Law of the Sea. I would like to sincerely thank Naomi Burke O'Sullivan, Alla Pozdnakova and Anne Saab for their helpful feedback on earlier drafts. All errors remain mine.

1 Paul Ekins, Joyeeta Gupta and Pierre Boileau (eds.), *Global Environmental Outlook GEO-6: Healthy Planet, Healthy People* (Cambridge: Cambridge University Press, 2019).

2 Jeannie Sowers, Ayner Vengosh and Erika Weinthal, 'Climate Change, Water Resources, and the Politics of Adaptation in the Middle East and North Africa' (2011) 104 *Climate Change* 599.

3 See Robbie Gramer, 'This country wants to tow icebergs from Antarctica to the Middle East' *Foreign Policy*, 5 May 2017, <www.foreignpolicy.com>; 'UAE firm planning to tow icebergs from Antarctica to start testing this year' *Arabian Business*, 7 July 2019, <www.arabianbusiness.com>; Caroline Winter, 'Towing an iceberg: One captain's plan to bring drinking water to 4 million people' *Bloomberg Businessweek*, 6 June 2019, <www.bloomberg.com>.

exploitation and preservation – support and limit such operations. Such questions remain underexplored in the literature.[4]

The use of icebergs for freshwater is not a novel idea. Arctic inhabitants, for instance the Greenlandic Inuit, have traditionally relied on icebergs for their freshwater needs, and icebergs continue to be used in Greenland, albeit on a relatively small scale.[5] Additionally, icebergs are used in producing luxury goods such as exotic bottled water or liquor in Canada, Norway and Denmark.[6] However, these are relatively small-scale demands on icebergs that would not merit questions on how to balance exploitation of icebergs with preservation of marine resources and environment. What prompted the writing of this chapter was the prospect of this 'cold rush' expanding, with proposals to use icebergs on industrial levels to supply freshwater for entire cities. This also is not an entirely new plan. As early as 1973 it was estimated that use of a mere 10 per cent of the icebergs calving off annually could supply freshwater to more than 500 million people annually.[7] Icebergs represent a substantial reserve of freshwater. In fact, some estimates indicate that the 16,000 icebergs formed annually roughly represent the same amount of freshwater as the annual water flow of all rivers on Earth.[8]

As around 70 per cent of all freshwater in the world is locked in the polar regions as ice,[9] the obvious locations from where icebergs could be towed are Antarctica and the Arctic regions. This means that the Antarctic Treaty System (ATS) and the UN Convention on the Law of the Sea (UNCLOS) are of relevance. Putting aside questions of technical feasibility,[10] this chapter engages with the rules and principles of the law of the sea that would regulate such activities. The aim is to examine how the current law of the sea may need to evolve to respond to a possible new demand on the oceans. As will be demonstrated, the legality of the use of icebergs for freshwater can be somewhat blurry. In fact, there has already been a dispute arising from this legal ambiguity when Denmark disputed the right of Canada to utilise icebergs found in Canadian waters, as they originated from Greenland's ice sheet.[11]

4 For valuable contributions see for instance Christopher Joyner, 'Ice-Covered Regions in International Law' (1991) 31 *Natural Resources Journal* 213; Jorge E. Viñuales, 'Iced Freshwater Resources: A Legal Exploration' (2009) 20 *Yearbook of International Environmental Law* 188.

5 Mathew H. Birkhold, '$166 water could dictate international iceberg law' *The Atlantic*, 31 October 2019, <www.theatlantic.com>.

6 Ibid.

7 J. L. Hult and N. C. Ostrander, *Antarctic Icebergs as a Global Freshwater Resource: Prepared for the National Science Foundation* (Santa Monica: Rand Corporation, 1973), v.

8 Laurence Boisson de Chazournes, *Freshwater in International Law* (Oxford: Oxford University Press, 2013), 41.

9 Pierre-Marie Dupuy and Jorge E. Viñuales, *International Environmental Law* (Cambridge: Cambridge University Press, 2018), 128.

10 For a brief study of technical feasibility see Evan Lubofsky, 'Can icebergs be towed to water-starved cities' Woods Hole Oceanographic Institution, 6 January 2021, <www.whoi.edu>.

11 Dupuy and Viñuales (n 9), 140.

Therefore, the discussions in this chapter are relevant for the debate on sustaining a fit-for-purpose rule of law for oceans for decades to come.

Section 9.2 lays out the current legal framework within which the proposed operations would take place. The section highlights the shortcomings of the regulatory capacities of international law to balance the exploitation and preservation of marine resources in the context of the proposed operations. Section 9.3 deals with the question of how international law could be adapted to deal with this possible new pressure on the natural resources of the oceans. Specifically, the section considers whether the ongoing negotiations on biodiversity beyond national jurisdiction (BBNJ) could be a suitable avenue for addressing gaps in the current legal framework.

9.2 REGULATING THE USE OF ICEBERGS WITHIN THE CURRENT FRAMEWORK OF INTERNATIONAL LAW

This part briefly lays out the general status of different types of ice under international law to contextualise the question how international law views icebergs. It then moves onto the more concrete legal questions that may arise if/when the proposed activities occur.

9.2.1 *Status of Ice under International Law*

Broadly speaking, there are three different categories of ice that may be regulated in different manners by international law: alpine glaciers, pack-ice (or sea ice) and continental glaciers.[12]

Alpine glaciers fall firmly within the confines of national State sovereignty. However, if glaciers are part of an international watercourse, their use may be subject to the UN Watercourses Convention with rules such as equitable and reasonable use and the duty to prevent significant harm to other States.[13] This may prove to be an increasingly accepted view as a watercourse has evolved from being narrowly defined as rivers and lakes to a broader concept of a drainage basin and its ecosystem.[14]

Pack-ice is relatively thin (normally only a few meters in comparison with the hundreds of meters of depth icebergs can reach), and forms over the seas, expanding

[12] Boisson de Chazournes (n 8), 39.

[13] Convention on the Law of the Non-Navigational Uses of International Watercourses, New York, 21 May 1997, in force 17 August 2014, 2999 UNTS, Doc. A/51/869, Arts. 5–7 [Watercourses Convention]. For further details on the law of international watercourses see Stephen C. McCaffrey, *The Law of International Watercourses* (3rd ed., Oxford: Oxford University Press, 2019).

[14] Dupuy and Viñuales (n 9), 129.

and contracting seasonally.[15] The only time UNCLOS mentions ice is in reference to pack-ice. Article 234 holds that States have the right to adopt laws and regulations to deal with the danger that navigation through ice-covered waters poses.[16] Apart from this, treatment of pack-ice is no different to the waters it is found in. Joyner argues that there is a consensus that pack-ice falls under the coastal State's jurisdictional zones due to its relatively short life-span.[17] Furthermore, pack-ice does not affect the delimitation of States' maritime zones,[18] and beyond the 200 nautical mile limit of the exclusive economic zone (EEZ), the principle of the freedom of the high seas will be applicable, meaning that States cannot claim sovereignty rights over pack-ice.[19] This principle will be discussed further in relation to icebergs found in the high seas.

Continental glaciers or ice sheets are very large ice formations that have been formed atop land, most importantly the Antarctic and Greenland ice sheets. Continental glaciers are of interest in this chapter as icebergs are calved off into the seas from their fringes (ice shelves). As continental glaciers are found atop land, States may claim sovereignty over them. Greenland is under Danish sovereignty, while Argentina, Australia, Chile, France, New Zealand, Norway and the United Kingdom all claim sovereignty over parts of Antarctica. It must be mentioned that their sovereignty claims are frozen by virtue of Article IV of the Antarctic Treaty,[20] the implications of which will be further discussed.

Icebergs, however, are not mentioned in UNCLOS. As discussed, ice is only mentioned in the context of Article 234. Icebergs are not mentioned in the Antarctic Treaty either. Therefore, the main question for this chapter is where international law places icebergs in the spectrum outlined earlier. This chapter supports the approach of treating ice as part of territory subject to the territorial sovereignty of a State.[21] If the ice is found at sea, it must be governed by the regime applicable to the maritime zone it is surrounded by. With pack-ice the provisions of UNCLOS are applicable just the same way as if the sea was not frozen, without the ice affecting the delimitation of States' maritime zones.[22]

Bearing the foregoing in mind, we can turn to the other two categories of ice analysed earlier to determine, or rather approximate, how international law views

[15] Joyner (n 4), 224.

[16] United Nations Convention on the Law of the Sea, Montego Bay, 10 December 1982, in force 16 November 1994, 1833 UNTS 3. For more information on Art. 234 see Jan Jakub Solski, 'The Genesis of Article 234 of the UNCLOS' (2021) 52 *Ocean Development & International Law* 1.

[17] Joyner (n 4), 224.

[18] UNCLOS, Art. 5; Joyner (n 4), 224.

[19] UNCLOS, Art. 88.

[20] Antarctic Treaty, Washington, 1 December 1959, in force 23 June 1961, 402 UNTS 71.

[21] M. Bedjauoi, 'Le status de la glace en droit international' in Eduardo Jiménez de Aréchaga and Manuel Rama-Montaldo (eds.), *Le droit international dans un monde en mutation, International Law in an evolving world, Liber Amicorum Eduardo Jimenez de Arechaga* (Montevideo: Fundacion de Cultura Universitaria, 1994), 715.

[22] UNCLOS, Art. 5; Joyner (n 4), 224.

icebergs. Although icebergs can be kilometres wide and long,[23] they are no longer capable of being claimed sovereignty over after they break off from the continental glaciers. Icebergs are also clearly not seen in the same light as alpine glaciers as they are not found attached to land under the sovereignty of States. However, an analogy can be drawn between how icebergs are to be treated and how the UN Watercourses Convention deals with international watercourses. Icebergs can be thought to be akin to the water flowing between States. In the context of international watercourses, an upstream State cannot claim sovereignty over water once it leaves its territory,[24] and downstream countries may use the water so long as they comply with principles such as reasonable utilisation,[25] no harm,[26] environmental protection and cooperation.[27] Similarly, the State where an iceberg originates cannot claim sovereign rights over it when it is found and used in another's territory. Therefore, the way in which international law views icebergs is mostly akin to pack-ice, though there are important nuances that will be discussed further.

9.2.2 *Rules and Principles Regulating Operations to Tow Icebergs*

This section deals with the application of current rules and principles to operations to tow icebergs in light of the findings of the previous section. The fundamental questions around such operations are: who can take icebergs, where can icebergs be taken from, is there a limit to the quantity of icebergs that can be exploited and are there any standards to be met in carrying out a towing operation? As icebergs would be taken from the Arctic or Antarctic area, the two legal regimes to analyse are UNCLOS and the ATS.

This section begins with UNCLOS. As discussed in the foregoing, UNCLOS only mentions ice in Article 234, which does not discuss ice as a resource, rather a risk factor to be managed. Although the operations in question were not foreseen by UNCLOS, there are still relevant provisions.

Regarding the questions of who can take icebergs and where they can be taken from, it is useful to think of the Denmark and Canada example mentioned in Section 9.1. If icebergs are found in the territorial waters of Canada, then they are under the sovereignty of Canada according to Article 2 of UNCLOS, despite originating in Denmark. As discussed, icebergs are not capable of being claimed sovereignty over, unlike continental glaciers but like pack-ice. If icebergs are found

[23] Jonathan Amos, '315 billion-tonne iceberg breaks off Antarctica' BBC News, 30 September 2019, <www.bbc.com>.

[24] For discussions on the now rejected 'absolute sovereignty' approach see Dupuy and Viñuales (n 9), 130. See also Watercourses Convention (n 13), Art. 5.

[25] Watercourses Convention (n 13), Arts. 5 and 6.

[26] Ibid., Art. 7.

[27] Ibid., Art. 20.

in Canada's EEZ, then Canada would enjoy sovereign rights according to Articles 55 and 56 of UNCLOS. Article 56(1) includes:

> sovereign rights for the purpose of exploring and exploiting, conserving and managing the natural resources, whether living or non-living, of the waters suprajacent to the seabed and of the seabed and its subsoil, and with regard to other activities for the economic exploitation and exploration of the zone, such as the production of energy from the water, currents and winds

It is true that ice is not mentioned in Article 56 as a specific sort of non-living resource. However, this term is quite wide and is bound to include freshwater that is different in its qualities to the sea water surrounding it. Furthermore, the utilisation of ice would most definitely be covered by the wording 'other activities for the economic exploitation and exploration of the zone'. This also means that Canada would not be able to tow the iceberg if it was still in the Danish EEZ, as Denmark may claim sovereign rights to utilise ice in their waters pursuant to Article 56. In this sense, icebergs are different from the waters they are found in, as they could be characterised as a resource. However, as ice does not fall into a *sui generis* category under UNCLOS, Denmark cannot claim continuous ownership over it even outside its waters.

The next question is the legality of towing icebergs that are found in the high seas. Are icebergs to be used according to the principle of freedom of the high seas?[28] Or should they be used in accordance with the concept of common heritage of mankind?[29] The essence of Part VII of UNCLOS is one of freedom of the high seas. Therefore, the fact that Article 87 or section 2 of Part VII do not specifically address ice and its utilisation cannot be construed to mean that States lack the right to utilise ice found in the high seas, as the principle of the freedom of the high seas is the fallback position. This is despite the argument that it would be unjust for developed States, who may have contributed more to climate change and indirectly to water scarcity, to be able to use icebergs without much heed to their common nature, while developing States would remain incapable of accessing this alternative freshwater resource.

Regarding the quantity of icebergs and the existence of standards for towing operations, Part XII of UNCLOS concerning protection and preservation of the marine environment is of relevance.[30] Article 192 contains a general obligation for States to protect and preserve the marine environment. Among these obligations Article 196 requires States to prevent pollution of the marine environment resulting

[28] UNCLOS, Art. 82.

[29] UNCLOS, Art. 136.

[30] See Catherine Redgwell, 'From Permission to Prohibition: The 1982 Convention on the Law of the Sea and Protection of the Marine Environment' in David Freestone, Richard Barnes and David Ong (eds.), *The Law of the Sea: Progress and Prospects* (Oxford: Oxford University Press, 2006).

from the use of technologies, Article 204(2) requires States to monitor activities that they permit to determine their impact on the environment and Article 206 requires States to communicate information regarding planned activities that have potentially significant harmful effects on the marine environment. These obligations limit the freedom of States in conducting operations for the utilisation of ice. However, this does not necessarily prohibit States from using icebergs as it is not evident that such utilisation is fundamentally against preservation and protection of the environment.

Having these discussions in mind, it is prudent to conclude that the use of icebergs is not prohibited under UNCLOS.[31] However, this is not due to a well thought-through regulatory approach in the codification of international law, but is arguably an example of the controversial *Lotus* principle in action.[32] UNCLOS does not give details as to the requirement or content of environmental impact assessments regarding operations to use icebergs,[33] and the general obligation to protect and preserve the environment seems too vague to have a meaningful impact on operations to use icebergs. These ambiguities and shortcomings in UNCLOS mean that UNCLOS is not capable of supporting, limiting and regulating the use of icebergs appropriately. This is why Section 9.3 discusses how the law of the sea may evolve to deal with this emerging demand on oceans.

This section now turns its attention to the legality of using icebergs under the ATS,[34] as both the UAE and South African proposals involved Antarctic icebergs.

The first issue is the moratorium on sovereignty claims pursuant to Article IV of the Antarctic Treaty. This moratorium may be of significance both for the question of from where icebergs can be taken and who can take them. However, as the subject of the moratorium is sovereignty claims, and as already mentioned icebergs cannot be claimed sovereignty over, the moratorium does not render the use of icebergs unlawful in and of itself.

Further instruments under the ATS may be relevant regarding the questions who can take icebergs and from where, such as prohibition of activities relating to mineral resources other than scientific research pursuant to the Protocol on

[31] Viñuales also concludes similarly. See Viñuales (n 4).

[32] See Armin von Bogdandy and Markus Rau, 'The Lotus' in Rüdiger Wolfrum (ed.), *Max Planck Encyclopedia of Public International Law* (Oxford Public International Law 2006), available at opil.oplaw.com.

[33] UNCLOS, Art. 206; see also E. Barritt and J. E. Viñuales, 'Legal Scan: A Conservation Agenda for Biodiversity beyond National Jurisdiction' (2016) Cambridge Centre for Environment, Energy and Natural Resource Governance, University of Cambridge, 68.

[34] When talking about the ATS one includes a number of instruments such as: the Antarctic Treaty; Convention for the Conservation of Marine Living Resources, Canberra, 20 May 1980, in force 7 April 1982, 1329 UNTS 47; Protocol on Environmental Protection to the Antarctic Treaty, Madrid, 4 October 1991, in force 14 January 1998, 30 ILM 1455 [Madrid Protocol]. For a useful analysis see Karen Scott and David Vanderzwaag, 'Polar Oceans and Law of the Sea' in Donald R. Rothwell et al. (eds.), *The Oxford Handbook of the Law of the Sea* (Oxford: Oxford University Press, 2015).

Environmental Protection to the Antarctic Treaty (Madrid Protocol).[35] As water and ice are not mineral resources that could be said to be under this prohibition pursuant to Article 7 of the Madrid Protocol, the prohibition does not impede the use of icebergs.

In terms of questions about the quantity of icebergs and the existence of any standards for towing operations, the ATS offers somewhat more concrete answers in comparison to UNCLOS. There is an important limitation to any operation to use icebergs as a freshwater resource in the Antarctic Treaty area. Although icebergs do not fall under the prohibition of the Madrid Protocol, Article 8 and Annex I of the Protocol do require States to carry out an environmental impact assessment if a proposed operation is deemed to involve risks of even minor or transitory impact on the Antarctic environment. As Article 3(2)(a) maintains: ‘activities in the Antarctic Treaty area shall be planned and conducted so as to limit adverse impacts on the Antarctic environment and dependent and associated ecosystems’. This is due to the realisation of State parties that the Antarctic environment is extremely fragile. As the threshold for requiring an environmental impact assessment is quite low, any operation to retrieve and tow icebergs that is carried out in the Antarctic Treaty area will likely need to be subjected to an environmental impact assessment (EIA).

These discussions show that although there are more stringent environmental protection requirements under the ATS, it shares the more general weakness with UNCLOS in not having explicit provisions that address or could anticipate the use of icebergs for freshwater. Furthermore, another shortcoming of the Antarctic Treaty, similar to many other agreements on Marine Protected Areas, is that it does not offer a buffer zone to protect the protected area from activities occurring outside their boundaries.[36] In other words, although the environmental standards for activities in the Antarctic area are high, activities that may affect Antarctica but occur outside the area are not dealt with appropriately.[37] It is fair to say that there is a rather iceberg-sized gap in international law.

The shortcomings of international law that were identified in this section are of significance for two reasons. First, a legal framework capable of regulating the use of icebergs is advantageous, as it would allow sustainable and careful use of icebergs to meet the dire demand for freshwater in areas struck with water scarcity. Second, an

[35] Madrid Protocol (n 34), Art. 7.

[36] R. Fletcher and others, *Biodiversity beyond National Jurisdiction: Legal Options for a New International Agreement* (Cambridge: UNEP-WCMC, 2017), 25; see also Barritt and Viñuales (n 33), 54.

[37] One must also think about the *pacta tertiis* rule, which means that international law does not compel adherence to a treaty or force States to become party to a treaty. Therefore, those aspects of the ATS that do not originate from customary law can be circumvented. See Art. 34 Vienna Convention on the Law of Treaties, Vienna, 23 May 1969, in force 27 January 1980, 1155 UNTS 331 [VCLT]; and for a discussion on the customary character of the Antarctic Treaty see Bruno Simma, ‘The Antarctic Treaty as a Treaty Providing for an Objective Regime’ (1986) 19 *Cornell International Law Journal*, 189.

appropriate legal framework would be capable of limiting and at times prohibiting the use of icebergs when there is a risk of environmental harm. This is a very important point in the context of the use of icebergs, as both Antarctica and the Arctic have fragile and vulnerable environments.[38] Unfortunately, due to a lack of environmental impact assessment of operations to utilise icebergs, this chapter cannot offer a comprehensive overview of the potential risks involved with the proposed operations. However, even a rather commonplace shipping accident, which will not be unlikely in the conduct of a precarious towing operation, could spell disaster for the fragile environments of the Arctic and Antarctic. This highlights the need for better regulation and gap filling. That is why the next section will discuss how international law could fill this regulatory gap.

9.3 FILLING AN ICEBERG-SIZED GAP IN INTERNATIONAL LAW

This section analyses how to fill gaps in the ATS and UNCLOS, starting with the ATS. Filling a regulatory gap in the ATS may be carried out through Antarctic Consultative Meetings and their ability to issue binding recommendations. There has already been one such recommendation of relevance. Recommendation XV-21 is focused on 'Exploitation of Icebergs'.[39] The preamble to the Recommendation acknowledges that technology may make utilisation of icebergs possible at some point in the future.[40] Concerns about uncontrolled exploitation of Antarctic icebergs that could adversely affect the Antarctic environment were envisaged at the Consultative Meeting.[41] However, the Recommendation merely maintains that it would not be desirable for the exploitation of ice to occur without prior examination by the Contracting Parties to the Antarctic Treaty.[42] Therefore, despite the fact that the Recommendation is binding generally and entered into force in 2004, the language does not render operations for towing icebergs to use for freshwater illegal under the Antarctic System, or introduce much of a regulatory framework for that matter. At this stage there does not seem to be any follow-up action regarding this issue in subsequent Consultative Meetings. However, the road to address the inadequacies of the ATS regulatory capacities seems clear.

Filling the regulatory gap in UNCLOS regarding the use of icebergs can be achieved in two ways. First, there is the possibility of subsequent practice and interpretation of UNCLOS provisions to better regulate the use of icebergs.

[38] See the stringent environmental provisions in the Madrid Protocol (n 34); see also Vito De Lucia, 'The Arctic Environment and the BBNJ Negotiations: Special Rules for Special Circumstances?' (2017) 86 *Marine Policy*, 235.

[39] Recommendation Antarctic Treaty Consultative Meeting XV-21, available at www.ats.aq/devAS/Meetings/Measure/190.

[40] Ibid., Preamble, recital 2.

[41] Ibid., Preamble, recital 2.

[42] Ibid., Preamble, recital 9.

However, as discussed, many of the relevant UNCLOS provisions are quite broad and vague.[43] Therefore, one must be aware of the limitations of stretching the meaning of broad provisions to regulate highly specific operations. One could argue that such subsequent interpretation may even be tantamount to all but modifying the treaty, which is arguably not wholly consistent with the law of treaties.[44] If, on the other hand, no action is taken, then the practice of the few countries capable of using icebergs may lead to the emergence of customary rules regarding the issue. However, this is not desirable for two reasons. First, there are fairness and equity issues in allowing a few States to overwhelmingly use a resource and influence the development of international law regulating a resource that may be found beyond the national jurisdiction of any country.[45] Furthermore, this approach would run into the problem of a lack of careful deliberation to regulate the optimal use of icebergs.

Therefore, the second avenue, that is, negotiations in the context of a new international legally binding instrument, would be preferable. As it happens, the negotiations on BBNJ are currently ongoing to address gaps in UNCLOS.[46] Although the issue of the use of icebergs is not directly related to biodiversity, there are indirect connections regarding protection of the marine environment in areas beyond national jurisdiction (ABNJ), where many of the icebergs ripe for the taking are located (i.e., the high seas adjacent to the Antarctic Treaty Area and the Arctic). Therefore, the rest of the section discusses how the BBNJ negotiations could address some of the gaps in answering the questions of who can take the icebergs, from where, limits on the quantity of icebergs and the existence of standards to be met in carrying out a towing operation. This analysis is possible in light of the BBNJ negotiations and the current draft text.[47]

The first issue relates to the question of whether the use of icebergs should be according to the principle of freedom of the high seas or the concept of the common

43 See for instance UNCLOS, Arts. 192 and 206 on environmental protection and environmental impact assessment.

44 See Art. 31(3) VCLT; see also Marcelo Kohen, 'Keeping Subsequent Agreements and Practice in Their Right Limits' in G. Nolte (ed.), *Treaties and Subsequent Practice* (Oxford: Oxford University Press, 2013), 35–36. Kohen mentions that the International Law Commission's proposal for the modification of treaties by subsequent practice was rejected in the VCLT in favour of the stability of treaties.

45 The same point is raised in the BBNJ context, see Rachel Tiller and others, 'The Once and Future Treaty: Towards a New Regime for Biodiversity in Areas beyond National Jurisdiction' (2019) 99 *Marine Policy*, 241.

46 Resolution on Development of an international legally binding instrument under the United Nations Convention on the Law of the Sea on the conservation and sustainable use of marine biological diversity of areas beyond national jurisdiction, GA Res 69/292 (2015); also see Tiller et al. (n 45), 240.

47 Revised draft text of an agreement under the United Nations Convention on the Law of the Sea on the conservation and sustainable use of marine biological diversity of areas beyond national jurisdiction, A/CONF.232/2020/3 (2019) [BBNJ Draft Text].

heritage of mankind, where there is benefit sharing for the use of common resources. In this regard, the BBNJ negotiations do not have a directly relevant contribution. However, the same question regarding benefit sharing is also relevant regarding marine genetic resources (MGR). The position of the developing nations is that the provisions of UNCLOS must not be seen as limiting benefit sharing only to seabed minerals, as the only reason MGRs were not included was ignorance regarding their value.[48] This issue is hotly contested. The current revised draft, at the time of writing this chapter, clearly shows that there is no agreement on whether benefit sharing is encouraged or mandated.[49] However, the principle of the common heritage of mankind, which underpins benefit sharing, has re-entered, albeit bracketed, the most recent draft.[50] If the arguments of the developing States carry the day, it would have positive consequences in terms of arguing for benefit sharing in the context of using icebergs. First, it gives weight to the benefit sharing camp in the debate against the principle of freedom of the high seas. Furthermore, the argument goes that exclusion of and silence on a common resource due to ignorance regarding its value should not mean that benefit sharing for that resource could not be required.

The second issue relates to from where icebergs would be taken and the possible limits to the quantity of icebergs to be used. The areas from where icebergs would be taken may have fragile and vulnerable environments. Icebergs located outside the Antarctic Treaty Area and in the Arctic, and outside national jurisdictions, fall directly under the BBNJ negotiations. Part III of the BBNJ Draft Text in particular provides for area-based management tools in ABNJ, where there is no relevant legal instrument or framework.[51] Apart from provision of an area-based management tool for ABNJ, there is an added benefit by way of proposals to have buffer zones outside protected areas (relevant in the context of icebergs outside the Antarctic Treaty Area) so that direct and indirect pressures on protected areas can be mitigated more effectively and prevent environmental harm.[52] This proposal would add to the protections for the fragile Antarctic environment. In this way, there are protections against dangerous activities that occur just outside the Antarctic Area. However, towing icebergs cannot be classified as a risky or dangerous activity unless a rigorous EIA is conducted.

This brings us to the third and final issue, the requirement of conducting EIAs. The challenge of the current rules is that the EIA requirement is vague both in terms of the threshold for mandating it and its content.[53] The current Draft Text shows some promising signs on this front, although there are many crucial points of contention. In terms of the threshold for conducting EIAs, along with the typical

[48] Tiller (n 45), 241.
[49] BBNJ Draft Text, Arts. 10–11.
[50] BBNJ Draft Text, Art. 5.
[51] BBNJ Draft Text, Art. 15.
[52] Fletcher (n 36), 25.
[53] Barritt and Viñuales (n 33), 79.

requirement of the risk of substantial or significant harm there is a proposal to lower the threshold to minor or transitory harm. In this debate, a very interesting proposal is to mandate a preliminary or simple EIA when the risk is minor or transitory, and mandate a full EIA when there is a risk of significant harm.[54] Even more relevant in terms of taking icebergs from the fragile environments of the Arctic and Antarctic is the proposal to lower the threshold for mandating EIAs in those areas.[55] In this context, it would be useful if future BBNJ drafts refer to the Madrid Protocol, which only requires minor or even transitory effects.[56]

Beyond the threshold, it has been pointed out that in the past activities that were not clearly identified would fall through the cracks of the fragmented regime as they were not predicted by pre-existing instruments.[57] Therefore, the academic suggestion has been that the new agreement should contemplate how to deal with unidentified activities yet to develop.[58] The Draft Text is contemplating an indicative list of activities that would require an EIA.[59] This list has not been drawn up at the time of writing this chapter. Therefore, there is an opportunity here to explicitly name use of icebergs as an activity requiring EIAs, to avoid questions of whether using icebergs as unidentified and unexpected activities do require EIAs or not. Lastly, it is noteworthy that the Draft Text also offers detailed suggestions in terms of the requirements for the content of the EIA. Namely, describing measures to avoid impacts, explaining uncertainties and gaps in knowledge, identifying sources of information, explicitly indicating predictive methods and underlying assumptions and the environmental record of the proponents of an activity.[60] These detailed suggestions certainly attempt to address problems with the current international rules, which are too vague and offer little assistance regarding the content of EIAs in ABNJ.[61] It remains to be seen how the final Agreement text mandates specific content.

9.4 CONCLUSION

This chapter has been one manifestation of the debates on the need for adequate legal frameworks to ensure that continuing and new demands on the oceans and the marine environment are checked by an adequate rule of law. It has discussed multiple angles to determine the legality of proposed plans to utilise icebergs as an alternative source of freshwater. The conclusions of this analysis are that, first,

54 BBNJ Draft Text, Art. 24.
55 BBNJ Draft Text, Art. 27.
56 Art. 3(2)(a); Art. 8 and Annex I Madrid Protocol (n 34).
57 Barritt and Viñuales (n 33), 67 and 79.
58 Barritt and Viñuales (n 33), 79–84.
59 BBNJ Draft Text, Art. 29.
60 BBNJ Draft Text, Art. 35.
61 Barritt and Viñuales (n 33), 66.

UNCLOS does not prohibit the use of icebergs for freshwater resources. Ice can be seen as yet another form of non-living resources that may be found in maritime zones under the national jurisdiction of States. The only limitations are that States cannot utilise ice that they find in the maritime zones of other States, and the obligations under Part XII of UNCLOS to protect the marine environment. Second, the chapter discussed the issue of the legality of using ice found in Antarctica. None of the instruments within the ATS indicate a prohibition against the use of icebergs found in Antarctica. The only limitation is one of EIA to ensure that the proposed operation does not harm the fragile Antarctic environment.

Although the ATS represents more stringent environmental standards, it also presents a vague and unclear general structure to deal with the question of utilisation of icebergs as it was not a foreseen demand on the Antarctic environment. Therefore, the chapter argued that there is a gap in the regulatory capacities of international law, which could become problematic for the rule of law if/when the use of icebergs for freshwater were to proliferate, leading to an imbalance between the need for exploitation of this potential new resource with preservation of the marine Antarctic environments. Thus, the chapter also discussed some of the ways in which international law could be adapted to fill the identified gaps, to ensure it is fit for purpose and that the rules that would regulate new demands are equitable. In particular, it has been shown that although the BBNJ negotiations may not at first sight seem relevant for filling this gap, there is interesting potential in the negotiations to flesh out many important rules and principles that are needed to adequately regulate the use of icebergs for freshwater when icebergs are taken from ABNJ.

10

The Precautionary Principle/Approach and the United Nations Convention on the Law of the Sea

Management of Living Resources

Maurus Wollensak

10.1 INTRODUCTION

The United Nations Convention on the Law of the Sea (UNCLOS or Convention)[1] is an international treaty among an excessive number of subjects of international law. These 168 subjects have committed themselves to adhere to international law established in the (almost) comprehensive system codified in the 320 articles and nine annexes.[2] The Convention strives to provide answers on 'all issues relating to the law of the sea'.[3] Hence, it is more than an ordinary convention – it is 'an international state of mind and a commitment to the rule of law'.[4] Accordingly, one may argue, the Convention reproduces a commitment 'to uphold legal order and stability, to provide equality of application of the law, . . . and to settle disputes before an independent legal body'.[5]

The author would like to thank the conference organizers Alla Pozdnakova and Froukje Maria Platjouw. Further, he wishes to extend gratitude to Professor Dr Alexander Proelß and Laura-Theresa Godau for their thoughtful comments on the present work.

1 1833 UNTS 3.

2 Cf. Tanaka, Y., *The International Law of the Sea*, 3rd ed. (Cambridge: Cambridge University Press, 2019), 38; von Vitzthum, W., 'Begriff, Geschichte und Rechtsquellen des Seerechts', in W. von Vitzthum (ed.), *Handbuch des Seerechts* (Munich: C.H. Beck, 2006), 46.

3 Preamble (para. 1) UNCLOS.

4 Galdorisi, G., 'The United States Freedom of Navigation Program: A Bridge for International Compliance with the 1982 United Nations Convention on the Law of the Sea?' (1996) 27 *Ocean Development & International Law*, 399–408, 399; cf. Oxman, B. H., 'The Rule of Law and the United Nations Convention on the Law of the Sea' (1996) 7 *European Journal of International Law*, 353–71, at 354f; Moore, J. N., 'The Rule of Law in the Oceans', in M. H. Nordquist and J. N. Moore (eds.), *Security Flashpoints: Oil, Islands, Sea Access and Military Confrontation* (Leiden: Martinus Nijhoff Publishers, 1998), 473.

5 For this definition of the 'international rule of law' see: McCorquodale, R., 'Defining the International Rule of Law: Defying Gravity?' (2016) 65 *International and Comparative Law Quarterly*, 277–304 at 303f.

More than two-thirds of the Earth is covered by seas and oceans[6] with about 90 per cent of the living biomass.[7] This living biomass, in particular fish, is of importance as a source of food (e.g., as a protein source) and raw materials.[8] As set out in the preamble of the UNCLOS, one of the Convention's objectives intends the 'equitable and efficient utilization' of the seas and oceans and 'conservation of their living resources'.[9] Nonetheless, stocks fished at a 'biologically unsustainable level' increased from 10 per cent in 1974 to almost 35 per cent in 2017.[10] Thus, from a bird's eye view, it seems that the Convention's impact is rather lean in respect of living resources.[11]

One way to counter such developments is the application of the precautionary principle/approach. Whilst the principle/approach is no stranger to, for example, the 1995 United Nations (UN) Fish Stocks Agreement,[12] the 1982 UNCLOS does not demand application of the precautionary principle/approach *expressis verbis*. Concluded after the UN Conference on the Human Environment (1972), but long before the UN Conference on Environment and Development (1992), the specific requirements of the precautionary principle/approach were not subject to a general scientific debate during the negotiations for the UNCLOS.[13]

More than 20 years ago, in the *Southern Bluefin Tuna* cases (SBT cases), the International Tribunal for the Law of the Sea (ITLOS) laid the cornerstone with respect to the precautionary principle/approach.[14] In the SBT cases between the States of Australia, New Zealand and Japan, both the ITLOS and an *ad hoc* arbitral

6 Moore, J. N., 'The United Nations Convention on the Law of the Sea: One of the Greatest Achievements in the International Rule of Law', in M. H. Nordquist, J. N. Moore and R. Long (eds.), *Legal Order in the World's Oceans* (Leiden: Martinus Nijhoff Publishers, 2018), 8; Oxman (n 4) 359.

7 Beyerlin, U. and Marauhn, T., *International Environmental Law* (Oxford: Hart Publisher, 2011), 133.

8 Cf. Matz-Lück, N., 'Meeresschutz', in A. Proelß (ed.), *Internationales Umweltrecht* (Berlin: De Gruyter, 2017), paras. 2, 23, 114; Beyerlin and Marauhn (n 7) 133.

9 Preamble (para. 4) UNCLOS.

10 FAO, *The State of World Fisheries and Aquaculture 2020: Sustainability in Action* (Rome: Food and Agriculture Organization, 2020), 47.

11 Cf. Beyerlin and Marauhn (n 7) 140.

12 Arts. 5(c), 6 Agreement for the Implementation of the Provisions of the United Nations Convention on the Law of the Sea of 10 December 1982 relating to the Conservation and Management of Straddling Fish Stocks and Highly Migratory Fish Stocks (FSA), 2167 UNTS 3.

13 Hassan, D. and Karim, M. S., 'Ocean Governance and Marine Environmental Conservation: Concepts, Principles and Institutions', in D. Hassan and M. S. Karim (eds.), *International Marine Environmental Law and Policy* (London: Routledge, 2018), 24; cf. Beyerlin, U., 'New Developments in the Protection of the Marine Environment: Potential Effects of the Rio Process' (1995) 55 *Zeitschrift für ausländisches öffentliches Recht und Völkerrecht*, 554; Proelß, A., *Meeresschutz im Völker- und Europarecht: Das Beispiel des Nordostatlantiks* (Berlin: Duncker & Humblot, 2004), 83.

14 Wolfrum, R. (2007), 'Statement on Agenda item 77 (A) at the Plenary of the Sixty-second Session of the United Nations General Assembly, New York, 10 December 2007', available at: www.itlos.org/fileadmin/itlos/documents/statements_of_president/wolfrum/ga_101207_eng.pdf.

tribunal (SBT Tribunal) (constituted in accordance with Annex VII of the UNCLOS) were confronted with Australia's and New Zealand's claims regarding the 'precautionary principle'.[15] Due to both tribunals' lack of jurisdiction with respect to the merits, they were unable to discuss the management of Southern Bluefin Tuna in detail. However, the ITLOS, whilst prescribing provisional measures, hinted broadly at the requirement of the precautionary application under the UNCLOS. It prescribed that the parties should act with 'prudence and caution', which may be seen as 'equivalent to [act] by applying a precautionary approach'.[16]

This chapter therefore undertakes an expedition through the UNCLOS, analysing its relationship with the precautionary principle/approach and addressing the two decades after the SBT cases and respective developments. This journey seeks to answer one question only:

Does the UNCLOS demand application of the precautionary principle/approach with respect to management of living resources *vel non*?

In answering this question, this chapter will briefly turn to the general notions of the precautionary principle/approach and management of living resources (2). Building on this, the most relevant provisions of the Convention and the corresponding jurisprudence are analysed (3).

10.2 PRECAUTIONARY PRINCIPLE/APPROACH, MANAGEMENT OF LIVING RESOURCES

10.2.1 *The Notion of the 'Precautionary Principle/Approach'*

Countless books, articles and judgments of national and international courts address the precautionary principle/approach. As law serves to set clear expectations regarding rights and obligations,[17] it is neither the intention nor a requirement to reproduce these colossal findings – it will suffice to identify the core elements of the principle/approach as a benchmark for the analysis of the UNCLOS in this chapter.

[15] Cf. Southern Bluefin Tuna (*New Zealand* v. *Japan*; *Australia* v. *Japan*), Request for the Prescription of Provisional Measures Submitted by Australia, available at: www.itlos.org/cases/list-of-cases/case-no-3-4/, para. 8; Southern Bluefin Tuna, Request for the Prescription of Provisional Measures Submitted by New Zealand, available at: www.itlos.org/cases/list-of-cases/case-no-3-4/, para. 8.

[16] Golitsyn, V. (2014), 'Statement on Agenda Item 74 (A) "Oceans and the Law of the Sea", New York, 9 December 2014', available at: www.itlos.org/fileadmin/itlos/documents/statements_of_president/Golitsyn/Statement_GA_09122014_FINAL_EN.pdf; different view: 'the Tribunal [in the SBT Order] did not speak of the precautionary principle/approach' MOX Plant (*Ireland* v. *United Kingdom*), Provisional Measures, Separate Opinion of Judge Wolfrum, Order of 3 December 2001, ITLOS Reports 2001, 95, 133f; cf. Zander, J., *The Application of the Precautionary Principle in Practice: Comparative Dimensions* (Cambridge: Cambridge University Press, 2010), 39.

[17] Cf. Moore, 'One of the Greatest Achievements' (n 6) 9.

The scope of the precautionary principle/approach is broad, and no universal definition exists.[18] The precautionary principle and precautionary approach are often used interchangeably[19] and even if not, there is no clear-cut differentiation.[20] As no significant legal relevance to the distinction may be identified,[21] hereinafter the term 'precautionary principle' is used, including the idea of an approach.[22]

The so-called Rio Declaration's Principle 15 and its underpinning definition can be regarded as accepted by a broad spectrum,[23] stating '[w]here there are threats of serious or irreversible damage, lack of full scientific certainty shall not be used as a reason for postponing cost-effective measures to prevent environmental degradation'.[24] In light of many similar international instruments,[25] three elements may be deduced: a threat of environmental harm, scientific uncertainty and action despite uncertainty.[26] Accordingly, a threat of environmental harm bundled with scientific uncertainty 'triggers' precautionary actions.[27]

18 For a detailed analysis see: Sandin, P., 'Dimensions of the Precautionary Principle' (1999) 5 *Human and Ecological Risk Assessment: An International Journal*, 889–907; Wiener, J. B., 'Precaution', in D. Bodansky, J. Brunnée and E. Hey (eds.), *The Oxford Handbook of International Environmental Law* (Oxford: Oxford University Press, 2007), 602–7.

19 Cf. Schröder, M., 'Precautionary Approach/Principle', in R. Wolfrum (ed.), *Max Planck Encyclopedia of Public International Law* (Oxford: Oxford University Press, 2014), para. 3.

20 Peel, J., 'Precaution a Matter of Principle, Approach or Process?' (2004) 5 *Melbourne Journal of International Law*, 483–501, 490; Schiffman, H. S., 'The Precautionary Approach at the International Tribunal for the Law of the Sea: The Southern Bluefin Tuna Cases' (2005) 5 *International Journal of Global Environmental Issues*, 78–95 at 81f.

21 Proelß, A., 'Prinzipien des internationalen Umweltrechts', in A. Proelß (ed.), *Internationales Umweltrecht* (n 8), 89; contra: Macdonald, J. M., 'Appreciating the Precautionary Principle as an Ethical Evolution in Ocean Management' (1995) 26 *Ocean Development & International Law*, 255–86.

22 The ITLOS uses the term 'precautionary approach'.

23 Sands, P., Peel, J., Fabra Aguilar, A. and Mackenzie, R., *Principles of International Environmental Law*, 4th ed. (Cambridge: Cambridge University Press, 2018), 230.

24 A/CONF.151/26 (1992), The Rio Declaration on Environment and Development.

25 E.g., Art. 3(f) Bamako Convention on the Ban of the Import into Africa and the Control of Transboundary Movement and Management of Hazardous Wastes within Africa, 2101 UNTS 177; Art. 3 United Nations Framework Convention on Climate Change, 1771 UNTS 107; Art. 2 (1)(a) Convention for the Protection of the Marine Environment of the North-East Atlantic, 2354 UNTS 67; Art. 3(2) Convention on the Protection of the Marine Environment of the Baltic Sea Area, 1507 UNTS 166; Art. 6 Convention on the Conservation and Management of Highly Migratory Fish Stocks in the Western and Central Pacific Ocean, 2275 UNTS 43; Art. 5 (2)(a) Convention on the Sustainable Management of Lake Tanganyika, 2338 UNTS 43.

26 Trouwborst, A., 'The Precautionary Principle in General International Law: Combating the Babylonian Confusion' (2007) 16 *Review of European Community & International Enviromental Law*, 185–95, 187, 191; for other, yet similar elements, see e.g., Wiener, J. B., 'Precautionary Principle', in L. Krämer and O. Emanuela (eds.), *Principles of Environmental Law* (Cheltenham: Edward Elgar Publishing, 2018), 179; delineation from the preventive principle see: Zanella, T. V. and Cabral, R. P., 'The Application of the Precautionary Principle in International Law: An Analysis of the Contribution of the International Tribunal for the Law of the Sea' (2017) 14 *Veredas do Direito*, 229–60 at 233–5.

27 Cf. Peel (n 20) 487.

As a side note, the features beyond the Rio Declaration ascribe and stipulate that the principle may be limited to mere authorization/legitimization to take measures[28] or go as far as having effects on the burden or standard of proof.[29]

10.2.2 *The Notion of 'Living Resources'*

Lacking a definition by the UNCLOS, two dominant views address the question of living resources. The first calls for a broad scope emphasizing 'living' as a differentiation from 'non-living'[30] to include all marine living resources, for example, corals and birds.[31] The second and narrower view relies on resources 'prone to exploitation for economic reasons'.[32] The latter view can be considered predominant[33] and, therefore, is adopted in this chapter; thus, primarily fish, cuttlefish, cetaceans, pinnipeds and sirenians comprise living resources.[34]

10.2.3 *The Notion of 'Management'*

Despite also being undefined in the UNCLOS, management may reflect 'human intervention in the dynamic processes . . . to maintain a particular desired pattern or series of processes'.[35] To 'manage one or more species of living marine resources' can be considered a management measure.[36]

[28] Wiener (n 26) 177.

[29] Southern Bluefin Tuna (n 15), Provisional Measures, Separate Opinion of Judge Laing, Order of 27 August 1999, ITLOS Reports 1999, 305, para. 14; Birnie, P. W., Boyle, A. and Redgwell, C., *International Law and the Environment*, 3 ed. (Oxford: Oxford University Press, 2009), 158; cf. Cançado Trindade, A. A., 'Principle 15 Rio Declaration', in J. E. Vinuales (ed.), *The Rio Declaration on Environment and Development: A Commentary* (Oxford: Oxford University Press, 2015), 407–9.

[30] Harrison, J. and Morgera, E., 'Article 61 UNCLOS', in A. Proelß (ed.), *United Nations Convention on the Law of the Sea: A Commentary* (Munich: C.H. Beck/Hart/Nomos, 2017), para. 2; Beyerlin, U., 'Different Types of Norms in International Environmental Law Policies, Principles, and Rules', in Bodansky, Brunnée and Hey (eds.), *The Oxford Handbook of International Environmental Law* (n 18), 340.

[31] Sands et al. (n 23) 506.

[32] Fuchs, J., 'Marine Living Resources, International Protection', in R. Wolfrum (ed.), *Max Planck Encyclopedia of Public International Law* (n 19), para. 6.

[33] Cf. Churchill, R., 'The UNCLOS Regime for Protection of the Marine Environment – Fit for the Twenty-First Century?', in R. G. Rayfuse (ed.), *Research Handbook on International Marine Environmental Law* (Cheltenham: Edward Elgar Publishing, 2015), 13f. See also Art. 119(b) UNCLOS.

[34] Rothwell, D. and Stephens, T., *The International Law of the Sea*, 2nd ed. (Oxford: Hart Publishing, 2016), 332; Matz-Lück (n 8), para. 115.

[35] Holdgate, M. W., 'Conservation in a World Context', in I. F. Spellerberg, F. B. Goldsmith and M. Morris (eds.), *The Scientific Management of Temperate Communities for Conservation* (Oxford: Blackwell, 1991), 1.

[36] Art. 1(b) FSA.

'Management' is often used together with 'conservation' but cannot be equated to it.[37] The World Conservation Strategy defines the latter as 'the management of human use of the biosphere ...',[38] combining both notions. Management has further been defined by, for example, Article 2 of the Geneva Convention on Fishing and Conservation of the Living Resources of the High Seas 1958[39] as 'the aggregate of the measures rendering possible the optimum sustainable yield ... to secure a maximum supply of food and other marine products'.

In sum, 'management' should be understood broadly so as to encompass human activities in general, including conservation measures.

10.3 THE PRECAUTIONARY PRINCIPLE IN REGARD TO THE MANAGEMENT OF LIVING RESOURCES 'WITHIN' THE UNCLOS

10.3.1 *Part V, Part VII and Article 290(1) UNCLOS*

Judge Laing, in his separate opinion in the SBT cases, articulated 'it cannot be denied that [the UNCLOS] adopts a precautionary approach'.[40] Hereby, the approach will be envisaged in Part V (Exclusive Economic Zone), Part VII (High Seas) and Article 290 (1) UNCLOS.[41]

Regarding Article 290(1) UNCLOS, the possibility to prescribe provisional measures 'to prevent serious harm to the marine environment' 'underscores the salience of the [precautionary] approach'.[42] Judge Treves also stated that 'a precautionary approach seems ... inherent in the very notion of provisional measures'.[43] Further, he suggested in the particular SBT cases that the requirement of 'urgency' in Article 290(5) UNCLOS 'is satisfied only in the light of such precautionary approach'.[44]

The question, however, is whether application of the precautionary principle is demanded. This seems not to be the case as courts and tribunals are not obliged to prescribe provisional measures.[45] They are, rather, provided with the possibility to do

[37] Cf. illustrated by the enumerations in Art. 65 UNCLOS.

[38] IUCN (1980), World Conservation Strategy: Living Resource Conservation for Sustainable Development, available at: https://portals.iucn.org/library/efiles/documents/WCS-004.pdf.

[39] 559 UNTS 286.

[40] SBT cases, ITLOS, Provisional Measures, Separate Opinion Laing (n 29), para. 17.

[41] Ibid.

[42] Ibid.

[43] Southern Bluefin Tuna (n 15), Provisional Measures, Separate Opinion of Judge Treves, Order of 27 August 1999, ITLOS Reports 1999, 316, para. 9.

[44] Ibid., para. 8.

[45] Treves, T., 'Article 290 UNCLOS', in A. Proelß (ed.), *United Nations Convention on the Law of the Sea: A Commentary* (n 30), para. 18; for more on the topic see: Tanaka, Y., 'The Impacts of the Tribunal's Jurisprudence on the Development of International Law', in International Tribunal for the Law of the Sea (ed.), *The Contribution of the International Tribunal for the Law of the Sea to the Rule of Law: 1996–2016 / La contribution du Tribunal international du droit de la mer à l'état de droit: 1996–2016* (Leiden: Martinus Nijhoff Publishers, 2018), 170–4.

so.[46] In any event, it seems doubtful whether provisional measures are the appropriate stage for applying the precautionary principle.[47] Therefore, Article 290 UNCLOS need not be further addressed.[48]

Addressing Part V and Part VII, the UNCLOS establishes a far-reaching system of marine resource management.[49] This system may be divided into a direct approach (addressing the living resource itself) and an indirect approach (addressing their habitat).[50] Further, it may be distinguished between a zonal[51] and a species-specific[52] management approach. However, not many arguments have been voiced regarding demand for application of the principle by the UNCLOS under Part V and Part VII.[53]

[46] Cf. M/V "Louisa" (*Saint Vincent and the Grenadines* v. *Kingdom of Spain*), Provisional Measures, Order of 23 December 2010, ITLOS Reports 2008–2010, 58, para. 83.

[47] Cf. MOX Plant, Provisional Measures, Separate Opinion Wolfrum (n 16), 134; MOX Plant (*Ireland* v. *United Kingdom*), Provisional Measures, Separate Opinion of Judge Treves, Order of 3 December 2001, ITLOS Reports 2001 (n 16) 137, para. 9.

[48] Of course, the elaborations here may be utilized when at the stage of provisional measures, cf. Fabra, A., 'The LOSC and the Implementation of the Precautionary Principle' (1999) 10 *Yearbook of International Environmental Law*, 15–24 at 22.

[49] Dupuy, P.-M. and Vinuales, J., *International Environmental Law*, 2nd ed. (Cambridge: Cambridge University Press, 2018), 114; Rosenne, S. and Yankov, A., 'Articles 192 to 278, Final Act, Annex VI', in M. H. Nordquist, N. S. Nandan, S. Rosenne and N. R. Grandy (eds.), *United Nations Convention on the Law of the Sea 1982: A Commentary* (Leiden: Martinus Nijhoff Publishers, 1990), para. 192.2.

[50] Cf. PCA, South China Sea Arbitration (*Republic of the Philippines* v. *People's Republic of China*), Award, Award of 12 July 2016, available at: https://pcacases.com/web/sendAttach/2086, para. 959; Czybulka, D., 'Article 192 UNCLOS', in A. Proelß (ed.), *United Nations Convention on the Law of the Sea: A Commentary* (n 30), para. 25.

[51] Tanaka, 'Law of the Sea' (n 2) 284–9; Rothwell and Stephens (n 34) 308; regarding the management of living resources in the internal waters, territorial sea, archipelagic waters and continental shelf, see: Matz-Lück, N. and Fuchs, J., 'Marine Living Resources', in D. Rothwell, A. O. Elferink, K. Scott and T. Stephens (eds.), *The Oxford Handbook of the Law of the Sea* (Oxford: Oxford University Press, 2015), 497ff; Harrison, J., *Saving the Oceans through Law: The International Legal Framework for the Protection of the Marine Environment*, 1st ed. (Oxford: Oxford University Press, 2017), 168ff.

[52] Tanaka, 'Law of the Sea' (n 2) 289–301.

[53] E.g. the term 'available' in Art. 119 UNCLOS may demand application of the precautionary approach – Verschuuren, J., *Principles of Environmental Law: The Ideal of Sustainable Development and the Role of Principles of International, European, and National Environmental Law* (Baden-Baden: Nomos, 2003), 120; Rayfuse, R. G., 'Article 119 UNCLOS', in A. Proelß (ed.), *United Nations Convention on the Law of the Sea: A Commentary* (n 30), para. 24; Nandan, N. S. and Rosenne, S., 'Articles 86 to 132 and Documentary Annexes', in M. H. Nordquist et al. (eds.), *United Nations Convention on the Law of the Sea 1982: A Commentary* (n 49), para. 119.7(c); cf. Marr, S., *The Precautionary Principle in the Law of the Sea: Modern Decision Making in International Law* (Leiden: Martinus Nijhoff Publishers, 2003), 135f; Winter, G. (ed.), Towards a Legal Clinic for Fisheries Management (IUCN Environmental Policy and Law Paper No. 74), available at: https://portals.iucn.org/library/sites/library/files/documents/EPLP-074.pdf.

10.3.2 *Part XII UNCLOS*

Beyond Judge Laing's claim, the UNCLOS is influenced by concepts such as sustainable development,[54] ecosystem-based approaches[55] and the precautionary approach. Whether the latter is incorporated in protection and preservation of the marine environment regime (Part XII) has been subject to debate in recent years.[56]

The UNCLOS does not define 'protection and preservation', or 'marine environment' as prescribed by Article 192 UNCLOS. Deriving from its heading and the overwhelming number of pollution-based provisions, Part XII might appear as limited to the prevention, reduction and control of pollution. Such assumption is reaffirmed by abstaining from using the wording 'conservation', as otherwise mostly utilized in connection with living resources.[57] However, Article 194(5) UNCLOS hints at an ecosystem and habitat focus.[58] In the SBT cases, the ITLOS stated that 'the conservation of the living resources of the sea is an element in the protection and preservation of the marine environment'.[59] In 2015, it confirmed this finding in its Request for an advisory opinion submitted by the Sub-Regional Fisheries Commission (SRFC AO).[60] Thus, Part XII must be regarded as (indirectly) applying to the management of marine living resources.[61]

54 Tanaka, 'Law of the Sea' (n 2) 301–3; cf. Gabčíkovo-Nagymaros Project (*Hungary/Slovakia*), Judgment of 25 September 1997, ICJ Reports 1997, 7, para. 140; Award in the Arbitration Regarding the Iron Rhine ('Ijzeren Rijn') Railway between the Kingdom of Belgium and the Kingdom of the Netherlands, Decision of 24 May 2005, RIAA XXVII, 35, para. 59.

55 Tanaka, 'Law of the Sea' (n 2) 303–6.

56 Other provisions may be e.g. Art. 145 UNCLOS, cf. Churchill (n 33) 21.

57 Nandan, N. S. and Rosenne, S., 'Article 1 to 85, Annexes I and II, Final Act, Annex II' (n 49) para. 61.12(a).

58 Wacht, F., *Mariner Umweltschutz durch Meeresschutzgebiete im jurisdiktionsfreien Raum der Hohen See* (Baden-Baden: Nomos, 2018), 218; cf. Czybulka, D., 'Article 194 UNCLOS' (n 30) para. 30; Gjerde, K. M., 'High Seas Marine Protected Areas: Participant Report of the Expert Workshop on Managing Risks to Biodiversity and the Environment on the High Seas, including Tools Such as Marine Protected Areas: Scientific Requirements and Legal Aspects Current Legal Developments: High Seas Marine Protected Areas' (2001) 16 *International Journal of Marine and Coastal Law*, 515–28 at 524.

59 Southern Bluefin Tuna (n 15), Provisional Measures, Order of 27 August 1999, ITLOS Reports 1999, 280, para. 70; cf. Proelß, A., 'The Contribution of the ITLOS to Strengthening the Regime for the Protection of the Marine Environment', in A. Del Vecchio and R. Virzo (eds.), *Interpretations of the United Nations Convention on the Law of the Sea by International Courts and Tribunals* (Berlin: Springer, 2019), 99.

60 Request for Advisory Opinion Submitted by the Sub-Regional Fisheries Commission (SRFC), Advisory Opinion, 2 April 2015, ITLOS Reports 2015, 4, para. 120.

61 Proelß, A. and Houghton, K., 'Protecting Marine Species', in R. G. Rayfuse (ed.), *Research Handbook* (n 33), 233; Guo, J. and Wang, P., 'Due Diligence and Overlooked Evidence in the South China Sea Arbitration: A Note' (2019) 50 *Ocean Development & International Law*, 235–42 at 240; cf. Wacht (n 58) 218–20; Tanaka, Y., 'Principles of International Marine Environmental Law', in R. G. Rayfuse (ed.), *Research Handbook* (n 33), 35; Boyle, A., 'The Environmental Jurisprudence of the International Tribunal for the Law of the Sea Symposium to Mark the Tenth Anniversary ITLOS: The Jurisprudence of the International Tribunal of the

10.3.2.1 The Precautionary Principle and Due Diligence/Obligations of Conduct

Taking one step back, in the 2010 *Pulp Mills* case, the International Court of Justice (ICJ) held 'that the principle of prevention, as a customary rule, has its origins in the due diligence'.[62] The Seabed Disputes Chamber in its 2011 Responsibilities and obligations of States with respect to activities in the Area advisory opinion (Seabed Mining AO) took this one step further.[63] The Chamber noted that 'the precautionary approach is also an integral part of the general obligation of due diligence', that due diligence and obligations of conduct are interrelated and the precautionary principle applies outside the International Seabed Authority's Regulations.[64] Further, the ITLOS linked due diligence and the precautionary principle in its SBT cases.[65] Although these cases do not deal with living resources, it may be noted that the overall concept of due diligence may include application of precaution/the precautionary principle.[66]

10.3.2.2 Due Diligence/Obligations of Conduct under the UNCLOS

Arguably, the idea of due diligence is reflected in the jurisprudence as early as the SBT cases.[67] The ITLOS determined that 'although the Tribunal cannot conclu-

Law of the Sea: Assessment and Prospects' (2007) 22 *International Journal of Marine and Coastal Law*, 369–82, 373; Rosenne and Yankov, Volume IV (n 49) para. 192.11(a).

62 Pulp Mills on the River Uruguay (*Argentina* v. *Uruguay*), Judgment of 20 April 2010, ICJ Reports 2010, 14, para. 101; ILC (2001), Draft Articles on Prevention of Transboundary Harm from Hazardous Activities, with Commentaries, Yearbook of the International Law Commission, 2001, Vol. II, Part Two, 146.

63 Responsibilities and Obligations of States with Respect to Activities in the Area, Advisory Opinion, 1 February 2011, ITLOS Reports 2011, 10, paras. 111–115.

64 Ibid., paras. 131f, cf. 242.3(B)(b); cf. Kelly, E., 'The Precautionary Approach in the Advisory Opinion Concerning the Responsibilities and Obligations of States Sponsoring Persons and Entities with Respect to Activities in the Area', in International Tribunal for the Law of the Sea (ed.), *The Contribution of the International Tribunal for the Law of the Sea to the Rule of Law* (n 45), 55; the other way around: Hey, E., *Advanced Introduction to International Environmental Law* (Cheltenham: Edward Elgar Publishing, 2016), 71f.

65 Seabed Mining AO (n 63), para. 132.

66 Oral, N., 'Implementing Part XII of the 1982 UN Law of the Sea Convention and the Role of International Courts', in N. Boschiero, T. Scovazzi, C. Pitea and C. Ragni (eds.), *International Courts and the Development of International Law: Essays in Honour of Tullio Treves* (The Hague: T. M. C. Asser Press, 2013), 419; Jaeckel, A. and Stephens, T., 'The Interpretation of Sustainable Development Principles in ITLOS', in M.-C. Cordonier Segger and C. G. Weeramantry (eds.), *Sustainable Development Principles in the Decisions of International Courts and Tribunals: 1992–2012* (London: Routledge, 2017), 348.

67 Cf. Chen, L., 'Realizing the Precautionary Principle in Due Diligence' (2016) 25 *Dalhousie Journal of Legal Studies*, 1–24, 22.

sively assess the scientific evidence presented by the parties', they should 'act with prudence and caution ... to prevent serious harm to the stock of southern bluefin tuna'.[68] Thus, in light of scientific uncertainty, the ITLOS ordered the parties to act with 'prudence and caution'.[69]

The ITLOS reaffirmed this notion of 'prudence and caution' in its MOX Plant case.[70] It considered employing it to require cooperation of the disputing parties.[71] The duty to cooperate 'is a fundamental principle in the prevention of pollution of the marine environment under Part XII'.[72] Judge Treves, in a separate opinion, hinted that procedural rights, including obligations to cooperate, may be 'relevant for complying with the general obligation of due diligence' in regard to environmental impacts.[73] This seemingly applies a principle of international (environmental) law, that is, the cooperation principle; and links 'prudence and caution' to that principle.[74]

The Seabed Mining AO determined that the 'responsibility to ensure' in Article 139(1) UNCLOS is one of conduct and of due diligence,[75] that is, a 'due diligence to ensure'.[76] Such diligence has flexible content and may change over time as measures 'may become not diligent enough'.[77] This entails all measures necessary, hence, all adequate means.[78] The AO further noted the obligation 'to ensure' can be found in Article 194(2) UNCLOS.[79] Hence, the findings have been considered as embracing the precautionary principle under the UNCLOS implicitly.[80]

[68] SBT cases, ITLOS, Provisional Measures (1999), para. 80, 77; passim: Land Reclamation in and around the Straits of Johor (*Malaysia* v. *Singapore*), Provisional Measures, Order of 8 October 2003, ITLOS Reports 2003, 10, para. 99; M/V "Louisa" (n 46), para. 77.

[69] Cf. Zanella and Cabral (n 26) 245.

[70] MOX Plant (*Ireland* v. *United Kingdom*), Provisional Measures, Order of 3 December 2001, ITLOS Reports 2001 (n 16) 95, para. 84; reiterated in: Land Reclamation (n 68), para. 92.

[71] MOX Plant, ITLOS, Provisional Measures (n 16), para. 84.

[72] Ibid., para. 82; repeated in: SRFC AO, ITLOS (n 60), para. 140.

[73] MOX Plant, ITLOS, Provisional Measures, Separate Opinion Treves (n 16), para. 9.

[74] Rashbrooke, G., 'The International Tribunal for the Law of the Sea: A Forum for the Development of Principles of International Environmental Law?' (2004) 19 *The International Journal of Marine and Coastal Law*, 515–36 at 526; Golitsyn, V., 'The Contribution of the International Tribunal for the Law of the Sea to the Progressive Development of International Environmental Law' (2016) 46 *Environmental Policy and Law*, 292–8 at 294.

[75] Seabed Mining (n 65), para. 110.

[76] Kelly (n 64) 52.

[77] Seabed Mining (n 65), para. 117.

[78] Ibid., para. 118.

[79] Ibid., para. 113.

[80] Cf. LaMotte, K. R., 'Introductory Note to the International Tribunal for the Law of the Sea: Responsibilities and Obligations of States Sponsoring Persons and Entities with Respect to the Activities in the Area (Request for Advisory Opinion Submitted to the Seabed Disputes Chamber)' (2011) 50 *International Legal Materials*, 455–93, 457; French, D., 'From the Depths: Rich Pickings of Principles of Sustainable Development and General International Law on the Ocean Floor: The Seabed Disputes Chamber's 2011 Advisory Opinion' (2011) 26 *The International Journal of Marine and Coastal Law*, 525–68, 547.

In 2015, the ITLOS held in the SRFC AO that flag States have a 'responsibility to ensure' that ships flying their flag comply with coastal State regulations and do not engage in illegal, unreported and unregulated fishing.[81] The Tribunal stressed this responsibility, reaffirming such obligation's character as being of conduct as well as due diligence.[82] Pursuant to Article 192 and 193 UNCLOS, this encompasses measures necessary to ensure, hence, a duty to 'do the utmost'.[83] This finding seems doubtful in the absence of 'to ensure' or similar language.[84]

According to Annex VII of the Tribunal in the South China Sea Arbitration (SCS Tribunal), Article 192 UNCLOS imposes a due diligence obligation on States to protect the marine environment.[85] Beyond prevention of direct harvesting of threatened species, the obligation further indirectly prevents harm to habitat 'that would affect depleted, threatened, or endangered species', this is 'given particular shape in the context of fragile ecosystems by Article 194(5)'.[86]

10.3.2.3 Beyond Today's Jurisprudence

Beyond the jurisprudence, it has been argued that the wording of Article 1(1)(4) UNCLOS, read in conjunction with the obligation under Articles 192, 206 UNCLOS, may be seen as implying application of the precautionary principle.[87] The definition of 'pollution of the marine environment' in Article 1(1)(4) UNCLOS stipulates that pollution is the introduction of substances or energy by humans, 'which results or is likely to result' in *inter alia* harm to living resources. Thus, such wording may be considered to be an 'embryonic' use of the precautionary principle.[88]

Further, it has also been argued that Article 196 UNCLOS 'clearly reflects the precautionary principle'.[89] This was particularly based on a 'fairly far-reaching' interpretation of the term 'which may cause significant and harmful changes'.[90] The word 'may' can be seen as incorporating an obligation to take measures 'before preventive measures have to be taken'.[91]

81 SRFC AO, ITLOS (n 60), paras. 124–6.
82 Ibid., paras. 127f.
83 Ibid., paras. 136, 29.
84 Cf. Guo and Wang (n 61) 236; Schatz, V., 'Fishing for Interpretation: The ITLOS Advisory Opinion on Flag State Responsibility for Illegal Fishing in the EEZ' (2016) 47 *Ocean Development & International Law*, 327–45, 333.
85 SCS Arbitration, Annex VII, Merits (2016), paras. 959, 64; critic: Schatz (n 84) 334.
86 SCS Arbitration, Merits (n 85), para. 959.
87 Proelß and Houghton (n 61) 232; cf. Marr (n 53) 52f; Proelß (n 59) 95f.
88 Churchill (n 33) 9.
89 Czybulka, D., 'Article 196 UNCLOS' (n 30) para. 9.
90 Ibid., para. 19.
91 Tsimplis, 'Alien Species Stay Home' 414.

However, these arguments reflected in literature seem difficult to accept. In the absence of an interpretation by a competent authority, their understandings of the meaning of the Convention are marginalized.

10.3.2.4 Conclusion

Summa summarum, the relationship between the precautionary principle, obligations of conduct/due diligence and obligations under the UNCLOS might be a plausible reason for future tribunals to interpret Article 192 UNCLOS so that it requires application of the precautionary principle.[92] Overall, should this be the case, the Convention will have come a long way.

10.4 FINAL REMARKS

This section returns to the original question of whether the UNCLOS requires application of the precautionary principle: recalling that the precautionary principle was only visible on the horizon during the negotiations.[93] It therefore appears the Convention originally did not require application. However, it seems that the principle now informs the normative content of the UNCLOS, and, thus, some may argue that the Convention does require its application after all.[94] If so, following the latter view, then such requirement may be considered indirect through the obligation to protect and preserve the marine environment (see Section 10.3.2). As Part XII covers all maritime zones,[95] a good argument may be made that direct approaches must be interpreted considering the obligations set out

[92] Cf. Mossop, J., 'Can We Make the Oceans Greener: The Successes and Failures of UNCLOS as an Environmental Treaty' (2018) 49 *Victoria University of Wellington Law Review*, 573–94, 588f; König, D., 'The Elaboration of Due Diligence Obligations as a Mechanism to Ensure Compliance with International Legal Obligations by Private Actors', in International Tribunal for the Law of the Sea (ed.), *The Contribution of the International Tribunal for the Law of the Sea to the Rule of Law* (n 45) 88.

[93] Kimball, L. A., 'The United Nations Convention on the Law of the Sea: A Framework for Marine Conservation (Part 1)', in D. M. Johnston, L. A. Kimball, P. Payoyo and P. M. Saunders (eds.), *The Law of the Sea: Priorities and Responsibilities in Implementing the Convention* (Gland: International Union for Conservation of Nature, 1995), 36; cf. Proelß (n 59) 95; Churchill, (n 33) 29.

[94] E.g., 'these principles cannot modify the UNCLOS', Rothwell and Stephens (n 34) 520; cf. Sage-Fuller, B., *The Precautionary Principle in Marine Environmental Law: With Special Reference to High Risk Vessels* (London: Routledge, 2013), 70.

[95] Oral (n 66) 405; Wolfrum, R., 'Preservation of the Marine Environment', in J. Basedow, U. Magnus and R. D. Wolfrum (eds.), *The Hamburg Lectures on Maritime Affairs 2011–2013* (Berlin: Springer, 2015), 12; Jakobsen, I. U., *Marine Protected Areas in International Law: An Arctic Perspective* (Leiden: Martinus Nijhoff Publishers, 2016), 76; for more details see: Czybulka, Article 192 (n 30) paras. 5–7.

in Part XII.[96] Therefore, it may well be argued that the UNCLOS requires application of the precautionary principle.

However, one must keep in mind, that (too much) 'coercion kills all noble, voluntary devotion'.[97] Many States have subjected themselves to the UNCLOS and the so called package deal.[98] This package is limited to an extensive but general framework.[99] Excessive pulling on the cords that hold the package together can lead to unforeseeable consequences.

96 Cf. Fabra (n 48) 22.

97 Translation by the author (originally: "Zwang tötet alle edle, freiwillige Hingebung"), Knigge, A. F., *Über den Umgang mit Menschen* (Leipzig: Reclam, 1878), 126.

98 See Art. 309 UNCLOS; cf. Moore, 'One of the Greatest Achievements' (n 6) 8f.

99 Cf. Beyerlin and Marauhn (n 7) 120.

11

A Regime Lost at Sea

Critical Reflections on the UNCLOS Conservation Regime and the Future of Marine Biodiversity Protection

Pierre Cloutier de Repentigny

11.1 INTRODUCTION

The oceans conjure powerful emotions: awe, fear, bewilderment and even love. Their immensity, resilience, aesthetic and brute force have inspired many in the arts and science. Oceans have also played a crucial role in feeding parts of humanity and on facilitating transportation. Overall, humanity has an intimate and complex relationship with the vast expanses of saltwater that give our planet its nickname of the 'blue planet'. Sadly, humanity's relationship with marine life has been detrimental to the latter and has led to a period of mass extinction.[1] The causes of this tragedy are multiple and include overfishing, habitat destruction, pollution, acidification and climate change.[2] Overfishing remains the main cause of marine life decline with approximately 31.4 per cent of fish stocks overfished or depleted, and 58.1 per cent fully fished.[3] Estimates have found that around 90 per cent of large marine animals, 65 per cent of wetland and seagrass habitats, 85 per cent of oyster reefs and 20 per cent of mangrove forests have disappeared.[4] The situation is so dire

[1] United Nations Environment Programme (UNEP) Regional Seas Programme, *Global Synthesis: A Report from the Regional Seas Conventions and Action Plans for the Marine Biodiversity Assessment and Outlook Series* (UNEP, 2010) 5–7.

[2] Ibid., 5; Census of Marine Life International Secretariat, *Scientific Results to Support the Sustainable Use and Conservation of Marine Life: A Summary of the Census of Marine Life for Decision Makers* (Consortium for Ocean Leadership, 2011) 5; Food and Agriculture Organization (FAO), *State of the World Fisheries and Aquaculture 2010* (FAO, 2010) 115.

[3] Philippe Sands and Jacqueline Peel, *Principles of International Environmental Law* (3rd ed., Cambridge: Cambridge University Press, 2012) 397–398; Food and Agriculture Organization, *State of the World Fisheries and Aquaculture 2016* (FAO, 2016) 38.

[4] Census of Marine Life International Secretariat (n 2) 4; Secretariat of the Convention on Biological Diversity, *Global Biodiversity Outlook 3* (CBD Secretariat, 2010) 46–48.

that some studies have predicted that harvested species of marine fish could disappear by 2048.[5]

Nonetheless, our relationship with the oceans and marine life is not a lawless one, as this book aptly demonstrates. It is structured by interconnected layers of rules that in turn are structured by the United Nations Convention on the Law of the Sea[6] (UNCLOS).[7] While conservation and associated norms have increased significantly in number and form over recent decades, their effectiveness at protecting marine biodiversity is in serious doubt.[8] Multiple regime flaws have been identified, including weak and/or vague obligations, limited and/or ineffective enforcement and compliance measures, and political unwillingness to implement or ratify existing obligations.[9] While these issues should not be ignored and underline important lacunae in the current marine biodiversity protection regime, they offer a limited perspective. In other words, they explore the symptoms (e.g., weak enforcement) rather than the causes of regime failure. Any serious reflections on the role and rule of law in the design of solutions to ocean and coastal problems must dive deeper and look at the structures that mould law to avoid adopting new rules that produce the same results.

This chapter analyses the inability of the law of the sea to slow down or halt marine biodiversity decline from a critical perspective, that of green legal theory (GLT). Its aim is to briefly demonstrate the entanglement of the UNCLOS marine conservation framework with economic growth and to begin reflecting on how to move past the limitations of this framework to build better rules for the protection of marine life. The chapter begins with a summary of GLT and its applicability to the law of the sea context. Then, it analyses the current law of the sea regime regarding conservation of marine life through a GLT lens. The chapter ends by looking forward and thinking through means of reimagining the regime, focusing on the

5 Boris Worm et al., 'Impacts of Biodiversity Loss on Ocean Ecosystem Services' (2006) 314(5800) *Science* 787.

6 Adopted 10 December 1982, entered into force 16 November 1994, 1833 UNTS 3 (UNCLOS).

7 Simone Borg, *Conservation on the High Seas: Harmonizing International Regimes for the Sustainable Use of Living Resources* (Cheltenham: Edward Elgar, 2012) 10–16; Alan Boyle, 'Further Development of the 1982 Convention on the Law of the Sea: Mechanisms for Change' in Richard Barnes, David Freestone and David M. Ong (eds.), *The Law of the Sea, Progress and Prospects* (Oxford: Oxford University Press, 2006).

8 Rebecca M. Bratspies and Anastasia Telesetsky, 'Marine Environmental Law: UNCLOS and Fisheries' in Shawkat Alam et al. (eds.), *Routledge Handbook of International Environmental Law* (Oxfordshire: Routledge, 2013) 260.

9 See Richard Barnes, 'The Convention on the Law of the Sea: An Effective Framework for Domestic Fisheries Conservation' in Barnes, Freestone and Ong, *The Law of the Sea, Progress and Prospects* (n 7) 234–235; Robin Churchill, 'The LOSC Regime for Protection of the Marine Environment: Fit for the Twenty-First Century?' in Rosemary Rayfuse (ed.), *Research Handbook on International Marine Environmental Law* (Cheltenham: Edward Elgar, 2015) 17–21; Michaela Young, 'Then and Now: Reappraising Freedom of the Seas in Modern Law of the Sea' (2016) 47(2) *Ocean Development & International Law* 165, 166; Bratspies and Telesetsky (n 8) 263–267.

future UNCLOS implementing agreement on biodiversity beyond national jurisdiction (BBNJ Agreement).

11.2 A GREEN LEGAL THEORY FRAMEWORK FOR THE LAW OF THE SEA

GLT builds on and inscribes itself in the 'green theory' movement, which stems from the application of broader scholarship on deep ecology and environmental philosophy to particular fields.[10] The reflections on human and societal relationship with 'nature' brought on by green theory have triggered various legal queries,[11] particularly examination of the role of law 'in both creating systemic unsustainability, and in impeding or facilitating its resolution. From this vantage point, *environmental* law must be assessed self-reflectively, both as a field of intellectual endeavour and as a vehicle for practical action, with particular attention to its often implicit theoretical underpinnings'.[12]

GLT uses the concept of 'constitutive processes' as its central tool to study environmental law. Through this concept, it 'seeks to re-orient the attention now directed to *downstream* "legal laws" to develop a new understanding of the *upstream* constitutive "dynamics" of material and cultural production that today lie largely undisturbed behind the environmental law paradigm'.[13] Constitutive processes do not simply inform law; they constrain law and other institutions; they act as a form of meta-normative framework for law and other aspects of society.[14]

Economic growth, and its parent philosophy, liberalism, is the main constitutive process studied by GLT. One of the central roles of the State within liberalism is to facilitate the exercise of economic freedoms, usually through the 'market'. The resulting economic growth can be used to generate revenues, which are in turn used to fund programmes that soften the harsher element of capitalist modes of production.[15] Economic growth thus acts as a meta-goal of the State, on which the rest of society is structured; it becomes a constitutive process. Challenging economic growth becomes challenging the liberal politico-juridical system itself.[16] Environmental law, within this system, is thus prevented from addressing the

[10] Michael M'Gonigle and Paula Ramsay, 'Greening Environmental Law: From Sectoral Reform to Systemic Re-Formation' (2004) 14 *Journal of Environmental Law and Practice* 333, 351–352; Andrew Dobson et al., 'Andrew Dobson: Trajectories of Green Political Theory. Interview by Luc Semal, Mathilde Szuba and Olivier Petit' (2014) 22 *Natures Sciences Sociétés* 132.

[11] See eg Vito De Lucia, 'Towards an Ecological Philosophy of Law: A Comparative Discussion' (2013) 4(2) *Journal of Human Rights and the Environment* 167.

[12] M'Gonigle and Ramsay (n 10) 335.

[13] Michael M'Gonigle and Louise Takeda, 'The Liberal Limits of Environmental Law: A Green Legal Critique' (2013) 30 *Pace Environmental Law Review* 1005, 1059.

[14] Ibid. 1060.

[15] Ibid. 1019–1020, 1059–1065 and 1109–1110.

[16] Ibid. 1062–1067.

underlying causes of environmental degradation: economic development. It acts, instead, as a way to mitigate the worst impacts of economic activities in order to render them more acceptable – to legitimise them – without going as far as seriously limiting growth. GLT calls this concept the law of mitigated production.[17]

GLT is a particularly apt framework of analysis for the marine biodiversity protection regime given the historical link between economic activities, use of the seas by the European powers and the international rules they have instituted for ocean governance.[18] It can help us better understand the place economic growth occupies, the role it plays, within the regime – even in provisions traditionally viewed as focused on conservation – and highlight how law can legitimate and facilitate the demands of economic growth.[19] While GLT was developed in a national context, it is an inherently flexible approach that resists legal boundaries, especially given the dominance of liberalism within the international legal system.[20] Moreover, international law is not only structured by liberalism but also serves as a vehicle for the propagation and imposition of liberalism throughout the globe through its imperialist, colonialist and globalising roots and effects.[21]

Such a critical perspective of the regime is necessary because it highlights the limits or the issues with a rule-of-law approach to marine biodiversity decline. GLT demonstrates that a thin understanding of the rule of law (i.e., ensuring States follow the law) is problematic given the role law plays in environmental degradation, and that a thick understanding (i.e., a substantive understanding based on criteria such as

17 Ibid. 1054–1059, 1067–1071 and 1081–1086; see also De Lucia (n 11) 169.

18 See Davor Vidas, 'The Anthropocene and the International Law of the Sea' (2011) 369(1938) *Philosophical Transactions of the Royal Society* A 909; Harry N. Scheiber, 'Economic Uses of the Oceans and the Impacts on Marine Environments: Past Trends and Challenges Ahead' in Davor Vidas and Peter Johan Schei (eds.), *The World Ocean in Globalisation: Climate Change, Sustainable Fisheries, Biodiversity, Shipping, Regional Issues* (Leiden: Martinus Nijhoff, 2011).

19 M'Gonigle and Ramsay (n 10) 345–347; Rémi Bachand, 'Pour une théorie critique en droit international' in Rémi Bachand (ed.), *Théories critiques et droit international* (Brussels: Bruylant, 2013) 128.

20 M'Gonigle and Ramsay (n 10) 349; Anthony Carty, 'Sociological Theories of International Law' in Rüdiger Wolfrum (ed.), *Max Planck Encyclopedia of Public International Law* (online ed., Oxford: Oxford University Press, 2008) para. 1, 4–8; Hélène Mayrand, 'Déconstruire et repenser les fondements du droit international de l'environnement' (2018) September Special Issue *Revue québécoise de droit international* 35, 39–40; Robert Knox, 'Marxist Approaches to International Law' in Anne Orford and Florian Hoffman (eds.), *The Oxford Handbook of the Theory of International Law* (Oxford: Oxford University Press, 2016) 319–322.

21 Antony Anghie, 'Imperialism and International Legal Theory' in Anne Orford and Florian Hoffman (eds.), *The Oxford Handbook of the Theory of International Law* (Oxford: Oxford University Press, 2016) 166–168; Carmen G. Gonzalez, 'Bridging the North-South Divide: International Environmental Law in the Anthropocene' (2015) 32 *Pace Environmental Law Review* 407, 413–416; Michael M'Gonigle, 'Between Globalism and Territoriality: The Emergence of an International Constitution and the Challenge of Ecological Legitimacy' (2002) 15(2) *Canadian Journal of Law and Jurisprudence* 159.

democracy and human rights) is insufficient if it does not challenge the constitutive processes that are preventing law from addressing ecological degradation.[22]

However, GLT goes further than critiquing and attempts to envision law – environmental law specifically – as a potential transformative tool. The ultimate, and perhaps utopic, goal of GLT is to re-form (re-create or re-constitute) the system entirely to purge it of its destructive or harmful elements and thus ensure good relations with the environment and within society. Before exploring what re-formation could look like for marine biodiversity, the next section identifies some of the key structural issues within the current legal regime for marine life conservation. This step is crucial in determining why the regime is failing and, consequently, how to proceed with its re-formation (i.e., how to avoid past mistakes).

11.3 ECONOMIC GROWTH AND UNCLOS' FRAMEWORK FOR MARINE BIODIVERSITY PROTECTION

UNCLOS and its implementing agreement, the United Nations Agreement Relating to the Conservation and Management of Straddling Fish Stocks and Migratory Fish Stocks (UNFSA),[23] form the current global conservation regime for 'marine living resources'.[24] UNCLOS codified States' jurisdiction over their coastal fisheries through the new Exclusive Economic Zone (EEZ) (up to 200 nautical miles (nm) except for the 12nm territorial sea).[25] Specifically, coastal States possess sovereign rights over natural resources, including 'marine living resources', in their EEZ.[26] The rest of the oceans are part of the high seas where States retain their freedom to fish, subject to applicable rules of international law.[27] The rights of States over living resources in their EEZ were counter-balanced by the establishment of conservation duties.[28] The general duties require States to set total allowable catches for stocks and set conservation measures, taking into account best available science, to ensure that such stocks are not endangered by overexploitation.[29] Conservation measures must also maintain or restore stocks at levels that can

[22] David V. Wright, 'Brief on Environmental Rule of Law: In Need of Coherence in Contested Terrain' (2020) 15(1) *McGill Journal of Sustainable Development Law* 1, 12–13.

[23] Adopted 4 August 1995, entered into force 11 November 2001, 2167 UNTS 3 (UNFSA).

[24] Part XII of UNCLOS also contains provisions relevant to the protection of marine biodiversity, and while they would also benefit from a GLT analysis, this chapter focuses on the conservation of 'marine living resources' to manage its scope and concentrates on the rules pertaining to the main cause of marine biodiversity decline: overexploitation.

[25] UNCLOS (n 6) Art. 3, 55, 57.

[26] Ibid. Art. 56.

[27] Ibid. Art. 87, 116.

[28] Francisco O. Vicuña, *The Changing International Law of High Seas Fisheries* (Cambridge: Cambridge University Press, 1999) 30.

[29] UNCLOS (n 6) Art. 61(1)(2).

produce the maximum sustainable yield (MSY) taking into account international standards, stocks' interdependence and the impact on associated species.[30]

Despite these obligations, commercial exploitation did not slow down.[31] Instead, the regime, pushed by the imperative of economic growth, led to an increase in the total amount of commercial exploitation.[32] The EEZ regime contains two internal indicia of its commercial nature. First, MSY is specifically allowed to be based, in part, on economic needs.[33] Second, the goal of the regime is the 'optimum utilization of the living resources', in other words to provide maximum economic outcomes.[34] These legal technologies result in immediate economic imperative taking precedence over any other considerations and exemplify the commercial nature of EEZ fisheries obligations.[35] The language of conservation in the regime acts as the law of mitigated production, that is, conservation measures (e.g., time and place of fishing or specifying the types of nets to use) are peripheral to the real concern (exploitation), which goes unanswered. Measures that could significantly reduce exploitation – such as reducing fishing fleets, prohibiting the harvesting of certain species, creating quotas based on food security and sovereignty and ecosystem health, favouring small-scale and subsistence fisheries, reducing and potentially limiting commercial exploitation altogether – are simply not on the table as they would have unacceptable economic consequences within the economic growth paradigm.

The EEZ regime is also anchored in the Eurocentric and imperialist conception of sovereignty,[36] which is reproduced in the concept of sovereign right over natural resources. M'Gonigle and Takeda specifically highlight sovereignty as an important structuring framework for environmental issues.[37] Their proposition is strengthened by Porras, Natarajan and Khoday, who have demonstrated how sovereignty is defined by and founded on States' ability to exploit their territories' resources.[38]

30 Ibid. Art. 61(3)(4).
31 Scheiber (n 18) 79–81.
32 Bratspies and Telesetsky (n 8) 265; Rachel Baird, 'Illegal, Unreported and Unregulated Fishing: An Analysis of the Legal, Economic and Historical Factors Relevant to Its Development and Persistence' (2004) 5 *Melbourne Journal of International Law* 299, 306–308.
33 UNCLOS (n 6) Art. 61(3).
34 Ibid. Art. 62(1). This objective is arguably inapplicable to marine mammals: Cameron S. G. Jefferies, *Marine Mammal Conservation and the Law of the Sea* (Oxford: Oxford University Press, 2016) 191.
35 Bratspies and Telesetsky (n 8) 263; Barnes (n 9) 241–242; Mayrand (n 20) 43–44.
36 See Antony Anghie, *Imperialism, Sovereignty and the Making of International Law* (Cambridge: Cambridge University Press, 2004).
37 M'Gonigle and Takeda (n 13) 1110.
38 Ileana Porras, 'Appropriating Nature: Commerce, Property, and the Commodification of Nature in the Law of Nations' (2014) 27 *Leiden Journal of International Law* 641; Usha Natarajan and Kishan Khoday, 'Locating Nature: Making and Unmaking International Law' (2014) 27 *Leiden Journal of International Law* 573, 586–588.

The EEZ regime transposes this logic of exploitation in the oceans by creating an imperative to exploit 'marine living resources' to assert States' (quasi)sovereignty in the EEZ as exemplified by the objective of optimum utilisation and the obligation to give to other States the ability to exploit the 'surplus' of resources when the coastal State is incapable of exploiting it.[39] The latter operates, in a sense, as a demonstration that sovereign rights are absolute (to the extent allowed by international law) only when coastal States are able to fully exploit their 'marine living resources'. In line with the narrative of economic growth, however, States have generally fully or 'optimally' exploited their stocks.[40]

In the high seas, freedom of fishing continues to be a significant obstacle to the preservation of marine life by providing legal justification for fairly unrestricted commercial fisheries.[41] The high seas' conservation duty – which must be fulfilled in cooperation with relevant States and/or regional fisheries management organisations (RFMOs)[42] – is based on the concept of MSY and thus suffers from the same issues described previously.[43] The duty to cooperate, being a duty of conduct rather than result,[44] is of little assistance in countering the economic growth narrative that permeates the law of the sea and the competitive nature of capitalism, especially since the duty assumes good faith.[45] Furthermore, conservation measures that result from cooperation are not automatically better than unilateral ones and are still subject to the logic of economic growth.

UNFSA implements the UNCLOS general conservation obligations regarding straddling and migratory stocks.[46] UNFSA emphasises the need to coordinate conservation measures between EEZs and the high seas, and makes participation in RFMOs mandatory for State parties.[47] It also establishes a list of conservation obligations including adopting measures based on the precautionary and ecosystem approaches.[48] Despite these advances, UNFSA has not been successful at stemming the decline of marine biodiversity.[49] The agreement's ineffectiveness is due in part to the fact that, while its language is more centred on biodiversity protection, it is

39 UNCLOS (n 6) Art. 62(1)(2); Pierre Cloutier de Repentigny, 'To the Anthropocene and Beyond: The Responsibility of Law in Decimating and Protecting Marine Life' (2020) 11(1–2) *Transnational Legal Theory* 180, 190–191.

40 Barnes (n 9) 245–246.

41 Young (n 9) 166.

42 UNCLOS (n 6) Arts. 117, 118; Young (n 9) 169–170; *Fisheries Jurisdiction Case (Federal Republic of Germany* v. *Iceland)* (Merits) [1974] ICJ Rep 175.

43 UNCLOS (n 6) Art. 119(1).

44 Young (n 9) 170.

45 Vicuña (n 28) 48.

46 UNCLOS (n 6) Arts. 63–64; UNFSA (n 23) Arts. 2, 4.

47 UNFSA (n 23) Arts. 7–10.

48 UNFSA (n 23) Art. 5(c)(d)(e)(g), 6, Annex II.

49 Borg (n 7) 50; Bratspies and Telesetsky (n 8) 265–266; Karin Mickelson, 'The Maps of International Law: Perceptions of Nature in the Classification of Territory' (2014) 27 *Leiden Journal of International Law* 621, 632.

very much still a resource management and exploitation agreement. UNFSA shares the same lacunae as UNCLOS concerning cooperation, and the need for conservation measures to 'promote the objective of [stocks'] optimum utilization' and be designed around the concept of MSY.[50] The approaches of the agreement, however, add new variables.

The precautionary approach – '[t]he absence of adequate scientific information shall not be used as a reason for postponing or failing to take conservation and management measures'[51] – has some potential as a legal technology regulating the uncertainties of human–environment interactions.[52] Its operationalisation in UNFSA is, however, limited. The agreement transforms the approach in a management tool centred on obtaining data on fish stocks, enhancing monitoring and setting reference points for stocks' health.[53] As with MSY, precautionary measures need to take into account 'existing and predicted … socio-economic conditions',[54] which in a context dominated by economic growth tends to favour short-term economic benefits. This language is part of neo-liberalism's modernisation of ecology; that is, an approach centred on techno-scientific and economic management in line with the primacy of economic growth.[55] Risk is managed by avoiding delaying conservation measures rather than prescribing necessary actions to prevent the risk from manifesting in the first place. Prevention means that in many respects fishing licences, for example, should simply not be issued unless the risk can be justified by concrete needs beyond purely economic considerations (e.g., to allow coastal population access to local food sources). However, such preventative measures are usually not 'cost-effective' as they require rejecting activities that generate profits and run counter to the optimum utilisation of the resource.[56]

The ecosystem approach – 'a strategy for the integrated management of land, water and living resources that promotes conservation and sustainable use'[57] – is in a similar boat. An ecocentric or similar conceptualisation of the approach holds a lot of potential in terms of shifting how we conceptualise conservation.[58] Nonetheless, UNFSA's use of the ecosystem approach is not spelled out; rather it is implied from several of its principles. It is thus undefined, which leaves considerable room for interpretation,

[50] UNFSA (n 23) Art. 5(a)(b).
[51] Scott Parsons, 'Ecosystem Considerations in Fisheries Management: Theory and Practice' (2005) 20 *International Journal of Marine and Coastal Law* 381, 386–388.
[52] See Geoffrey Garver, 'The Rule of Ecological Law: The Legal Complement to Degrowth Economics' (2013) 5 *Sustainability* 316, 329.
[53] Ibid. art. 6, Annex II. See Borg (n 7) 134–135.
[54] UNFSA (n 23) Art. 6(3)(c).
[55] Mayrand (n 20) 49.
[56] M'Gonigle and Takeda (n 13) 1072–1074.
[57] Secretariat of the Convention on Biological Diversity, 'Ecosystem Approach' (*Convention on Biological Diversity*, 8 August 2019) <www.cbd.int/ecosystem/>.
[58] See Vito De Lucia, 'Competing Narratives and Complex Genealogies: The Ecosystem Approach in International Environmental Law' (2015) 27 *Journal of Environmental Law* 91, 104–106.

especially considering the inherently ambiguous nature of the approach.[59] Soft law instruments offer a more precise picture; one where ecosystem considerations are subordinated to human interests, especially economic considerations.[60] The ecosystem approach is even considered by the Food and Agriculture Organisation as compatible with typical fisheries management practices, which are based on the (economic) production framework responsible for depletion of stocks.[61] The approach is thus relegated to a management tool of ecological modernisation aimed at 'tackling the negative externalities of industrial modernity, preserve the resource base necessary to sustain global production and consumption patterns, and thus legitimate contemporary ecological regimes of accumulation'.[62] In the end, the UNSFA is a sophisticated law of mitigated production: it paints a picture of conservation and sustainable management, adding legitimacy to the regime, without fundamentally addressing the issue of economic exploitation of marine life, the root cause of the problem. It remains firmly situated with the constitutive process of economic growth.

Overall, the UNCLOS conservation regime is simply incapable of meaningfully dealing with the fundamental causes of fisheries decline.[63] In other words, the law of the sea's first aim is to create a regime permitting and even encouraging the exploitation of marine life, with a subsidiary aim of attempting to ensure the 'sustainability' of the former. Therefore, calls for States to simply 'obey' the law or even for substantive reforms without challenging the economic growth paradigm, have a high risk of simply reproducing the flaws identified by GLT. If we are to use ocean law as a mean to engender or participate in the re-formation of constitutive processes beyond economic growth and towards ecological sustainability, we need to think strategically about how we push or advocate for the 'rule of law', as doing so uncritically could hinder paradigmatic shifts and potentially result in further marine biodiversity decline.

11.4 FORGING A NEW FUTURE FOR MARINE BIODIVERSITY PROTECTION: STRATEGIC REVOLUTION AND THE LAW

Offering a diagnosis is often easier than suggesting effective remedies. One thing is clear: legal reforms – adopting more conservation rules within the current system – are insufficient to initiate the type of deep cultural and structural changes

[59] Ibid. 97–99; Parsons (n 51) 388.

[60] Convention on Biological Diversity, COP 5 Decision V/6 (May 2000); Food and Agriculture Organisation, 'Fisheries Management: 2. The ecosystem approach to fisheries' (2003) *FAO Technical Guidelines for Responsible Fisheries* 4 Supp 2, 14; De Lucia (n 58) 106–113.

[61] FAO (n 60) 11–14.

[62] De Lucia (n 58) 104.

[63] See Patricia Birnie, Alan Boyle and Catherine Redgwell, *International Law and the Environment* (3rd ed., Oxford: Oxford University Press, 2009) 751–752; Sands and Peel (n 3) 447–448; Bratspies and Telesetsky (n 8) 260, 265–266; Baird (n 32) 308–309.

needed to address wicked problems such as marine biodiversity decline.[64] The typical option for massive radical change is revolution. However, revolution seems unlikely, at least in the short term, as 'the structural transformation of the capitalist growth economy and the consumer culture … regard[ed] as indispensable if large-scale catastrophe and social collapse are to be averted, is nowhere in sight'.[65] This binary of absolute – reform or revolution – is not only false but counterproductive. As Knox suggests, instead of focusing on this binary, we should focus on strategy and tactics: 'in a long-term, structural, and strategic sense, we wish to overthrow the existing order. But in a short-term, conjunctural, tactical sense it is necessary to work within it. The task, then, is to figure out how these interrelate'.[66] De Lucia goes in the same direction, suggesting that such an approach

> should perhaps be conceptualized as a form of internal resistance and as a strategy, one that may need to be discarded as soon as it becomes a hindrance. Such an understanding arguably keeps alive the important tension between practical action and radical cultural change – which is the level and kind of change essential for a deep, long-term shift of our cultural vision and of our juridical forms.[67]

This thinking fits perfectly within the GLT pragmatic approach to the re-formation of law.[68] This approach, which can be named strategic revolution, does not abandon (international) environmental law, but instead contextualises it, provides it with a better understanding of the hegemonic structures in which it operates, and thus allows the strategic use of law, in addition to other social actions, to instigate deeper changes and challenge existing constitutive processes.[69] There is no precise method or way of undertaking strategic revolution in law. Rather, such actions are simply guided by their aim of re-formation and by a need for flexibility, as some actions may become inefficacious and would need to be replaced. Typically, however, a constellation of actions is needed, as only rarely will one change to the law be able on its own to push back against existing constitutive processes.

Measures that could qualify as strategic revolution within the law of the sea have already begun to be explored by a burgeoning scholarship.[70] The proposed or existing legal measures have a common element, one that makes them re-formative: they all seek to displace economic growth as a constitutive process. For example,

64 See Bachand (n 19) 118–120; M'Gonigle and Ramsay (n 10) 354.
65 Ingolfur Blühdorn, 'A Much-Needed Renewal of Environmentalism? Eco-politics in the Anthropocene' in Clive Hamilton, Christophe Bonneuil and François Gemenne (eds.), *The Anthropocene and the Global Environmental Crisis: Rethinking Modernity in a New Epoch* (Oxfordshire: Routledge, 2015) 156.
66 Knox (n 20) 326.
67 De Lucia (n 11) 190.
68 M'Gonigle and Takeda (n 13) 1112–1113; M'Gonigle and Ramsay (n 10) 352.
69 M'Gonigle and Ramsay (n 10) 356.
70 See Cloutier de Repentigny (n 39) 193–195.

Indigenous law offers a completely different paradigm based on deep kinship, spiritual and cultural connections to the environment that behave, in a way, as their own constitutive process. Allowing Indigenous peoples to govern the marine spaces that are part of their territory and adapting non-Indigenous law along the same lines – e.g., based on notions of Earth Jurisprudence – could offer an emerging counter-process to economic growth.[71] The current negotiation for a BBNJ Agreement offers a potential avenue to introduce such elements of strategic revolution in the marine biodiversity protection regime.

The current draft of the BBNJ Agreement (18 November 2019 version) creates three mechanisms: (1) area-based protection and management measures (ABPMM) with a focus on marine protected areas (MPA); (2) environmental impact assessments (EIA); and (3) sustainable use of genetic resources.[72] The EIA provisions act as a detailed implementation of the UNCLOS EIA obligations.[73] These types of provisions are useful in providing information on marine activities and their impact on the marine environment. Beyond that, they are a perfect example of ecological modernisation, focusing on mitigating potential impacts, technocratic input and managing economic activities to make them 'greener' without questioning the activities themselves.[74] EIA focuses on procedure more than substance and, ultimately, the agreement does not provide a clear limit on activities; in other words, it does not impose a firm answer as to what projects are environmentally unacceptable and thus which projects should be rejected.[75] The marine genetic resources provisions offer even less of a potential for strategic revolution.[76] The provisions conceptualise marine biodiversity as a source of genetic resources that produces economic benefits and can be appropriated in the form of intellectual property, rather than intrinsically valued, accessible to all and for the benefit of all.[77] This approach fits squarely in the commercialisation of marine life and the narrative of economic growth.

The provisions on ABPMM offer more re-formative potential.[78] The BBNJ Agreement would create a mechanism to establish ABPMM in areas beyond

71 Ibid.

72 Intergovernmental Conference on an international legally binding instrument under the United Nations Convention on the Law of the Sea on the conservation and sustainable use of marine biological diversity of areas beyond national jurisdiction, Revised draft text of an agreement under the United Nations Convention on the Law of the Sea on the conservation and sustainable use of marine biological diversity of areas beyond national jurisdiction, 4th sess., Annex, UN Doc A/CONF.232/2020/3, 18 November 2019 (Draft BBNJ Agreement).

73 UNCLOS (n 6) Arts. 204–206.

74 Draft BBNJ Agreement (n 72) Part IV.

75 See M'Gonigle and Ramsay (n 10) 336–337.

76 Draft BBNJ Agreement (n 72) Part II.

77 See A. B. M. Vadrot, A. Langlet and I. Tessnow-von Wysockim 'Who Owns Marine Biodiversity? Contesting the World Order through the "Common Heritage of Humankind" Principle' (2021) 31 *Environmental Politics* 226–250 DOI: 10.1080/09644016.2021.1911442.

78 Draft BBNJ Agreement (n 72) Part III.

national jurisdiction. State parties will be able to propose ABPMM to be adopted by the conference of parties (COP). ABPMM are to be identified based on, inter alia, the ecosystem approach, and best available science and, potentially, Indigenous peoples' traditional knowledge. Once an ABPMM is adopted, State parties must conform to it, but are allowed to adopt more stringent measures. Notwithstanding the issue of participation, which could make or break the agreement, there are some areas of concern with the proposed ABPMM. First, the agreement does not define the ecosystem approach, which is problematic as the approach is susceptible to being captured by the narrative of economic growth.[79] There is also potentially problematic language in the objective provisions regarding 'sustainable use' and 'socioeconomic objectives'.[80] While the use of marine biodiversity is not per se problematic (rather it is the hegemonic conceptualisation of use as economic exploitation that is problematic), this language is often interpreted or conceptualised through the lens of economic growth and serves to legitimise exploitation through the language of sustainability. Second, the Agreement is currently framed as not prejudicing the rights and obligations under UNCLOS and has to be implemented so as not to undermine other global or regional agreements (e.g., UNFSA and RFMOs).[81] This is concerning given the GLT critique of the UNCLOS conservation regime. If the Agreement cannot address the main cause of marine biodiversity decline – overexploitation, which is not adequately addressed by the current regime – its ability to instigate positive change within the regime is in question.

Nonetheless, the potential of ABPMM, especially MPA, should not be dismissed; State parties will ultimately determine their normative content and have a certain degree of leeway to use these measures strategically. Their strength lies in their ability to create a legal 'bubble' or 'space' where 'normal' rules do not apply. In these spaces, different rules based on considerations other than economic growth can be implemented with the flexibility needed due to the complexity and interconnected nature of marine ecosystems. Sensitive or vulnerable ecosystems can obtain robust protection through MPAs, where the prime objective is ecological integrity. MPAs can then be interconnected through networks of other MPAs and other, less stringent, ABPMM. These other ABPMM could better accommodate human needs without the pressures of economic growth and within the limits of ecosystems. These spaces could eventually demonstrate that better cohabitation with the marine environment is possible. The BBNJ Agreement could eventually serve as a central

79 Ibid. Art. 5(f). See Vito De Lucia, 'The Ecosystem Approach and the Negotiations towards a New Agreement on Marine Biodiversity in Areas beyond National Jurisdiction' [2019:2] *Nordic Environmental Law Journal* 7.

80 Draft BBNJ Agreement (n 72) Art. 2, 14(a)(c)(d).

81 Ibid. Art. 4. See Vito De Lucia, 'A very quick look at the revised draft text of the new agreement on marine biodiversity in areas beyond national jurisdiction' (*EJIL: Talk!*, 23 January 2020) <www.ejiltalk.org/a-very-quick-look-at-the-revised-draft-text-of-the-new-agreement-on-marine-biodiversity-in-areas-beyond-national-jurisdiction/#more-17849>.

institution that ensures a form of global marine spatial planning for marine biodiversity, in tandem with other relevant institutions, to ensure maximum efficacy and coordination with national measures.[82] Hopefully, the eventual success of the regime could push States to re-form fisheries conservation along the same lines.

States can begin this work by 'testing' measures within their jurisdiction and using their success to push for change at the international level through various channels, including BBNJ Agreement measures. These could include fleet reduction, blocking the fisheries trade from overexploiting States, establishing a moratorium on certain commercial fisheries while reducing others, evaluating population needs for 'living resources', establishing networks of ABPMM within their EEZ, and the like. Some measures may start as unilateral measures that go against the established legal order.[83] This is why strict adherence to the (thin) rule of law is counter-productive to strategic revolution and ultimately the safeguard of marine biodiversity. To put it differently, the law may have to be 'broken' (to a certain extent) to be 'rebuilt'. This is likely a necessary step given the incompatibility of the liberal paradigm of contemporary international law with effective ecological protection. Unilateral and multilateral measures through the BBNJ Agreement could, step by step, create a new paradigm for the law of the sea, a new rule of law for the oceans detached from the demands of economic growth. Ultimately, whether the BBNJ Agreement can be an instrument of strategic revolution will depend both on the final text and its subsequent implementation by State parties individually and through the COP.

11.5 CONCLUSION

Marine life, treated as a commodity or a 'living resource', is currently subject to the rule of economic growth through the law of the sea. Conservation obligations are simply mobilised to increase the legitimacy of the regime by mitigating negative effects (symptoms) without challenging our destructive relationship with marine life (the disease). Overall, as highlighted by GLT, economic growth is omnipresent within the UNCLOS 'marine living resources' regime, and its influence should not be underestimated by anyone who cares about the state of marine biodiversity and the biosphere more generally. The move towards a law of the sea capable of reversing marine biodiversity decline is not easy or straightforward. Simply demanding respect for the law or insisting on an uncritical rule of law will lead to more of the same. To strategically mobilise the rule of law, we will need concerted

[82] See Brice Trouillet and Stephen Jay, 'The Complex Relationships between Marine Protected Areas and Marine Spatial Planning: Towards an Analytical Framework' (2021) 127 *Marine Policy* 104441.

[83] This is not a new tactic as Canada's unilateral fisheries enforcement actions against foreign vessels and the subsequent adoption of UNFSA demonstrate: see Vicuña (n 28) 112–117.

and constant efforts to shift the liberal paradigm of law through various actions challenging the constitutive process of economic growth; this will require strategic legal revolution. The BBNJ Agreement may offer a starting point, but global pressure on States to prioritise marine biodiversity over economic growth will be needed. In the words of Angela Davis: '[y]ou have to act as if it were possible to radically transform the world. And you have to do it all the time'.[84] That goes for our socio-political and legal actions concerning the oceans.

[84] 'Angela Davis' in Eugenia O'Neal (ed.), 113 *Black Voices: Speaking Truth to Power* (Saint Mary: Maiden Hall Press, 2019) 52.

12

Fisheries Redistribution under Climate Change

Rethinking the Law to Address the 'Governance Gap'?

Mitchell Lennan

12.1 INTRODUCTION

Climate change is altering the ocean through warming, acidification, deoxygenation and other stressors. Taking the troubling state of global fish stocks[1] and the decline in global biodiversity levels[2] into account, this paints an alarming picture.[3] A pervasive yet overlooked issue is the impact of climate change on the distribution of fish stocks and other marine species (marine living resources or MLRs), which causes governance issues and threatens the rule of law for the oceans. For example, when fish move across static jurisdictional and management boundaries, they may become unregulated and risk being overexploited.[4] Shifting fish stocks threaten the certainty, predictability and stability of the international fisheries legal framework. They also undermine conservation and management measures (CMMs) by coastal States and regional fisheries management organisations or arrangements (RFMO/As), impeding sustainable exploitation and conservation of global fish stocks.[5]

To address these challenges, the legal framework applicable to fisheries and marine biodiversity must be flexible and adaptive in response to redistribution of fish stocks across scales, or risk undermining the rule of law. Since this framework

1 D. Pauly and D. Zeller, 'Catch Reconstructions Reveal that Global Marine Fisheries Catches Are Higher than Reported and Declining' (2016) 7 *Nature Communications* 10244.

2 S. Diaz et al. (eds.), *Summary for Policymakers of the Global Assessment Report on Biodiversity and Ecosystem Services for the Intergovernmental Science-Policy Platform on Biodiversity and Ecosystem Services* (Bonn: IPBES, 2019).

3 UN Environment, 2020: A crunch year for the biodiversity and climate emergency, Press Release 23 December 2019 <www.unenvironment.org/news-and-stories/story/2020-crunch-year-biodiversity-and-climate-emergencies>.

4 M. Pinsky et al., 'Preparing Ocean Governance for Species on the Move' (2018) 360 *Science* 1189–1191.

5 IPCC, 'Summary for Policymakers' in H.-O. Pörtner et al. (eds.), *IPCC Special Report on the Ocean and Cryosphere in a Changing Climate* (IPCC 2019) 12.

does not directly account for species shifts, it has been argued to constitute a 'governance gap' requiring urgent attention.[6]

This chapter assesses whether and to what extent the international legal framework adequately places an obligation on States to adapt to the complexities caused by MLRs shifting their location, in order to ensure legal certainty, stability and predictability and maintain the rule of law. First, it outlines the main issues caused by fisheries redistribution (Section 12.2). Second, it assesses whether the key principles and obligations within the international legal framework are fit for purpose to address these issues (Section 12.3). A systemic interpretation of relevant provisions from the United Nations Convention on the Law of the Sea (UNCLOS),[7] the Fish Stocks Agreement (UNFSA),[8] the Convention on Biological Diversity (CBD),[9] the Convention on Migratory Species (CMS),[10] as well as the international climate law regime,[11] indicate a general obligation on States, either individually or through RFMO/As to adapt management and conservation of MLRs to the effects of climate change. Section 12.4 explores potential solutions that might strengthen adaptive responses to fisheries redistribution within this framework, thereby helping to maintain the rule of law.

12.2 FISHERIES REDISTRIBUTION UNDER CLIMATE CHANGE

This section provides a brief overview of the ever-growing body of scientific literature on marine species redistribution under climate change, followed by the jurisdictional and managerial challenges this causes, which constitute the so-called governance gap that the international legal framework must address to maintain the rule of law in response to environmental change.

12.2.1 *Causes and Consequences*

The ocean has been warming faster than previously estimated,[12] and has become more acidic, particularly at higher latitudes.[13] Extreme marine temperature events

[6] Pinsky et al. (n 4).
[7] United Nations Convention on the Law of the Sea (UNCLOS), Montego Bay, 10 December 1982, in force 16 November 1994, 1833 UNTS 3.
[8] Agreement for the Implementation of the Provisions of the United Nations Convention on the Law of the Sea of 10 December 1982 relating to the Conservation and Management of Straddling Fish Stocks and Highly Migratory Fish Stocks (UNFSA), New York, 4 August 1995, in force 11 November 2001, 2167 UNTS 3.
[9] United Nations Convention on Biological Diversity (CBD), Rio de Janeiro, 22 May 1992, in force 29 December 1993, 1760 UNTS 79.
[10] Convention on the Conservation of Migratory Species of Wild Animals (CMS), Bonn, 23 June 1979 in force 1 November 1983, 1651 UNTS 333.
[11] United Nations Framework Convention on Climate Change (UNFCCC), New York, 9 May 1992, in force 21 March 1994, 1771 UNTS 107; Paris Agreement, Paris, 12 December 2015, in force 4 November 2016, UN Doc. FCCC/CP2015/L.9/Rev/1.
[12] Ê. Plagányi, 'Climate Change Impacts on Fisheries' (2019) 363 *Science* 930–931.
[13] IPCC, 'Summary for Policymakers' (n 5) 24.

are also increasing in frequency and duration,[14] as are warming "'hotspots' in different regions of the ocean.[15]

Generally, the response of marine species to changes in temperature is to shift location poleward, or into deeper waters, towards their preferred environmental conditions.[16] This results in the redistribution of species from their historical locations and across maritime boundaries, causing complications for conservation, management and exploitation of MLRs.[17] Species shifting poleward due to temperature changes may encounter unsuitable acidity and/or oxygen levels, leaving them squeezed between extremes, causing local extinctions or decreases in abundance.[18] Latest estimates suggest that on average, fish and other marine species have shifted into new areas at a rate of 70 kilometres per decade.[19] It has been predicted that 892 MLRs of commercial importance are expected to shift their distribution in the future.[20]

Complications from these changes in distribution and abundance are numerous. They include species leaving designated conservation areas and thus limiting the efficacy of marine protected areas (MPAs).[21] Inter- and intra-State conflicts can occur over quota allocations as they move across management jurisdictions[22] and into deeper waters.[23] Problems also arise when the distribution of a fish stock becomes less predictable, and 'are compounded when States act unilaterally to exploit the resultant windfall'.[24] Conflicts and breakdowns in cooperation can lead to overexploitation of MLRs and environmental damage, undermining the legal objectives of conservation and sustainable use.[25]

[14] E. C. J. Oliver et al., 'Longer and More Frequent Marine Heatwaves over the Past Century' (2018) 9 *Nature Communications* 1324.
[15] A. Hobday and G. Pecl, 'Identification of Global Marine Hotspots: Sentinels for Change and Vanguards for Adaptation Action' (2014) 24 *Reviews in Fish Biology and Fisheries* 415–425.
[16] E. S. Poloczanska et al., 'Global Imprint of Climate Change on Marine Life' (2013) 3 *Nature Climate Change* 919–925.
[17] Pinsky et al. (n 4).
[18] W. W. L. Cheung et al., 'Modelling Future Oceans: The Present and Emerging Future of Fish Stocks and Fisheries' in R. Caddell and E. Molenaar (eds.), *Strengthening International Fisheries Law in an Era of Changing Oceans* (Oxford: Hart, 2019) 13–23, 15.
[19] Poloczanska et al. (n 16).
[20] Pinsky et al. (n 4).
[21] Ibid.
[22] A. Østhagen et al., 'Collapse of Cooperation? The North-Atlantic Mackerel Dispute and Lessons for International Cooperation on Transboundary Fish Stocks' (2020) 19 *Maritime Studies* 155–165.
[23] J. Spijkers et al., 'Marine Fisheries and Future Ocean Conflict' (2018) 19 *Fish and Fisheries* 789–806.
[24] Pinsky et al. (n 4) 1189.
[25] Østhagen et al. (n 22); Spijkers et al. (n 23).

12.2.2 *The Case for Adaptation*

Marine species shifts and their consequences will persist at current rates or accelerate, depending on levels of future warming.[26] The social and ecological benefits of keeping climate warming to a minimum have been outlined extensively.[27] Implementation of the 2°C temperature goal in Article 2 of the Paris Agreement (PA) would benefit 75 per cent of coastal States through stabilised or increased catch of MLRs, ~90 per cent of which would occur in developing countries.[28] Even if current climate warming targets are met, however, some level of environmental change is guaranteed.[29] Adverse changes cannot be prevented by emission reductions alone, and further warming and acidification of the ocean is unavoidable, making adaptation a necessity.[30]

This considered, the need for international law relating to fisheries and the marine environment to facilitate adaptation to environmental change is necessary to promote resilience to climate change impacts on the oceans and their biodiversity. Though present in the international climate legal regime from the outset, climate adaptation is enshrined in the global goal on adaptation in the PA.[31] Climate adaptation in anthropogenic systems is considered as 'the process of adjustment to actual climate and its effects, in order to moderate harm or exploit beneficial opportunities'.[32] Fisheries are anthropogenic, social-ecological systems, where management decisions and fishing activities undertaken by humans impact marine ecosystems.[33] Several forms of climate adaptation can take place, that is, 'planned adaptation' defined as '[a]daptation that is the result of a deliberate policy decision, based on an awareness that conditions have changed or are about to change and that action is required to return to, maintain, or achieve a desired state'.[34] This is the definition of adaptation used throughout the rest of the chapter.

26 Cheung et al (n 18).

27 IPCC, *Climate Change 2007: The Synthesis Report: Summary for Policy Makers. Fourth Assessment Report for the Intergovernmental Panel on Climate Change* (Bonn: IPCC Secretariat, 2007).

28 U. R. Sumalia et al., 'Benefits of the Paris Agreement to Ocean Life, Economies, and People' (2019) 5 *Science Advances* 3855.

29 IPCC, *Climate Change* 2007 (n 27).

30 Ibid., 19; IPCC, 'Summary for Policymakers' (n 5), 415.

31 Paris Agreement (n 11), Art. 7.

32 C. B. Field et al. (eds.), *Managing the Risks of Extreme Events and Disasters to Advance Climate Change Adaptation: Special Report of the Intergovernmental Panel on Climate Change* (Cambridge: Cambridge University Press, 2007), 556.

33 C. Folke, 'Social-Ecological Systems and Adaptive Governance of the Commons' (2007) 22 *Ecological Research* 14–15; C. Folke et al., 'Social-Ecological Resilience and Biosphere-Based Sustainability Science' (2016) 21 *Ecology and Society* 41–57.

34 M. L. Parry et al. (eds.), *Climate Change 2007: Impacts, Adaptation and Vulnerability: Contribution of Working Group II to the Fourth Assessment Report of the Intergovernmental Panel on Climate Change* (Cambridge: Cambridge University Press, 2007), 869.

Several complications face the conservation, management and exploitation of MLRs, complications that result from shifts in distribution due to climate change. Since the applicable international legal framework does not directly account for these, this has been argued as constituting a gap in law and governance,[35] which undermines legal certainty. Climate change causes uncertainty, instability and change in marine social-ecological systems, that is, fisheries, making adaptation a necessity. Conventional legal and governance frameworks aim to provide certainty and stability, and fisheries redistribution challenges this. Climate change pressurises these frameworks by requiring them to adapt to climate impacts (normative adaptation) so that adaptive action can be taken (practical adaptation). The role of law here is to facilitate action to increase resilience and adaptive capacity of social-ecological systems to climate change, in order to maintain stability and the rule of law.[36] The next section assesses whether the international legal framework is adequate to facilitate an adaptive response by States to the complexities caused by marine species shifting their location.

12.3 THE INTERNATIONAL LEGAL FRAMEWORK: FIT FOR PURPOSE?

Several international legal instruments constitute the framework governing States' rights and obligations with respect to the use of oceans and their resources, including fisheries and protection of the marine environment. Regional agreements and their commissions, including RFMO/As, play a similar role in regional seas or in areas beyond national jurisdiction (ABNJ), providing finer detail for cooperative management needs specific to a certain region. However, the fact that 'the current legal framework for the international regulation of fisheries does not directly account for fluctuating or changing distributions'[37] has been argued to constitute a gap in the law and governance regime applicable to MLRs, risking conflict and overexploitation of species and undermining the rule of the law for the oceans.

Working with the legal instruments already at hand in response to such pressing issues is vital, considering the urgent need to adapt. In assessing whether the international legal framework is fit for purpose, this section outlines its relevant features that could facilitate effective adaptation to marine species redistribution. The framework is presented as key obligations and principles within several multilateral instruments. This is done to stress the importance of systemic and evolutive interpretation of the international legal framework to address new challenges to the marine environment, maximise efficiency of existing fragmented legal rules and address and avoid governance gaps, thereby strengthening the rule of law.

[35] Pinsky et al. (n 4).

[36] R. K. Craig et al., 'Balancing Stability and Flexibility in Adaptive Governance: An Analysis of Tools Available in U.S. Environmental Law' (2017) 22 *Ecology and Society* 3–18.

[37] Pinsky et al. (n 4) 1190.

12.3.1 *Protection and Preservation of the Marine Environment*

Part XII of UNCLOS obliges States to protect and preserve the marine environment. This is a general obligation of conduct, of 'due diligence' applying to all maritime areas regardless of jurisdiction.[38] This obligation is *erga omnes*, and jurisprudential developments over the past twenty years support a progressive, evolutionary interpretation with the provisions covering, inter alia, MLRs.[39] UNCLOS places responsibility for the conservation and management of fish stocks on coastal States within their exclusive economic zones (EEZs),[40] and adopting CMMs for all MLRs within their EEZ is mandatory and an 'integral element' in the protection and preservation of the marine environment.[41] States have an obligation to ensure that MLRs within their jurisdiction are not overexploited.[42] Through this obligation, there is the possibility that national regulations could contribute to far-sighted sustainable management of fish stocks that move into, or straddle, waters in an adjacent State's jurisdiction due to climate change.[43] Should new fish stocks appear in a coastal State's EEZ, that State is under a positive obligation to introduce CMMs for those stocks, cooperating with any neighbouring States whose waters that stock may also inhabit. This can include designation of transboundary or regional MPAs. Cooperation is discussed in greater detail later in Section 3.3.

The CBD is a crucial interpretive tool in this context. Parties must read CBD provisions consistently with UNCLOS,[44] and these provisions inform and strengthen the marine environmental protection obligations in Part XII.[45] Parties have adopted commitments to increase MPA coverage by 10 per cent by 2020 as one of the Aichi Biodiversity Targets,[46] as well as other effective area-based conservation measures.[47] However, while quantitative progress has been made in meeting the 10 per cent target of MPAs, the qualitative aspect, that is, MPAs that are ecologically representative, well connected and equitably managed, has not received adequate

[38] *Request for an Advisory Opinion Submitted by the Sub-Regional Fisheries Commission* (Fisheries Advisory Opinion), Advisory Opinion of 2 April 2016, ITLOS Reports (2015), para. 120; *South China Sea Arbitration* (*Philippines* v. *China*), PCA Award of 12 July 2016, para. 940.

[39] *Southern Bluefin Tuna (New Zealand* v. *Japan; Australia* v. *Japan)*, Provisional Measures Order of 27 August 1999, ITLOS Reports 1999, 280 para. 70; *Chagos Marine Protected Area Arbitration (Mauritius* v. *United Kingdom)*, Award of 18 March 2015, PCA Case No. 2011-03, paras. 320 and 583; *South China Sea Arbitration* (n 38) para. 945.

[40] UNCLOS (n 7), Art. 56.

[41] *Southern Bluefin Tuna* (n 39) para. 96; *Fisheries Advisory Opinion* (n 38) para. 120.

[42] UNCLOS (n 7), Arts. 61.3; 191(1)(a).

[43] Pinsky et al. (n 4) 1190.

[44] CBD (n 9), Arts. 6–10, 22.

[45] *South China Sea Arbitration* (n 38) para. 908.

[46] CBD (n 9), Aichi Biodiversity Targets <www.cbd.int/sp/targets/>.

[47] CBD Decision X/2; Aichi Biodiversity Target 11; CBD (n 9), Art. 8(a) obliges parties to establish a system of protected areas.

attention.[48] Moving forward, the first draft of the Post-2020 Global Biodiversity Framework proposes to increase protection to 30 per cent and contribute to climate change mitigation and adaptation through ecosystem-based solutions.[49]

Obligations under the CBD relating to conservation and sustainable use of biological diversity apply to fisheries, fishing activities and conservation of marine biodiversity. Parties have indicated the necessity for further implementation and improvement of the ecosystem approach to fisheries (EAF).[50] Parties have also committed to achieving Aichi Target 6,[51] which outlines that by 2020 all fish and invertebrate stocks are managed and harvested legally and sustainably, applying ecosystem-based approaches, so that overfishing is avoided, recovery plans and measures are in place for all depleted species, fisheries have no significant adverse impacts on stocks and species and ecosystems are within safe ecological limits.[52]

With this commitment, parties are expected to engage in sustainable management practices framed by the EAF.[53] Logically, this should include adaptive management to species redistribution.

Aichi Target 10 commits to minimising additional multiple anthropogenic pressures on vulnerable marine ecosystems already impacted by climate change to maintain their function and integrity.[54] Implementation of this target can include reduction of overexploitation and harvesting;[55] for example, in response to arrival of new species, fisheries managers in Tasmania introduced 'proactive management policies to limit catch of several new species through the introduction of bag limits for recreational fishers, to allow new fish populations to become established'.[56] While these are helpful components of international legal tools to adapt marine conservation and management to climate change, there are some issues.

[48] B. Erinosho et al., 'Transformative Governance in Ocean Biodiversity' in I. J. Visseren-Hamakers and M. Kok (eds.), *Transforming Biodiversity Governance* (Cambridge: Cambridge University Press, 2021) <https://papers.ssrn.com/sol3/papers.cfm?abstract_id=3853886>; D. Diz et al., 'Mainstreaming Marine Biodiversity into the SDGs: The Role of Other Effective Area-Bases Conservation Measures (SDG14.5)' (2018) 93 *Marine Policy* 251–261; S. Rees et al., 'Defining the Qualitative Elements of Aichi Biodiversity Target 11 with Regard to the Marine and Coastal Environment in Order to Strengthen Global Efforts for Marine Biodiversity Conservation Outlined in the United Nations Sustainable Development Goal 14' (2018) 93 *Marine Policy* 241–250.

[49] CBD, First Draft of the Post-2020 Global Biodiversity Framework, 5 July 2021, CBD/WG2020/3/3 <www.cbd.int/doc/c/abb5/591f/2e46096d3f0330b08ce87a45/wg2020-03-03-en.pdf>.

[50] CBD Decision X/2, CBD Decision XI/18, para. 2; CBD Decision XIII/2.

[51] CBD, *Aichi Target 6: Technical Rationale* <www.cbd.int/sp/targets/rationale/target-6/>.

[52] CBD Decision X/2.

[53] Ibid.

[54] CBD, *Aichi Target 10: Technical Rationale* <www.cbd.int/sp/targets/rationale/target-10/>.

[55] Ibid.

[56] B. R. Scheffers and G. Pecl, 'Persecuting, Protecting or Ignoring Biodiversity under Climate Change' (2019) 9 *Nature Climate Change* 581–586, 582.

The CBD places considerable weight on return to historical conditions and in situ conservation, which could potentially be a barrier to successful adaptive management in response to marine species redistribution. Though inexplicit, the CBD definition of in situ[57] reflects the ecosystem approach (EA),[58] which parties have committed to applying.[59] Article 8 provides an exhaustive 'toolkit of measures to be applied case-by-case to achieve conservation in situ, including inter alia establishing protected areas, rehabilitation of degraded ecosystems and legislation for protection of threatened species.[60] The definition of in situ has yet to be addressed by CBD parties, and it is recommended that a shift in objective is needed to account for climate change consequences in the environment.[61] With this in mind, could 'time-bound', 'temporary' or 'flexible MPAs be an adaptive response? CBD Article 10 on sustainable use of components of biological diversity supports the notion that MPAs with this characteristic could maintain resilient protection of marine species as they shift location. Since in situ reflects the EA, which, depending on local, regional, national or global conditions, integrates differing legal and management strategies,[62] it is by nature an adaptive and anticipatory approach.[63] This considered, MPAs could either be adaptive in the sense that they are not geographically fixed, and can move in response to shifts in distribution, spread across an interconnected 'patchwork' or simply be large enough and spread across management jurisdictions that they can accommodate shifts in marine species.

Like the CBD, another interpretative tool of UNCLOS Part XII is the CMS. The CBD has recognised the CMS as a lead partner in the conservation and sustainable use of migratory species over their entire range.[64] CMS parties are obliged to take necessary steps to conserve migratory species and their habitats.[65] Article III(4) of the CMS arguably covers climate adaptation and mitigation measures through the obligation to 'prevent, reduce or control factors that are endangering or are likely to further endanger'[66] species listed in Appendix I, which includes several species of

57 CBD (n 9), Art. 2
58 P. Birnie et al., *International Law and the Environment*, 3rd ed. (Oxford: Oxford University Press, 2009) 639.
59 CBD Decisions V/6 & VII/11.
60 CBD (n 9), Arts. 8(a), 8(d), 8(f), 8(k).
61 A. Trouwborst, 'Climate Change Adaptation and Biodiversity Law' in J. Verschuuren (ed.) *Research Handbook on Climate Adaptation Law* (Cheltenham: Edward Elgar, 2013) at 298–332; Pinsky et al. (n 4); Erinosho et al. (n 48).
62 CBD Decision V/6; CBD Decision VII/11.
63 E. Morgera, 'Far Away, So Close: A Legal Analysis of the Increasing Interactions between the Convention on Biological Diversity and Climate Change Law' (2011) 2 *Climate Law* 85–115; Erinosho et al. (n 48).
64 CBD Decision VI/20.
65 CMS (n 10), Art. II.
66 CMS (n 10), Art. III(4).

shark and ray.[67] This obligation has been elaborated,[68] including through Resolution 12.21, obliging parties to 'take into account potential social and environmental impacts on migratory species when developing and implementing relevant climate change mitigation and adaptation action'.[69] Parties are invited to interpret Article I(1)(c)(4) on 'favourable conservation status' in light of climate change 'particularly with a view to climate-induced range shifts' and 'action beyond the historic range of species is compatible with, and maybe be required' to meet CMS obligations.[70] This furthers the argument that States have a positive obligation to adapt management and conservation of shifting marine biodiversity. For context, Trouwborst and Blackmore have argued that this is enough to facilitate the necessary climate adaptation measures for large terrestrial carnivores, that is, protected areas, connectivity and dealing with non-climate threats can be achieved through implementation of this obligation.[71] The same can be argued with regard to international legal obligations to adapt conservation and management of marine species in response to climate change.

12.3.2 *UNCLOS Part XII and International Climate Law*

The UN Framework Convention on Climate Change and its subsequent instruments constitute the body of international climate law.[72] UNCLOS obligations for the protection and preservation of the marine environment include atmospheric pollution.[73] Part XII is informed by other applicable rules of international law,[74] and any breaches of 'generally accepted international regulations' are a breach of Part XII.[75] Article 212 on pollution of the ocean from or through the atmosphere, for example, brings the PA 'within the scope of Part XII'.[76] The supportive

[67] CMS (n 10), Appendix I <www.cms.int/sites/default/files/basic_page_documents/appendices_cop13_e_0.pdf>.

[68] CMS Resolution 11.16.

[69] CMS Resolution 12.21, para. 3.

[70] Ibid. para. 9.

[71] A. Trouwborst and A. Blackmore, 'Hot Dogs, Hungry Bears and Wolves Running Out of Mountain: International Wildlife Law and the Effects of Climate Change on Large Carnivores' (2020) 23 *Journal of International Wildlife Law & Policy* 212–238.

[72] D. Bodanksy et al., *International Climate Change Law* (Oxford: Oxford University Press, 2017) 10–11.

[73] M. McCreath, 'Report of the Conference on Climate Change and the Law of the Sea: Adapting the Law of the Sea to Address the Challenges of Climate Change, Centre for International Law, National University of Singapore, 13–14 March 2018' (2018) 33 *The International Journal of Marine and Coastal Law* 836–846; J. Harrison, *Saving the Oceans through Law* (Oxford: Oxford University Press, 2017) 246–274.

[74] *South China Sea Arbitration* (n 38) paras. 945–946.

[75] Ibid. para. 1083.

[76] A. Boyle, 'Climate Change, Ocean Governance and UNCLOS' in J. Barret and R. Barnes (eds.) *Law of the Sea: UNCLOS as a Living Treaty* (London: British Institute of International and Comparative Law, 2016) 211–230, 215; Harrison (n 73), 256; C. Redgwell, 'Treaty Evolution,

interpretation of the two regimes has focused primarily on climate mitigation. The connection with adaption provisions in the climate regime and UNCLOS is not as clear-cut.[77] As before, there is no direct obligation to adapt to changes in the marine environment due to climate change under UNCLOS; however, adaptation is included as a key response in the international climate change regime.[78] While it can be argued that these adaptation provisions do inform the obligations of UNCLOS Part XII, they are, unlike climate mitigation provisions, not target-based in nature.

Article 7 of the PA establishes the global goal on adaptation, enhancing adaptive capacity, strengthening resilience and reducing vulnerability to climate change, and parties have recognised that there is significant need for adaptation.[79] Understandably, the goal is general and does not point to specific targets, or how much or how little adaptation a party should undertake. Parties are obliged to strengthen their cooperation on adaptation enhancement through the Cancún Adaptation Framework, with sharing of information and practices, institutional arrangements, scientific knowledge, assisting developing countries in identifying adaptation practices and improving the effectiveness and durability of adaptation action.[80] Regional cooperation on adaptation is also specified in Article 7(7) of the PA.

Since the PA is universal in scope and applies to the ocean, parties can include adaptation to the effects of the marine environment within their national determined contributions (NDCs) – a set of national targets to inter alia reduce emissions and adapt to the effects of climate change. Some parties have already done this; however, only 33 per cent of NDC adaptation components submitted in early 2021 referred to the ocean, while 39 per cent mentioned fisheries as a specific adaptation sector or priority.[81] This suggests greater effort is needed by States in including marine issues into climate adaptation, let alone species redistribution.

Adaptation and Climate Change: Is the LOSC "Enough" to Address Climate Change Impacts on the Marine Environment?' (2019) 43 *The International Journal of Marine and Coastal Law* 1–18, 10; A. Boyle, 'Law of the Sea Perspectives on Climate Change' (2012) *The International Journal of Marine and Coastal Law* 831–838, 836.

77 R. K. Craig, 'Mitigation and Adaptation' in E. Johansen et al. (ed.), *The Law of the Sea and Climate Change: Solutions and Constraints* (Cambridge: Cambridge University Press, 2021) 49–80; A. Boyle, 'Protecting the Marine Environment from Climate Change' in Johansen et al., 81–103, 84.

78 UNFCCC (n 11), Art. 4(1); Paris Agreement (n 11), Arts. 7–10.

79 Ibid. Art. 7(6).

80 Paris Agreement (n 11), Art. 7(8).

81 *National Determined Contributions under the Paris Agreement* UN Doc. FCCC/PA/CMA/2021/2; M. Lennan, 'Climate change and the oceans: NDC synthesis report suggests greater work to be done to mainstream marine issues into climate adaptation' (2021) <https://oneoceanhub.org/climate-and-the-oceans-ndc-synthesis-report-suggests-more-work-to-be-done-to-mainstream-climate-adaptation-and-oceans/>.

With regard to international fisheries management, recent analysis has shown that decisions by some RFMO/As do consider climate change legal developments, which has increased over time since 2002.[82] However, the majority of these decisions have been focused on learning climate issues, rather than active management decisions in response to climate change.[83] It is clear that adaptive action to climate change is necessary to adequately fulfil the obligation to protect and preserve the marine environment; however, this obligation must be informed at national level by States in their interpretation and application of the adaption provisions of the climate legal regime.

12.3.3 *Cooperation with Relevant States*

International cooperation is vital for effective governance of marine species redistribution. Adaptation-based management must be achieved through increasing international and inter-State cooperation to either maintain or create transboundary agreements on conservation and exploitation of MLRs that may appear in new jurisdictions due to climate change.[84] Cooperation is considered fundamental in fulfilling the obligations of Part XII,[85] and enshrined in terms of conservation and exploitation of MLRs on a global or regional basis, considering regional features and protection of the marine environment in UNCLOS Article 197. Where a coastal State borders an enclosed or semi-enclosed sea, Article 197 is achieved through cooperation directly or through a regional organisation.[86] An example of fulfilling this duty would be through joining and participating in a regional marine environment body such as the Convention for the Protection of the Marine Environment in the North-East Atlantic, which facilitates international cooperation on environmental protection in that area.[87] CBD Article 5 outlines obligations to cooperate for the conservation and sustainable use of biological diversity.[88] Article 10(e) encourages cooperation between government authorities and the private sector in developing

[82] J. Sumby et al., 'Hot Fish: The Response to Climate Change by Regional Fisheries Bodies' (2021) 123 *Marine Policy* 104284.

[83] Ibid.

[84] Scheffers and Pecl (n 56) 584.

[85] *The MOX Plant Case (Ireland* v. *United Kingdom)*, Provisional Measures Order of 3 December 2000, ITLOS Reports 2001, para. 82; *Case Concerning Land Reclamation by Singapore in and around the Straits of Johor (Malaysia* v. *Singapore)*, Provisional Measures, Order of 8 October 2003, ITLOS Reports 2003, para. 92; *Fisheries Advisory Opinion* (n 38) para. 140.

[86] *South China Sea Arbitration* (n 38) paras. 984–986.

[87] Convention for the Protection of the Marine Environment of the North-East Atlantic, Paris, 22 September 1992, in force 25 March 1998, 2354 UNTS 67.

[88] CBD (n 9), Art. 5; *See also* CBD (n 9). Art. 13(b) on cooperation with other States and international organisations in the development of educational and public awareness programmes concerning the conservation and sustainable use of biological diversity.

methods for sustainable use of biodiversity.[89] Parties to the CMS are obliged to cooperate in the conservation of species and habitat of migratory species.[90] As previously, these obligations should be read to support UNCLOS Part XII.

States bear 'both an individual and collective duty to cooperate'[91] in the conservation of MLRs,[92] and in the management, conservation and exploitation of transboundary fish stocks existing in the EEZs of two or more coastal States,[93] and on the High Seas.[94] Importantly, the biological unity of transboundary stocks is considered in their management, requiring cooperation across international and regional scales. Article 8 UNFSA elaborates and institutionalises this duty through establishment or joining of RFMO/As.[95] States are also required to cooperate within these organisations to improve their effectiveness in establishing and implementing CMMs for straddling and HM fish stocks.[96] Some RFMO/As conventions uphold the duty to cooperate,[97] and some have made a conscious effort to cooperate between organisations in response to species redistribution, though active improvement is necessary.[98]

12.3.4 *Use of the Best Available Science*

Scientific research is central to developing and maintaining knowledge and understanding of the marine environment. This is necessary for informing natural resource managers' decisions and solutions. States are obliged under UNCLOS and the UNFSA to use the best science available in managing fish stocks within their jurisdiction,[99] and for transboundary stocks.[100] Molenaar argues that 'a qualified obligation on climate-change adaptation can be derived' from this obligation.[101] In addition, to implement the precautionary principle and the EA, States are obliged to improve the decision-making process for MLR conservation and management by

89 CBD (n 9), Art. 10(e).
90 CMS (n 10), Art. II.
91 R. Rayfuse, 'Regional Fisheries Management Organizations' in D. Rothwell and T. Stephens (eds.), *Oxford Handbook on the Law of the Sea* (Oxford: Oxford University Press, 2017) 439–462, 440.
92 UNCLOS (n 7), Arts. 117–118.
93 Ibid. Arts. 63–4.
94 Ibid. Art. 118; UNFSA (n 8), Art. 8.
95 UNFSA (n 8), Art. 8.
96 Ibid. Art. 13.
97 Convention on the Conservation and Management of High Seas Fisheries Resources in the South Pacific Ocean (SPRFMO) (2009) Art. 3; Convention on the Conservation of Antarctic Marine Living Resources (CCAMLR) (1980), Preamble.
98 R. Rayfuse, 'Addressing Climate Change Impacts in Regional Fisheries Management Organizations', in R. Caddell and E. Molenaar (n 18) 247–268.
99 UNCLOS (n 7), Art. 61(1–2).
100 Ibid. Art. 119(1)(a); UNFSA (n 8), Art. 5(b).
101 E. J. Molenaar, 'Integrating Climate Change in International Fisheries Law', in Johansen (n 77) 263–288, 271.

obtaining and sharing the best available scientific information, as well as improving and implementing techniques dealing with risks and uncertainty.[102] States must also determine stock-specific reference points based on the best science available and action to be taken when exceeded.[103] Emergency measures too must be based on the best available science.[104] UNFSA and RFMO/A conventions contain obligations to promote cooperation in utilisation of the best science.[105] The CMS also obliges States to use the best scientific evidence available to indicate that a migratory species is endangered.[106]

12.3.5 *Interim Conclusions*

This section sought to outline the relevant international legal obligations to address the question of whether the international legal framework is fit for purpose in fostering adaptation by States to the complexities caused by fish and other marine species shifting their location across management jurisdictions. The author is inclined to answer in the affirmative, considering that there are no barriers on States in the framework that prevent or discourage adaptation in this context. However, the lengths that States go to in implementing adaptation measures is dependent on their interpretation and application of the relevant provisions in international climate law, and how these are applied to the marine environment. Adaptation measures must be informed by use of the best scientific evidence available, and of course cooperation between relevant States as MLRs shift across management boundaries. As such, the framework is adequate, but the efficacy of the framework to facilitate adaptation, and maintain the rule of law, depends on implementation of the obligations outlined in this section. The final section explores solutions that may aid in this.

12.4 ADAPTIVE RESPONSES TO FISHERIES REDISTRIBUTION: STRENGTHENING SOLUTIONS

Having attested to the adequacy of the international legal framework to facilitate adaptation to fisheries shifting distribution under climate change, this section briefly outlines two potential solutions that reflect the urgency of the need to adapt, and could help further strengthen the rule of law in this area.

The first involves exploiting the potential of the precautionary principle and EAF in implementing the obligations outlined earlier. The precautionary principle in combination with the obligation to cooperate could help in pushing States to agree pre-emptively to ensuring bi- or multi-lateral fisheries agreements for a stock that

[102] UNFSA (n 8), Art. 6.3(a).
[103] Ibid. Art. 6.3(b).
[104] Ibid. Art. 6.7.
[105] Ibid. Art. 14; CCAMLR (n 97), Art. 15; SPRFMO (n 97), Art. 3.
[106] CMS (n 10), Art. 3.

may become transboundary. This could prevent conflicts arising when a fish stock shifts primarily into the jurisdiction of one State, which might be inclined to exploit that stock unilaterally.[107] Considering the EAF, which is widely accepted and called for in various international instruments,[108] aims to apply a holistic approach and account for ecosystem structure and function, and considers transboundary species and ecosystems,[109] is an important feature in addressing the problem of climate driven shifts. However, since depletion of some and arrival of new species due to climate change creates novel ecosystems, this complicates application of the EAF. In order to address this, guidelines on the application and implementation of the EAF should be revisited in light of climate change.[110]

The second taps into the role of the Food and Agriculture Organization of the United Nations (FAO) and its role in developing the international legal framework for fisheries and the marine environment. The FAO has developed a plethora of scientific and technical documents on the impacts of climate change and fisheries,[111] as well as on the EAF,[112] and also provides technical assistance to RFMO/As. The FAO Committee on Fisheries (COFI) recommended its members to strengthen efforts to assess change in distribution of fish species in response to climate change.[113] The FAO has adopted many legally binding and non-legally binding instruments that aid various fisheries and marine environmental obligations. COFI has requested development of guidelines that focus on climate change impacts on fisheries in recent years.[114] These could perhaps aid in developing the EAF vis-à-vis climate change, facilitate cooperative management both bilaterally and within an RFMO/A context, and as such would be incredibly valuable in assisting States in implementing their obligations to adapt fisheries management in response to climate change.

To conclude, the international legal framework can facilitate adaptation to marine species redistribution under climate change, and can be described as adequate at best, and not a barrier at worst. There is a greater need for States and legal researchers to engage with the jurisdictional and managerial problems created by the redistribution of fisheries and other marine species. In terms of state practice,

[107] See text after n 21; Østhagen (n 22); Spijkers (n 23).
[108] CBD, Decision V/6.
[109] FAO, 'The Ecosystem Approach to Fisheries' *FAO Fisheries Technical Paper* 443 (2003).
[110] CBD Decision X/2; CBD Decision XI/18, para. 2.
[111] FAO, 'Climate Change Implications for FISHEries and Aquaculture: Overview of Current Scientific Knowledge' *FAO Fisheries and Aquaculture Technical Paper* 530 (2009); FAO, 'Impacts of Climate Change on Fisheries and Aquaculture' *FAO Fisheries and Aquaculture Technical Paper* 627 (2018).
[112] FAO (n 109).
[113] Report of the 29th Session of FAO Committee on Fisheries (2011), para. 40a.
[114] Report of the 32nd (2016) COFI Session, paras. 16 and 114; Report of the 33rd COFI Session (2018), para. 101; See also Molenaar (n 101) 274.

a regional approach and cooperation through appropriate regional bodies such as RFMO/As and FAO is vital for effective adaptive management. Further, these regional bodies must enable adaptive management through inter-institutional cooperation, and engagement with research. In terms of research, the need is for greater multi- or cross-disciplinary research exploring the role of dynamic management of marine biodiversity while ensuring the law applicable to it is still robust enough to provide safeguards for marine species conservation facing climate impacts.

13

Defining Marine Genetic Resources

Navigating through the Sea of Uncertainties

Jakub Ciesielczuk

13.1 INTRODUCTION

Recent technological advances have provided scientists with more opportunities to explore the richness of marine life.[1] One particular element of marine biodiversity that has sparked interest within scientific circles is the utilisation of marine genetic resources (MGRs).[2] While international law and literature lack a universal definition of MGRs, there is growing interest among States in MGRs, which can be depicted by the ongoing negotiations on an international legally binding instrument on the conservation and sustainable use of marine biological diversity of areas beyond national jurisdiction (BBNJ) under the auspices of the 1982 United Nations Convention on the Law of the Sea (UNCLOS).[3] It is pivotal to examine the implications of divergences in meanings of MGRs, as a universal definition of that term might also be of potential importance to several existing regimes.[4]

Understanding the elements of the definition of MGRs and its scope is a way forward to better protecting marine biodiversity, as managing MGRs without full

I wish to thank Professor Elizabeth A. Kirk for the very useful comments on earlier drafts.

1 J. Mark Cock and others, 'Marine Genomics and the Exploration of Marine Biodiversity', in Carlos M. Duarte (ed.), *The Exploration of Marine Biodiversity: Scientific and Technological Challenges* (Bilbao: Fundación BBVA, 2006), 117–139.

2 David Leary and others, 'Marine Genetic Resources: A Review of Scientific and Commercial Interest' (2009) 33 *Marine Policy* 183–194, at 184–188.

3 United Nations Convention on the Law of the Sea (UNCLOS), Montego Bay, 10 December 1982, in force 16 November 1994, 1833 UNTS 397; see also, Intergovernmental Conference on marine biological diversity of areas beyond national jurisdiction available at: www.un.org/bbnj/ (last accessed 27 February 2020).

4 See e.g., Convention on Biological Diversity, Rio de Janeiro, 22 May 1992, in force 29 December 1993, 1760 UNTS 69; Convention on International Trade in Endangered Species of Wild Fauna and Flora, Washington, 3 March 1973, in force 1 July 1975, 993 UNTS 243.

comprehension of their nature is challenging. A compass in the form of a working definition of MGRs will help navigate the sea of uncertainties and strengthen the rule of law. At its most basic level, the rule of law means that no one is above the law; in other words, all individuals are subject to the law.[5] In the international arena, the rule of law supports the argument that parties to multilateral environmental treaty regimes need to act in a manner that renders application of their legal provisions equally among them. In order to achieve that, some key values of the rule of law should be taken into consideration while drafting texts of treaty regimes. It is evident from the literature that rule of law values include, but are not limited to, predictability, clarity, certainty, coherence and stability.[6] In the context of this chapter, the rule of law is understood as ensuring legal clarity and legal certainty in environmental regimes regulating to MGRs. Definitions that provide legal clarity and legal certainty and are interpreted in 'good faith in accordance with the ordinary meaning' in line with the 1969 Vienna Convention on the Law of Treaties (VCLT) ensure that parties within treaty regimes can predict their obligations and rights according to the provisions embedded in the text of those regimes.[7] Providing a clear, working definition of MGRs will help with a universal understanding of MGRs across existing and future MGR-related regimes and relationships between rules included in those regimes.

The chapter is divided into five sections and begins with a brief review of the role of the definition of genetic resources in defining MGRs, before moving on to a review of the material scope (i.e., the nature of MGRs) of the definition of MGRs. The following section discusses the geographical scope (i.e., areas in which MGRs are found) of the definition of MGRs. The last section provides a working definition of the term 'MGRs' and the future outlook.

13.2 STARTING POINT: GENETIC RESOURCES

Neither law nor literature provides a definition of the term 'MGRs'. What might appear surprising to some is that the UNCLOS, which has often been referred to as 'a constitution for the oceans' does not define MGRs. However, a consensus exists among scholars that Article 2 of the Convention on Biological Diversity (CBD), which defines genetic resources, should be a starting point in defining what

5 Albert Venn Dicey, *Introduction to the Study of the Law of the Constitution* (5th ed., London: MacMillan, 1897) [1885], 42.

6 See e.g., Lon Fuller, *Morality of Law*, rev. ed. (New Haven, CT: Yale University Press, 1969), 39; Friedrich A. Hayek, *Constitution of Liberty* (Chicago: University of Chicago Press, 1960), 156.

7 Vienna Convention on the Law of Treaties, Vienna, 23 May 1969, in force 27 January 1980, 1155 UNTS 331; (1969) 8 ILM 679; UKTS (1980) 58, Arts. 31 and 32.

constitutes MGRs.[8] States' delegations in the ongoing BBNJ negotiations also agree that the definition of MGRs in the future treaty should be built on Article 2 of the CBD.[9]

Under the CBD, genetic resources are defined as 'genetic material of actual or potential value', in which 'genetic material' contains 'any material of plant, animal, microbial or other origin containing functional units of heredity'.[10] The term 'genetic resources' was not commonly used as a legal concept prior to adoption of the CBD.[11] However, after its inclusion in the operative text of that regime, the term has been invoked in a few international treaties, debates, negotiations and documents.[12]

It should be stressed that the CBD is one of the most widely ratified treaties in international law (i.e., as of 2022, the CBD has 196 members and 168 signatories). The work of its Committee of Parties and subsidiary bodies has contributed significantly to the understanding of marine biodiversity.[13] However, the definition of genetic resources included in Article 2 of the CBD raises some concerns about its legal clarity and legal certainty as the elements of that definition are not explained in the text of the CBD.[14] Thus various actors might act in different ways in response to an ambiguous law, which hinders the normative effect of the law. For example,

8 See e.g., Konrad J. Marciniak, 'Marine Genetic Resources: Do They Form Part of the Common Heritage of Mankind Principle?', in Lawrence Martin and others (eds.), *Natural Resources and the Law of the Sea: Exploration, Allocation, Exploitation of Natural Resources in Areas under National Jurisdiction and Beyond* (Juris Publishing, 2017), 374; Gaute Voight-Hanssen, 'Current Light and Heavy Options for Benefit-Sharing in the Context of the United Nations Convention on the Law of the Sea' (2018) 33 *The International Journal of Marine and Coastal Law* 683–705, 685; Rabone Muriel and others, 'Access to Marine Genetic Resources (MGR): Raising Awareness of Best-Practice through a New Agreement for Biodiversity beyond National Jurisdiction (BBNJ)' (2019) 6 *Frontiers in Marine Science*, 3.

9 See, Revised draft text of an agreement under the United Nations Convention on the Law of the Sea on the conservation and sustainable use of marine biological diversity of areas beyond national jurisdiction (27 November 2019).

10 Art. 2 Convention on Biological Diversity Home | Convention on Biological Diversity (cbd.int).

11 Fridtjof Nansen Institute, 'The Concept of "Genetic Resources" in the Convention on Biological Diversity and How It Relates to a Functional International Regime on Access and Benefit-Sharing' UNEP/CBD/WG-ABS/9/INF/1 (19 March 2010), 6.

12 See e.g., the work of the Intergovernmental Commission on Genetic Resources, Traditional Knowledge and Folklore, available at www.wipo.int/tk/en/igc/ (last accessed 27 February 2020); Draft Decision to enhance mutual supportiveness between the TRIPS Agreement and the Convention on Biological Diversity, TN/C/W/59 (19 April 2011); International Treaty on plant genetic resources for food and agriculture, Rome, 3 November 2001, in force 29 June 2004, 2400 UNTS 303.

13 See e.g., the 'Jakarta Mandate' agreed to by the Parties to the Convention on Biological Diversity at their Second Conference in Jakarta in November 1995. UNEP/CBD/COP/2/19 (30 November 1995).

14 Morten Walløe Tvedt and Tomme Young, Beyond Access: Exploring Implementation of the Fair and Equitable Sharing Commitment in the CBD ABS, ABS Series No. 2, IUCN Environmental Policy and Law Paper No. 67/2 (2007), 54.

there may be confusion regarding the access and benefit sharing (ABS) provisions embedded in the CBD. Users (e.g., industry researchers including agriculture, cosmetic and pharmaceutical industries, or research institutes) and providers (i.e., States with sovereign rights over natural resources under their jurisdiction) of natural resources might have different interpretations of elements of the definition of genetic resources, which are not clearly elaborated.

The drafting history of the CBD does not provide further clarification of the definition of genetic resources provided by Article 2 of the CBD.[15] Against this backdrop, it is necessary to untangle elements of definitions included in Article 2 of the CBD. While some terms used in the definition of genetic resources in Article 2 of the CBD are self-explanatory, that is, plant (e.g., floating and rooted plants), animal (e.g., mammals, birds, fish, reptiles, amphibians), microbial (e.g., bacteria, yeasts) or other origin (e.g., fungi), other terms need further elaboration.[16] Three separate elements that should be analysed are; 'functional units of heredity', 'of actual or potential value' and 'material'.[17] Examining these building blocks of the definition of genetic resources is worthwhile, as they have significant implications on defining MGRs. All three terms are discussed in the next section under the material scope of the definition of MGRs.

13.3 MATERIAL SCOPE

13.3.1 *'Material'*

The CBD does not define the term 'material'. According to its ordinary meaning, the term 'material' should be defined as something physical or tangible (i.e., samples which physically contain genetic material).[18] The question then becomes: should digital sequence information (DSI) be included within the MGR definition?

Consensus among experts is lacking on whether the definition of genetic resources under Article 2 of the CBD includes DSI. For example, the Commission on Intellectual Property of the International Chamber of Commerce argues that 'material' within the definition of 'genetic resources' refers to tangible or

[15] Lyle Glowka, Françoise Burhenne-Guilmin and Hugh Synge in collaboration with Jeffrey A. McNeely and Lothar Gündling, A Guide to the Convention on Biological Diversity (1994) Environmental Policy and Law Paper No. 30, IUCN-ELC.

[16] Tvedt and Young (n 14), 53–57.

[17] Ibid.; see also, Peter Johan Schei and Morten Walløe Tvedt, 'Genetic Resources' in the CBD. The Wording, the Past, the Present and the Future, Fridtjof Nansen Institute Report 4/2010 (n 11).

[18] See e.g., Tade M. Spranger, Expert opinion on the applicability of the Convention on Biological Diversity and the Nagoya Protocol to digital sequence information, submitted on behalf of the German Federal Ministry of Education and Research, Berlin 2017, at 16; International Chamber of Commerce (ICC) Commission on Intellectual Property, Report on Digital Sequence Information, 2017, 1 ICC Commission on Intellectual Property, Report on Digital Sequence Information, 2017, available at https://iccwbo.org/content/uploads/sites/3/2017/05/ICC-IP-position-paper-on-digital-sequence-information.pdf (last accessed 30 November 2021).

physical material, and given that DSI is intangible by nature it is not covered by that definition.[19] The Global Genome Biodiversity Network points out 'the CBD and Nagoya Protocol explicitly cover genetic material, not information about this material'.[20] Others claim DSI comes under the scope of the definition of genetic resources and point to the words 'or other origin' and 'value' in Article 2 of the CBD.[21] Further, parties to the CBD and 2010 Nagoya Protocol on Access to Genetic Resources and the Fair and Equitable Sharing of Benefits Arising from their Utilization to the Convention on Biological Diversity (Nagoya Protocol) also appear to disagree as to whether DSI comes under the scope of these instruments.[22] The challenges of defining what exactly constitutes DSI go beyond the regimes on biodiversity, as indicated by similar discussions within various other UN processes and such regimes as the 2001 International Treaty on Plant Genetic Resources for Food and Agriculture (ITPGRFA), the Pandemic Influenza Preparedness Framework and the BBNJ negotiations.[23]

Most policy processes that have addressed DSI have struggled to provide a clear definition and scope of the term.[24] DSI is a placeholder term, which lacks a globally accepted definition.[25] The Ad Hoc Technical Expert Group (AHTEG) report on Digital Sequence Information on Genetic Resources, established under the CBD

[19] ICC, Report on Digital Sequence Information, 1, available at https://iccwbo.org/content/uploads/sites/3/2017/05/ICC-IP-position-paper-on-digital-sequence-information.pdf (last accessed 30 November 2021).

[20] Global Genome Biodiversity Network, Letter to the CBD on Digital Sequence Information (7 September 2017), 1, available at www.cbd.int/abs/DSI-views/GGBN-DSI.pdf (last accessed 30 November 2021).

[21] See e.g., India's submission on Digital Sequence Information on Genetic Resources in response to CBD notification 2019-012 dated 5 February 2019 pursuant to decisions 14/20 and NP-3/12, available at www.cbd.int/abs/DSI-views/2019/India-DSI.pdf (last accessed 30 November 2021).

[22] See Submissions of views and information on Digital Sequence Information on Genetic Resources on Digital Sequence Information on Genetic Resources in response to CBD notification 2019-012 dated 5 February 2019 pursuant to decisions 14/20 and NP-3/12, available at www.cbd.int/dsi-gr/2019-2020/submissions/ (last accessed 28 February 2020). See e.g., contrasting views expressed by submissions of India and Switzerland.

[23] Elisa Morgera, 'Fair and Equitable Benefit-Sharing in a New Treaty on Marine Biodiversity: A Principled Approach towards Partnership Building?' (2018) 7 *Maritime Safety and Security Law Journal* 48–77 at 60, 66, available at Morgera_MSSLJ_2018_Fair_and_equitable_benefit_sharing_in_a_new_treaty_on_marine.pdf (strath.ac.uk); International Treaty on plant genetic resources for food and agriculture, Rome, 3 November 2001, in force 29 June 2004, 2400 UNTS 303.

[24] Ad Hoc Technical Expert Group on Digital Sequence Information on Genetic Resources, 'Report of the Ad Hoc Technical Expert Group on Digital Sequence Information on Genetic Resources' CBD/DSI/AHTEG/2020/1/7 (20 March 2020), 66.

[25] Ad Hoc Technical Expert Group on Digital Sequence Information on Genetic Resources, 'Digital Sequence Information on Genetic Resources: Concept, Scope and Current Use' CBD/DSI/AHTEG/2020/1/3 (29 January 2020), 10.

and its Nagoya Protocol, provides a list of potential forms of DSI.[26] For example, these could include: 'the nucleic acid sequence reads', 'amino acid sequences' or 'cellular metabolites'.[27]

Analysis of ongoing policy processes on DSI (i.e., the ITPGRFA, the CBD and Nagoya Protocol) demonstrates the existence of a growing practice of relying on DSI in bio-based research, and DSI has 'potential for generating high-value products, and thus monetary and non-monetary benefits, with the increasing use of synthetic biology technologies in the future'.[28] On the other hand, it is difficult to identify the provenance of DSI and assess its value and contributions.[29] There is also a growing concern that few countries worldwide have the capacity and funds to maintain databases of DSI and derive benefits from it.[30] Consequently, the potential exclusion of DSI from the definition of MGRs could trigger inequalities in the form of biotechnology companies profiting from DSI without sharing benefits with less developed States, which have reduced technological capacity.[31]

Given the far-reaching implications of DSI for the ABS framework in the future BBNJ treaty, and the growing reliance on DSI in bio-based research and its potential in developing new products, DSI should be captured by the working definition of MGRs. However, the precise scope and definition of that term require further research.

13.3.2 *'Functional Units of Heredity'*

The term 'functional units of heredity' can be perceived as a qualifying element of the definition of 'genetic material'. Unfortunately, no explanation of that term can

26 Ad Hoc Technical Expert Group on Digital Sequence Information on Genetic Resources, 'Report of the Ad Hoc Technical Expert Group on Digital Sequence Information on Genetic Resources' 9.

27 Ibid., 9; see also Jakub Ciesielczuk and Elizabeth A. Kirk, 'Sustainable Use of Marine Genetic Resources', in W. Leal Filho, A. M. Azul, L. Brandli, A. Lange Salvia and T. Wall (eds.), *Life below Water. Encyclopedia of the UN Sustainable Development Goals* (Cham: Springer 2021) 4–5.

28 Eric W. Welch, Margo Bagley, Todd Kuiken and Sélim Louafi, 'Potential Implications of New Synthetic Biology and Genomic Research Trajectories on the International Treaty for Plant Genetic Resources for Food and Agriculture' (2017) FAO, vi.

29 Ad Hoc Technical Expert Group on Digital Sequence Information on Genetic Resources, 'Fact-Finding and Scoping Study on Digital Sequence Information on Genetic Resources in the Context of the Convention on Biological Diversity and the Nagoya Protocol' CBD/DSI/AHTEG/2018/1/3 (12 January 2018), 14.

30 Ad Hoc Technical Expert Group on Digital Sequence Information on Genetic Resources, 'Synthesis of views and information on the potential implications of the use of digital sequence information on genetic resources for the three objectives of the Convention and the objective of the Nagoya Protocol' CBD/DSI/AHTEG/2018/1/2 (9 January 2018), 13; Welch, 'Potential Implications' (n 29).

31 See e.g., Ad Hoc Technical Expert Group on Digital Sequence Information on Genetic Resources, 'Fact-Finding and Scoping Study', 46.

be found in the CBD wording. The ordinary meaning of this term does not provide any guidance either. Some genetic resources experts posit that the term 'functional units of heredity' was selected by policymakers, rather than geneticists.[32] In effect, this term is not purely scientific and can be viewed from two different perspectives, namely political and technical. Scientists interpret 'functional units of heredity' as genes or deoxyribonucleic acid (DNA) and ribonucleic acid (RNA).[33] While relying on the wording of the CBD in the context of the definition of MGRs is desirable, rethinking the terms invoked to construct that definition could be considered. The usage of the term 'functional units of heredity' in the text of the CBD epitomises the issue of relying on technical terminology in legal instruments. The interpretation of such a problematic term, which may affect implementation of the regime, relies on the audience. For example, national, non-technical bodies tasked with implementing the regime may interpret terms differently than technical bodies. Substituting the term 'functional units of heredity' with 'DNA' or 'RNA' could potentially clarify the definition of MGRs. However, a more thorough understanding of such a substitution and its implications would be required, from both the scientific and legal perspectives. Although such inquiry falls outside the scope of this chapter, it provides potential for further research.

From the political perspective, the lack of clarity around the term 'functional units of heredity' within the definition of genetic resources provides the opportunity for wide interpretations contingent on national interests.[34] Legal clarity and legal certainty of definitions in treaty regimes are often subject to political disagreement. This can be depicted by the ongoing BBNJ negotiations, which include a debate on whether derivatives should come under the scope of the definition of MGRs.[35]

A derivative can be understood in at least two ways: as a naturally occurring biochemical compound or as a chemical compound synthesised through human intervention.[36] The former could be labelled as unmodified chemical compounds, other than DNA or RNA, resulting from metabolic processes of genetic resources, such as aromas, resins and snake venoms.[37] From that perspective, derivatives might be studied, and scientific research of them might lead to development of products. The latter could be regarded as DNA or RNA, or a chemical compound, modified

[32] Tvedt and Young (n 15), 53.

[33] See e.g., Bevis Fedder, *Marine Genetic Resources, Access and Benefit Sharing: Legal and Biological Perspectives* (London: Routledge, 2013) 36.

[34] Jonas Ebbesson, 'The Rule of Law in Governance of Complex Socio-Ecological Changes' *Global Environmental Change* (2010) 20 (3), 414–422, 415.

[35] Arts. 2 and 8 of the Revised draft 2019 (n 10).

[36] Lyle Glowka, A Guide to Designing Legal Frameworks to Determine Access to Genetic Resources (1998) IUCN, Environmental Policy and Law Paper No. 34, 35.

[37] Thomas Greiber, An Explanatory Guide to the Nagoya Protocol on Access and Benefit-sharing (2012) IUCN Environmental Policy and Law Paper No. 83, 65.

or synthesised via human intervention from genetic resources. Examples might include a breeder's hybrid seed or a synthetic version of an extracted biochemical.[38]

A derivative is defined by Article 2 of the Nagoya Protocol as a 'naturally occurring biochemical compound resulting from the genetic expression or metabolism of biological or genetic resources, even if it does not contain functional units of heredity'. This definition clearly reflects the first type of derivatives discussed. The second type of derivatives, alongside a myriad of other interpretations, was excluded from the definition included in Article 2 of the Nagoya Protocol.[39] It can be noticed that the definition of derivatives under Article 2 of the Nagoya Protocol does not require derivatives to contain 'functional units of heredity' as stipulated by Article 2 of the CBD. However, it is understood that as long as derivatives possess genetic material (i.e., smaller than DNA or RNA) that can be utilised and is of actual or potential value, they come under the definition of MGRs.[40]

Derivatives within the meaning of Article 2 of the Nagoya Protocol are included in the working definition of MGRs offered by this chapter, as there appears to be no scientific basis for their exclusion.[41] The literature supports the conclusion that the second type of discussed derivatives should be excluded from the scope of the definition of MGRs.[42]

13.3.3 *'Of Actual or Potential Value'*

Another building block of the definition of genetic resources is the term 'of actual or potential value'. As with 'material' and 'functional units of heredity' the CBD is silent on what is meant by 'of actual or potential value'. However, it is evident from the definitions provided by Article 2 of the CBD that genetic resources are a subset of genetic material.[43] Consequently, what turns genetic material into genetic

38 Glowka, 'A Guide to Designing Legal Frameworks' (n 36), 35.

39 Ad Hoc Open-Ended Working Group on Access and Benefit Sharing, Report of the Meeting of the Group of Legal and Technical Experts on Concepts, Terms, Working definitions and Sectoral Approaches, UNEP/CBD/WG-ABS/7/2 (12 December 2008), 9.

40 Ad Hoc Technical Expert Group on Digital Sequence Information on Genetic Resources, 'Digital Sequence Information' (n 25), 12.

41 See e.g., Rabone (n 8), 'Raising Awareness of Best-Practice'.

42 Harriet Harden-Davies, 'Deep-Sea Genetic Resources: New Frontiers for Science and Stewardship in Areas beyond National Jurisdiction' (2017) 137 *Deep-Sea Research Part 2: Topical Studies in Oceanography* 504–513, 506; Jeffrey J. Marlow and others, 'The Full Value of Marine Genetic Resources (MGR)' (2019) *Deep Ocean Stewardship Initiative Policy Brief*, 3.

43 Lyle Glowka, Françoise Burhenne-Guilmin, Hugh Synge, Jeffrey A. McNeely, Lothar Gündling, 'A Guide to the Convention on Biological Diversity' International Union for Conservation of Nature, IUCN 1994, 22; Fridtjof Nansen Institute, 'The Concept of "Genetic Resources"' (n 11), 13.

resources is actual or potential value. This value must be linked to the inherited genetic components of a species.[44]

The decision to incorporate the words 'actual' and 'potential' in determining the value of genetic resources could be interpreted as a reflection of current and future scientific knowledge and technological advancement.[45] The word 'actual might refer to the value of genetic resources that can be determined using techniques and knowledge currently available. The word 'potential' might relate to the future value of genetic resources, which could be determined alongside available technological and genetic developments.[46] A simple scenario illustrates the practical application of this interpretation: marine species collected from the ocean in 2021 may be stored in a research centre for 50 years and may only be of 'actual' value after analysis using new technology not available at time of collection.

That scenario raises questions concerning the length of time a species is considered to have 'potential value' and how its genetic material is identified as being potentially valuable. The problem with the word 'potential' lies in the argument that all genetic material could be categorised as of 'potential' value, unless proven otherwise.[47] Use of the word 'potential' in the context of the definition of MGRs raises concerns regarding legal clarity and legal certainty. Where can one draw a clear line on what types of genetic material should be regarded as of 'potential' value? While the word 'potential' may be praised for rendering the definition of genetic resources dynamic and allowing it to keep abreast of rapid scientific and technological developments, its legal utility is questionable. Definitions of genetic resources and genetic material read in conjunction indicate that it would be possible at the time of collection of marine species to distinguish between biological resources and genetic resources relying on its actual or potential value for its functional units of heredity. However, it is simply not the case, as normally, the value of collected material can only be determined via the research process in labs.[48] On many occasions, material that is considered to be of potential value might turn out not to be of use for its genetic characteristics.[49] The opposite might also be possible; units of heredity previously labelled as junk (i.e., '*junk-DNA*') might at some future point be considered of value.[50] However, given that science advances much faster than law, and the law should reflect those advances, the word 'potential' is kept in the working definition of MGRs.

44 Tvedt and Young (n 14), at 55.
45 Fridtjof Nansen Institute, 'The Concept of "Genetic Resources"' (n 11), 8.
46 Ibid.
47 Glowka et al., 'A Guide to the Convention on Biological Diversity' (n 15) 22; Fridtjof Nansen Institute, 'The Concept of "Genetic Resources"' (n 11), 13.
48 Ad Hoc Technical Expert Group on Digital Sequence Information on Genetic Resources, 'Digital Sequence Information' (n 25), 12.
49 Fridtjof Nansen Institute, 'The Concept of "Genetic Resources"' (n 11), 9.
50 Ibid., 10.

Another point to consider linked with the concept of actual or potential value is the nature of utilisation. Actual or potential value within the context of Article 2 of the CBD comes to light when the genetic material of biological resources is utilised in a manner that takes advantage of the genetic characteristics viz., functional units of heredity.[51] That is supported by the definition of utilisation of genetic resources under Article 2 of the Nagoya Protocol that refers solely to conducting research and development based on genetic and/or biochemical material from genetic resources. Utilisation of genetic resources as a commodity is not included within that definition.[52]An example will be used to illustrate that distinction better. Commercial fishing designed to obtain large quantities of fish to sell as food, although constituting utilisation of biological resources found in the marine environment, should not be regarded as utilisation of MGRs. On the other hand, synthesising a DNA sample from a fish found in the marine environment and using it for research designed to develop a new drug falls under utilisation of MGRs.

While it is generally accepted that utilisation of biological resources in bulk and as commodities lies outside the scope of definitions provided by Article 2 of the CBD, the line between utilisation of resources for their genetic properties and more conventional purposes is often blurred.[53] The ideal scenario where commercial fishing expeditions and researchers are always working separately and do not impact each other might not be the case. In reality, some scientists might be tempted to use resources that were not specifically collected for their genetic material. Nothing stops researchers from acquiring marine resources from commercial fishing companies or even shops and then utilising them for their genetic material. In that scenario, marine resources were harvested to sell them, for which they should be considered a commodity, but were then utilised for their genetic properties. Exclusion of these resources from the scope of the definition of MGR would create a loophole, permitting unfair use of MGRs. A possible way forward to remedy that issue is to focus on the point of access of MGRs rather than the point of collection in determining the nature and purpose of utilisation.[54] 'Point of access' is understood as a moment when marine resources are utilised in relation to their genetic characteristics. In the definition of MGRs offered by this chapter, it is encapsulated in the phrase 'accessed for'.

[51] Biological resources are defined by Art. 2 CBD as containing 'genetic resources, organisms or parts thereof, populations, or any other biotic component of ecosystems with actual or potential use or value for humanity'.

[52] See also Art. 2 of International treaty on plant genetic resources for food and agriculture (n 23).

[53] Fridtjof Nansen Institute, 'The Concept of "Genetic Resources"' (n 11), 13.

[54] IUCN Comments on International legally binding instrument under the United Nations Convention on the Law of the Sea on the conservation and sustainable use of marine biological diversity of areas beyond national jurisdiction (15 August 2019), at 13, available at www.iucn.org/sites/dev/files/iucn_comments_on_bbnj_draft_text_-_august_2019_1.pdf (last accessed 30 November 2021).

Further, to underline the distinction between utilisation of marine resources for their genetic properties and as a commodity, the phrase 'of actual or potential value' should be linked with the term 'genetic material' in the context of drafting a working definition of MGRs. Thus, within the proposed definition, it is phrased as 'actual or potential value of their genetic material'.

13.4 GEOGRAPHICAL SCOPE

Defining the term 'marine' and establishing the limits of the area covered by that term is a prerequisite for drafting a working definition of MGRs. The word 'marine' has common definitions. The Cambridge Dictionary defines the word marine as 'related to the sea or sea transport',[55] whereas the Léxico Dictionary defines it as 'relating to or found in the sea'.[56] Both definitions are similar in that they point towards the correlation between the word marine and sea.

While the UNCLOS does not define the term 'marine', protection and preservation of the marine environment are one of the main aims of that regime.[57] As a legal treaty that has codified pre-existing customary international law on the law of the sea, the UNCLOS had been drafted to regulate seas and oceans.[58] Thus, in the context of the UNCLOS, the word 'marine' extends to oceans as well. The term 'marine' can be found in the substantive texts of the Antarctic treaty and the Convention on the Conservation of Antarctic Marine Living Resources,[59] where it also should be interpreted as referring to the oceans. In addition, the word 'marine' refers to the seas within the texts of many regional sea conventions.[60] Thus, contingent on the geographical scope of the legal instrument the word 'marine' might denote seas and/or oceans. Combining this conclusion with the definition of the word 'marine' provided by the Léxico Dictionary (i.e., 'relating to or found in the

55 Cambridge Dictionary, available at https://dictionary.cambridge.org/dictionary/english/marine (last accessed 28 February 2020).

56 Léxico Dictionary, available at https://en.oxforddictionaries.com/definition/marine (last accessed 28 February 2020).

57 Para. 4 Preamble to the United Nations Convention on the Law of the Sea, available at www.un.org/depts/los/convention_agreements/texts/unclos/closindx.htm (last accessed 30 November 2021).

58 Paras. 1, 4 Preamble to the United Nations Convention on the Law of the Sea, available at www.un.org/depts/los/convention_agreements/texts/unclos/closindx.htm (last accessed 30 November 2021); see also Joanna Mossop, 'Can We Make the Oceans Greener: The Successes and Failures of UNCLOS as an Environmental Treaty' (2018) 49 *Victoria University of Wellington Law Review* 573, 575–578.

59 Convention on the Conservation of Antarctic Marine Living Resources, Canberra, 20 May 1980, in force 4 April 1982, 1329 UNTS 47, Art. 1.

60 See e.g., Convention for the Protection of the Marine Environment and the Coastal Region of the Mediterranean, Barcelona, 10 June 1995, in force 09 July 2004, 1102 UNTS 27, Art. 4; Convention on the Protection of the Marine Environment of the Baltic Sea Area, Helsinki, 09 April 1992, in force 17 January 2000, 2009 UNTS 197, Art. 1; Convention for the Protection of the Marine Environment of the North-East Atlantic, Paris, 22 September 1992, in force 25 March 1998, 2354 UNTS 67, Art. 1.

sea') offers the following working definition 'found in or originating from sea or ocean'.

However, a few potential issues arise with the proposed definition. First, the status of anadromous species (e.g., salmon), catadromous species (e.g., eel) and certain species of marine birds might be difficult to determine under the scope of the proposed working definition of the term 'marine'.[61] Given that those species do not spend their whole life in the seas and oceans, the question arises of whether they should be regarded as MGRs. Another issue to consider is the status of living organisms found on, in or under the subsoil of the seas or ocean; should those be regarded as MGRs?

Although these issues are legal (i.e., separate legal regimes, marine zones) from the scientific point of view, all these species could most likely be categorised as MGRs, as they are found in marine environments. While these issues constitute potential for further research, they are beyond the scope of this chapter. It appears that it is not possible at this time to determine the precise limits of the term 'marine' for the working legal definition of MGRs. Thus, the broad definition of 'marine' is adopted, namely 'found in or originating from sea or ocean'.

13.5 CONCLUSION AND OUTLOOK

The chapter arrives at the following definition of MGRs;

> any material of plant, animal, microbial or other origin, found in or originating from sea or ocean containing functional units of heredity, and their derivatives, which are accessed for the actual or potential value of their genetic material.

As conservation and sustainable use of MGRs without fully understanding or agreeing on their nature is challenging, providing a working definition of MGRs is a crucial step forward in strengthening the rule of law and its role in protecting marine biodiversity. While the proposed definition resolves some questions surrounding the scope of MGRs, it still leaves certain issues to be addressed through future research. For example, precision is needed in delineating the boundaries of seas and oceans and uncertainties surrounding the status of anadromous, catadromous and sedentary species.

The proposed definition relies on the text of Article 2 of the CBD but adjusts it to reflect current scientific reality and to address issues with utilisation of the definition of genetic resources under the CBD. The amendments to the definition of genetic resources provided by Article 2 of the CBD should not cause negative fragmentation

[61] See e.g., Ekaterina Popova and others, 'Ecological Connectivity between the Areas beyond National Jurisdiction and Coastal Waters: Safeguarding Interests of Coastal Communities in Developing Countries' (2019) 104 *Marine Policy Journal* 90–102; Michael S. Webster and others, 'Links between Worlds: Unraveling Migratory Connectivity' (2002) 17 *Trends in Ecology & Evolution* 76–83.

of law in the form of duplication or conflicts between environmental standards. On the contrary, the proposed definition of MGRs still follows the key elements of the definition of genetic resources included in Article 2 of the CBD; it also fits with the approach taken in other regimes regulating genetic resources. It is clearly visible that other regimes follow the definition of genetic resources provided by Article 2 of the CBD.

Looking ahead, an apparent way to ensure conservation and sustainable use of MGRs is to adopt a clear definition of MGRs in the future BBNJ treaty. The working definition provided by this chapter should be used. The future BBNJ treaty has the potential of setting an example for existing and future MGR-related treaties regarding making sure that the important terms are defined, adhering to legal clarity and legal certainty. Political disagreements in negotiations leading to adoption of a future BBNJ treaty should not result in loss of legal clarity and legal certainty in the text of that treaty.

It is also pivotal that further research is conducted to keep the definition of MGRs up to date with scientific developments. A balance must be maintained to keep the definition dynamic whilst ensuring it has legal clarity, legal certainty, and thus enforceability. One potential solution to achieve that is to facilitate interdisciplinary dialogue between the various actors within MGR-related regimes, which can lead to informed decisions on proposed legal definitions.[62] This fits with the broader argument that participation by various actors in decision-making processes can improve the quality of decisions.[63]

[62] Nordberg and Minssen, 'Cutting edges and weaving threads in the gene editing (Я)evolution', 83. For the example of initiative involving various actors see e.g., Ad Hoc Technical Expert Group on Digital Sequence Information on Genetic Resources, 'Report'.

[63] See e.g., National Research Council, *Public Participation in Environmental Assessment and Decision Making* (Washington, DC: The National Academies Press 2008), 50; Thomas C. Beierle and Jerry Cayford (eds.), *Democracy in Practice: Public Participation in Environmental Decisions* (Oxfordshire: Routledge 2010), 43.

PART IV

Paths towards Effective Ocean Governance, Implementation and Compliance

14

Legitimacy and EU Marine Governance

David Langlet

14.1 INTRODUCTION

Great expectations are pinned on marine governance,[1] including protecting the marine environment while promoting sustainable growth in 'blue sectors'.[2] At the same time, marine governance is widely recognised as being complex and characterised by fragmentation.[3] Many of the challenges associated with the marine environment and marine space have been described as 'wicked', implying that science does not provide clear answers and that addressing them is liable to generate winners and losers.[4]

It is well established that measures taken in pursuit of marine policy objectives can have significant implications for the social, economic and cultural interests and identities of individuals as well as groups of people. This applies, for example, to the establishment of marine protected areas (MPAs),[5] measures taken to combat

[1] United Nations General Assembly (UNGA). Our ocean, our future: call for action. Resolution A/RES/71/312, July 6, 2017; L. Schøning, 'More or Less Integrated Ocean Management: Multiple Integrated Approaches and Two Norms' (2020) 51:2 *Ocean Development & International Law* 95–115.

[2] P. Ehlers, 'Blue Growth and Ocean Governance: How to Balance the Use and the Protection of the Seas' (2016) 15 *WMU Journal of Maritime Affairs* 187–203.

[3] S. J. Boyes and M. Elliott, 'Marine Legislation: The Ultimate "Horrendogram": International Law, European Directives & National Implementation' (2014) 86 *Marine Pollution Bulletin* 39–47; K. Scott, 'Integrated Oceans Management: A New Frontier in Marine Environmental Protection', in D. Rothwell, A. G. Oude Elferink, K. N. Scott and T. Stephens (eds.), *The Oxford Handbook of the Law of the Sea* (Oxford: Oxford University Press, 2015) 463–490, 464.

[4] L. Mee, P. Cooper, A. Kannen, A. Gilbert and T. O'Higgins, 'Sustaining Europe's Seas as Coupled Social Ecological Systems' (2015) 20 *Ecology and Society* 1–10, 1.

[5] A. Charles and L. Wilson, 'Human Dimensions of Marine Protected Areas' (2008) 66 *ICES Journal of Marine Science* 6–15.

invasive marine species[6] or regulation of marine aquaculture.[7] Not surprisingly, recent years have seen increasing calls for paying more attention to the political dimensions and societal implications of marine policy and management processes in addition to the predominately natural science perspectives traditionally applied.[8]

In an EU context, the last two decades have seen the development of a comprehensive legal framework that aims to protect the marine environment, promote sustainable growth of maritime economies and ensure efficient use of marine space. The main elements of this framework are three directives: the Water Framework Directive (WFD) adopted in 2000,[9] the 2008 Marine Strategy Framework Directive (MSFD)[10] and the Maritime Spatial Planning Directive (MSPD) of 2014.[11] The immediate implications of some marine environmental objectives were also strengthened by the 2015 ruling of the Court of Justice of the EU (CJEU) in the so-called *Weser* case.[12] In this case, the CJEU established that the core environmental objectives of the WFD are binding in relation to individual projects, including many industries, infrastructure facilities and public utilities.

Against this background, it is important to pose questions about the legitimacy of the EU's marine law and governance, not least as a fundamental element of an effective and rule of law-based legal regime for the marine realm. There are numerous ways of approaching issues of legitimacy. The approach here is one focusing on legal texts, inquiring in particular as to what extent and how they address aspects of legitimacy as well as on any guidance provided for dealing with legitimacy in the implementation or operationalisation of legal requirements. Legitimacy of EU marine law and governance is a multidimensional issue. In addition to more generic aspects, it raises questions that are particular to the EU as a unique form of regional legal and policy integration, as well as issues that are more or less specific to activities in the marine domain. Before engaging with

6 A. Novoa, K. Dehnen-Schmutz, J. Fried and G. Vimercati, 'Does Public Awareness Increase Support for Invasive Species Management? Promising Evidence across Taxa and Landscape Types' (2017) 19 *Biological Invasions* 3691–3705.

7 G. Krause and others, 'Visualizing the Social in Aquaculture: How Social Dimension Components Illustrate the Effects of Aquaculture across Geo-Graphic Scales' (2020) 118 *Marine Policy* 103985.

8 S. Linke, M. Gilek, M. Karlsson and O. Udovyk , 'Unravelling Science-Policy Interactions in Environmental Risk Governance of the Baltic Sea: Comparing Fisheries and Eutrophication' (2014) 17 *Journal of Risk Research* 505–523, 517.

9 Directive 2000/60/EC of the European Parliament and of the Council of 23 October 2000 establishing a framework for Community action in the field of water policy, OJ 2000 No. L327/1.

10 Directive 2008/56/EC of the European Parliament and of the Council of 17 June 2008 establishing a framework for community action in the field of marine environmental policy (Marine Strategy Framework Directive), OJ 2008 No. L164/19.

11 Directive 2014/89/EU of the European Parliament and of the Council of 23 July 2014 establishing a framework for maritime spatial planning, OJ 2014 No. L257/1.

12 Case C-461/13, *Bund für Umwelt und Naturschutz Deutschland* ECLI:EU:C:2015:433.

legitimacy in this particular context, some reflection is needed on legitimacy, as such, and how it may be understood.

14.2 ON LEGITIMACY

Much like 'rule of law', legitimacy is a challenging concept since it can be defined in many ways and used in various contexts. When talking about legitimacy in relation to law and governance it tends to relate broadly to 'the justification and acceptance of political authority',[13] thus indicating a close connection to rule of law as a form of protection against capricious and unjustified exercise of power. Legitimate law-making and wider exercise of public authority is closely linked to ideas about democracy.[14] Effective democratic governance arguably requires that the governing organs are widely perceived as legitimate.[15] Legitimacy is also associated with more instrumental values. It is widely accepted that rules and decisions meet with higher acceptance and are better complied with if they are seen as legitimate.[16] This in turn should decrease the need for and thus the cost of monitoring, control and enforcement.[17] In this sense, legitimacy is a means of increasing compliance while reducing costs.

Discussions about legitimacy tend to approach the subject either from a theoretical perspective, often grounded in philosophy or political science, or a more sociological one. Whereas theoretical approaches are generally concerned with defining and testing various criteria for what may constitute legitimacy, the sociological ones rather aim to determine to what extent institutions, laws and decisions are de facto perceived as legitimate by those affected.[18]

Many attempts have been made at defining or classifying different forms or versions of legitimacy. A common division is that between output legitimacy and input legitimacy.[19] Simply put, input legitimacy relates to participation and

[13] D. Bodansky, 'The Concept of Legitimacy in International Law', in R. Wolfrum and V. Röben (eds.), *Legitimacy in International Law. Beiträge zum ausländischen öffentlichen Recht und Völkerrecht*, vol. 194 (Berlin, Heidelberg, New York: Springer, 2008) 309–317, 310.

[14] G. Davies, 'Democracy and Legitimacy in the Shadow of Purposive Competence' (2015) 21:1 *European Law Journal* 2–22; V. A. Schmidt, 'Democracy and Legitimacy in the European Union', in E. Jones, A. Menon and S. Weatherill (eds.), *The Handbook on the European Union* (Oxford: Oxford University Press, 2012) 661–672; W. Voermans, J. M. R. Hartmann and M. Kaeding, 'The Quest for Legitimacy in EU Secondary Legislation' (2014) 2:1 *The Theory and Practice of Legislation* 5–32.

[15] T. R. Tyler, 'Psychological Perspectives on Legitimacy and Legitimation' (2006) 57:1 *Annual Review of Psychology* 375–400, 380.

[16] Bodansky (n 13) 310; Voermans, Hartmann and Kaeding (n 14) 7.

[17] J. Raakjær Nielsen, 'An Analytical Framework for Studying: Compliance and Legitimacy in Fisheries Management' (2003) 27:5 *Marine Policy* 425–432, 428.

[18] Bodansky (n 13) 313.

[19] F. Scharpf, *Governing in Europe: Effective and Democratic?* (Oxford: Oxford University Press, 1999).

representation in decision-making and the reflection of citizens' concerns and values in adopted laws and policies. Output legitimacy relates to the performance and effective delivery of laws and policies.[20] In the words of Lord and Magnette, in a democracy, 'elections provide input legitimacy and the delivery of voter preferences secures output legitimacy'.[21]

A related concept is 'throughput' legitimacy, which is used to refer to the openness, accountability, transparency and efficacy of decision-making processes. Whereas this dimension is important – since, for example, incompetent or corrupt governance practices can undermine legitimacy – throughput legitimacy is no substitute for missing input or output legitimacy.[22] In practice, however, the perceived fairness of relevant institutions and procedures seems to have a strong impact on the extent to which the rules and decisions produced are in fact deemed legitimate and on the propensity of people to voluntarily defer to them.[23]

In relation to EU law-making, input legitimacy is associated with a major discussion on the 'democratic deficit' associated with, among other things, the partial bypassing of national parliaments and the strong position of the unelected European Commission in law-making, as well as the general lack of a 'collective political identity' underpinning EU law.[24] These aspects of legitimacy are largely generic to EU law in general and will not be the focus here,[25] although they should be borne in mind when engaging with legitimacy in relation to more specific measures or policy areas.

Although the present chapter will not, for reasons of space, attempt a systematic assessment of EU marine law and governance according to the different forms of legitimacy outlined in this section, they still constitute a useful backdrop for discussing issues of legitimacy in the more specific context of the EU's marine legal frameworks.

14.3 LEGAL FRAMEWORKS FOR EU MARINE GOVERNANCE

Questions of legitimacy can be pertinently posed in relation to virtually any law or policy affecting the interests of groups or individuals or somehow arbitrating between competing objectives or values. Legal aspects of EU marine governance can in principle cover areas such as chemicals law, rules on species and habitats protection, as well as regulation of specific activities such as fishing or water

[20] Schmid (n 14) 662; Voermans, Hartmann and Kaeding (n 14), 12.

[21] C. Lord and P. Magnette, 'E Pluribus Unum? Creative Disagreement about Legitimacy in the EU' (2004) 42:1 *Journal of Common Market Studies* 183–202, 187.

[22] Schmidt (n 14) 662.

[23] Tyler (n 15) 394.

[24] Voermans, Hartmann and Kaeding (n 14) 6.

[25] See instead e.g., Schmidt (n 14); Voermans, Hartmann and Kaeding (n 14).

treatment plants. In order to enable a more focused discussion, the analysis here deals with legitimacy in relation to EU legal acts that have a comprehensive aim in that they potentially apply to all or most activities in a particular marine area or those that affect the marine environment or marine space generally. This entails a focus on the three framework directives presented in the introduction, that is, the WFD, the MSFD and the MSPD. In the following, the three directives are briefly described with a focus on features that are particularly pertinent from the perspective of legitimacy. In addition to looking for provisions that explicitly address issues of legitimacy and fairness, those that have a clear potential to affect people's (perceived) rights and interests, including trade-offs between rights or interests, are highly pertinent. The same goes for rules on participation and decision-making. That is followed by a more comparative analysis that also tries to point out how legitimacy may be enhanced where needed.

14.3.1 *The Water Framework Directive*

The WFD has several purposes, among which is to prevent further deterioration and protect and enhance the status of aquatic ecosystems and to promote sustainable water use.[26] The Directive is relevant for marine areas not only because it aims to regulate the quality of water in the rivers, streams as well as groundwater that feed into the sea, but also because it is applicable to coastal waters.[27]

Under the Directive, all river basins within the territory of a Member State, together with their associated groundwaters and coastal waters, must be assigned to river basin districts. For each such district a river basin management plan must be adopted,[28] and programmes of measures need to be drawn up for all basins.[29] These programmes, which are central to the governance model of the WFD, should include measures necessary to achieve at least good water status as measured at the level of individual bodies of surface water such as a stream or discrete stretch of coastal water.[30] Good surface water status requires that both the ecological status and chemical status of the particular water body are at least 'good' on a scale from high to bad.[31] As regards ecological status, 'good' signifies that relevant biological quality elements for the specific surface water body type show low levels of distortion resulting from human activity and deviate only slightly from those normally associated with undisturbed conditions.[32]

[26] Directive 2000/60/EC, Art. 1.
[27] Ibid., Art. 2.
[28] Ibid., Art. 13.1.
[29] Ibid., Arts. 4 and 11(1).
[30] Ibid., Arts. 4 and 2, point 10.
[31] Ibid., Art. 2, point 18.
[32] Ibid., Annex V, Section 1.2.

However, since the CJEU decision in the *Weser* case, it is clear that the Member States cannot just implement the measures set out in programmes of measures. There is also a binding obligation to refuse authorisation for any project that will result in deterioration of the status of a water body or even jeopardise attainment of good surface water status, unless the project is covered by a derogation recognised by the WFD.[33] While logical from an environmental perspective, the strict application of objectives in individual cases rather than within broader programmes of measures can decrease the potential for designing protective measures in ways that are cognizant of social and cultural effects as well as broader environmental or climate concerns. While broad programmes of measures allow for some spatial and temporal variation in the way that objectives are pursued, that possibility tends to be lost or at least decreased when a specific standard or objective has to be met in each individual case. This also limits the ability to give extra weight to a competing interest in a particular situation or context, even if the effect of that can be compensated through other measures covered by the programme of measures.

The WFD itself does not use terms such as legitimacy, fairness or justice, nor does it apparently deal with many distributional, social or cultural effects of water governance.[34] Instead it is strongly focused on natural science concepts, while governance structures and processes are described in a technical, ostensibly value free manner. There are, however, some elements of a 'social dimension' in the WFD that may more clearly relate to different forms of legitimacy.

One such area is rules on recovery of costs for water services. While requiring Member States to put in place water-pricing policies that provide adequate incentives for users to use water resources efficiently, the Directive allows regard to be had to 'the social, environmental and economic effects of the recovery' when doing so.[35] There should also be an economic analysis of water use for each river basin district.[36] While the WFD itself says little about the purpose or nature of such analyses, a short annex on economic analysis clearly places the emphasis on cost-effectiveness and calculation of costs of water services so as to enable cost recovery.[37] However, non-binding guidance documents developed as part of the so-called Common Implementation Strategy (CIS), set up by the Member States, the European Commission and Norway, convey a partly different message. A guidance document on 'Economics and the Environment' talks about the need for understanding the trade-offs at stake, for identifying 'the losers' and 'the gainers' when assessing the economic impact of proposed programmes, and potentially

33 Case C-461/13, para. 50.

34 'Legitimate' occurs once in the Directive, but then only in the definition of pollution, and in a way that is of little relevance to the present discussion. Directive 2000/60/EC, Art. 2, point 33.

35 Ibid., Art. 9.1.

36 Ibid., Art. 5.

37 Ibid., Annex III.

addressing the need for specific measures to compensate losers.[38] However, the economic principles, approaches and tools highlighted in the document are strongly focused on cost-effectiveness and water pricing, without much explicit concern for social dimensions, equity or legitimacy.

The CIS guidance document on the planning process of the WFD talks about planning as having the capacity to increase the legitimacy of decisions. This is to be achieved by enabling 'open and wide dialogue between the public, interest groups and authorities'.[39] This is in line with the general conclusion that in EU water and marine governance the 'social dimension' is predominantly seen as a matter of consultation and dialogue.[40] Although public participation is not explicitly referred to in the WFD, the Directive requires the Member States to 'encourage the active involvement of all interested parties' in its implementation.[41] Referring to this, the CIS guidance on participation mentions the prospect of making the management of natural resources more sustainable and socially acceptable by involving the people that depend on them for their livelihood.[42] However, this is not much elaborated. It is also emphasised, however, in the guidance document on the planning process that, among other things, equity, redistribution and social welfare can be issues equally important as economic efficiency and that water planning processes should involve reasonable alternatives and evaluate their economic, environmental, political and social impacts.[43]

According to the Directive, socioeconomic needs can in some instances play a role in the justification of achieving less stringent environmental objectives than would normally be required.[44] Probably most important for the current discussion is the possibility to justify failure to achieve 'good' status or to prevent deterioration of a body of surface water when it results from new modifications to the physical characteristics of the water body, or if, in the case of failure to prevent deterioration from 'high' status to 'good' status, it is the result of new sustainable human development activities. The reasons for making the modifications or alterations must be of overriding public interest and/or the benefits to the environment and to society of achieving the environmental objectives must be outweighed by the benefits of the new modifications or alterations to human health, to the maintenance of human

38 Common Implementation Strategy for the Water Framework Directive (2000/60/EC), Guidance Document No 1, 'Economics and the Environment', European Communities, 2003, 8.
39 Common Implementation Strategy for the Water Framework Directive (2000/60/EC), Guidance Document No 11, 'Planning Process', European Commission, 2003, 11.
40 D. Langlet and A. Westholm, 'Realizing the Social Dimension of EU Coastal Water Management' (2021) 13 *Sustainability* 2261.
41 Directive 2000/60/EC, Art. 14.
42 Common Implementation Strategy for the Water Framework Directive (2000/60/EC), Guidance Document No 8, 'Public Participation in relation to the Water Framework Directive', European Communities, 2003, 52.
43 Guidance Document No 11, 'Planning Process' (n 39) 12.
44 Directive 2000/60/EC, Art. 4 (5).

safety or to sustainable development. With respect to water bodies that have a 'high' status, this introduces some flexibility to accept new activities that are deemed sustainable, as long as they do not result in a fall of status below 'good'. For bodies of water that are currently below 'high' status, it is only modifications to the physical characteristics of the water body, for example, through dredging or construction of port infrastructure, that can be justified in this way.

While these exceptions can invite excessive and unjustified use, they also enable, when applied in good faith, social needs broadly construed to be given priority in specific cases so as to avoid extensive and seemingly unfair consequences of the WFD in a particular location or for a particular group of people.

14.3.2 *Marine Strategy Framework Directive*

The MSFD aims broadly to ensure the integration of environmental concerns into policies, agreements and legislative measures that have an impact on the marine environment.[45] It is intended to deliver the 'environmental pillar' of the EU's wider Integrated Maritime Policy,[46] which also aims to stimulate, inter alia, increased marine research, better use of marine space and blue growth.[47] The MSFD applies to all marine waters of the EU Member States,[48] but coastal waters are only covered to the extent that a particular aspect of the environmental status is not already addressed through the WFD or other EU legislation.[49]

Under the MSFD, the Member States are required, subject to some exceptions,[50] to take the necessary measures to achieve or maintain good environmental status (GES) in the marine environment.[51] The Directive contains a lengthy and rather vague definition of GES.[52] In practice, what constitutes GES is determined on the basis of eleven qualitative descriptors set out in an annex.[53] All of these relate to the status of the natural environment, and make no direct reference to social aspects. Rather than assessing the status of individual water bodies as under the WFD, the MSFD is concerned with achieving GES at the level of so-called marine regions or sub-regions. These are large areas such as the Baltic Sea, the Black Sea or the Western Mediterranean.[54]

45 Directive 2008/56/EC, Art. 1.
46 Ibid., preambular para. 3.
47 Communication from the Commission – An Integrated Maritime Policy for the European Union, COM (2007) 574 Final.
48 Directive 2008/56/EC, Art. 2.
49 Ibid., Art. 3, point 1.
50 Ibid., Art. 14.
51 Ibid., Art. 3.
52 For this definition, see ibid., Art. 3.
53 Ibid., Art. 9.
54 Ibid., Art. 4.

The method for achieving GES is the development and implementation of marine strategies by each Member State.[55] In many respects, the MSFD takes a similar approach to environmental management as the WFD but does so on a larger scale and in a partly less detailed manner. Like the WFD, it is based on an implementation cycle comprising assessment, defining a desired state of the environment, implementing measures and monitoring.[56]

Concepts such as legitimacy and justice are hardly used in the MSFD. It does, however, refer to 'fairness and feasibility' as reasons to make provision for cases where it would be impossible for a Member State to achieve the level of ambition of the environmental targets set or to achieve or maintain GES.[57] In this vein, and similar to the WFD, the MSFD allows for modifications or alterations to the physical characteristics of marine waters brought about by actions taken for reasons of overriding public interest that outweigh the negative impact on the environment, even if they result in the environmental targets or GES not being achieved.[58]

Social dimensions potentially relevant for legitimacy are more explicitly addressed in the MSFD compared to the WFD. Assessments of the environmental status of marine waters are to include 'an economic and social analysis of the use of those waters and of the cost of degradation of the marine environment'.[59] In a similar vein, programmes of measures drawn up to achieve or maintain GES must give due consideration to sustainable development and, 'in particular, to the social and economic impacts of the measures envisaged'.[60] Additionally, in setting targets and associated indicators due consideration should be taken of social and economic concerns.[61] The guidance developed on economic and social analysis for initial assessment for the MSFD is largely focused on economic aspects, and the methods proposed relate to costs valuation and distribution of the economic effects of measures.[62] While opening up for criticism for not including other social dimensions,[63] this is at least a clear recognition of the fact that the marine governance measures have social and economic impacts that need a cognizant approach.

As for participation, the MSFD obliges the Member States to ensure that all interested parties are given early and effective opportunities to participate in implementation. How this is to be done is not further specified beyond the fact that it is to

55 Ibid., Art. 1.

56 M. Cavallo, Á. Borja, M. Elliott, V. Quintino and J. Touza, 'Impediments to Achieving Integrated Marine Management across Borders: The Case of the EU Marine Strategy Framework Directive' (2019) 103 *Marine Policy* 68–73.

57 Directive 2008/56/EC, preambular para. 29.

58 Ibid., Art. 14.

59 Ibid., Art. 8.

60 Ibid., Art. 13.

61 Ibid., Annex 4.

62 Marine Strategy Framework Directive (MSFD), Common Implementation Strategy, 'Economic and Social Analysis for the Initial Assessment for the Marine Strategy Framework Directive', MSFD Guidance Document 1, European Commission, 2018.

63 Langlet and Westholm (n 40).

be in accordance with other relevant EU legislation.[64] This becomes particularly important in view of the fact that the MSFD, to a large extent, is a mechanism for the integration of environmental concerns into existing policies, agreements and legislative measures that have an impact on the marine environment.[65] In this sense, the MSFD is layered on existing regulation at national, EU and international levels,[66] which often means that the legitimacy aspects of the MSFD get mixed with similar aspects of those other legal measures.

14.3.3 *Maritime Spatial Planning Directive*

Compared to both the WFD and the MSFD, the MSPD is intended to take a more comprehensive approach to marine activities and resources by establishing a framework for maritime spatial planning (MSP), which aims to promote the sustainable growth of maritime economies, sustainable development of marine areas and sustainable use of marine resources.[67] It requires Member States to set up maritime spatial plans identifying the spatial and temporal distribution of relevant existing and future activities and uses.[68] Through these plans, the Member States are to aim to contribute to a number of objectives, including sustainable development of energy sectors at sea, maritime transport and the fisheries and aquaculture sectors, as well as preservation, protection and improvement of the environment. They may also pursue additional objectives, such as sustainable tourism and sustainable extraction of raw materials.[69]

When pursuing these objectives through planning processes, the Member States must, inter alia, take into account environmental, economic and social aspects as well as ensuring involvement of stakeholders.[70] As for public participation, the only specific requirements in the MSPD are that means of public participation must be established by informing all interested parties and by consulting the relevant stakeholders and authorities, and the public concerned, at an early stage in the development of maritime spatial plans and in accordance with relevant provisions of EU legislation.[71] The word legitimacy does not feature in the Directive, nor do equity or fairness.

In its 'Roadmap for MSP', published in 2008, the European Commission refers to MSP as a tool for achieving sustainable use of marine resources and as providing

64 Directive 2008/ 56/ EC, Art. 19.
65 Ibid., Art. 1.
66 J. van Leeuwen and others, 'Implementing the Marine Strategy Framework Directive: A Policy Perspective on Regulatory, Institutional and Stakeholder Impediments to Effective Implementation' (2014) 50 *Marine Policy* 325–330, 327.
67 Directive 2014/89/EU, Art. 1.
68 Ibid., Art. 8.
69 Ibid., Art. 5.
70 Ibid., Art. 6.
71 Ibid., Art. 9.

legal certainty and predictability.[72] However, the strong framework character and very general obligations of the MSPD as eventually adopted leave the attainment of such effects almost entirely to the individual Member States. The Directive is explicitly 'without prejudice to the competence of Member States to determine how the different objectives are reflected and weighted' in their plans,[73] and its implementation should also to the greatest extent possible build on existing rules and mechanisms.[74] Not surprisingly, it has been questioned whether the MSPD has the ability to steer relevant spatial planning practices in a sustainable direction.[75]

A further important limitation of the effect of the Directive is that coastal waters that are subject to a Member State's town and country planning are exempted from its purview, provided that this is communicated in the relevant national maritime spatial plans.[76] Since coastal waters are where most maritime activities occur, this can significantly limit the effect of the Directive. However, if MSP is to be ecosystem based and consider land–sea interactions, as required by the MSPD, close coordination between existing town and country planning processes and planning undertaken according to the Directive is evidently needed.[77]

While MSP in principle has the potential to help reconcile different spatial demands and democratise marine governance, warnings have increasingly been raised that it can also be used to entrench pre-existing power imbalances, cloak the interests of elite actors in ostensibly democratic processes and potentially even be an instrument for so-called ocean grabbing.[78] Due to the nature of the MSPD, the extent to which such effects will materialise in an EU context depends on the ways in which Member States chose to implement the Directive and the nature of their planning processes and traditions.

The EU legislator could be accused of not seriously engaging with the legitimacy aspects of MSP, but instead leaving all hard choices and trade-offs to the Member States. However, if the Member States are regarded as generally better suited to

[72] Communication from the Commission, 'Roadmap for Maritime Spatial Planning: Achieving Common Principles in the EU', COM (2008) 791 final, 2 and 3.

[73] Directive 2014/89/EU, Art. 5.

[74] Ibid., preambular para. 12.

[75] N. Soininen and F. M. Platjouw, 'Resilience and Adaptive Capacity of Aquatic Environmental Law in the EU: An Evaluation and Comparison of the WFD, MSFD, and MSPD', in D. Langlet and R. Rayfuse (eds.), *The Ecosystem Approach in Ocean Planning and Governance* (Leiden: Brill Nijhoff, 2019) 17–79, 43.

[76] Directive 2014/89/EU, Arts. 1 and 2.

[77] Langlet and Westholm (n 40) 12.

[78] W. Flannery, N. Healy and M. Luna, 'Exclusion and Non-Participation in Marine Spatial Planning' (2018) 88 *Marine Policy* 32–40, 39; B. Queffelec and others, 'Marine Spatial Planning and the Risk of Ocean Grabbing in the Tropical Atlantic' (2021) *ICES Journal of Marine Science* fsab006, no page; J. Behagel and E. Turnhout, 'Democratic Legitimacy in the Implementation of the Water Framework Directive in the Netherlands: Towards Participatory and Deliberative Norms?' (2011) 13:3 *Journal of Environmental Policy & Planning* 297–316, 299.

make such decisions, both in terms of subsidiarity – being closer to the relevant trade-offs and potential synergies – and due to their overall greater democratic legitimacy, this may not be negative for legitimacy. It does, however, make it hard to evaluate the MSPD as such from the perspective of legitimacy.

14.4 CONCLUDING DISCUSSION

Legitimacy is not a notion that is explicitly addressed by core EU marine legislation, although the potential of planning and participatory processes to enhance legitimacy is highlighted in some guidance documents. Interestingly, the WFD, which is likely to have the most tangible effects on the economic and social conditions of individuals, is least clear on how to deal with these dimensions of marine and water governance.

An important aspect of so-called output legitimacy is the extent to which politically agreed results are actually delivered. The WFD sets out substantive requirements that are – at least for those capable of comprehending the details – reasonably precise and liable to have a direct impact on what environmental quality to expect. It also enables individuals to rely on the quality standards of the Directive and to challenge individual authorisations that are inconsistent with their achievement.[79] The *Weser* case increased the effects of the Directive's environmental objectives in relation to individual projects. Still, there are challenges with complexity, making it hard to understand what rights or duties actually follow from the WFD, as well as insufficient implementation by Member States. The MSFD is in this regard similar to the WFD but vaguer in its requirements, not least due to the larger spatial scales of application and higher level of aggregation, making it harder to know at a local level what to expect from the Directive and to judge if it has delivered. This problem also tends to be exacerbated by time lags between measures and effects in many natural systems.

The binding nature and partly direct applicability of environmental objectives decided at EU level could also pose a challenge to legitimacy by decreasing the ability to balance different interests and consider 'the bigger picture'.[80] Overall, both the WFD and the MSFD have a strong focus on the environmental dimension of sustainability, and other aspects are mostly possible to accommodate through specific exemptions or the flexibility that is inherent to national implementation processes. This has the advantage of clarity; these legal acts primarily aim to protect the environment while other considerations require specific justifications or must be pursued without infringing on the environmental objectives. On the other hand, it

[79] L. Squintani and H. van Rijswick, 'Improving Legal Certainty and Adaptability in the Programmatic Approach' (2016) 28 *Journal of Environmental Law* 443–470, 461.

[80] Davies (n 14) 2–22, 2.

may invite the criticism that prioritisation and decisions on trade-offs have already been made at EU level, leaving only technical details to the (hopefully) more transparent and participatory national implementation processes. In practice, however, there tends to be rather significant room for decisions on trade-offs at the national level, in particular beyond the situations covered by the *Weser* decision.

The need for legal frameworks dealing with ecosystems to be flexible and adaptive has itself the potential to decrease legitimacy by undermining legal certainty and foreseeability.[81] All three marine directives apply the programmatic approach which entails flexibility that can be used for adaptation and enables a fair allocation of economic development and costs for environmental protection but at the same time makes it harder to know what will be required in the longer term. Indeed, there is a considerable literature debating the challenges of reconciling traditional legal virtues such as rule of law and legal certainty with the flexibility required by adaptive governance models.[82] In practice, however, law is not static and is always subject to interpretation. Hence, intentionally adaptive legal structures are not inherently different from more traditional legal arrangements.[83] They can even make the inevitable adjustments to changing circumstances more transparent and easier to anticipate.

The MSPD, which is much more comprehensive in its aim than the two other directives, is also so vague in terms of substantive requirements that it hardly restricts the scope of (legitimate) national or local balancing of objectives. On the other hand, it is prone to criticism for being too thin on substance, making it impossible to know what to expect as a result of its implementation.

While the MSPD most explicitly recognises the need for considering multiple interests and objectives in marine governance, none of the marine directives is particularly clear on how to address the 'wicked' aspects of marine governance. Although the MSFD mandates consideration of social and economic impacts of targets and measures and a non-binding guidance to the WFD makes reference to the need for identifying and possibly compensating 'the losers', there is little clarity as to how this can or should be done and what results to expect. In some ways, this may be positive. The EU legislator may not be best placed to legitimately arbitrate between complex interests, and the WFD and the MSFD are explicitly focused mainly on ecological dimensions. At the same time, one could at least have expected clearer demands on the principles and processes to be used for dealing with such challenges in a transparent and legitimate way. Now, this is almost entirely left to individual Member States, making outcomes as well as processes very different between countries. Reasonably, the legitimacy of EU legal acts can

81 Squintani and van Rijswick (n 79) 444.

82 See, e.g., J. Ebbesson, 'The Rule of Law in Governance of Complex Socio-Ecological Changes' (2010) 20:3 *Global Environmental Change* 414–422; Soininen and Platjouw (n 75).

83 Ebbesson (n 82) 415.

suffer if what they are seen to deliver varies considerably across the Union. Both the WFD and the MSFD have also been criticised for being silent on access to justice as they do not ensure that the public have legal means to challenge the validity of an adopted programme of measures.[84]

As noted previously, the perceived fairness of decision processes has clear implications for the extent to which management is deemed legitimate. This lends support to the argument that increased attention to and transparency about actual and perceived trade-offs among users and interests are important, not least in maritime planning.[85] To better address such aspects, the use of a 'sociocultural approach' has been proposed, dealing with issues such as procedural justice, social inclusion and knowledge pluralism.[86] However, the Member States already have tools they can employ to increase transparency and quality in the way they deal with social dimensions of marine governance. These include social impact assessment and stakeholder perceptions and interest assessment.[87]

All three directives largely rely on participation for dealing with core legitimacy dimensions. While participation can be a way of enhancing both input and throughput legitimacy, participation as a provider of legitimacy is not unproblematic. Challenges pertain inter alia to defining who has a legitimate say in decision-making processes,[88] and to ensuring that participation can be genuine, with stakeholders understanding what can and cannot be changed through a participatory process as well as seeing that their participation is meaningful and can affect the outcome.[89] Sufficient time must also be allowed for deliberations and integration of varied interests and different kinds of knowledge.[90]

84 Squintani and van Rijswick (n 79) 459.

85 B. S. Halpern, 'Near-Term Priorities for the Science, Policy and Practice of Coastal and Marine Spatial Planning (CMSP)' (2012) 36 *Marine Policy* 198–205, 201.

86 M. Gilek, F. Saunders and I. Stalmokaitė, 'The Ecosystem Approach and Sustainable Development in Baltic Sea Marine Spatial Planning: The Social Pillar, a "Slow Train Coming"', in D. Langlet and R. Rayfuse (eds.), *The Ecosystem Approach in Ocean Planning and Governance* (Leiden: Brill Nijhoff, 2019), 160–194, 186–187.

87 F. Vanclay, 'The Potential Application of Social Impact Assessment in Integrated Coastal Zone Management' (2012) 68 *Ocean Coastal Management* 149–156; I. Lukic and others, *Stakeholder Profiles*, MUSES Project, Deliverable No. 4.1, 2017.

88 K. Soma and C. Haggett, 'Enhancing Social Acceptance in Marine Governance in Europe' (2015) 117 *Ocean & Coastal Management* 61–69, 62.

89 Gilek, Saunders and Stalmokaitė (n 86) 165.

90 A. Cliquet, F. Kervarec, D. Bogaert, F. Maes and B. Queffelec, 'Legitimacy Issues in Public Participation in Coastal Decision Making Processes: Case Studies from Belgium and France' (2010) 53 *Ocean & Coastal Management* 760–768, 768.

15

Recognition of Maritime Environmental Crimes within International Law

A New Global Paradigm for the Protection and Preservation of the Marine Environment

Vasco Becker-Weinberg

15.1 INTRODUCTION

Maritime environmental crimes are perpetrated in every part of the ocean and include a vast array of activities, mostly related to ship-source pollution, particularly accidental and wilful oil discharges, which are a major threat to the marine environment and human health, accounting for most of the oil pollution in the ocean. These crimes take place across the whole shipping sector, from unseaworthy vessels engaged in illegal, unreported and unregulated fishing, to oil tankers and luxury cruise liners.[1]

Despite a decline in accidental and intentional discharges in recent years, the impact of human-produced incidents greatly offsets natural processes, given the large volumes of oil that can be released in a single incident. It is estimated that 53 per cent of all petroleum reaching the marine environment is human-produced and occurs near coastlines, while natural processes account for the rest.[2] It is also estimated that most of the 2.1Mt of oil discharged every year into the sea goes undetected.[3]

Moreover, as a result of the ocean being interconnected and impermeable to any political or legal divisions, maritime environmental crimes happening in one part of

1 'Japanese Shipping Company Fined $1.5 Million for Concealing Illegal Discharges of Oily Water': www.justice.gov/opa/pr/japanese-shipping-company-fined-15-million-concealing-illegal-discharges-oily-water; 'Cruise Line Ordered to Pay $40 Million for Illegal Dumping of Oil Contaminated Waste and Falsifying Records': www.justice.gov/opa/pr/cruise-line-ordered-pay-40-million-illegal-dumping-oil-contaminated-waste-and-falsifying 'Marine pollution: thousands of serious offences exposed in global operation': www.europol.europa.eu/newsroom/news/marine-pollution-thousands-of-serious-offences-exposed-in-global-operation (last accessed August 2021).

2 S. Polinov, R. Bookman and N. Levin, 'Spatial and temporal assessment of oil spills in the Mediterranean Sea' (2021) 167 *Marine Pollution Bulletin*, 1, 8.

3 N. Giovannini L. Melica, E. Cukani, M. Giannotta and M. Zingoni, 'Addressing environmental crimes and marine pollution in the EU: legal guidelines and case studies' (2013) *Droit au Droit*, 36.

the ocean will affect the whole ocean. No single State is able to tackle the causes and consequences of these crimes on its own. Indeed, the existing legal rules addressing spatial and functional jurisdiction at sea result in complex multijurisdictional challenges that can cause conflict of jurisdictions and, consequently, the ineffectiveness of international law to prevent and combat maritime environmental crimes. Specific legal rules addressing maritime environmental crimes are also lacking.

The harm and damage caused by maritime environmental crimes to vast areas of the ocean and coastlines, together with destruction of vulnerable and fragile marine ecosystems and devastation of marine life, affect the livelihood of many coastal communities and have an impact on economic activities that depend on the ocean, including international navigation. They also cause psychological distress and can seriously affect the wellbeing of entire populations. Despite improvements in oil-spill response, cleanup and restoration methods, restitution of affected areas is generally very difficult, in addition to being extremely costly and time consuming, lasting for several decades.[4] In some cases, damage is simply irreparable.

Maritime environmental crimes are committed to avoid compliance with international rules and regulations, thus obtaining substantial financial gain by not calling into port to use the necessary facilities and avoiding procedures established under national and/or international law, which are time-consuming and entail significant costs. These crimes are a quick and inexpensive solution, and the chances of criminals getting caught, prosecuted or convicted are very small.[5] Indeed, perpetrators are organized and act in a concerted and evasive manner, with the aim of committing these crimes at sea, taking advantage of existing gaps and overlaps in international law.

No specific data record the value of maritime environmental crimes, but they do pay off.[6] The rewards of maritime environmental crimes can be seen, for example, in the fact that illegal disposal can save a ship owner anywhere from US$80K–220K every year, depending on the size and age of the ship, the number of days at sea and how well it is maintained, which can represent 5–12 per cent of a ship's operating costs.[7]

Maritime environmental crimes are a global problem that has been severely overlooked. This is chiefly due to lack of awareness but also to absence of a clear

[4] This is the case of the pollution caused by the 1989 *Exxon Valdez* oil spill disaster, which has taken several decades to clean up: www.justice.gov/opa/pr/united-states-and-state-alaska-opt-not-recover-additional-damages-exxon-mobil-under-reopener (last accessed August 2021).

[5] B. Vollaard, 'Temporal displacement of environmental crime: evidence from marine oil pollution' (2017) 82 *Journal of Environmental Economics and Management*, 169, 172.

[6] Overall, Europol estimates the annual value of transnational environmental crime to be worth US$70–213B. See EnviCrimeNet Intelligence Project on Environmental Crime Report on Environmental Crime in Europe (2015): www.envicrimenet.eu/images/docs/ipec_report_on_environmental_crime_in_europe.pdf (last accessed August 2021).

[7] Vollaard (n 5).

sense of direction by States to address these crimes and to do so in a collective manner, in order to improve the international legal response to maritime environmental crimes. These include, for example, the proposal for recognition of ecocide as a new international crime.[8]

This chapter suggests that a new global paradigm is needed for protection and preservation of the marine environment, in the shape of a rule of law that is able to deliver improved collective and effective legal responses to address maritime environmental crimes, in other words: departing from the law as it stands.

15.2 CONCEPTUALIZATION

Maritime environmental crimes can be broadly defined as acts committed at sea that breach national and/or international law, causing harm or damage to the marine environment. This broad definition includes acts perpetrated within and beyond national jurisdiction, as well as pollution[9] from different sources, including ship-source pollution, such as illegal dumping,[10] especially of oil and oil-bunkering, or pollution from offshore installations and structures or cables and pipelines.

Notwithstanding, there is no set definition of maritime environmental crimes, nor does international law criminalize acts or conduct considered as such. Criminalization only exists under national law, subject to States' discretion.[11] Maritime environmental crimes are not permitted under international law, but they are also not subject to collective and international criminal suppression, despite the fact that they are a major threat facing the marine environment and humankind.

The proposed concept of maritime environmental crimes must be based on the recognition that individually or collectively, environmental rights are an extension of human rights. These include the right to a healthy environment, but also the right of access to information, public participation in decision-making and access to

[8] STOP Ecocide Foundation, Independent Expert Panel for the Legal Definition of Ecocide: Commentary and Core Text, June 2021: https://static1.squarespace.com/static/5ca2608ab914493c64ef1f6d/t/60d7479cf8e7e5461534dd07/1624721314430/SE+Foundation+Commentary+and+core+text+revised+%281%29.pdf (last accessed August 2021).

[9] Art. 1(1)(4) UNCLOS defines 'pollution of the marine environment' as the introduction by man, directly or indirectly, of substances or energy into the marine environment, which result or are likely to result in such deleterious effects as harm to living resources and marine life, hazards to human health, hindrance to marine activities, including fishing and other legitimate uses of the sea, impairment of quality for use of sea water and reduction of amenities.

[10] Art. 1(1)(5) UNCLOS defines 'dumping' as any deliberate disposal of wastes or other matter from vessels, aircraft, platforms or other man-made structures at sea, and of vessels, aircraft, platforms or other man-made structures at sea. It excludes incidental disposals or those resulting from normal operations or the placement of matter for a purpose other than the mere disposal thereof, provided that such placement is not contrary to the aims of the Convention.

[11] In the case of the European Union, Member States are subject to specific obligations under EU law: Directive 2009/123/EC of the European Parliament and of the Council of 21 October 2009, amending Directive 2005/35/EC on ship-source pollution and on the introduction of penalties for infringements.

justice in environmental matters, all of which reinforce the connection between the human element and the environment.

Currently, several international and regional human rights instruments include references to the environment, but no international human rights legal instrument expressly mentions the ocean.[12] Furthermore, although there is clearly a collective interest in protection and preservation of the marine environment,[13] international law has not made the right of each State to intercede on behalf of the marine environment in areas subject to the jurisdiction or sovereignty of other States. One State may only seek legal action against another State based on the latter's responsibility for damage suffered, and not representing any community or collective interest, or on the basis of an *actio popularis* as a result of such interest being affected.[14] This is most remarkable in the high seas, where all States have a clear interest in protecting and preserving the marine environment.[15]

Therefore, development of the notion that marine environmental rights are an extension of human rights will undoubtedly reinforce the theoretical basis of the new paradigm, which will, in turn, support the concept of maritime environmental crimes. Recognition of maritime environmental crimes must also be based on the acknowledgement that these crimes are a global problem and not one exclusively subject to national jurisdiction. Indeed, consistent with the notion in the law of the sea that problems of the ocean are interrelated and must be considered as a whole, an environmental crime committed at sea is a crime against the whole ocean. It is the marine environment and ultimately humanity that are at stake.

[12] I. Papanicolopulu, *International Law and the Protection of People at Sea* (Oxford: Oxford University Press, 2018), 84–87, 99; V. Becker-Weinberg, 'Time to get serious about combating forced labour and human trafficking in fisheries' (2020) 36 *The International Journal of Marine and Coastal Law*, 1–26.

[13] Art. 30 Charter of Economic Rights and Duties of States, UNGA Resolution 3281 (XXIX), 12 December 1974. The International Court of Justice recognized 'that the environment is not an abstraction but represent the living space, the quality of life and the very health of human beings, including generations unborn'. See *Legality of the Threat or Use of Nuclear Weapons, Advisory Opinion*, I.C.J. Reports 1996, para. 29; *Gabčíkovo-Nagymaros Project (Hungary/Slovakia)*, Judgment, I.C.J. Reports 1997, para. 140.

[14] See M. Fitzmaurice, 'International responsibility and liability', in: D. Bodansky, J. Brunnée and E. Hey (eds.), *The Oxford Handbook of International Environmental Law* (Oxford: Oxford University Press, 2007), 1020–1022. For an interpretation of Art. 288(1) UNCLOS allowing a State to pursue a case based on community interests see R. Wolfrum, 'Enforcing community interests through international dispute settlement: reality or utopia', in: Ulrich Fastenrath, Rudolf Geiger, Daniel-Erasmus Khan, Andreas Paulus, Sabine Von Schorlemer and Christoph Vedder (eds.), *From Bilateralism to Community Interest: Essays in Honour of Judge Bruno Simma* (Oxford: Oxford University Press, 2011), 1132–1145; Also *see* B. Simma, 'From bilateralism to community interest in international law' (1994) 250 *Recueil de cours de l'Académie de Droit Internationale de La Haye*, 217–384.

[15] Art. 87(2) UNCLOS. See *Request for an Examination of the Situation in Accordance with Paragraph 63 of the Court's Judgment of 20 December 1974 in the Nuclear Tests (New Zealand v. France) Case*, I.C.J. Reports 1995, para. 64.

International environmental law is a combination of fragmented international legal instruments and general principles and rules, included in both binding and non-binding instruments. No overarching normative framework applies to international environmental law, despite the fact that there have been calls for adoption of 'a comprehensive and unifying international instrument that gathers all the principles of environmental law'.[16]

However, like most, if not all, fields of international law, international environmental law suffers from several gaps and shortcomings. These are mostly the result of lack of political compromise and consensus between States, as well as the fact that implementation of international environmental law at national level varies and, consequently, hinders the possibility of ensuring a coherent international legal system. Yet, despite sparse customary international environmental law, certain rules and principles have become widely accepted and recognized by international courts and tribunals as part of the legal corpus that forms international environmental law, such as the obligation not to cause transboundary harm or damage.[17]

With respect specifically to protection and preservation of the marine environment, the entry into force of the United Nations Law of the Sea Convention (UNCLOS)[18] altered the perception of the relation between States and the ocean, giving way to awareness of the interconnectivity of different marine ecosystems and an understanding of the duty to cooperate as a fundamental principle in preventing pollution of the marine environment. The Convention also replaced the previously dominant reactive approach towards protection and preservation of the marine environment, with adoption of preventive measures and control of the sources of pollution. Moreover, UNCLOS comprises the notion that the obligation to protect and preserve the marine environment is connected with States' exercise of sovereignty and jurisdiction.

Nonetheless, at present no international legal regime specifically criminalizes and/or requires States to criminalize and punish acts and conduct that cause harm or damage to the marine environment.[19] Indeed, although protection and preservation of the marine environment has rightly captured global attention, little or no

[16] United Nations, Report of the Secretary-General, Gaps in International Environmental Law and Environment-related Instruments: Towards a Global Pact for the Environment, 30 November 2018, ref. UN Doc A/73/419, 2.

[17] In the context of the law of the sea, see Art. 194(2) UNCLOS. Also see V. Becker-Weinberg. *Joint Development of Hydrocarbon Deposits in the Law of the Sea* (Berlin, Heidelberg: Springer-Verlag, 2014), 116–120.

[18] 1833 UNTS 3.

[19] The International Convention for the Prevention of Pollution from Ships of 1973, as modified by the Protocol of 1978 (MARPOL 73/78), 1340 UNTS 62, includes certain provisions requiring some form of sanctioning, although not comprehensively. Customary international law does not make damage a requirement for state liability, see *Responsibilities and obligations of States sponsoring persons and entities with respect to activities in the Area, Advisory Opinion (Request for Advisory Opinion submitted to the Seabed Disputes Chamber)*, 1 February 2011, Case n. 17, paras. 178, 179, 210.

consideration has been given to the recognition of maritime environmental crimes in international law. Furthermore, in addition to the absence of an international effective response to tackle these crimes, the multijurisdictional challenge resulting from the intricate legal rules applicable to spatial and functional jurisdiction at sea have contributed to a permissive setting in which maritime environmental crimes take place, often going unreported, undetected and unpunished.

15.3 THE MULTIJURISDICTIONAL CHALLENGE

In order to overcome the multijurisdictional challenge caused by the rules on spatial and functional jurisdiction at sea, it is necessary to tackle existing gaps and overlapping rules that cause conflict of jurisdictions and, consequently, the ineffectiveness of international law to prevent and combat maritime environmental crimes. In this regard, the *M/V "Norstar"* Case *(Panama* v. *Italy)* addressed the possibility of non-flag States exercising prescriptive jurisdiction on the high seas where flag States traditionally enjoy freedom of navigation.[20] This development in the interpretation and application of international law reinforces the ground-breaking approach required for development of a new paradigm, which, together with innovative solutions available in State practice, could have a game-changing effect, such as the exercise of extraterritorial jurisdiction over maritime environmental crimes.[21]

15.3.1 *Spatial Jurisdiction*

Depending on where maritime environmental crimes are committed and the location of the infringing vessel, the applicable law and jurisdiction can vary. This can result in crimes being committed out of sight of any national authority and/or beyond the reach of any law enforcement arm. It can also lead to near-impossible timely and effective law enforcement operations.

The ocean is divided into areas that are subject to some measure of jurisdiction by coastal States and areas that cannot be claimed by or allocated to any State. Areas within national jurisdiction are the territorial sea, internal waters, international straits, archipelagic waters, contiguous zones, exclusive economic zones (EEZ) and the continental shelf.[22] The measure of jurisdiction enjoyed by States in these areas varies. In some cases (for example, the territorial sea and internal waters) coastal States have rights of sovereignty; in others (such as the continental shelf,

[20] *The M/V 'Norstar' case (Panama* v. *Italy)*, Judgment, 10 April 2019, ITLOS Case No. 25, www.itlos.org/fileadmin/itlos/documents/cases/case_no.25/Judgment/C25_Judgment_10.04.pdf (last accessed August 2021). See V. Becker-Weinberg, 'The M/V "Norstar" Case (Panama v. Italy)', in: *Il Diritto Maritimo* (2019), 760–766.

[21] D. Guilfoyle, 'Article 92', in: A Proelss (ed.), *United Nations Convention on the Law of the Sea (UNCLOS) A Commentary* (Munich: C.H. Beck Verlag, 2017), 234.

[22] Arts. 2, 8, 34, 46, 33, 55 and 76 UNCLOS.

the EEZ and, where established, the contiguous zone) they may exercise only limited sovereign and jurisdictional rights. Maritime areas beyond national jurisdiction are the high seas and the Area.[23]

The rights of foreign ships or vessels – terms not defined and used interchangeably in UNCLOS – vary from one maritime zone to the other. Most importantly, a foreign ship enjoys the right of innocent passage through the territorial sea on condition that passage is innocent.[24] This also means that a foreign ship does not engage in 'any act of wilful and serious pollution contrary to the Convention'.[25] That seems to preclude accidental pollution, in addition to creating uncertainty as to the meaning of 'wilful' and 'serious pollution', giving room for some level of discretion.[26] In the EEZ and the high seas the principle is that of freedom of navigation. There is no general right of innocent passage in internal waters; there, the coastal State may board a foreign ship and enforce its laws against the vessel and those on board.[27]

15.3.2 *Functional Jurisdiction*

Central to the challenge caused by functional jurisdiction at sea is the principle of flag State pre-emption. On the one hand, a flag State enjoys the 'monopoly'[28] of law enforcement at sea regarding ships flying its flag. On the other hand, the increasing number of ships at sea and the growing facilitation of movement of persons and goods across borders make it impossible for any flag State to monitor all ships flying its flag, as well as ensure compliance with national laws on pollution and enforcing the law.[29] This is even more challenging in the case of flags of convenience, where

[23] Arts. 1(1) (Part XI) and 86 UNCLOS. Arts. 1(1) UNCLOS defines 'Area' as 'the seabed and ocean floor and subsoil thereof, beyond the limits of national jurisdiction.' Provisions governing the Area are contained in Part XI UNCLOS. The high seas are governed by provisions of Part VII. According to 86 UNCLOS thereof, Part VII applies to 'all parts of the sea that are not included in the exclusive economic zone, in the territorial sea or in the internal waters of a State, or in the archipelagic waters of an archipelagic State.'

[24] Arts. 17, 18, Art. 19(1), (2)(a), 24(1), 52(1) and 54 UNCLOS. Similarly, Arts. 38, 39 and 45 UNCLOS recognize the rights of all ships to enjoy transit passage in straits used for international navigation.

[25] Art. 19(2) lit. h) UNCLOS. Also see Art. 211(4) UNCLOS.

[26] R. Barnes, 'Article 19', in: A. Proelss (ed.), *United Nations Convention on the Law of the Sea* (n 21), 194–195.

[27] The exception is provided in Art. 8(2) UNCLOS.

[28] Freedom of navigation is not an absolute freedom, being subject to exceptions: Arts. 92(2), 58 (1), (3), 78(2), 87(1)(a) and (2) UNCLOS. The most established exception is the universal jurisdiction to seize ships engaged in piracy, see Art. 105 UNCLOS. See *SS Lotus (France v. Turkey)*, 1927, Permanent Court of International Justice (PCIJ), Ser A, No 9, 25 (7 Sept), paras. 64–5. Also, MARPOL 73/78 determines that violation of its requirements shall be prohibited, and sanctions shall be established by flag States.

[29] Art. 211(2) UNCLOS.

there is no genuine link between the flag State and the ship. In these cases, flag States are simply unable and/or unwilling to enforce international law.[30]

There are also challenges facing coastal States and port States, as both are subject to specific obligations under the law of the sea to protect and preserve the marine environment, although they have limited prescriptive and enforcement jurisdiction within national maritime areas. Accordingly, coastal States have restrictive powers when a flag State fails to fulfil its obligations regarding protection and preservation of the marine environment, which are dependent on adoption of certain safeguards.[31]

Moreover, flag States that fail to protect and preserve the marine environment under domestic law are subject to the principle of state responsibility for breach of their general obligation to protect and preserve the marine environment.[32] In these cases, the basis for responsibility lies in obligations inherent to the concept of sovereignty as both control and responsibility are considered in the context of international accountability.

15.3.3 *Conflict of Jurisdictions*

A difficult legal and multijurisdictional challenge arises when a coastal State or a flag State is unable to enforce its own jurisdiction. In these cases, it is possible to have an overlap or conflict of jurisdictions that may inevitably result in ineffectiveness of international law. For example, a coastal State having evidence that a vessel is polluting in its territorial sea or EEZ may be unable to exercise its enforcement powers if the flag State exerts its prerogative to exercise jurisdictional pre-emption, even if the latter effectively fails to do so in practice.[33] Alternatively, the flag State of a vessel engaged in pollution in the territorial sea or EEZ cannot intervene if such conduct is tolerated by the coastal State, because any enforcement action in the territorial sea or EEZ without the consent of the coastal State would be a breach of the law of the sea.

In both cases, one of the States is (willingly or unwillingly) creating a permissive environment for maritime environmental crimes to take place. The result is international law becoming ineffective, despite existing legal rules allowing for the exercise of jurisdiction and enforcement powers. In these cases, crimes would go unpunished, despite being detected and reported.

[30] Art. 91(1) UNCLOS.

[31] Arts. 19(2)(h), 21(1)(f), 25, 27(5), 42(1)(b) and (2), 56(1)(b)(iii) and (2), 73(1), 87(2), 94(3)(a), 109 (4), 110, 111, 194(3)(b) and (4), 211, 218, 220, and 224–227 UNCLOS. On safeguards, see V. Becker-Weinberg, 'Article 223' to 'Article 233', in: A. Proelss (ed.), *United Nations Convention on the Law of the Sea* (n 21) 1527–1566.

[32] Art. 192 UNCLOS.

[33] Arts. 27(3) and 27(1) and 73 UNCLOS. See R. Barnes, 'Article 27', in: A. Proelss (ed.), *United Nations Convention on the Law of the Sea* (n 21), 234; and J. Harrison, 'Article 73', in: A. Proelss (ed.), *United Nations Convention on the Law of the Sea* (n 21) 556.

15.4 THE IMPORTANCE OF INTERNATIONAL COOPERATION

Important differences exist between environmental crimes taking place at sea and those on land. The maritime dimension of environmental crimes is a departure from the factual and legal reality of environmental crimes taking place on land, within the territory of one single State or across the territory of more than one State. On land, evidence of environmental crime, such as illegal transportation of waste, most notably hazardous waste and increasingly of plastic,[34] is more ample and easily obtained. Likewise, existing legal regimes addressing environmental crimes on land are greatly advanced and provide a more efficient response, particularly regarding responsibility and liability, including that of corporations.

Perpetrators use deceit and concealment as part of their modus operandi. In most cases, crimes occur while the vessel is on route, taking advantage of growing maritime traffic and avoiding detection, as well as during nighttime when visibility is low, seeing that detection of oil discharges relies on visual inspection.[35] Moreover, damage at sea is not always easily detected.[36] Even in situations of accidental pollution, ships often fail to report for fear of legal and financial repercussions.

Establishing causation can also be extremely difficult and is dependent on States cooperating by sharing information and intelligence, in addition to collaborating at operational level together with international law enforcement agencies. Also relevant in this regard is the need to ensure a certain level of harmonization with respect to the standard of evidence admissible under different national jurisdictions.[37]

In 2018, Interpol headed an international operation involving 276 law enforcement and environmental agencies across 58 States and a global network of 122 national coordinators. This operation lasted one month and carried out 5, 200 inspections that resulted in approximately 185 investigations and detected more than 500 offences, including illegal discharges of oil and garbage from vessels, shipbreaking, breaches of ship emissions regulations and pollution in rivers and land-based runoff to the sea.[38]

The following year, in 2019, Interpol led an operation encompassing sixty-one States and regional law enforcement partners, which identified thousands of illicit activities behind severe marine pollution. The preliminary results of this concerted operation that lasted one month, gathering more than 200 enforcement authorities worldwide across all continents, revealed more than 3,000 offences, detected during

[34] 'INTERPOL report alerts to Sharp rise in plastic waste crime': www.interpol.int/News-and-Events/News/2020/INTERPOL-report-alerts-to-sharp-rise-in-plastic-waste-crime (last accessed August 2021).

[35] Vollaard (n 5), 169.

[36] Ibid., 171.

[37] Ibid.

[38] 'Marine pollution crime: first global multi-agency operation, 13 November 2018': www.interpol.int/News-and-Events/News/2018/Marine-pollution-crime-first-global-multi-agency-operation (last accessed August 2021).

17,000 inspections. These offences were committed primarily to avoid the cost of compliance with environmental legislation.[39]

These examples highlight the vital importance of international cooperation between States and international law enforcement entities, such as Interpol[40] and Europol,[41] for gathering and sharing data and evidence, establishing causation and acting in a coordinated, timely and effective manner. However, the prevailing interpretation of applicable international law is that criminal acts and conduct that constitute maritime environmental crimes are subject to the exclusive jurisdiction of national law, even though only a few States have legislation on maritime environmental crimes and even fewer exercise jurisdiction. The United States is one of those States that has efficiently exercised prescriptive and enforcement jurisdiction. In addition to accepting and rewarding collaboration by whistleblowers,[42] the United States established exterritorial jurisdiction through the Oil Pollution Act of 1990, in addition to the well-known Aliens Tort Claims Act of 1789.[43]

Lastly, regarding international cooperation, it should be noted that there is no international body to monitor maritime environmental crimes or measure performance and progress, and identify ways to enhance cooperation between States. Existing organizations such as the International Maritime Organization or the United Nations Office on Drugs and Crime do not have the competence to tackle these crimes, despite the natural contiguity of their mandates in terms of protection and preservation of the marine environment[44] and combating transnational

[39] 'Marine pollution: thousands of serious offences exposed in global operation, 16 December 2019': www.interpol.int/News-and-Events/News/2019/Marine-pollution-thousands-of-serious-offences-exposed-in-global-operation (last accessed August 2021).

[40] See nn 38 and 39.

[41] Europol provides a regional law enforcement response to several cross-border aspects of transnational environmental crime. Europol–Environmental Crime: www.europol.europa.eu/crime-areas-and-trends/crime-areas/environmental-crime (last accessed August 2021).

[42] The Act to Prevent Pollution from Ships of 1980 allows a Court to issue a monetary award for up to one half of any imposed criminal fine to whistleblowers. See Whistleblower News Network, 'Whistleblower Detection Credited in 76% of Last 100 APPS Cases': https://whistleblowersblog.org/2018/05/articles/whistleblower-news/environmental-whistleblowers/whistleblower-detection-credited-in-76-of-last-100-apps-cases/ (last accessed August 2021).

[43] An action under the Aliens Tort Claims Act can be brought for torts (civil wrongs) against transnational corporations for violations of international human rights committed abroad, thus creating a tool to increase corporate accountability, even though it is only applicable to internationally agreed and recognized rights. This Act has become an opportunity for transnational legal action and the possibility for adjudication when other national legal systems have failed.

[44] Convention on the International Maritime Organization, Geneva, 6 March 1948, in force 17 March 1958, 289 UNTS 3. An example of expansion of the action of the IMO is the amendment of the Convention for the Suppression of Unlawful Acts against the Safety of Maritime Navigation and Protocol for the Suppression of Unlawful Acts Against the Safety of Fixed Platforms Located on the Continental Shelf, 1678 UNTS 201. See R. Balkin, 'The International Maritime Organization and Maritime Security' (2006) 30 *Tulane Maritime Law Journal*, 22–31.

organized crime or providing maritime law enforcement capacity building.[45] Consequently, important governance gaps exist between different organizations and a lack of aggregated information regarding the full impact of maritime environmental crimes throughout the world.

In short, lack of cooperation results in the ineffectiveness of international law to prevent and effectively combat maritime environmental crimes.

15.5 IS THERE ROOM FOR MARITIME ENVIRONMENTAL CRIMES WITHIN INTERNATIONAL LAW?

Despite the shortcomings of international law for not including specific rules on maritime environmental crimes, this does not mean no room is available for maritime environmental crimes in international law. It is necessary to consider the unity of international law and the need to achieve the functional systemic integration of different legal regimes. No international legal instrument is a self-contained regime and is certainly not impermeable to other legal regimes. Systemic integration can help fill the gaps and maximize efficiency of fragmented legal rules.

In order to deliver an improved collective and effective legal response to address maritime environmental crimes, it is necessary to go beyond the law of the sea and into other sources of international law. This is because maritime environmental crimes straddle different fields of international law. *Prima facie*, these include the law of the sea, international environmental law and international criminal law but also human rights law, as environmental rights are also human rights.[46] Indeed, international law has gradually widened the range and reinforced protection of environmental rights. This is the case for the 1998 Convention on Access to Information, Public Participation in Decision-Making and Access to Justice in Environmental Matters (Aarhus Convention),[47] which has influenced national and regional legislation on recognition of procedural environmental rights, as is the case for the European Union and its Member States.[48]

[45] United Nations Convention Against Transnational Organized Crime, 2225 UNTS 209. The UN Office on Drugs and Crime (UNODC) Global Maritime Crime Programme aims to provide maritime law enforcement capacity building, including techniques for conducting a vessel 'visit, board, search and seizure' process. In this regard, maritime crimes include piracy, fisheries crime, trafficking in persons and smuggling of migrants.

[46] The European Court of Human Rights, Case of *Mangouras* v. *Spain*, Judgment 28 September 2010.

[47] Aarhus, 25 June 1998, in force 30 October 2001, 2161 UNTS 447.

[48] Regulation (EC) No 1367/2006 of the European Parliament and of the Council of 6 September 2006 on the application of the provisions of the Aarhus Convention on Access to Information, Public Participation in Decision-making and Access to Justice in Environmental Matters to Community institutions and bodies; Directive 2003/35/EC of the European Parliament and of the Council of 26 May 2003 providing for public participation in respect of the drawing up of certain plans and programmes relating to the environment and amending with regard to public

The international legal framework on protection and preservation of the marine environment consists of several international legal instruments, in addition to regional frameworks and non-binding guidelines and recommendations from different international and regional organizations. The most relevant instruments addressing ship-source pollution are UNCLOS and the 1973 International Convention for the Prevention of Pollution from Ships, as modified by the 1978 Protocol (MARPOL 73/78).[49] These instruments were drafted in the wake of the 1967 'Torrey Canyon' and the 1978 'Amoco Cadiz' disasters involving oil tankers, which revealed the urgent need for improvement and enforcement of preventive measures in light of a rapidly expanding shipping sector and new developments in the field of marine pollution control. This called for adoption of more stringent requirements for ships entering or nearing States' waters in order to eliminate substandard ships.[50]

Although international legal instruments are not directly applicable to maritime environmental crimes, they bear relevance. In addition, when integrated with other sources of international law they can substantially improve the international response to maritime environmental crimes. Moreover, international liability rules in relation to environmental damage are still developing, notwithstanding general principles of international law that impose responsibility and liability for illegal acts, or the adverse consequences of lawful activities, many of which are included in the 2001 International Law Commission Draft Articles on State Responsibility, and some are considered to reflect customary international law.[51] In this regard, a new paradigm will enable establishment of communication veins where none exist at the moment as a result of the gaps caused by fragmentation of international law.

Perhaps the strongest example of the ability to establish communication veins can be found in the Rome Statute of the International Criminal Court (ICC), by clearly establishing a link between international criminal law and the environment. In the definition of war crime the Statute considers 'intentionally launching an attack in the knowledge that such attack will cause ... widespread, long-term and severe damage to the natural environment which would be clearly excessive in relation to

participation and access to justice Council Directives 85/337/EEC and 96/61/EC; Directive 2003/4/EC of the European Parliament and of the Council of 28 January 2003 on public access to environmental information and repealing Council Directive 90/313/EEC; Directive 2001/42/EC of the European Parliament and of the Council of 27 June 2001 on the assessment of the effects of certain plans and programmes on the environment; Directive 2000/60/EC of the European Parliament and of the Council of 23 October 2000 establishing a framework for Community action in the field of water policy: https://ec.europa.eu/environment/aarhus/legislation.htm (last accessed August 2021).

49 The International Convention for the Prevention of Pollution from Ships of 1973 (n 19).

50 UNCLOS III, Memorandum by the President of the Conference on Document A/CONF.62/WP.10 (UN Doc. A/CONF.62/WP.10/ADD.1), (1977), OR VIII, 65. Also see: Third Committee UNCLOS III, 31st Meeting (UN Doc. A/CONF.62/C.3/SR.31) (1976), OR VI, 100; Third Committee UNCLOS III, 32nd Meeting (UN Doc. A/ CONF.62/C.3/SR.32) (1976), OR VI, 106.

51 ITLOS, *Responsibilities and obligations of States* (n 19), para. 169.

the concrete and direct overall military advantage anticipated'.[52] In this regard the proposal to introduce 'ecocide'[53] as a new international crime under the Rome Statute,[54] in addition to a new preambular paragraph and amending Article 5, can undoubtedly contribute towards a change of paradigm.[55]

In order to achieve the ultimate goals of recognition of maritime environmental crimes within international law, no distinction should be drawn as to whether these crimes are committed in wartime or in peacetime. Instead, there should be integral protection of the environment under international criminal law.[56] Nonetheless, the underlying rationale of the example provided by the Rome Statute could be expanded, *mutatis mutandis*, and possible communication veins replicated between different legal regimes that are not sufficient, on their own, to support the concept of maritime environmental crimes within international law.

However, since international law is essentially state-centric, one could question how environmental rights can be interpreted and protected under the existing rules, when there is no international legal instrument establishing international criminal responsibility of natural or legal persons for maritime environmental crimes. This question exposes the deep disconnect between international law and protection of the marine environment from criminal acts, particularly as most maritime environmental issues are global in nature and not the specific problems of one or a group of persons.

Also challenging under international law is the need to demonstrate that pollution has had a harmful effect on the rights of persons and not simply a general deterioration of the environment.[57] With respect to individual criminal responsibility, it should be noted that Article 25 of the Rome Statute determines that the ICC wields jurisdiction over natural persons. So, should 'ecocide' be recognized as a new international crime within the jurisdiction of the ICC, the Court would have jurisdiction over a person who commits ecocide and, consequently, who would be individually responsible and liable for punishment under the Rome Statute, without

[52] Art. 8(2) lit. b) (iv) of the Rome Statute of the International Criminal Court, done in Rome on 17 July 1998 and entered into force on 1 July 2002, published in 2187 UNTS 90. Also see Art. 20 lit. g) of the International Law Commission Draft Code of Crimes against the Peace and Security of Mankind.

[53] STOP Ecocide Foundation (n 8).

[54] Art. 8 ter (1) defines 'ecocide' as unlawful or wanton acts committed with knowledge that there is a substantial likelihood of severe and either widespread or long-term damage to the environment being caused by those acts.

[55] On different proposals for a new crime against the environment and an analysis of 'ecocide', see A. Bustami and M.-C. Hecken, 'Perspectives for a New International Crime against the Environment: International Criminal Responsibility for Environmental Degradation under the Rome Statute' 11(1) *Goettingen Journal of International Law* (2021), 170–185.

[56] Ibid., 163–165.

[57] The European Court of Human Rights, Case of *Kyrtatos* v. *Greece*, Judgment 22 August 2003, paras. 52–53.

prejudice to the responsibility of States under international law. However, the Rome Statute does mention corporate criminal responsibility.

Regarding the need to show harmful effect, it should be noted that with recognition of maritime environmental crimes comes a new perspective, one that envisages protection of the environment for its own sake and ultimately that of humanity.[58] As mentioned in the introductory remarks, there is a need for a new global paradigm that is able to deliver an improved collective and effective legal response to address maritime environmental crimes, departing from what the law currently is and contributing towards progressive development of international law. In this regard, the inter-normative dialogue between international and national law could make a significant contribution. Indeed, although international environmental criminal law is an emerging field of international environmental law, there are examples of state practice involving prescription of maritime environmental crimes.

Similar to the development and progressive codification of international law, national legislative developments are also connected with environmental disasters that too often demonstrate the inadequacy of protection regimes to deter and prevent environmental crimes but also to punish those responsible and provide adequate remedies. This was the case of the US Oil Pollution Act of 1990, adopted following the 1989 *Exxon Valdez* oil spill disaster off the coast of Alaska, and the US Act to Prevent Pollution from Ships of 1980 in order to implement MARPOL 73/78.

National laws addressing environmental crimes vary considerably. Some are very lenient and others very stringent. Some impose strict liability, while others do not. Very often States adopt a complex system where environmental criminal law coexists with civil liability and administrative regulation, as is applicable to natural persons and/or to legal persons, namely corporations. In this regard the 1999 *Erika* and 2002 *Prestige* disasters involving oil tankers, respectively off the coasts of France and Spain, are a clear reminder of how lack of inter-normative dialogue can lead to conflict between different sources of law and pose serious liability and jurisdictional challenges. It also demonstrates the many obstacles facing environmental criminal law when these incidents take place at sea and the difficulty in applying international and national law.[59]

Therefore, development of the new paradigm should also focus on the inter-normativity and reciprocal influence between international, regional and national law, taking into consideration the growing expansion of both international and regional law with respect to the marine environment. For example, by establishing extraterritorial jurisdiction with respect to maritime environmental crimes States are able to extend the applicability of the law and the use of penalties beyond national

[58] Butami and Hecken (n 55), 166–168.

[59] V. Frank, 'Consequences of the Prestige Sinking for European and International Law' (2005) 20(1) *The International Journal of Marine and Coastal Law*, 1–64.

borders. This is the case of the US Oil Pollution Act of 1990, which provides that its criminal provisions may apply to foreign nationals beyond its territory, giving the USA a broader range for action than provided under international law. These and other similar national legislative developments regarding the exercise of prescriptive and enforcement jurisdiction at sea can significantly influence international law.

15.6 CONCLUSIONS AND OUTLOOK

The ocean is getting busier. The increasing number of ships at sea and the growing facilitation of movement of persons and goods across borders constitute a serious challenge to individual flag States in regulating and monitoring all ships flying their flag. This is also a challenge for coastal and port States, because of the limitations imposed by spatial and functional jurisdiction at sea.

Moreover, the shipping industry is entering a new era, with the introduction of unmanned ships. Likewise, there are new usages and activities in the ocean, in addition to global threats, such as climate change, sea level rise and ocean acidification. These pressures are having a significant impact on the marine environment and humankind, but none more so than maritime environmental crimes.

The body of rules and principles applicable to protection and preservation of the marine environment, drafted in the 1970s and early 1980s during the III United Nations Conference on the Law of the Sea and other codification efforts, does not meet current expectations and the environmental rights discourse. Simply put, existing international legal rules do not echo the overall concern for protection and preservation of the marine environment, and neither do they meet the expectations of those looking for implementation and enforcement of more stringent and effective rules. There is no international legally binding rule, body of rules or principle that criminalizes or establishes an obligation for States to criminalize transnational organized maritime environmental crime.

Consequently, recognition of and adherence to the notion of transnational organized maritime environmental crime would have the effect that criminalization would no longer be dependent solely on domestic law, even though it would be difficult to overcome the limitations resulting from the existing legal framework applicable to prescriptive, and especially enforcement, jurisdiction at sea. In this regard, proposals for a new international crime such as 'ecocide' could potentially lead the way for further development of international law and of the legal tools necessary to ensure a collective and effective legal response to maritime environmental crimes.

In the meantime, under the current international regime, States have very limited powers of enforcement when a flag State fails to fulfil its obligations regarding protection and preservation of the marine environment, despite the fact that, arguably, flag States that fail to protect and preserve the marine environment under domestic law are subject to the principle of state responsibility. In these cases, the basis for responsibility lies in the obligations inherent to the concept of sovereignty as both control and responsibility, taking into account the context of international accountability.[60] States remain responsible for lack of due diligence and ultimately for allowing the persistence of permissive circumstances for acts of pollution to occur and remain unpunished. A difficult legal challenge arises when a coastal State or a flag State with jurisdiction is unable to enforce its own jurisdiction.

Therefore, States must lawfully and legally assert their maritime jurisdiction, both spatial and functional. This should also include extraterritorial jurisdiction.

Following the exercise of prescriptive jurisdiction, States must also establish the situations and conditions for the exercise of enforcement jurisdiction, or maritime law enforcement, in accordance with international law and in particular the law of the sea, including with respect to boarding, detention, arrest, search and seizure of a ship. States must further provide internal remedies and access to justice.

Lastly, international cooperation is essential to ensure effective protection and preservation of the marine environment, as well as to address circumstances favourable to organized crime, such as the presence of corruption, bribery and obstruction of justice. Law enforcement cooperation and the sharing of investigative tools and evidence and intelligence are particularly important, including for the purpose of enforcement and prosecution.

60 International Commission on Intervention and State Sovereignty (ICISS), *The Responsibility to Protect: Report of the International Commission in Intervention and State Sovereignty* (International Development Research Centre, 2011), 12.

16

Mending the Net

State Responsibility for Nationals Engaged in IUU Fishing?

Pieter van Welzen

16.1 INTRODUCTION

Illegal, unreported and unregulated (IUU) fishing is a serious threat to the world's food resources, frustrates efforts to conserve and protect marine living resources and ecosystems, and threatens geopolitical stability.[1] The resources and economies of developing States, in particular, are badly affected by IUU fishing operations in their EEZs.[2] The purpose of this chapter is to consider whether it can be argued that States whose nationals are owners or operators of fishing vessels involved in IUU fishing activities have an obligation to act against those persons.[3]

Although a considerable number of international, governmental and non-governmental organisations are involved in the fight against IUU fishing, it still occurs on a large scale, and the rules, as currently applied, have for various reasons not proven to be very effective. For example, the UN Convention on the Law of the Sea (UNCLOS)[4] imposes primary responsibility on coastal States to regulate fishing operations in their EEZ and to enforce such regulations. However, States, in particular developing States, may not have the resources and capacity to regulate fishing in their EEZ and to enforce such regulations meaningfully. Moreover,

[1] See for an explanation of the meaning of 'illegal', 'unreported' and 'unregulated' in the definition of IUU fishing, for example G. Oanta, 'Illegal fishing as a criminal act at sea', in Hague Academy of International Law, *The Centre for Studies and Research in International Law and International Relations* (Leiden/Boston: Brill Nijhoff, 2014), 157.

[2] The damaging impact of IUU fishing is for example described in M. Palma, M. Tsamenyi and W. Edeson, *Promoting Sustainable Fisheries: The International Legal and Policy Framework to Combat Illegal, Unreported and Unregulated Fishing* (Leiden/Boston: Martinus Nijhoff, 2010), 9; and A. Shaver and S. Yozell, *Casting a Wider Net: The Security Implication of Illegal, Unreported and Unregulated Fishing* (Washington, DC: Stimson, 2018), 7, 11.

[3] This question appears still unanswered. See V. Schatz, 'The contribution of fisheries access agreements to flag State responsibility' (2017) 84 *Marine Policy*, 318.

[4] United Nations Convention on the Law of the Sea, Montego Bay, 10 December 1982, in force 16 November 1994, 1833 UNTS 3.

although international law gives flag States an important role in the fight against IUU fishing, not all flag States are willing to fulfil this task or capable of doing so. This is often the case with States that offer flags of convenience.[5] However, there are also more established flag States whose vessels are regularly involved in IUU fishing, without the flag State appearing to take much visible action against such activities.[6]

A further reason, intertwined with the failure of coastal States and flag States to act against IUU fishing operations, is the relationship between these operations and the involvement of transnational corporations that are active 'behind the scenes', often as operators or beneficial owners of the vessels involved in these operations. Given the profits that can be made by engaging in IUU fishing, these corporations are willing to take considerable risks. Therefore, the sanctions that can be imposed by coastal States for IUU fishing infractions are not treated as a deterrent but as a cost of doing business.[7] Often advantage is taken of weaknesses in the administrative and enforcement systems of coastal States and port States.[8] The financial interests involved also result in the use of more sophisticated methods for circumventing applicable regulations, such as trans-shipment of fish from fishing vessels to refrigerated transport vessels or by reflagging vessels on a regular basis.[9] Corporations that engage in IUU fishing are sometimes involved in other, related, criminal activities such as forced labour, corruption, human trafficking, smuggling or drug running.[10]

By prohibiting persons from being involved in IUU fishing activities, for example as operators or owners of vessels, and imposing appropriate sanctions in the case of breach of the prohibition, fewer incentives will exist for IUU fishing operations.

5 North Atlantic Fisheries Intelligence Group, *Chasing Red Herrings: Flags of Convenience and the Impact on Fisheries Crime Law Enforcement* (Copenhagen: The Nordic Council of Ministers, 2017); and UN Office on Drugs and Crime (UNODC), *Rotten Fish –A Guide to Addressing Corruption in the Fisheries Sector* (Vienna: United Nations, 2019).

6 Shaver and Yozell (n 2), 8.

7 See for example M. Beke, R. Ackermann and R. Blomeyer, *The Common Fisheries Policy: Infringement Procedures and Imposed Sanctions throughout the EU, Committee on Fisheries* (Brussels: European Parliament, 2014), 62.

8 A. Telesetsky, 'Laundering fish in the global undercurrents: Illegal, unreported, and unregulated fishing and transnational organized crime' (2014) 41(4) *Ecology Law Quarterly*, 939, 960; and M. Beseng, 'Cameroon's choppy waters: The anatomy of fisheries crime in the maritime fisheries sector' (2019) 108 *Marine Policy*, 4.

9 V. Mundy, *The Impact of the EU IUU Regulation on Seafood Trade Flows: Identification of Intra-EU Shifts in Import Trends Related to the Catch Certification Scheme and Third Country Carding Process* (Brussels: Environmental Justice Foundation, Oceana, The Pew Charitable Trusts, WWF, 2018), 60.

10 For example: INTERPOL Environmental Security Directorate, *Study on Fisheries Crime in the West African Coastal Region* (Paris: INTERPOL, 2014), 21; and North Atlantic Fisheries Intelligence Group (n 5), 26.

16.2 IUU FISHING: CURRENT FRAMEWORK

16.2.1 *UNCLOS*

UNCLOS has created various maritime zones, each with distinct rights and responsibilities.[11] With regard to the EEZ, UNCLOS contains provisions that deal with fishing activities by vessels flying the flag of another State. Article 56(1)(a) UNCLOS grants sovereign rights to a coastal State for exploring and exploiting, conserving and managing marine resources in its EEZ. Paragraph (b) of the same provision grants a coastal State jurisdiction for protection and preservation of the marine environment. Article 62(4) UNCLOS describes, on a non-enumerative basis, the topics of the laws and regulations that a coastal State may impose in connection with fishing and related activities in its EEZ. Next to these rights, UNCLOS also imposes obligations on coastal States, requiring them to promote the objective of optimum utilisation of the living resources in their EEZ[12] and to apply proper conservation and management measures so that the living resources in their EEZ are not endangered by over-exploitation.[13] A coastal State must also cooperate with other States for the conservation of marine species and stocks that are shared with such other States.[14] Article 192 UNCLOS applies to all maritime zones created by UNCLOS, including the EEZ, and obligates States to protect and preserve the marine environment.[15]

Under Article 58(3) UNCLOS, for example, a State that exercises its rights in the EEZ of another State must comply with the laws and regulations adopted by that other State. Although this rule is addressed to States, it has been interpreted as an obligation on a State to ensure that its nationals, when fishing in the EEZ of another State, observe the regulations of the coastal State.[16] Pursuant to Article 62(4) UNCLOS nationals of States fishing in the EEZ must comply with the conservation and other fisheries-related measures of the EEZ coastal State. If a vessel breaches the coastal State's fisheries regulations, that State can, pursuant to Article 73(1) UNCLOS, act against the relevant vessel and its crew, including boarding,

[11] See for a more detailed description: N. Matz-Lücke and J. Fuchs, 'Marine living resources', in D. Rothwell et al., *The Oxford Handbook of the Law of the Sea* (Oxford: Oxford University Press, 2015), 497; and R. Churchill and A. Lowe, *The Law of the Sea* (Manchester: Manchester University Press, 1999), 288.

[12] Art.62(1) UNCLOS.

[13] Art.61(2) UNCLOS.

[14] Arts. 63 to 67 UNCLOS.

[15] For a more general discussion regarding this provision, see D. Czybulka, 'Article 192: General obligation', in A. Proelss (ed.), *The United Nations Convention on the Law of the Sea: A Commentary* (Munich, Oxford and Baden-Baden: C.H. Beck/Hart/Nomos, 2017), para. 18; and J. Mossop, 'Can we make the oceans greener: The successes and failures of UNCLOS as an environmental treaty' (2018) 49(4) *Victoria University of Wellington Law Review*, 558.

[16] A. Proelss, Article 58: Rights and duties of other States in the exclusive economic zone in Proelss, *UNCLOS Commentary* (n 15), para. 24.

inspection and arrest of the vessel and initiation of judicial proceedings.[17] However, the arrested vessel and its crew must be promptly released upon the posting of a reasonable bond or other security.[18] Sanctions imposed on crew members may not include imprisonment or any form of corporal punishment.[19]

16.2.2 *ITLOS Advisory Opinion*

Since UNCLOS contains no specific provisions about the responsibility of flag States for fishing in the EEZ of another State, the question arose whether a coastal State could hold a flag State liable for IUU fishing by vessels flying its flag in that coastal State's EEZ. The Sub-Regional Fisheries Commission, whose membership consists of a number of West African States that suffer from IUU fishing in their EEZs, requested the International Tribunal for the Law of the Sea (ITLOS) for an opinion on this question, which ITLOS provided in April 2015 (the ITLOS Advisory Opinion).[20] ITLOS stated therein that the primary responsibility for taking the necessary measures to prevent, deter and eliminate IUU fishing in the EEZ rests with the EEZ coastal State.[21] However, this primary responsibility does not release other States from their obligations in this respect.[22] With regard to the role of flag States whose vessels conduct IUU fishing activities in the EEZ of another State, ITLOS observed that UNCLOS contains general obligations for the conservation and management of marine living resources, set out in its Articles 91, 92, 94, 192 and 193, which are to be met by flag States in all maritime areas regulated by UNCLOS, including the EEZ of another State. It also noted that Articles 58(3) and 62(4) contain specific obligations in this respect with regard to fishing activities conducted by nationals of a flag State in the EEZ of another State.[23]

ITLOS held that a flag State must ensure compliance by its vessels with the relevant conservation measures enacted by a coastal State for its EEZ.[24] This is a due diligence obligation and not an obligation of result.[25] Accordingly, a flag State's liability under international law in connection with IUU fishing arises from its

[17] The measures are described in more detail in Palma, Tsamenyi and Edeson (n 2), 147.
[18] Art.73(2) UNCLOS.
[19] Art.73(3) UNCLOS.
[20] ITLOS, Request for an Advisory Opinion submitted by the Sub-Regional Fisheries Commission (SRFC) (2015) ITLOS Case No. 21. See for a critical analysis: V. Schatz, 'Fishing for interpretation: The ITLOS advisory opinion on flag state responsibility for illegal fishing in the EEZ' (2016) 47 *Ocean Development & International Law*, 327.
[21] ITLOS Advisory Opinion (n 20), paras. 96 and 106.
[22] Ibid., para. 108.
[23] Ibid., para. 111.
[24] Ibid., para. 120.
[25] Ibid., para. 129.

failure to comply with the due diligence obligation and, therefore, a flag State is not liable for IUU fishing in the EEZ of another State by vessels flying its flag if it has taken all necessary and appropriate measures to meet this obligation.[26]

The ITLOS Advisory Opinion focuses on the obligation of vessels to comply with a coastal State's fisheries regulations. However, the vessel is generally not the addressee of such regulations. These are typically directed at persons who control the movements of the vessel and the activities in which the vessel is involved, such as the master, crew members, owner and operator of the vessel.[27] These persons are often not nationals of or resident in the flag State concerned. This means that, for enforcement of its regulations against foreign owners, operators and crew members of the vessel, a flag State will be dependent on cooperation from other States, which may not be forthcoming. It is not clear whether ITLOS considered this point when concluding that the flag State was responsible for IUU fishing activities conducted by vessels flying its flag as well as by its nationals.[28] There is no reference in the ITLOS Advisory Opinion to the responsibilities of states of which owners or operators of fishing vessels are nationals.

16.2.3 *Other Instruments*

Recognising that relying on flag and coastal States to fight IUU fishing may not be sufficient, other ways to act against IUU fishing must be considered. One could prohibit landing fish that originate from IUU fishing, which is the main purpose of the Agreement on Port State Measures (PSMA).[29] The PSMA allows, and in some cases requires, a State to refuse entry to its ports[30] or use of port services[31] by a vessel that has been or is suspected to have been engaged in IUU fishing. Other measures, such as those adopted by the EU[32] and the United States,[33] are market

[26] Ibid., paras. 146–148.

[27] For example, in a West African context the laws of Cameroon, Gambia, Ghana, Guinea Bissau, Liberia and Senegal impose vicarious liability on the owner of a vessel for breaches of its fisheries regulations. Operators of the vessel can be held liable under the laws of Cabo Verde, Gabon, Ghana, Guinea Bissau, Guinea Conakry, Liberia, Mauritania, Nigeria, Senegal and Sierra Leone.

[28] ITLOS Advisory Opinion (n 20), para. 124.

[29] Agreement on Port State Measures to Prevent, Deter and Eliminate Illegal, Unreported and Unregulated Fishing, Rome, 22 November 2009, in force 5 June 2016, 55 ILM 1157.

[30] Ibid., Art. 9.

[31] Ibid., Art. 11.

[32] Council Regulation (EC) No 1005/2008 of 29 September 2008 establishing a Community system to prevent, deter and eliminate illegal, unreported and unregulated fishing, amending Regulations (EEC) No 2847/93, (EC) No 1936/2001 and (EC) No 601/2004 and repealing Regulations (EC) No 1093/94 and (EC) No 1447/1999, OJ 2008 No L 286, 29 October 2008 (EU IUU Regulation).

[33] The Magnuson–Stevens Fishery Conservation and Management Act (16 U.S.C. 1801 – 1891(d)) (2014). See further A. Telesetsky, 'U.S. seafood traceability as food law and the future of marine fisheries' (2017) 47 *Environmental Law*, 765.

focused[34] and enable the competent authorities to restrict the import of fish that has been caught by vessels flagged to a State that condones IUU fishing activities.[35] However, the impact of EU and US measures appears to be limited as a result of a lack of implementation and application.[36]

There have also been suggestions to characterise IUU fishing as organised crime under the United Nations Convention against Transnational Organized Crime (UNTOC).[37] If it is considered as a 'serious crime' under UNTOC, then a legal basis would exist for extradition, mutual legal assistance and law enforcement cooperation. However, since Article 73(3) UNCLOS prohibits imposition by a coastal State of prison sentences on crew members involved in IUU fishing, it is questionable whether a coastal State can qualify IUU fishing by foreign vessels in its EEZ as a form of organised crime as defined in UNTOC.[38]

It has also been suggested that if it is not possible to act against IUU fishing activities themselves, one could consider prosecuting the offenders for other, related criminal activities, which may be easier to characterise as organised crime.[39] This alternative is, however, not so straightforward. First, there must have been such a related criminal activity. Second, a State should have regulatory and enforcement jurisdiction to prosecute the crime. If reliance is placed on the flag State of the vessel or the affected coastal State, similar capacity issues as mentioned earlier in the context of IUU fishing offences may arise.

[34] However, it is not clear to what extent these market restrictions are compatible with GATT/WTO rules. See for example, A. Telesetsky, 'Scuttling IUU fishing and rewarding sustainable fishing: Enhancing the effectiveness of the Port State Measures Agreement with trade-related measures' (2015) 38 *Seattle University Law Review*, 1267.

[35] K. Wyman, 'Unilateral steps to end high seas fishing' (2018) 6(1) *Texas A&M Law Review*, 259; and Palma, Tsamenyi and Edeson (n 2), 173.

[36] European Commission, Commission Staff Working Document Impact Assessment Accompanying the document Proposal for a Regulation of the European Parliament and of the Council Amending Council Regulation (EC) No 1224/2009, and amending Council Regulations (EC) No 768/2005, (EC) No 1967/2006, (EC) No 1005/2008, and Regulation (EU) No 2016/1139 of the European Parliament and of the Council as regards fisheries controls, SWD/2018/280 final, 30 May 2018; and Natural Resources Defense Council, 'On the Hook: How the United States Enables Illegal, Unreported, and Unregulated Fishing', January 2021, 14.

[37] United Nations Convention against Transnational Organized Crime, Palermo, 12 December 2000, in force 29 September 2003, 40 ILM 335 (2001).

[38] Art.2(b) UNTOC defines 'serious crime' as 'conduct constituting an offence punishable by a maximum deprivation of liberty of at least four years or a more serious penalty'. However, other States, such as flag States, market States and States whose nationals are involved in IUU fishing, are not bound by the limitation of Art. 73(3) UNCLOS.

[39] See, for example, Telesetsky, 'Laundering fish' (n 8), 939; and P. Bondaroff, N. Teale et al., *The Illegal Fishing and Organized Crime Nexus: Illegal Fishing as Transnational Organized Crime'* (Geneva: The Global Initiative against Transnational Organized Crime and the Black Fish, 2015), 36.

16.3 CHALLENGING THE PERSONS BEHIND THE SCENES

16.3.1 *Owners, Operators and Other Beneficiaries*

It is recognised by law enforcement agencies and non-governmental organisations that if the international community wants to fight effectively against IUU fishing, action needs to be taken against the persons and organisations that operate behind the scenes of IUU fishing and on whose behalf their activities are undertaken, such as the operators and beneficial owners of vessels.[40] Various actions could be taken against these persons. More traditional criminal and administrative sanctions could be imposed.[41] In particular, where financial sanctions are not substantial, these could be combined with confiscation of (estimated) profits.[42] Alternative sanctions could include withdrawal of subsidies or tax benefits, tax increases,[43] revocation of licences,[44] restrictions on insurability or voidance of existing insurance policies.[45] These alternative sanctions can be useful in situations where the activities of the persons themselves are legitimate. As a result of these measures, their activities will become more expensive or riskier. They will, however, have limited impact on activities by criminal organisations that do not pay taxes or are not beneficiaries of subsidies.

The effectiveness and impact of sanctions is largely dependent on the ease with which sanctions can be imposed and the ability to enforce them effectively.[46] The owners and operators of vessels involved in IUU fishing may be located in States that are potentially in a better position in terms of capacity and experience to take enforcement action than the affected developing coastal or flag State.[47] From that perspective, it would be desirable if the State where the persons are located were able to exercise both regulatory and enforcement jurisdiction.

[40] Bondaroff et al. (n 39), 70; Shaver and Yozell, (n 2), 29; OECD Trade and Agriculture Directorate – Fisheries Committee, *Combatting Illegal, Unreported and Unregulated Fishing: Where Countries Stand and Where Efforts Should Concentrate in the Future*' (Paris: OECD Secretariat, 2018), 12, 38, 42.

[41] Art. 44 EU IUU Regulation (n 32). See also N. Noval, *The Spanish Legal Process for Prosecuting Illegal Fishing: A Story of Success?* (Madrid: ClientEarth, 2019).

[42] See Arts. 44 and 46 EU IUU Regulation (n 32); Bondaroff et al., (n 40), 70.

[43] P. Bender and G. Lugten, 'Taxing illegal fishing (A proposal for using taxation law to reduce profiteering from IUU fishing offences)' (2007) 22(4) *The International Journal of Marine and Coastal Law*, 517.

[44] See Art. 45 EU IUU Regulation (n 32).

[45] D. Miller, 'Cutting a lifeline to maritime crime: Marine insurance and IUU fishing' (2016) 7 *Frontiers in Ecology and the Environment*, 357.

[46] Bondaroff et al. (n 40), 50.

[47] For the role of EU Member States as operators or beneficial owners of vessels engaged in IUU fishing see, for example: Environmental Justice Foundation, *Pirate Fishing Exposed: The Fight Against Illegal Fishing in West Africa and the EU* (London: Environmental Justice Foundation, 2012), 31.

It is acknowledged that transnational corporations involved in IUU fishing typically operate through a network of nominee companies, thereby making it more difficult to create a direct link between the registered owner of a vessel that is engaged in IUU fishing and its beneficial owner.[48] However, the use of 'big data', anti-tax evasion and anti-money laundering regulations make it easier nowadays to identify the beneficial owners of companies.[49]

Furthermore, if being involved in IUU fishing as owners and operators of vessels is already sanctionable, it may not be necessary to prove a direct link between particular illegal fishing activities of a vessel in a State's EEZ (with an *in flagrante* arrest of the vessel), and other forms of evidence could be used, such as an involvement in the organisational or financial aspects of IUU fishing operations, the marketing of the resulting fish or fish products, or documentary inconsistencies. The State where the corporations are located could also treat their involvement in IUU fishing as a form of organised crime so that the cooperation arrangements of UNTOC would apply.[50]

16.3.2 *Exercise of Jurisdiction*

A State whose nationals are involved in IUU fishing as owners or operators of a fishing vessel could have a meaningful role to fulfil in the fight against IUU fishing. What jurisdictional basis could it use for this purpose? First, it could do so by applying the so-called active personality principle.[51] On the basis of this principle, a State can assert criminal jurisdiction over the conduct of its nationals abroad.[52] This personality link could be extended from nationality to residence or domicile if the connection is strong enough to meet the jurisdictional purposes in question.[53] It may also be possible for a State to create jurisdiction over activities connected to IUU fishing that have taken place or are deemed to have taken place within its territory.[54] It could, for example, provide that it is illegal within its territory to organise, direct or finance activities that result in a breach of the

48 Telesetsky, 'Laundering fish' (n 8), 989; North Atlantic Fisheries Intelligence Group (n 5), 24; and A. Brush, *Strings Attached: Exploring the Onshore Networks behind Illegal, Unreported, & Unregulated Fishing* (New York: C4ADS, 2019).

49 See for example OECD, *Fighting Tax Crime: The Ten Global Principles* (Paris: OECD, 2017).

50 Such state is not bound by the limitations that follow from Art. 73(3) UNCLOS.

51 Palma, Tsamenyi and Edeson (n 2), 102.

52 A. Mills, 'Rethinking jurisdiction in international law' (2014) 84(1) *British Yearbook of International Law*, 198.

53 C. Blattner, 'The unexplored: Direct extraterritoriality', in Charlotte E. Blattner (ed.), *Protecting Animals Within and Across Borders: Extraterritorial Jurisdiction and the Challenges of Globalization* (Oxford: Oxford University Press, 2019), 173.

54 Mills (n 52), 196.

fishing laws of another State. This will create territorial jurisdiction of the State concerned.

A number of States already have legislation in place that addresses nationals who are involved in IUU fishing operations. For example, the EU IUU Regulation provides that nationals who are subject to the jurisdiction of a Member State should neither support nor engage in IUU fishing, including by engagement on board or as operators or beneficial owners of fishing vessels included in the EU IUU vessel list.[55] It also provides that Member States must take appropriate action with regard to nationals identified as supporting or engaged in IUU fishing.[56] Spain and Portugal have included provisions in their legislation that implement these obligations.[57] Other States, such as New Zealand and Australia, also prohibit the involvement of their nationals in IUU fishing.[58]

Another interesting example is the US Lacey Act.[59] In the context of IUU fishing, this prohibits the import, export, transport, sale, receipt, acquisition or purchase in inter-state or foreign commerce of any fish or wildlife taken, possessed, transported or sold in violation of any law or regulation of any State or in violation of any foreign law.[60] It therefore targets US nationals involved in the supply chain of illegally caught fish. Since the Lacey Act refers to foreign law generally, it covers IUU fishing in another State's EEZ.[61] It was applied in a case involving the import into the United States of lobster that was illegally caught in South Africa's territorial waters and EEZ. In 2017, after extended legal proceedings, the person who directed the illegal activities, a certain Mr Bengis, was given a prison sentence of 57 months. The courts also imposed a forfeiture order of USD 37 million. A substantial part of the funds recovered from Mr Bengis was handed over to South Africa as compensation for the losses that it suffered due to these illegal fishing activities.[62]

[55] Art. 39(1) EU IUU Regulation (n 32).

[56] Ibid., Art. 39(3).

[57] Spain: Art. 2 Royal Decree 1134/2002 of 31 October; and Art. 101(k) and (l) Law 3/2001 of 26 March; Portugal: Art. 9 Decree Law 35/19.

[58] New Zealand: Art. 113A(1) Fisheries Act 1996, Public Act 1996 No 88; Australia: Arts. 105F and 105FA Fisheries Management Act 1991, No. 162, 1991. See also G. Rose and M. Tsamenyi, *Universalizing Jurisdiction over Marine Living Resources Crimes* (Gland: World Wide Fund for Nature, 2013), 58.

[59] Lacey Act (18 USC 42-43; 16 USC 3371-3378). See also G. Arevalo, 'Free trade agreements and the Lacey Act: A carrot and stick approach to prevent and deter trade in IUU fisheries' (2015) 10 *Florida A & M University Law Review*, 349.

[60] 16 USC Section 3372(a)(2)(A).

[61] The US courts interpret 'foreign law' quite broadly. See M. White, 'Overcriminalization based on Foreign Law: How the Lacey Act incorporates foreign law to overcriminalize importers and users of timber products' (2013) 12(2) *Washington University Global Studies Law Review*, 388.

[62] See C. Dutot, 'Hout Bay and the illegal lobster trade: a case study in recovering illicit proceeds of IUU fishing and wildlife trafficking' (Basel: Basel Institute on Governance (Green Corruption Case Study), 2021). For a detailed description of the facts and the initial proceedings, see M. Asner, 'To catch a wildlife thief: Strategies and suggestions for the fight against illegal wildlife trafficking' (2016) 12 *University of Pennsylvania Asian Law Review*, 4.

16.4 OBLIGATION TO ACT AGAINST NATIONALS INVOLVED IN IUU FISHING?

16.4.1 *UNCLOS and Responsibility for IUU Fishing Operations*

States whose nationals (or residents) are engaged in IUU fishing operations can take measures against those persons. The next question is whether they have an obligation under international law to do so.[63] There are indeed grounds for arguing that there is such an obligation. It may in this context be useful to look at the provisions of UNCLOS that are relevant to fishing and the conservation of marine resources in a State's EEZ. As mentioned previously, Article 192 applies to all States that are a party to UNCLOS, Article 62(4) applies to the nationals of other States who are fishing in a coastal State's EEZ and Article 58(3) to all States with an activity or interest in the coastal State's EEZ. Therefore, although the ITLOS Advisory Opinion links the obligation to comply with conservation measures to flag States (also as a result of the questions that ITLOS was asked), the provisions to which it refers are not limited to flag States. Although applying to the high seas only, Article 117 UNCLOS is another provision with a reference to 'nationals'. It has been suggested that the term 'national' should extend to individuals and entities who operate behind the scenes, including by piercing the corporate veil.[64]

Article 62(4) UNCLOS refers to nationals of other States fishing in another State's EEZ.[65] The question here is whether 'other States' refers only to vessels and nationals of the vessel's flag State or whether it could also include other States, for example the States of which the operators or owners of the vessel are nationals. As mentioned earlier, there are various States whose fisheries laws include provisions that apply to the owner or operator of a vessel or provide that an owner or operator can be held liable for breaches of its fisheries laws. The 'other States' to which Article 62(4) UNCLOS refers should therefore in my view also include the States of which such owners and operators are nationals.[66]

63 Although not possible to analyse it in this chapter, the 'no harm' principle (*sic utere tuo ut alienum non laedas*) could also support such an obligation on a more general basis.

64 R. Rayfuse, 'Article 117: Duty of States to adopt with respect to their nationals measures for the conservation of living resources of the high seas', in Proelss, *UNCLOS Commentary* (n 15), para. 35.

65 Its first sentence reads as follows: 'Nationals of other States fishing in the exclusive economic zone shall comply with the conservation measures and with the other terms and conditions established in the laws and regulations of the coastal State'.

66 Various examples of regulations that a coastal State can impose as listed in Art. 62(4) UNCLOS would typically be directed at the owners and operators of the vessel rather than the vessel itself or its crew.

16.4.2 *Obligation to Act against Nationals Involved in IUU Fishing?*

According to the ITLOS Advisory Opinion, Article 192 UNCLOS imposes on all States parties to UNCLOS an obligation to protect and preserve the marine environment. This applies to all maritime areas, including those encompassed by an EEZ.[67] This provision was also discussed in the South Chinese Sea Arbitration award,[68] where the arbitral tribunal considered it well established that Article 192 UNCLOS entails a positive obligation to take active measures to protect and preserve the marine environment, and by logical implication, the negative obligation not to degrade the marine environment. The arbitral tribunal emphasised that Article 192 UNCLOS sets forth obligations not only in relation to activities directly undertaken by States and their organs but also also obligations to ensure that activities within their jurisdiction and control do not harm the marine environment.[69] This could imply that a State is required to take action against persons (such as owners and operators of vessels involved in IUU fishing operations) under its jurisdiction who adversely affect the marine environment in an area under the control of another State, such as another State's EEZ.

The notion that States have a general obligation to ensure that their nationals are not involved in IUU fishing (and therefore not limited to vessels flying its flag) can further be found in paragraph 18 of the FAO International Plan of Action to Prevent, Deter, and Eliminate Illegal, Unreported and Unregulated Fishing (IPOA IUU), which provides policy guidance for States to support national efforts to combat IUU fishing.[70] This paragraph calls on all States to take measures or cooperate to ensure that their nationals do not support or engage in IUU fishing and to cooperate in identifying those nationals who are the operators or owners of vessels involved in IUU fishing. In its technical guidelines for the implementation of this paragraph, the FAO observes that the measures to be taken could include laws prohibiting nationals from engaging in IUU fishing, even if the activity in question takes place aboard a foreign vessel or in waters under the jurisdiction of another State.[71]

In line with the IPOA IUU, in the proceedings leading to the ITLOS Advisory Opinion, New Zealand argued that similar duties to those imposed on flag States may also fall on other States in certain circumstances. Such duties are then imposed in order to address evasion of legal responsibility by operators that deliberately

67 ITLOS Advisory Opinion (n 20), para. 120.

68 *South China Sea Arbitration, Philippines* v. *China*, Award, PCA Case No 2013-19, ICGJ 495 (PCA 2016), 12 July 2016, Permanent Court of Arbitration.

69 South China Sea Award, ibid., para. 944.

70 FAO International Plan of Action to Prevent, Deter and Eliminate Illegal, Unreported and Unregulated Fishing, adopted by FAO's Committee on Fisheries on 2 March 2001 and endorsed by the FAO Council on 23 June 2001.

71 FAO Fisheries Department, *Implementation of the International Plan of Action to Prevent, Deter and Eliminate Illegal, Unreported and Unregulated Fishing. FAO Technical Guidelines for Responsible Fisheries*, No. 9 (Rome: FAO, 2002), 12.

choose to flag their vessels in States that fail to properly discharge their duty of effective control. New Zealand stated that in such circumstances, there is concurrent responsibility on the part of the State of nationality of those operating the vessel. It also held that States also have a responsibility to exercise effective control over their nationals, including the beneficial owners or operators of vessels, in order to prevent and deter them from engaging in IUU fishing.[72]

Moreover, the UN General Assembly regularly adopts resolutions in relation to IUU fishing.[73] In its unanimously adopted resolution of 8 December 2020, it

> [u]rges States to effectively exercise jurisdiction and control over their nationals, including beneficial owners, and vessels flying their flag, in order to prevent and deter them from engaging in illegal, unreported and unregulated fishing activities or supporting vessels engaging in illegal, unreported and unregulated fishing activities, including those vessels listed by regional fisheries management organisations or arrangements as engaged in those activities, and to facilitate mutual assistance to ensure that such actions can be investigated and proper sanctions imposed.[74]

Although General Assembly resolutions are as such not considered to have binding effect, this resolution's unanimous adoption, the fact that it repeats the principles set out in previous resolutions and its translation into state practice as described earlier would suggest that it reflects at least the development of a norm.[75]

16.5 CONCLUSION

The traditional approach of combating IUU fishing, with strong reliance on flag State enforcement, has proven not to be effective due to use of flags of convenience and stateless vessels and the involvement of internationally operating organisations with considerable financial interests in IUU fishing. This chapter suggests involving other States in the fight against IUU fishing, in particular those States in which owners and operators of vessels engaged in IUU fishing activities are located. Although the focus under UNCLOS for challenging IUU fishing in a State's EEZ

[72] International Tribunal for the Law of the Sea (Case No. 21) (n 20), Request for an Advisory Opinion submitted by the Sub-Regional Fisheries Commission (SRFC), Written Statement of New Zealand, 27 November 2013, paras. 32 and 33.

[73] See for an overview: United Nations, 'Oceans and the Law of the Sea in the General Assembly of the United Nations, General Assembly resolutions and decisions', available at www.un.org/Depts/los/general_assembly/general_assembly_resolutions.htm (accessed on 3 June 2021).

[74] Resolution adopted by the General Assembly on 8 December 2020; A/RES/75/89 -Sustainable fisheries, including through the 1995 Agreement for the Implementation of the Provisions of the United Nations Convention on the Law of the Sea of 10 December 1982 relating to the Conservation and Management of Straddling Fish Stocks and Highly Migratory Fish Stocks, and related instruments, para. 83.

[75] S. Schwebel, 'The effect of resolutions of the U.N. General Assembly on Customary International Law' (1979) 73 *American Society of International Law Proceedings*, 305.

has been on coastal States and flag States, it can be argued that UNCLOS also obliges States whose nationals are directly or indirectly involved in the fisheries sector to ensure that those nationals do not engage in or support IUU fishing. Such obligations could be based on the ITLOS Advisory Opinion, that is, a due diligence obligation to ensure that a State's nationals refrain from being involved in IUU activities, including as operator or owner of a vessel engaged in fishing in the EEZ of another State, and to comply with the conservation measures applying to that EEZ.[76]

[76] ITLOS Advisory Opinion (n 20), para. 131.

17

The Advisory Jurisdiction of the ITLOS

From Uncertainties to Opportunities for Ocean Governance

Carlos A. Cruz Carrillo

17.1 INTRODUCTION

The advisory function of the plenary of the International Tribunal for the Law of the Sea (ITLOS or Tribunal) has existed since the first rules of the Tribunal, adopted in October 1997, pursuant to Article 16 of the Statute of the ITLOS. This judicial function remained disused and undisputed until 2015 when the Tribunal delivered the advisory opinion *Request for Advisory Opinion submitted by the Sub-Regional Fisheries Commission* (*SRFC Advisory Opinion*).[1] On that occasion, the ITLOS considered that the legal basis for its advisory function derived from the foundational agreement of the requesting entity, in connection to Article 21 of its Statute and Article 138 of its Rules. As explained in this contribution, many States and scholars criticized the Tribunal for exercising this judicial function whereas others supported the decision to do so. Notwithstanding the debate, the advisory function prevails as a tool to enhance the rule of law for oceans and adapt it to tackle new challenges. Indeed, after nearly forty years since the adoption of the United Nations Convention on the Law of the Sea (UNCLOS),[2] new challenges call for re-interpreting and calibrating UNCLOS. For example, climate change alone poses legal challenges that were even unthinkable during the Third Conference on the Law of the Sea, including the rise in sea levels[3] or ocean

[1] *Request for Advisory Opinion Submitted by the Sub-Regional Fisheries Commission* (*SRFC Advisory Opinion*), Advisory Opinion, 2 April 2015, ITLOS Reports 2015, 4.

[2] Montego Bay, 10 December 1982, in force 16 November 1994, 1833 UNTS 397.

[3] See: International Law Commission (ILC), *Sea-Level Rise in Relation to International Law: First Issues Paper* (by Bogdan Aurescu and Nilüfer Oral) UN Doc. A/CN.4/740, (2020); C. Hioureas and A. Camprubì, "Legal and Political Considerations on the Disappearance of States due to Sea Level Rise", in T. Heidar (ed.), *New Knowledge and Changing Circumstances in the Law of the Sea* (Leiden: Brill/Nijhoff, 2020), 407–426; D. Vidas, "International Law at the Convergence of Two Epochs: Sea Level Rise and the Law of the Sea for the Anthropocene", in C. Espósito, J. Kraska, H. N. Scheiber and M. S. Kwon (eds.), *Ocean Law and Policy: 20 Years under UNCLOS* (Leiden: Brill Nijhoff, 2017), 101–123.

acidification.[4] Similar complex issues derive from technological advances and the quest for natural resources and maritime power. In this context, understanding the advisory function of the ITLOS stands as a tool in enhancing ocean governance.

This chapter aims at elucidating the scope of the advisory function of the ITLOS plenary. In particular, it revises the configuration of this judicial function and underscores the potential use of ad hoc jurisdictional agreements to request advisory opinions. To that end, this contribution will first present the utility of advisory opinions to strengthen the rule of law for oceans; second, it will then examine ambiguities within the legal basis of the advisory function of the ITLOS to determine the plausibility of using special agreements to request advisory opinions..

17.2 ADVISORY OPINIONS AND OCEAN GOVERNANCE

Since the Permanent Court of International Justice, certain international judicial bodies can exercise the judicial function of delivering advisory opinions.[5] These can be defined as a judicial service to assist with comprehension and compliance with international obligations.[6] This function allows identification of the abstract field in which the rules apply, their application to concrete situations and the legal consequences flowing from their application.[7] The main difference with a contentious jurisdiction is that the outcome of an advisory jurisdiction is not binding and thereby does not entail stigmatization as in contentious proceedings.[8] Exceptions to this are particular cases where an advisory opinion functions as a preliminary ruling,[9] as a

4 D. Bialek and J. Ariel, "Ocean Acidification: International Legal Avenues under the UN Convention on the Law of the Sea", in M. B. Gerrard (ed.), *Threatened Island Nations: Legal Implication of Rising Seas and Changing Climate* (Cambridge: Cambridge University Press, 2013), 15–54; IOC, *Global Ocean Science Report: The Current Status of Ocean Science around the World* (IOC-UNESCO, 2017), 46.

5 M. Samson and D. Guilfoyle, "The Permanent Court of International Justice and the "Invention" of International Advisory Jurisdiction", in M. Fitzmaurice and C. Tams (eds.), *Legacies of the Permanent Court of International Justice* (Leiden: Brill/Nijhoff, 2013), 41–68.

6 *SRFC Advisory Opinion* (n 1), para. 77; IACtHR, *The Environment and Human Rights*, Advisory Opinion OC-23/17, 15 November 2017, [2017] IACtHR Series A No. 23, para. 23; *Legality of the Threat or Use of Nuclear Weapons*, Advisory Opinion, 1. C.J. Reports 1996, 226; *Interpretation of Peace Treaties with Bulgaria, Hungary and Romania*, First Phase, Advisory Opinion, ICJ Reports 1950, 71.

7 R. Kolb, *The International Court of Justice* (Oxford: Hart Publishing, 2013), 1020.

8 See: T. Buergenthal, "The Inter-American Court of Human Rights", *The American Journal of International Law*, 76(2) (1982), 245; See also: *Interpretation of Peace Treaties*, Advisory Opinion: ICJ Reports (n 6), 65, para. 71.

9 E.g., the advisory function of the European Court of Human Rights. See: *Protocol No. 16 to the Convention on the Protection of Human Rights and Fundamental Freedoms*, adopted on 2 October 2013, Council of Europe Treaty Series – No. 214; See: M. Dicosola et al., "The Prospective Role of Constitutional Courts in the Advisory Opinion Mechanism before the European Court of Human Rights: A First Comparative Assessment with the European Union and the Inter-American System", *German Law Journal*, 16 (6) (2015), 1387–1428.

dispute settlement mechanism[10] or as an appeal instance,[11] entailing a compulsory effect.

Notwithstanding its non-binding nature, an advisory opinion entails authoritative statements that contribute to clarification of the applicable law and, in so doing, help to prevent disputes from arising.[12] Likewise, the legal findings in advisory opinions are generally authoritative for the members of a legal system and even foster judicial cross-fertilization between courts and tribunals.[13] As stated by the ITLOS, judicial determinations in advisory opinions carry no less weight and authority than those in judgments.[14] Therefore, advisory opinions have the same value under Article 38 (1) (d) of the Statute of the International Court of Justice. Furthermore, they might prove to be useful in designing international and domestic public policies, or as suggested, preventing future disputes.

In the context of the law of the sea, recent challenges are finding new legal vacuums in the UNCLOS. Put differently, it seems unclear whether this treaty provides guidance or if it is necessary to adopt new rules. Far from fostering an amendment to the Convention, the advisory function stands as a significant tool to shed light on how to interpret and apply UNCLOS to recent issues. An urgent example is climate change and its effects on the rule of law for oceans such as ocean acidification, ocean deoxygenation or rising sea levels.[15] The International Law

[10] See: *Convention on the Privileges and Immunities of the United Nations*, adopted on 13 February 1946, UNTS 4, Art. VIII, section 30; UNCLOS, Art. 188 (2) (a) and (b); C. Dominicè, "Request for Advisory Opinions in Contentious Cases?", in L. Boisson de Chazournes et al. (eds.), *International Organizations and International Dispute Settlement: Trends and Prospects* (Transnational Publishers, Leyden 2002), 91–104.

[11] *Judgment No. 2867 of the Administrative Tribunal of the International Labour Organization upon a Complaint Filed against the International Fund for Agricultural Development*, Advisory Opinion, ICJ Reports 2012, 10, paras. 27 and 29; *Application for Review of Judgement No. 158 of the United Nations Administrative Tribunal*, Advisory Opinion, ICJ Reports 1973, 166, para. 39.

[12] Cf. S. Rosenne, *The International Court of Justice: An Essay in Political and Legal Theory* (A.W. Sijthoff, Leyden 1957), 492–493; L. Boisson de Chazournes, "Advisory Opinions and the Furtherance of the Common Interest of Mankind", in L. Boisson de Chazournes et al. (eds.), *International Organizations and International Dispute Settlement – Trends and Prospects* (n 10), 107.

[13] For example, the IACtHR relied on previous ITLOS advisory opinions to elucidate the content of environmental obligations. See: IACtHR, *The Environment and Human Rights*, Advisory Opinion OC-23/17 (n 6), footnotes: 171, 237,140, 278, 335.

[14] *Dispute Concerning Delimitation of the Maritime Boundary between Mauritius and the Maldives in the Indian Ocean (Mauritius/Maldives)*, Preliminary Objections, Judgment 28 January 2021, ITLOS Reports 2021–2021, in p.17 para. 203.

[15] See in this volume: C. Voigt (Chapter 2); M. Lennan (Chapter 12). Also see: L. Mayer, "Climate Change and the Legal Effects of Sea Level Rise: An Introduction to the Science", in T. Heidar (ed.), *New Knowledge and Changing Circumstances in the Law of the Sea* (n 2); C. Redgwell, "Treaty Evolution, Adaptation and Change: Is the LOSC 'Enough' to Address Climate Change Impacts on the Marine Environment?", *The International Journal of Marine and Coastal Law*, 34(3) (2019), 440–457; A. Boyle, "Law of the Sea Perspectives on Climate Change", *The International Journal of Marine and Coastal Law*, 27 (2012), 834.

Commission (ILC) is already considering the topic within its agenda.[16] In this regard, an advisory opinion on the legal consequences of sea-level rise might assist the ILC's work on the issue by identifying applicable rules and, perhaps, providing novel interpretations.[17] Moreover, an opinion could provide factual and legal statements that later can foster international climate change litigation.[18] Another example is marine litter and plastic pollution, which entail cross-cutting legal considerations in international law. An advisory opinion on this point might provide important material for negotiating a new global instrument. In this context, Article 55 ter of the draft text of the ABNJ agreement introduces a jurisdictional clause for requesting advisory opinions from the ITLOS.[19] If accepted in the final text, Article 55 ter will be helpful in interpreting the provisions of the agreement in the context of technical and scientific changes. Judge Lijnzaad proposes the possibility of an ITLOS Special Chamber on Marine Biodiversity bestowed with an advisory function.[20]

Another aspect to consider is the utility of two previous ITLOS advisory opinions, which resulted in main inputs to global ocean governance and the development of international law.[21] The first opinion entails valuable considerations on the scope and content of environmental obligations towards the marine environment in the context of deep seabed mining.[22] Some authors consider this opinion to be the most comprehensive treatment of international environmental law by any international

16 ILC (n 3).

17 The opinion came after the author raised a question during a conference regarding sea-level rise, displacement, migration and human rights, held online on 28 May 2020.

18 See: A. Boyle, "Litigating Climate Change under Part XII of the LOSC", *The International Journal of Marine and Coastal Law*, 34(3) (2019), 458–481; P. Sands, "Climate Change and the Rule of Law: Adjudicating the Future in International Law", *Oxford Journal of Environmental Law*, 28 (2016), 29.

19 Intergovernmental conference on ABNJ, *Revised Draft Text of an Agreement under the United Nations Convention on the Law of the Sea on the Conservation and Sustainable Use of Marine Biological Diversity of Areas beyond National Jurisdiction*, UN Doc. A/CONF.232/2022/5, available at https://undocs.org/Home/Mobile?FinalSymbol=A%2FCONF.232%2F2022%2F5&Language=E&DeviceType=Desktop&LangRequested=False

20 L. Lijnzaad, "Dispute Settlement for Marine Biodiversity beyond National Jurisdiction: Not an Afterthought", in H. Ruíz Fabri, M. Benatar et al., *A Bridge over Troubled Waters: Dispute Resolution in the Law of International Watercourses and the Law of the Sea* (Leiden: Brill/Nijhoff, 2020) 177.

21 V. Golitsyn, "The Role of the International Tribunal for the Law of the Sea in Global Ocean Governance", in S. Minas and J. Diamond (eds.), *Stress Testing the Law of the Sea: Dispute Resolution, Disasters and Emerging Challenges* (Leiden: Brill, 2018), 17.

22 *Responsibilities and Obligations of States with Respect to Activities in the Area*, Advisory Opinion, 1 February 2011, ITLOS Reports 2011, 10, 46; See: E. Kelly, "The Precautionary Approach in the Advisory Opinion Concerning the Responsibilities and Obligations of States with Respect to Activities in the Area", in ITLOS, *The Contribution of the International Tribunal for the Law of the Sea to the Rule of Law: 1996–2016* (Leiden: Brill/Nijhoff, 2017).

court or tribunal.[23] The second advisory opinion provided legal inputs for tackling illegal, unreported and unregulated fishing.[24] Thus, advisory opinions indeed stand as a judicial mechanism to enhance the rule of law for oceans. Nevertheless, in the particular case of the ITLOS plenary, the architecture of its advisory function places legal questions on its operation by potential requesting entities.

17.3 ARCHITECTURE OF THE ITLOS ADVISORY FUNCTION: VACUUMS AND OPPORTUNITIES

In international law, everything exists because of the consent of subjects of international law. Among other aspects, States can agree to establish an international tribunal with particular judicial functions to bring legitimacy to the norms and institutions created by a regime where they will perform its judicial functions.[25] Consent operates as a legal condition of jurisdiction imposed by the mandate providers and the parties to a specific dispute; and as an important factor in legitimating the operation of international courts and tribunals.[26] Therefore, international judicial bodies can exercise those functions conferred by their creators. In the case of the advisory function of the ITLOS plenary, this statement calls for analysing its legal basis and operation.

This section elaborates on four points: (1) The legal basis of advisory jurisdiction; (2) the scope of the 'international agreements' requirement; (3) special agreements for advisory proceedings; (4) the discretionary powers of the ITLOS.

17.3.1 *The Legal Basis of the Advisory Function*

The legal architecture for the advisory function was the subject of debate among States, scholars and practitioners, following the *SRFC Advisory Opinion*. The discussion pointed to the lack of express reference to this function in UNCLOS and its annexes; *ultra vires* action by the ITLOS while drafting its rules of procedure, among others.[27] Arguably, the advisory jurisdiction of the ITLOS derives from

[23] A. Boyle, C. Redgwell and P. Birnie, *International Law and the Environment* (Oxford: Oxford University Press, 2021), 266.

[24] *SRFC Advisory Opinion* (n 1).

[25] Y. Shany, *Assessing the Effectiveness of International Courts* (Oxford: Oxford University Press, 2014), 137; A. Orakhelashvili, "The Concept of International Judicial Jurisdiction: A Reprisal", *The Law and Practice of International Courts and Tribunals*, 3 (2003), 504–505.

[26] Y. Shany, *Questions of Jurisdiction and Admissibility before International Courts* (Cambridge: Cambridge University Press, 2016), 7, 34.

[27] See: M. Lando, "The Advisory Jurisdiction of the International Tribunal for the Law of the Sea: Comments on the Request for an Advisory Opinion Submitted by the Sub-Regional Fisheries Commission", *Leiden Journal of International Law*, 29 (2016), 441–461; T. Ruys and A. Moon Soete, "'Creeping' Advisory Jurisdiction of International Courts and Tribunals? The Case of the International Tribunal for the Law of the Sea", *Leiden Journal of International Law*, 29 (2016), 155–176; Y. Tanaka, "Reflections on the Advisory Jurisdiction of ITLOS as a Full Court:

Article 21 of its Statute. According to this provision, the jurisdiction of the ITLOS 'comprises all disputes and all applications submitted to it in accordance with the convention and all matters specifically provided for in any other agreement which confers jurisdiction on the Tribunal'.[28] The advisory jurisdiction may be expressly absent from Article 21, however: in the *SRFC Advisory Opinion* the ITLOS considered that the phrase 'all other matters' must include advisory opinions.[29] The Tribunal endorsed this interpretation in 1997 when it adopted its first rules of procedure. Let us remember that the Tribunal has to frame rules for carrying out its functions, in particular, rules of procedure, pursuant to Article 16 of the Statute.[30] In this regard, it has been established that the rules of procedure are a source of law that reflects the consent of States and the judicial body´s conception of the rules and powers needed to carry out its functions.[31] Bearing this in mind, the 1997 Rules of the ITLOS included Article 138, as a step to regulate the advisory function encompassed in Article 21 of its Statute. Therefore, Article 138 of the Rules elaborated on the requirements in order to request an advisory opinion, namely: the existence of an international agreement related to the purposes of UNCLOS; a legal question; and submission of a request by an authorized body.[32]

As a judicial body, the ITLOS is bestowed with inherent powers that exist *ipso facto* for any judicial body,[33] whose function is to safeguard its judicial functions.[34] Among these powers, the principle of *compétence de la compétence* enables the Tribunal to determine the scope of its jurisdiction.[35] The ICJ established that in the absence of any agreement to the contrary, an international tribunal has the right to decide as to its own jurisdiction and has the power to interpret for this purpose the

The ITLOS Advisory Opinion of 2015", *The Law and Practice of International Courts and Tribunals*, 14 (2015), 318–339.

28 *Annex VI of the United Nations Convention for the Law of the Sea*, UNTS 31363, adopted on 10 December 1982, Montego Bay, Art. 21 (The Statute of ITLOS).

29 *SRFC Advisory Opinion* (n 1) para. 56.

30 *The Statute of ITLOS* (n 28) Art. 16.

31 C. Brown, *A Common Law of International Adjudication* (Oxford: Oxford University Press, 2007), 39.

32 *Rules of the International Tribunal for the Law of the Sea*, adopted on 28 October 1997, last amendment on 25 September 2018, ITLOS/8, Art. 138 (Rules of the ITLOS); *SRFC Advisory Opinion* (n 1) paras. 54–56; S. Lekkas, "Article 21, Part XI The Area", in A. Proelss (ed.), *United Nations Convention on the Law of the Sea: A Commentary* (München: Verlag C. H. Beck, 2017), 2381.

33 See: *Nuclear Tests* (*Australia* v. *France*), Judgement, I.C.J. Reports 1974, p. 253, para. 23; F. Weiss, "Inherent Powers of National and International Courts: The Practice of the Iran-US Claim Tribunal", in C. Binder et al. (eds.), *International Investment Law for the 21th Century: Essays in Honour of Christoph Schreuer* (Oxford: Oxford University Press, 2009), 191.

34 C. Brown, "The Inherent Powers of International Courts and Tribunals", *British Yearbook of International Law*, 76(1) (2005), 228.

35 H. Thirlway, *The Law and Procedure of the International Court of Justice: Fifty Years of Jurisprudence* (Oxford: Oxford University Press, 2013), Vol II, 39.

instruments that govern the jurisdiction.[36] In the present case, no prohibition is established in UNCLOS or in the Statute for the Tribunal to exercise an advisory function. Moreover, in the *SRFC Advisory Opinion*, the ITLOS clarified that the basis of the advisory jurisdiction is an international agreement conferring this judicial function on the Tribunal, and that Article 138 of the Rules mainly elaborates on the requirements to seise jurisdiction.[37] Therefore, the scope of the advisory function under analysis derives from the Statute and the Rules. Yet, it is the international agreement where States will consent to confer this function on the Tribunal.

17.3.2 *The Requirement of 'International Agreement': A Restrictive or Broad Approach?*

In 2015, the ITLOS underscored that Article 21 of the Statute did not itself establish the advisory jurisdiction but rather the other agreement conferring jurisdiction on the Tribunal. It recognized that the other agreement and Article 21 are interconnected and constitute the substantive legal basis for the advisory jurisdiction under analysis.[38] It is possible to affirm that under Article 21 of the Statute and Article 138 of the Rules, an international agreement is the cornerstone to the advisory jurisdiction. It is the international agreement that encompasses the advisory jurisdictional clause, the relation to the object and purpose of UNCLOS and the body authorized to request an opinion. Yet the question arises whether all types of international agreement can establish this jurisdiction; and if yes, what kind of control should be exercised by the Tribunal. In international law, an international agreement must be concluded between States/international organizations in written form[39] and governed by international law, whether embodied in a single instrument or in two or more related instruments, whatever its particular designation.[40] Thereby, any international agreement complying with these requirements and those others envisaged in Article 138 of the ITLOS Rules could be the basis for the advisory function of the ITLOS. In order to consider possible consequences, it is pertinent to analyse this terminology under a restrictive and a broad approach.

17.3.2.1 Restrictive Approach

Under this approach, the wording 'international agreement' should comprise exclusively those substantive agreements encompassing a jurisdictional clause in favour of the ITLOS. By substantive agreement, this research considers that the following would

[36] *Nottebohm case* (Preliminary Objections), Judgment of November 18th, 1953: ICJ Reports 1953, p. III, p. 119. See also: *Interpretation of the Greco-Turkish Agreement*, Advisory Opinion, PCIJ Rep, Series B No 16 (1920), 18.

[37] *SRFC Advisory Opinion* (n 1) paras. 58–59.

[38] *SRFC Advisory Opinion* (n 1) para. 58.

[39] In some cases, non-written forms may entail legal consequences for the parties. See: C. Eckart, *Promises of States in International Law* (Oxford: Hart, 2012).

[40] *Maritime Delimitation in the Indian Ocean (Somalia v. Kenya)*, Preliminary Objections, Judgment, ICJ Reports 2017, 3, para 42.

qualify: foundational instruments for international or regional organizations (e.g., regional fisheries management organizations), multilateral agreements related to the purposes of the UNCLOS (e.g., the forthcoming ABNJ agreement) or bilateral treaties regulating determined maritime areas. Following a restrictive approach will require two main tasks for requesting an advisory opinion: first, finding a treaty containing a jurisdictional clause, and if missing, exploring the institutional channels to amend the treaty to include a jurisdictional clause, or creating a new organization comprising a jurisdictional clause in its constitutive instruments. Second, it will require observing the internal procedure established in that treaty to request an opinion from the ITLOS, such as discussing in the plenary of the organization the possibility of requesting an advisory opinion and the legal questions to be submitted.

Let us remember that the advisory jurisdiction of the ITLOS in the *SRFC Advisory Opinion* emanated from Article 33 of the Convention on the Determination of the Minimal Conditions for Access and Exploitation of Marine Resources within the Maritime Areas under Jurisdiction of the Member States of the Sub-Regional Fisheries Commission.[41] In that case, the Conference of Ministers of the SRFC enabled the Permanent Secretary to request an advisory opinion from the ITLOS. An interesting development in this regard happened during the 26th Conference of the Parties of the United Nations Framework Convention on Climate Change (UNFCCC).[42] Antigua and Barbuda, and Tuvalu signed an agreement to establish the Commission of Small Island States on Climate Change and International Law (COSIS).[43] *Inter alia*, COSIS aims at developing and implementing fair and just global environmental norms and practices. Moreover, COSIS will be able to request advisory opinions from the ITLOS on the legal responsibility of States for carbon emissions, marine pollution and rising sea levels. Despite the early stage of COSIS, its foundational agreement complies with a restrictive reading of Article 21 of the Statute and Article 138 of the Rules to establish the advisory jurisdiction.

17.3.2.2 Broad Approach

Under a broad approach, the terminology 'international agreement' should encompass those instruments that can be characterized as a treaty under the rules of international law, such as those reflected in Article 2 (1) (a) of the 1969 and 1986

[41] *SRFC Advisory Opinion* (n 1) paras. 61–63; *Convention on the Determination of the Minimal Conditions for Access and Exploitation of Marine Resources within the Maritime Areas under Jurisdiction of the Member States of the Sub -Regional Fisheries Commission*, adopted in Dakar, Senegal, on 8 June 2012, Art. 33.

[42] UNFCCC, *Antigua and Barbuda, Tuvalu*, Press Conference, 1 November 2021. Available at < https://unfccc-cop26.streamworld.de/webcast/antigua-barbuda-tuvalu>

[43] UNFCCC, *Antigua and Barbuda, Tuvalu, Press Conference*, 1 November 2021. Available at https://unfccc-cop26.streamworld.de/webcast/antigua-barbuda-tuvalu; D. Freestone, R. Barnes and P. Akhavan, 'Agreement for the Establishment of the Commission of Small Island States on Climate Change and International Law' (2022) 37 (1) *International Journal of Marine and Coastal Law* 175–178.

Vienna Conventions on the Law of Treaties[44] and the jurisprudence.[45] Moreover, pursuant to Article 138 of the Rules of the ITLOS, the additional requirement is that the agreement should be related to the object and purpose of the UNCLOS and should contain a jurisdictional clause. Therefore, the broad approach of the international agreement may include substantive agreements, foundational instruments and any other type of agreement fulfilling the requirements of law. This opens some opportunities not only for international organizations but also to States willing to use the advisory function of the ITLOS. Among these possibilities is the use of agreements on filing a request for an advisory opinion. Judge Wolfrum endorsed this interpretation, but it points to the relevance of identifying the question to be raised.[46] This scenario could foster a judicial dialogue among States, international organizations and the Tribunal concerning the application and interpretation of UNCLOS. At the same time, it is crucial to explore the scope and limits of using ad hoc jurisdictional agreements to request advisory opinions.

17.3.3 *Ad Hoc Jurisdictional Agreements: Requirements and Foresights*

Following the broad approach, the use of ad hoc jurisdictional agreements seems feasible to seise the ITLOS. The use of these instruments may enhance the rule of law for oceans due to the plurality of actors that can request advisory opinions without engaging in institutional processes to obtain authorization. This section examines the requirements and the limits of ad hoc jurisdictional agreements.

According to Professor Thirlway, a special agreement or *compromis* is an agreement for the immediate reference of a specific dispute to settlement by a judicial or arbitral body.[47] Special agreements reflect the consent of the parties to submit disputes to a judicial body voluntarily. In doing so, the parties can delimit or not the jurisdiction of the tribunal.[48] In the context of the advisory jurisdiction of the ITLOS, an ad hoc jurisdictional agreement should consider the requirements contained in Article 138 of the Rules of the ITLOS. In that context, this section

[44] *Vienna Convention on the Law of Treaties*, adopted on 23 May 1969, entered into force on 27 January 1980, UNTS 18232, Vol.1155, p.331, Art. 2(1); *Vienna Convention on the Law of Treaties between States and International Organizations or between International Organizations*, adopted on 21 March 1986, not yet in force, Art. 2(1).

[45] *Maritime Delimitation in the Indian Ocean* (*Somalia* v. *Kenya*), Preliminary Objections, Judgment, ICJ Reports 2017, 3, para. 42.

[46] R. Wolfrum, "Advisory Opinions: Are they a Suitable Alternative for Settlement of International Disputes?", in R. Wolfrum and I. Gätzschmann (eds.), *International Dispute Settlement: Room for Innovations?* (Berlin/Heidelberg: Springer, 2013), 54; P. Chandrasekhara Rao and Philippe Gautier, *The International Tribunal for the Law of the Sea: Law, Practice and Procedure* (Cheltenham: Edward Elgar Publishing, 2018), 164.

[47] H. Thirlway, *Compromis* (Max Planck Encyclopedias of Public International Law, 2006), para. 1.

[48] Chandrasekhara Rao and Philippe Gautier (eds.), *The International Tribunal for the Law of the Sea: Law, Practice and Procedure* (n 45) paras. 3.083 and 3.084.

will address four points. First, the minimum requirements for establishing the advisory jurisdiction in a special agreement. Second, the personality to conclude *special agreements*. Third, the configuration of the legal question. And fourth, the relevance of the discretionary power of the ITLOS as a tool in contentious matters.

17.3.3.1 Minimum Requirements

Considering the wording of Article 21 of the Statute and 138 of the Rules of the ITLOS, an ad hoc agreement should fulfil two main points. First, the agreement should be related to the purposes of the UNCLOS. Second, it should contain a jurisdictional clause granting an advisory function to the ITLOS.

Let us remember that, according to the preamble of UNCLOS, its object and purpose is to establish a legal order for the seas and oceans that will facilitate international communication, and will promote peaceful uses of the seas and oceans, equitable and efficient utilization of their resources, conservation of their living resources, and study, protection and preservation of the marine environment.[49] Bearing this in mind, the parties to an intended ad hoc agreement should underscore the relevance of requesting an advisory opinion as a means to interpret UNCLOS provisions and fulfil its obligations. For example, an ad hoc agreement to request an advisory opinion on the sea-level rise could highlight the importance for the parties to clarify Articles 5, 7, 13 or 121 of UNCLOS as a mechanism to guarantee equitable use of the oceans in the context of climate change. As will be shown, this aspect is closely related to the legal question, and both should synergize to demonstrate the utility of an opinion for the requesting entity.

Regarding the second point, the ITLOS recognized in 2015 that its advisory jurisdiction derived from an international agreement providing for that jurisdiction.[50] Thereby, in an ad hoc jurisdictional agreement, the jurisdictional clause is the cornerstone. The jurisdictional clause expresses the consent of the parties to grant advisory jurisdiction to the ITLOS. Moreover, the clause can comprise some parameters for seising the tribunal, for example, the exhaustion of a particular internal process, such as having previous consultations among the members or the filing of a request by a determined entity. This aspect of the clause may differ according to whether the requesting entity is a State, international organization or both.

17.3.3.2 Personality to Conclude Special Agreements

One of the central issues when considering 'special agreements' is who among the subjects of international law can conclude an ad hoc jurisdictional agreement. Article 20 of the Statute of the Tribunal offers some clues:

[49] *United Nations Convention for the Law of the Sea* (n 2), Preamble.
[50] *SRFC Advisory Opinion* (n 1) paras. 58–59.

> 1. The Tribunal shall be open to *States Parties*.
> 2. The Tribunal shall be open to entities *other than States Parties* in any case expressly provided for in Part XI or in any case submitted *pursuant to any other agreement conferring jurisdiction on the Tribunal* which is accepted by all the parties to that case.[51] [Author's italics]

In principle, State parties to the UNCLOS can bring proceedings to ITLOS. However, the second paragraph of Article 20 broadens the *ratione personae* scope of this provision with the wording 'entities other than States Parties'. This opens the floor to include international organizations that are not entitled to participate in proceedings (e.g., International Maritime Organization (IMO), Intergovernmental Oceanographic Commission of UNESCO (IOC-UNESCO), Commission on the Limits of the Continental Shelf (CLCS), among others). Similarly, one may wonder if a State that is not a party to the UNCLOS (e.g., the United States, Turkey or Colombia) could trigger the jurisdiction of the ITLOS.[52] In the context of a special agreement, what matters under Article 21 (2) is that the legal instrument conferring jurisdiction to the ITLOS identifies the entities authorized to seise jurisdiction and reflect their consent.

On this issue, Article 138 (2) of the Rules establishes: 'A request for an advisory opinion shall be transmitted to the Tribunal by whatever body is authorized by or in accordance with the agreement to make the request to the Tribunal'.[53] A literal interpretation of this provision provides for two assumptions. In the first place, a request for an advisory opinion should be filed by a body authorized under the agreement. This assumption encompasses a scenario where an international agreement is the foundational instrument for an international organization. Thereby, as occurred in the *SRFC Advisory Opinion*, it requires the international or regional organization to previously identify and authorize a body or an office within it to perform the function of requesting entity before the Tribunal. The second assumption is that the request for an advisory opinion should be transmitted to the Tribunal in accordance with the agreement. Under this assumption, the personality is open to whatever entities – States and organizations – are identified and authorized by an international agreement, in this case, a special agreement. Likewise, this allows for the agreement to establish any institutional precondition to trigger the advisory jurisdiction (e.g., previous consultation between States or within an international organization). In this vein, academic discussion entails divergent opinions on the topic. In the first place, Professor Rosenne considered that the requirement for a

[51] *The Statute of ITLOS* (n 28) Art. 20.

[52] See: P. Gautier, "Two Aspects of ITLOS Proceedings: Non-State Parties and Costs of Bringing Claims", in N. Scheiber and J. H. Paik (eds.), *Regions, Institutions and Law of the Sea: Studies in Governance* (Leiden: Brill/Nijhoff, 2013), 77; T. Treves, "UNCLOS and Non-Party States before the International Court of Justice", in Carlos Espósito et al. (eds.), *Ocean Law and Policy* (Leiden: Brill, 2016), 367–378.

[53] *Rules of the ITLOS* (n 32), Art. 138 (2).

request to be transmitted to the Tribunal by a duly authorized body does not permit a State, or a group of States, to initiate advisory proceedings otherwise than through a duly authorized body.[54] Conversely, Professor Gautier and Judge Jesus propose that nothing in the wording of Article 21 of the Statute or Article 138 of the Rules restricts the possibility for States to conclude an international agreement.[55]

Hence, the question of personality in the advisory jurisdiction remains open for international and regional organizations and States. This plurality of actors will increase the judicial dialogue among different actors to enhance the UNCLOS system. As part of this dialogue, the public interest is another factor that will foster identification of issues and a subsequent request for an advisory opinion. However, the issue of personality needs to be tested by the different actors and assessed by the Tribunal to avoid abuses attempting to circumvent the principle of consent to adjudication.

17.3.3.3 Legal Question: The Functional and Legitimate Tests

Under international law, a legal question is framed in terms of law, from which it derives problems of international law and is susceptible to a reply based on law.[56] In this regard, the legal question should follow the logic in a manner that the answer delivered by the Tribunal represents assistance to the requester and the entire legal system while performing its international obligations.[57]Article 130 of the Rules of the ITLOS, applicable *mutatis mutandis* to advisory proceedings of the ITLOS plenary, states that the Tribunal must consider whether a request for an advisory opinion relates to a legal question pending between two or more parties.[58] If this is the case, the interested parties may appoint a judge ad-hoc to act during the proceedings,[59] a practice also present in other jurisdictions.[60]

54 S. Rosenne, "International Tribunal for the Law of the Sea: 1996–97 Survey", *International Journal of Marine and Coastal Law*, 13(4) (1998), 507.

55 P. Gautier, "The International Tribunal for the Law of the Sea: Activities in 2006", *Chinese Journal of International Law*, 6(2) (2007), 389–402, para. 32; J. L. Jesus, "Article 138", in P. Chandrasekhara and P. Gautier, *The Rules of the International Tribunal for the Law of the Sea: A Commentary* (Leiden: Brill, 2006), 394.

56 *Legal Consequences of the Construction of a Wall in the Occupied Palestinian Territory*, Advisory Opinion, ICJ Reports 2004, 136, para. 37; *Responsibilities and Obligations of States with Respect to Activities in the Area* (n 22), 10, at 25, para. 39.

57 IACtHR, *Advisory Opinion OC-21/14* of 19 August 2014. Series A No. 21, para. 25; IACtHR, *Advisory Opinion OC-22/16* of 26 February 2016. Series A No. 22, para. 21.

58 *Rules of the ITLOS* (n 32), Art. 130 (2); J. L. Jesus, "Article 130", in P. Chandrasekhara and P. Gautier, *The Rules of the International Tribunal for the Law of the Sea: A Commentary* (n 55), 375–377.

59 *Statute of the ITLOS* (n 28), Art. 17; Rules of the ITLOS (n 32), Art. 130 (2).

60 *Rules of the International Court of Justice*, Adopted on 14 April 1978, Rule 102 (3); *Western Sahara*, Order of 22 May 1975, I.C.J. Reports 1975, p. 6. See: E. Jiménez de Aréchaga, "Judges Ad-Hoc in Advisory Proceedings", *Heidelberg Journal of International Law*, 31 (1971), 697–711

In the context of a special agreement, the legal question is relevant for identifying the legitimate interest and the general purpose of the advisory opinion. Both aspects are elements that the ITLOS should consider in the admissibility analysis of the request. Regarding the first aspect, the legal question must relate to the duties performed by the international organization or to the obligations performed by States. This is in line with Article 131 (1) of the Rules of the ITLOS.[61] In the *SRFC Advisory Opinion*, the ITLOS assessed whether the legal questions were related to the performance of the obligation encompassed in the MCA Convention.[62] In the case of States requesting an advisory opinion, it should be enough to address the importance and necessity of obtaining an advisory opinion for the performance of rights and duties enshrined in UNCLOS. Likewise, the legal question should pursue an answer that may be useful for the entire system. That is, whether the legal questions addresses an issue of major relevance for the international community with particular consequences on the requesting States (e.g., the effects of climate change in the ocean), the general purpose of the opinion may be accredited and will open the floor for other entities to present their views during the written and oral proceedings. For example, in its advisory opinion on human rights and the environment, the Inter-American Court of Human Rights (IACtHR) estimated that an opinion on the topic would 'be of real value for the countries of the region because it will identify, clearly and systematically, the State obligations in relation to the protection of the environment within the framework of their obligation to respect and to ensure the human rights of every persons subject to their jurisdiction'.[63]

The formulation of the legal question is perhaps the more complex stage of requesting an advisory opinion from any judicial body. Drafting a legal question implies an examination of the purposes of requesting an advisory opinion and how it will be useful for the requesting entity. As mentioned, this process will comprise previous consultations among the members of the requesting entity, mainly a debate between States. There should be a consensus on the goal pursued with the opinion, the drafting and content of the legal question and, perhaps, an assessment of the possible scenarios that a judicial body may take when issuing an opinion.

17.3.3.4 Discretionary Power of the ITLOS

An important feature of the advisory jurisdiction among international judicial bodies is their discretionary power to decide on whether they exercise its jurisdiction in

[61] *Rules of the ITLOS* (n 32), Art. 130 (1).

[62] *SRFC Advisory Opinion* (n 1), paras. 67–68; *Legality of the Use by a State of Nuclear Weapons in Armed Conflict*, Advisory Opinion, ICJ Reports 1996, 66, at 77, para. 22.

[63] IACtHR, *The Environment and Human Rights*, Advisory Opinion OC-23/17 (n 6), para. 23.

light of a compelling reason.[64] These powers have been described as a wider margin of appreciation of the general considerations of admissibility of requests for advisory opinions to protect the integrity of judicial functions.[65] In the particular case of the ITLOS, Article 138 of the Rules confers these powers on the Tribunal to consider exercising its advisory function even when the conditions of jurisdiction are satisfied, if there is a compelling reason.[66] The literature and the jurisprudence identify as main compelling reasons: lack of consent of an interested party, lack of factual documentation and evidence, and the highly political nature of the question.[67] From among all of these grounds, perhaps the question of consent to adjudication is the most relevant. The ICJ has stated that the consent of an interested State is relevant not for the Court's competence but for an appreciation of the property of giving an opinion, for instance, if the request aims at circumventing the principle of consent to adjudication.[68] On this point, it has been considered that to determine whether a request is circumventing the lack of consent to adjudication, it is necessary to compare the subject matter of the bilateral dispute with the legal question presented by the request.[69] The ITLOS should then assess whether the legal question and the reasons behind the request may transgress the principle of consent to jurisdiction. As mentioned, analysing the context and the scope of the legal question are relevant for this assessment. While ensuring this, the Tribunal will be safeguarding its legitimacy as a judicial body within the UNCLOS.

17.4 CONCLUSIONS

Following the 2015 *SRFC Advisory Opinion*, the advisory jurisdiction of the ITLOS plenary has not been used despite the vast legal uncertainties arising from new

[64] *Legal Consequences of the Separation of the Chagos Archipelago from Mauritius in 1965*, Advisory Opinion ICJ, (2019), para. 65; *Accordance with International Law of the Unilateral Declaration of Independence in respect of Kosovo*, Advisory Opinion, I.C.J. Reports 2010 (II), p. 416, para. 30; *SRFC Advisory Opinion* (n 1), para. 71.

[65] G. Abi-Saab, "On Discretion: Reflections on the Nature of the Consultative Jurisdiction of the International Court of Justice", in P. Sands and L. Boisson de Chazournes (eds.), *International Law, the International Court of Justice and Nuclear Weapons* (Cambridge: Cambridge University Press, 1999), 45.

[66] *SRFC Advisory Opinion* (n 1), para. 71.

[67] H. Thirlway, *The Law and Procedure of the International Court of Justice: Fifty Years of Jurisprudence* (n 33), Vol II, 1724–1731; P. d'Argent, "Commentary to Article 65", in A. Zimmermann et al. (eds.), *The Statute of the International Court of Justice: A Commentary* (3rd ed., Oxford: Oxford University Press, 2019), para. 45.

[68] *Interpretation of Peace Treaties*, Advisory Opinion: I.C.J. Reports 1950, p. 65, p.71; *Western Sahara*, Advisory Opinion, I.C.J. Reports 1975, p. 12, at p 25, paras. 32 and 33.

[69] *Legal Consequences of the Separation of the Chagos Archipelago from Mauritius in 1965*, Dissenting Opinion of Judge Donoghue, (2019), para. 10.

challenges to ocean governance. One may wonder whether the reason behind this inaction is lack of knowledge on how to trigger the advisory jurisdiction or just a way to avoid awakening the debate on the advisory jurisdiction triggered in 2015. Drawing on the *lex lata* governing the advisory jurisdiction of the ITLOS plenary, this chapter examined the opportunities offered by this judicial function, as well as the limits that the ITLOS should set.

As a first remark, the advisory function stands as a valuable tool to enhance the UNCLOS system and foster strengthened global governance in the ocean. In other jurisdictions, advisory opinions are demonstrable guidance in the interpretation and application of law. Yet, it should be clear that advisory opinions will not by themselves resolve an issue; rather, they are a complement to a parallel effort. However, their legal effects entail opportunities for stakeholders to reach concrete solutions following the law. In this context, stakeholders should consider the opportunities and the limits of the advisory jurisdiction of the ITLOS to seek legal guidance on how to tackle current challenges in the law of the sea.

Considering the guidance provided by the ITLOS in the *SRFC Advisory Opinion* on the requirements for triggering the advisory jurisdiction, this research underscores the role of an international agreement as the cornerstone of the advisory function. In this regard, this chapter proposes that the terminology 'international agreement' should mean that this jurisdiction emanates from multilateral, regional, bilateral and substantive treaties. Yet the terminology likewise enables the use of ad hoc jurisdictional agreements to request an advisory opinion. As established, a group of States and international organizations can conclude an ad hoc jurisdictional agreement to request an advisory opinion. However, this agreement should comply with the minimum requirements under Article 21 of the Statute and Article 138 of the Rules. These minimum requirements could function as a standard to provide legitimacy to the ITLOS. Nevertheless, the use of ad hoc jurisdictional agreements requires meticulous consideration by the ITLOS to avoid potential abuses. In this vein, the discretionary powers of the ITLOS stand as the main mechanism of control that the Tribunal should employ to prevent abuses when using the advisory jurisdiction. The ITLOS should determine whether there are compelling reasons that will menace judicial propriety. Among these compelling reasons, the Tribunal should pay special attention in protecting the principle to consent to adjudication, mainly due to the particular architecture of its advisory jurisdiction.

As mentioned, Antigua Barbuda, and Tuvalu created COSIS to inter alia trigger an advisory proceeding before the ITLOS on questions concerning climate change and the oceans. This new entity will remain open for other States to join the efforts.[70] The question is whether this agreement will fulfil the requirements

70 At the moment of writing, only Tuvalu, Antigua and Barbuda and Palau are members of this Commission.

imposed by Article 138 of the Rules to seise advisory jurisdiction. Drawing on the analysis of this chapter, the answer will depend on the legal question submitted to the ITLOS and the utility of an advisory opinion for the requesting states. Furthermore, COSIS will open a new chapter in the understanding and operation of the advisory jurisdiction of the ITLOS. It will be on the Tribunal and States to determine the outcome of a new request for an advisory opinion.

18

Could the WTO Save the Oceans?

An Inquiry into the Role of the WTO in the Future of Fisheries Policies

Leonila Guglya

18.1 INTRODUCTION

The fisheries subsidies mandate of the World Trade Organisation (WTO) recently celebrated its twentieth birthday. Somewhat clarified and reshaped over the years, the mandate remains only partially fulfilled.[1] The 12th WTO Ministerial Conference (MC12), scheduled to take place in November–December 2021, at which the negotiations were hoped to finally be concluded, was postponed indefinitely due to a new outbreak of the COVID virus. While fish stocks are at risk of further depletion in the face of increasingly capable fleets, among other hazards, the WTO Members need to take pragmatic yet ambitious steps as a matter of urgency, in order to be able to contribute to the search for solutions.

Analytical reflections, whenever they are present, are fully the author's own, as are possible mistakes in the assessment.

[1] Substantive work on this chapter was concluded before the "light" version of a self-standing Fisheries Subsidies Agreement was adopted as a rushed part of the WTO MC12 outcomes on 17 June 2022, being integrated in the Annex 1A to the WTO Agreement. The text of the Fisheries Subsidies Agreement could be found in the Annex to the dedicated WTO Ministerial Decision (WT/MIN(22)/33WT/L/1144, 22 June 2022). The instrument regulates subsidies contributing to IUU fishing and subsidies regarding overfished stocks offering generous yet time barred SDT exemptions. The WTO Members were not able to reach consensus on the third, key, substantive pillar – subsidies contributing to overcapacity and overfishing. As a result, only some elements thereof (the prohibition of all subsidies to fishing or fishing related activities in the unregulated high seas and the due restraint provision relating to subsidies to vessels not flying the flag of the subsidizing Member) have entered the text. According to Article 12 of the Agreement, read in conjunction with paragraph 4 of the Ministerial Decision, the longevity of the new treaty is subject to agreeing on "additional provisions that would achieve a comprehensive agreement on fisheries subsidies, including through further disciplines on certain forms of fisheries subsidies that contribute to overcapacity and overfishing", subject to effective special and differential treatment. In case no agreement on this open agenda would be reached within 4 years, the Fisheries Subsidies Agreement shall automatically terminate. Accordingly, most of the points raised in this Chapter retain their relevance.

The WTO is authorised to reduce (or even eliminate) fisheries subsidies through new rules to be integrated in its framework and enforceable via its own dispute settlement mechanism (DSM). This task is not common for a body mostly concerned with trade regulation rather than sustainability (which is treated in a somewhat restricted manner through exceptions), or, even more broadly, the law of the sea. However, if accomplished, it would contribute to current ocean governance through restricting financial inflows into enhancement of the fishing effort, which is damaging for stocks.

Meanwhile, lacking fishing management-related experience or capacity to develop it, the WTO is bound to rely on the procedures and findings of specialist fisheries management bodies as triggers for its disciplines. This requires efficient interaction with other ocean governance players not only throughout negotiations but also (or even more so) during implementation of a future agreement. Similarly, the WTO is inevitably put into the network of the core law-of-the-sea notions embodied in the United Nations Convention on the Law of the Sea (UNCLOS) and related binding and soft law instruments, as well as their implementation.

Having first addressed the impediments encountered by the WTO Negotiating Group on Rules (NGR) despite mounting pressure to deliver, which the Group faces (I), this chapter will further proceed with briefly outlining the history of fisheries subsidies negotiations at the WTO (II); present the factors attracting fisheries subsidies issues to the Organisation (III); explore the potential for integration of disciplines-to-be within the WTO framework already regulating subsidies (IV); and detail and analyse the three key disciplines under discussion, assessing the viability and enforceability of their potential contributions to the Rule of Law for the oceans (V).

18.2 THE [POORLY SHAPED] PRESSURE TO DELIVER: IMPEDIMENTS FACED BY WTO NGR NEGOTIATORS

An aspiring wish list for the future WTO Fisheries Subsidies Agreement includes numerous and varied entries. In particular, the outcome is expected to (to name a few): respect the mandate(s); show due care for fish; account for developing concerns; duly interplay with the other Sustainable Development Goals (SDGs) and their targets;[2] integrate into both the legal framework of the WTO (its Single [Legal] Undertaking) and that of the other fora concerned with fisheries management; be [immediately] implementable; balance the three groups of sustainability concerns (i.e., environmental, social and economic); and prove the ongoing relevance of the multilateral trading system (MTS) embodied in the WTO.[3] In the meantime, one

[2] Among those – selected targets of the SDG 1, 2, 5, 8, 9, 10, 14, 16 and 17. See UN, 2015. Transforming Our World: The 2030 Agenda for Sustainable Development, A/RES/70/1.

[3] WTO 2019 Public Forum Working Session "How Millennials could be of help in understanding and resolving the hurdles of the multilateral trading system, making it [more] inclusive and development-oriented?" Closing remarks. WTO, 10 October 2019.

other objective – attesting that SDG [early] deadlines could be respected – was missed when the negotiators were unable to reach a deal by the end of 2019.

Despite enhanced attention to future fisheries subsidies disciplines, their sense, scope and dimensions are not well known or understood outside of the WTO negotiating rooms. Even more so, WTO and fisheries experts are each often able to see only part of the picture (e.g., 'subsidies' and 'fisheries', respectively), whereas other stakeholders demand delivery 'as is', not paying enough attention to the manifold technicalities that have so far emerged along the way. Lack of transparency over the progress of negotiations for over a decade[4] has contributed towards misperceptions and misunderstandings and, arguably, inhibited the establishment of working relationships between the WTO and other international organisations and arrangements operating in fisheries and/or fisheries management. These issues were partially addressed through publication of the evolving NGR chair's draft texts in May,[5] June[6] and November[7] 2021, the explanatory notes thereto[8] and the draft text of the agreement, expected to be considered during the MC12,[9] also accompanied by an explanatory note.[10] Nonetheless, the documents evidenced the existence of numerous disagreements, reflected in square brackets and placeholders.

Interaction between the WTO and the other 'fisheries' players will be necessary in implementation of the new agreement. The negotiators have indeed benefited from the knowledge shared by fisheries experts invited to participate in the technical sessions of the fisheries subsidies negotiations clusters and in the side events, as well as through studies and datasets on specific topics prepared in support of the negotiations. However, this is a 'one-way street' since news pertaining to progress in developing WTO fisheries rules did not necessarily spread. As a result, effective

4 TN/RL/W/213, 30 November 2007, Negotiating Group on Rules, Draft Consolidated Chair Texts of the Antidumping and Subsidies and Countervailing Measures Agreements, and TN/RL/W/232, Page C-1, Annex C – Fisheries Subsidies.

5 TN/RL/W/276, 11 May 2021, Negotiating Group on Rules, Fisheries Subsidies: Draft Consolidated Chair Text.

6 TN/RL/W/276/Rev.1, 30 June 2021, Negotiating Group on Rules, Fisheries Subsidies: Revised Draft Consolidated Chair Text: revision.

7 TN/RL/W/276/Rev.2, 8 November 2021, Negotiating Group on Rules, Fisheries Subsidies: Revised Draft Text: revision.

8 TN/RL/W/276/Add.1, 11 May 2021, Negotiating Group on Rules, Fisheries Subsidies: Draft Consolidated Chair Text. Chair's Explanatory Note Accompanying TN/RL/W/276. Addendum. With corrections made on 9 June 2021; TN/RL/W/276/Rev.1/Add.1, 30 June 2021, Negotiating Group on Rules, Fisheries Subsidies: Revised Draft Consolidated Chair Text. Chair's Explanatory Note Accompanying TN/RL/W/276/Rev.1. Addendum; TN/RL/W/276/Rev.2/Add.1, 8 November 2021, Negotiating Group on Rules – Fisheries subsidies – Revised draft text – Chair's explanatory note accompanying TN/RL/W/276/Rev.2. Addendum.

9 WT/MIN(21)/W/5, 24 November 2021, Ministerial Conference - Twelfth Session – Geneva, 30 November – 3 December 2021 – Agreement on fisheries subsidies – Draft text.

10 WT/MIN(21)/W/5/Add.1, 24 November 2021, Ministerial Conference – Twelfth Session – Geneva, 30 November – 3 December 2021 – Agreement on fisheries subsidies – Draft text – Addendum.

contributions from many of the fisheries specialists were disabled. Worse, the risk is that the outcome might make those same specialists somewhat reluctant to participate in implementing an unknown deal, fearing that its design might have a negative impact on the other initiatives.

The same prolonged lack of transparency has also made academic inquiry into the matter more complicated. This is because most of the submissions and communications by the Members, as well as other working papers, are restricted. In addition, in the past (up until May 2021, when the first version of the new NGR chair's consolidated text was shared beyond WTO walls), summaries or updates rarely reached the public domain. In combination, these factors were impeding holistic and objective analysis from being accomplished and/or published.

18.3 FISHERIES SUBSIDIES AT THE WTO: THE HISTORY

The history of WTO fisheries subsidies negotiations dates back to 1995. Then, right after establishment of the Organisation, issues related to the harmful effects of these subsidies on fish stocks were raised before the WTO Committee on Trade and Environment. The Committee started by updating itself on recent developments in the area, for instance, through studying Articles 11.2 and 11.3 of the Food and Agriculture Organisation of the United Nations (FAO) Code of Responsible Fisheries, devoted to responsible trade; laws and regulations relating to the fish trade and addressing sanitary and phytosanitary (SPS) measures, technical barriers to trade (TBT) measures, tariffs and non-tariff measures, relevant technology transfer requirements, transparency and cooperation.[11]

Inquiring into the core of the phenomenon, one of the proponents of establishing the disciplines in the area recognised: 'Fisheries subsidies, irrespective of whether they take the form of cost reduction or price supports, encourage increased fishing effort. Thus, fisheries subsidies exacerbate the already serious common property problem of ocean fisheries ... '.[12] On the other hand, an alternative approach has also started to crystalise. This approach – supported by Japan, among others – emphasises fisheries management rather than fisheries subsidies, as a result, advocating in favour of establishing considerably more modest and selective effect-based disciplines.[13]

[11] Brought to the attention of the WTO Members by the Note of the WTO Secretariat on Trade measures for environmental purposes taken pursuant to multilateral environmental agreements: recent developments, WT/CTE/W/15, 15 December 1995.

[12] WT/CTE/W/111, 11 March 1999. On the Environmental Impact of Fisheries Subsidies, A short report by the Icelandic Ministry of Fisheries, 1 February 1999, Submission by Iceland.

[13] WT/GC/W/221, 28 June 1999, Preparations for the 1999 Ministerial Conference, Negotiations On Forestry And Fishery Products, Communication From Japan; and PRESS/TE/036, 6 July 2001, UNEP and MEAs Participate In CTE Information Session on Compliance and Dispute Settlement. CTE Discusses WTO-MEA Relationship, Domestically Prohibited Goods, Biodiversity Convention and TRIPS Agreement, Eco-Labelling, and Fisheries Subsidies Reform.

Numerous submissions – mostly by the Friends of Fish: Iceland, New Zealand, the United States, Australia, Chile, Peru and Norway – have addressed many of the core points, including a drastic lack of transparency over fisheries subsidies granted by WTO Members,[14] posing real difficulties in terms of estimating the true impact of those subsidies. As a result, the first ever draft version of the WTO fisheries subsidies mandate, introduced during the MC3 in Seattle (yet never adopted), comprehensively captured most of the important elements of the discussions-to-be. It addressed 'certain subsidies that may contribute to over-capacity in fisheries and over-fishing'; provided that 'the work on fisheries subsidies shall be carried out in cooperation with the FAO and drawing also on relevant work under way within other intergovernmental bodies, including RFMOs' and included 'identification and examination of subsidies which contribute to over-capacity in fisheries and over-fishing' and 'the clarification and strengthening, as appropriate of disciplines under the Agreement on Subsidies and Countervailing Measures (SCM) with respect to such subsidies ... '.[15] However, it is important to note that the mandate as drafted had an additional, purely 'trade-related' facet, which has gradually disappeared as the work progressed. Namely, it was also dealing with fisheries subsidies that 'cause other adverse effects to the interests of Members' and 'have trade-distorting effects'.[16] The only area not addressed by the Seattle fisheries draft, which has later become a central element of the mandate, was that of development.

After the failure of the Seattle Ministerial to deliver,[17] unrelated to fisheries subsidies, a much more modest version of the relevant mandate was introduced in paragraph 28 of the Doha Ministerial Declaration.[18] This referred to clarification and improvement of the 'WTO disciplines on fisheries subsidies, taking into account the importance of this sector to developing countries' within the framework of 'negotiations aimed at clarifying and improving disciplines under the Agreements on Implementation of Article VI of the GATT 1994 and on Subsidies and Countervailing Measures'. This provision was supplemented by a broadly phrased undertaking to negotiate on 'the reduction or, as appropriate, elimination of tariff and non-tariff barriers to environmental goods and services' (non-specific to fisheries subsidies) in paragraph 31 (iii) of the same Declaration. The dual – trade and environmental – emphasis was thus, for the moment, preserved.

A largely identical mandate was restated in paragraph 28 of the 2005 Hong Kong Ministerial Declaration.[19] However, in paragraph 9 of its Annex D, the same instrument, in addition, explicitly referred to 'prohibition of certain forms of fisheries

[14] David J. Doulman, An Overview of World Fisheries: Challenges and Prospects for Achieving Sustainable Resource Use, April 1996, 16, quoted in ITEM 6, fisheries sector – submission by New Zealand, WT/CTE/W/52, 21 May 1997.

[15] Seattle (MC3) draft ministerial declaration, Para II(3)(a).

[16] Ibid.

[17] Report of the Third Ministerial Meeting of WTO, CUTS International, available at https://cuts-citee.org/report-of-the-third-ministerial-meeting-of-wto/.

[18] WT/MIN(01)/DEC/1, 20 November 2001.

[19] WT/MIN(05)/DEC, 22 December 2005.

subsidies that contribute to overcapacity and over-fishing', also containing a much more elaborate special and differential treatment (SDT) clause.

The NGR chair's Draft 2007,[20] even if not having normative value, is also worth a mention, since it has influenced the future of the negotiations in at least two respects. The first is by offering a definition of fisheries subsidies, containing an explicit reference to their 'specificity' (by suggesting, in Article I.1, that '... the following subsidies within the meaning of paragraph 1 of Article 1, to the extent they are specific within the meaning of paragraph 2 of Article 1, shall be prohibited'. The second is by introducing an extra negotiation track for subsidies to fishing on overfished stocks (Article I.2: 'In addition to the prohibitions listed in paragraph 1, any subsidy referred to in paragraphs 1 and 2 of the Article 1 [listing varied types of capacity-enhancing subsidies] the benefits of which are conferred on any fishing vessel or fishing activity *affecting fish stocks that are in an unequivocally overfished condition shall be prohibited*' (emphasis added). Both these items remain on the agenda up until today.

The situation evolved in late 2015 with adoption of SDG's, in particular, SDG 14.6, designed to 'by 2020, prohibit certain forms of fisheries subsidies which contribute to overcapacity and overfishing, and eliminate subsidies that contribute to IUU fishing, and refrain from introducing new such subsidies ... '. The prohibitory language of SDG 14.6 was picked up by the Ministerial statement of the 10th WTO Ministerial Conference (MC10), supported by some twenty-six WTO Members[21] and, later, the Ministerial Decision on Fisheries Subsidies[22] of the 11th WTO Ministerial Conference (MC11) in which, expanding the prior mandate, the Members agreed 'to continue to engage constructively in the fisheries subsidies negotiations building up on the progress already made ..., with a view to adopting, by the Ministerial Conference in 2019, an agreement on comprehensive and effective disciplines that prohibit certain forms of fisheries subsidies that contribute to overcapacity and overfishing, and eliminate subsidies that contribute to IUU-fishing ... '. This way, the mandate was supplemented by reference to Illegal, Unreported and Unregulated (IUU) fishing, and now contains two de-jure and three de-facto substantive elements.

In addition to these elements, the exact language of the mandate clearly evidences its evolution, starting from 'clarification' and reaching achieving agreement on new 'comprehensive and effective disciplines'.

18.4 FACTORS ATTRACTING THE ISSUE TO THE WTO AGENDA

The initial reason for introducing fisheries subsidies on to the WTO agenda seems to be clear. That is: the [once] strong dispute settlement that could extend to

[20] TN/RL/W/213, 30 November 2007, Draft Consolidated Chair Texts on the AD and SCM Agreements, Annex VIII, Fisheries Subsidies, 87–93.
[21] WT/MIN(15)/37, 19 December 2015, para. 2.
[22] WT/MIN(17)/64, WT/L/1031, 18 December 2017.

ensuring compliance with these trade-related obligations,[23] albeit mostly grounded in environmental sustainability. Redress for violating the fisheries governance rules is underexplored elsewhere, especially as far as the domain of capacity-enhancing subsidies is concerned, the one originally submitted for creation of the WTO rules-to-be. In this area, fisheries management plans, quasi-voluntary in nature, currently predominate. This leaves States questioning their neighbours' conservation efficiency to resort either to a) reinforcing it through technical assistance and enhancing cooperation within the framework of free trade agreements (FTAs) or fishing access agreements (FAAs), or b) adopting unilateral trade-restrictive measures, some of which were even contested before the General Agreement on Tariffs and Trade (the GATT) and WTO panels,[24] also featuring parallel counter-proceedings elsewhere.[25] In this light, the desire to legitimise at least some conservation measures within the global trade order looks justified, at least beyond the capriciousness of the GATT Article XX(g) exception. The situation with the IUU disciplines, joined to the WTO fisheries subsidies mandate, appears to be similar. However, arguably, these are already subject to harsher enforcement mechanisms. Despite the recent entry into force of the UN Port State Measures Agreement (PSMA),[26] as of now, such arrangements are predominantly of a unilateral nature.

Other factors of attraction – though arguably of comparatively less significance – include, for example, the nature of the measure, bearing in mind that the GATT, followed by the WTO, has significant experience in putting together, implementing and enforcing varied subsidies rules, proving that the subject matter of the new deal – fisheries/fish – is not foreign to the WTO, having been subject to market access measures, including tariffs and non-tariff measures (NTMs), such as SPS, TBT, transit and export/import restrictions. It might be also argued that the rules on fisheries subsidies could potentially benefit from peer pressure enhancing compliance, ensured by the institutional structure of the WTO. Finally, after the change of circumstances these days, in particular, the demise of the WTO Appellate Body (AB) and the resulting crisis of the WTO dispute settlement mechanism as a whole, the mandate remains on the agenda thanks to the *pacta sunt servanda* principle, supported by the efforts made in clarifying it earlier.

[23] Jaemin Lee, Looking for a Panacea in the SCM Agreement? Systemic Challenges for Post-Bali Fisheries Subsidies Discussion and Some Food for Thought to Overcome Them (2014) *Asian Journal of WTO & International Health Law and Policy*, Vol. 9, 477.

[24] EU – Measures on Atlanto-Scandian Herring: Request for Consultations by Denmark in Respect of the Faroe Islands, WT/DS469/1, G/L/1058 and Chile–Measures Affecting the Transit and Importation of Swordfish: Request for Consultations by the European Communities, WT/DS193/1, G/L/367. Both cases were settled before establishment of a panel.

[25] M. A. Orellana, The Swordfish Dispute between the EU and Chile at the ITLOS and the WTO (2002) *Nordic Journal of International Law*, Vol. 77, Issue 1, 55–81.

[26] Agreement on Port State Measures to Prevent, Deter, and Eliminate Illegal, Unreported, and Unregulated Fishing 2009, UNTC, vol. 54133.

18.5 SQUARING THE NEW SUBSIDIES WITH WTO SUBSIDIES DISCIPLINES

If adopted, the Agreement on Fisheries Subsidies would become the fourth covered agreement addressing subsidy matters at the WTO, after the GATT, the Agreement on Agriculture (AoA) and the Agreement on Subsidies and Countervailing Measures (SCM). It should be noted that the principle of effectiveness requires that the 'provisions [of the WTO agreements] are read in a coherent and consistent manner which gives full and effective meaning to all of their terms'.[27] Remarkably, while both the SCM and the AoA have adopted different regulatory approaches and structural solutions, they seem to overlap in attributing different weight to different types of subsidies, the SCM – through the 'traffic light' approach, while the AoA – via its boxes. This results in stricter treatment of the most trade-distorting measures. In the SCM, more restraining treatment is, for instance, reserved for the case of export subsidies, which, together with import substitution subsidies, forms the 'prohibited subsidies' category. While the SCM prohibited such subsidies from the start by virtue of its Article 3(1)(a), the AoA in its Part V (Articles 8-11) first subjected them to detailed regulation. This, however, was also later followed by the prohibition introduced through the Ministerial Decision on Export competition in the Bali Ministerial package,[28] which is now subject to gradual implementation. The typologies are closely linked to the issue of enforceability, with the more stringent disciplines being subject to better streamlined procedures.

Even should the Fisheries Subsidies Agreement be integrated into the SCM, its distinctive character and pursuit of non-trade objectives would certainly make it stand out as a *lex specialis* with respect to the other, general, subsidies rules incorporated therein. Fisheries (like other) subsidies are already covered by the SCM disciplines as far as their trade-related effects are concerned. Most of these subsidies are actionable, which means that a Member contesting a measure should be able, as per Part III of the SCM, to show (and quantify) adverse trade effects. As was suggested by Australia, Chile, Ecuador, Iceland, New Zealand, Peru, Philippines and the United States during early elaboration of the Doha Mandate,

> subsidised production reduces the access of existing and potential participants to fisheries, as well as to markets. Subsidies that limit others' access to stocks are trade-distorting, because in altering production patterns they necessarily alter trade patterns. ... The effects of such subsidies might be to keep unsubsidised catches

[27] AB Report, US – Upland Cotton, paras. 549–550; AB Report, EC – Large Civil Aircraft, para. 1054, and Debra P. Steger, The Subsidies and Countervailing Measures Agreement: Ahead of Its Time or Time for Reform? (2010) *Journal of World Trade*, Vol. 44, Issue 4, 779–796, at 782.

[28] WT/MIN(13)/40 and WT/L/915, 11 December 2013.

at low levels where they would otherwise have increased. ... If subsidised fishers deplete a shared stock, all other fishers lose access to that stock, not merely those competing alongside the subsidised product at market.[29]

The same submission further noted that the distortions caused by the fisheries subsidies might be difficult to address under the SCM Agreement, operating the notions of price cuts and import impediments or displacements.[30] The proponents also pointed out that the task of identifying market distortions by fisheries subsidies is made more difficult by the diversity in nature of fisheries products and of the economic structures used by the industrial segment concerned.[31]

This might suggest the reasons why no cases challenging fisheries subsidies provided by a Member were ever raised before the WTO panels and the AB. The same structure proves highly impracticable if 'trade' effects are replaced by 'environmental' concerns. Nor would it meet the mandate, unambitiously calling for no less than 'prohibition'. The fisheries subsidies rules, which are being elaborated, are not directly aimed at disciplining trade restrictive measures otherwise resorted to by the Members in the fisheries sector, such as import, export and transit restrictions. Those would likely continue their parallel existence, even though, indeed, they might be impacted by synergies created by better fisheries management practices, the introduction of which might be catalysed by the Fisheries Subsidies Agreement, or even a run-up thereto, and, where applicable, the other WTO rules disciplining trade restrictions. What is suggested is an alternative avenue. Lastly, the fisheries subsidies disciplines might be relevant in interpreting the text of GATT Article XX(g) as applied to other trade restrictive measures taken to meet conservation ends.

18.6 WHAT THE NEGOTIATIONS ARE REALLY ABOUT: THE THREE ELEMENTS OF A FUTURE DEAL

Even if it might be argued that at the core of the ongoing negotiations are disciplines tackling overcapacity and overfishing, two other additional issues are on the table. One of those – subsidies to fishing overfished stocks – was added de facto, not de jure. These three substantive areas will be assessed next.

18.6.1 *Capacity-Enhancing Subsidies (e.g., Contributing to Overcapacity and Overfishing)*

Input of overcapacity into overfishing is clear (see Chart 18.1) and widely recognised. Moreover, as the term 'contributing' itself suggests, even if this is not the only cause of overfishing, it remains an important one. In addition, overcapacity is the area

[29] TN/RL/W/3, 24 April 2002. Para. 15.
[30] Ibid., para 16.
[31] Ibid.

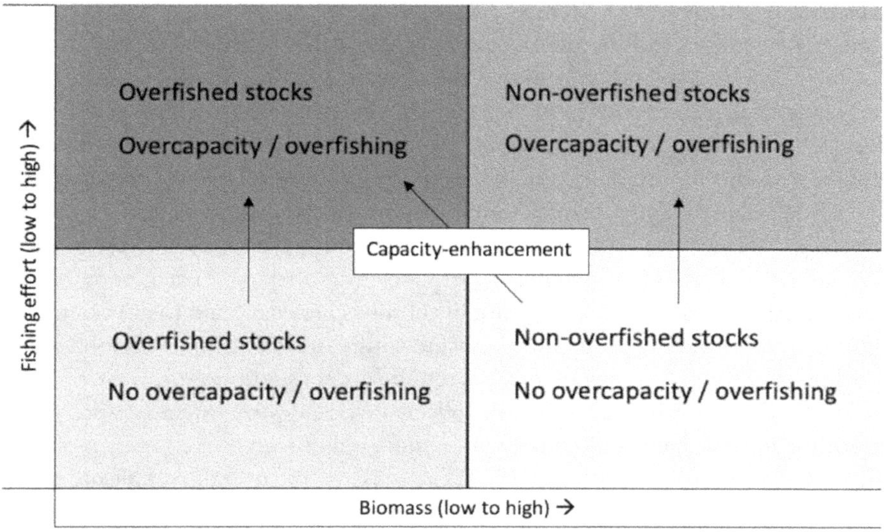

CHART 18.1. Impact of capacity-enhancing subsidies on fish stocks (on adjusted Kobe Plot)

offering most comfort to the WTO negotiators, since it largely relies on economic terms and indicators, to which they are accustomed. The impact of capacity-enhancing subsidies on the conditions of fish stocks is demonstrated on the adjusted version of the Kobe (or the phase) plot. This constituted part of the Report of the first joint meeting of the tuna RFMOs, which is used to evaluate the status of a stock based on fishing mortality (F) and biomass (B) associated with maximum sustainable yield (MSY; FMSY and BMSY).

Subsidies increasing capacity – even more so when coupled with poor or inexistent fisheries management practices – appear also to contribute to IUU. Thus, overcapacity disciplines could, in addition, curtail IUU fishing, which, as noted by Lee, is a by-product rather than a subject of subsidisation.[32] Tackling a broader perspective, prohibition of certain overcapacity subsidies would make an important contribution to fisheries governance overall, since this particular issue is not pre-empted by the existing framework. That is especially so with respect to fishing on the high seas – outside the areas/ species covered by the RFMO/As, or even within them – since the measures taken by different organisations and arrangements are not identical in their efficiency. Finally, considering the migrating, straddling and shared nature of many fish stocks, which make management efforts particularly difficult, blocking enhancement of fisheries effort could be a viable addition or alternative.

[32] Lee (n 22).

Even though the WTO Members seem to agree that subsidies contributing to overcapacity and overfishing have to be curtailed, reaching consensus over the way in which this result could be achieved has proven to be a difficult task. The three main approaches suggested and debated are as follows. First, the positive list approach, according to which most harmful types of capacity-enhancing fisheries subsidies would be identified and so listed and prohibited. Second, the negative effect test, according to which only capacity-enhancing subsidies negatively impacting stocks would face prohibition. And third, the approach establishing (scheduling) subsidy caps, specific to particular Members or their groups, which would limit the total allowable amount of subsidies provided, and might be subject to further reductions. These approaches were considered alone and in combination.

While the list and the caps approaches require consensus upfront – in establishing the lists and quantifying the caps respectively – the negative effect test postpones determination of what is prohibited to the future – as a matter of a highly problematic step in light of the ongoing WTO DSM impasse, the overall complexity of the WTO DSM and particular challenges fisheries subsidies might contribute thereto.

The blended approach, embodied in the latest Chair's draft, relies on the stabilised demonstrative list of prohibited subsidies (subsidies for fixed and operational costs, including fuel), followed by effect-based flexibility and exceptions incorporating certain elements used in elaborating the capping proposals. The design of these provisions implies that the setting of action is the territorial sea, EEZ or RFMO/A area. Special provisions prohibit subsidies contingent on fishing on the high seas in whole or in part, as well as subsidies to vessels flying a flag of a different Member. The flexibility tolerates capacity-enhancing subsidisation 'if the subsidising Member demonstrates that measures are implemented to maintain the stock or stocks in the relevant fishery or fisheries at a biologically sustainable level'. Meanwhile, the exceptions reflected (save for the one devoted to disaster relief and available to all Members) are targeting low income, resource-poor or livelihood fishing, or fishing-related activities of the developing Members and LDCs in their territorial seas or EEZs. These exceptions are not only time-limited but are also subject to exemptions from eligibility, referring to the Member's share of the annual global marine capture fish production and, potentially, other indicators.

18.6.2 *Subsidies to Fishing on Overfished Stocks*

A separate stream of disciplines related to prohibition of subsidies to fishing on overfished stocks, not explicitly forming a part of the mandate, were first introduced by the chair's Draft in late 2007. These are the disciplines that have faced the most impressive dynamics, having moved from the non-existent and, next, redundant, to the core and most stringent disciplines among the proposed prohibitions.

The idea behind subsidies to fishing on overfished stocks is plausibly based on 'not going from bad to worse', that is, not depleting already 'suffering' stocks still further. Nevertheless, the drafting solutions suggested by the Members in this respect initially tended to tweak the main aim of these disciplines by, rather, using the latter as a shield safeguarding their right to continue to subsidise fishing on overfished stocks, subject to the set conditions, for instance – a post-factum negative effect test. Unsurprisingly, this solution appeared somewhat far-fetched. The chair's Draft contains a clear prohibition on subsidising fishing on overfished stocks, subject to flexibility allowing stock-rebuilding subsidies only, conditional on compliance with [enhanced] transparency requirements. In a sense, flexibility is structured so that it is more likely to be invoked in practice by developed countries. The disciplines are also subject to highly restrictively phrased time-limited exceptions for low-income, resource-poor or livelihood fishing or fishing-related activities in the territorial seas by developing Members and LDCs. Technically, the overfished stocks disciplines feature a very high level of reliance on stock assessment and management domains, which might seriously hamper their already limited efficiency.

Finally, after years of heated debates, Members appear to have decided not to retain the presumption of overfishing with respect to unassessed stocks. Thus, the overfishing disciplines would not apply to those stocks. While the final provisions in the draft encourage Members to exercise due restraint with respect to subsidisation of such stocks, this solution is rather weak and might disincentivise stock assessment.

18.6.3 *Subsidies to IUU Fishing*

The late-comer to the WTO fisheries subsidies mandate – 'elimination of subsidies to Illegal, Unreported and Unregulated (IUU) fishing' as well as fishing-related activities in support of such fishing – has an accessory flavour. The framework developed at the WTO so far, even if having accumulated a high degree of consensus, remains weak and heavily dependent on external IUU determinations by coastal States (including port States), flag States and RFMO/As. Obligations are limited to adopting, implementing and notifying to the WTO the national laws prohibiting the grant of subsidies to vessels and/or operators determined to be engaged in IUU fishing. The IUU determination triggering the prohibition is subject to positive evidence and should be conducted in line with due process standards. The expected impact of the disciplines is not fully clear and, in any case, appears to be quite modest due to the prospective injunctive (as opposed to retrospective compensatory) nature of WTO remedies. However, despite its practical insignificance, elimination of IUU subsidies discipline could conceivably be useful in supporting relevant measures taken elsewhere.[33]

[33] For an overview of such measures, see S. Widjaja, T. Long, H. Wirajuda et al. 2019. Illegal, Unreported and Unregulated Fishing and Associated Drivers. Washington, DC: World Resources Institute. Available online at www.oceanpanel.org/iuu-fishing-and-associated-drivers.

18.6.4 *The Effective Way Forward*

While the framework of the new agreement appears to be largely in place, the Members are working on aligning their positions on several outstanding details. Key among those are the scope of flexibilities and exceptions (namely those reflecting the 'appropriate and effective' SDT), as well as institutional matters, in particular, the extent of the transparency obligation and adjustments to the WTO DSM to duly accommodate fisheries subsidies disputes. The short transitional periods, now proposed for the prohibition of subsidies to fishing on overfished stocks disciplines, seem to be based on a presumption of quick recovery of unsustainable stocks, which might be over-optimistic. Instead, a closer look might be taken at the gradual diversification in the occupational focus of the coastal communities engaged in livelihood fishing, especially in developing countries and LDCs, to allow their members to decrease their dependence on catches, even if temporarily. This might require not only additional time but also a creative strategy joined by suitable technical assistance.

In line with the considerations presented earlier in this chapter, the text, as it stands, has largely omitted stock management tasks, albeit reliance on their results as a trigger inevitably remains. This, once again, suggests that implementation of the WTO Fisheries Subsidies Agreement, when adopted, would necessitate cooperation between the WTO and the national fishing management authorities, RFMOs and RFMAs, as well as the FAO. Moreover, coordination with the work being accomplished by the UN (UNECE and UNCTAD), the OECD and the World Bank would also be useful. A key feature of this process would be to understand variable areas of competence and divide tasks, without undue usurpation of those by the 'new' player (WTO). If duly implemented, this approach would shape positive synergies.

18.7 CONCLUDING REMARKS

The contours of the potential contribution by the WTO to the Rule of Law for the Oceans are largely defined by now. It will include rules contributing to minimising financial inflows supporting enhancement of the fishing effort and so damaging stocks. These rules would be divided into three streams, shaped as prohibitions of: a) subsidies contributing to overcapacity and overfishing; b) subsidies for fishing on overfished stocks; and c) subsidies to vessels and/or operators involved in IUU fishing. Reflecting the accessory role of the WTO in ocean governance and once again emphasising that the WTO does not exist in a clinical isolation, the new disciplines are built around law of the sea notions and are relying on the efforts taken and findings made by fisheries management organisations and arrangements as triggers.

While the oceans are well-inscribed into the environmental sustainability pillar of a future agreement, which appears to feature a higher degree of convergence, the other two – social and economic sustainability – elements, are still subject to heated discussion. Indeed, a reduction in the usual state support might have a considerable impact on fishers and their communities, especially in the short term. On the other hand, the impossibility of investing in fleets could interfere with the industrialisation strategies of developing countries and LDCs, most of which, nowadays, are responsible for only an insignificant share of subsidisation due to their restricted relevant budgets. Mutually acceptable solutions to these issues are hoped to be found by the MC12, now postponed to March 2022 at the earliest due to the COVID pandemic.

The WTO fisheries subsidies negotiations are a marathon rather that a sprint. Another lap or several might be required to make sure that the agreement is ripe for delivery and subsequent implementation. On this track, every step forward is of importance to both the WTO and the oceans. A win-win outcome might well be achievable: through establishing the new, sustainability-driven subsidies rules, the WTO could help the oceans to recover, while the progress and the eventual successful conclusion of the fisheries subsidies negotiations could affirm that the WTO remains relevant and could meaningfully deliver on trade-related issues of global concern.

19

Improving Compliance with International Fisheries Law through Litigation

Solène Guggisberg

19.1 INTRODUCTION

As recognized by the UN General Assembly, the rule of law requires that States 'abide by all their obligations under international law'.[1] Against this standard, the traditional regime regulating international fisheries appears inadequate, since many States are unwilling or unable to respect their relevant obligations. This issue is enabled or compounded, at the global level, by the absence of a well-established, inter-governmental compliance mechanism to hold them accountable.[2] Such a mechanism would be tasked, first, to verify, independently, whether States are respecting their obligations and then, if needed, to take measures to trigger modification of behaviour.

This chapter examines the potential of using litigation to increase compliance with existing norms in the field of fisheries. International courts and tribunals are indeed important contributors to the rule of law,[3] be it by solving the specific dispute in front of them[4] or clarifying the law.[5] Existing research has examined case-law

1 United Nations General Assembly (UNGA), Declaration of the High-level Meeting of the General Assembly on the Rule of Law at the National and International Level, A/Res/67/1, para. 37.

2 On this, see S. Guggisberg, "Verifying and Improving States' Compliance with Their International Fisheries Obligations", in A. M. Cisneros-Montemayor, W. W. L. Cheung and Y. Ota (eds.), *Predicting Future Oceans* (Amsterdam: Elsevier, 2019) 453–464.

3 UNGA, Resolution A/Res/67/1 (n 1), paras. 31–32.

4 Statute of the International Court of Justice (ICJ), Article 38. On this role more generally, see for example A. von Bogdandy and I. Venzke, "On the Functions of International Courts: An Appraisal in Light of Their Burgeoning Public Authority" (2012) ACIL Research Paper No 2012–10 1, 6.

5 On other uses of international courts and tribunals, see e.g., V. Lowe, "The Function of Litigation in International Society" (2012) 41 *ICLQ* 209, 214.

relevant to fisheries or the marine environment more generally,[6] and has analysed the potential of litigation for environmental purposes.[7] The present chapter aims to add to this body of literature by analysing the potential of and obstacles to using litigation in three specific fisheries-focused scenarios: litigation against a flag State, against a coastal State and against a fishing State.

The adjudicative bodies examined in the present chapter focus on public international law, leaving aside trade law as a more discrete field. In addition to references to contentious cases in front of the International Court of Justice (ICJ), the International Tribunal for the Law of the Sea (ITLOS) and arbitral tribunals, the chapter considers advisory opinions and conciliation commissions. Litigation is hence understood in an expansive fashion.

It is worth noting at the outset that the main framework for the law of the sea, the United Nations Convention on the Law of the Sea (UNCLOS), establishes a robust and compulsory system for the settlement of disputes. Part XV of that nearly global treaty contains dispute settlement procedures applicable to all parties to the treaty since reservations are not allowed under the Convention, unless provided otherwise in specific provisions. Disputes regarding interpretation or application of the Convention can, if certain conditions are fulfilled, be submitted unilaterally to third-party dispute settlement.

19.2 LITIGATION AGAINST A FLAG STATE

A first possibility to improve compliance with existing obligations would be to focus litigation strategy on flag States, which are central players in maritime activities, including fisheries.

The obligations of the flag State are, inter alia, to control vessels flying its flag, both on the high seas and in the Exclusive Economic Zone (EEZ) EEZs of third States, and to ensure that they respect applicable conservation and management

6 R. R. Churchill, "The Jurisprudence of the International Tribunal for the Law of the Sea Relating to Fisheries: Is There Much in the Net?" (2007) 22 *IJMCL* 383–424; N. Klein, "Litigation over Marine Resources: Lessons for the Law of the Sea, International Dispute Settlement and International Environmental Law" (2009) 28 *Aust YBIL* 131–179; D. R. Rothwell, "The Contribution of ITLOS to Oceans Governance through Marine Environmental Dispute Resolution", in T. M. Ndiaye and R. Wolfrum (eds.), *Law of the Sea, Environmental Law and Settlement of Disputes: Liber amicorum Judge Thomas A. Mensah* (Leiden: Nijhoff 2007) 1007–1024; T. Stephens, "Marine wildlife and ecosystems", in T. Stephens (ed.), *International Courts and Environmental Protection* (Cambridge: Cambridge University Press 2009) 196–244; T. Treves, "Fisheries disputes: Judicial and arbitral practice since the entry into force of UNCLOS", in R. Wolfrum, M. Seršić and T. Šošić (eds.), *Contemporary Developments in International Law* (Leiden: Brill 2015) 328–336.

7 P. Sands, "International Environmental Litigation and Its Future" (1999) 32 *U Rich L Rev.* 1619–1641. See also, more generally, T. Stephens (ed.), *International Courts and Environmental Protection* (n 6).

measures (CMMs). The obligation is provided for in Article 94 of UNCLOS[8] and further elaborated, in relation to the fisheries sector, in other treaties.[9] This obligation of due diligence does not imply that a flag State will be held responsible for each violation of applicable rules by one of its vessels, but that it must 'take all necessary measures to ensure compliance and to prevent IUU [illegal, unreported and unregulated] fishing by fishing vessels flying its flag'.[10]

While this is an obligation of conduct rather than result, it should not be underestimated; the order of the oceans, in particular on the high seas, is based on assigning jurisdiction to the flag State. Unfortunately, the issue of flags of non-compliance is widespread in the fisheries field.[11] In that light, the potential impact of addressing this issue would be considerable. The law of the sea is not so much a legal regime with major gaps as a legal regime insufficiently implemented and enforced.

19.2.1 *Standing*

A potential challenge with this strategy would be in determining the entity competent to bring a case to a court or a tribunal. In contentious cases, only those States whose legal interests are infringed have standing to initiate proceedings in front of international courts.[12] It is indeed generally accepted that a State 'should be able to establish a legal interest in respect of the claim brought before an international tribunal'[13] and that 'a mere interest' is insufficient.[14] Traditionally, States with

8 United Nations Convention on the Law of the Sea (UNCLOS), Montego Bay, 10 December 1982, in force 16 November 1994, 1833 *UNTS* 396.

9 Agreement to Promote Compliance with International Conservation and Management Measures by Fishing Vessels on the High Seas, Rome, 24 November 1993, in force 24 April 2003, 2221 *UNTS* 120; Agreement for the Implementation of the Provisions of the United Nations Convention on the Law of the Sea of 10 December 1982 relating to the Conservation and Management of Straddling Fish Stocks and Highly Migratory Fish Stocks (UNFSA), New York, 4 August 1995, in force 11 December 2001, 2167 *UNTS* 88.

10 *Request for an Advisory Opinion Submitted by the Sub-Regional Fisheries Commission (SRFC), Advisory Opinion, 2 April 2015, ITLOS Reports 2015.*

11 C. Goodman, "The Regime for Flag State Responsibility in International Fisheries Law: Effective Fact, Creative Fiction, or Further Work Required" (2009) 23 *A&NZ Mar LJ* 157, 164; D. D. Miller and U. R. Sumaila, "Flag Use Behavior and IUU Activity within the International Fishing Fleet: Refining Definitions and Identifying Areas of Concern" (2014) 44 *Marine Policy* 204–211; D. Warner-Kramer, "Control Begins at Home: Tackling Flags of Convenience and IUU Fishing" (2004) 34 *Golden Gate ULRev* 497, 499–502.

12 P. Birnie, A. Boyle and C. Redgwell, *International Law and the Environment* (3rd ed. Oxford: Oxford University Press 2009) 252.

13 P. Okowa, "Issues of Admissibility and the Law on International Responsibility" in M. D. Evans (ed.), *International Law* (3rd ed. Oxford: Oxford University Press 2010) 472.

14 *Case Concerning the Barcelona Traction, Light and Power Company, Limited (Belgium v. Spain) – Second Phase, Judgment, 5 February 1970, I.C.J. Reports 1970*, para. 46; C. J. Tams, *Enforcing Obligations Erga Omnes in International Law* (Cambridge: Cambridge University Press 2005) 29–31.

standing are defending their rights or legal interests, not those of the international community generally.[15]

A category of States with clear standing are injured States, as defined in Article 42 of the International Law Commission (ILC) Articles on the Responsibility of States.[16] However, as the relevant obligations of flag States are not owed to any particular State, a State wanting to invoke a flag State's responsibility would have to be 'specially affected' or the situation would have to be such that 'each party's performance is effectively conditioned upon and requires the performance of each of the others'.[17] The former case could be that of a coastal State if a flag State did not control its vessels fishing in the coastal State's EEZ. The latter could, arguably, be invoked more generally by one State against another State whose conduct enables free-riding by vessels flying its flag, leading to the total fishing pressure on a stock exceeding sustainable levels.

A second category of States with potential standing are those that are not injured by the actions they may want to combat in court. That would be, for example, a State deciding to bring a well-known flag of non-compliance to court, in a situation where the applicant's interest is to fight impunity rather than to see a specific violation against its own interests remedied. De *lege lata*, the existence of a general right for a State to act for protection of the international community's rights and on its behalf, in what is called an *actio popularis*, is still controversial and unsettled even in relation to obligations owed to the international community.[18]

In terms of obligations relying on multilateral treaties, that is, obligations *erga omnes partes*, standing might actually not be an issue. Some compromissory clauses provide a basis for standing without the need to show any special interest.[19] Hence, States wishing to react to a breach of these conventional frameworks do not have to demonstrate an injury.[20] Article 286 of UNCLOS is one such clause that does not require the applicant to have directly or particularly suffered an injury. It provides that 'any dispute concerning the interpretation or application of this Convention shall . . . be submitted at the request of any party to the dispute'.

[15] M. Fitzmaurice, "The International Court of Justice and International Environmental Law" in C. J. Tams and J. Sloan (eds.), *The Development of International Law by the International Court of Justice* (Oxford: Oxford University Press 2013) 354.

[16] Articles on the Responsibility of States for Internationally Wrongful Acts, (2001) vol. II-2 *YILC*, Art. 42.

[17] Ibid., commentary on Art. 42, para. 13.

[18] R. Wolfrum, "Enforcing Community Interests through International Dispute Settlement: Reality or Utopia" in U. Fastenrath and others (eds.), *From Bilateralism to Community Interest: Essays in Honour of Bruno Simma* (Oxford: Oxford University Press 2011) 1132.

[19] *Questions Relating to the Obligation to Prosecute or Extradite (Belgium* v. *Senegal), Judgment, 20 July 2012 I.C.J. Reports 2012*, p. 422, para. 69; see also G. Gaja, "Obligations and Rights Erga Omnes in International Law: Preparatory Work" (2005) 71-I *Annuaire de l'Institut de Droit International* 117 at 123.

[20] Tams (n 14) 125.

Even for cases started on other jurisdictional bases, there are general signs that an international court or tribunal may be willing to hear a case related to obligations *erga omnes partes*. In particular, in the *Whaling* case, the applicant State, Australia, was not directly injured by the actions of Japan. Both States were parties to the International Convention for the Regulation of Whaling, the provisions of which Australia claimed that Japan had breached. The basis of jurisdiction relied on by the Applicant was unilateral declarations under Article 36(2) of the ICJ Statute. Japan did not raise an objection regarding Australia's standing to bring the case to the ICJ, which in turn did not consider the question.[21] When addressing matters of jurisdiction and admissibility, the ICJ must examine any potential issue *proprio motu* and its silence on the question of a non-injured State's standing seems to imply that it did not see this as an impediment to hearing the case on the merits.

As for obligations *erga omnes*, that is, not treaty-reliant but rather of a customary international law nature, the situation may be more precarious. On the one hand, the ILC acknowledged, in its Articles on the Responsibility of States, that a non-injured State can invoke a wrongdoing State's responsibility in order to protect collective interests, hence pointing to the possibility for such an *actio popularis*.[22] On the other hand, the consequences of a non-injured State's ability to invoke responsibility were acknowledged in the Commentary to be a progressive development of international law,[23] and the relevant provision more generally was controversial during the drafting process.[24] Hence, courts and tribunals might be reluctant to allow a case started by a non-injured State to proceed if the obligations binding the parties are not treaty-based. The practical impacts of this probable absence of standing are likely limited since UNCLOS is a nearly global treaty. Nonetheless, some noteworthy non-parties remain, such as the United States, which are not bound by Part XV.

19.2.2 *Jurisdiction*

After settling the question of standing, a court or tribunal would examine the question of jurisdiction. An issue may arise, in relation to cases started under the compulsory dispute settlement mechanism set up under UNCLOS, if both applicant and respondent are also parties to the same regional fisheries management

21 *Whaling in the Antarctic (Australia* v. *Japan: New Zealand intervening), Judgment, I.C.J. Reports* 2014, 226.

22 Articles on the Responsibility of States for Internationally Wrongful Acts, Art. 48. On this, see e.g., J. R. Crawford, "State responsibility" *MPEPIL*, para. 46; Institut de Droit International (IDI), Resolution on the Obligations and rights erga omnes in international law, Session de Cracow 2005.

23 Articles on the Responsibility of States for Internationally Wrongful Acts, commentary on Art. 48, para. 12.

24 E. B. Weiss, "Invoking State Responsibility in the Twenty-First Century" (2002) 96 *AJIL* 798 at 805.

organization (RFMO). These are the main bodies entrusted with conservation and management of straddling and highly migratory species. Article 281 of the Convention gives precedence to other dispute settlement mechanisms, if so agreed by the parties.[25]

Most RFMOs have agreed to some sort of dispute settlement in their founding treaties. Hence, depending on the interpretation given to the terms of Article 281(1), an applicant might be precluded from accessing compulsory dispute settlement procedures under UNCLOS and instead be limited to potentially non-binding procedures. The arbitral tribunal in the *Southern Bluefin Tuna* cases brought by Australia and New Zealand against Japan found that the procedure established under the convention establishing the Commission for the Conservation of Southern Bluefin Tuna (CCSBT) precluded recourse to compulsory jurisdiction provided by UNCLOS. While the relevant provision of that treaty[26] does not explicitly prohibit referral of a dispute to ITLOS, the ICJ or an arbitral tribunal under Part XV of UNCLOS, the Arbitral Tribunal found that it did not have jurisdiction because the agreement between the Parties excluded any further procedure.[27]

This decision has been widely criticized.[28] Instead of a binding compulsory mechanism under UNCLOS, a legally weaker mechanism took priority. If this decision were to serve as a precedent, it would exclude a number of treaties that could otherwise fall *ratione materiae* under UNCLOS dispute settlement procedures but have a clause related to some dispute settlement mechanism – usually a weak one – of their own.[29] Indeed, the convention establishing the CCSBT is not the only RFMO treaty with such a provision: at least three others include similarly worded articles in their founding treaties.[30]

However, the questionable reasoning found in the *Southern Bluefin Tuna* cases has been reversed in the more recent *South China Sea* case. In the decision on jurisdiction and admissibility, the Arbitral Tribunal examined Article 281 and found

[25] UNCLOS, Art. 281(1).

[26] Convention for the Conservation of Southern Bluefin Tuna, Canberra, 10 May 1993, in force 20 May 1994, 1819 *UNTS* 359, Art. 16.

[27] *Southern Bluefin Tuna (New Zealand* v. *Japan, Australia* v. *Japan)*, Arbitral Award, 4 August 2000, Arbitral Tribunal, (2006) *XXIII RIAA* 1, paras. 53–59, 72.

[28] A. Boyle, "The Southern Bluefin Tuna Arbitration" (2001) 50 *ICLQ* 447 at 451; J. Peel, "A Paper Tiger Which Dissolves in the Rain? The Future for Resolving Fisheries Disputes under UNCLOS in the Aftermath of the Southern Bluefin Tuna Arbitration" (2002) 3 *Melb J Int Law* 53–79; C. Romano, "The Southern Bluefin Tuna Dispute: Hints of a World to Come . . . Like It or Not" (2001) 32 *ODIL* 313, 331.

[29] D. L. Morgan, "Implications of the Proliferation of International Legal Fora: The Example of the Southern Bluefin Tuna Case" (2002) 43 Harv Int'l *LJ*. 541, 550; R. Salama, "Fragmentation of International Law: Procedural Issues Arising in Law of the Sea Disputes" (2005) 19 A&NZ *Mar LJ* 24, 36–37.

[30] Convention on the Conservation of Antarctic Marine Living Resources, Canberra, 20 May 1980, in force 4 April 1982, 1329 *UNTS* 47, Art. XXV; General Fisheries Commission for the Mediterranean Convention, Art. 19; Inter-American Tropical Tuna Commission Convention, Washington, 31 May 1949, in force 3 March 1950, 80 *UNTS* 3, Art. XXV.

that, for the dispute settlement mechanisms established under UNCLOS not to be applicable pursuant to that provision, an express exclusion was required.[31] Under this interpretation of Article 281, most RFMO founding documents could not be used to preclude a dispute about UNCLOS provisions from being examined by an international court or tribunal. The line of argumentation in the recent award is certainly more convincing, but it will remain to be seen whether future courts and tribunals decide to widely follow it, in particular in light of the political considerations surrounding the *South China Sea* case.[32] The decision on competence in the *Timor Sea conciliation* is, in that sense, encouraging.[33] In any event, since the potential issue of jurisdiction is related to Article 281 of UNCLOS, cases started under other bases of jurisdiction would not be at risk.

19.3 LITIGATION AGAINST A COASTAL STATE

A second possibility to improve compliance with existing obligations would be to focus litigation strategy on coastal States, whose waters are the most productive in the oceans, and where most fishing occurs.[34]

Coastal States must ensure that the resources under their jurisdiction are not over-exploited.[35] To do so, they must set a total allowable catch, taking into account the best scientific evidence and adopting measures to maintain or restore stocks to a level where they can produce maximum sustainable yield.[36] Failings by the coastal State may be due to unwillingness and/or inability, as managing vast expenses of waters is a costly endeavour. Since a large proportion of stocks are overfished,[37] it seems clear that the obligation to avoid overexploitation is not properly respected.

31 *The South China Sea Arbitration (The Republic of Philippines* v. *The People's Republic of China)*, Award, 12 July 2016, paras. 223–224.

32 The People's Republic of China has clearly and incessantly worked on the international scene to discredit the award (see for example the press release of the Embassy of the People's Republic of China in the USA <www.china-embassy.org/eng/zt/abc123/> [last accessed 27 July 2021]) and the long special issue of the *Chinese JIL* on the award ((2018) 17 "The South China Sea Arbitration Awards: A Critical Study"; on this see D. Guilfoyle, "A New Twist in the South China Sea Arbitration: The Chinese Society of International Law's Critical Study" (2018) *EJIL: Talk!* <www.ejiltalk.org/a-new-twist-in-the-south-china-sea-arbitration-the-chinese-society-of-international-laws-critical-study/> [last accessed 27 July 2021]).

33 *Timor Sea Conciliation (Timor-Leste* v. *Australia)*, Decision on Australia's Objections to Competence, 19 September 2016, paras. 56–58.

34 U. Rashid Sumaila et al., "Winners and Losers in a World Where the High Seas Is Closed to Fishing" (2015) 5 *Scientific Reports* 8481 <https://doi.org/10.1038/srep08481>.

35 UNCLOS, Art. 61(2).

36 Ibid., Art. 61(1).

37 Over 33 per cent of stocks are overfished (Food and Agriculture Organization (FAO), *The State of the World Fisheries and Aquaculture* (Rome 2018) 6).

19.3.1 *Scope of Jurisdiction*

A major problem with the strategy of bringing a coastal State to court is to be found in the limitations to UNCLOS' compulsory jurisdiction. Issues related to a coastal State's sovereign rights 'with respect to the living resources in the exclusive economic zone or their exercise, including its discretionary powers for determining the allowable catch ... and the terms and conditions established in its conservation and management laws and regulations' are indeed listed in the automatic exceptions to the compulsory dispute settlement principle found in UNCLOS.[38]

In certain cases concerning fisheries, conciliation is possible under Annex V section (2) of UNCLOS. This procedure is open in specific situations when a coastal State 'manifestly failed' its conservation obligations and marine living resources in its EEZ are 'seriously endangered'.[39] This mechanism is clearly intended only for extreme situations.[40] Moreover, the coastal States' discretion is not to be put into question.[41] In any case, the results of a conciliation procedure are non-binding.[42]

Notwithstanding these limitations, Annex V conciliations remain an open avenue, and a precedent now exists for the establishment of a conciliation commission: the *Timor Sea* conciliation. While this concerned issues of maritime delimitations and oil and gas exploitation, rather than fisheries, it is nevertheless an interesting precedent. In particular, Australia objected to the competence of the conciliation commission,[43] an issue that may arise in the present scenario, due to the qualified wording of Article 297(3)(b) and the potential existence of other treaties between the parties. That the commission proceeded to hold hearings on the matter and issued a decision asserting jurisdiction[44] – which Australia did respect – is proof that this procedure is able to deal with complex issues. The format followed in that conciliation, where Australia and Timor-Leste were negotiating to find a mutually acceptable solution, requires the constructive involvement of both parties. It may consequently not be a viable way forward in the case of tense and confrontational relations. Nonetheless, one could envisage a conciliation of

[38] UNCLOS, Art. 297(3)(a); E. Scalieri, "Discretionary Power of Coastal States and the Control of Its Compliance with International Law by International Tribunals" in A. Del Vecchio and R. Virzo (eds.), *Interpretation of the United Nations Convention on the Law of the Sea by International Courts and Tribunals* (Berlin, Heidelberg, New York: Springer 2019) 349–381.

[39] UNCLOS, Art. 297(3)(b)(i-iii).

[40] Churchill (n 6) 389.

[41] J. G. Merrills, *International Dispute Settlement* (5th ed. Cambridge: Cambridge University Press 2007) 172.

[42] UNCLOS, Art. 297(3)(b)(c) and annex V, Arts. 7(2) and (14).

[43] *Timor Sea Conciliation (Timor-Leste v. Australia)*, Decision on Australia's Objections to Competence, 19 September 2016, paras. 13–20.

[44] Ibid., para. 111.

a different type, with a decision issued by the commission, similar to an arbitration but of a non-binding nature.

In light of the potential challenges to starting litigation-like proceedings vis-à-vis a coastal State under UNCLOS, it may be worth considering having recourse to other bases of jurisdiction, such as unilateral declarations recognizing the competence of the ICJ, if available. In such cases, UNCLOS would still be the applicable law, but not the source of jurisdiction. The limits to the competence of the ICJ would consequently only be those included in the States' declarations.

19.3.2 *Remedies*

Even in the case of contentious litigation against a coastal State, questions related to the availability of remedies – and their adequacy – would arise. The remedies envisioned under the ILC Articles on the Responsibility of States are, inter alia, cessation and reparation. Remedies can be available for environmental damage, as illustrated by a case between Costa Rica and Nicaragua in front of the ICJ.[45] In a separate phase of this case addressing environmental damage in a disputed area between the two countries, the Court indeed awarded compensation to be paid to Costa Rica for the impairment or loss of environmental goods and services and for restoration costs.[46]

Cessation would be the first remedy – and the only one available if there is no injured State,[47] a situation quite likely in fisheries disputes. This might not actually solve the problem, especially if the violation has been ongoing for a long period of time and stocks are in need of support to re-establish themselves. Cessation could nonetheless include remedial measures if the violation of a positive obligation such as that 'to maintain or restore populations of harvested species at levels which can produce the maximum sustainable yield'[48] were to be found by a court or tribunal.

Reparations are due for injury caused, which 'includes any damage, whether material or moral, caused by the internationally wrongful act'.[49] They may, however, not be fully adequate, even if a State could show that it was victim of an injury. Restitution, which is the preferred form of reparation, requires knowing how the situation actually was before the wrongful act took place, in order to re-establish that situation – such information might not be available if a coastal State has not managed the stocks under its jurisdiction at all. Restitution is also conditional on not being 'materially impossible [nor...] involv[ing] a burden out of all

45 *Certain Activities Carried Out by Nicaragua in the Border Area (Costa Rica* v. *Nicaragua), Compensation, Judgment, I.C.J. Reports 2018.*

46 Ibid., para 157 (1).

47 Gaja (n 19) 138.

48 UNCLOS, Art. 61(3).

49 Articles on the Responsibility of States for Internationally Wrongful Acts, Art. 31.

proportion'.[50] Re-improving the status of stocks after unsustainable fishing does not appear an easy task and may be disproportionate to the expected benefit. A suitable alternative remedy might be compensation. In that respect, it may be possible – even easy – to quantify damage to target species, which have a market price attached to them, but it may prove more difficult for associated and dependent species, or even for the marine environment.

Finally, and in any case, one could wonder whether traditional remedies are appropriate to the actual issue of mismanagement of fisheries resources. A cause of – or at least an important factor in – such unsustainable practices is often the coastal State's inability to manage stocks, rather than its unwillingness to do so.[51] Hence, in the case of many developing States, facilitative measures will be more likely to lead to improvements than punitive measures.

19.4 LITIGATION AGAINST A STATE FISHING SHARED STOCKS

A third litigation possibility to improve compliance with existing obligations would be to address the duty that States involved in fishing transboundary, straddling or highly migratory fish stocks have to cooperate in conserving these resources.

Both coastal States – when dealing with fish stocks not exclusively located in their waters – and the flag States of vessels active on the high seas are under an obligation to cooperate in the conservation of marine living resources.[52] The obligation found in UNCLOS is further developed in the United Nations Fish Stocks Agreement (UNFSA), which provides that States shall cooperate with the relevant RFMO – or in the absence of one establish one – before they are allowed to fish straddling and highly migratory fish species in the high seas.[53] In practice, RFMOs adopt CMMs, which member States and cooperating parties are supposed to comply with – except if they have opted out, although this option only applies to parties.

This double obligation of cooperation and conservation stemming from UNCLOS is particularly crucial in areas beyond national jurisdiction, as, in its absence, the regime is one of free-for-all, leading to a potential tragedy of the commons.[54] The worrisome state of fish stocks, in particular in the high seas, speaks volumes as to the existence of problems in the regional management of these marine resources.

50 Ibid., Art. 35.

51 C. Mora et al., "Management Effectiveness of the World's Marine Fisheries" (2009) 7(6) *PLOS Biol* e1000131, <https://doi.org/10.1371/journal.pbio.1000131>.

52 UNCLOS, Arts. 118–119.

53 UNFSA, Art. 8.

54 Shared stocks in general appear to be more likely to be overexploited (S. F. McWhinnie, "The Tragedy of the Commons in International Fisheries: An Empirical Examination" (2009) 57 *J Environ Econ Manage* 321–333).

19.4.1 *Content of Relevant Obligation*

Litigation might be used to tackle individual States' breaches of their obligation to cooperate in the conservation of fish stocks. A clear target would be a flag State that allows or enables its vessels to fish in the area under the mandate of an RFMO without cooperating with this regional organization. The flag State would need to actively permit such fishing or at the very least show a pattern of not responding to the RFMO's communications regarding the vessel. The mere fact that a vessel flying a non-member State flag is fishing within the area of an RFMO would indeed not necessarily entail the international responsibility of the flag State, as the actions of a vessel are not, as such, attributable to the flag State.[55]

The main issue in such a litigation strategy would be whether this behaviour is actually illicit. The content of the obligation to cooperate in the conservation of shared marine living resources is indeed somewhat lacking in clarity. Whereas UNCLOS Articles 118–119 are recognized as customary international law and hence binding on all States, the same cannot be said with certainty about the relevant provisions of the UNFSA.[56] Indeed, on the one hand, Article 8 of that latter treaty may be seen as customary international law in its own right, or as implementing UNCLOS provisions and hence being applicable through it. On the other hand, it can also be considered as further development of international law, since it effectively intends to put an end to the high sea's freedom of fishing. If the potential respondent is not a party to the UNFSA, in the absence of an authoritative decision with regard to the status of that rule, a State may be wary of starting proceedings with no certainty of outcome.

Another situation that might breach a single State's obligation to cooperate is that of an RFMO member violating CMMs or repeatedly opting out of those that have been adopted. While starting proceedings against a party to an RFMO for acting in breach of relevant CMMs could successfully contribute to the rule of law, doing so for opting out of CMMs might be more complicated. On the one hand, by repeatedly objecting to measures, a State could arguably be said to be an internal free-rider, endangering the mandate and functioning of the RFMO. On the other hand, it may be difficult to prove that such behaviour amounts to illicit non-cooperation, especially when opting out is formally allowed and reasons for doing so may be varied.

A solution to these issues of legal uncertainty could be to encourage an RFMO to request an advisory opinion respectively on the legal status of non-cooperating,

[55] *Request for an Advisory Opinion Submitted by the Sub-Regional Fisheries Commission (SRFC), Advisory Opinion, 2 April 2015, ITLOS Reports 2015*, para. 129. see also Y. Takei, "Assessing Flag State Performance in Legal Terms: Clarifications of the Margin of Discretion" (2013) 28 *IJMCL* 97, 130.

[56] On this, see the author's discussion in a previous publication (S. Guggisberg, *The Use of CITES for Commercially-Exploited Fish Species* (Berlin, Heidelberg, New York: Springer 2016) 43–49).

non-contracting parties that are fishing in the areas under its mandate and on the relationship between cooperation and repeated objections. Provision of an advisory opinion is not *per se* a legal novelty, but until ITLOS declared that it was competent in relation to the Sub-Regional Fisheries Commission's request for an advisory opinion in 2013, the bodies allowed to make such a demand were limited.[57] It was originally unclear whether ITLOS was empowered to issue advisory opinions of a general nature (in opposition to those related to the deep seabed),[58] but ITLOS found an implied power to give such an advisory opinion. This opened the door to other occurrences where an international organization is entrusted with the mandate to request authoritative interpretations from ITLOS. In practice, before requesting an advisory opinion, an RFMO may have to amend its founding treaty, in order to prove that it has clear competence to do so.

19.4.2 *Bilateral Proceedings v. Complex Multilateral Reality*

An applicant State could also start proceedings against several RFMO members for their joint failure to cooperate in conservation of fish stocks, demonstrated by the adoption of unsustainable CMMs. Only cases where CMMs egregiously depart from scientific advice might be considered. Indeed, Article 119 of UNCLOS acknowledges that the maximum sustainable yield can be 'qualified by relevant environmental and economic factors, including the special requirements of developing States ... ', giving States much leeway in adopting CMMs.

Even in a case of States manifestly disregarding conservation, litigation might be unsuccessful, in light of the procedural rules of courts and tribunals as these presently stand. There are no avenues under traditional international law to bring to court a group of States for their joint behaviour. Such limitation would be at odds with the multilateral nature of the issue, that is, of several States, through their negotiating processes, having failed to deliver on their obligations. Indeed, the applicant would need to start proceedings against several States, *separately* – while proving that, *jointly*, these States failed to cooperate. If past cases are to go by, the unsuccessful attempt by the Marshall Islands to litigate against nuclear-weapon States for their failure to negotiate denuclearisation[59] shows that international courts and tribunals are not well equipped for such cases. While the ICJ reached a decision on its lack of competence on the absence of a dispute at the critical date,[60] many

[57] Statute of the ICJ, Art. 65; Charter of the UN, Art. 96; ICJ, "Organs and Agencies Authorized to Request Advisory Opinions", <www.icj-cij.org/en/organs-agencies-authorized> [last accessed 27 July 2021].

[58] UNCLOS, Art. 191; Statute of ITLOS, Art. 40(2).

[59] See the cases started by the Marshall Islands at the ICJ against nine nuclear-weapon States on the Obligations concerning Negotiations relating to Cessation of the Nuclear Arms Race and to Nuclear Disarmament.

[60] *Obligations Concerning Negotiations Relating to Cessation of the Nuclear Arms Race and to Nuclear Disarmament (Marshall Islands* v. *India) / (Marshall Islands* v. *Pakistan) / (Marshall*

other grounds brought up in the objections of the Respondents, such as the absence of indispensable third parties, could also, arguably, have led to the same decision.[61] Similar arguments are bound to be raised if several members of an RFMO are targeted by a case for their joint management decisions.

This issue is related to the questioned adequacy of a judicial dispute settlement mechanism for public interest matters.[62] Dispute settlement in front of international courts is indeed typically aiming at solving bilateral disputes, while questions related to fisheries – the same as most global environmental issues – might rather need to be considered multilaterally.[63]

19.5 CONCLUSION

In light of the long-standing issue of non-compliance in the fisheries field and the resulting unsustainable management of stocks, litigation is an option that should be considered by States. As examined, recent cases have clarified that many avenues are open, even if some issues, such as jurisdictional restrictions or adequacy of remedies, may remain. Having recourse to litigation in some of the situations examined in this chapter would be beneficial for the rule of law, in that it could bring an end to specific violations, hence tackling the most egregious cases of non-compliance. By doing so, it would provide a strong message against impunity, hopefully serving as a deterrent against similar behaviour by others. In particular, cases with a non-negligible impact and which are likely to succeed are those against notorious flags of non-compliance. Moreover, bringing a case to a court or a tribunal may also enable clarification of certain obligations, especially by way of advisory opinions. In that respect, one should consider a request for an advisory opinion to clarify the content of the obligation to cooperate in the conservation of shared stocks.

However, litigation has serious limitations. First and foremost, it is costly to start proceedings against another State, in both monetary and political terms. Hence, it will remain a rarity, especially if States are not reacting to direct injury but acting on behalf of the international community. Moreover, beyond the indirect deterrent effect on third States, a case will only ever solve a specific bilateral dispute, thus coming nowhere close to a comprehensive review of States' compliance with their obligations in the fisheries field. Furthermore, litigation cannot replace well-functioning science-based management: judges are not scientists, and a case is

Islands v. *United Kingdom), Preliminary Objections, Judgment, I.C.J. Reports 2016*, respectively paras. 56(1) / 56(1) / 59(1).

61 See Judge Xue's Declaration, for example, in the case against the United Kingdom, paras. 9–11.

62 M. Bothe, "Compliance" *MPEPIL* para. 45; P. Okowa, "Environmental Dispute Settlement: Some Reflections on Recent Developments" in M. D. Evans (ed.), *Remedies in International Law: The Institutional Dilemma* (Oxford: Hart Publishing 1998) 166–167.

63 R. R. Churchill and G. Ulfstein, "Autonomous Institutional Arrangements in Multilateral Environmental Agreements: A Little-Noticed Phenomenon in International Law" (2000) 94 *AJIL* 623, 644–645.

brought *ex post*, instead of focusing on prevention of damage. Finally, litigation is only able to successfully address non-compliance due to lack of willingness. It is not geared towards solving the large(r) problem of lack of capacity.

Hence, while litigation may certainly have a role to play in the field of fisheries, and even if several cases were started in front of international courts and tribunals, other mechanisms should also be developed and/or strengthened. Compliance procedures under global or regional frameworks should serve for comprehensive, in-depth and regular review of States' compliance with their obligations. As established procedures, they furthermore have the advantage of not relying on a particular State's willingness to invest resources in litigation against another State. In comparison to the ad hoc nature of litigation, this characteristic of compliance procedures has the potential to add much-needed objectivity, impartiality and comprehensiveness to the pursuit of accountability.

PART V

Strengthening the Rule of Law in Regional Seas and Oceans

20

Regional Cooperation for the Conservation of Marine Biodiversity in the Eastern Tropical Pacific

A Rule of Law Perspective

Sarah Ryan Enright

20.1 OCEAN GOVERNANCE AND THE RULE OF LAW

Governance depends on cooperation to succeed, building on partnerships and interactions across multiple domains and actors.[1] It is not a clear-cut notion, and is often characterized by flexibility and dynamism in contrast to the static structures usually associated with law.[2] Ocean governance is now a field in its own right reflecting the 'need and desire to pursue a holistic, integrated, and/or cross sectoral approach to the management of the oceans'.[3] It has been defined as 'the way in which ocean affairs are governed, not only by governments, but also by local communities, industries and other "stakeholders". It includes national and international law, public and private law as well as custom, tradition and culture and the institutions and processes created by them'.[4] It is clear that law is an essential element of ocean governance given that the system created by the United Nations Law of the Sea Convention (UNCLOS)[5] provides the overarching framework for management of the global ocean. Yet the precise relationship between the law of the

The author's PhD research is funded by the Irish Marine Institute as part of the Navigate project on Ocean Law and Marine Governance (Grant-Aid Agreement No. PBA/IPG/17/01). The author would like to thank Dr Anne Marie O'Hagan and Professor Owen McIntyre for comments on an earlier draft.

1 C. Blanchard, 'Fragmentation in High Seas Fisheries: Preliminary Reflections on a Global Oceans Governance Approach' (2017) 84 *Marine Policy* 327, 329.

2 Ibid.

3 E. J. Molenaar, 'Chapter 40 – Ocean Governance beyond Boundaries: Origins, Trends, and Current Challenges' in Andrés M. Cisneros-Montemayor, William W. L. Cheung and Yoshitaka Ota (eds.), *Predicting Future Oceans* (Amsterdam: Elsevier 2019), 419.

4 As defined by Elisabeth Mann Borgese in *Ocean Governance: Legal, Institutional and Implementation Considerations*, Ocean Policy Research Institute Report No. 5 (The Nippon Foundation, 2002), cited in D. Werle and others, *The Future of Ocean Governance and Capacity Development* (Leiden: Brill Nijhoff 2019), 6.

5 United Nations Convention on the Law of the Sea 1833 UNTS 397 (1982).

sea and ocean governance remains contested, with the law of the sea naturally more concerned with legally binding norms.[6]

The field of ocean governance itself has become increasingly complex with a diverse array of laws, actors and institutions involved. UNCLOS divided the ocean into arbitrary zones (e.g., areas beyond national jurisdiction (ABNJ) *versus* areas under national jurisdiction), which are regulated under different regimes and subject to different management standards. These are essentially geo-political divisions and do not correspond with ecological boundaries, which tend to group similar species and habitats together, often as controlled by climatic and oceanographic parameters.[7] This mismatch between the law of the sea and the ecological reality of the ocean has generated serious challenges from a rule of law perspective. It has been described as a 'paradox with which lawyers have to grapple'[8] and a 'serious deficiency' in ocean governance.[9] Consequences include significant regulatory gaps[10] and negative outcomes for ocean health.[11] Therefore, the 'rule of law'[12] as it currently applies to the oceans is clearly far from satisfactory.

Some scholars have argued that elements of good governance, such as cross sectoral cooperation and coordination and science-based decision-making, could be engaged to enhance the existing legal framework.[13] These 'less politicized' forms of governance are seen as offering a more holistic way to address the transboundary

6 For more in-depth discussion on this subject, see Y. Takei, 'A Sketch of the Concept of Ocean Governance and Its Relationship with the Law of the Sea', in C. Ryngaert, E. J. Molenaar and S. Nouwen (eds.), *What's Wrong with International Law?* (Leiden: Brill Nijhoff 2015), 58–60.

7 M. V. Lomolino and others, *Biogeography* (fourth ed., Sunderland, MA: Sinauer Associates Inc. 2010).

8 P. W. Birnie, A. E. Boyle and C. Redgwell, *International Law and the Environment* (third ed., Oxford: Oxford University Press 2009), 704.

9 Y. Tanaka, *The International Law of the Sea* (second ed., Cambridge: Cambridge University Press 2015), 4.

10 See e.g., K. M. Gjerde, N. A. Clark and H. R. Harden-Davies, 'Building a Platform for the Future: The Relationship of the Expected New Agreement for Marine Biodiversity in Areas beyond National Jurisdiction and the UN Convention on the Law of the Sea' (2019) 33 *Ocean Yearbook Online* 1, 4–5.

11 See e.g., The First Global Integrated Marine Assessment (United Nations World Ocean Assessment I), UN Doc. A/70/112, 22 July 2015 Available at www.un.org/regularprocess/content/first-world-ocean-assessment and the annual Ocean Health Index global assessments at http://ohi-science.org/ohi-global/

12 The 'rule of law' is a very broad concept. The Secretary General of the United Nations describes it as a 'principle of governance' in which 'all persons, institutions and entities, public and private, including the State itself, are accountable to laws that are publicly promulgated, equally enforced and independently adjudicated, and which are consistent with international human rights norms and standards. It requires, as well, measures to ensure adherence to the principles of supremacy of law, equality before the law, accountability to the law, fairness in the application of the law, separation of powers, participation in decision-making, legal certainty, avoidance of arbitrariness and procedural and legal transparency'. United Nations. Guidance Note of the Secretary General. *UN Approach to Rule of Law Assistance*. April 2008. On the rule of law more generally, see T. Bingham, *The Rule of Law* (London: Penguin UK 2011).

13 Takei (n 6) 61.

challenges particular to the marine environment.[14] It has also been asserted that regional cooperation and coordinated responses are key for managing the transboundary reality of many activities and processes in the marine environment.[15] This chapter will argue that regional cooperation has the potential to contribute to a more effective rule of law for the oceans by filling some of the gaps left by the 'chronic fragmentation'[16] of international ocean governance, especially if embedded within an overarching regional and global strategy.

First, the emergence of regional ocean governance as a subfield within the broader sphere of ocean governance will be introduced, along with its main implementing mechanisms, followed by a case study on State-led regional cooperation efforts in the Eastern Tropical Pacific to create the first transboundary network of marine protected areas (MPAs) in Latin America. Finally, specific rule of law challenges faced by this initiative will be discussed, such as the lack of a legally binding cooperation agreement, limited sectoral participation, the vast scale and the lack of a cohesive regional ocean governance framework in the region.

20.2 A REGIONAL APPROACH TO OCEAN GOVERNANCE

The international community has recognized the need for a move towards a more integrated approach to ocean management through its endorsement of the ecosystem approach.[17] While implementation of the ecosystem approach in practice remains an ongoing challenge,[18] regional ocean governance (ROG) efforts have shown promise by enabling cooperation and coordination across territorial and sectoral boundaries, which could help to link disconnected areas of regulation arising from fragmentation.[19]

14 Blanchard (n 1) 329.

15 See e.g., J. Palacios-Abrantes and others, 'The Transboundary Nature of the World's Exploited Marine Species' (2020) 10 *Nature Scientific Reports* 1.

16 M. Ntona and E. Morgera, 'Connecting SDG 14 with the Other Sustainable Development Goals through Marine Spatial Planning' (2018) 93 *Marine Policy* 214, 215.

17 The Convention on Biological Diversity (CBD) in COP 5 Decision V/6 (2000) defines the Ecosystem Approach (EA) as 'a strategy for the integrated management of land, water and living resources that promotes conservation and sustainable use in an equitable way'. For an overview of the EA in a marine context, see further S. R. Enright and B. Boteler 'The Ecosystem Approach in Marine Environmental Law and Governance' in T. O'Higgins, M. Lago and T. H. DeWitt (eds.), *Ecosystem-Based Management and Ecosystem Services: Theory, Tools, and Practice* (Cham: Springer 2020).

18 See e.g., D. Langlet and R. Rayfuse 'Challenges in Implementing the Ecosystem Approach: Lessons Learned' in D. Langlet and R. Rayfuse (eds.), *The Ecosystem Approach in Ocean Planning and Governance. Perspectives from Europe and beyond* (Leiden: Brill Nijhoff 2018).

19 G. Wright and others, 'Partnering for a Sustainable Ocean: The Role of Regional Ocean Governance in Implementing SDG14' (2017) Partnership for Regional Ocean Governance (PROG): IDDRI, IASS, TMG & UN Environment, 11.

The duty to cooperate regionally flows from the well-established general duty to cooperate in international law.[20] In the 1970s the notion that seas with multiple coastal States could be governed or managed regionally first appeared,[21] and by 1982, a legal obligation to cooperate on a regional basis for the protection and preservation of the marine environment was explicitly included in the text of UNCLOS.[22] The 1992 Convention on Biological Diversity (CBD) also promotes regional cooperation for the conservation and sustainable use of biological diversity.[23] The international community has continued to formally recognize the importance of regional levels of governance. For example, the 2030 Agenda for Sustainable Development underlines the importance of regional cooperation and coordination in order to achieve the Sustainable Development Goals (SDGs).[24] Enhanced ROG and a greater role for regional agreements has been proposed as a specific means of achieving the targets associated with SDG 14, which aims to 'conserve and sustainably use the oceans, seas and marine resources'.[25] It has been recommended that regional seas should have a key implementing role in the Post-2020 Global Biodiversity Framework, given that they are in a 'unique position to support States to achieve ocean-related elements',[26] and it is also very likely that ROG will have increased prominence under a new international treaty for biodiversity beyond national jurisdiction (BBNJ), which is currently under negotiation.[27]

From a global governance perspective, the main mechanisms for ROG at present include Regional Seas Programmes (RSP), Regional Fishery Bodies (RFB) and

[20] See e.g., *MOX Plant*, ITLOS case No. 10 (2001). See also Principle 4 of the 'Declaration on Principles of International Law Concerning Friendly Relations and Cooperation among States in accordance with the Charter of the United Nations', General Assembly Res. 2625 (XXV), 26 October 1970.

[21] L. M. Alexander, 'Regionalism and the Law of the Sea: The Case of Semi-Enclosed Seas' (1974) 2 *Ocean Development & International Law* 151, cited in N. Oral, 'Forty Years of the UNEP Regional Seas Programme: From Past to Future', *Research Handbook on International Marine Environmental Law* (Cheltenham: Edward Elgar Publishing 2015), 341.

[22] Art. 197 UNCLOS. Art. 123 UNCLOS specifically requires States bordering enclosed and semi-enclosed seas to cooperate with each other 'directly or through an appropriate regional organization'.

[23] Convention on Biological Diversity 1760 UNTS 79 (1992). Preamble.

[24] United Nations, *Transforming Our World: The 2030 Agenda for Sustainable Development,* UNGA Resolution A/RES/70/1 United Nations, New York, 2015, para. 21.

[25] Agenda 2030, 14, 23–24. See further https://sdgs.un.org/goals/goal14.

[26] United Nations Environment Programme, *Regional Seas Biodiversity under the post-2020 Global Biodiversity Framework* (Nairobi, 2021), 4.

[27] Resolution 72/249 adopted by the United Nations General Assembly on 24 December 2017 on an International legally binding instrument under the United Nations Convention on the Law of the Sea on the conservation and sustainable use of marine biological diversity of areas beyond national jurisdiction. UN doc A/Res 74/249. New York: United Nations General Assembly. For further discussion see e.g., N. A. Clark 'Institutional Arrangements for the New BBNJ Agreement: Moving beyond Global, Regional, and Hybrid' (2020) 122 *Marine Policy* 104–143.

Large Marine Ecosystem (LME) mechanisms.[28] The RSP and RFBs are intergovernmental bodies made up of State parties, whereas LME mechanisms are usually projects that bring together coastal States of the LMEs, international agencies and regional bodies.[29] The United Nations Environment Program (UNEP) established the RSP in 1974 to serve as the mechanism for promoting cooperation among States sharing a common regional marine space.[30] For each RSP, an action plan serves as the basis for regional cooperation, and many also decide to adopt legally binding instruments and framework conventions.[31] The framework conventions typically provide general terms and conditions and an overall direction for States to follow. However, they are usually too vague to lead to decisive actions, and parties must therefore negotiate specific agreements, known as protocols.[32] The mandates of the different RSPs have evolved from an initial focus on pollution to encompass biodiversity conservation, particularly through the creation of MPAs.[33] Several RSPs have adopted a separate protocol for protection of marine biodiversity,[34] which require State parties, either individually or cooperatively, to establish protected areas for fragile and vulnerable ecosystems.[35]

RFBs are regional mechanisms, established under UNCLOS, through which States cooperate on the sustainable use and conservation of marine living resources.[36] Considerable differences exist in the geographical mandates of RFBs, and they may cover both high seas areas and coastal maritime zones.[37] As with the RSP, the geographic scopes of the RFBs have been driven by a mix of scientific and political considerations and opportunism, rather than by a goal to demarcate ocean regions.[38] Regional Fishery Management Organizations (RFMOs) are a subset of

[28] J. Rochette and others, 'Regional Oceans Governance Mechanisms: A Review' (2015) 60 *Marine Policy* 9.

[29] R. Billé and others, *Regional Oceans Governance: Making Regional Seas Programmes, Regional Fishery Bodies and Large Marine Ecosystem Mechanisms Work Better Together* (UNEP Regional Seas Reports and Studies No 197 2016), 42.

[30] Oral (n 21) 339.

[31] Billé and others (n 29) 3.

[32] Ibid., 25.

[33] Ibid.

[34] The Caribbean, Mediterranean and Eastern Africa regions, the Red Sea and the Gulf of Aden, the Black Sea, the South East Pacific and the ROPME sea area. Cited in Oral (n 21) 353.

[35] Ibid.

[36] Art. 118 UNCLOS. See also Art. 8(1) of the Agreement for the Implementation of the Provisions of the UN Convention on the Law of the Sea of 10 December 1982 relating to the Conservation and Management of Straddling Fish Stocks and Highly Migratory Fish Stocks, 4 August 1995 (in force 11 December 2001) 2167 UNTS 3.

[37] Billé and others (n 29) 35.

[38] R. M. Warner, 'Conserving Marine Biodiversity in Areas beyond National Jurisdiction: Coevolution and Interaction with the Law of the Sea' (2014) 1 *Frontiers in Marine Science* 6, 4.

RFB with a management mandate and the power to establish legally binding conservation and management measures, such as temporary closures.[39]

These outlined approaches are complemented by other regional initiatives, such as those taken by political and economic organizations,[40] leaders and heads of State, non-governmental organizations, coastal communities and individuals.[41] A recent global study of ROG arrangements found that the majority of regional arrangements are 'indigenous', meaning developed by the countries of the region as opposed to being promoted by an external agency.[42] Given that most previous consideration of ROG has focused on the RSP and RFBs,[43] this discovery has important implications for ocean governance. The following sections of this chapter will focus on a case study of such an 'indigenous' regional cooperation agreement and its associated rule of law challenges.

20.3 REGIONAL COOPERATION IN THE EASTERN TROPICAL PACIFIC OCEAN

The decline of marine biological diversity worldwide, due to anthropogenic causes, has led to calls for more legally protected areas. International targets, which previously aimed for protection of 10 per cent of global waters by 2020, are due to be increased to 30 per cent by 2030 under the Post-2020 Global Biodiversity Framework.[44] Networks of MPAs,[45] including cross-jurisdictional boundaries, are now seen as increasingly necessary due to ecological connectivity between marine ecosystems.[46] Cross-jurisdictional coordination and regional cooperation are

[39] Billé and others (n 29) 37. RFBs that do not have a mandate to adopt binding measures are known as advisory RFBs. Currently there are forty-one marine RFBs worldwide, comprising twenty-one RFMOs and twenty advisory RFBs. See further www.fao.org/in-action/vulnerable-marine-ecosystems/background/regional-fishery-bodies/en/

[40] E.g., the European Union, the African Union (AU), Association of Southeast Asian Nations (ASEAN) and the Caribbean Community (CARICOM). See further Wright and others, 'Partnering for a Sustainable Ocean: The Role of Regional Ocean Governance in Implementing SDG14' (n 19) 16–18.

[41] D. E. Johnson and others, 'Building the Regional Perspective: Platforms for Success' (2014) 24 (S2) *Aquatic Conservation: Marine and Freshwater Ecosystems* 75–93, 75.

[42] R. Mahon and L. Fanning, 'Regional Ocean Governance: Polycentric Arrangements and Their Role in Global Ocean Governance' (2019) 107 *Marine Policy* 103590, 4, 11.

[43] Ibid.

[44] Target 3 of First Draft of the Post-2020 Global Biodiversity Framework, CBD/WG2020/3/3, 5 July 2021. Available at www.cbd.int/conferences/post2020/wg2020-03/documents

[45] Networks of MPAs have been defined as 'a collection of individual MPAs operating cooperatively and synergistically, at various spatial scales, and with a range of protection levels, in order to fulfil ecological aims more effectively and comprehensively than individual sites could alone'. IUCN World Commission on Protected Areas (IUCN-WCPA) *Establishing Marine Protected Area Networks: Making It Happen* (Washington, DC: IUCN-WCPA, National Oceanic and Atmospheric Administration and the Nature Conservancy 2008), 3.

[46] See e.g., D. Laffoley and others, 'Evolving the Narrative for Protecting a Rapidly Changing Ocean, Post COVID-19' (2020) 31, 1512–1534 *Aquatic Conservation: Marine and Freshwater Ecosystems* 4.

considered essential for their management.[47] The United States National Oceanic and Atmospheric Administration (NOAA) defines ecological networks of MPAs as 'systems of core habitats connected by ecological corridors that are established, restored, and/or maintained to conserve biological diversity in systems that have been fragmented'.[48] Ecological corridors are therefore important tools in the creation of an effective network of MPAs. Regional organizations, such as the European Union, now require integration of ecological corridors into MPA networks.[49]

The Eastern Tropical Pacific Marine Corridor (CMAR)[50] is regarded as a leading example of regional cooperation for the creation of a network of MPAs.[51] It is located within the Eastern Tropical Pacific Ocean (ETPO), which has exceptional levels of biodiversity, unique oceanographic conditions and large numbers of endemic, native and migratory species.[52] The proposed marine corridor encompasses the national waters, coasts and islands of Ecuador, Colombia, Costa Rica and Panama and contains five world-renowned MPAs: Galapagos (Ecuador), Cocos (Costa Rica), Coiba (Panama), Malpelo and Gorgona (Colombia) (Figure 20.1).

All of the MPAs, except for Gorgona, are UNESCO World Heritage Sites,[53] two are Ramsar Sites (Galapagos and Cocos)[54] and the International Maritime Organization (IMO) has designated Galapagos and Malpelo as Particularly Sensitive Sea Areas (PSSAs).[55] In further recognition of its biological value, CMAR was recognized in 2016 as an Ecologically and Biologically Significant Area (EBSA) by parties to the CBD, who considered it 'important for the connectivity of species on their migratory routes and at other times of their life cycles (e.g., mating, birth, feeding)'.[56] Despite its immense ecological value, the region faces a number of governance challenges, including illegal, unreported and unregulated

[47] P. J. S. Jones and S. D. Long, 'Analysis and Discussion of 28 Recent Marine Protected Area Governance (MPAG) Case Studies: Challenges of Decentralisation in the Shadow of Hierarchy' (2021) 127 *Marine Policy* 104362, 12; J. A. Guerreiro da Silva and others, 'Transboundary MPAs: A Challenge for the Twenty-First Century' (2012) 23 *Management of Environmental Quality: An International Journal* 328, 329.

[48] NOAA Ecological Connectivity for Marine Protected Areas, available at https://marineprotectedareas.noaa.gov/

[49] European Commission EU Biodiversity Strategy for 2030: Bringing nature back into our lives COM (2020) 380 final, 4.

[50] CMAR is the Spanish acronym and refers to Corredor Marino del Pacifico Este Tropical.

[51] Johnson and others (n 41) 80.

[52] See e.g., P. C. Fiedler and M. F. Lavín, 'Oceanographic Conditions of the Eastern Tropical Pacific' in P. W. Glynn, D. P. Manzello and I. C. Enochs (eds.), *Coral Reefs of the Eastern Tropical Pacific* (Berlin, Heidelberg, New York: Springer 2017), 59–83.

[53] https://whc.unesco.org/en/list/

[54] www.ramsar.org/sites/default/files/documents/library/sitelist.pdf

[55] www.imo.org/en/MediaCentre/HotTopics/PSSA/Pages/default.aspx

[56] CBD-COP Decision XII 22.

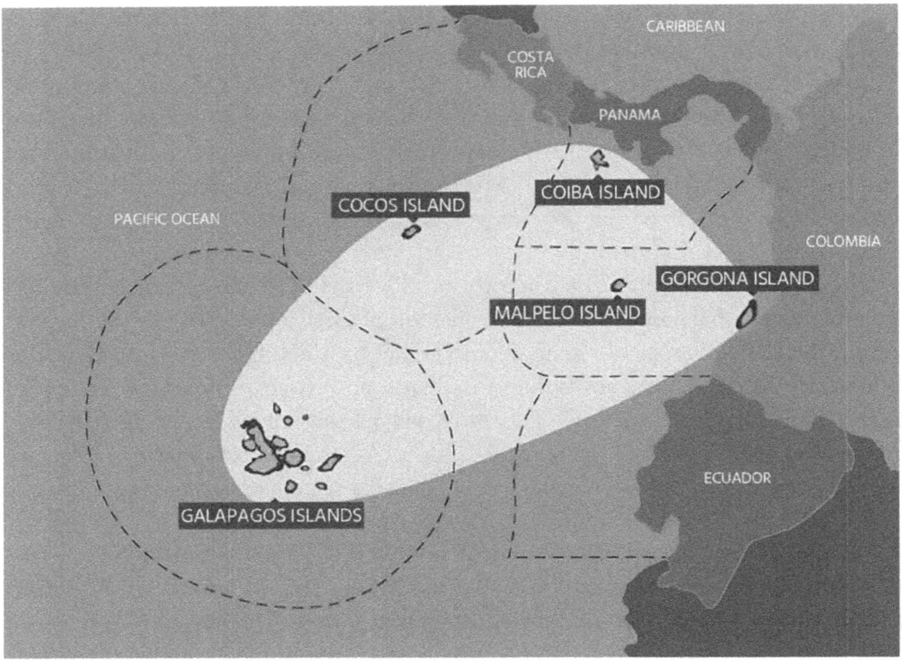

FIGURE 20.1. Proposed Eastern Tropical Pacific Marine Corridor (CMAR)
This map has been created for illustrative purposes only, and is based on the map available on the CMAR website at http://cmarpacifico.org/donde-trabajamos/pacifico-este-tropical. The official geographic delimitation of CMAR remains pending. Information provided by Ricardo Meneses-Orellana, CMAR Technical Secretariat.

(IUU) fishing, overfishing, pollution and coastal development.[57] Climate change[58] and weak governance[59] are overarching, aggravating factors.

In response to these pressures, CMAR was formally established in 2004 by the San Jose Declaration (SJD),[60] a non-binding regional cooperation

[57] See e.g., J. J. Alava and F. Paladines 'Illegal Fishing on the Galápagos High Seas' (2017) 357 *Science (Am. Assoc. Adv. Sci.)* 1362 and L. F. Ramirez, 'Marine Protected Areas in Colombia: Advances in Conservation and Barriers for Effective Governance' (2016) 125 *Ocean & Coastal Management*. 49–62.

[58] Intergovernmental Science-Policy Platform on Biodiversity and Ecosystem Services (IPBES) *Global Assessment Report on Biodiversity and Ecosystem Services* (2019). Summary for policy-makers, 4.

[59] R. Arauz and others, *Migramar. Science for the Conservation of Migratory Marine Species in the Eastern Pacific* (MigraMar 2017); WildAid, *An Analysis of the Law Enforcement Chain in the Eastern Tropical Pacific Seascape* (2010) Preface, 1. Available at www.issuelab.org/resources/26036/26036.pdf

[60] Declaración de San José sobre el corredor marino de Conservación del Pacifico este Tropical Entre las Islas Coco – Galápagos – Malpelo – Coiba – Gorgona, el 2 de abril del 2004. Available at http://cmarpacifico.org/web-cmar/quienes-somos/que-es-el-cmar/

agreement signed by Ecuador, Costa Rica, Panama and Colombia. The Action Plan for 2019–2024 defines CMAR as 'a regional initiative for conservation and sustainable use which seeks, via an ecosystem approach, the adequate management of the biodiversity, marine and coastal resources of the Eastern Tropical Pacific, through regional governmental strategies, jointly supported by civil society, nongovernmental organizations and international cooperation, with the MPAs of Cocos, Galapagos, Malpelo, Gorgona and Coiba considered core areas'.[61]

In order to achieve its objectives, the SJD provides for the establishment of a regional mechanism, made up of political and technical components. The political element consists of a Regional Ministerial Committee (RMC), which is made up of representatives of the Ministry of Environment of each State.[62] It issues guidelines and supports the process of implementation politically in accordance with the conservation priorities for CMAR, the policies of each participating State and the relevant international framework.[63] It is the main decision-making body for CMAR.[64] The RMC meets once a year and its Presidency has a rotating character between the four participating States, each term lasting three years.[65] The Foreign Ministries of each State also play an advisory role with regard to matters of international relations between the States.[66] The technical component of CMAR is made up of a Regional Technical Committee (RTC), which is responsible for defining the actions needed to implement CMAR.[67] It meets twice a year and acts as the advisory body to the RMC. It is made up of a delegate of each State's Ministry of Environment, who is often a director of one of the core MPAs.[68] In terms of decision-making, each State has one vote, yet all decisions are adopted by consensus.[69] The RTC is supported by a Secretariat in charge of carrying out CMAR management actions and coordinating cooperation between the four participating States and any involved international organizations and NGOs.[70]

61 Corredor Marino del Pacífico Este (CMAR) *Plan de acción 2019–2024* (San José, Costa Rica 2019), 8. Quoted text translated from Spanish to English by author.
62 San Jose Declaration (n 60) para 4.a.
63 Ibid.
64 CMAR Action Plan 2019–2024, 10.
65 Ibid.
66 Ibid.
67 San Jose Declaration (n 60) para. 4.b.
68 CMAR Action Plan 2019–2024, 10.
69 Corredor Marino del Pacífico Este (CMAR) Technical Document *Corredor marino de conservación y desarrollo sostenible del pacifico este tropical entre las islas Coco – Galápagos – Malpelo – Coiba – Gorgona. Antecedentes y consideraciones técnicas para su definición* (San José, Costa Rica 2004), 30.
70 CMAR Action Plan 2019–2024, 10.

20.4 RULE OF LAW CHALLENGES

MPA managers within CMAR territories have identified several limiting factors from a governance perspective, including overlapping or interfering jurisdiction between authorities, lack of coordination between authorities, lack of resources, lack of political will regarding conservation and institutional weakness in the government environmental sector.[71] While these are issues impeding effective ocean and coastal management more generally in CMAR member States, the following discussion will focus on four specific challenges faced by the marine corridor itself.

20.4.1 *Lack of a Legally Binding Agreement*

CMAR is a voluntary, political initiative between four States and therefore not legally binding.[72]

Voluntary, non-binding commitments have become a popular tool in international environmental governance, including in an ocean sustainability context.[73] They have been considered particularly useful in the context of transboundary governance, where competing sovereign interests can delay the negotiation of intergovernmental agreements.[74] As a political initiative, CMAR offers the possibility to harmonize national positions in the region with respect to marine environmental protection. On the other hand, the lack of any binding force has significant implications for compliance and enforcement. Voluntary commitments are often critiqued for lacking appropriate monitoring and evaluation strategies and not providing sufficient evaluation of their own effectiveness.[75] The lack of a legally binding agreement also implies no dedicated funding mechanism, which obviously impacts on critical issues such as institutional infrastructure, implementation and capacity for monitoring and enforcement. At a 2004 CMAR Regional Ministerial meeting, it was decided that the Secretariat would be funded by support from other interested governments, international organizations and NGOs,[76] creating circumstances that have not been conducive to financial sustainability. The Secretariat does not yet have a permanent physical infrastructure and currently rotates between each State every three years, concurrently with the Presidency. The State that exercises the Presidency covers the cost of operating the Secretariat with funds

[71] Wild Aid *An Analysis of the Law Enforcement Chain in the ETP Seascape*, 4 and K. Cremers, G. Wright and J. Rochette, 'Options for Strengthening Monitoring, Control and Surveillance of Human Activities in the Southeast Pacific Region' (2020) *STRONG High Seas Project* 11.

[72] CMAR Technical Document, 29.

[73] B. Neumann and S. Unger, 'From Voluntary Commitments to Ocean Sustainability' (2019) *Science* 363, 35–36.

[74] M. Voyer and others, 'The Role of Voluntary Commitments in Realizing the Promise of the Blue Economy' (2021) 71 *Global Environmental Change* 102372, 5.

[75] Ibid., 2.

[76] CMAR Technical Document, 30.

provided by that government's budget or via international cooperation.[77] In acknowledgement of the weaknesses inherent in the current non-binding model, the Action Plan for 2019–2024 recommends evaluating the possibilities for transforming CMAR into a legally binding agreement.[78]

20.4.2 *Limited Sectoral Participation*

Another governance challenge for CMAR is that it was not framed in a multi-sectoral manner from the outset. To create a level of sectoral engagement, Regional Working Groups and National Commissions are provided for within the structure of CMAR. The working groups cover five key thematic areas identified as priorities for conservation in the region (Tourism, MPAs, Science, Fisheries and Communications) and are made up of representatives from government institutions, NGOs, research and academia.[79] The purpose of the National Commissions[80] is to deal with any CMAR-related matters in a national context, and in conjunction with the working groups, incorporate the viewpoints of the different groups carrying out activities in the ETP.[81] Yet the private sector is notably absent from both. CMAR has acknowledged that interaction with the fishing sector has been limited due to the restricted capacity of CMAR to take political or institutional decisions affecting this sector.[82]

20.4.3 *Scale*

The scale of a project like CMAR involving transboundary marine management across four jurisdictions is a significant governance challenge. It is the first such undertaking in the region, and progress on formalizing the initiative has been slow due to the legal and institutional complexities involved in managing shared biological resources over such a large geographical area and the limited amount of resources available.[83] Given that the four CMAR States have already faced significant challenges in effectively managing MPAs within their national jurisdictions, it remains to be seen how this can effectively be done on a larger scale, especially in the absence of a wider supporting ROG strategy. CMAR has not yet been officially delimited from a geographical or jurisdictional perspective.[84] It is likely that the eventual delimitation of CMAR will only cover an area within the Exclusive Economic Zones (EEZs) of the respective member States,

[77] S. R. Enright, R. Meneses-Orellana and I. Keith, 'The Eastern Tropical Pacific Marine Corridor (CMAR): The Emergence of a Voluntary Regional Cooperation Mechanism for the Conservation and Sustainable Use of Marine Biodiversity within a Fragmented Regional Ocean Governance Landscape' (2021) 8 *Frontiers in Marine Science*. 674825, 5.

[78] CMAR Action Plan 2019–2024, 45.

[79] Ibid., 10.

[80] Only Colombia has established a National Commission thus far, in 2012. Ibid.

[81] Enright and others (n 77) 5.

[82] CMAR Action Plan 2019–2024, 11–12.

[83] CMAR Technical Document, 9.

[84] CMAR Action Plan 2019–2024, 11.

not the high seas pocket included in Figure 20.1.[85] This is due to the absence of a regional or internationally agreed legal framework with the power to establish protected areas in the high seas. However, the BBNJ negotiations, which aim to address such governance gaps, may result in a new international legal framework for the establishment of high seas MPAs.[86] The impact this may have on the ETP region remains unclear and will be discussed further in Section 20.4.6.

20.4.4 *Fragmented Regional Ocean Governance*

The wider ROG framework in the region is fragmented, with limited cross sectoral cooperation, differing membership compositions and varying mandates and geographic coverage. There is no RSP covering the Eastern Tropical Pacific region. While there is the Antigua Convention for the North East Pacific,[87] which was signed by Panama, Costa Rica, Colombia and several other Central American States in 2002,[88] it has not yet entered into force.[89] Out of the CMAR participating States, only Ecuador, Colombia and Panama are parties to the Lima Convention for the South East Pacific.[90] The Lima Convention applies to the territorial seas and the EEZs of its member States with a narrow mandate in the adjacent high seas, restricted to pollution.[91] However, its Executive Secretariat, a role held by the Permanent Commission for the South Pacific (CPPS),[92] has expressed a desire to expand its interests in the high seas.[93]

The CPPS could be considered weak from a rule of law perspective. It has an advisory mandate only and no management authority.[94] This means it does not have

85 However, in this context, it should be noted that Ecuador has declared its right to extend its continental shelf to 350nm measured from the baselines of the Galapagos Archipelago and made a joint submission with Costa Rica to the Commission on the Limits of the Continental Shelf in December 2020. Available at www.un.org/Depts/los/clcs_new/submissions_files/submission_criecu_86_2020.htm

86 The treaty negotiations are limited to four issues: marine genetic resources, including benefit-sharing, area-based management tools, including marine protected areas, environmental impact assessments and capacity building and marine technology transfer.

87 Convention for Cooperation in the Protection and Sustainable Development of the Marine and Coastal Environment of the Northeast Pacific. Adopted on 18 February 2002. (Not yet in force). Available at www.ecolex.org (TRE-001350)

88 Mexico, El Salvador, Honduras, Nicaragua and Guatemala.

89 The Convention needs at least four country ratifications to come into force and only two countries (Guatemala and Panama) have ratified it thus far. Available at www.unenvironment.org/explore-topics/oceans-seas/what-we-do/working-regional-seas/regional-seas-programmes/north-east-o

90 Convention for the Protection of the Marine Environment and Coastal Area of the South-East Pacific, 12 November 1981, in force 19 May 1986, 1648 UNTS 3 (Lima Convention).

91 Ibid., Art. 1.

92 CPPS is the Spanish acronym for Comisión Permanente del Pacifico Sur. Available at www.cpps-int.org/index.php/home/cpps-historia

93 http://cpps.dyndns.info/consulta/index.php/asambleas/ordinarias/86-x-asamb-ord-2012/358-comp-galapagos

94 UNEP-WCMC, 'Governance of areas beyond national jurisdiction for biodiversity conservation and sustainable use: Institutional arrangements and cross-sectoral cooperation in the

the power to establish legally binding conservation measures such as MPAs. However, it has a lot of support in the region as a cross-sectoral coordinating mechanism.[95] For example, it has signed bilateral cooperation agreements for the purposes of improving conservation with competent RFMOs in the region, the Inter-American Tropical Tuna Commission (IATTC),[96] of which all four CMAR States are members, and the South Pacific RFMO,[97] of which Ecuador is a member and Panama is a non-contracting Party. Given the importance of the fishing sector in the region, this type of cooperation is a positive step forward, especially given that the RFMOs have a management mandate and the power to establish legally binding conservation and management measures.

However, in general, cooperation between the key actors within this region is not well developed and enthusiasm for enhanced collaboration is varied. For example, the Memorandum of Understanding between CPPS and IATTC expired in 2020 and cooperation efforts have since stalled.[98] IATTC has previously expressed concerns that cross-sectoral area-based planning initiatives may compromise its ability to adopt a flexible approach to species protection.[99] Given that fishing is a fundamentally important socio-economic activity in the region, there has been reluctance by some authorities to commit to sharing data and information on those resources.[100] Therefore, it is not surprising that at the time of adoption of the SJD in 2004, the creation of a new regional mechanism was criticized as premature prior to adequately exploring the scope for working with existing bodies in the region, such as the CPPS, navies and the fishing sector.[101]

20.5 THE ROAD AHEAD

A key challenge from a rule of law perspective stems from the overlaps and gaps in the mandates of the applicable governance arrangements in the ETP. Previous studies examining ROG arrangements in the ETP region identified ten different governance arrangements but with no overarching integration mechanism in

Western Indian Ocean and the South East Pacific' (Cambridge: UN Environment Programme World Conservation Monitoring Centre 2017), 75.

95 Ibid., 79.

96 IATTC Memorándum de Entendimiento y Cooperación entre la Comisión Permanente del Pacifico Sur (CPPS) y la Comisión Interamericana del Atún Tropical (CIAT), 2015. Available at www.iattc.org/IATTCDocumentsENG.htm

97 SPRFMO Memorandum of Understanding Between the Permanent Commission of the South Pacific (CPPS) and the South Pacific Regional Fisheries Management Organization (SPRFMO), signed 13 March 2019. Available at www.sprfmo.int/cooperation/mous

98 Enright and others (n 77) 8.

99 UNEP-WCMC, 'Governance of Areas beyond National Jurisdiction' (n 94) 83.

100 Ibid., 81.

101 R. Bensted-Smith and H. Kirkman, *Comparison of Approaches to Management of Large Marine Areas*. (Cambridge: Fauna & Flora International 2010), 98.

place.[102] It is arguable that CMAR emerged 'indigenously' as a response to the lack of an appropriate governance mechanism to facilitate transboundary marine governance in the region. However, it suffers from several of the same weaknesses that afflict ROG more generally, including a lack of interaction with important sectors such as fisheries, lack of resources and political instability among some participating States.[103] While bottom-up, State-led regional approaches such as CMAR do appear to engage more active participation of coastal States,[104] it is submitted that underpinning the marine corridor with a legally binding framework and integrating it within the broader ROG context would significantly strengthen CMAR.

CMAR has had limited interaction with other regional bodies operating in the region. However, cooperation efforts have increased in recent years. CMAR and CPPS have similar action plans and are currently working towards a cooperation agreement,[105] and there may be scope for a cooperation agreement with the IATTC in the future.[106] There have been calls for increased cross-sectoral cooperation in this region more generally, with a recent report recommending adoption of an agreement between the CPPS, IATTC and SPRFMO for the purposes of cooperating on data collection, data analysis, joint monitoring and enforcement actions in the Southeast Pacific.[107]

Integration is of course challenging when the applicable ROG framework remains fragmented. It has been claimed that fixing problems of fragmentation in ocean governance requires attention to all levels of policy processes and all types of interaction, but especially coordinating ones.[108] For this reason, CPPS has been suggested as the best-placed institution to play an integrating role in the region given its long history of facilitating cooperation.[109] However, the fact that it does not cover the entirety of the ETP could be a sticking point.[110] A clear benefit that CPPS offers

102 Mahon and Fanning (n 42) 5.

103 For a general critique on ROG, see Rochette and others (n 28).

104 For some concrete examples in the context of CMAR, see Enright and others (n 77) 11.

105 Ibid., 9.

106 Ibid. To date, CMAR has participated as an observer in IATTC committee meetings and meetings of the Parties.

107 Cremers and others (n 71) 40.

108 L. Fanning and R. Mahon, 'Governance of the Global Ocean Commons: Hopelessly Fragmented or Fixable?' (2020) 48 *Coastal Management* 1–7, 530 citing M. Zurn and B. Faude, 'On Fragmentation, Differentiation, and Coordination' (2013) 13(3) *Global Environmental Politics* 119–130.

109 UNEP-WCMC, 'Governance of Areas beyond National Jurisdiction for Biodiversity Conservation and Sustainable Use' (n 94) 79–80.

110 R. Mahon and L. Fanning, 'Regional Ocean Governance: Integrating and Coordinating Mechanisms for Polycentric Systems' (2019) 107 *Marine Policy* 103589, Supplementary material, 4. Bensted-Smith and Kirkman (n 101) 131, observed that the CPPS mechanisms of decision-making and implementation can be quite cumbersome and it does not get involved in programmes involving only some of its members.

is the institutional support provided by the RSP (which has an explicit mandate for marine biodiversity conservation) such as common regional frameworks for monitoring, assessing and reporting on the state of the marine environment, which can provide a useful baseline for tracking progress against globally agreed goals and targets, such as MPA coverage.[111] This, in turn, should help to encourage the development of a coherent regional approach to design and implementation of MPA networks. The RSP also provides a useful platform for regions to engage with global ocean governance processes via its association with a UN body; in this way it plays an essential linking role between global and national levels of governance.[112]

While the regional scale has been acknowledged as the most appropriate for the management of biodiversity elements such as networks of MPAs and highly mobile species,[113] the new BBNJ instrument has the potential to help address some of the governance gaps in the ETP by introducing a legal mechanism at the global level for MPAs, which could potentially provide a legal basis for the designation of MPAs in ABNJ and a set of overarching governance principles to guide oversight and coordination of a global network of MPAs. While the final text of the treaty, and therefore the precise role of ROG organizations, remains under negotiation,[114] it is understood that existing regional and sectoral ocean governance bodies, as well as cross sectoral cooperation and coordination, will have a critical role to play in its effective implementation.[115] It has even been suggested that the new agreement should specifically recognize regional cooperative agreements, as part of an ecosystem approach.[116] This makes sense given that 'indigenous', State-led regional arrangements such as CMAR have the potential to mainstream ocean sustainability horizontally at the national level and link upwards into the broader ocean governance field by applying globally and regionally agreed standards.[117] Given the likelihood of increased visibility

[111] Johnson and others (n 41) 76–77.

[112] J. Rochette and others, 'The Regional Approach to the Conservation and Sustainable Use of Marine Biodiversity in Areas beyond National Jurisdiction' (2014) 49 *Marine Policy* 109–117, 109.

[113] United Nations Environment Programme, Regional Seas Biodiversity under the post-2020 Global Biodiversity Framework, 6.

[114] The current draft text can be found at www.un.org/bbnj/ .For analysis see K. Cremers and others, 'A preliminary analysis of the draft high seas biodiversity treaty' (2020) IDDRI, *Study* N°01/20.

[115] K. M. Gjerde and S. S. Yadav, 'Polycentricity and Regional Ocean Governance: Implications for the Emerging UN Agreement on Marine Biodiversity Beyond National Jurisdiction' (2021) 8 *Frontiers in Marine Science*. 704748.

[116] K. M. Gjerde and G. Wright, 'Towards Ecosystem-Based Management of the Global Ocean: Strengthening Regional Cooperation through a New Agreement for the Conservation and Sustainable Use of Marine Biodiversity in Areas beyond National Jurisdiction' (2019) *STRONG High Seas Project*, 18.

[117] Mahon and Fanning (n 110), 1.

and roles for the regional level of ocean governance under BBNJ and the Post-2020 Global Biodiversity Framework, the time is ripe for a strengthening of existing ROG arrangements in the ETP, including CMAR itself, in order to enable the diverse range of applicable instruments to function as an effective, cohesive whole, in line with a 'multi-level', polycentric approach to governance.[118]

[118] Gjerde and Yadav (n 115) 2; Fanning and Mahon (n 108).

21

Oil Pollution Control Regulations in the Baltic Sea

The Effect of Institutional Interplay on Implementation of the Ecosystem Approach

Kirsi White

21.1 INTRODUCTION

The importance of the ocean for safeguarding a habitable Earth system is key. This means that careful management of our Earth's most valuable natural resource is central. This is a fact that has recently gained more recognition as global warming has become apparent with unprecedented extreme weather and climate events caused by climate change.[1] The importance of sustainably managing marine ecosystems is well recognised, and implemented in different policy instruments such as the United Nations Sustainable Development Goals[2] (the United Nations 2030 Agenda for Sustainable Development), the United Nations Convention on Biological Diversity 1992[3] and the European Green Deal and the Biodiversity Strategy, aiming to halt the loss of marine biodiversity and to move towards a zero-pollution society.[4] However, it has remained a challenge to halt the continuing degradation of marine ecosystems and to manage this global resource sustainably. Regardless of the awareness that regional regulation of the marine environment has been considered as key in addressing these challenges, and despite the long-standing efforts of institutions such as the Baltic Marine Environment Protection Commission (HELCOM), the ability to halt degradation of the marine environment at regional sea level has not been achieved.[5] Therefore questions arise. What are the challenges facing the rule

1 The Intergovernmental Panel on Climate Change.

2 United Nations Sustainable Development Goals, SDG 14 'Life Below Water'.

3 United Nations Convention on Biological Diversity 1992.

4 Communication from the Commission to the European Parliament, The Council, the European Economic and Social Committee and the Committee of the Regions on a new approach for a sustainable blue economy in the EU Transforming the EU's Blue Economy for a Sustainable Future COM/2021/240.

5 Marine messages II; Navigating the course towards clean, healthy and productive seas through implementation of an ecosystem-based approach (2019) European Environment Agency Report 17.

of law in ecosystem-based management of marine ecosystems? Are the current legislative measures in force such that they will strengthen the rule of law central to achieving sustainability and environmental goals to safeguard the marine environment?[6] The aim of this chapter is to consider these questions in the context of the Baltic Sea, one of the world's most regulated seas, with specific emphasis on regulation of ship source oil pollution. The first part of the chapter will briefly discuss the Baltic Sea marine environment and the concerns introduced by shipping in general. Then, consideration will be given to the current legislative framework to regulate oil pollution and the concept of the ecosystem approach in the fragmented and multi-layered legislative framework specifically at regional sea level.

The Baltic Sea is a small enclosed sea surrounded by nine nation States. Eight of these are Member States of the European Union – the Russian Federation being the exception. Anthropogenic pressures on the ecological status of the Baltic Sea are all prioritised in legislative frameworks at national, regional and European contexts as major environmental problems.[7] There is a general trend in increasing global seaborne trade volumes, the Baltic Sea being no exception to this trend. Increasing traffic volumes will undoubtedly have an effect on the marine environment.[8] Of the total annual tonnage of maritime transport globally, carriage of crude oil and oil products accounts for around 3,000 million tonnes.[9] It is estimated that the number of vessels in the Baltic Sea is to double in the next twenty years, and that of oil-carrying vessels in particular, due to a predicted increase in demand for maritime oil transport. This increase will also be influenced by the European Commission introducing intermodal maritime-based logistics chains as a more sustainable and commercially efficient alternative to road-only transport ('Motorways of the Sea').[10] The increase in maritime traffic volume as well as the increase in vessel sizes, added to sectoral competition for space in the already narrow and shallow Baltic Sea, will continue to challenge regulation of shipping activities and their effect on the vulnerable marine ecosystem.

Oil released from shipping into the Baltic Sea marine ecosystem occurs through intentional or negligent actions: emptying of tanks, bilge water dumping or accidents.[11] The International Maritime Organization (IMO) construction regulations on oil pollution have introduced vessel design features, as well as regulation for on-

6 IUCN World Declaration on the Environmental Rule of Law.

7 M. Gilek, M. Karlsson et al., *Environmental Governance of the Baltic Sea* (Berlin, Heidelberg, New York: Springer, 2016).

8 United Nations Conference on Trade and Development, Review of Maritime Transport 2018.

9 United Nations Conference on Trade and Development, Review of Maritime Transport 2020.

10 Corrigendum to Decision No 884/2004/EC of the European Parliament and of the Council of 29 April 2004 amending Decision No 1692/96/EC on Community guidelines for the development of the trans-European transport network (OJ L 167, 30 April 2004. Corrected version in OJ L 201, 7 June 2004).

11 HELCOM core indicator report (HELCOM 2018).

board requirements including adequate competency of seafarers,[12] and the 'Shipboard Oil Pollution Emergency Plan'.[13] Measures such as the phasing-out of single-hull construction of vessels[14] and 'Goal Based Standards' for ship construction introduced by the International Convention for the Safety of Life at Sea (SOLAS), to regulate oil tankers and bulk carriers, encouraging innovation in ship design and promoting safety,[15] have been considered by some as highly successful in regulating accidental oil pollution to date.[16] As one of the most recent measures at regional sea level, accidental oil pollution from shipping is also managed through the introduction of 'Traffic Separation Schemes' and utilisation of 'Ship Reporting Systems'.[17] These measures take into consideration the specific typographic features of the Baltic Sea, which has also been established as among the 'Particularly Sensitive Sea Areas' (PSSAs) by the IMO to regulate ship-source pollution. PSSAs are areas requiring special protection by action through the IMO because of their significance for recognised ecological, socio-economic or scientific attributes, where such attributes may be vulnerable to damage by international shipping activities.[18] The Baltic Marine Environmental Protection Commission (HELCOM) has compiled data on fifty-two different anthropogenic pressures affecting the Baltic Sea.[19] Since monitoring started, there have been 4,420 illegal oil discharges and 216 other discharges.[20] The HELCOM Monitoring and Assessment Strategy outlines the core indicators that form the basis for marine environmental assessment in the Baltic Sea. In relation to oil pollution, the estimated oil introduced to the Baltic Sea is considered to be an indicator threshold value of a defined reference period. Oil contamination of the marine environment has been identified as one of the large-scale environmental problems in the Baltic Sea.[21] As the Baltic Sea marine environment is a complex adaptive system, it should be regulated as a whole, rather than having different regulatory regimes for the different components.[22] This is also

[12] International Convention on Standards of Training, Certification and Watchkeeping for Seafarers 1978.

[13] MARPOL Annex I, Regulation 37.

[14] MARPOL Annex I, Regulations 19 and 20.

[15] The International Association of Classification Societies, *Annual Review. Celebrating 50 Years*. (2018).

[16] B. Hassler, 'Accidental versus Operational Oil Pollution in the Baltic Sea: Risk Governance and Management Strategies' (2011) *AMBIO* 40, 170–178.

[17] HELCOM. The Clean Shipping Guide 2016.

[18] Resolution A.982(24), Revised Guidelines for the Identification and Designation of the Particularly Sensitive Areas. 2005.

[19] HELCOM. Towards a tool for quantifying anthropogenic pressures and potential impacts on the Baltic Sea marine environment: A background document on the method, data and testing of the Baltic Sea Pressure and Impact Indices, Balt. Sea Environ. Proc. No. 125.

[20] HELCOM Map and Data service, http://maps.helcom.fi/website/mapservice/index.html.

[21] O. Udovyk and M. Gileck, 'Coping with uncertainties in science-based advice informing environmental management of the Baltic Sea' (2013) *Environmental Science & Policy* 29, 12–23.

[22] F. M. Platjouw, *Environmental Law and the Ecosystem Approach: Maintaining Ecological Integrity through Consistency in Law* (Oxfordshire: Routledge, 2018).

recognised by the regional legislative measures currently in force, setting ecological targets as an objective, aiming to move away from sectoral management of the different marine ecosystem components. However, attempts to manage a large sectoral variety successfully through joint objectives has proven to be a challenge, as in order to achieve success, there must be an understanding of both ecosystem dynamics and socio-ecological interactions.[23] This understanding must be taken into consideration in environmental decision-making, and law plays a central role in interacting with socio-ecological resilience.[24]

21.2 ECOSYSTEM APPROACH IN THE CONTEXT OF BALTIC SEA MARINE PROTECTION

Central to the legislative instruments in force in the Baltic Sea regulating the use of aquatic systems, as with many global instruments on ocean management, is the concept of the ecosystem approach. As a feature of marine environmental protection, the ecosystem approach can be considered a fairly new concept. The first explicit utilisation was in 1980 in the Convention on the Conservation of Antarctic Marine Living Resources, recognising the importance of safeguarding the environment and protecting the ecosystem integrity of the seas surrounding Antarctica.[25] Ecosystem Based Management (EBM) is based on agreed indicators and reference points to monitor the status of the marine environment. As stated by the United Nations Open-ended Informal Consultative Process on Oceans and the Law of the Sea in 2006, ecosystem-based approaches to management require integrated information and knowledge within and among ocean sectors, which generally do not sufficiently exist. The current science knowledge base hinders more informed decision-making and implementation of EBM.[26] In relation to management of the marine environment in the Baltic Sea, it is apparent that it is not just ecological and social complexity hindering management but also lack of scientific interdisciplinary interaction to assess the risks. The multitude of institutions and fragmented policy instruments with a mismatch between the ecological processes of the marine ecosystem and the legislative framework hinders successful management of marine

[23] H. Österblom, A. Garmark et al., 'Making the Ecosystem Approach Operational: Can Regime Shifts in Ecological- and Governance Systems Facilitate the Transition?' (2010) *Marine Policy* 34, 1290–1299.

[24] A. Garmestani, C. R. Allen and M. Benson, 'Can Law Foster Social-Ecological Resilience?' (2013) *Ecology and Society* 18(2), 37.

[25] V. De Lucia, 'Competing Narratives and Complex Genealogies: The Ecosystem Approach in International Environmental Law' (2015) *Journal of Environmental Law* 27, 91–117.

[26] G. Piet, F. Culhane et al., 'An Integrated Risk-Based Assessment of the North Sea to Guide Ecosystem-Based Management' (2019) *Science of the Total Environment* 654, 694–704.

ecosystems.[27] The ecosystem approach is also a concept that is somewhat new in law, with some uncertainty as to how such a concept may be compatible with, and incorporated into, law.[28] EBM has evolved through non-binding soft law principles, with the result that implementation and application lack legal clarity. This can be seen as weakening the rule of law.

The central features of the ecosystem approach discussed in this section, which take into consideration scale dependency, scientific knowledge, participation and adaptive management, will be considered in Section 21.3 in relation to the legislative instruments currently in force in the Baltic Sea. This consideration is used to determine explicit or implicit evidence of the existence of EBM.

21.3 ECOSYSTEM APPROACH IN THE BALTIC SEA

International environmental protection has been characterised as 'regime dense',[29] and marine environmental governance is no exception – it consists of complex multilevel and multi-sectoral integration.[30] Regulation of the marine ecosystem in the Baltic Sea may be divided into three interrelated levels, including global governance (e.g., the International Maritime Organization), regional (e.g., the EU and HELCOM) and national (e.g., port authorities).[31] Such multilevel governance structures are considered desirable in the Baltic Sea.[32] The EU legislative provisions in relation to sustainable management of the marine ecosystem use the ecosystem approach, which is key to EU environmental policy. Central to EU marine law is achieving or maintaining set quality standards, such as the concept of 'good environmental status' through adoption of programmes entailing regular assessments.

21.3.1 *United Nations Convention on the Law of the Sea (UNCLOS) and International Convention for the Prevention of Pollution from Ships (MARPOL)*

The United Nations has been at the heart of developing the only global treaty framework for protection of the marine environment since the Stockholm

[27] A. V. V. Nanda, J. Rijke, L. Beesley, B. Gersonius, M. R Hipsey and A. Ghadouani, 'Matching Ecosystem Functions with Adaptive Ecosystem Management: Decision Pathways to Overcome Institutional Barriers' (2018) *Water* 10(6), 672.

[28] A. K. Nilsson and B. Bohman, 'Legal Prerequisites For Ecosystem-Based Management in the Baltic Sea Area: The Example of Eutrophication' (2015) *AMBIO* 44(Suppl 3), 370.

[29] O. R. Young, 'Institutional Linkages in International Society: Polar Perspectives' (1996) *Global Governance* 2(1), 1–24.

[30] M. Gilek and K. Kern (eds.), *Governing Europe's Marine Environment. Europeanization of Regional Seas or Regionalization of EU Policies?* (Hampshire: Asghate Publishing, 2015).

[31] B. Hassler, 'Accidental versus Operational Oil Spills from Shipping in the Baltic Sea: Risk Governance and Management Strategies' (2011) *AMBIO* 40(2), 170–178.

[32] Gilek and Karlsson, Environmental Governance of the Baltic Sea (n 7).

Conference on the Human Environment in 1972.[33] The United Nations Convention on the Law of the Sea of 1982 (UNCLOS), which came into force in 1994 with the objective of codifying pre-existing treaties and conventions, may be considered the 'constitution for the oceans',[34] providing an authoritative framework for regulation of marine affairs.[35] UNCLOS is in force in the whole of the Baltic Sea, and all of the Baltic Sea States as well as the EU are parties to the Convention. The relevance of maritime zones for the Baltic Sea is that all of the sea areas are defined as 'territorial' or 'exclusive economic zones' of the coastal States that have jurisdiction over regulation and enforcement – there are no 'high seas' in the Baltic Sea. UNCLOS also stipulates that the 'flag State' has the main responsibility for ships flying their flag. In addition to regulating at global scale, UNCLOS gives specific consideration to regional seas, such as recognition and allocation of 'Special Areas' and 'Special Sensitive Sea Areas'. EBM of the oceans is to be implemented holistically as stated in the preamble to the UNCLOS, 'Conscious that the problems of ocean space are closely interrelated and need to be considered as a whole'. According to Article 197 State parties to the Convention must co-operate both globally as well as regionally when necessary, directly or through a competent international organisation to protect and preserve the marine environment. However, the maritime zones set by the Convention do not take into consideration maritime ecosystem boundaries.

The International Maritime Organisation (IMO), established by the Convention on the International Maritime Organisation of 1948, has been central to negotiation of the key legislative measures regulating all sources of shipborne pollutants. Regulating specifically shipping-induced oil pollution by introduction of technical standards is the International Convention on the Prevention of Pollution from Ships 1973 (MARPOL 73/78) as amended in 1978, coming into force in 1983 with the aim of regulating marine pollution caused by operational activities and accidents. Regulation of shipborne pollution in general differs from other sources of marine environmental pollution due to the IMO being the central regulator in this field of activity. Ecosystem-based management has been incorporated into MARPOL – it establishes 'Particularly Sensitive Sea Areas' based on ecological and socio-economic importance. In relation to institutional interaction within the legislative framework, it is noteworthy that IMO legislative measures have at times been influenced by and negotiated as a response to EU measures.[36] In relation to vertical

33 R. Rayfuse (ed.), *Research Handbook on International Marine Environmental Law* (Cheltenham: Edward Elgar Publishing, 2017).

34 R. Churchill, The LOSC Regime for the Protection of the Marine Environment: Fit for the Twenty-First Century? In R. Rayfuse (ed.), *Research Handbook on International Marine Environmental Law* (3–30) (Cheltenham: Edward Elgar Publishing, 2017).

35 H. Ringbom, 'Regulation of Ship-Source Pollution in the Baltic Sea' (2018) *Marine Policy* 98, 246–254.

36 H. Ringbom and M. Joas, 'Concluding Article: The Changing Regulatory Landscape of the Baltic Sea – An Analysis' (2018) *Marine Policy* 98, 317–324.

fragmentation and governance of ship-source oil pollution, the UNCLOS 1982 and MARPOL 73/78 have been incorporated into regional seas conventions such as the Helsinki Commission (HELCOM), and into the national legislatures of the Baltic Sea nation States.[37] However, it is noteworthy that the EU has developed instruments regarding shipping control due to general dissatisfaction with the IMO regulations and the apparently weak connection to national maritime administrators, leading to broadly discretionary practices.

21.3.2 *The Convention on the Protection of the Marine Environment of the Baltic Sea Area 1992 and the HELCOM Baltic Sea Action Plan*

The Convention on the Protection of the Marine Environment of the Baltic Sea Area 1992 (the Helsinki Convention) came into force on 17 January 2000. With ten Contracting Parties, including all of the Baltic Sea States and the EU, it applies to the Baltic Sea only.[38] A key area in the work of HELCOM is addressing sea-based pollution sources.[39] Every ship entering the Baltic Sea is 'urged' to comply with the anti-pollution regulations of HELCOM, irrespective of the flag State or being a party to the Convention.[40] The convention text refers to MARPOL provisions but also includes specific shipborne pollution regulations, and is amended when necessary to take into consideration developments in international law (last amended 1 July 2014[41]). HELCOM also acts as the coordination platform regarding implementation of the Directive 2008/56/EC of the Parliament and of the Council of 17 June 2008 establishing a framework of community action in the field of marine environmental policy (Marine Strategy Framework Directive, MSFD), and the programme of measures under the Directive contributes directly to implementation of HELCOM agreements. The Contracting Parties also agreed in 2017 to use HELCOM as the coordinating platform for regional implementation of the UN Sustainable Development Goals related to the oceans. Assessment of the status of the environment, in terms of pressures as well as ecosystem components, is based on HELCOM core indicators, each of which have a set threshold value against which the current status is assessed – on an 'achieved or 'failed' basis. HELCOM also introduces Recommendations, of which there are to date over 260.[42] These usually reinforce international obligations with more detail in relation to implementation in

[37] M. Elliot, 'Integrated Marine Science and Management: Wading through the Morass' (2014) *Marine Pollution Bulletin*, 86(1–2), 1–4.

[38] Convention on the Protection of the Marine Environment of the Baltic Sea Area 1992. Art. 2.

[39] HELCOM Assessment on maritime activities in the Baltic Sea 2018. Baltic Sea Environment Proceedings No.152. Helsinki Commission, 253pp.

[40] HELCOM, The Clean Shipping Guide 2016.

[41] In accordance with HELCOM Recommendation 34E/3, Annex VII 'Response to Pollution Incidents' is amended with substantial changes to Regulation 1 (1), Regulation 2, Regulation 8 (1a), Regulation 10 (1a, 1b, 1c, 2 and 3) to explicitly include response on the shore.

[42] HELCOM.

the Baltic Sea.[43] Deployment of EBM is stated in the preamble: 'Acknowledging, that the ecosystem approach is based on an integrated management of all human activities impacting on the marine environment and, based on best available scientific knowledge about the ecosystem and its dynamics, identifies and leads to actions improving the health of the marine ecosystem thus supporting sustainable use of ecosystem goods and services'.

The Baltic Sea Action Plan (BSAP), guiding the policy actions of HELCOM, was adopted in 2007. Its aim is restoration of good ecological status of the Baltic Sea marine ecosystem by 2021, by introducing innovative management approaches into policy implementation – including that of the ecosystem approach, and supporting the contracting States in fulfilling their national, European and international obligations. The BSAP refers to the ecosystem approach, integrated management, stakeholder participation and understanding interactions between social and ecological systems.[44] It has the specific goals of achieving a Baltic Sea unaffected by eutrophication, undisturbed by hazardous substances, having environmentally friendly maritime activities and favourable status of biodiversity. The BSAP also has detailed provisions for shipping activities. In relation to oil pollution of the marine environment from shipping, the objective is to stop illegal spills. Implementation of the HELCOM Recommendations is reported regularly, most recently being 'Implementation of the Baltic Sea Action Plan 2018: Three years left to reach good environmental status'. The ecological objectives of the Action Plan, and that of reaching favourable conservation status of Baltic Sea biodiversity, a holistic controlling element, can only be achieved by taking into consideration all of the human activities affecting the Baltic Sea marine ecosystem. The Helsinki Convention has been seen as a catalyst for the MSFD,[45] discussed in more detail in Section 21.3.3.

21.3.3 *Marine Strategy Framework Directive*

The Marine Strategy Framework Directive, a goal-oriented legislative tool implementing EBM at regional sea level, was adopted in 2008 with the main objective of achieving 'good environmental status' of EU marine waters by 2020. Included in the Directive are eleven qualitative descriptors in Annex I, which will aid the Member States in their interpretation of what the term 'good environmental status' entails. Key in achieving good environmental status is the regulatory objective to protect marine biodiversity by establishing European marine regions and sub-regions. The Directive lists the pressures related to human activities on the marine environment,

[43] HELCOM, Implementation of the Baltic Sea Action Plan 2018.

[44] M. Boström, S. Grönholm and B. Hassler, The Ecosystem Approach to Management in Baltic Sea Governance: Towards Increased Reflexivity? In Gilek and Karlsson, *Environmental Governance of the Baltic Sea* (n 7).

[45] Österblom et al. (n 23).

and is implemented in conjunction with detailed criteria and methodological standards, which guide the Member States in implementation,[46] using existing regional institutional structures in doing so. Each Member State is to develop a strategy specific to its own marine waters, also reflecting the overall perspective of the marine region or sub-region concerned (Article 11). The Directive thus also places importance on the BSAP as an already existing provision. The MSFD emphasises the importance of addressing all the human actions that have an impact on the marine ecosystem in order to succeed in conservation and sustainable use. The EBM is explicitly mentioned as a means of attaining the goals of the MSFD, in support of the priority to conserve ecosystem structure and function as well as resilience. The MSFD requires application of the ecosystem approach in the marine strategies of the Member States, and thus makes it a legally binding principle in the management of marine ecosystems.[47] The MSFD is a regulatory tool, which transitions marine governance from the national and supranational arenas towards the transnational arena of the regional seas,[48] emphasising cross-border and cross-sectoral integration. It aims to regulate the whole of the marine environment rather than just activities taking place in the Baltic Sea and introduces the concepts of 'marine region' and 'regional co-operation'. The Directive creates an obligation to fulfil the requirements of certain international agreements and commitments related to protection of the marine environment from pollution such as the Convention on the Protection of the Marine Environment of the Baltic Sea Area.[49] To aid in uniform implementation of the Directive, the Commission passed a Commission Decision laying down criteria and methodological standards on good environmental status of marine waters and specifications and standardised methods for monitoring and assessment.[50] This was based on the need for a clearer, more coherent and comparable set of good environmental status criteria and methodological standards, which became apparent after the first implementation cycle. As to implementation of the MSFD and the BSAP, this is addressed in parallel,[51] and due to the complementarities between these two, the BSAP was seen as a pilot providing

[46] Commission Decision (EU) 2017/848 of 17 May 2017 laying down criteria and methodological standards on good environmental status of marine waters and specifications and standardised methods for monitoring and assessment, and repealing Decision 2010/477/EU.

[47] Report from the Commission to the European Parliament and the Council on the implementation of the Marine Strategy Framework Directive (Directive 2008/56/EC) COM(2020) 259 final.

[48] J. Tatenhove, 'How to Turn the Tide: Developing Legitimate Marine Governance Arrangements at the Level of the Regional Seas' (2013) *Ocean & Coastal Management* 71, 296–304.

[49] Approved by Council Decision 94/157/EC.

[50] (EU) 2017/848 of 17 May 2017.

[51] H. Backer, J. M. Leppänen, et al., 'Helcom Baltic Sea Action Plan – A Regional Programme of Measures for the Marine Environment Based on the Ecosystem Approach' (2010) *Marine Pollution Bulletin* 60(5), 642–649.

the experience on which to build the MSFD.[52] The MSFD may be considered key in the EU delivering on its global commitments on marine environment protection.[53]

21.4 INSTITUTIONAL INTERPLAY AND THE ECOSYSTEM APPROACH

As discussed previously, the ecosystem approach in marine policy was initiated at global level and further adopted in marine ecosystem regulation by the UN Law of the Sea, as well as the EU in its marine policy and regionally by HELCOM through its Baltic Sea Action Plan. This adaptation has been influenced by institutional interaction between regimes. Successful implementation of EBM in achieving the objective of reducing concentrations of hazardous substances close to natural levels by keeping to a minimum the release of oil into the marine environment in accordance with the Baltic Sea Action Plan and the Marine Strategy Framework Directive[54] is dependent on integrating this concept in policies, and linking regional governance to a global framework.[55] It is also of importance to consider the interlocking structure of international governance institutions and EU legislative instruments.[56] As the legislative instruments discussed previously do not function in a vacuum, the success of multilevel arrangements is influenced by horizontal and vertical interplay, as well as integration of non-member States of the EU.[57] Therefore, it is also of importance to consider the influence of one institution on another in the Baltic Sea. Institutional interaction may create synergy, or it may undermine or disturb the effectiveness of policies.[58] Resultant links between institutions may generate consequences that are benign, such as regional regimes, which gain strength from being nested into global regimes. Such interaction between regional and global institutions in relation to shipping governance in particular may be essential but has not received enough attention in academic discussion.[59]

52 S. Gänzle, 'The European Union's Strategy for the Baltic Sea Region (EUSBSR): Improving Multilevel Governance in Baltic Sea Cooperation?' (2017) *Journal of Baltic Studies* 48(4), 407–420.

53 Report from the Commission to the European Parliament and the Council on the implementation of the Marine Strategy Framework Directive (Directive 2008/56/EC) COM/2020/259.

54 Directive 2008/56/EC of the European Parliament and of the Council of 17 June 2008 establishing a framework for community action in the field of marine environmental policy.

55 B. Hassler, Oil Spills from Shipping: A Case Study of the Governance of Accidental Hazards and Intentional Pollution in the Baltic Sea. In Gilek and Karlsson, *Environmental Governance of the Baltic Sea* (n 7), 125–146.

56 S. Oberthur and T. Gehring, *Institutional Interaction in Global Environmental Governance Synergy and Conflict among International and EU Policies* (Cambridge: Cambridge University Press, 2006).

57 Gilek and Kern (n 30).

58 Oberthur and Gehring (n 56).

59 O. Stokke 'Regime Interplay in Arctic Shipping Governance: Explaining Regional Niche Selection' (2013) *International Environmental Agreements: Politics, Law and Economics* 13(1), 65–85.

Thus, in order to appreciate the conditions required for legitimate and integrated marine governance arrangements in the Baltic Sea, a key to understanding is the multi-level dynamics of marine governance, the institutional setting where these policies are developed and implemented, and interaction between institutions.[60]

Institutional interplay has been recognised as an important feature of global environmental governance since 1998,[61] and the effectiveness of a specific institution is a culmination of its own features as well as its interaction with other institutions.[62] International regimes and organisations, as well as the EU, may be considered institutions that involve States as the main actors addressing issues in specific areas.[63] The term 'institution' may be defined to include international regimes and organisations as well as EU legislative instruments. Institutional interplay may be defined as one institution affecting the contents, operations and consequences of another.[64] It refers to a causal relationship between two institutions where the 'source' institution exerts influence on the 'target' institution,[65] affecting its development or performance. Institutional interplay may also cluster around certain issues and institutions jointly addressing a particular problem, as is the case with oil pollution control, contributing to the effectiveness of governance in that specific area.[66] Institutional interplay may take the form of horizontal or vertical interplay, where the former is interplay between institutions at the same level of governance, and the latter concerning the interaction between global and regional institutions. In considering the institutional interplay of the regimes, the conceptual framework developed by Oberthür and Gehring, where there is no implication that influence runs back and forth between institutions, but where the causal influence implies that influence runs unidirectionally from the source to the target, is deployed.[67] Thus, in order to establish a causal relationship there must be a source institution and its rules establishing influence, a target institution and a specific issue area subject to the influence of the source institution, as well as unidirectional causal pathways connecting the institutions.[68] Interplay through cognition, as one of the three forms of interplay identified by Obenthür and Gehring, is a transfer of knowledge and ideas taking place in the agenda-setting phase and during implementation from one institution to the other. In the case of more complex interplay through cognition, joint learning and development of converging policies in the

60 Tatenhove (n 48) 296–304.

61 O. R. Young, *Institutional Dimension of Global Environmental Change Science Plan*, Public Administration and Public Policy, Vol. II, No. 9, 16 (Bonn: IHDP Report, 1999/2005).

62 S. Oberthur and O. Stokke, *Managing Institutional Complexity: Regime Interplay and Global Environmental Change* (Cambridge: MIT Press, 2011).

63 Ibid.

64 Ibid., 144.

65 Ibid.

66 Ibid.

67 Ibid., 229.

68 Ibid., 228.

different institutions may result. The second type of interplay is through commitment, where one institution affects the decision making of another by normative commitments. In overlapping issue areas commitments of one institution will result in a change of preference in the other, leading to different outputs. This is a type specifically relevant to nested institutions such as the IMO and the EU, interdependent in regulating environmental aspects of shipping. The EU may not have formal control of the IMO but may influence it due to overlapping regulations and compliance procedures in place. Finally, interplay through compliance is present in the implementation phase, when institutions have overlapping issue areas, and where the output of one institution effects a behavioural change further altering implementation and resulting in behavioural change in another institution. If an additional means of implementation is activated by diffusion of an obligation between institutions with similar identical objectives, this will increase the effectiveness of both institutions involved. Institutional interplay also has an effect on implementation of the ecosystem approach to management in the Baltic Sea.

Regarding the ecosystem approach in marine management, cognitive interplay was initiated at international level as discussed previously and evolvement of which is evident between the MSFD and the HELCOM BSAP, as the MSFD was based on knowledge contained in the BSAP. Cognitive interaction is also clear between the EU and the HELCOM BSAP in relation to the MSFD,[69] the MSFD being influenced by the HELCOM BSAP, and based on its existing knowledge. The MSFD is clear on the requirement of ecosystem-based management. The difference in learning between organisations may have an effect on how a concept such as the ecosystem approach to management may form during the process.[70] Interaction through commitment plays an important role within nested institutions such as the IMO and the EU as a commitment within one affects the decision making process in the other.[71] In the Baltic Sea the ecosystem approach has generated synergies due to transforming the non-binding recommendations of HELCOM into EU law through the MSFD. Institutional interaction through compliance in relation to the IMO and the EU manifests in binding standards[72] and their enforcement mechanisms,[73] by implementation of IMO obligations into EU law, creating synergies. For shipping regulation, interplay through compliance of IMO regulations and

69 Tatenhove (n 48) 296–304.

70 K. Kern, 'Governance for Sustainable Development in the Baltic Sea Region' (2011) *Journal of Baltic Studies* 42(1), 21–35.

71 J. van Leeuwen and K. Kern, 'The External Dimension of European Union Marine Governance: Institutional Interplay between the EU and the International Maritime Organization' (2013) *Global Environmental Politics* 13(1), 69–87.

72 European Parliament legislative resolution of 13 March 2019 on the proposal for a directive of the European Parliament and of the Council on port reception facilities for the delivery of waste from ships, repealing Directive 2000/59/EC and amending Directive 2009/16/EC and Directive 2010/65/EU.

73 Port State Control Directive (2009/16/EC).

the EU is of utmost importance. The institutional interplay between the IMO and the EU has been affected by recognition of the pressing need to protect the Baltic Sea with more urgent measures than IMO procedures may accommodate, and different EU initiatives have led to more stringent shipping standards. In addition, unilateral EU initiatives have influenced formation of decentralised institutional complexes as part of institutional interplay management. The institutional interplay between the HELCOM BSAP and the EU Strategy for the Baltic Sea Region (EUSBSR) can be seen from the aforementioned strategy's BSAP implementation recommendation. Thus, it may be argued that the distinctive institutional features present in the Baltic Sea make regional marine governance particularly suited to conducting knowledge-building and capacity-enhancement in the international governance system for shipping. This may be considered a regime 'niche' that a regime can specialise in within a larger institutional complex.[74]

21.5 REFLECTIONS AND SUGGESTIONS FOR IMPROVEMENT

International legislative measures have been considered traditionally as the most efficient in regulating global sectors such as shipping. The current legislative measures in force regulating marine ecosystems have introduced a more holistic management approach, moving away from a top-down sectoral approach with the aim of managing the marine ecosystem as a whole. Fragmented management at regional sea level, with different sectors having their own independent and different governance arrangements, may have hindered successful implementation of the ecosystem approach into legislative measures safeguarding marine ecosystems. Therefore, it is the development of institutional interlinkages between polycentric governance arrangements that may facilitate common policy objectives, decision-making and implementation of sectoral measures in support of the ecosystem approach. In relation to ship source pollution, the core problem with the IMO has been considered to be its weak connection to national maritime administrators, leading to broadly discretionary practices.[75] In shipping, regionalisation may enable dynamic interplay and synergies between the IMO and EU shipping regulations: and it is this synergy that can be described as complementary with each other.[76] The use of 'soft' modes of governance has become central in the globally centralised regulation of ship-source oil pollution, which leaves practical implementation and enforcement to the individual States. This as such may weaken the rule of law. However, use of these modes is of specific importance in a polycentric governance system as a tool for steering policy implementation by introduction of innovative

[74] Stokke (n 59) 65–85.
[75] O. F. Knudsen and B. Hassler, 'IMO Legislation and Its Implementation: Accident Risk, Vessel Deficiencies and National Administrative Practices' *Marine Policy* (2011) 35(2), 201–207.
[76] Kern (n 70).

practices, learning and co-ordination. The role of non-governmental organisations (NGOs) and port authorities in regulating oil pollution may be considered key, as well as stakeholder-inclusive collaborative learning platforms at the regional (or sub-basin) level, with a clear mandate and aim of spatially relevant dynamics.[77] Key to management of the Baltic Sea marine ecosystem is institutional interaction, reinforcing international and European governance by activating an additional layer of enforcement by the actors involved to realise their desired objectives.[78] Thus, success in implementing EBM in the Baltic Sea is influenced by the involvement of stakeholders, as this may help inconsistencies in implementation of legislative measures by way of bottom-up initiatives in the existing framework created by 'top-down' enabling legislation. The often-wide discretion of implementing EBM may well benefit from regional regulation and soft law instruments. Therefore, regional regulation in the Baltic Sea may be utilised as an implementation tool bringing added value through local implementation;[79] in this the EU occupies a central role, which is also apparent from the institutional synergies present. It is these synergies, which may be described as complementary to each other, that have the potential to fill possible regulatory gaps.[80] Regional institutions may be seen as having a key role in strengthening international regulation of oil pollution based on IMO regulations. Regional regulation of this global environmental threat may also be central to strengthening the rule of law by enabling enactment and implementation of enforceable and effective legislative measures.

77 Österblom et al. (n 23).
78 Oberthur and Stokke (n 62).
79 Gilek and Kern (n 30).
80 T. Hickmann, H. Van Asselt, S. Oberthür, L. Sanderink, O. Widerberg and F. Zelli, Institutional Interlinkages. In F. Biermann and R. Kim (eds.), *Architectures of Earth System Governance: Institutional Complexity and Structural Transformation* (119–136) (Cambridge: Cambridge University Press, 2020).

22

The International Law of the Sea and Arctic Governance

Paving the Way to Integrated Ecosystem-Based Marine Management

Andrey Todorov

22.1 INTRODUCTION

The existing framework for Arctic Ocean governance is an excellent example of the law of the sea as a legal framework, which, on the one hand, supports stability and predictability in regional relations and, on the other hand, has to evolve in tune with emerging challenges and structural changes. By endorsing the 2008 Ilulissat declaration,[1] the five Arctic coastal States – Canada, the Kingdoms of Denmark and Norway, Russia and the United States – agreed that an extensive international legal framework applies to the Arctic Ocean. This framework, with the 1982 United Nations Convention on the Law of the Sea (UNCLOS[2]) at its core, provides the basis for orderly settlement of any potential overlapping claims and the main types of ocean use. Since the Arctic Ocean consists of both areas under sovereignty and jurisdiction of the coastal States and areas beyond national jurisdiction (ABNJ), UNCLOS is crucially important for defining the rights and obligations of the Arctic coastal States and non-regional States, as well as for regional cooperation.

However, the existing concept of management of marine use, which is the same for the Arctic maritime areas as for the rest of the world ocean, is facing a crisis. As anthropogenic pressure and threats stemming from climate change increase, traditional management of ocean resources is widely considered insufficient and ineffective.[3] This gives rise to a clear global trend to replace conventional sectoral

[1] The Ilulissat Declaration, adopted in Ilulissat, Greenland on 28 May 2008, available at: ttps://arcticportal.org/images/stories/pdf/Ilulissat-declaration.pdf.

[2] United Nations Convention on the Law of the Sea of 10 December 1982 (UNCLOS), entered into force 16 November 1994.

[3] Long, R. D., Charles, A. and Stephenson, R. L., 'Key principles of marine ecosystem-based management' (2015) *Marine Policy* 57, 53–60. doi:10.1016/j.marpol.2015.01.013, 53; Katsanevakis, S., Stelzenmüller V., South A. et al., 'Ecosystem-based marine spatial management: Review of concepts, policies, tools, and critical issues' (2011) *Ocean & Coastal Management* 54(11), 807–820. doi:10.1016/j.ocecoaman.2011.09.002, 808.

regulation of different maritime activities with a more holistic approach known as Integrated Ecosystem-Based Marine Management (IEBMM).[4]

In this context, the Arctic is also on the threshold of a paradigm shift. Due to climate change and sea ice decline, the Arctic Ocean[5] is becoming more accessible, with new shipping lanes opening for trade and tourism, opportunities for fisheries and the mining industry multiplying. The negative side of the same processes consists in new challenges to the safety of life at sea, a fragile environment and the local population, resulting from oil spills, ship collisions, overexploitation of living resources and so on. Accordingly, new legal instruments are being introduced: the Polar code,[6] which provides standards for safety at sea and pollution prevention in the polar seas; the first three binding agreements under the auspices of the Arctic Council (AC);[7] and others. But are these instruments sufficient for the Arctic region today to keep up with constant changes and challenges?

The main purpose of this chapter is to discuss how the instruments and tools of the IEBMM could be used to improve ocean governance in the Arctic. Given that the ecosystems of the Arctic are cross-boundary and include waters under the national jurisdiction of two or more Arctic States, as well as ABNJ,[8] the key rule-of-law question to be addressed in this regard is how to ensure that IEBMM-related tools and measures are adopted and enforced in a holistic cross-border manner in full compliance with international law. While the waters within 200 nautical miles (nm) and continental shelf fall within the national jurisdiction of the Arctic coastal States, whose competence to adopt and enforce binding decisions with respect to these marine areas is not disputed, a number of freedoms and rights are enjoyed by all States in the vast ABNJ in the region that can be restricted only in limited cases

4 Long et al., (n 3), 53; Halpern, B. S., McLeod, K. L., Rosenberg, A. A. and Crowder, L. B., 'Managing for cumulative impacts in ecosystem-based management through ocean zoning' (2008) *Ocean & Coastal Management* 51(3), 203–211. doi:10.1016/j.ocecoaman.2007.08.002; Elliott, M., 'Integrated marine science and management: Wading through the morass' (2014) *Marine Pollution Bulletin* 86(1–2), 1–4. doi:10.1016/j.marpolbul.2014.07.026 ,1.

5 The term 'Arctic Ocean' is used in this chapter as defined by the International Hydrographic Office, covering the East Siberian Sea, the Laptev Sea, the Kara Sea, the Barents Sea, the White Sea, the Greenland Sea, the Norwegian Sea, the Iceland Sea, the Davis Strait, Hudson Strait, Hudson Bay, Baffin Bay, the Lincoln Sea, the North Western Passages, the Beaufort Sea and the Chukchi Sea. See IHO (International Hydrographic Office), 'Limits of Ocean and Seas'.

6 International Code for Ships Operating in Polar Waters, adopted in November 2014 and May 2015.

7 Agreement on Cooperation on Aeronautical and Maritime Search and Rescue in the Arctic, adopted 12 May 2011, entered into force 19 January 2013; Agreement on Cooperation on Marine Oil Pollution Preparedness and Response in the Arctic, adopted 15 May 2013, entered into force 25 March, 2016; Agreement on Enhancing International Arctic Scientific Cooperation, adopted 11 May 2017, entered into force 23 May 2018.

8 'Guidelines for Implementing an Ecosystem Approach to Management of Arctic Marine Ecosystems. Arctic Council Joint PAME, CAFF, AMAP, SDWG Ecosystem Approach Expert Group' (2019), 6.

and through relevant international mechanisms. Other important problems to address are finding the best way of engaging third States in implementing regional IEBMM tools for ABNJ and achieving the cross-sectoral nature of the regulations.

The second section of this Chapter gives a brief overview of the concept of integrated ecosystem-based marine management, as well as the challenges it implies specifically for ABNJ. The third part provides a comparative study of how IEBMM tools (in particular, creation of marine protected areas) are implemented in other regions with a focus on those regional mechanisms that to some extent have succeeded in implementingthe IEBMM in ABNJ. Despite the unique challenges of the Arctic Ocean, some achievements of other regional instruments in implementing the IEBMM could be valuable for the Arctic. Therefore, an attempt is made in the fourth part to refer the results of the comparative study to Arctic Ocean governance. The work concludes with some recommendations on possible ways forward.

22.2 INTEGRATED ECOSYSTEM-BASED MARINE MANAGEMENT

The concept of integrated ecosystem-based marine management has evolved as an alternative to the traditional sector-by-sector approach, where each type of human activity is managed separately.[9] Ecosystem-based management is a place-based approach, focusing on a specific ecosystem and the range of human activities affecting it, rather than considering single industries or species in isolation. This entails cross-boundary and cross-sectoral regulation of all types of economic activity in certain sea areas, where they might result in negative impacts on the marine environment, and development of a holistic strategy for all parties and industries concerned. IEBMM is implemented through different tools: key among these are Marine Spatial Planning (MSP), Marine Protected Areas (MPAs) and Ocean Zoning (OZ).[10]

Implementation of IEBMM requires solution of several major legal and organizational questions. The boundaries of ecosystems do not, as a rule, overlap with the boundaries of national jurisdiction of coastal States. The zonal approach enshrined in the UNCLOS implies a variable balance between coastal State sovereignty and jurisdiction, and third-State rights and freedoms. Thus, relevant policies of IEBMM in various sea areas with different legal status and regime should be coordinated. Most of the efforts to develop IEBMM deal with areas of national jurisdiction (within 200 miles)[11] and therefore require either commitment by one coastal State or cooperation between several neighbouring coastal States. However, the case of the Arctic Ocean is a special one since it covers the vast ABNJ. Consequently, a

9 Halpern et al. (n 4), 203.
10 Katsanevakis et al. (n 3).
11 Ibid.

crucial challenge in this regard is how to make regional measures in ABNJ binding and ensure compliance by non-Arctic stakeholders.

UNCLOS contains provisions that oblige all States to prevent marine environmental pollution (in particular, Articles 192, 196). These obligations are supplemented by the provisions of the 1992 Convention on Biological Diversity,[12] which set out the responsibility of States to cooperate for the sustainable use of biological diversity, including in ABNJ (e.g., Articles 3,4, 7). However, there is a condition that regional agreements are not to affect the basic principles of the UNCLOS (Article 311), including freedom of the high seas, without the explicit consent of the States concerned. Members of regional mechanisms can establish a regime modifying the common legal framework, thus restricting freedom of the high seas for those persons subject to their respective jurisdiction. Nevertheless, they are not entitled to limit the rights of third States absent their express consent.[13]

This challenge could to some extent be addressed through different global management organizations, which are allowed to adopt decisions related to ABNJ, binding on all States. However, the mandates of relevant international bodies are fragmented and may be considered insufficient for an effective IEBMM.[14] There is no clear answer to the question how ecosystem-based policies are to correlate with measures developed by sectoral international organizations.

The problem of IEBMM has been the focus of growing attention from global international organizations. The most comprehensive effort came from the United Nations, which launched negotiations on a possible new UNCLOS implementing agreement related to biodiversity in marine areas beyond national jurisdiction (the BBNJ Agreement). Although many complicated issues have not been resolved so far,[15] the BBNJ Agreement could be a major contribution to establishing a global framework for the implementation of IEBMM, creating a set of unified principles for this purpose.

22.3 REGIONAL EXPERIENCE

It should be noted that the Arctic does not play a pioneering role in terms of implementing the concept of IEBMM on the regional level. Yet, although some regions have achieved significant progress, the IEBMM concept has been applied mainly to areas within national jurisdiction. Only a few regional organizations have

[12] Convention on Biological Diversity, adopted in 1992 (entered into force on 29 December 1993).

[13] Tanaka, Y., 'Reflections on high seas marine protected areas: A comparative analysis of the Mediterranean and the North-East Atlantic models' (2012) *Nordic Journal of International Law* 81, 295, 316.

[14] Wright, G., Gjerde, K. M., Johnson D. E. et al., 'Marine spatial planning in areas beyond national jurisdiction' (2019) 132 *Marine Policy*, https://doi.org/10.1016/j.marpol.2018.12.003.

[15] For the progress of negotiations see the UN official website www.un.org/bbnj/

developed IEBMM tools in marine ABNJ.[16] For the purposes of this chapter, it would be useful to look into the experience of some of these regional mechanisms to identify optimal responses to the questions raised in this study (engaging third States in implementing IEBMM regulations for ABNJ and achieving the cross-sectoral aspect of such regulations) in the context of Arctic governance. Special focus is on the practice of using such IEBMM tools as designation of MPAs, for it has been successfully implemented in the ABNJ in some regions.

22.3.1 *CAMLR Commission*

The Commission for the Conservation of Antarctic Marine Living Resources (CAMLR Commission) is a regional organization in the Southern Ocean acting within the framework of the 1980 CAMLR Convention.[17] Though the CAMLR Convention is an independent international instrument managing the living resources of the Antarctic, it is an integral part of the Antarctic Treaty System (ATS). It is important to note that, taking into account the special status of the Antarctic, the overwhelming majority of marine areas within the CAMLR Commission mandate constitute ABNJ.[18]

The South Orkney Islands MPA established in 2009 by a decision of the CAMLR Commission became the first MPA in world history to cover ABNJ.[19] All types of commercial fishing activities, dumping of any type of waste and trans-shipment activities are prohibited within the area. This makes it an MPA with one of the highest levels of protection in the world.[20] In 2017 a decision of CCAMLR came into effect establishing another MPA in the Ross Sea, which is the largest marine protected area in the world and covers zones with different levels of protection with the aim of conserving krill resources.[21] The CCAMLR has also developed proposals for MPAs in other regions of the Southern Ocean.[22]

It is clear that the CCAMLR has significantly contributed to the promotion of IEBMM and marine spatial planning. However, this is possible not least because of the special status of the Antarctic region. Being an integral part of the Antarctic

[16] Regional Seas programmes covering Areas beyond National Jurisdictions. UNEP Regional Seas Reports and Studies No. 202, 2017 // UN. Available at: www.un.org/Depts/los/biodiversityworkinggroup/Regional_seas_programmes_ABNJ.pdf; Wright et al. (n 14), 4.

[17] The Convention on the Conservation of Antarctic Marine Living Resources, adopted in 1980, entered into force 7 April 1982.

[18] Sothieson, D., '*Marine Protected Areas in the North-East Atlantic Ocean And Southern Ocean: The Role of Regional Organisations in Areas beyond National Jurisdiction*', LLB Degree thesis, Victoria University of Wellington (2014), 38–39.

[19] Ibid., 15.

[20] Ibid., 16.

[21] 'Marine Protected Areas (MPAs)', CCAMLR official website. Available at: www.ccamlr.org/en/science/marine-protected-areas-mpas

[22] Ibid.

Treaty System, which to a large extent represents *lex specialis* towards the provisions of UNCLOS[23] and was designed as an integrated framework, the CCAMLR holds a broad mandate, including adoption of legally binding decisions related to marine ABNJ. This gives the ATS and CCAMLR a significant advantage in promoting integrated ecosystem management.[24] Since most of the marine areas of the Arctic are governed by UNCLOS with the traditional sectoral approach and significant freedoms of States in ABNJ are implied, the experience of the CCAMLR and ATS could hardly be considered relevant for the Arctic.

22.3.2 *Mediterranean Instrument*

Another quite efficient regional mechanism is the Mediterranean instrument run under the UNEP Regional Seas Program and based on the 1976 Barcelona Convention[25] and Protocols thereto. The Barcelona Convention also applies to ABNJ (high seas) until all of the coastal States in the region establish their EEZ.[26] In 1999 in Rome, France, Monaco and Italy concluded an agreement for the establishment of a sanctuary for marine mammals (PELAGOS Agreement[27]) in the form of SPAMI. Today it is the only MPA in the Mediterranean to cover ABNJ (potential EEZ).[28] Any taking of marine mammals (except for the purpose of scientific research) is prohibited in that MPA (Article 7a of the PELAGOS Agreement), along with some other human activities (in particular, high-speed vehicle competitions – Article 9). Parties are to take measures to prevent marine pollution (Article 6).

Although the experience of the Barcelona mechanism could seem useful in terms of applying IEBMM in ABNJ in the Arctic, a specific feature of the Mediterranean Sea considerably distinguishes it from the Arctic Ocean – namely, the distance between the opposite coasts in the Mediterranean does not exceed 400 nautical miles. To date, not all of the coastal States bordering the Mediterranean Sea have

[23] Rothwell, D., 'A maritime analysis of conflicting international law regimes in Antarctica and the Southern Ocean' (1995) *Australian Year Book of International Law* 16, 168.

[24] Molenaar, E., 'Managing biodiversity in areas beyond national jurisdiction' (2007) *The International Journal of Marine and Coastal Law* 22(1), 89–124. doi:10.1163/157180807781475263, 95.

[25] The Convention for the Protection of the Mediterranean Sea Against Pollution, adopted on 16 February 1976 in Barcelona, entered into force in 1978.

[26] 'Note on the legal framework for the protection of marine biological diversity in Mediterranean Sea areas beyond national jurisdictions (BBNJ) or for which the limits of sovereignty or jurisdiction have not yet been defined'. UNEP(DEPI)/MED WG.431/Inf.9, 25 April 2017. Available at: www.rac-spa.org/nfp13/documents/02_information_documents/wg_431_inf_9_note_on_legal_framework_for%20bbnj.pdf

[27] Agreement related to the creation of a Sanctuary for marine mammals in the Mediterranean Sea, adopted in 1999, entered into force in 2002.

[28] Sothieson (n 18), 51.

claimed EEZ\CS,[29] leaving some ABNJ. Still, this situation implies that in case (if, or rather– when) all coastal States establish their 200 nm EEZ, there will be no ABNJ. Legally, this would mean the extension of national jurisdiction of coastal States, related to protection and conservation of the marine environment, to the entire Mediterranean Sea, thus eliminating one of the main challenges to IEBMM – namely, the legality of imposing regulatory measures on third States in ABNJ. The Law of the Sea furnishes coastal States with sufficient rights and jurisdiction to adopt and enforce measures related to protection of the marine environment within EEZ (e.g., Articles. 56, 211, 216, 234). Moreover, the fact that the total area of the Mediterranean Sea is covered by national jurisdiction makes it redundant to coordinate regional IEBMM measures with relevant global organizations such as the International Maritime Organization (IMO), or the International Seabed Authority (ISA). Therefore, inter-organizational coordination in the Mediterranean, in reality, is limited to ad hoc cooperation with the General Fisheries Commission for the Mediterranean.[30] Since the Arctic Ocean is not entirely covered by 200-nm zones of the coastal States, it is practically impossible to form a regional mechanism in the Arctic similar to that of the Barcelona model.

22.3.3 *OSPAR*

In contrast, the OSPAR model seems to perfectly fit the criteria of the Arctic Ocean. The 1992 OSPAR Convention[31] covers various economic activities in the North-East Atlantic that could have adverse effects on marine ecosystems and biodiversity. However, the Convention provides two major exceptions from OSPAR's jurisdiction – fisheries management and certain limitations for the regulation of shipping. OSPAR has made great efforts to implement IEBMM tools in ABNJ, given that the North-East Atlantic is not entirely covered by national jurisdiction zones of coastal States. OSPAR has its own MPA Network, which covers 5.9 per cent of the OSPAR Maritime Area,[32] including ten MPAs beyond the EEZ of its parties.[33] Some MPAs seek to conserve the biological diversity of the seabed and superjacent waters, while others aim to conserve the biological diversity of the water superjacent to the sites.[34]

A solution by the OSPAR mechanism (the OSPAR Commission) of the key challenges of the IEBMM in ABNJ, raised in this chapter, seems to originate from its commitment to active cooperation with regional and global sectoral organizations

[29] 'Maritime Space: Maritime Zones and Maritime Delimitation'. The United Nations. Available at: www.un.org/Depts/los/LEGISLATIONANDTREATIES/europe.htm

[30] Sothieson (n 18), 51.

[31] Convention for the Protection of the Marine Environment of the North-East Atlantic, adopted on 22 September 1992, entered into force on 25 March 1998.

[32] Ibid.

[33] Status Report of the OSPAR Commission on the OSPAR Network of Marine Protected Areas (2018). Available at: www.ospar.org/documents?v=40944

[34] See Tanaka (n 13), 311ff.

and mechanisms governing different maritime activities. The OSPAR Commission has signed memoranda of understanding (MoU) with The North East Atlantic Fisheries Commission (NEAFC), ISA, the IMO and other organizations.[35] Close coordination with these institutions provides the OSPAR Commission with a range of important benefits. First, this enhances the legitimacy of OSPAR's regulatory measures in ABNJ, in particular aimed at marine environmental protection. The IMO and ISA have indisputable authority to legally restrict different sectors of States' marine use, including in ABNJ. The same effect is achieved by cooperation with NEAFC, which can legally impose measures on third States under the 1995 Fish Stock Agreement[36] (inspections of fishing vessels and putting on the blacklist of IUU fishing).

Second, active collaboration with sectoral organizations enables the regime to achieve a cross-sectoral effect. While shipping and fisheries fall outside the OSPAR regulatory regime, coordination with the IMO and NEAFC fills this gap. The ISA mandate to regulate exploitation of mineral resources of the Area also takes precedence over regional efforts, so that coordination with ISA increases the efficiency of regulations adopted by OSPAR.

And finally, this provides a great possibility to engage a wide range of third States. Membership of global international organizations, such as the IMO or ISA, is much wider than that of any regional mechanism. Coordination with these organizations enables the OSPAR Commission to indirectly involve States non-parties to the OSPAR Convention in regulation related to ABNJ. The legitimacy of the duty to comply with the measures developed by these international organizations is indisputable for the States parties thereto. On the other hand, a difficulty that may arise in this respect is coordination of measures in the region for a State that is a party to different international organizations in case the decisions of these organizations are not harmonized between each other.[37]

22.4 POSSIBLE SOLUTIONS TO IEBMM CHALLENGES IN THE ARCTIC OCEAN

The experience of other regional instruments dealing with IEBMM, including in ABNJ, allows us to propose the following measures related to implementation of IEBMM in the Arctic region.

[35] Memoranda of Understanding and Cooperation Arrangements. *OSPAR*. Available at: www.ospar.org/about/international-cooperation/memoranda-of-understanding

[36] Agreement for the Implementation of the Provisions of the United Nations Convention on the Law of the Sea of 10 December 1982 relating to the Conservation and Management of Straddling Fish Stocks and Highly Migratory Fish Stocks, New York, 4 August 1995. In force 11 December 2001.

[37] Molenaar, E. J., and Elferink, A. G. O., 'Marine protected areas in areas beyond national jurisdiction: The pioneering efforts under the OSPAR Convention' (2009) *Utrecht Law Review* 5(1), 19.

22.4.1 *Efficient Regional Management Organization*

The efficiency of a regional mechanism depends to a large extent on the efficiency of its main body responsible for carrying out the entire workload related to IEBMM. This implies that there should be a strong executive body endowed with a wide mandate to implement IEBMM measures – whether it is the OSPAR Commission or the CCAMLR.

As is widely acknowledged, the main intergovernmental forum for regional cooperation in the Arctic is the Arctic Council. Since its establishment in 1996, the AC has considerably contributed to collaboration among the eight Arctic States with the active involvement of third States-observers and representatives of Arctic Indigenous Peoples. The focus of its work has been protection of the marine environment and sustainable development of the region. Under its auspices, three legally binding agreements have been signed.[38]

Despite some progress achieved by the AC on IEBMM-related issues,[39] today the Arctic Council is facing serious challenges. Put in a nutshell, these relate to the following:[40]

- legally, the AC is not an international organization and is not allowed to adopt legally binding decisions – a significant impediment for implementing the tools of a regional IEBMM;
- the AC suffers from a lack of proper instruments for measuring the effectiveness of numerous projects and programmes the AC undertakes;
- funding is inadequate: almost all projects are funded on an *ad hoc* basis by the States who advocate for them, but the AC has insufficient programmatic and discretionary funding;
- issues of environmental protection outbalance the problems of sustainable development.

This gives room for fears that the AC would not be able to succeed in promoting the concept of IEBMM in the Arctic[41] and lead the AC further away from the OSPAR model. However, it would surely be easier to work with existing instruments than to create new ones from ground zero. Proceeding from that assumption, there is a compelling need for significant expansion of the competence and mandate of the

[38] See (n 7).

[39] See Guidelines for Implementing an Ecosystem Approach to Management of Arctic Marine Ecosystems (n 6).

[40] See Exner-Pirot, H., Ackrén, M., Loukacheva, N. et al., 'Form and function: The future of the Arctic Council' (2015) *The Arctic Institute*. Available at: www.thearcticinstitute.org/form-function-future-arctic-council/; Balton D. and Ulmer F., 'A Strategic Plan for the Arctic Council: Recommendations for Moving Forward', Working Paper (Wilson Center, Harvard Kennedy School, 2019).

[41] Balton, D. and Zagorski, A., 'Implementing Marine Management in the Arctic Ocean', Russian International Affairs Council, Woodrow Wilson International Center, 2020, 23.

AC and its bodies. In particular, this would imply moving towards endowing the Arctic Council and its Secretariat with international legal personality; establishing a subsidiary body with a broad mandate comparable to that of the OSPAR Commission, or transforming the Secretariat into an 'Arctic Council Commission'; authorizing that subsidiary body to initiate discussions on relevant issues in the decision-making bodies of the Arctic Council (Ministerial meetings); a substantial increase of financing of the subsidiary body (the 'AC Commission').

22.4.2 *Coordination with Sectoral Organizations*

The experience of OSPAR and other regional mechanisms shows that the most effective and legitimate (if not the only) way to ensure the cross-sectoral synergy of regulative measures is to cooperate and coordinate efforts with global international organizations responsible for different types of marine use. The most rapidly growing sector of marine activities in the Arctic is shipping. This has drastically risen in the region over the past two decades and is expected to intensify further as northern routes become increasingly accessible.[42] Bearing that in mind, in the short-term period Arctic States (through the Arctic Council) will need to develop a joint position in the IMO. This is not a new challenge for the AC, though. For instance, the AC supported the work on a legally binding Polar Code, negotiated within the framework of the IMO, which is reflected in the decisions of Ministerial meetings.[43] However, technically the initiative in the IMO was put forward by individual members of the AC.[44]

The process of coordinating positions in global organizations is not settled among the AC member States. Notably, the relatively successful implementation of IEBMM tools by OSPAR relies not least on cohesion and a spirit of shared interest among the States-parties.[45] However, for the AC it could be a hard task to fulfil, mainly due to a lower level of members' cohesion in the AC compared to OSPAR.

As far as other sectoral organizations are concerned, the urgency of coordination is less evident. Emergence of the Area in the Arctic Ocean governed by ISA directly depends on accomplishing the process of establishing coastal States' extended continental shelf. Since this process takes much time, collaboration with ISA is an

[42] 'Ocean and Cryosphere in a Changing Climate', Special Report of the Intergovernmental Panel on Climate Change (2019), Chapter 3, section 3.2.4.3.

[43] Report of the Senior Arctic Officials to the Ministers of the Arctic Council Member States, adopted May, 2011. Available at: https://oaarchive.arctic-council.org/bitstream/handle/11374/1535/SAO_Report_to_Ministers_-_Nuuk_Ministerial_Meeting_May_2011.pdf?sequence=1&isAllowed=y; Report of the Senior Arctic Officials to the Ministers of the Arctic Council Member States, adopted 15 May 2013. Available at: https://oaarchive.arctic-council.org/bitstream/handle/11374/848/MM08_Kiruna_SAO_Report_to_Ministers_Final_formatted.pdf?sequence=1&isAllowed=y

[44] IMO Document MSC 86/23/9, adopted on 24 February 2009.

[45] Sothieson (n 18), 28.

issue of a more distant perspective. Issues relating to conservation and regulation of fisheries in the central part of the Arctic Ocean could be partly dealt with within the framework of the 2018 Agreement on prevention of unregulated fisheries on the high seas in the Central Arctic Ocean,[46] which directly or indirectly involves (through participation in the EU) all member States of the AC and major non-Arctic fishing powers (China, the EU, Japan, Iceland, South Korea). In future, the agenda could include cooperation between the AC and NEAFC over a small area in the central part of the Arctic Ocean, covered by the NEAFC's mandate.

22.4.3 *Greater Involvement of Non-Arctic States*

As mentioned previously, in order to ensure that the IEBMM mechanism works well in the entire Arctic region, including in ABNJ, where non-regional States enjoy certain freedoms and rights, it should engage a wide group of non-Arctic stakeholders. Certainly, cooperation of the Arctic regional mechanism with global and regional sectoral organizations would contribute to resolving this problem, since their membership is much broader than that of the Arctic Council. But apart from that the AC has another powerful resource to tackle this challenge – the pool of its observer States.

To date, thirteen non-Arctic nations as well as twenty-seven international and non-governmental organizations are observers to the AC. Observers are invited to meetings and other activities of the Arctic Council and contribute to its work primarily at the level of working groups.[47] However, the role of observers has recently become an issue of major concern both for the Arctic States and for third countries. The scope of their capabilities in the AC is significantly limited. They may, at the discretion of the chair, make statements after the Arctic States and Permanent Participant. Observers are not entitled to participate in the decision-making process and to propose projects independently, while total financial contributions from all observers to any given project may not exceed the financing from Arctic States.[48] What is more important in relation to IEBMM: observers are not invited to participate in negotiations of legally binding agreements under the auspices of the AC. All three agreements mentioned here were signed by the eight Arctic States only. Though the 2018 Fishery Agreement for the Central Part of the Arctic Ocean was negotiated with non-Arctic States, it was concluded outside of the AC. Few observers seem to be satisfied with their position in the Council, with some

[46] Agreement to Prevent Unregulated High Seas Fisheries in the Central Arctic Ocean, signed 3 October 2018.

[47] Arctic Council Rules of Procedure as revised by the Arctic Council at the Eighth Arctic Council Ministerial Meeting, 15 May 2013.

[48] Ibid.

of them calling for greater transparency, better communication and more opportunities to engage in the work of the AC.[49]

Limitations on the role of observers may be largely motivated by fear on the part of the 'Arctic Eight' to surrender to non-members too much influence over Council activities. On the one hand, this is a natural concern on the part of regional nations. But on the other, the AC could make better use of its observers to implement IEBMM measures for the Arctic Ocean. This could facilitate engagement of third States in implementing decisions developed by the AC or within other regional fora, as well as in promoting joint initiatives in international organization, provided that observers are more intensively involved in discussion and development of recommendations within the working bodies of the AC. To start with, the Arctic Council could consider promoting global awareness of issues related to sustainable development of the Arctic and polar competence-building in the observer States.

22.4.4 *Coordination of Research Efforts in the Arctic*

One of the main prerequisites of a potent IEBMM mechanism is support by scientific groups. The Arctic Council's definition of the Ecosystem Approach implies that integrated management of human activities should be based on 'best available scientific and traditional knowledge about the ecosystem and its dynamics, in order to identify and take' management actions.[50] This principle can also be traced to the practice of other regional instruments.

A wide range of scientific groups are active in the Arctic: ICES, PICES, the Pacific Arctic Group (PAG) of the International Arctic Science Committee (IASC), bilateral Russian-US and Russian-Norwegian Fisheries Commissions and the like. However, it is often recognized[51] that none of them is dedicated to coordinating integrated marine science activity throughout the entire Arctic Ocean, as well as transferring research results to regional institutions for management decision-making (except for ICES[52]). For instance, the geographic area of ICES, with all the eight Arctic States being parties to it, covers the Atlantic Ocean with an explicit emphasis on the North Atlantic and touches only a part of the Arctic.[53] PICES is an

[49] Balton and Ulmer (n 40), 7.

[50] Report submitted to the Senior Arctic Officials by the Expert Group on Ecosystem-Based Management, May 2013. Available at: https://oaarchive.arctic-council.org/bitstream/handle/11374/1210/Doc3-7a_EBM_Experts_Group_Report_to_SAOs.pdf?sequence=1&isAllowed=y

[51] Baker, B., 'ICES, PICES, and the Arctic Council Task Force on Arctic Marine Cooperation' (2016) *UC Irvine Law Review* 6(1), 4.

[52] 'ICES stocktaking of its role and capabilities in ocean and coastal sustainability', Report of the International Council for the Exploration of the Sea (2012). Available at: https://perma.cc/KJ7Y-UPW3, 1.

[53] Convention for The International Council for the Exploration of the Sea, adopted 12 September, 1964.

organization similar to ICES, active in the Northern Pacific, which adjoins only three Arctic States. Besides, unlike ICES, it does not provide management advice to competent authorities. Despite the fact that the area of IASC covers the entire marine Arctic and the range of research issues is quite wide, this scientific organization was created 'bottom-up' – by scientists' initiative and efforts. This is a nongovernmental organization with all relevant challenges in funding, especially for research across national boundaries.[54]

Today, discussion is ongoing on the issue of how to proceed towards coordinating and accumulating marine scientific research for the purposes of IEBMM.[55] Some experts believe that, despite notable efforts by various research organizations in the Arctic, currently gaps remain in scientific understanding of the marine Arctic, especially in its central part. In that light, they suggest that there is a need to establish a new stand-alone coordination mechanism.[56] Others consider such a measure premature and suggest amending the mandates of existing mechanisms, in particular, ICES, instead of establishing an entirely new scientific organization.[57]

It would certainly seem feasible to work towards a comprehensive integrated regional programme within the Arctic Council for scientific research for the purpose of adopting scientific-based decisions related to spatial planning in the Arctic Ocean. Both national scientific organizations of the AC member States and external international scientific organizations and programmes could participate in such initiatives, including IASC and ICES, among others. A good starting point could be establishment of the mechanism under the 2018 Agreement on prevention of unregulated fisheries in the central part of the Arctic Ocean. This could provide a platform for a subsequent build-up of coordinated research of marine ecosystems in the region.

22.5 WAYS FORWARD

Implementation of integrated ecosystem-based marine management in the Arctic will be associated with major challenges, both legal and organizational. This refers to the need to ensure that ecosystem-based measures are in full compliance with international law, especially in terms of ABNJ, finding ways to engage non-regional countries in complying with IEBMM measures in ABNJ, as well as tackling the problem of achieving a cross-sectoral effect of ecosystem-based management by coordination among different marine industries.

54 Van Pelt, T., Huntington, H. P., Romanenko, O. V. et al., 'The missing middle: Central Arctic Ocean gaps in fishery research and science coordination' (2017) *Marine Policy* 85, 79–86. doi: 84.10.1016/j.marpol.2017.08.008, 84.

55 See, e.g., ibid., 85; Baker, 'ICES, PICES' (n 51) 19.

56 Van Pelt et al. (n 54), 85; Balton and Zagorski (n 41), 18.

57 Baker, 'ICES, PICES' (n 51) 19.

Solutions to these challenges would seem to lie in unfolding the Arctic Council's potential. Efficient implementation of IEBMM tools is possible through a significant build-up of the AC: moving towards endowing the AC with international legal personality; transforming the AC Secretariat into an authoritative Commission with relevant functions similar to that of the OSPAR Commission. Bearing in mind, however, the limited possibilities of the Arctic Council to adopt binding decisions restricting third States' rights and freedoms in marine ABNJ, additional measures would also be reasonable. The AC could play the central role in coordinating IEBMM tools (such as applying marine spatial planning or creation of marine protected areas) with global and regional sectoral organizations active in the Arctic. This includes: the IMO in relation to shipping; the NEAFC and possible future mechanisms under the 2018 Agreement on fisheries in the central part of the Arctic Ocean; and the ISA in relation to exploration and exploitation of the resources of the Area (long-term perspective). Collaboration with these institutions with much broader membership would also provide compliance with AC policies by third States parties to these organizations. However, the mandates of global and regional sectoral organizations do not cover all economic activities that could pose a potential threat to the marine environment in the Arctic. This refers to reduction of marine environmental pollution from land-based sources, the oil and gas industries, construction of artificial islands and installations, laying cables and so on, which should be the subject of further consideration.

A more rational use by the AC of its observers could also serve the purposes of IEBMM: observers could be involved to a larger extent in discussions on relevant regional regulations; they could be allowed to participate in negotiations of legally binding agreements and to sign them. Synergetic effects could be further increased by establishing a regional scientific programme within the AC (or under its auspices) aimed at systematic planning, coordination and integration of scientific research for the purpose of introducing the integrated approach to marine management.

23

Understanding Japan's Resumption of Commercial Whaling under International Law

Constantinos Yiallourides[*]

23.1 WHALING UNDER INTERNATIONAL LAW: AN ONGOING DEBATE

On 1 July 2019, Japan officially withdrew from the International Convention for the Regulation of Whaling (ICRW)[1] and resumed commercial whaling after nearly 31 years.[2] On this very date, the Japanese government announced that a maximum of 383 minke, Bryde's and sei whales would be caught during its first annual whaling tour within its exclusive economic zone (EEZ) of 200 nautical miles.[3] The Japanese whaling fleet, which had been conducting scientific whaling in the high seas, has resumed commercial whaling but limited to the Pacific coasts of Japan and not the Sea of Japan or the East China Sea. All other whaling operations are conducted on Japan's Pacific side except for areas off the coasts of Hokkaido that face the Sea of Okhotsk.[4] This maritime area is much narrower compared to Japan's previous whaling area in the Antarctic Ocean (see Figure 23.1).

On 8 October 2019, the whaling fleet 'Nisshin Maru' reportedly returned having captured 187 Bryde's whales (about 1,171 tons), 25 sei whales (about 232 tons) and 11 minke whales (about 23 tons), totalling approximately 1,426 tons of whale meat.[5]

* Arthur Watts Research Fellow in the Law of the Sea, British Institute of International & Comparative Law. Email: c.yiallourides@BIICL.ORG.

1 International Convention for the Regulation of Whaling (adopted 2 December 1946, entered into force 10 November 1948) UNTS Vol 161 (72).

2 Ministry of Foreign Affairs of Japan (26 December 2018); Press Secretary of the Ministry of Foreign Affairs, 'Japan Is Committed to the Conservation of Whales' (*New York Times*, 11 January 2019).

3 Minke whale: 171; Bryde's whale: 187; Sei whales: 25, Fisheries Agency Statement of 1 July 2019 <www.jfa.maff.go.jp/j/press/kokusai/190701.html>.

4 Junko Sakuma, 'Gains and Loses of Japan's Withdrawal from the International Whaling Commission' (*Asahi*, 9 January 2019).

5 'Commercial Whaling Vessel Nisshin Maru Returned to Port' (Keizai Daily News, 8 October 2019) [translation from Japanese] <https://bit.ly/2vpD5YE>.

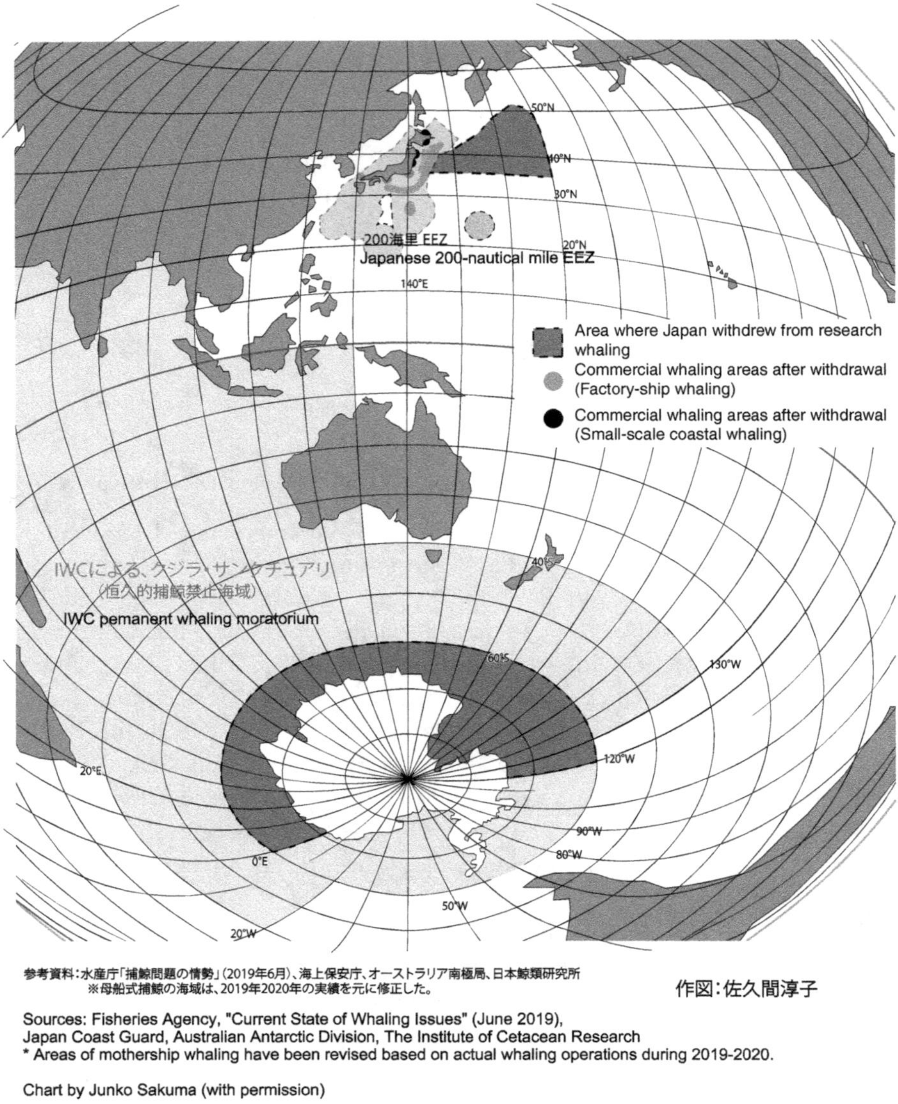

FIGURE 23.1. Japan's past and current whaling areas

On 24 February 2020, the fleet embarked on a new whaling tour in Japan's South-Eastern EEZ. The first 2020 catch was announced on 3 March: a Bryde's whale (about 14.85 tons).[6] In July 2020, the Japanese government released the 2020 catch

[6] 'First Catch in 2020' (*Blog of Kyodo Senpaku*, 3 March 2020).

quotas for Minke, Bryde's and Sei whales and stated that these are 'substantially equal to those for 2019'.[7]

The literature has detailed the rules and objectives of the ICRW;[8] the work of the International Whaling Commission (IWC), which was established in 1948 to implement the ICRW;[9] and litigation under the ICRW.[10] This chapter builds on existing scholarship and presents the reasons for, and possible implications of, Japan's decision to withdraw from the ICRW and resume commercial whaling in its EEZ from 1 July 2019.[11] This chapter places the issue of whaling within the overall environmental law debate and explains that promotion of the international rule of law in the field of commercial whaling calls for positive cooperation at the international level to promote the conservation and sustainable use of whale stocks. To illustrate this, the discussion provides an overview of Japan's approach towards environmental conservation and living resources management in the light of the applicable rules of international law, especially under UNCLOS and the ICRW. The chapter argues that, despite its withdrawal from the ICRW, Japan remains under a continuing obligation to cooperate meaningfully with other States through the appropriate international organizations, including the IWC, for the conservation and management of the marine natural resources presented by whales. Equally, other interested States remain under a continuing obligation to cooperate with Japan for the same purpose. Nevertheless, the degree or means of cooperation required by Japan and other interested States to fulfil their legal duty to cooperate under international law lacks clarity. It is further argued that whilst Japan is under a positive duty to adopt a precautionary approach to whaling within its EEZ, application of the precautionary approach does not generally prescribe what measures must be taken at the national level. The lessons that ought to be learnt from Japan's withdrawal by the global protagonists of whaling and the rule of law implications in light of unclarity in the applicable legal framework have been articulated as concluding remarks.

7 Government of Japan, Fisheries Agency, 'Fisheries White Paper, 5 June 2020' Government of Japan, Fisheries Agency, 'Whaling Catch Quotas 2020' <www.jfa.maff.go.jp/e/whale/attach/pdf/index-7.pdf>

8 Malgosia Fitzmaurice, 'International Convention for the Regulation of Whaling and International Whaling Commission: Conservation or Preservation – Can the Gordian Knot Be Cut (or Untangled)' (2013) 5 *Yearbook of Polar Law* 451.

9 William C. G. Burns and Geoffrey Wandesforde-Smith, 'The International Whaling Commission and the Future of Cetaceans in a Changing World' (2002) 11(2) *Review of European Community & International Environmental Law* 199.

10 Malgosia Fitzmaurice, *Whaling and International Law* (Cambridge: Cambridge University Press 2015) 88–122.

11 Atsuko Kanehara, 'Japan's Withdrawal from the International Convention for the Regulation of Whaling' (2019) 62 *Japanese Yearbook of International Law* 376–387.

23.2 WHALING IN RELATION TO MARINE ENVIRONMENTAL PROTECTION

Pro-whaling nations, such as Japan, and anti-whaling nations and environmental non-governmental organizations (NGOs), such as Australia and Greenpeace respectively, have fundamentally different approaches to the matter. Anti-whaling parties' rhetoric is largely focused on emotion and ethics: the whale is presented as a beautiful and highly intelligent living creature that should not be exploited.[12] An image has been created of a 'super whale' drawing on all whale species: the whale is the largest animal on earth (the blue whale); it has the largest brain on earth (the sperm whale); it sings nicely (the humpback whale); it is friendly (the grey whale); it is endangered (the blue whale); and the like. Some States that favour whaling, such as Norway and Japan, criticize this emotional approach. They assert that the core issue for natural resource sustainability is neither the animal per se nor its appearance or intelligence, but protection and conservation of the marine environment, its flora and its fauna.[13] Such States posit the key question: should the management, conservation and sustainable use of the marine natural resources be (re)presented by whales? These States argue this is a legal and scientific question on protection of the marine environment and, in particular, the sustainable management of whale stocks.

These two approaches embody, according to Fitzmaurice, 'the tension between, or the binary of, on the one hand, the expressly commercial objective of conserving and managing whale stocks in order to provide for the "orderly development of the whaling industry", and on the other the recognition that whales are a "general trust" to be safeguarded for future generations'.[14] Ethical issues, including surrounding animal rights and cultural diversity, permeate the whaling debate.[15] Some animal rights theories suggest whaling should be banned altogether as animals enjoy a full right to life.[16] Conversely, theories based on cultural diversity or cultural identity assert the need to protect the cultural rights

[12] Michael Heazle, *Scientific Uncertainty and the Politics of Whaling* (Washington, DC: University of Washington Press 2006) 170.

[13] As Morishita explains, 'There are more than 80 different species of cetaceans and the statement ["whales are endangered"] is as wrong as stating that "birds are endangered"', Joji Morishita, 'Multiple Analysis of the Whaling Issue: Understanding the Dispute by a Matrix' (2006) 30 *Marine Policy* 802, 803.

[14] Fitzmaurice, *Whaling and International Law* (n 10) 34.

[15] Morishita (n 13) 802–808; Fitzmaurice, *Whaling and International Law* (n 10) 123–181.

[16] Anthony D'Amato and Sudhir Chopra, 'Whales: Their Emerging Right to Life' (1991) 85 *American Journal of International Law* 21; Catherine Redgwell, 'Life, the Universe and Everything: A Critique of Anthropocentric Rights' in Alan Boyle and Michael Anderson (eds.) *Human Rights Approaches to Environmental Protection* (Oxford: Oxford University Press 1996) 71–75.

of nations that have historically engaged in whaling.[17] Many other theories relevant to environmental policy, which draw for instance on moral philosophy and bioethics, cannot be explored fully in this chapter.[18] These theories are largely relative and depend on one's standpoint, personal views and emotions. Their application within UNCLOS, the ICRW and other relevant environmental treaties is not without problems.[19] Ethical values and attitudes differ among people and States, including depending on whether they practise whaling. There are strong emotions on all sides of the ethical and cultural whaling debate.[20]

What Japan and other pro-whaling States see as essential is not blanket preservation of individual animals based on emotions and ethics, but protection of the holistic whole, the marine environment, based on law and science.[21] International law takes an expansive view of 'marine environmental protection'. The totality of Articles 192–196 of the UNCLOS indicates that protection and preservation of the marine environment encompasses protection of ecosystems and conservation of living resources and depleted or endangered species of marine life.[22] Thus, the task at hand is to weigh those pro-whaling States' legal and scientific evidence of conservation and sustainable use against the competing evidence of anti-whaling States in light of applicable rules and principles of international law.

As the present chapter argues, promoting the international rule of law in the field of whaling lies in compromise and meaningful cooperation between the global protagonists of whaling. Maintaining inflexible assertions without being prepared to make concessions in pursuit of common ground neither conserves nor protects fragile whale stocks for generations to come. Instead, it alienates key whaling players, thus undermining whatever chances for meaningful international cooperation may have existed while rendering existing legal instruments incapable of implementation and enforcement.[23]

17 Fitzmaurice, *Whaling and International Law* (n 10) 148–149.

18 Ibid., 123.

19 Ibid., 168.

20 Ibid., 147.

21 D'Amato and Chopra (n 16) 451, 455; Fitzmaurice *Whaling and International Law* (n 10) 147.

22 In the South China Sea arbitration, the Annex VII tribunal noted that ' … the obligations in Part XII apply to all States with respect to the marine environment in all maritime areas, both inside the national jurisdiction of States and beyond it', *The South China Sea Arbitration (Philippines* v. *China)* (Merits) (Award of 12 July 2016) para. 940.

23 Malgosia Fitzmaurice, 'International Convention for the Regulation of Whaling' (United Nations Audiovisual Library of International Law 2017) <https://legal.un.org/avl/pdf/ha/icrw/icrw_e.pdf>.

23.2.1 *Legality of Whaling and the Precautionary Approach*

Under present international law, whales are an exploitable marine living resource and States possess, in principle, 'a legal right to whale'.[24] The UNCLOS preamble endorses the 'equitable and efficient utilization' of marine living resources in conformity with 'protection and preservation of the marine environment'.[25] A coastal State has a legal right to authorize and regulate exploitation of marine living resources, including whales, within its territorial sea[26] and EEZ.[27] This right is subject to due regard obligations and a legal duty to cooperate 'with a view to ensuring conservation and promoting the objective of *optimum utilization*' (emphasis added) of highly migratory species listed in Annex I of UNCLOS.[28] Category 17 of Annex I encompasses seven families of whales: sperm, blue, humpback, minke, bowhead, grey and narwhal whales. UNCLOS also allows the sustainable exploitation of marine living resources on the high seas.[29]

States decide whether or not they wish to harvest whales. The IWC determines which and how many whale species member States can harvest. The ICRW preamble includes 'the proper conservation of whale stocks and . . . the orderly development of the whaling industry' as an aim.[30] Similarly to UNCLOS, the ICRW discusses sustainable exploitation by employing expressions such as achieving the 'optimum level of whale stocks', 'confined to those species best able to sustain exploitation' and safeguarding for future generations 'the great natural resources represented by the whale stocks'.[31] The ICRW preamble further recognizes that 'whale stocks are susceptible of natural increases if whaling is properly regulated, and that increases in the size of whale stocks will permit increases in the number of whales which may be captured without endangering these natural resources'.[32] It adds that 'it is in the common interest to achieve the optimum level of whale stocks as rapidly as possible without causing widespread economic and nutritional distress'.[33] The ICRW seeks to balance the objective of protecting and conserving whale stocks against the objective of managing and utilizing whale stocks, thus

[24] Steinar Andresen, 'The International Whaling Regime: Order at the Turn of the Century?' in Davor Vidas and Willy Østreng (eds.) *Order for the Oceans at the Turn of the Century* (Dordrecht: Kluwer Law 1999) 215, 218.

[25] Preamble, UNCLOS.

[26] Art. 2 UNCLOS provides that the sovereignty of a coastal State extends to the territorial sea.

[27] Art. 56 UNCLOS gives coastal States 'exclusive sovereign rights' for the purpose of exploring and exploiting, conserving and managing the living resources occurring within their EEZ subject to 'due regard' for obligations with respect to the rights and duties of other States.

[28] Art. 7(1)(b) UNCLOS.

[29] Art. 120 UNCLOS.

[30] Preamble, ICRW.

[31] Ibid.

[32] Ibid.

[33] Ibid.

preserving the whaling industry.[34] The International Court of Justice (ICJ) found that these objectives had remained essentially unchanged in the *Whaling in the Antarctic* case.[35]

Can commercial whaling take place without severely depleting whale stocks and, hence, without harming the marine environment of which whales form an inalienable part? This is the chief question when ascertaining the legality of exploiting whale resources under UNCLOS and the ICRW. The answer is not straightforward. Science has not so far provided definite answers about the population dynamics of certain whale species and the impact of human-related and climatic factors on those species.[36] Scientists remain unsure of how many whales exist, how marine pollution disturbs their habitat, how declining fisheries affect their food supply and how whaling impairs their ability to survive.[37] Other scientists argue that 'difficulties in dealing with uncertain data were exacerbated by strong personal philosophies, which in some cases were influenced by national positions'.[38] Morishita, Japan's leading marine scientist, writes that 'with greatly advanced scientific knowledge about whales and wildlife management and new technologies available today, sustainable whaling is possible'.[39]

Even in the absence of conclusive scientific evidence linking commercial whaling to permanent environmental damage, it may be argued that the precautionary approach is applicable to exploitation of whales as a means of ensuring effective conservation and preventing serious harm to whale stocks.[40] This is particularly true in light of the *Southern Bluefin Tuna* case.[41] There, ITLOS's references to 'scientific uncertainty' focused on the relevance of the precautionary approach to the interpretation and application of UNCLOS.[42] Judges Laing and Treves stressed this point

[34] Fitzmaurice, *Whaling and International Law* (n 10) 43–45.

[35] *Whaling in the Antarctic (Australia v Japan: New Zealand intervening)* (Judgment) [2014] ICJ Rep 226 paras. 56–58; Fitzmaurice, *Whaling and International Law* (n 10) 178.

[36] Fitzmaurice, 'Can the Gordian Knot Be Cut (or Untangled)' (n 8) 51–54.

[37] Cinnamon Pinion Carlane, 'Saving the Whales in the New Millennium: International Institutions, Recent Developments and the Future of International Whaling Policies' (2005) 24 *Virginia Environmental Law Journal* 1, 32–45.

[38] Joji Morishita and Dan Goodman, 'Role and Problems of the Scientific Committee of the International Whaling Commission in terms of Conservation and Sustainable Utilization of Whale Stocks' (2005) 9(2) *Global Environmental Research* 157–166.

[39] Joji Morishita, 'Resumption of Whaling and the Principle of Sustainable Use' (2002) *Ship and Ocean Newsletter* No 4, 10.

[40] *Whaling in the Antarctic* (Sep Op Charlesworth) ICJ Rep 226, 455; *Responsibilities and Obligations of States with Respect to Activities in the Area* (Advisory Opinion, 1 February 2011) ITLOS Reports 2011; *Gabcikovo-Nagymaros Project (Hungary v. Slovakia)* (Judgment) (Sep Op Judge Weeramantry) reprinted in (1998) 37 *International Legal Materials* 162, 215.

[41] *Southern Bluefin Tuna (New Zealand v. Japan; Australia v. Japan)* (Provisional Measures) (1999) ITLOS Rep 280 para. 70.

[42] Ibid., para. 74.

in their separate opinions: environmental legal instruments should be interpreted and applied in light of the precautionary approach.[43]

The IWC halted commercial whaling by adopting 'zero quotas' on whale hunting in 1982. Some commentators viewed this blanket moratorium as application of the precautionary approach to commercial whaling: preventive action should be taken even in the absence of clear evidence as to the necessity for such measures before damage has been determined.[44] Voigt describes several factors that are not directly associated with the exploitation of whales and make a prediction of impacts on marine life, and hence whale populations, virtually impossible.[45] Such factors include climate change (global warming affects oceanographic conditions and harms zooplankton species krill, whales' primary source of food in the Southern Hemisphere) and chemical and noise pollution (marine contaminants and underwater noise pollution may pose long term threats to marine mammals' living conditions, but the precise impact of these threats must be further investigated).[46]

23.2.2 *Whaling in Japan's Environmental and Ocean Policy*

Understanding Japan's approach towards commercial whaling requires starting from Japan's legal system for protection of the marine environment and conservation of marine natural resources. The Japanese legal system takes an expansive view of the definition of the environment, be it terrestrial or maritime. The Japanese Basic Environment Law of 1993 states that its principal purpose is to promote 'environmental conservation' to prevent among others 'decrease in wildlife species and others which are caused by human activities and affect the environment of the entire globe or a large part of it . . .'[47] The same law stipulates that 'environmental harm or damage' (*kogai* in Japanese) includes any interference with environmental conservation 'as a result of business and other human activities, which cause damage to human health or the living environment (including property closely related to human life, as well as fauna and flora closely related to human life and their living environment)'.[48]

43 Ibid. (Sep Op Judge Laing) paras. 16–19 and (Sep Op Judge Treves) para. 9.

44 Fitzmaurice, 'Can the Gordian Knot Be Cut (or Untangled)' (n 8) 453–454.

45 Christina Voigt, 'A Precautionary Approach to the Whaling Convention: Will the ICJ Challenge the Legality of Scientific Whaling?' in Inge Lorange Backer, Ole Kristian Fauchald, and Christina Voigt (eds.) *Pro Natura: Festskrift til Hans Christian Bugge* (Oslo: Universitetsforlaget 2012) 557, 575–781 <https://papers.ssrn.com/sol3/papers.cfm?abstract_id=2430723>

46 Ibid.

47 Art. 1, Basic Environmental Law (Law No 91 of 1993) (JPN) <https://www.env.go.jp/en/laws/policy/basic/index.html>.

48 Ibid., Art. 2(3); Yumiko Nakanishi (ed.), *Contemporary Issues in Environmental Law: The EU and Japan* (Berlin, Heidelberg, New York: Springer 2016) 1–13.

Japan's Basic Act on Ocean Policy of 2007 (Ocean Act) introduces a utilitarian approach to marine environmental conservation.[49] The Ocean Act connects, on the one hand, marine biological diversity and marine environmental protection to, on the other, the prosperity of the Japanese people and development of the Japanese economy. It states: 'securing marine biological diversity and conserving the marine environment are the basis of the existence of mankind and also *indispensable for prosperous and affluent lives of the citizenry*' (emphasis added).[50] This connection is likely truer for Japan than other G-20 countries, given Japan's heavy reliance on seafood to support its national economy and society. Commentators defend Japan's position on whaling on the basis of whaling's contribution to Japan's 'food self-sufficiency'.[51] Others note that appetite for whale meat is 'embedded in the Japanese psyche' and should therefore continue to be a source of food.[52] However, whaling is no longer a major industry in Japan, and whale meat consumption in the country had declined even before the 1982 moratorium.[53] Whale constituted around 3 per cent of overall meat consumption in 1981.[54] Japanese government subsidies keep the country's whaling industry on life-support and current trends suggest commercial whaling may become unprofitable in the long term.[55]

The Ocean Act sets out the general principles and objectives guiding the development and use of Japan's waters and marine natural resources 'in harmonization of the peaceful and positive development and use of the oceans with ... conservation of the marine environment'.[56] This aspires to 'contributing to the sound development of the economy and society', 'supporting industries bearing the development, use and conservation of the oceans' (referred to as 'Oceanic Industries') and improving 'the stability of the lives of citizens'.[57] The Ocean Act states that the Japanese government undertakes three policy objectives. First, to promote the 'sound development of Japan's Ocean Industries'.[58] The central Government, through the Ministry of Agriculture, Forestry and Fisheries (MAFF) and its Fisheries Agency,

49 Basic Act on Ocean Policy <www8.cao.go.jp/ocean/english/act/pdf/law_e.pdf>.

50 Art. 2, ibid.

51 Kate Barclay and Charlotte Epstein, 'Securing Fish for the Nation: Food Security and Governmentality in Japan' (2008) 37(2) *Asian Studies Review* 215.

52 Arne Kalland, 'Aboriginal Subsistence Whaling: A Concept in the Service of Imperialism' in Georg Blichfeldt (ed.) *11 Essays on Whale and Man* (2nd ed., High North Alliance 1994) 5; Yasuo Lino and Dan Goodman, 'Japan's Position in the International Whaling Commission' in William C. G. Burns and Alexander Gillespie (eds.) *The Future of Cetaceans in a Changing World* (Transnational Publishers 2003) 3, 7–8.

53 Junko Sakuma, 'The Repercussions of the Documentary Film *The Cove*: Unravelling the Real Nature of the Whaling Problem the Film and the Two Counter-Movies Failed to Uncover' (2018) 60 *Journal of Applied Sociology* 251 (in Japanese).

54 Credit: Junko Sakuma (2018).

55 Annual Budget Report, Cetacean Research Institute (Estimated Budget for 1 April 2019; to 31 March 2020); Kanehara (n 11) 384.

56 Art. 1, Basic Act on Ocean Policy (n 49).

57 Ibid.

58 Art. 5, Basic Act on Ocean Policy (n 49).

have a legal duty to ensure the proper conservation and management of fisheries resources; secure a stable supply of fishery products; and support the development of the fishing industry. As whaling is part of fisheries in Japanese law, the Government has a legal duty to promote its sound development.[59] Of note here, the ICRW also uses the expression 'whale fisheries', which raises the 'assumption of similarity in nature' between whaling and commercial fishing.[60]

Second, to improve 'scientific knowledge of the oceans' through 'ocean science and technology' programmes as an 'indispensable [condition] for the proper development and use of the oceans and conservation of the marine environment'.[61] Scientific programmes on the study, conversation and development of whale stocks fall under this policy objective.

Third, to 'formulate a basic plan with regard to the oceans'.[62] This plan would prescribe necessary measures for the 'conservation and management of living aquatic resources, conservation and improvement of the growing environment for aquatic plants and animals, increase of fishing ground productivity'.[63] The Basic Plan on Ocean Policy was published for the first time in 2008 and was revised in 2013 and 2018. The first edition (2008) recognized that 'realization of sustainable use of finite major fishery resources has become an urgent issue for international society'.[64] It further added that 'it is important for Japan to make efforts to gain the understanding and support of the international society widely for its basic stance to seek sustainable use of marine living resources'.[65]

The second edition (2013) first repeated the long-established maxim that 'the development and use of the oceans are the basis of existence for the economy and society of [the Japanese] State'.[66] It then directs the Japanese government to '*elicit the potential of the sea to the maximum extent* in order to bring wealth and prosperity to [the] country ... while seeking to harmonize the development and use of the oceans with conservation of the marine environment' (emphasis added).[67] The Ocean Plan, conscious of issues raised by Japan's whaling activities, also called on the Government to: '[s]afely conduct whale research programmes, and continually implement initiatives to gain a wider international understanding of Japan's stance to realize sustainable use of whale stocks based on scientific evidence'.[68]

[59] See also Art. 24, Basic Act on Ocean Policy (n 49); under Japanese law, marine mammals, including whales, are excluded from the regulations of the Wildlife Protection and Hunting Law and come under the jurisdiction of the Fisheries Agency and the Fishery Resource Conservation Law.
[60] Preamble and Art. II (6), ICRW.
[61] Arts. 4 and 23, Basic Act on Ocean Policy (n 49).
[62] Ibid., Art. 16.
[63] Ibid., Art. 17.
[64] Basic Plan on Ocean Policy (March 2008) 20.
[65] Ibid., 20–22.
[66] Basic Plan on Ocean Policy (April 2013) 2.
[67] Ibid.
[68] Ibid., 20.

The third and most recent edition of the Ocean Plan (2018) directs the Government, through global initiatives 'to lead the world on measures to protect the environment and to promote the integrity of environmental protection and the sustainable use and development of the ocean by cultivating sound marine industries'.[69] The Plan stresses that: 'It is necessary to increase the effectiveness of environmental protection and to develop a *win-win relationship with sustainable development and environmental protection*' (emphasis added).[70] The Ocean Plan envisages the expansion of 'ocean-based businesses', including the fishing industry, as contributors to national economic growth.[71] On commercial whaling, the Ocean Plan states that, in anticipation of resumption of commercial whaling, Japan will continue discussing the issue of whaling with stakeholder countries and conducting scientific whaling based on Japanese law.[72]

23.2.3 *Public Opinion on Whaling and Implications on Policy-Making in Japan*

Japanese public opinion on whaling is an important factor, which is not directly relevant to Part XII of UNCLOS but which impacts Japan's ocean policy-making and has played a crucial role in its decision to resume commercial whaling. Several nationwide opinion polls have included questions concerning whaling.[73] A 2011 survey by the Associated Press asked whether commercial whaling and the subsequent sale of whale meat were supported: 52 per cent said yes, 35 per cent were indifferent and only 13 per cent said no.[74] Thus, while only a small fraction of the Japanese public consumes whale meat, a majority supports commercial whaling to produce whale meat.[75]

Reasons underpinning this discrepancy are unclear. Holm writes that despite a sharp decline in whale meat consumption, the Japanese public has in recent years become more involved in traditional whaling culture.[76] Whaling is seen as the 'symbolic continuation of a genuine whaling culture from the Edo period and has become more significant for the Japanese population and politicians in recent years'.[77] Indeed, many Japanese coastal communities, so-called whaling towns, 'have

69 Basic Plan on Ocean Policy (March 2018) 15.

70 Ibid., 15–16 and 22.

71 Ibid., 29.

72 Ibid., 77; Act No. 76 of 2017 (JPN).

73 Data provided to the author by Junko Sakuma (March 2018).

74 The 2011 public survey results can be accessed here: <https://search.e-gov.go.jp/servlet/Public?CLASSNAME=PCMMSTDETAIL&id=550002675&Mode=2> (in Japanese).

75 Amy L. Catalinac and Gerald Chan, 'Japan, the West, and the Whaling Issue: Understanding the Japanese Side' (2005) 17(1) *Japan Forum* 133, 148–149.

76 Fynn Holm, 'Japan's Walfangpolitik: Die Gründe für den Austritt aus der Internationalen Walfangkommission' in Chiavacci and Wieczorek (eds.) *Japan 2019: Politik, Wirtschaft, Gesellschaft* (München: Iudicium 2019) 126.

77 Ibid.

inextricably linked the continued existence and rebuilding of their towns with coastal whaling operations'.[78] The Japanese delegation has made repeated efforts before the IWC to allow these communities to carry out limited small-scale coastal whaling to protect their traditional lifestyle and ensure their economic survival.[79] These efforts have been unsuccessful, despite the conclusions of a scientific report suggesting that the IWC create a 'separable and definable category' of small-scale whaling with overlapping elements of both aboriginal and commercial whaling.[80]

Other authors suggest that constant anti-whaling campaigns by Western environmental NGOs since the 1960s have contributed to growing 'whale nationalism (*kujira nashonarizumu*).[81] As Maekawa and Fukuda explain, although the Japanese public should be indifferent to whaling in general, 'it is a recent characteristic that when foreigners criticize the whale issue, strong nationalistic calls such as "this is the arrogance of the West" or "Japanese food culture must be protected" suddenly appear'.[82]

At any rate, if the Japanese public – for whatever reasons – broadly supports whaling and if Japanese basic ocean policy is to support Japan's oceanic industries, the Japanese government has a vested interest in acting on this mandate.

23.3 JAPAN'S RESUMPTION OF COMMERCIAL WHALING UNDER INTERNATIONAL LAW

Japan has resumed commercial whaling within its EEZ and emphasized in its domestic laws, regulations and public rhetoric that whaling will only be conducted in a sustainable and transparent manner based on science.[83] This is in essence what the international rule of law in the maritime domain calls for, according to Japan. Indeed, Japan's whaling policy is based on a straightforward principle: 'being a food resource, if whale populations can sustain a controlled harvest then there is no reason to prohibit their utilization for human consumption'.[84] The government of Japan was legally entitled to leave the ICRW: Article XI of the ICRW expressly

[78] Fynn Holm, 'After Withdrawal from the IWC: The Future of Japanese Whaling' (2019) 17(4) *The Asia-Pacific Journal* 1–16.

[79] Fitzmaurice, *Whaling and International Law* (n 10) 78–87, 121.

[80] Tomoya Akimichi and others, *Small-Type Coastal Whaling in Japan: Report of an International Workshop* (Alberta: University of Alberta Press 1988) 84.

[81] Ben Dooley and Hisako Ueno, 'Do People in Japan Actually Want Commercial Whaling to Resume After Three Decades?' (*The Independent*, 2 July 2019).

[82] Yūsuke Maekawa and Masahiko Fukada, 'The Fate of Whaling: Future of Japanese Whaling Driven into Difficult Situation' (*Newsweek*, 15 April 2014) (in Japanese).

[83] Kanehara (n 11) 380.

[84] Catalinac and Chan (n 75) 133, 153.

provides for the ability of a State party to withdraw from the ICRW.[85] Japan gave formal notice of its withdrawal on 26 December 2018 and, hence, stopped being bound by the ICRW on 30 June 2019.[86] So, what are the possible rule-of-law ramifications of Japan's decision to resume commercial whaling?

Despite its withdrawal, Japan remains under a general obligation to cooperate with other States 'either directly or through appropriate subregional or regional organizations' for the conservation and management of species occurring across jurisdictions (Article 63 of UNCLOS) and of highly migratory species, including several whale species (Article 64 of UNCLOS and Annex I).[87] The obligation to cooperate in relation to marine environmental protection is reinforced by Article 65 of UNCLOS, which notably provides that:

> States shall cooperate with a view to the conservation of marine mammals and in the case of cetaceans shall in particular *work through the appropriate international organizations* for their conservation, management and study (emphasis added).[88]

Article 65 is UNCLOS's 'principal marine mammal provision'.[89] However, this provision is subject to important ambiguities and limitations. Two points merit highlighting. The first concerns the meaning of the 'appropriate international organizations'. UNCLOS does not specify which body, or bodies, is 'the appropriate international organization' through which States must cooperate with respect to the management and conservation of whales.[90] The literature shows some consensus on whaling regulation: the IWC, that is, the body entrusted with implementation of the ICRW, is the principal international organization.[91] Section 17 of Agenda 21 of the Rio Conference expressly refers to the IWC as the competent international organization for the conservation and management of whale stocks and regulation of whaling.[92] In addition to the IWC, other international organizations may also have a mandate to conserve and manage whales and, thus, fall within Article 65. The United Nations Division for Ocean Affairs and the Law of the Sea (DOALOS) note

85 Art. XI, ICRW.

86 Art. 70 (1–2), Vienna Convention on the Law of Treaties (23 May 1969) 1155 United Nations Treaty Series 331.

87 Philippe Sands and others, *Principles of International Environmental Law* (4th ed., Cambridge: Cambridge University Press 2018) 215–216.

88 Ted L. Mcdorman (1998) 'Canada and Whaling: An Analysis of Article 65 of the Law of the Sea Convention' (1998) 29(2) *Ocean Development & International Law* 179–194; Patricia W. Birnie, 'Marine Mammals: Exploiting the Ambiguities of Article 65 of the Convention on the Law of the Sea and Related Provisions: Practice under the International Convention for the Regulation of Whaling' in David Freestone, Richard Barnes and David Ong (eds.) *The Law of the Sea: Progress and Prospects* (2006) 261–280; Fitzmaurice, Whaling and International Law (n 10) 214–216.

89 Mcdorman (n 88) 179, 181.

90 Birnie (n 88) 309, 323.

91 Fitzmaurice, 'Can the Gordian Knot Be Cut (or Untangled)' (n 8) 451, 471.

92 United Nations Conference on Environment and Development (1992). www.un.org/Depts/los/consultative_process/documents/A21-Ch17.htm.

these organizations could include the Food and Agricultural Organization (FAO) and the United Nations Environment Programme (UNEP).[93]

Additionally, DOALOS has suggested that 'some organisations may become "competent" in the future' with respect to whaling regulation.[94] Insofar as Article 65 does not specify a single international organization with exclusive authority on whales, other international organizations could reasonably be established for the conservation, management and study of whales.[95] This is particularly important if one considers 'the prevalent atmosphere of confrontation and mistrust among member governments' within the IWC, which has led, according to the Chair and Vice-Chair of the IWC, 'to little progress being made on key practical matters of conservation and management since the early 1990s despite advances at scientific level'[96]. The ongoing lack of consensus within the IWC 'contributes to its declining credibility among member States and the wider international community, and encourages the development of other "appropriate international organizations"'.[97] Indeed, Iceland, the Faroe Islands, Greenland and Norway established the first whaling regional organization in 1992 by expressly invoking Article 65: the North Atlantic Marine Mammal Commission (NAMMCO).[98] Japan has repeatedly emphasized the importance of regional environmental organizations, its intention to maintain and strengthen its observer role within NAMCCO and its aim to lead regional efforts to establish another international organization relating to the conservation and management of whale stocks.[99]

Another fundamental limitation in Article 65 relates to the meaning of 'work[ing] through' the appropriate international organizations. To 'work through' entails some form of inter-State cooperation with a view to managing and conserving marine living resources, including whales and other marine mammals.[100] How a State would fulfil its obligation to 'work through' the appropriate organization(s) is,

[93] Office for Ocean Affairs and Law of the Sea (1996) 31 Law of the Sea Bulletin 79, see Table at 82. www.un.org/Depts/los/doalos_publications/LOSBulletins/bulletinpdf/bulletinE31.pdf.

[94] Ibid., 79.

[95] Mcdorman, (n 88) 182–183.

[96] IWC, Proposed Consensus Decision to Improve the Conservation of Whales from the Chair and Vice-Chair of the Commission (28 April 2010) 57, cited Goodman (2011) 63–74.

[97] Steven Freeland and Julie Drysdale, 'Co-Operation or Chaos? Article 65 of United Nations Convention on the Law of the Sea and the Future of the International Whaling Commission' (2005) 2(1) *Macquarie Journal of International and Comparative Environmental Law* 1, 10–11.

[98] Agreement on Cooperation in Research, Conservation and Management of Marine Mammals in the North Atlantic thereby establishing the North Atlantic Marine Mammals Commission ('NAMMCO') (Signed 9 April 1992, entered into force 8 July 1992) <www.fao.org/faolex/results/details/en/c/LEX-FAOC024298/>.

[99] Alex Kirby, Japan Plans Pro-Whaling Alliance (BBC News, 14 July 2004) http://news.bbc.co.uk/1/hi/sci/tech/3892909.stm.

[100] Seokwoo Lee and Jeong Woo Kim, 'UNCLOS and the Obligation to Cooperate: International Legal Framework for Semi-Enclosed Seas Cooperation' in Keyuan Zou (ed.) *Maritime Cooperation in Semi-Enclosed Seas* (Leiden: Brill 2019) 11–29.

however, unclear. UNCLOS does not clarify the substantive elements of the positive duty to 'work through'. Taken plainly, to 'work through', means 'to manage a problem that has many different parts step by step'.[101] It may be suggested that Article 65 does not give rise to a legal obligation on States to become members of the relevant international organizations or to adhere to the regulations adopted by these organizations.[102] Article 65 may be satisfied 'through consultation with scientific bodies'[103] or 'active engagement in the organization as observers'.[104] On the other hand, the requirement to 'work through' cannot be narrowed to mere scientific consultation. Article 65 would oblige States 'to defer to the appropriate international organizations to set minimum conservation and management measures for cetaceans'.[105] In the specific context of Japanese whaling, the obligation to 'work through the appropriate international organizations' is insufficient to determine the degree or means of cooperation required by the Japanese government to fulfil its legal duties under Article 65 of UNCLOS.[106]

Japan expressly recognizes its duty to cooperate over whaling matters and has publicly committed to engage meaningfully with other States directly and through the appropriate international organizations in good faith. First, Japan has indicated that it would maintain observer status within the IWC.[107] Second, Japan has stated it would strictly monitor all whaling operations within its EEZ by having government officials at each landing base and onboard factory ships and by observing vessels' locations through satellite communication devices. All relevant information about operations and the number of whales caught would then be shared publicly. Third, all catch quotas within Japanese waters will be calculated in accordance with the calculation formula unanimously adopted by the IWC Scientific Committee for setting sustainable catch limits and preventing any adverse effects on whale stocks.[108] This formula, known as the Revised Management Procedure (RMP),[109] was the culmination of several years of research and extensive simulation testing by the IWC

[101] Cambridge Dictionary, https://dictionary.cambridge.org/dictionary/english/work-through-sth

[102] Ray Gambell, 'International Management of Whales and Whaling: An Historical Review of the Regulation of Commercial and Aboriginal Subsistence Whaling' (1993) 46(2) *Arctic* 97, 105.

[103] Mcdorman (n 88) 183.

[104] James Harrison and Elisa Morgera, 'Commentary to Articles 61–65' in Alexander Proelß (ed.) *United Nations Convention on the Law of the Sea: A Commentary* (Oxford: Hart 2017) 480–526.

[105] Kimberly Davis, 'International Management of Cetaceans under the New Law of the Sea Convention' (1985) 3 *Boston University International Law Journal* 477, 505–506.

[106] Ibid.

[107] Ministry of Foreign Affairs of Japan, Statement by Chief Cabinet Secretary (26 December 2018) <www.mofa.go.jp/ecm/fsh/page4e_000969.html>.

[108] *Minutes of the Committee on Agriculture, Forestry and Fisheries, House of Councilors, 198th Session* No 4 (April 9, 2019) 10, cited in Kanehara (n 11) 376, 382.

[109] This presents 'a scientifically robust method of setting safe catch limits for certain stocks (groups of whales of the same species living in a particular area) where the numbers are plentiful' IWC, 'The Revised Management Procedure' <https://iwc.int/index.php?cID=581&cType=html&zenario_sk_return=zenario__content/panels/content_types/item//html//item//en//html_1>.

Scientific Committee based on quantifiable 'politically agreed management objectives' set by the IWC in the event of the moratorium being lifted or relaxed.[110] According to Japan's Fisheries Agency, this calculation formula is 'extremely conservative' and confirms 'that continuous harvest of calculated number of animals for 100 years would have no harmful effect on the targeted stock'.[111] However, despite the RMP's scientific soundness and unanimous endorsement by the IWC Scientific Committee, the proposal to lift the moratorium did not attract the required three-quarters majority for adoption; hence the moratorium remained in place.[112]

In all, Japan's obligation to engage meaningfully with other States and the IWC does not constitute an obligation to agree to or adopt unconditionally every IWC regulation.[113] How other States delineate the substantive content of Japan's duty to 'work through' with the IWC and other international organizations under Article 65 of UNCLOS remains to be seen.[114]

23.3.1 *Whaling within Japan's EEZ Lawful if Conducted Sustainably*

Japan's decision to resume commercial whaling may be unpopular for anti-whaling States and environmental NGOs. Yet, it is existing legal instruments governing whaling that provide the legal pathways to whaling.[115] For instance, Norway, which opted out of the moratorium, has been conducting commercial whaling in its EEZ 'perfectly legally', according to New Zealand's Commissioner to the IWC, Sir Geoffrey Palmer.[116] The ICRW provides an option for States members to avoid being bound by a particular proposed new regulation simply by objecting to them under Article V(3) of the Schedule of the ICRW.[117] Japan also objected to the moratorium but was later persuaded by the United States to drop its objection. Iceland left the ICRW in 2002 and later re-joined with a reservation against the moratorium.

[110] Justin Cooke, Russell Leaper and Vassili Papastavrou, 'Science Should not be Abandoned in a Bid to Resolve Whaling Disputes' (2009) 5(5) *Biology Letters* 614–616.

[111] 'The catch limit calculated by this method is always less than 1% of he estimated abundance of the targeted stock', Fisheries Agency of Japan, 'Resumption of Commercial Whaling' (1 July 2019).

[112] Ibid.

[113] Mika Hayashi, 'The Whaling Judgment and the Challenges of Dynamic Treaty Regimes' in Malgosia Fitzmaurice and Dai Tamada (eds.) *Whaling in the Antarctic: Significance and Implications of the ICJ Judgment* (Leiden: Brill 2016) 221, 232.

[114] Freeland and Drysdale (n 97) 1–33.

[115] Fitzmaurice, 'Can the Gordian Knot Be Cut (or Untangled)' (n 8) 456–458, 464–465; Geoffrey Palmer, 'Whales and Humans: How Whaling Went from Being a Major Industry to a Leading Environmental Issue then Landed Japan in the International Court of Justice for the First Time' (2015) 13 *New Zealand Yearbook of International Law* 107, 111.

[116] Palmer (n 115).

[117] Art. V(3), ICRW.

Thus, it would appear that under the current rules, Japan could lawfully pursue whaling outside the ICRW, thereby pursuing the benefits sought for its economy and citizens, and not be bound to abstain from whaling as long as it conducts commercial whaling sustainably and does not lead species to overexploitation. Nevertheless, this is not an uncomplicated endeavour. Overexploitation is not the only concern for whale sustainability. Today, whales are subjected to simultaneous threats, not associated with whaling per se, including climate change, marine contamination, and biological and habitat degradation.[118] Scientific research, in part led by Japan, gives clues on how human activities may impact certain marine mammals, but, as Voigt writes, 'knowledge is far from complete, and it appears that there is no understanding of how such activities will affect cetaceans when they are synergistically exposed to them'.[119] Scientists are not always able to precisely quantify the short- or long-term scale of such impacts.

At any rate, application of the precautionary approach does not generally prescribe what measures must be taken at the national level. Instead, the precautionary approach can be applied 'in different ways and different contexts'.[120] Thus, in practice, States – whilst under a positive duty to adopt a precautionary approach – what sort of action the precautionary approach prescribes may differ significantly from State to State and, thus, whether a State interprets the precautionary approach in light of scientific uncertainty as requiring either a complete ban or regulated hunting is part of the State's lawful discretion: it may mean an open-ended blanket ban on all whale species or controlled hunting of certain species known to be abundant in the target areas, subject to stricter conditions and constant monitoring.[121]

23.4 TOWARDS SOLUTIONS

This chapter has shown that whaling is intimately connected to the broader environmental law debate. The legal and regulatory approach to whaling is, first and foremost, about environmental protection and sustainable use of marine living resources. Therefore, clearer guidance is required as to what will promote sustainable whaling in any given situation. One possibility, which may be unpopular in certain countries, is to allow limited, but internationally monitored, whaling in specific places. In other places, whaling could be stopped altogether. As Freeland

[118] Voigt (n 45) 557, 579.
[119] Ibid.
[120] Ibid.
[121] Yoshifumi Tanaka, 'The Changing Approaches to Conservation of Marine Living Resources in International Law' (2011) 71 *ZaöRV* 291, 315.

writes, if complete cessation of whaling cannot be achieved, at least in the short term, 'the only rational and pragmatic response is to ensure that as few whales as possible are taken'.[122] The only way for that to happen is for IWC members to agree a compromise based on widely accepted environmental principles such as sustainability.

Further research should be conducted to allow an adjustment of those approaches based on science. This necessarily makes discussions more complex than a straightforward binary decision to allow or ban whaling. Yet it also allows for urgently needed constructive international engagement. In some places, whaling will be off the table because of its not being supported by the public (hence being politically unviable) – but that applies on the side of the proponents of a global whaling ban as much as on the side of its opponents, such as Japan and Norway, where whaling is still popular and supported politically.[123] As we have seen, the Japanese government has a vested national interest in safeguarding whaling, even if it is not a major industry in Japan.

Independent scientific research, uncompromised by the economic, social and political interests of those concerned with whaling, is urgently needed to ensure decisions are based on the scientific evidence produced.[124] As scientific knowledge advances and whale stock management theories become even more complex, scientific advice may not necessarily produce clear-cut answers. In situations of scientific uncertainty, the precautionary principle can allow for rational decisions – provided that the principle is not misinterpreted and transformed into 'a principle of inaction' by insisting on the status quo and refusing to consider alternative courses of action.[125] The precautionary approach serves precisely to enable meaningful decisions in the face of uncertainty. This ensures that decision-making is not stifled in every instance of uncertainty and reflects the reality that uncertainty may remain unavoidable in the foreseeable future. The search for a desirable compromise will inevitably involve some risk.

Decisions must be multi-dimensional, grounded on good science and international environmental cooperation. Such cooperation should be conducted in good faith and presupposes, according to the ICJ, 'a genuine attempt … to engage in discussions with the other disputing party, with a view to resolving the

[122] Steven Freeland, 'With a Less Confrontational Approach to Whaling, More Whales Could be Saved' (The Conversation, 7 November 2016) <www.abc.net.au/news/2016-11-07/a-less-confrontational-approach-to-whaling/8001302>.

[123] Ian Hurd, 'Almost Saving Whales: The Ambiguity of Success at the International Whaling Commission' (2012) 26(1) *Ethics & International Affairs* 1, 6–7.

[124] Shigeki Sakamoto, 'ICJ Judgment in the Antarctic: Its Significance and Implications: The Whaling in the Antarctic from a Japanese Perspective' (2015) 58 *Japanese Yearbook of International Law* 247.

[125] Gail Charnley, 'Risk Analysis under Fire' (2000) 20(1) *RISK Newsletter* 3.

dispute'.[126] This duty of cooperation, which stands at the heart of international environmental law, is an obligation of means and not of result. It does not mandate that all negotiations succeed: it is effectively a duty of 'meaningful cooperation'.[127] The International Law Commission has confirmed in its work that meaningful cooperation requires that discussions be conducted in good faith 'and must take into account each other's legitimate interests'.[128] This arguably includes a willingness to alter one's approach in light of the other party's legitimate interests and views as opposed to insisting on maintaining the status quo despite the existence of reasonable and satisfactory alternatives. After the IWC imposed its blanket moratorium on whaling in 1982, Japan argues that it spent 30 years trying to negotiate a compromise based on scientific evidence of sustainability; it repeatedly proposed amending the moratorium to allow limited and internationally controlled whaling under the ICRW; and it only decided to withdraw on realizing that such a compromise would not be reached.[129] One may suggest that Japan genuinely sought compromise and that the onus is on other IWC member States to show that they have duly fulfilled their duty of meaningful cooperation. Meaningful cooperation in good faith goes both ways. So does respect for ethical and cultural values. In essence, this is the perennial challenge of whaling regulation, which insists on and facilitates open disputes between parties with seemingly irreconcilable interests and assessing the relative positions.

[126] *Application of the International Convention on the Elimination of All Forms of Racial Discrimination (Georgia* v. *Russian Federation)* (Preliminary Objections) (Judgment) [2011] ICJ Rep 70 para. 157; On the requirement that negotiations ought to be meaningful, see *North Sea Continental Shelf Cases (Federal Republic of Germany* v. *Denmark and Netherlands)* (Judgment) [1969] ICJ Rep 3 para. 85; *Gabcíkovo-Nagymaros Project (Hungary/Slovakia)* (Judgment) [1997] ICJ Rep 7 para 141; *Pulp Mills on the River Uruguay (Argentina* v. *Uruguay)* (Judgment) [2010] ICJ Rep 14 para. 146.

[127] *North Sea Continental Shelf* (n 126) para. 85.

[128] International Law Commission, 'Draft Articles on Prevention of Transboundary Harm' Commentary on Article 9 (Yearbook of the International Law Commission, 2001, Volume II, Part Two), 148–170, 160, <https://legal.un.org/ilc/texts/instruments/english/commentaries/9_7_2001.pdf>.

[129] Holm, (n 76) 126.

24

Failing Rule of Law

The Case of the South China Sea

Agnes Chong

24.1 INTRODUCTION: THE RULE OF LAW

Overlapping claims in the South China Sea (SCS)[1] are at fundamental odds with States complying with their obligations to cooperate to protect the environment and to have due regard for rights and interests in the SCS. This conundrum invites the question 'is the rule of law for the oceans fit for purpose?'[2] Contestations over fishing, oil exploration, land reclamation, freedom of navigation rights and interests in the SCS have not been resolved by the rule of law; but rather have been subjects of political hostilities and confrontations that escalated and eased, and threatened the rule of law.[3] The rule of law was reinstated when the Permanent Court of Arbitration (PCA) adjudicated on the maritime entitlements between the Philippines and China in the *South China Sea Arbitration*. Amid open conflicts in the SCS, the ruling is primarily seen as countering a powerful political campaign initiated by China on its SCS neighbours to accept the legitimacy of China's

[1] The SCS comprises Thailand, Cambodia, Vietnam, China, Taiwan, the Philippines, Singapore, Malaysia, Brunei and Indonesia. Six states have overlapping claims over the SCS namely, China, Taiwan, Vietnam, the Philippines, Malaysia and Brunei.

[2] The theme of The Rule of Law for Oceans Conference 4–5 November 2019 (University of Oslo/Norwegian Institute for Water Research).

[3] For background to the SCS conflict, see Clive Schofield, Untangling a Complex Web: Understanding Competing Maritime Claims in the South China Sea in Cheng-Yi Lin and Ian Storey (eds), *The South China Sea Dispute* (Singapore: ISEAS-Yusof Ishak Institute, 2016), 21–46; Robert C. Beckman, ASEAN and the South China Sea Dispute in Pavin Chachavalpongpun (ed), *Entering Unchartered Waters ASEAN and the South China Sea* (Singapore: Institute of Southeast Asian Studies 2014), 15–35; Kun-Chin Lin and Andres Villar Gertner, China and the Emerging Order in the East and South China Seas (Chatham House, The Royal Institute of International Affairs, Research Paper, July 2015), available at 20150731MaritimeSecurityAsiaPacificLinGertner-0.pdf (chathamhouse.org); and Hayley Roberts, Current Legal Developments South China Sea, Responses to Sovereign Disputes in the South China Sea, 30 *The International Journal of Marine and Coastal Law*, 2015, 199–211.

maritime expansion.[4] It also sets a precedent for SCS States to comply with the rule of law and establish a rules-based order in the SCS.[5] The United Nations Convention on the Law of the Sea (UNCLOS)[6] is the normative framework for a global legal order for the oceans. Its goal is to maintain peace and security and uphold an equitable system of balancing the rights and obligations of coastal States and non-coastal States.[7] UNCLOS essentially shifts a system of unilateralism to multilateralism through the Convention's duties to cooperate, consult and obtain approval from various sea authorities such as the International Maritime Organisation and the International Seabed Authority, as well as mandates to resolve disputes by arbitration or adjudication.[8]

This chapter has four sections, following this opening one. Following this introduction, Section 24.2 discusses the *South China Sea Arbitration* that emphasised the obligations of cooperation and due regard. Section 24.3 highlights the cooperation regime of the SCS, and Section 24.4 discusses the obligation of due regard. Both of these fundamental mechanisms are structurally disabled due to the conflict over maritime claims. Section 24.5 addresses the difficulty of exercising the obligation to cooperate and at the same time have due regard to the rights and obligations of other States and recommends that the ASEAN Code of Conduct (COC) must enable radical action of States to adhere to their international obligations in marine protection of the SCS.

24.2 THE SOUTH CHINA SEA ARBITRATION AND PART XII OF UNCLOS

The PCA ruling is highly significant for marine protection in the SCS: it reinforced Part XII of UNCLOS and determined the legal rights and obligations of States in relation to the SCS.[9] *The South China Sea Arbitration* between the Philippines and China concerned legal maritime entitlements in the SCS and the lawfulness of certain actions by China decided by the PCA in accordance with UNCLOS.[10]

[4] Douglas Guilfoyle, The Rule of Law and Maritime Security in the South China Sea, 95(5) *International Affairs*, 2019, 999–1017, 1016.

[5] The term 'rules-based order' has become politicised and associated with curbing China's expansion in the SCS, which is an incidental outcome of enforcing the rule of law in the SCS, but it is not the main goal. See Hitoshi Nasu and See Seng Tan, A Rules-Based Order in the Asia-Pacific in Prospects for the Rules-Based Global Order, The Australian National University, The Centre of Gravity Series Paper No. 34, 2017.

[6] United Nations Convention on the Law of the Sea (UNCLOS), Montego Bay, 10 December 1982, in force 16 November 1994, 1833 UNTS 397.

[7] Preamble to UNCLOS.

[8] Bernard H. Oxman, The Rule of Law and the UN Convention on the Law of the Seas, 7 *EJIL*, 1996, 353–371, 356.

[9] Duncan French, In the Matter of the South China Sea Arbitration: *Republic of Philippines* v. *People's Republic of China*, 19(1) *Environmental Law Review*, 2017, 48–56.

[10] South China Sea Arbitration (*The Philippines* v. *China*) PCA Case No 2013–19 (12 July 2016).

China did not take part in the proceedings, and the hearings continued with China in absentia.[11]

While the arbitration decided the legal issues in the case,[12] it importantly upholds the rule of law for oceans in the face of contemporary challenges and enforcement of global rules. By emphasising UNCLOS as the constitution of the oceans to balance interests, the tribunal disregarded non-legal interests, that is, ultimately extinguishing historical claims in the EEZ[13] to focus on territorial entitlements protected by law. Furthermore, the tribunal upheld the authority of international treaties in respect to the compulsory procedure for dispute settlement in the present case.[14] Not only should there be a governance framework for the management of overlapping maritime claims and integrated management of the environment and marine resources but also any such framework must be rooted in the rule of law.[15]

The tribunal's ruling on maritime entitlements and the status of maritime features through interpretation of Article 121(3)[16] was guided by the notion of 'universalism in the law of the sea' – not only safeguarding the benefit of the local population in the EEZ and protecting the ocean as the common heritage of mankind but also countering unilateralism as demonstrated by China's claim in the SCS.[17] UNCLOS should be an effective constitution for the oceans in the legal sense and not just the political sense.[18]

[11] For discussion on China's non-participation in the proceedings, see Stefan Talmon, The South China Sea Arbitration: Observations on the Award on Jurisdiction and Admissibility, 15(2) *Chinese Journal of International Law*, 2016, 309–391.

[12] Among the issues, the Court determined the obligations on the marine environment in respect of the following activities by China, namely: (i) harmful fishing practices; (ii) construction of artificial islands, structures and installations; and (iii) harvesting endangered species. See *South China Sea Arbitration* (n 11), 386–388.

[13] Vincent P. Cogliati-Bantz, Current Legal Developments: The South China Sea Arbitration, 31 (4) *International Journal of Marine and Coastal Law*, 2016, 759–774, 772.

[14] Alfredo C. Robles Jr, *Endangered Species and Fragile Ecosystems in the South China Sea, The Philippines v. China Arbitration* (London: Palgrave 2020), 139–141. See contrasting view by Tsu-Sung Hsieh, Issue of Non-Participation in the South China Sea Arbitration in Tsu-Sung Hsieh (ed), *The South China Sea Disputes: Historical, Geopolitical and Legal Studies* (Singapore, Hackensack, NJ: World Scientific Publishing Co, 2018), 189–191.

[15] Vu Thanh Ca, A Regional Ocean Governance Framework for the Integrated Management of the Environment and Biological Resources in the South China Sea in Truong T. Tran, John B. Welfield and Thuy T. Le (eds), *Building a Normative Order in the South China Sea: Evolving Disputes and Expanding Options* (Cheltenham: Edward Elgar, 2019), 197.

[16] The definition of maritime features is provided in Art. 121(3) which states 'rocks which cannot sustain human habitation or economic life of their own shall have no EEZ or continental shelf.'

[17] Yoshifumi Tanaka, Reflections on the Interpretation and Application of Article 121(3) in the South China Sea Arbitration (Merits), 48(3–4) *Ocean Development and International Law*, 2017, 36–385, 376–379.

[18] Tommy B. Koh, 'A Constitution for the Oceans', Remarks, President of the Third United Nations Conference for the Law of the Sea, 1982, available at Ses1-6.-Tommy-T.B.-Koh-of-Singapore-President-of-the-Third-United-Nations-Conference-on-the-Law-of-the-Sea-_A-Constitution-for-the-Oceans_.pdf (nus.edu.sg).

This is the case for protection of the marine environment as UNCLOS has an integrated and holistic framework to enable application of provisions to protect the marine environment under its Part XII.[19] The provisions that were most relevant in the SCS were UNCLOS Articles 123 (duty to cooperate bordering semi-enclosed seas), 192 (duty to prevent significant harm), 194(5) (duty to protect marine ecosystems) as well as Article 204 (duty to monitor pollution effects), Article 205 (duty to publish monitoring results) and Article 206 (duty to conduct environmental impact assessments).[20] These articles were examined in the tribunal's determination of China's island-building programme where the court emphasised that cooperation may enable States to manage the risks of damage to the environment.[21] The regime supports the requirement to communicate and coordinate development plans under Article 123 where the tribunal effectively ruled that non-communication, non-coordination and non-cooperation were in breach of the substantive and procedural aspects of the obligation to cooperate.

The *South China Sea Arbitration* affirmed that China had a duty to cooperate under Articles 123 and 197 in prevention of marine harm, and in this regard international jurisprudence is continually developing to define the obligation.[22] The primary mechanisms to avoid conflicts and keep within the rule of law are: (i) cooperation; and (ii) due regard; these enable States to observe a rules-based oceans governance when exercising rights, interests and obligations in an EEZ.[23]

UNCLOS is crucial to ensure the rule of law for the oceans in managing the challenges of ocean governance and the need to balance concurrent rights and obligations.[24] The tribunal acknowledged

> the articles [governing] the exclusive economic zone were (as with much of the Convention) a compromise and intended to balance the interests of the peoples of coastal developing States with the interests of the traditional maritime States . . . and the Convention [contributes] to the realisation of a just and equitable international economic order which takes into account the interests and needs of mankind as a whole . . . [25]

19 Nilufer Oral, *The South China Sea Arbitral Award, Part XII of UNCLOS and the Protection and Preservation of the Marine Environment in The South China Sea Arbitration, The Legal Dimension*, edited by S. Jayakumar, Tommy Koh, Robert Beckman, Tara Davenport and Hao D. Phan (Cheltenham: Edward Elgar, 2018), 224.

20 Ibid., 373–379. The tribunal examined these provisions in deciding on the protection of the marine environment obligations under Part XII of UNCLOS.

21 Ibid., 394–395.

22 Chie Kojima, South China Sea Arbitration and the Protection of the Marine Environment: Evolution of UNCLOS Part XII through Interpretation and the Duty to Cooperate, 21 *Asian Yearbook of International Law*, 2015, 178.

23 Tanaka Yoshifumi, *The South China Sea Arbitration: Toward an International Legal Order in the Oceans* (Oxford: Hart, 2019), 331–333.

24 Ibid., 319–397 and 399–415.

25 Note 42, 216. See discussion by Yoshifumi Tanaka, Reflections on the Interpretation and Application of Article 121(3) in the *South China Sea Arbitration* (n 19) 36–385, 376–379.

Under Articles 56(2) and 58(3) of UNCLOS, coastal and non-coastal States are required to have regard to the rights and obligations of other States when utilising the seas in an EEZ.[26] The objective of this balancing mechanism is to ensure conciliation between overlapping rights, interests and obligations.[27] However, the due regard mechanism is not a voluntary undertaking but is an obligation to be complied with when a State exercises its right in an EEZ.[28] Implementation of due regard requires cooperation and willingness of the States in question. Separately, States have an obligation to cooperate to prevent environmental harm and to conserve marine ecosystems.[29] UNCLOS's cooperation provisions provide the measure by which States are required to cooperate in the conservation and management of marine resources through a mechanism of notification and development of contingency plans.[30] This includes exchange of scientific information, monitoring risks as well as agreeing on measures to prevent harm.[31]

24.3 THE INTERNATIONAL COOPERATION REGIME IN THE SCS

UNCLOS contains several provisions on the obligation to cooperate, which provide substantive and procedural obligations implicit in the duty to cooperate.[32] The Convention on Biological Diversity (CBD), an outcome from the Rio Summit held in June 1992, affirms States' commitments to sustainable development.[33] The CBD and its relevant provisions complement the environmental obligations in UNCLOS, which provide for States to cooperate on marine protection (at a general level) and on marine ecosystem and biodiversity preservation (at a specific level).[34]

[26] Arts. 56 and 58 UNCLOS.

[27] Mathias Forteau, The Legal Nature and Content of 'Due Regard' Obligations in Recent International Case Law, 34(1) *The International Journal of Marine and Coastal Law*, 2019, 25–42.

[28] Tullio Scovazzi, 'Due Regard' Obligations, with Particular Emphasis on Fisheries in the Exclusive Economic Zone, 34(1) *The International Journal of Marine and Coastal Law*, 2019, 56–72.

[29] The South China Sea Arbitration (n 11); ICJ, The Gabcikovo-Nagymaros Project (*Hungary* v. *Slovakia*), Judgment of 25 September 1997, ICJ Reports, 88-119; Pulp Mills on the River Uruguay (*Argentina* v. *Uruguay*), Judgment, ICJ Reports 2010; ITLOS, Mox Plant Case (*Ireland* v. *United Kingdom*), Number 10, ITLOS, Order, November 13, 2001.

[30] Arts. 197, 198, 199.

[31] Arts. 200 and 201.

[32] See Arts. 61, 64–66, 177–120, 198, 199, 200, 201, 242, 243, 244, 246, 247, 268, 269 and 270 and Part XII.

[33] Rio Declaration on Environment and Development, Report of United Nations Conference on Environment & Development (UNCED), Rio de Janeiro, 3–14 June 1992, and UNCED Agenda 21, Rio de Janeiro, Brazil, 3–14 June 1992.

[34] Rudiger Wolfrum, *Means of Ensuring Compliance with and Enforcement of International Environmental Law* (Leiden: Brill, 1998), Vol. 272, 16.

The basis of conservation cooperation can reverse the deteriorating SCS environment[35] – including: Article 3 of the CBD on the obligation to prevent harm to the marine environment; Article 5 of the CBD on the duty to cooperate in the conservation and sustainable utilisation of resources; Article 123 of UNCLOS on cooperation by States in semi-enclosed seas in the exploitation of natural resources and the protection of its marine environment; Article 192 of UNCLOS on the obligation to protect and preserve the marine environment of the seas; Article 194 (1)–(4) of UNCLOS on the obligation to prevent pollution of the marine environment; Article 194(5) of UNCLOS on protection of marine ecosystems; and Article 197 of UNCLOS on the general obligation to cooperate.

International courts are increasingly upholding prevention of environmental harm through cooperation,[36] and are adjudicating on the extent of cooperation required to fulfil the obligation. In *Chagos*, the tribunal decided that the United Kingdom's failure to resume talks after Mauritius called off meetings with the United Kingdom to discuss the development of marine protected areas on Chagos Island did not constitute reasonable cooperation.[37] Furthermore, the United Kingdom failed to comply with its environmental obligations in the circumstances as its actions in the present case fell short of the actions of the United Kingdom cooperating with the United States on similar environmental obligations.[38] Environmental cooperation must not be superficial and must be accompanied by firm policies and action.

Cooperation between semi-enclosed seas as applicable to SCS under Article 123 complements the requirement for parties to make further agreements relating to protection of the marine environment and is consistent with the principles and objectives of Article 237.[39] The complementarity of UNCLOS with CBD (both of which have universal ratification) reinforces the obligation to cooperate on marine protection and is reflected in non-binding regional instruments such as the 1976 ASEAN Treaty of Amity and Cooperation in Southeast Asia (TAC)[40] and the 2002 China–ASEAN Declaration on Conduct of the Parties in the SCS (DOC). These legal instruments establish a regional framework for effective ecological cooperation in the SCS. Notwithstanding the non-bindingness of the TAC and

35 See also, John W. McManus, Toward Establishing a Spratly Islands International Marine Peace Park: Ecological Importance and Supportive Collaborative Activities with an Emphasis on the Role of Taiwan, 41(3) *Ocean Development and International Law*, 2010, 270–280, 273.

36 See (n 31).

37 PCA, The Chagos Marine Protected Area Arbitration (*Mauritius* v. *Great Britain*), Award, March 18, 2015, 205–206, para. 525.

38 Ibid., 209–210, paras. 528–536. For a study of MPAs in the South China Sea, see Vu Hai Dang, *Marine Protected Areas Network in the South China Sea: Charting a Course for Future Cooperation* (Leiden: Martinus Nijhoff, 2014).

39 Alan Boyle, Further Developments of the Law of the Sea Convention: Mechanisms for Change, 54 *International and Comparative Law Quarterly*, 2005, 563–584, 575.

40 Treaty of Amity and Cooperation in Southeast Asia, Denpasar, Bali, 26 February 1976, in force 15 July 1976, 1025 UNTS 297.

DOC, ASEAN[41] has a distinctive long history of cooperation that has promoted coordinated resource planning and policymaking.[42] Among regional multilateral fora, ASEAN has historically played a key role in diffusing conflicts in the SCS.[43]

In respect to overlapping claims in the SCS EEZs, the ASEAN forum was utilised by SCS States to enter into a non-binding instrument between ASEAN and China – the DOC. The DOC sets out the commitment to form a future binding COC.[44] This was the culmination of efforts to settle maritime conflicts since 1992 and was a compromise when the parties could not agree on a binding treaty.[45] The DOC reaffirms the purpose of maintaining international peace and security as codified in the UN Charter, UNCLOS and the ASEAN TAC through which is realised in the 'building of trust and confidence ... on the basis of equality and mutual respect',[46] that is, the principle of sovereign equality. The TAC promotes cooperation and mutual assistance in areas of economic, social, scientific and technical matters.[47] The broad cooperation requirement is specified in areas such as the economy, society and the environment.[48]

Article 4 of TAC and Article 6(a) of the Draft Negotiation Text of DOC reflect the environmental provisions in UNCLOS and CBD. Article 4 of the TAC provides for the duty of cooperation in broad terms promoting 'economic, social, technical, scientific and administrative fields as well as common ideals and aspirations of international peace and stability in the region and all other matters of common interest'.[49] Cooperation on the environment feasibly falls within Article 4 of TAC and complements the specialised area of cooperation on marine environmental protection in Article 6(a) of the Draft Negotiation Text of DOC, which the latter leaves the specific details of bilateral and multilateral cooperation to be agreed by the parties.[50]

Prevention of marine harm in Article 192 of UNCLOS and Articles 3 and 5 of the CBD complement Article 4 of TAC and Article 6(a) of the Draft Negotiation Text of

41 ASEAN Member States are Brunei Darussalam, Cambodia, Indonesia, Lao PDR, Malaysia, Myanmar, Philippines, Singapore, Thailand and Vietnam.

42 Jeffrey David Wilson, *International Resource Politics in the Asia-Pacific: The Political Economy of Conflict and Cooperation* (Oxford: Edward Elgar, 2017).

43 Alan H. Yang, The South China Sea Arbitration and Its Implications for ASEAN Centrality, 21 *Asian Yearbook of International Law*, 2015, 83–95, 86.

44 Art. 10 Draft Negotiation Text of the DOC. See also, Ramses Amer and Li Jianwei, From DOC to COC, A Regional Rules-Based Order, in Zou Keyuan (ed), *Routledge Handbook of the South China Sea* (Abingdon: Routledge, 1st ed., 2021).

45 A Blueprint for a South China Sea Code of Conduct, AMTI, 11 October 2018.

46 Art. 2 Draft Negotiation Text of the DOC 2018.

47 Art. 4, 1976 ASEAN TAC.

48 Edward Best and Thomas Christiansen, *Regionalism in International Affairs in the Globalization of World Politics: An Introduction to International Relations*, edited by John Baylis, Steve Smith and Patricia Owens (Oxford: Oxford University Press, 2020), 375.

49 Art. 4, 1976 ASEAN TAC.

50 Art. 6 Draft Negotiation Text of the DOC 2018.

the DOC, thus allowing a broad and effective cooperation framework that protects the SCS environment. However, political will is essential to implement cooperation grounded in the international rule of law.[51] Thus, compliance and cooperation is contingent on States agreeing to do so. Hence, the rule of law must be the impetus that functions as a means to achieve the outcome of cooperation and place normative constraints on policies that are contrary to the law.[52] The rule of law is not applied in a vacuum but rather in a 'thick common moral framework' based on values that confirm States' criteria for membership of the international system, that is, are peace-loving States and willing to carry out international obligations under the UN Charter?[53] Hence, the underlying normative requirement to prevent marine harm through cooperation is reinforced through the SCS cooperation regime consisting of UNCLOS, CBD, DOC and TAC, and aligned with progress in international jurisprudence on marine protection.[54] In upholding the rule of law, the cooperation regime must be applied by States bilaterally and multilaterally. Broadly, the international and regional instruments relating to environmental protection of the SCS and developments in international jurisprudence should form the basis of marine protection in a future detailed and binding COC.

24.4 DUE REGARD

International treaty provisions contain the requirement to have due regard to other States, which has an important function of balancing various rights, interests and obligations.[55] Due regard is the substantive and procedural mechanism that balances the rights and duties of States in their use of a shared natural resource to

[51] Robert C. Beckman and Clive H. Schofield, Defining EEZ Claims from Islands: A Potential South China Sea Change, 29 *The International Journal of Marine and Coastal Law*, 2014, 193–243, 194.

[52] This is in line with rule of law's 'equality before the law' that places constraints on a State's exercise of power. See Simon Chesterman, An International Rule of Law, 331 *American Journal of Comparative Law*, 2008, 331–362, 360.

[53] Douglas Guilfoyle, The Rule of Law and Maritime Security: Understanding Lawfare in the South China Sea, 95(5) *International Affairs*, 2019, 1001; James D. Fry and Agnes Chong, Conditions of Admission of a State to Membership in the United Nations, Advisory Opinion [1948] ICJ Rep 57 in *Leading Decisions in the Law of International Organisations*, edited by Cedric Ryngaert, Ige Dekker, Ramses A. Wessel and Jan Wouters (Oxford: Oxford University Press, 2016), 138–155.

[54] See discussion on the progress of marine environmental jurisprudence in Joanna Mossop, Can We Make the Oceans Greener? The Successes and Failures of UNCLOS as an Environmental Treaty, 49 *Victoria University of Wellington Law Review*, 2018, 473–593.

[55] See UNCLOS (n 7), Convention on the Law of the Non-navigational uses of International Watercourses (UN Watercourses Convention), New York, 21 May 1997, in force 17 August 2014, 2999 UNTS 77, Treaty on Principles Governing the Activities of States in the Exploration and Use of Outer Space, including the Moon and other celestial bodies (the Outer Space Treaty) London/Moscow/Washington, 19 December 1966, in force 10 October 1967, 610 UNTS 205and Convention on International Civil Aviation (Chicago Convention), Chicago, 7 December 1944, in force 4 April 1947, 15 UNTS 295.

ensure that States as sovereign equals may enforce their rights and duties within the international legal regime.[56] There is no definition of due regard. However, in UNCLOS it exists as a legal obligation for coastal States and non-coastal States to pay due regard to each other's rights and obligations in the exercise of their own rights and freedoms. States carrying out their due regard obligations when exercising their rights and freedoms forms the basis of a type of 'mandatory multilateralism enshrined in UNCLOS.[57] Under Article 87 of UNCLOS the high seas are open and free to both coastal and non-coastal States but their right to the freedom of the high seas is subject to other freedoms provided in UNCLOS including those in Article 87(1) of UNCLOS.[58] States must have due regard to the interests of other States when exercising the freedom of the high seas and the rights in the convention.[59]

SCS States are obliged under UNCLOS to have due regard for the rights and obligations of both coastal States and non-coastal States when using exclusive economic zones (EEZs), which incidentally are the areas of contention in the SCS.[60] The due regard obligation obliges States to balance their interests with the interests of other States in the use of shared sea resources. As the majority of the SCS constitutes EEZs, which are neither sovereign territories nor the high seas, the due regard regime contained in Articles 56(2) and 58(3) applies.[61] Article 56(2) provides that when exercising its rights and performing its duties, a coastal State must have due regard for the rights and duties of other States.[62] The rights and duties of other States are laid out in Article 58 such as the freedoms of navigation, overflight, laying submarine cables and pipelines and other lawful freedoms associated with ships, aircraft and submarine cables.[63] When exercising their rights, States must have due regard for the rights and duties of coastal States.[64]

International jurisprudence on 'due regard' includes environmental protection of EEZs, thus bringing in greater regulation of activities in EEZs.[65] Sea activities of coastal States in EEZs under Article 56(1)(b)(iii) (protection and preservation of the marine environment) and non-coastal States under Article 58(3), must have due regard for the protection, preservation and sustainability of the seas.[66] The

56 ICJ, Fisheries Jurisdiction Case (*UK* v. *Iceland*), Merits, Judgment of 25 July 1974, paras. 67–68; and Chagos Marine Protected Area Arbitration (n 38), 517; and South China Sea Arbitration (n 11), 515.

57 Evan J. Criddle and Evan Fox-Decent, Mandatory Multilateralism, 3 *AJIL*, 2019, 272–375, 303.

58 Art. 87(1) provides the freedom of navigation; overflight; lay submarine cables and pipelines; construct artificial islands and other installations; fishing; and scientific research.

59 Art. 87(2) UNCLOS.

60 Beckman and Schofield (n 52) 193–243, 198.

61 Art. 55 UNCLOS.

62 Art. 56(2) UNCLOS.

63 Art. 58(1) UNCLOS.

64 Art. 58(3) UNCLOS.

65 See South China Sea Arbitration (n 11) 319–397 and 399–415.

66 See international case law (n 57).

jurisprudence to date reinforces the principle that due regard is both a substantive and procedural obligation.

Enforcing a due regard regime requires a degree of cooperation and compliance. The EU's framework for Maritime Spatial Planning (MSP) requires States to have due regard to the particularities of marine regions, relevant activities and their impacts and land–sea interactions under Article 4(5) and 8 of the MSP Directive EC 2014, and in this regard States must cooperate when considering the relevant interactions required under the Directive.[67] In *Whaling in the Antarctic* the ICJ considered the obligation of due regard within the framework of the duty to cooperate and ruled that Japan's duty to cooperate should include paying due regard to the International Whaling Commission (IWC) and the Scientific Committee's recommendations on non-lethal research methods.[68] The intrinsic link between due regard and cooperation is demonstrated by the fact that the obligation of due regard is not fulfilled without cooperation and compliance by the State parties.

The due regard mechanism is vital to balance concurrent rights, interests and obligations within any cooperation arrangement in practice, and to reverse the effects of the deteriorating SCS marine environment.[69] The ensuing maritime conflicts and competition for resources are worsening the prospects of cooperation in protecting and preserving the SCS marine environment.

Various ongoing issues in the SCS include the legal status of the EEZ arising from overlapping claims, the legality of foreign military activities in EEZs and freedom of navigation in the SCS,[70] all of which may affect the willingness not to view interests in the SCS as a zero-sum game making it difficult to comply with due regard. The enforcement jurisdiction in the EEZ also relies on compliance and cooperation among individual coastal States. However, any resolution for greater cooperation must be centred on marine conservation.[71] A future ASEAN COC should place a moratorium over the claims in the SCS in order to urgently address marine preservation as a collective security matter and place legal and institutional

67 Lynne McGowan, Stephen Jay and Sue Kidd, *Scenario-Building for Marine Spatial Planning in Maritime Spatial Planning, Past, Present and Future*, edited by Jacek Zaucha and Kira Gee (Oxford: Palgrave, 2018), 327–351, 330.

68 ICJ, Whaling in the Antarctic (*Australia* v. *Japan*: New Zealand intervening), Judgment, ICJ Reports 2014, 35.

69 United Nations, UNEP Project to Reverse Environmental Degradation Trend in South China Sea and the Gulf of Thailand, UNEP/87, March 29, 2001; *South China Sea Arbitration* (n 11), 823; Camilo Mora, Iain R. Caldwell, Charles Birkeland, and John W. McManus, Dredging in the Spratly Islands: Gaining Land but Losing Reefs, 14(6) *PLOS Biology*, 2016; and S. Tiezzi, South China Sea Ruling: China Caused 'Irreparable Harm' to Environment, *The Diplomat*, 15 July 2016.

70 U.S.–China Strategic Competition in South and East China Seas: Background and Issues for Congress, Congressional Research Service, updated 6 February 2020.

71 Aldo Chircop, Regional Cooperation in Marine Environmental Protection in the South China Sea: A Reflection on New Directions for Marine Conservation, 41(4) *Ocean Development & International Law*, 2010, 334–356.

frameworks for implementing the level of cooperation required to effectively reduce marine harm and restore the health of the SCS.

24.5 RESORT TO THE RULE OF LAW: COOPERATION AND DUE REGARD

The foundation of the international legal order to have due regard for other States' rights and duties is to ensure sovereign equality and ability to enforce all (not a few) States' rights and duties within a system.[72] The rule of law for the seas rejects unilateral actions (as with China's nine-dash line claim in the *South China Sea Arbitration*, Iceland's legislation that denies the UK its fishing rights in the *Fisheries Case (UK* v. *Iceland)*).[73] The legal order requires equitable balancing – hence, due regard is an obligation – which is not void of content.[74] UNCLOS, as a binding framework convention, provides the substantive and procedural rules as well as the framework for future agreements to cooperate on the marine environment of the SCS. The due regard mechanism for equitable balancing '[lacks] the precision of bright-line rules',[75] and requires cooperation among the parties to negotiate in good faith and conform to their agreement in upholding the rule of law. In the fragile geopolitical climate in the SCS, resorting to rule of law compliance may be the best way to diffuse tensions.[76]

Koskenniemi notes '[t]he fight for an international Rule of Law is a fight against politics, understood as a matter of furthering subjective desires and leading into an international anarchy. Though some measure of politics is inevitable, it should be constrained by non-political rules'.[77] The state of affairs in the SCS where the dominant trend is to repudiate or avoid rules is reminiscent of John Locke's phrase 'wherever law ends, tyranny begins'.[78] Failures to enforce the SCS Arbitral Award weaken bona fide attempts to cooperate in good faith, and moreover, challenge the underlying foundations of the rule of law ideal in undermining the legal equality of States by disregarding other States' rights and freedoms of the seas.[79]

Notwithstanding that cooperation and competition are polar opposites, scholars have recommended strategies of cooperation amidst overlapping maritime claims. One strategy is to establish a network of marine protected areas (MPAs) in the SCS

[72] Brad Roth, *Sovereign Equality and Moral Disagreement: Premises of a Pluralist International Legal Order* (Oxford: Oxford University Press, 2011), 273–274.

[73] Fisheries Jurisdiction (*United Kingdom* v. *Iceland*) (Merits, Judgment) [1974] ICJ Rep. 3 (n 57).

[74] See South China Sea Arbitration (n 11) 312.

[75] Ibid.

[76] Katherine Morton, China's Ambition in the South China Sea: Is a Legitimate Maritime Order Possible? 92(4) *International Affairs*, 2016, 909–940, 912–914.

[77] Martti Koskenniemi, The Politics of International Law, 1 *EJIL*, 1990, 4–32, 5.

[78] John Locke quoted in Tom Bingham, *The Rule of Law* (London: Penguin, 2011).

[79] Douglas Guilfoyle, The Rule of Law and Maritime Security in the South China Sea, 95(5) *International Affairs*, 2019, 999–1017, 1015–1016.

that may support different ecosystems as well as preserve areas from human impact to allow natural resources to recover from stress.[80] This strategy requires cooperation and political will to suspend maritime claims.[81] A less ambitious suggestion is for China and Vietnam to establish an MPA in the same location in the Paracel Islands under their respective national laws.[82]

Another recommendation is to resolve uncertainties over the parties' overlapping EEZ claims, following which joint development areas could be established.[83] It has been suggested that China declare an EEZ from the largest islands in the Spratly Islands and Paracel Islands and issue charts setting out the outer limit of its EEZ claims so that other ASEAN claimants would be able to clarify their claims.[84] These recommendations are dependent on setting aside territorial disputes, which requires cooperation and mutual trust. These strategies, however, are feasible where there is a moratorium over claims, at the very least, an urgent collective focus on marine protection that takes precedence over State claims in the SCS.

24.6 CONCLUSION: LOOKING TO THE FUTURE

The SCS illustrates that the rule of law is failing to protect the marine environment. Competing claims and antagonistic behaviour hinder the SCS States from cooperating and carrying out their obligations to conserve and protect the marine environment. Competition for maritime claims is at odds with the requirement to cooperate in good faith and to pay due regard to other States' rights and freedoms in the EEZs. Failure to uphold marine protection and preservation obligations has caused the SCS marine environment to deteriorate drastically. Legal mechanisms relying on State-to-State cooperation are unlikely to be successful. However, there are steps that can be taken by the parties to ameliorate the parlous state of the rule of law in the SCS, potentially leading to better outcomes for the environment.

The *South China Sea Arbitration* ruling has implications for all SCS States. It reflects the environmental standard expected of States in carrying out sea-related activities, as highlighted in other international cases.

The present regime incorporates environmental principles and balances the freedom of utilisation of marine resources with the requirement to preserve and

80 Hai Dang Vu, Towards a Regional MPA Network in the South China Sea: General Perspectives and Specific Challenges, 26 *Ocean Yearbook*, 2012, 291–316, 292–293.

81 David L. VanderZwaag and Hai Dang Vu, Regional Cooperation in the South China Sea and the Arctic: Lessons to Be Learned? in *The Regulation of International Shipping: International and Comparative Perspectives* (2012), 171–205; and Donald R. Rothwell, The Polar Regions and the Law of the Sea in Polar Geopolitics, edited by Richard Powell and Klaus Dodds (Oxford: Edward Elgar, 2014), 19–37.

82 Vu (n 80) 207–244, 216.

83 Beckman and Schofield (n 52) 193–243, 235.

84 Ibid.

protect the marine environment implicit in the term 'sustainable use'.[85] The COC must address the fundamental challenges of marine environmental protection and incorporate a requirement to cooperate reflecting the standard in international jurisprudence. A legally binding COC ensures compliance and counters the predominance of *realpolitik* in the SCS.[86] A moratorium over the claims in the SCS is the best chance for real cooperation.

Through some combination of these initiatives, the rule of law order may be restored with the hope that this may bring the benefits of the rule of law and stability to the SCS States, and ultimately result in more effective protection of the marine environment.

85 Kjell Griip, International Marine Environmental Governance: A Review, 46(4) *Springer Ambio*, 2017, 413–427.

86 Leszek Buszynski, Law and Realpolitik: The Arbitral Tribunal's Ruling and the South China Sea, 21 *Asian Yearbook of International Law*, 2015.

PART VI

Concluding Remarks

25

Legal Solutions for Oceans in Change

Mapping Out the Way Forward

Froukje Maria Platjouw and Alla Pozdnakova

The main aim of the book is to take the further, crucial, step of identifying and critically examining areas of law that need to change or evolve in order to respond to the challenges of governing the oceans of the future. Our ambition is thus not only to explain ocean-related environmental, legal and governance problems but to propose solutions on how to deal with those problems. Throughout the book, the chapters have discussed whether legal frameworks are sufficiently effective and adequate to address (new) challenges and pressures threatening the resilience of our oceans. Several pressures and challenges have been identified as currently insufficiently addressed under existing legal frameworks and in severe need of improvement to strengthen the rule of law for oceans in those areas. These include, for example, climate change and its interaction with and impact on ocean dynamics and functioning; emissions from ships; plastic pollution; fisheries and other exploitative use of living resources affecting biodiversity; as well as novel activities and uses of oceans such as geoengineering and spaceflight activities.

Four main questions have guided the contents of this book as well as its underlying structure: (1) How should law deal with existing and novel pressures on the marine environment?; (2) How should we balance exploitation and protection of oceans to ensure long-term resilience of marine ecosystems?; (3) How could we improve implementation, compliance and enforcement?; (4) What challenges and solutions exist in regional seas and ocean areas? Overall, these perspectives provide novel insights into the adequacy of our current legal, governance and compliance mechanisms and identify solutions needed to strengthen the rule of law for oceans from a broad range of viewpoints. Specific solutions and recommendations will be summarized in the second part of this chapter.

25.1 CROSS-CUTTING ISSUES AFFECTING THE RULE OF LAW FOR OCEANS

Despite the comprehensiveness of the book and its diversity of viewpoints, several cross-cutting rule of law challenges can be identified among chapters. The first major challenge is the tension between the need for flexibility and adaptivity in law and governance while the rule of law ideally requires predictability, coherence, legal certainty, stability and accountability. The level of scientific uncertainty related to the functioning of most marine ecosystems, the cascading effects of human-induced and natural changes, and the rapidity of change necessitate a cautious and adaptive approach in policymaking and decision-making on any marine ecosystem. This might be an argument for designing law and legislation with a certain level of generality to enable adapting and applying it to a broad variety of circumstances. However, this often entails a risk of law failing to be fit for purpose to address specific challenges and pressures. It appears that for many specific environmental problems, a fit-for-purpose and adequate legal framework is lacking. This significantly weakens the rule of law for oceans and has been identified as a key problem by several authors in this book.

Indeed, many authors emphasize that international treaties do not offer clear solutions for complex problems. The interaction between climate change and ocean dynamics is largely left unaddressed in both the United Nations Convention on the Law of the Sea (UNCLOS) and the United Nations Framework Convention on Climate Change (UNFCCC). Several authors discuss international treaties and their interaction, highlighting the need for dynamic or expanded interpretation as well as for developing new agreements as a possible solution to cover current gaps and weaknesses in law. International treaties for global problems such as plastics are important, but often need to be complemented by more specific measures, including trade regulatory measures, subsidies or tariffs, to enhance their effectiveness. On a regional level, there is also a need for regional treaties or other binding instruments to regulate certain challenges more effectively.

A second and slightly related cross-cutting issue is lack of clarity related to definitions, general provisions and principles, and how we should take decisions in the face of new scientific knowledge. Several authors have discussed UNCLOS Part XII provisions and the challenge of applying general provisions to specific activities. Legal uncertainties have been identified with respect to addressing fluctuating or changing distributions of fish stocks, and uncertainties with regard to the definition of marine genetic resources. Certain concepts and principles have also been under discussion by the authors. Application of the precautionary principle has been assessed in the context of management of living resources, and the concept of 'risks' in the context of restoration. These unclarities may lead to different interpretations by States and other users, to increased fragmentation and possibly to a weakening of the rule of law for the oceans. Of special importance is the role and use of scientific knowledge for regulating both new as well as existing activities. Divergent perceptions may exist of risks and benefits related to new technologies for use in the marine domain. Legal unclarity and uncertainty need to be resolved with regard to how to utilize new scientific knowledge related to certain technologies and activities, and how to balance different benefits and costs.

A third cross-cutting issue is the need for cooperation and coordination to enhance the rule of law for oceans. Several authors have emphasized the importance, scope and legal relevance of cooperation and coordination for moving forward. As noted by Voigt, for example, there is a need 'not only in creating a global level playing field that avoids free riding, but in creating the legal structure for a coordinated response commensurate with these global challenges'.[1] Thorough discussion has been given to institutions, such as the UN Environment Program, the International Maritime Organization and regional organizations, together with their roles for facilitating coordination and interaction. Authors have also emphasized the need for inter-institutional integration at national level, for example between national bodies and international bodies. Another suggestion was to clearly define the competencies of different players, both those long established and others newly joining the field (such as the WTO), with a view to improving synergy between their actions and avoiding unnecessary overlaps and duplications. In addition, enhanced coordination between international entities and forums has been highlighted, especially in regional areas.

A fourth cross-cutting issue is the importance of including diverse actors or groups in order to foster implementation and enforcement of international, regional and local rules. In general, legitimacy has been identified as critical. Perceived fairness of decision-making has clear implications for the extent to which management is deemed legitimate. Industrial actors and other stakeholders that consider processes legitimate may increase compliance with set rules and requirements. Various authors also emphasize the role of private actors and stakeholders as crucial to ensure tackling environmental problems adequately. Pollution from fisheries and plastic pollution require everyone to come on board, including private actors. Increasingly, plans aim to include the entire life cycle engaging stakeholders, including industry, through fit-for-purpose technical standards and certificates to tackle marine plastic pollution.

25.2 MAPPING OUT THE WAY FORWARD

25.2.1 *Strengthening the Rule of Law through Improved Regulation and Governance of Existing and Novel Pressures*

The book has highlighted three pressures and concerns that are in critical need of sounder legal solutions. These are, first, climate change and the interactions

[1] Voigt, Chapter 2 in this volume.

between climate change dynamics, greenhouse gas emissions and ocean dynamics (Voigt and Testa); second, marine plastic pollution (Jung and Telesetsky); and third, matters not (yet) adequately regulated such as marine pollution from spaceflight activities (Pozdnakova).

To better address the relationship between climate change and the ocean ecosystem, *Christina Voigt* recommends including ocean-based activities in the Nationally Determined Contributions (NDCs) of parties to the Paris Agreement. NDCs can play a critical role in supporting acceleration of renewable energy by sending clear, consistent signals to the private sector. Including this in the NDCs means that (through domestic planning and regulatory as well as enforcement measures) greater legal machinery will be set in motion. Decarbonization of ocean transport is another way by which ocean-related aspects might contribute to climate solutions. Ocean transport currently stands for about 3 per cent of global greenhouse gas emissions, with a rising trend. Increased energy efficiency, maximizing the overall operational efficiency of new and existing ships, as well as promoting or prescribing low and zero carbon fuels, could mitigate this contribution. International work through the International Maritime Organization (IMO) and regional organizations might be necessary; this should also increase possibilities for enforcement of norms. Here, too, including ocean transport in parties' NDCs could be an effective way forward. Voigt stresses that such changes would draw ocean governance under the transparency requirements of the Paris Agreement, enhancing their visibility, legitimacy and – potentially – coordination. International coordination through the IMO, or in processes related to Marine Biodiversity of Areas Beyond National Jurisdiction (BBNJ), might be beneficial in this context.

More specifically focusing on ocean transport and greenhouse gas emissions from shipping, *David Testa* recommends complementing the UNCLOS provisions by more technical fit-for-purpose rules to reduce greenhouse gas emissions from the ocean transport sector. The IMO's Initial Strategy is a welcome preliminary step towards giving meaningful content and substance to UNCLOS general provisions. Moving ahead, it is clear, however, that the Strategy will need to be followed up by substantive greenhouse gas emission reduction measures that are sufficiently ambitious in nature. In line with UNCLOS, these measures will require systemic integration with the wider international environmental law framework and will need to be informed by the relevant goals under the UN Climate Change regime. Ensuring both coherence and effectiveness through adequate rules and standards will contribute to development of an effective regime for reduction of greenhouse gas emissions from shipping.

Additionally, marine plastic pollution has been thoroughly discussed as a pressure that remains sorely in need of better regulation. *Dawoon Jung* stresses that although the 2019 amendment to the annexes of the Basel Convention amounts to notable progress in regulating plastic waste, the current legal framework for marine plastics pollution is still criticized as a patchwork of instruments that are fragmented and ineffective in tackling the marine plastics issue. To strengthen the rule of law, including legal certainty and implementation, she recommends improved cooperation and coordination between sector-specific instruments and between the multiple layers of regulations at global, regional and national levels in order to promote coherent regulations and implementation. Simultaneously, existing weaknesses within the legal framework need to be remedied. Jung emphasizes the importance of applying a holistic approach governing all the lifecycle phases of plastics. For that reason, a possible new global treaty should also incorporate this concept, ensuring that all phases of plastics are effectively regulated. To foster implementation, multi-stakeholder partnerships should be promoted to facilitate the emergence of initiative solutions throughout the entire lifecycle of plastics from design to recyclability.

Anastasia Telesetsky takes this idea one step further and proposes concrete measures to ensure the operationalization of such a lifecycle approach to plastics. She argues that the main challenge to the rule of law in the context of plastics is the role of powerful industry, such as corporations, and emphasizes the importance of 'thick' laws that contain sufficient substantive contents and tools for implementation to ensure a fundamental change in the current packaging industry. To realise such a change, Telesetsky proposes introducing effective and global multilateral tax measures that would reflect the costs of the environmental externalities of the industry. Economic instruments such as tariffs offer additional choices of tools beyond direct regulation and voluntary instruments.

While truly international tariffs have not been negotiated, they would provide an efficient means of pricing externalities that States are forced to absorb either in the form of additional investment in waste management or in damage to marine resources. Adopting an international tariff would be politically challenging but would address the gap in the existing rule of law where there is no real accountability in terms of addressing single-use plastics as a growing source of carbon emissions or as a global environmental health and public health threat. Additionally, a truly global carbon tax could change the calculus of operation for major energy-intensive industries such as the chemicals and plastics sectors. In the interim – before a global carbon tax catalyses system-wide changes across all industries – States should respond to citizens' demands for a first step towards implementing the circular economy in both the packaging industry and the fishing industry by placing tariffs on specific non-essential plastic products contributing to marine pollution. This will remedy the current accountability gap and enhance the rule of law for oceans.

A relatively unregulated pressure on the marine environment is pollution from spaceflight activities. In the absence of fit-for-purpose rules that regulate this pressure, the rule of law for oceans is under threat. *Alla Pozdnakova* points out that an effective environmental legal regime in the space sector needs to be developed through active cooperation between States. Such cooperation should first be aimed at gathering scientific knowledge about the marine environmental impact of spaceflights and strengthening the international institutional framework before any substantive provisions on prevention of pollution can feasibly be developed. She also highlights the importance of an internationally coordinated approach through an institution responsible for international legal development in the space sector, such as the Committee on the Peaceful Uses of Outer Space (COPUOS), supplemented by inter-institutional cooperation with other competent international organizations. This is indispensable to paving the way for prospective harmonization steps.

She recommends continuation of the work initiated by the IMO and UN COPUOS to evaluate expansion of the London Convention to the spaceflight sector and accordingly to amend the 1996 Protocol in order to include disposal of jettisoned space objects into the maritime environment.

25.2.2 *Strengthening the Rule of Law through a Better Balance between Exploitation and Protection of Our Oceans*

The book addresses the question how to ensure a proper balance between exploitation and protection of oceans, including preservation of marine biodiversity and marine living resources. The authors have identified several challenges, including novel types of balancing in the context of marine restoration (Roland Holst); the effects of climate change on fish stock redistribution, which requires adaptation (Lennan); unclear, vague or silent international legal frameworks, definitions, concepts or environmental principles (Bohman and Ringbom, Shams); the BBNJ process and its potential for regulating marine living resources (Wollensak) and its potential to foster an ecological sustainability path (Cloutier de Repentigny).

To deal with the existing level of marine plastic pollution, marine restoration activities have received increased interest. *Rozemarijn Roland Holst* sheds light on the legal challenges raised by the use of new technologies for marine environmental restoration purposes, using as a case study The Ocean Cleanup's (TOC) plastic cleanup activities in areas beyond national jurisdiction. This initiative entails a novel type of balancing where complex 'risk trade-offs' need to be taken in balancing the impacts of plastic debris with the risks of technology-driven clean-up of plastics. Perhaps the biggest challenge for the rule of law in governing restoration activities like TOC lies in dealing with uncertainty and knowledge gaps regarding both the benefits and risks involved in employing a new technology in a complex environment, and how to approach environmental risk/risk trade-offs when perceptions of these risks diverge. To fill this gap, she stresses the importance of relying on extra-legal knowledge, such as scientific data, to add content to legal standards. Scientific knowledge and understanding of the technology and its consequences are crucial to ensuring that legal rules, tools and principles such as best available technology, best available science and best practices are not devoid of meaningful content.

The balancing required in policymaking and decision-making increasingly involves different environmental concerns. *Brita Bohman and Henrik Ringbom* discuss this challenge, but in the context of sea-based measures (marine geoengineering) to abate eutrophication. Sea-based measures refer to different technological innovations that may be implemented at sea to target pollution that has already been released. These have a purely environmental objective, which complicates balancing between the interests concerned. The risk of further escalating eutrophication with all its consequences, and to continue only with land-based measures, has to be balanced against the risks that sea-based measures may exert on the ecosystem. Yet due to their novelty and because they have not been sufficiently tested in relation to environmental risks, the measures are not subject to any specific regulation, while environmental principles, such as the precautionary principle, do not provide sufficient legal guidance. Bohman and Ringbom conclude that it is both important and appropriate to focus on developing a new framework or guidelines, inspired by the Assessment Framework developed under the London dumping regime, to learn more about sea-based measures and to coordinate policies among the Baltic Sea States, thereby helping permit authorities in their tasks. With the recent adoption of the (voluntary) HELCOM Guidelines, this process appears to be well under way.

Another gap in law has been discussed by *Aref Shams* in the context of utilizing icebergs as an alternative source of fresh water, which may be an emerging demand on oceans and therefore in need of adequate rule of law. Neither UNCLOS nor the Antarctic Treaty System (ATS) indicate a prohibition against the use of icebergs. Although the ATS represents more stringent environmental standards, it also presents a vague and unclear general structure in terms of dealing with the question of utilizing icebergs as this was not foreseen as a demand on Antarctic resources. Therefore, Shams stresses that a gap exists in the regulatory capacities of international law, which could become problematic for the rule of law if/when the use of icebergs for fresh water were to proliferate, leading to an imbalance between the need to exploit this potential new resource with the need to preserve the marine environment.

Shams discusses some of the ways in which international law could be adapted to fill the gaps identified and ensure it is fit for purpose, particularly in the context of the BBNJ negotiations. Three key requirements of importance for utilizing icebergs would be: benefit sharing as a better solution to the high seas regime; limiting the quantity taken and on location through area-based management tools provisions; and a requirement to conduct Environmental Impact Assessments.

The rule of law for oceans is strengthened by clear and coherent rules. Currently, however, marine governance – indeed, environmental governance in general – is to a large extent also steered by environmental principles that should guide authorities and actors on sustainable pathways. These environmental principles could provide additional guidance to the overall legal framework and as such strengthen the rule of law in that field. *Maurus Wollensak* studies management of living resources under the UNCLOS, with particular focus on the precautionary principle/approach. Stocks fished at a 'biologically unsustainable level' have increased over the years, and it appears that UNCLOS has limited impact on protecting living resources against exploitation. One way to counter such developments is to apply the precautionary principle/approach, which UNCLOS does not demand *expressis verbis*. Wollensak explores two decades of developments and jurisprudence, arguing that the principle now appears to inform the normative content of UNCLOS. For that reason, it should be more effectively respected in the context of protecting preservation of the marine environment and managing marine living resources.

Another chapter discussing marine living resources is provided by *Mitchell Lennan*, who discusses whether the international legal framework adequately obliges States to adapt to complexities caused by marine living resources shifting their location, that is, redistribution of fish stocks due to climate change. He reasons that shifting fish stocks threaten the certainty, predictability and stability of the international fisheries legal framework, as well as undermining conservation and management measures by coastal States and regional fisheries management organizations. Since the legal framework does not directly account for species shifts, it has been argued as constituting a 'governance gap' requiring urgent attention. Lennan proposes several solutions, including using the Convention on Biological Diversity as a crucial interpretive tool to be read consistently with UNCLOS. In situ conservation objectives should be applied in a way that accounts for climate change consequences to the environment. Obligations to adapt also follow from the Convention on Migratory Stocks and the UNFCCC and Paris Agreement, which also apply to the oceans. He further recommends exploring the potential of the precautionary principle and Ecosystem Approach to Fisheries in implementing obligations, in combination with the obligation to cooperate. Bodies such as Regional Fisheries Management Organizations or Arrangements and the Food and Agriculture Organization must enable adaptive management through inter-institutional cooperation, and engagement with research.

Currently, diverse pressures and challenges exert a significant impact on the oceans. Is law as an instrument actually adequate to protect marine biodiversity? *Pierre Cloutier de Repentigny* analyses the UNCLOS through the lens of green legal theory to demonstrate the entanglement of the UNCLOS marine conservation framework with economic growth. He points out the importance of addressing the causes rather than the symptoms of regime failure. If we are to use ocean law as a means of engendering or participating in the re-formation of constitutive processes beyond economic growth and towards ecological sustainability, it is time to think more strategically about how to strengthen the 'rule of law'. He examines BBNJ and points out that the draft provisions conceptualize marine biodiversity as a source of genetic resources, indicating economic benefits, which is a narrative of economic growth. The provisions on Area-Based Protection and Management Measures (ABPMM) could, however, offer more re-formative potential. The BBNJ Agreement would create a mechanism to establish ABPMM in areas beyond national jurisdiction. State parties will be able to propose ABPMM to be adopted by the conference of parties. ABPMM are to be identified based, for example, on the ecosystem approach, and best available science and – potentially – Indigenous peoples' traditional knowledge. Once an ABPMM is adopted, State parties must conform to it but are allowed to adopt more stringent measures. Unilateral and multilateral action through the BBNJ Agreement could, step by step, create a new paradigm for the law of the sea, a new rule of law for the oceans detached from the demands of economic growth.

A final area for improvement discussed in this part of the book is related to marine genetic resources. *Jakub Ciesielczuk* explains that recent technological advances have provided scientists with more opportunities to explore the richness of marine life and in particular marine genetic resources. International law and literature, however, lack a universal definition of marine genetic resources. To strengthen the rule of law in this field, and in particular legal clarity and legal certainty, a clear working definition of marine genetic resources will help with a universal understanding of these resources across existing and future marine genetic resources-related regimes and relationships between the rules included in those regimes. Ciesielczuk develops and proposes a working definition that relies on the text of Article 2 of the Convention on Biological Diversity but adjusts it to reflect current scientific reality and to address identified genetic utilization challenges. The proposed working definition will ensure coherence between the Convention on Biological Diversity and other regimes regulating genetic resources. Looking ahead, he further recommends that ensuring conservation and sustainable use of marine genetic resources would clearly require adoption of a clear definition of marine genetic resources in the future BBNJ treaty, based on his proposed working definition.

25.2.3 *Strengthening the Rule of Law through Improved Implementation, Compliance and Enforcement*

The book explores various tools and mechanisms – and the lack thereof – that are important for effective governance, compliance and enforcement. This part of the book provides perspectives on the role of legitimacy in law (Langlet); criminalization of maritime environmental crimes (Becker-Weinberg); dynamic interpretations of UNCLOS to regulate and enforce prohibitions of Illegal, unreported and unregulated (IUU) fishing against fishing operators or owners of vessels (Van Welzen); the potential for using litigation to increase compliance with existing fisheries norms (Guggisberg); the potential of an advisory jurisdiction of the plenary of the International Tribunal for the Law of the Sea (Cruz Carrillo); and the role of the World Trade Organization, which is trying to establish new, sustainability-driven rules limiting certain forms of state support at sea under the auspices of the WTO Fisheries Subsidies Agreement (Guglya).

David Langlet explains that recent years have seen increasing calls to pay more attention to the political dimensions and societal implications of marine policy and management in addition to the predominately natural science perspectives traditionally applied. He reasons that the legitimacy and fairness of EU marine law and governance is a fundamental element of an effective and rule of law-based legal regime for the marine realm. Aspects of legitimacy, such as participation, representation, effective delivery of policies and laws, openness, accountability, transparency and efficacy of decision-making processes, can enhance the implementation or operationalization of legal requirements, thereby strengthening the rule of law for oceans. Langlet assesses the degree of legitimacy and fairness in the context of three EU framework directives important for the European seas: the Water Framework Directive, the Marine Strategy Framework Directive and the Maritime Spatial Planning Directive. All three directives largely rely on participation for dealing with core legitimacy dimensions. Several challenges need to be resolved, though, including defining who has a legitimate say in decision-making, ensuring that participation can be genuine, with stakeholders understanding what can and cannot be changed through a participatory process as well as seeing that their participation is meaningful and can affect the outcome. Sufficient time must also be allowed for deliberations and integration of diverse interests and knowledge.

In addition to enhancing the legitimacy and fairness of laws and policies to foster their implementation, other tools and solutions may also be sought to ensure an ecologically sustainable pathway. *Vasco Becker-Weinberg* emphasizes the strong need for criminalization of maritime environmental crimes, such as ship-source pollution through accidental and wilful oil discharges, which are currently one of the main causes of destruction of marine ecosystems and devastation of marine life. Maritime environmental crimes are committed in order to avoid compliance with international rules and regulations, thus obtaining substantial financial gain from avoiding procedures established under national and/or international law that are time-consuming and entail significant costs. He stresses the urgency of adopting an international, global approach to marine environmental crime so that criminalization would no longer depend on domestic laws only. International cooperation and joint law enforcement operations can be highly effective in reducing maritime crimes. However, this requires addressing the current jurisdictional limitations under the law of the sea and flag State jurisdiction that affect the fitness of existing laws and their enforcement. Proposals for a new international crime such as 'ecocide' could potentially lead the way for further development of international law and of the legal tools necessary to ensure a collective and effective legal response to maritime environmental crimes.

Pieter van Welzen addresses another challenge that needs improved compliance and enforcement. In examining the issue of illegal fishing, he argues that persons who organize these illegal fishing operations, such as the operators and owners of vessels, often use flags of convenience and take advantage of the weak legal systems of flag States and coastal States. He proposes that, in addition to coastal, port and flag States, the States of which such owners and operators are nationals also have a role to fulfil in the fight against illegal fishing. Although the focus under UNCLOS for challenging IUU fishing in a State's exclusive economic zone has been on coastal States and flag States, arguably UNCLOS also obliges States whose nationals are directly or indirectly involved in the fisheries sector to ensure that those nationals do not engage in or support IUU fishing. Such obligations could be based on the International Tribunal for the Law of the Sea (ITLOS) Advisory Opinion, that is, a due diligence obligation to ensure that its nationals refrain from being involved in activities, including as operator or owner of a vessel engaged in fishing in the exclusive economic zone of another State, to comply with conservation measures applying to that exclusive economic zone. Van Welzen thus points out that an international ruling and advisory opinion by ITLOS interprets UNCLOS provisions as imposing responsibility on States to exercise effective control over their nationals, which arguably includes responsibility to exercise control over beneficial owners and operators of vessels.

Carlos Cruz Carrillo discusses the potential of the advisory jurisdiction of the plenary of the International Tribunal for the Law of the Sea to strengthen ocean governance. The advisory function prevails as a tool to enhance the rule of law for oceans, as its legal effects entail opportunities for stakeholders to reach concrete solutions following the law. Advisory opinions can also provide guidance on how to interpret and use the law of the sea to tackle new challenges, such as climate change, ocean acidification and other complex issues that have emerged through technological advances and the quest for natural resources and maritime power. To strengthen the rule of law for oceans in this context, Cruz Carillo recommends revising the configuration of this judicial function and underscores the potential use of ad hoc jurisdictional agreements to request advisory opinions. At the same time, he advises that jurisdiction to give advisory opinions should be exercised only after careful evaluation of compelling reasons announced for such an opinion, also in light of protecting the principle to consent to adjudication.

Leonila Guglya explores the role of new rules reducing or eliminating subsidies to certain forms of fishing and fishing-related activities at sea, currently under elaboration by the World Trade Organization (WTO), as a possible accessory tool capable of helping exhausted fish stocks recover. If adopted, the new multilateral agreement integrated into the legal framework of the WTO would restrict financial inflows into enhancement of the fishing effort, which is damaging for stocks. The new disciplines would be divided into three streams, shaped as prohibitions of: (a) subsidies contributing to overcapacity and overfishing; (b) subsidies for fishing on overfished stocks; and (c) subsidies to vessels and/or operators involved in IUU fishing and fishing-related activities. Nevertheless, fisheries subsidies negotiations have been ongoing already for over two decades and face considerable challenges. The fisheries mandate is atypical for an organization mostly dealing with concerns directly related to trade, while its interaction with players implicated in fisheries management remains limited. Reduction in the usual state support might have a significant impact on fishers and their communities, while banning investment in fleets could interfere with the industrialization strategies of developing countries and least developed countries, most of which, nowadays, are responsible for only an insignificant share of subsidization due to restricted budgets. In spite of numerous impediments, Guglya sees a potential for a win-win outcome. While new and ambitious sustainability-driven subsidies rules, if adopted, could help oceans recover, progress in and eventual successful conclusion of fisheries subsidies negotiations could also affirm that the WTO remains relevant by, for example, addressing acute beyond-trade concerns.

Again related to fisheries, *Solène Guggisberg* addresses the challenge that the traditional regime regulating international fisheries appears inadequate at ensuring the rule of law, since many States are unwilling or unable to respect their relevant obligations, prolonging the long-standing issue of non-compliance in the fisheries field and the resulting unsustainable management of stocks. She stresses and examines the potential of using litigation to increase compliance with existing fisheries norms, in particular to address issues with flag States, coastal States and States involved in the fishing of shared stocks. Despite several limitations, litigation can play an important role in strengthening the rule of law for oceans in that it could bring an end to specific violations, hence tackling the most egregious cases of non-compliance. She notes that it is important, though, to supplement litigation with regular compliance procedures under global or regional frameworks that ensure comprehensive, in-depth and regular review of States' compliance with their obligations. This adds much-needed objectivity, impartiality and comprehensiveness to the pursuit of accountability.

25.2.4 *Strengthening the Rule of Law in the Regional Seas and Oceans*

In this final part of the book, the authors shed light on the rule of law for regional seas and oceans by providing a variety of perspectives on the challenges and solutions to strengthening the rule of law for the Eastern Pacific (Enright), the Baltic Sea (White), the Arctic Ocean (Todorov), Japan (Yiallourides) and the South China Sea (Chong). Their perspectives can be divided into two categories. The three authors in the first category emphasize the role of cooperation and coordination and provide solutions anchored in efforts to integrate environmental governance at the regional level. The two authors in the second category address unilateral conduct and decisions by States that result from disagreements and difficulties that have emerged during cooperation efforts and processes. Both categories are closely interrelated, and both have an impact on the rule of law and the effectiveness of environmental governance in regional seas and oceans.

Sarah Ryan Enright analyses State-led regional cooperation efforts in the Eastern Tropical Pacific Ocean (ETPO) to create a transboundary marine corridor linking five Marine Protected Areas across four jurisdictions. She stresses that regional ocean governance efforts have shown promise by enabling cooperation and coordination across territorial and sectoral boundaries, which in turn could help to link disconnected areas of regulation arising from fragmentation. The Eastern Tropical Pacific Marine Corridor is currently regarded as a leading example of regional cooperation for creation of a network of marine protected areas. Specific rule of law challenges faced by this initiative, however, include lack of a legally binding cooperation agreement, limited sectoral participation, the vast scale of the project and lack of a cohesive overarching regional ocean governance framework. A key challenge from a rule of law perspective stems from overlaps and gaps in the mandates of the applicable governance arrangements in the Eastern Tropical Pacific. She highlights that the new BBNJ instrument has the potential to help address some of the governance gaps in the Eastern Tropical Pacific by introducing a legal mechanism at the global level for Marine Protected Areas (MPAs). This could potentially provide a legal basis for the designation of MPAs in areas beyond national jurisdiction and a set of overarching governance principles to guide oversight and coordination of a global network of MPAs. Additionally, regional institutions, such as the Permanent Commission for the South Pacific, could play an important integrating role in the region, and their engagement should be further encouraged.

Again addressing the importance of cooperation and coordination, *Kirsi White* emphasizes that the development of institutional interlinkages between polycentric governance arrangements may facilitate common policy objectives, decision-making and implementation of sectoral measures. She argues that while soft modes of governance may weaken the rule of law, use of these modes is of specific importance in a polycentric governance system as a tool for steering policy implementation by introducing innovative practices, learning and coordination. More specifically, she highlights as key the role of non-governmental organizations and port authorities in regulating oil pollution in the Baltic Sea, as well as stakeholder-inclusive collaborative learning platforms at the regional (or sub-basin) level, with a clear mandate and the aim of spatially relevant dynamics. She addresses implementation of the ecosystem approach in overlapping legislative measures regulating ship source oil pollution in the Baltic Sea and recommends stronger interaction within the regional multi-layered regulatory system as well as among regional institutions to strengthen the rule of law in the area.

In the Arctic, *Andrey Todorov* also highlights the importance of integration and coordination. He stresses that it is feasible to work towards a comprehensive integrated regional programme within the Arctic Council for the purpose of adopting scientific-based decisions related to spatial planning in the Arctic Ocean. Legal and organizational challenges arise from the need to implement integrated ecosystem-based marine management in the Arctic. Todorov argues that solutions to the challenges uncovered lie in unfolding the potential of the Arctic Council and significantly building it up. His suggestions include moving towards endowing the Arctic Council with international legal personality, transforming the Arctic Council Secretariat into an authoritative Commission with relevant functions similar to that of the OSPAR Commission. In addition to these, the Arctic Council could also play the central role in coordinating Integrated Ecosystem-Based Marine Management tools (such as applying marine spatial planning or creation of marine protected areas) with global and regional sectoral organizations active in the Arctic. This includes: the International Maritime Organization in relation to shipping; the North East Atlantic Fisheries Commission and possible future mechanisms under the 2018 Agreement on fisheries in the central part of the Arctic Ocean; and the International Seabed Authority in relation to exploration and exploitation of the resources of the Area (long-term perspective).

The final two chapters (Chapters 23 and 24) provide another perspective on the issue of regional coordination and integration. These chapters shed light on the impacts of unilateral conduct and decisions of States resulting from disagreements and difficulties faced during the process of cooperation. The chapters show that this may have a significant impact on the rule of law in regional seas and oceans.

Constantinos Yiallourides is critical of the duty to cooperate, as it lacks clarity and insufficiently guides cooperation between States when there are divergent, or even opposite, views among States, on how to reconcile the commercial objectives of conserving and managing living resources (in this case, whale stocks) with environmental protection. Yiallourides explains the importance of whaling for Japan as a cultural and traditional activity and in terms of the economic survival of Japanese coastal communities. He explains that several perspectives and interests, such as those related to ethics and animal rights but also traditional ways of living and cultural diversity, are also relevant in the international debate. Japan recognizes the importance of regional cooperation and the duty to cooperate, but it has chosen to withdraw from the ICRW, arguably as a result of these divergences and inability to achieve a compromise. Yiallourides recommends allowing limited – but internationally monitored – whaling in specific locations, while stopping whaling altogether in other locations. This approach could be adjusted based on independent and politically uncompromised scientific evidence. That said, however, as scientific knowledge advances and whale stock management theories become more complex, scientific advice may not necessarily produce clear-cut answers. In situations of scientific uncertainty, the precautionary principle can inform rational decisions.

In the context of the South China Sea, *Agnes Chong* highlights that overlapping claims in the South China Sea are at fundamental odds with States complying with their obligations to cooperate to protect the environment and to have due regard for rights and interests in the South China Sea. This weakens both the rule of law and protection of the marine environment in this regional sea area. Possible solutions encompass strategies of cooperation amidst overlapping maritime claims.

One strategy is to establish a network of marine protected areas in the South China Sea that may support different ecosystems as well as preserve areas from human impact to allow natural resources to recover from stress. This strategy requires cooperation and political will to suspend maritime claims. A less ambitious suggestion is for China and Vietnam to establish an MPA in the same location in the Paracel Islands under their respective national laws. Another recommendation is to resolve uncertainties over the parties' overlapping EEZ claims, following which joint development areas could be established. She underlines that a binding ASEAN Code of Conduct is also a possible avenue to enforce a moratorium over claims and drive urgent cooperation based on Part XII UNCLOS to reverse the fast-deteriorating maritime environment of the South China Sea.

25.3 FUTURE OUTLOOK FOR THE RULE OF LAW FOR OCEANS

Currently, many seas and oceans are under threat due to the cumulative impacts of maritime activities, climate change, biodiversity loss and more. This book has shed light on the various environmental, governance and legal challenges that exist in different parts of the world. Despite the complexity of certain challenges and difficulties, this book has also demonstrated that many opportunities and solutions can be devised to strengthen the environmental rule of law in order to ensure better protection of our seas and oceans. The authors have provided future-oriented perspectives on how law should evolve to better protect the oceans against increasing pressures and demands. All chapters incorporate novel insights and ideas for legal solutions that might inspire scholars, actors, authorities, citizens and communities around the globe. Further research might be needed, but we hope this book encourages the further exploration and realization of suggested legal solutions, as well as initiation of similar projects that critically examine the rule of law for a better protection of our seas and oceans.

Index

For EU product safety concerns, contact us at Calle de José Abascal, 56–1°,
28003 Madrid, Spain or eugpsr@cambridge.org.

www.ingramcontent.com/pod-product-compliance
Lightning Source LLC
LaVergne TN
LVHW010916300926
849194LV00025B/247
* 9 7 8 1 0 0 9 2 5 3 7 2 7 *